W9-BZG-639

The Human Meaning of Social Change

The Human Meaning of Social Change

Edited by
Angus Campbell
and
Philip E. Converse

RUSSELL SAGE FOUNDATION
NEW YORK

PUBLICATIONS OF RUSSELL SAGE FOUNDATION

Russell Sage Foundation was established in 1907 by Mrs. Russell Sage
for the improvement of social and living conditions in the United States.
In carrying out its purpose the Foundation conducts research
under the direction of members of the staff or in close collaboration
with other institutions, and supports programs designed to develop
and demonstrate productive working relations between
social scientists and other professional groups.
As an integral part of its operations, the Foundation from time to time
publishes books or pamphlets resulting from these activities.
Publication under the imprint of the Foundation
does not necessarily imply agreement by the Foundation, its Trustees,
or its staff with the interpretations or conclusions of the authors.

Standard Book Number: 87154–193–9
Library of Congress Catalog Card Number: 75–169837

Russell Sage Foundation
230 Park Avenue
New York 10017

© 1972 by Russell Sage Foundation. All rights reserved.
Printed in the United States of America
by Connecticut Printers, Inc., Hartford, Connecticut.

301.24
C187h

The Contributors

Angus Campbell

Professor of Psychology and Sociology
Director, Institute for Social Research
The University of Michigan

Philip E. Converse

Professor of Political Science and Sociology
Program Director, Center for Political Studies
Institute for Social Research
The University of Michigan

Herbert H. Hyman

Professor of Sociology
The John E. Andrus Center for Public Affairs
Wesleyan University

Robert L. Kahn

Professor of Psychology
Director, Survey Research Center
Institute for Social Research
The University of Michigan

George Katona

Professor of Economics and Psychology
Program Director and Research Coordinator, Survey Research Center
Institute for Social Research
The University of Michigan

Rolf B. Meyersohn

Professor of Sociology
Graduate Center
The City University of New York,
and Lehman College

Albert J. Reiss, Jr.

Professor of Sociology
The Institute of Social Science
Yale University

John P. Robinson

Assistant Professor of Journalism
Study Director, Survey Research Center
Institute for Social Research
The University of Michigan

Peter H. Rossi

Professor of Sociology
Chairman, Department of Social Relations
The Johns Hopkins University

Melvin Seeman

Professor of Sociology
University of California at Los Angeles

Marvin B. Sussman

Professor of Sociology
Director, Institute on the Family
and the Bureaucratic Society
Case Western Reserve University

124554

Contents

Preface

In October 1966 Russell Sage Foundation convened a meeting of its Advisory Committee on Social Indicators to discuss its various activities relating to the measurement of social trends. The manuscript for its volume *Indicators of Social Change* was approaching completion and at that time its contents, dealing primarily with structural changes in American society, were reviewed. The discussion, which covered a number of developments in social reporting then under way in the universities and the federal government, brought to light the fact that none of these enterprises was giving primary attention to the psychological aspects of social change. There appeared to be great interest in the ways in which the structure of society was changing, but no specific concern with the attitudes and experiences which precede and result from these changes. From this discussion the present volume was born.

This book has had a long period of gestation. The scholars whom we asked to contribute chapters were all very busy people, some so busy they finally had to withdraw from their agreements. The manuscripts came in at a slow pace, so slow in fact that the chapters completed by Melvin Seeman and Herbert Hyman at the end of 1968 had aged for more than two years before the last of the contributions arrived. Fortunately these gentlemen acceded to our plea that they not insist on rewriting their chapters in order to capture all of the new literature which had appeared in the interim. We are, of course, grateful to all of the authors, early or late, and we trust that the appearance of this book will convince them that their efforts were expended to good purpose.

The initiative for this work came from Eleanor Bernert Sheldon of Russell Sage Foundation and Wilbert E. Moore, University of Colorado, Denver, formerly of Russell Sage Foundation. They saw the opportunity to emphasize an aspect of social reporting which previously had not been given specific attention and they persuaded their Board of Trustees to make the necessary investment to bring this about. As editors we were entirely responsible for the specific content of the volume and the recruitment of authors. The scope of the book will not satisfy èveryone and there are specific omissions which we regret. We hope the readers will agree, however, that the individual chapters deal with important aspects of the total problem with which the book is concerned. Taken together the contributions present an agenda for research on the human meaning of social change which is truly formidable.

The preparation of this volume has depended on the talents and energies of many people other than the authors. Without attempting to name all of the research assistants, secretaries, programmers, and others who assisted in the preparation of the various chapters, we simply acknowledge their contribution and thank them for it. Mrs. Ellen Seiler, former Editor for Russell Sage Foundation, accomplished the transformation of the typewritten manuscript into print with a minimum of confusion. In the Institute for Social Research office, Mrs. Betty Jennings has managed all of the administrative details, proofread the manuscript, prepared the index, and taken general responsibility for getting the successive versions of the manuscript to the Foundation office. We are grateful for the efficient and intelligent manner with which she has completed these assignments.

Angus Campbell
Philip E. Converse

1

Social Change and Human Change

Angus Campbell and Philip E. Converse

That life in America is changing is a ubiquitous fact. That the population is growing, that it is shifting from the farms to the cities and from the cities to the suburbs, that incomes are increasing and consumption is expanding, that children stay in school through high school or longer and go out into jobs which are increasingly likely to be in service occupations: these are facts of life apparent to everyone in the 1970's.

They are also aspects of American life for which our federal agencies provide substantial statistical documentation. The growing demand for objective data regarding these structural changes and the increasing sophistication of analytical methods have brought about a widening array of quantitative information from which it is possible to plot the changes that are taking place in the population, the work force, the economy, the health, and other basic attributes of our society. The 1968 Russell Sage Foundation volume, *Indicators of Social Change,* reviews the current status of these measurements and reveals the scope and depth of the total program of social reporting which this country supports.[1]

The contributors to the 1968 volume did not believe, however, that the indicators of change which they reviewed were adequate to what they took to be the needs of society, and they specified the kinds of extension they wished to see undertaken. In 1969, the Department of Health, Education, and Welfare issued a bulletin entitled *Toward a Social Report* which also emphasized the fact that "the nation has no comprehensive set of statistics reflecting social progress or retrogression" and described "the social statistics and indicators" necessary for

---

[1] W. E. Moore and E. B. Sheldon, *Indicators of Social Change.* Russell Sage Foundation, New York, 1968.

"a regular system of social reporting" with which "we can better measure the distance we have come and plan for the way ahead."[2]

The current pressure for the development of a "social report" to parallel the annual report of the Council of Economic Advisers undoubtedly reflects the growing sense of unease at the various manifestations of disturbance and social disorder now prominent on the American scene. Trends in the last 25 years, during a period of unprecedented rise in national income, have severely shaken traditional trust in economic indicators as measures of national well-being. The rising rates of public disorder, violence, crime, and drug use have made it clear that affluence is not the total answer to society's problems. The country's efforts to reduce the incidence of poverty, while partially successful, have produced some very disturbing side effects. There is no suggestion that the Economic Report to the President should be contracted or de-emphasized, but there is a growing feeling that the formation of intelligent social policy requires more information about the state of the nation than can be learned from economic data alone.

Although the ferment of interest in social reporting is growing both in this country and abroad, there is no agreement as to the priority of items that should be included in a system of social accounts. Duncan speaks of "the swelling chorus of proposals concerning social reporting" as a social movement which is at present in a situation of "transition from the early stage of excitement and incubation to the intermediate stage of rational debate undertaken to sort out and test alternatives."[3] In the course of this transition it will be necessary to come to an understanding of what the term "social indicators" implies and what the essential characteristics of social indicators are. For some, the present enthusiasm may amount to no more than a call for a major expansion of the kinds of social bookkeeping and social research which have been gaining momentum since the Enlightenment. In our view, at least two distinctive emphases ought to be associated with the definition of social indicators and provide it with unique connotations.

First, the term is intended to convey a stress on descriptive measurement which is much more "dynamic" than most social science research has been to date. Limited both by vision and resources, much of its empirical work has been devoted to the "one-shot" study of this or that phenomenon, on the assumption that enough would be learned from such forays to assemble useful middle-range empirical theories about key features of social systems. As time has worn on, however, it has become more and more apparent that relationships assessed at a single point in time are only uncertain indicators of more dynamic trends. It

---

[2] Department of Health, Education, and Welfare, *Toward a Social Report*. Government Printing Office, Washington, D.C., 1969.

[3] O. D. Duncan, *Toward Social Reporting: Next Steps*. Russell Sage Foundation, New York, 1969.

now seems clear that any strong causal inference requires longitudinal measurement, or continued "monitoring" of a system over time. One thrust of the "social indicators movement," then, is to bring social science into a more direct confrontation with problems of social change.

Second, and perhaps more notable, the call to arms represented by the social indicators movement lays a heavy stress on policy relevance. Indeed, it is not at all discontinuous with the cry of college students for "relevance," or the pressing of the question: Knowledge for what? Advocates of a broad-gauge social indicators program assume that, among the myriads of possible social variables that might be measured, high priority should be given to those that seem on the one hand most central in any assessment of the evolving quality of American social life and, on the other, that are amenable to manipulation through policy change.

We live in an age when confidence that man can eventually control and shape the social forces about him has risen significantly. Such control has come to be exercised over the physical environment with spectacular success and has changed the nature of human life to its core. Rapid strides have been made in controlling the biological environment, and further stunning developments are imminent. There are even signs of marked progress in the control of economic forces, as witnessed by the reduction of large-scale disasters in that sector.

The notion of intelligent control is, moreover, a central thread in cybernetic visions of a future society carefully guided toward more and more ambitious goals. The image is that of the helmsman who knows where he is, as well as where he ultimately wants to arrive. He does not exercise perfect control, so that he can move his craft in a simple straight line. The winds, tides, and currents continually push him to one side or the other. But by taking repeated bearings he can progressively adjust his course to changes in these uncontrollable forces so that his goal is achieved.

What is important for us in the image is the notion of repeated measurements to check on progress, as well as a clear cognizance of some ultimate goal. The former is the hallmark of social indicators proposals, and the setting of long-range social goals has become an increasing preoccupation of the federal government.[4] Furthermore, although it remains only implicit in the image, the helmsman must depend not only upon his current bearings and knowledge of the goal in order to set his course, but he must also have a clear understanding of the way to go about setting the course and propelling his craft along it. This is to say that he needs some clear grasp of causal relationships involved among those variables such as the angle of the tiller or the fullness of the sails that he can expect to control, as well as their interaction with forces beyond his control. Such contextual understanding is as critical to the development of proper ad-

[4] See a statement by President Richard M. Nixon on the "Establishment of a National Goals Research Staff," July 13, 1969.

justments in course as is a knowledge of "current bearings." The social indicators movement has been most directly concerned with the establishment of current bearings, and less explicitly with contextual understanding. Nevertheless, it is not difficult to see the accumulation of "bearings" measurements under different conditions over time as a vital ingredient in the development of such understanding, and it is probably by some such route that the helmsman first learned his art.

Purpose of This Volume

This volume has been assembled to play a specific role in the accumulating literature on social indicators. Of the numerous publications devoted to this subject the most significant appear to be the two monographs, *Toward a Social Report* by the Department of Health, Education, and Welfare and *Toward Social Reporting: Next Steps* by Otis Dudley Duncan; and three volumes, *Social Indicators* edited by Raymond Bauer,[5] *Social Intelligence for America's Future* edited by Bertram Gross,[6] and *Indicators of Social Change* edited by Wilbert E. Moore and Eleanor B. Sheldon. Of the three books, the most ambitious is the volume of essays assembled by Moore and Sheldon for Russell Sage Foundation, which attempts to provide an overview of basic indicators in time-series form across a wide range of domains important in the nation's development and life. Each expert commissioned to cover a particular domain attempted to provide a critical review of central time-series material already available, and to suggest points at which to improve existing series and to initiate urgently needed measurements. The focus of the volume is on basic properties and parameters of the economic and social structure of the nation; although some variation exists from chapter to chapter, attention is largely restricted to consideration of the types of information assembled by the federal government in connection with its census activities or its many other social and economic programs. This means in turn that the bulk of the volume is dedicated to what is sometimes regarded as "hard" data: housing starts, numbers of pupils processed through various levels of the education system, morbidity rates, rates of poverty, consumption patterns, population trends, distribution of the labor force.

Among major lessons that might be drawn from *Indicators of Social Change* is the fact that not only are many obviously important types of measurement utterly missing, but many of those more or less fragmentary time series concerning the nation's structure and welfare that do exist are crude and ambiguous for most of the interpretive purposes required by intelligent policy formation. Often these series are downright misleading, as may well be the case in

[5] R. A. Bauer, *Social Indicators.* MIT Press, Cambridge, 1966.

[6] B. M. Gross, *Social Intelligence for America's Future.* Allyn and Bacon, Boston, 1969.

long-term assessments of national crime rates. Frequently it can be shown that subtle changes have occurred over time in the modes or intensity of measurement in ways that vitally affect the behavior of apparent trends. In short, upon close examination, their validity tends to be unsettlingly limited.

One difficulty is that in most of the domains only a handful of measurements with any longitudinal depth is available, and these are subjected to a severe interpretive overload. Some suffer fundamental flaws in validity or reliability; but most of those that are relatively free of problems, and can be said to measure what they claim to measure, cannot be said to measure very much. Nevertheless, since they are all we have, an absurd range of inferences has been squeezed from them. Annual statements of gross national product do indeed say something about the state of the economy, or at least some of the more significant portions thereof. But most economists would agree that these figures tend to be wildly overinterpreted; they are much better than nothing, but it would be patently foolish to try to hinge a nation's economic planning on this single time series.

There is, of course, much to be said for tightening the validity of many measures on which we now depend. However, one of the classic ways to upgrade both reliability and validity is to broaden and proliferate the measurement base. As concurrent measurements are drawn of more and more interrelated variates within a particular domain, one begins to achieve a kind of clarification and specification of meaning closely akin to what Campbell and Fiske have discussed under the heading of the "multi-trait, multi-method" approach to problems of validity and reliability in psychological measurement.[7] This kind of triangulation is the surest cure for overinterpretation of any single measure taken alone, and represents a giant step toward the development of those causal insights that are necessary for any intelligent "steering" of the society.

The present volume was commissioned by Russell Sage Foundation as a companion piece to *Indicators of Social Change.* In some degree it is concerned with proliferations of measurement in various domains of the type which explicates and triangulates. But its main focus is upon a *special class* of such indicators that were largely bypassed by design in the original volume. Whereas the parent volume was concerned with various kinds of hard data, typically sociostructural, this book is devoted chiefly to so-called softer data of a more social-psychological sort: the attitudes, expectations, aspirations, and values of the American population.

Obviously, this emphasis is not intended to be competitive with that of the first volume, but in a very vital sense complementary to it. Indeed, it is for this reason that many of the broad structural trends under discussion in the first vol-

---

[7] D. T. Campbell and D. W. Fiske, "Convergent and Discriminant Validation by the Multi-Trait, Multi-Method Matrix," *Psychological Bulletin,* vol. 56, 1959, pp. 81–105.

ume will be subject to frequent reference here, because we are intensely interested in what sense people make of them, as well as the way these changes shape and determine the fine grain of human lives and gratification: in sum, the *human meaning* that these changes may be said to have.

We see it as imperative to maintain and greatly expand the kinds of measurements at issue in the first volume, but it is our conviction that they will achieve their greatest significance, both theoretically and at the practical policy level, only when supplemented by parallel series of the more subjective information to be considered here. The argument can be made in a variety of ways. Let us proceed first by example.

It has been apparent for several decades that the rate of divorce has been showing a rapid increase in modern industrial societies, including the United States. Attempts to estimate exact rates of family dissolution are flawed by such things as common-law marriage, *de facto* separations, and other intrusions on routine social bookkeeping that often differ systematically by social class and probably have varied in their prevalence over time as well. Still, the brute fact of increased divorce is in little dispute and seems, on the face of the matter, a very significant one.

The meaning of divorce for the growing numbers of people involved—children as well as spouses—has been left largely to speculation and dispute, however. For some time sociologists tended to view the trend with general alarm, taking for granted that it tokened a dangerous level of breakdown in family life, reflecting misery of the participants and undermining the fundamentals of child socialization. Later, other observers suggested that increased ease of divorce and its greater social acceptance might well mean that many people who otherwise would be locked into thoroughly corrosive marriages could now escape them and find some better arrangement, and indeed it could be shown that the rate of remarriage was substantial. What is important for our purposes is that the impressive change in rates, while a critical datum in itself, can be interpreted in very different ways when questions of human meaning of the change come to be asked. Studies have been made of people emerging from divorce, the effects of broken homes on children, and other aspects of divorce. They have been carried out, however, on haphazard samplings of parochial or specialized populations, and provide little in the way of a long-range or generalizable view of consequences. The few national studies that have attempted to assess human happiness have consistently shown that people who are divorced at the time of the interview indicate they are quite unhappy, and statistics linking divorce and suicide are well known. To our knowledge, however, none of these studies has ascertained whether the respondents now married had ever been divorced at an earlier point, and hence they are unable to address some of the major differences in interpretation of the meaning of the phenomenon for the quality of the lives involved.

This instance is merely symptomatic of most of our knowledge where large-scale, complex social phenomena are concerned. If we are lucky, we know something of central but skeletal rates; but beyond this point, the door is opened wide to speculation, which occurs in profusion. We know that the face of the nation, and indeed the planet, is being remade by rapid urbanization, yet there is little in the way of systematic information on historically significant populations as to the balance of perceived attractions and liabilities that the city represents, or the kinds of gratifications and frustrations that are experienced by its actual residents. Students of occupation structure in the United States are well aware of increased numbers of women flowing into various niches in the active labor force, but the motives involved or the social-psychological consequences of such change on the women, their families, and their work groups have largely been left to more casual surmise, often in quite contradictory veins, according to the prejudices of the observer. This volume contains a range of other examples in which crude "behavioral" rates are known, but little more.

In addition, there are numerous fragments of social speculation that have attracted wide attention since their suggestion, which feature social-psychological states or tendencies as their central terms, and are only indirectly addressed at best to any "harder" behavioral rates. Karl Marx's expectation of increasing alienation of the working class is one of the more famous of these. David Reisman's hypothesis of a shift from an inner-directed to an other-directed modal personality type is another. Further examples are yielded by such theories as those that attempt to link social comparison processes and the sense of relative deprivation with recent epidemics of civil disorder. In all of these cases variations in the central social-psychological terms are presumed to influence a variety of the "harder" behavioral rates in relevant domains; indeed, this is why the theories are important. Yet it is surely a weak procedure to scan the skies for changes in the behavioral rates thought to be affected, without giving any attention to measurement of change in the social-psychological terms themselves which, after all, can also be assessed and summarized in the form of rates.

It can plausibly be argued, moreover, that it will be more important in the future to understand actors' images, or psychological definitions of complex social situations, than it may have been in the past. We have entered an era of rapidly expanding choice on the part of the individual about matters that are vital to him but which are of prime collective importance as well. In the late eighteenth century, Thomas Malthus generated a theory of population change based on a knowledge of some bare vital statistics, consideration of various external constraints, and a substantial structure of supposition.[8] The Malthus theory now seems primitive and at some points clearly wrong, including its inattention to a number of rudimentary forms of collective family-planning and

---

[8] Thomas Malthus, *An Essay in the Principle of Population,* 1798.

population-control mechanisms of even the dim past. Yet, as a first rough approximation, it had some virtue in accounting for population balances over the bulk of human history. However, there can be no denying that the ease with which families are "planned," and the prevalence of such careful and conscious choice practices, has increased enormously over the past century, rendering Malthus increasingly irrelevant. Moreover, the advent of such expanded choice has stirred a lively interest among demographers as to the social and psychological definitions and preference hierarchies that underlie these family-size choices.

The scope of individual choice seems to have burgeoned in a surprising number of domains over the past few centuries, including choice of political leaders, place of residence, marriage partner, family size, forms of leisure-time activity, consumer durables, and vacation sites. It is likely to continue to increase, with the choice of sex or genetic characteristics of one's children being merely among the more dramatic examples. And wherever individual definitions and preferences are key mediating terms between environmental givens and behavioral choice, we must learn more about them in a systematic way, monitoring their unexpected changes while developing more capacious theories.

We generally know very little about the detailed interplay between objective situations and the way people assess them subjectively, if the situations involved display much complexity at all. This fact can itself be put forward as a further argument for fresh study of this interplay. Such an argument would have little force if, as some thinkers have presumed, these subjective states are epiphenomenal, with behavior completely predictable given sufficient knowledge of the objective situations that underlie it. Recent social history has done little to reinforce this kind of philosophical position, however. We have become deeply impressed at the degree to which subjective states can "pull apart" from what might be deduced on the basis of our current ways of understanding objective situations.

For example, it seems on one hand that the species is remarkably adaptable to whatever objective situations present themselves. Mercifully, perhaps, people are often quite unaware of what, from a broader historical perspective, they may be lacking. Although the truth can never be known, it seems likely that people in earlier eras, when life was quite "nasty, brutish and short," found tolerable levels of contentment and sources of gratification, and would be astonished to know that other people, socialized into the expectations of later times, might consider their existence little better than a living death. On the other hand, man is not so locked into circumstances but that he can display bitter discontentment with objective situations that, by any retrospective standards, are overflowing with abundance. Both the fact of dislocation between the subjective and the objective, as well as the towering social importance of such dislocations, has been well illustrated in recent decades by the "revolution of rising expectations." Discontentment with objective conditions has appeared to be increasing over exactly the same period that those conditions have at most points and by almost all criteria been improving, a discrepancy with portentous social and political implications.

To imagine that these subjective reactions could in principle be predicted from sufficiently sophisticated and detailed knowledge of patterns of objective conditions remains a tenable philosophical position. But the frequency with which these apparent dislocations occur should warn us that we are very far from possessing that knowledge at this time. And while we might ignore subjective states on principle, trying to piece together patterns of objective conditions in ways that become more reliably intelligible, there seems little point in doing so. Surely it is a short cut to study these subjective states more directly, with particular emphasis on how they interact with changes in objective circumstance. It is this latter interest that links this volume most firmly with the concerns of the preceding one.

Finally, the importance of understanding social-psychological perceptions and evaluations can scarcely be denied if we consider how closely they are interwoven with the cybernetic vision of the purposively guided society. The helmsman must have a goal, current bearings, and a contextual understanding of the forces about him. In varying degree, all three involve these subjective states.

For the social indicators movement, "current bearings" are often assumed to be constituted of no more than updated knowledge of various skeletal rates of the "hard" variety. However, we have argued above that they should include some direct monitoring of key social-psychological states of the population as well. We trust that the remainder of this volume lends weight to this insistence. Social-psychological terms are equally important in forming the firm contextual understanding needed if social phenomena are to be manipulated intelligently. Perceptions of complex social situations, as well as the expectations, hopes, and frustrations of the participants facing them, constitute the classic "intervening variables" so vital in explicating behavioral correlations that otherwise are often perplexing or ambiguous. Subjective data are basic in selecting between rival diagnoses that would lead to quite different practical prescriptions as to how any specific goal might be attained.

Finally, the goal of the helmsman itself must, in its early stages, be no more than a psychological image. Here there are basic questions as to how such goals are formed in the mind. There are also basic questions as to who forms them and for whom. In some few instances these questions may not be urgent because there is little controversy about the narrowly defined goals involved: most people would, for example, see increased health and education as unquestionable values. In many instances, however, the case is less clear and the questions cannot be sidestepped.

In one extreme model, the helmsman formulating the goals is a leadership elite, and in the other, the "public" in general. Both extremes can be made quite unpalatable. The first smacks of paternalism, and because of the uncertain relation between objective conditions and subjective states, poses the specter of an elite which grandly misreads the needs and aspirations of the population at large. But the democratic mode, if pushed to its populist extreme, runs aground on a parallel reef, already mentioned: people are often unaware of alternatives that they might find highly attractive and fulfilling on closer view, and elites are more likely to have some grasp of the range of possibilities. Clearly some mixed model is required. However, it is hard to imagine any enlightened mixed model that fails to provide leadership with a much more specific and current view of the distribution of aspirations in the public than has been technologically feasible in the past. To stop short of this kind of input information is to court the kind of current impasse, where the provision of greater and greater abundance of material goods seems to some increasingly irrelevant. What we must recognize is that the overarching new goal of higher "quality of life" is a more intensely psychological destination than the real-world helmsman has ever tried to find.

With all these considerations in mind, we have risked entitling this volume *The Human Meaning of Social Change,* despite the fact that the reader will not find in these pages any direct expository discourse on so broad a topic, but instead a series of essays largely devoted to some of the kinds of measurement not now being carried out that could begin in the future to shed much more light on the subject. It is this focus on human meaning that most clearly distinguishes this volume from its predecessor. We are interested in human meaning from at least two prime points of view. First, we are interested in the human meaning which human beings attribute to the complex and multifarious social environment in which they find themselves enmeshed: their communities; their lives at work and leisure; their understandings of group relations, the political process, and the consumer economy in which they participate; and so on. Second, we are interested in the impact that the various alternatives offered by the environment have on the nature of their lives, and the fulfillment of those lives. Throughout, we are concerned with the significance that broad-scale changes in those alternatives have for them—the meaning such changes have *to* them, on the one hand, and *for* them, on the other.

For the purposes of this volume, then, we are willing to imagine that the ultimate unit of meaning for all social structure, economic organization, technological development, and policy is the individual as the consumer in the largest sense of the word. This is not to deny for a moment the awesome reality of collective interrelationships, or the momentum and autonomy from individual concerns that so frequently seem to characterize the ponderous superstructures of the various social orders. But it is to say that if we seek a yardstick which might be brought to bear to gauge large-scale collective performance in any of these domains, it is likely to involve large sets of individuals in the final analysis. The good helmsman is one who strives to maximize individual fulfillment within the constraints of available resources.

Overview of the Book

In bringing together this collection of essays we aspired to set forth an inclusive statement of the most significant dimensions of psychological change, a review of the state of our present information regarding them, and a projection of the measurements needed to improve our understanding of these changes in the future. We assume that the changes with which we are concerned come about as the result either of changes in people or of changes in the environment within which people find themselves. Thus Negro agitation for civil rights is preceded by a lifting of Negro aspiration levels; the aspiration levels have been lifted by changes in federal law which promise greater equality in civil rights. Behavior change follows attitudinal change which has been brought about by changes in the environment. It is in the psychological situation, the nexus of the individual and his environment, that we look for the explanation of psychological change.

Of course every individual lives in many environments, each with its distinctive cluster of roles. As a citizen he responds to a world of legal and political demands and restraints; as a father he is moved by special duties, rewards, and hazards of parenthood; as a worker he reacts to a totally different set of circumstances. This division of an individual's world into major areas suggested a congenial mode of organization for the core of the volume, since it is the basis on which most of the data with which we will be concerned are organized, and provides no little parallelism with the companion Russell Sage Foundation volume on structural change.[9] While the number of such major life areas to be considered is somewhat arbitrary, we proposed to limit it to eight and the volume in fact includes seven.

Whereas these seven areas form the bulk of the volume, we were equally interested in developing initial and terminal sections intimately related to this core, but crosscutting it in at least a logical sense. In addition to an introductory chapter, we wished to consider the way in which the individual distributes his attention across life areas, particularly as represented in the way he allocates his time. Second, since it is well known that involvement in various life areas, as well as the roles played within them, vary dramatically for individuals as a function of their position in the life cycle, we wanted to devote a third chapter to

[9] Indeed, one domain that would have been highly appropriate to this volume—religious values and perceptions in the population—was set aside because it had been so well covered in these terms in the preceding volume. See N. V. Demerath, III, "Trends and Anti-Trends in Religious Change," Chap. 8 in Moore and Sheldon, *op. cit.*

systematic psychological changes associated with this temporal variable of great structural significance.

This prefatory section leads in a natural way to a consideration of the various life areas taken separately, over the central portion of the book. However, we also envisioned a closing section of the volume drawing together a few of the psychological themes most recurrent in the core of the book. The status of this section is interesting, for the organization around social-psychological themes is what one might expect of a full volume of this type at some future time when a wider range of data would hopefully be available. For now, the closing section is limited to the development of two such themes at chapter length, chosen on the grounds of richness of information in hand, frequency of use in the rest of the volume, and ultimate conceptual importance.

As the reader will discover, the book does not contain all the chapters we had projected. Either because of failure to find a qualified author or the inability of overburdened authors to complete their assignments, there are obvious lacunae in the total presentation. Of the two chapters we had planned for the first section, we have only one, "Social Change Reflected in the Use of Time." This chapter, written primarily by John P. Robinson, is concerned not only with the ways in which people use their 24 hours each day but with the meaning these activities have for them—their motive-serving, their replaceability, their satisfaction-giving. The difficulties of establishing time series are well illustrated in Robinson's review of the scattering of studies of time use, based on differing populations, methods of recording, and definitions of terms. Fortunately the 1966 national study of time use (Converse and Robinson) described in this chapter will now serve as a substantial baseline for subsequent measurement.

The chapter we had projected on "The Impact of Social Change Through the Life Cycle" is missing. This is a serious loss since there is little doubt that social change has different meaning to people at different ages. There are occasional references to age differences throughout the following chapters but we are not able to present a systematic statement of how change influences experience in the various areas of the life-space for people at different stages of the life cycle.

In Chapter 3, the first chapter devoted to specific areas of social life, Peter H. Rossi discusses the difficult concept of community. Rejecting more global definitions of the term, he chooses to speak of the residential locality, with its solidarity (the identification of the residents with the locality), its integration (the extent to which the residents are linked by ties of exchange), and its political autonomy (its ability to make collective decisions which are binding on the residents). Rossi reviews the various ways in which the quality of a residential locality may be assessed and suggests an ordering of priorities of social indicators to provide measurements of change in such communities.

Chapter 4 was written by Marvin B. Sussman and is entitled "Family, Kinship, and Bureaucracy." Dr. Sussman describes the functions of the family and the kinship network, especially in their linkage with the bureaucratic systems with which the family members must deal. He proposes research on the effect on the family of the developing value of "personal happiness," on the changing roles of husbands and wives with the increasing employment of women, and on the experimental family forms which have sprung up as part of the "counterculture." It was our original hope that this chapter would be accompanied by an essay on childhood but this turned out to be our second casualty. In view of the current concern about changing values and behavior in the preadult generation, this is a loss which we were regrettably unable to replace.

In Chapter 5, Robert L. Kahn considers the meaning of work, the area of life which has perhaps been subjected to more empirical study than any other. Dr. Kahn discusses the inadequacies of this extensive body of research, its difficulties in definition, its scatteration of methods and, in particular, its failure to establish trend lines. In proposing the development of indicators of the personal strains and rewards of the work life he suggests that the evaluation of work may be shifting from an almost exclusive interest in the contribution of work to economic production to a growing concern with its psychological consequences for the worker.

The chapter on work is followed by Rolf Meyersohn's essay on leisure, which is Chapter 6. The study of leisure, like most of the areas of experience treated in this book, suffers from a failure of systematic accumulation of research evidence. Although in Dr. Meyersohn's discussion the essential distinction between leisure and "free time" lies in the meaning of the leisure experience, in the ability of leisure to provide human satisfactions, the bulk of the available research is limited to counts of the activities which fill the individual's free time. Dr. Meyersohn proposes a redirection of emphasis toward a concern with the experienced quality of leisure rather than with its content and duration.

In Chapter 7, George Katona discusses the human factor in economic affairs. Dr. Katona's research over the past 25 years provides an impressive illustration of a continuing study of the interrelationships between structural changes and individual response. The great increase since the Second World War in the proportion of the population with "discretionary income" has led to rising aspirations and changing patterns of behavior. Consumers, who were taken for granted by an earlier school of economics, now contribute an important influence on the course of the nation's economy. Dr. Katona reviews research findings regarding the nature of change in economic attitudes and behavior and urges the integration of these data with other social indicators.

The participation of the American population in democratic politics is one of the rare areas outside of economic affairs that has left any long-term quantitative record in the country's annals. Fairly complete aggregate voting statistics are extant for all but the beginnings of national history. In addition, a periodic monitoring of the electorate through sample surveys has greatly enriched this record for the past 20 or 30 years. In Chapter 8, we consider aspects of both phases of this record for the light they may shed on important trends in the nature of the democratic response to government. For the deeper historical period, we focus on a cluster of major changes in the character of voting statistics which co-occurred around the turn of this century, and consider the severe problems of interpretation that the skeletal record taken alone seems to pose. We then summarize some of the insights provided by survey research evidence concerning a few of the most imposing recent changes in the nature of the electorate, including the political mobilization of the black population, the erosion of the Solid South, the educational upgrading of the electorate, and the increase in political alienation of the late 1960's.

Chapter 9 deals with the complexities of change in the social and psychological characteristics of that part of the population which is Negro. Although over the years there have been thousands of titles published on the subject of race relations in this country, social science has failed to provide the systematic monitoring of change in the social psychology of American Negroes which the importance of the problem would appear to justify. Herbert H. Hyman has reviewed those fragments of data that are available and outlined the kinds of dimensions on which measurement should be periodically taken. These include aspiration levels, sense of deprivation, feelings of hate and distrust, specific grievances and dissatisfactions, expectations and preferences regarding integration and separatism. Hyman urges the special study of influentials as well as of the general public and the comparative analysis of age cohorts as an indicator of change.

Chapter 10 is concerned with the phenomenon of criminal activity and its relationship to the quality of life. Albert J. Reiss, Jr., reviews an extensive literature describing the institutions of public order, the services they perform, the behavior of public officials performing the service, and the responses of those who are served. This literature has the same shortcomings as we have seen in other chapters of this volume and Dr. Reiss outlines the major features of the criminal justice systems which deserve more disciplined investigation than they have received. He would concentrate immediate research effort into continuing assessment of victimization by crime, the quality of discretionary authority and service for citizens, and the accountability of public servants.

As we indicated at an earlier point in this introduction, we proposed to close this volume with a set of chapters that would have expanded on major themes that recurred in the central section of the book. Two such chapters are presented. The first of these, entitled "Aspiration, Satisfaction, and Fulfillment," concerns itself with the concept of quality of life, emphasizing the subjective experience of life rather than the objective conditions in which people live. Utilizing Abraham Maslow's well-known theory of hierarchy of needs, the chapter undertakes to lay out a program of measurements that would provide indicators of the extent to which people find their lives to be stimulating, rewarding, and fulfilling. These psychological indicators are considered to be an essential accompaniment to the more conventional social indicators as the basis of assessing the nature of change in the nation's well-being.

The final chapter, written by Melvin Seeman, discusses the critical problem of alienation. Alienation is a term to which a variety of meanings have been attributed and a human condition which is held accountable for a great many social ills. Dr. Seeman stresses the necessity of specific definition of the distinguishable components of alienation and develops the construction of the concept which has grown out of his own research. Although he does not believe these indicators of alienation are sufficiently well developed at present to serve in a comprehensive system of social accounting, he indicates the kinds of improvement in measuring techniques and study design that are needed and suggests a program of research on the patterns and the consequences of alienation.

Conclusions

It will be apparent to the reader that this volume does not fully attain its rather pretentious aspirations. While it concerns itself with numerous significant dimensions of psychological change, it has obviously omitted various others. These failures are regrettable and the book would have been a more satisfying statement if we had been able to overcome them. We do not believe, however, that additional chapters are needed to demonstrate what is surely the central message of this book, that there has been very little systematic accounting of the meaning which recent social changes have had for the people of this country. We have been far more vigilant about monitoring changes in the objective conditions of life than in the subjective experience of life.

Despite the extraordinary growth of the behavioral sciences in this country since the Second World War, there are few examples to be found of continuing programs of research devoted to repeated measurements of the psychological characteristics of the American people. Such data are not produced in the ordinary routines of governmental accounting which make available such voluminous records of large-scale structural changes in society. Our two chapters on changes in economic and political expectations and attitudes draw heavily from research conducted over the past 20 years at the Survey Research Center but these two programs are virtually *sui generis* in their national scope, their continuity in design and methods, the frequency of their measurements, and the length of time they have continued. As the reader will observe, in most of the chapters of this book the authors have struggled to find coherence in data gathered from a variety of different populations, based on measuring instruments of all kinds, and seldom graced by any disciplined replication over time. It is not surprising that their proposals for research to be undertaken far exceed in scope and programmatic character the actual research which they are able to report.

If this country is to move seriously toward the establishment of a program of psychological indicators of the kind our authors suggest there will clearly have to be a major commitment of resources and energy. No doubt some set of priorities could be agreed upon so that the more important series of measurements would be given precedence, but eventually the program would require a level of support that the behavioral sciences do not at present receive. We believe that in due course this support will be forthcoming. As a nation we have long since decided that our system of economic accounting is worth paying for; we are now moving strongly toward a program of social indicators and an annual social report. As we increasingly come to realize that these measures do not tell us all we need to know about changes in the quality of American life, we will inevitably have to develop the kinds of psychological measurements which the contributors to this volume prescribe.

2

Social Change Reflected in the Use of Time

John P. Robinson and Philip E. Converse

How human beings allocate their time in daily life has been a matter of recurrent fascination for observers of society. Questions surrounding the interplay of labor and leisure were of frequent concern for the ancients. As an empirical social science emerged a century ago, the collection of family financial budgets was among the first forms of systematic social research on a mass scale, and with only some lag, interest broadened to include how time as well as money was expended.[1] Yet this interest has been sporadic, particularly in the West, and in 1962 a panel of distinguished social scientists, commissioned by the President's Scientific Advisory Commission to assess information needs of the behavioral sciences, noted that "there are many significant aspects of behavior about which systematic data are almost completely lacking. We know something of how people spend their money, but almost nothing of how they spend their time. . . ."[2]

The scattered nature of this interest in time use springs from a number of rather obvious attractions of such information along with a set of somewhat less evident limitations. On the face of it, the way time as a resource is used would seem to give the theorist a unique view of the intersection between the imperatives of the human condition and the range of individual choice. Much of the 24-hour day that contains all human experience is tightly constrained by the physiology of the species and the impress of the immediate economic environ-

---

[1] A useful summary of these developments is provided in Alexander Szalai, "Trends in Comparative Time Budget Research," *American Behavioral Scientist*, vol. 9, May, 1966, pp. 3–8.

[2] Behavioral Sciences Subpanel of the President's Scientific Advisory Committee, "Strengthening the Behavioral Sciences," *Science*, vol. 136, April 20, 1962, p. 239.

ment. The details of these limits are of interest in themselves. Yet, in addition, margins of discretionary time remain in the daily round for most men of most eras, and here the patterns of allocation can be taken to reflect the differentiation of individual tastes, values, and life styles.

Even in a static sense, moreover, exhaustive catalogues of what individuals do over a fixed period of time appear to bring the analyst face to face with the individual as a totality. The study of economics focuses on the small fractions of daily existence in which man behaves as an economic animal in the narrow sense of the word; the study of politics examines those relatively rare moments in which he relates himself to the political system; various sociological specialties are concerned with their respective clusters of the social roles through which he moves from hour to hour. Another capital attraction of time-budget studies for the theorist, then, has been the promise of putting these fragments of experience back together again in their realistic composite.

These expectations, demonstrably exaggerated, have contributed in the past to disappointment and lapses of theoretical interest. Attempts to deal with the human being as totality have tended to mean an inadvertent superficiality of treatment across the myriad of parts, particularly at the measurement and analysis stages. Moreover, empirical quantities in time-budget tabulations take on full meaning only as they are related to conceptual developments in much narrower subdisciplines. Hence, time-use information, when gathered at all, has served most obviously the function of "substrate data," a backdrop or reference library of momentary interest to a great variety of more specialized interests ranging from welfare economists to population demographers, engineers of transportation systems, sociologists of the family, market analysts, and civil defense administrators.

This is, of course, no mean function. Indeed, the multifarious practical utility of time-budget statistics undoubtedly accounts for the fact, so startling to Western sociologists, that this type of investigation has been and is enjoying a central position and relative continuity of development in the empirical social research of the socialist countries. In the Eastern setting, such research is more directly motivated by the immediate exigencies of large-scale social planning. For the administrator or social engineer, time budgets can make clear who is where, when, and under what circumstances. They give a kind of time-and-motion study writ large that may be indispensable in the planning of collective facilities and the formation of policies affecting social and industrial organization.

Szalai has presented several examples of the utility of time-budget research in economic planning in the East.[3] One study is of double interest to us, as it is the prime example of historical comparison of data on time use from different eras, reflecting social change. In 1959, Prudensky replicated a time-budget study

---

[3] Szalai, *op. cit.,* p. 4.

carried out in 1924 by Strumilin among Soviet urban workers. The data showed that, despite a shorter workweek and the freeing of Russian women of almost an hour of housework over the intervening 35 years, the amount of discretionary "leisure" time had increased only slightly among women and had actually declined for men. The decreases in work and housework time had been absorbed by marked increases in the amount of time spent waiting in queues and shopping, as well as traveling to and from work. Findings of this sort contributed to Soviet alarm over the efficiency of the distribution system, a concern that has generated various remedial efforts at the policy level. Similarly, estimates based on time-budget studies of some 100 billion annual man-hours going into primitive household work in the Soviet Union, a significant fraction of which could be regained by production of work-saving consumer durables, have constituted another potent input to national economic planning.

Although we in the United States are less well equipped with long-term empirical data for comparisons, the rejuvenation of sociological interest in trends and processes of social change has been accompanied by a resurgence of interest in the interplay between time and social change.[4] Of course, detailed information on the use of time by individuals constitutes but one aspect of this more general concern, as Heirich has elaborated.[5] Yet the theoretical attractions of time budgets, statistically drawn as a single "slice of life," are compounded when one imagines rigorously comparable data through repeated measurement over longer periods. Physiological needs vary only within narrow limits for an aggregate. But other types of time allocation should be responsive to changes both in the social and economic environment and in specific tastes and values. One would expect to see reflected in time use the upthrust of major technological innovations showing broad diffusion, such as the automobile, radio and television, or even running water and central heating. Broad changes in the structure of society, for example, the progression of women into the active labor force or the movement of populations from farm to city, should be chronicled with some sensitivity by collective displacements in time budgets. Although we do not have to look to time budgets to know that such changes have occurred, it can be argued that the impact of these changes on daily time allocations is one way of bringing us a step closer to the understanding of their

---

[4] Among excellent recent treatments are Wilbert Moore, *Man, Time and Society*. Wiley, New York, 1963; Max Heirich, "The Use of Time in the Study of Social Change," *American Sociological Review*, vol. 29, June, 1964, pp. 386–397; Robert MacIver, *The Challenge of the Passing Years: My Encounter with Time*. Simon & Schuster, New York, 1962; Wilbert Moore, *Social Change*. Prentice-Hall, Englewood Cliffs, N.J., 1965, Chap. 2; Carle Zimmerman, "No Time for Sociology—a Review Study," *Social Science*, vol. 42, April, 1967, pp. 88–93.

[5] Heirich, *op. cit.*, lists four other aspects of time use that would be of prime interest to social theorists: time in its social meaning, time as a causal link in the explanation of change, time as a measure of quantitative relationships, and time as a qualitative measure of change.

human meaning. And other kinds of more subtle change in sentiments and values—attention to religious practice, for example, or dependence on family interaction—may quite possibly be detected as readily and reliably by time-use information as by any other means. In a still longer run, analysis of the currents of response and nonresponse to various types of environmental changes in time budgets may etch more clearly the pattern of plasticities and constant needs in the human make-up.

All these are at the moment unfulfilled aspirations. They may well encounter disillusionment in the future, and probably would if time-budget information were limited to the type collected a generation ago. But there is room to believe that some of the skeletal quality of older time-budget work derived from mechanical and conventional limitations that are no longer problematic. Certainly the richness of information gathered on the nature of activities engaged in by respondents is on the increase. Instead of a bare set of a dozen or so gross activities such as sleeping, eating, working, and reading captured in the past, it is becoming customary to proliferate the number of activities discriminated and to fill in such further information as locus of the activity, social partners involved, concurrent secondary activities, and the like. In some instances, efforts are made to monitor even such things as the content of communications and aspects of the psychological meaning of the transaction for the actor. Many of these elaborations would be wasted without new facilities for data analysis. In an earlier period, even the compiling of average durations of a modest array of activities for a few gross subgroups was tedious, and more elegant statistical manipulations were out of the question. The advent of the computer has opened remarkable new horizons for the content analysis of activities, as well as for the reduction of data masses in fresh ways which are only now coming to be explored. Therefore, it would be rash to restrict the expected significance of time-budget information to some meager role as a grab bag of primitive parameters, solely on the basis of the limited insights yielded by the method in the past.

Later in this chapter we shall consider the range of enrichments of time-use information that seem conceptually important to cultivate on a more systematic basis in the future. The first order of business, however, is to examine some of the common obstacles to the assessment of even the simplest facts of time allocation in large aggregates and, in particular, those obstacles that have tended to make historical comparisons difficult. For with time use, as with so many other domains treated in these volumes, there is much reason for dissatisfaction with the reliability and meaningfulness of many past efforts at study. Wilensky[6] and de Grazia[7] have recently provided stimulating efforts to reconstruct some of the more vital changes in the human condition over the past mil-

[6] Harold Wilensky, "The Uneven Distribution of Leisure: The Impact of Economic Growth on 'Free Time,' " *Social Problems,* vol. 9, Summer, 1961, pp. 32–56.
[7] Sebastian de Grazia, *Of Time, Work, and Leisure.* Twentieth Century Fund, New York, 1962.

lennium, with strong focus on time allocation as a major indicator. Yet it is depressing to see the amount of scholarly talent consumed in the drudgery of estimating merely the gross and central balance between labor and leisure for even the most recent decades, given the abysmal incomparabilities and fragmentation of the records available.

Any attempt to work out solid comparisons between current information and studies from earlier periods remains by far the most effective way to become sensitized to the standardization needs of the future, however. In the following section we depend upon our experience in this regard to survey common obstacles to reliability and comparability. Although many of the precautions we cite seem embarrassingly obvious, few among them have not at one time or another escaped the attention of the fine minds of yesteryear.

This section on methodological problems serves as a set of caveats for the ensuing section where we turn to a review of the few major substantive trends in time use in the United States over the past few decades that seem to stand out above the general noise level imposed by methodological ambiguities. Finally, we consider some of the more elaborated ways of dealing empirically with time use from the perspective of greatest interest for the study of social change.

Problems of Measurement and Comparability in Past Studies

In view of the fact that the gathering of data on allocations of time to various activities is a relatively old empirical preoccupation, at least as compared with most forms of social research beyond the vital statistics of government censuses, we should be able to probe more deeply into the historical record with these indicators than with many other types. Yet, despite considerable amounts of such work even in the United States, systematic material from the past presents an incredibly mixed bag with respect to modes of data elicitation, tactics of sampling, and categorization of activities. The vast majority of these studies in retrospect seem haphazardly executed and/or confined to relatively narrow classes of activities (like housework, or industrial time-and-motion studies) or specialized samples (farmers, students, executives, rural housewives). Although, on occasion, these studies yield suggestive estimates, the marginal returns from their close examination tend to be low. At best, perhaps a half-dozen studies scattered over the past 35 years were sufficiently rigorous and multipurpose in nature to be of much interest, and even here methodological defects and incomparabilities abound. In virtually all instances, the coded data as well as the raw protocols have disappeared, so that the flexibility of secondary analysis to tighten comparisons must be foregone, leaving us dependent on whatever summary tabulations may have been printed at the time. What was perhaps the most useful study of the 1930's, conducted by Robert Merton, was never reported, and no trace is left save the knowledge it was carried out.

Modes of Data Elicitation. A certain number of studies make no attempt to pin down detailed quantitative estimates of time use. Instead, they focus on the incidence of selected activities reported by the respondent for some extended time period, such as the regularity of church attendance or the frequency with which he has attended movies over the preceding year. Such data are not without interest and can in their own terms afford useful historical comparisons. Nevertheless, information of this kind is limited to certain forms of relatively salient, unusual, and temporally "chunked" activities. Such an approach may thus be ideal for ascertaining in a gross way the disposition of an annual vacation or the nature of infrequent trips away from home, and can be a useful complement to a more detailed and focused time-budget schedule. But for less salient activities, frequent but irregularly spaced in time, distortions of recall accumulate rapidly. Moreover, the most natural colloquial expressions of frequency ("much of the time," "several times a year") are characteristically vague, yet various enough that no pair of investigations without deliberate coordination is likely to have chosen exactly the same response categories.

All told, studies of this type yield an extremely limited contribution to our immediate interests. We have done some experimentation with comparisons of information derived by these methods and evidence of activity incidence from more conventional time-budget material. Where the two data bases can be compared at all, mild discrepancies in inference are frequent, and upon occasion become blatant. If particular activities show marked seasonality and the time budgets provide an inadequate sampling across seasons, the retrospective estimates of incidence are obviously more accurate, suggesting again their use as complements to time budgets. But for most purposes it is reasonable to assume that the time budgets themselves, if properly gathered, are the more reliable source.[8]

Therefore, for comparative purposes we can make specific reference to a single "frequency" study, one brought to light by de Grazia.[9] Conducted by the Opinion Research Corporation (ORC) in the early summer of 1957, i warrants sustained attention primarily because it is one of the few time-use studies on a national sample, and because it focuses not on long-term recall of participation, but rather on activities done "yesterday." A national probability sample of 5,000 persons over 15 years of age was given a check list of 20 activities and then was asked which of these they had engaged in on the day prior to the interview.

Within the domain of more ambitious studies that aim at some *seriatim* cataloguing of activities and their durations in time, further choices clearly remain open to investigators as to the time span to be covered or sampled, as well as the observation techniques to be used. Broadly speaking, such catalogues or

---

[8] These comments, along with numerous others in this section, rest on work to be more fully reported in a forthcoming monograph on time use in the United States under preparation by the current authors.

[9] de Grazia, *op. cit.,* pp. 460–463.

"time budgets" can be recorded by the subject himself, directly observed by some second party, or elicited by subsequent interview. Where reliability is concerned, direct observation clearly recommends itself, but suffers obvious limitations of practicality and possibilities of contamination. Its only use has been with unrepresentative, small-scale "captive" populations. Interviews, which must refer to some prior period of time, thereby encounter the fundamental problem that memory is remarkably fleeting about specific sequences of events and precise durations. Time budgets elicited by interview tend to be of the "yesterday" type; they attempt to account for the allocation of time over the preceding 24-hour cycle, or over some portion thereof, without pressing recall further. The keeping of time diaries by the subject "on the spot" as events transpire has clear advantages over interview recall. With samples of cross-section populations, however, problems of functional illiteracy, variations in personal compulsiveness about the detail of events captured, and variations in general motivation to cooperate often arise.

The primary studies we shall use for longitudinal comparison are "yesterday" interviews of either the diary or interview type. The most recent study was conducted by the present authors in 1965 and 1966 through the facilities of the Survey Research Center (SRC) of the University of Michigan; it was deliberately planned as a "bench-mark" study for comparative use in future decades. Here an attempt was made to combine the respective advantages of diaries and interviews. Respondents were asked to maintain diaries for a 24-hour period on a simple printed schedule, but demands for detail were kept ·elatively light in order to limit the complexity of the task and maximize cooperation. By prearrangement, the subject was then visited on the ensuing day for a full-scale interview which used the diary as an explicit guide, probing for detail to bring the record up to a relatively standard level and extending the description of activities in various directions, as well as attempting to tap further generalized attitudes toward time and its use.

While the SRC 1965–66 study attempted to cover only a single 24-hour period in the respondents' lives, other major studies of historical interest have often tried to span at least slightly longer periods. Aside from the ORC study in 1957, the next most recent information comes from the large-scale study of time use conducted in 1954 on a national probability sample of 7,000 households by the J. A. Ward Company for the Mutual Broadcasting System. For the purposes of this study, respondents kept diaries over a consecutive two-day period; entries were made for every quarter hour of activity between 6 A.M. and 11 P.M. The early morning hours were not monitored. This study provides what are unquestionably the most solid "historical" reference points for temporal comparisons, and it is extremely unfortunate that neither the data cards nor the original reports have been saved.[10]

[10] Descriptive material from the study survives in de Grazia, *op. cit.*

The only other faintly comparable studies of any magnitude which would give glimpses into earlier periods in the United States are two studies dating from the 1930's. Given the state of the art at the time, neither provides a very adequate population sample; each of the samples were local and haphazardly selected. In 1935, Sorokin and Berger managed to extract almost thirty-five hundred diary days from a meager sample of 176 Bostonians, few of whom were male, employed, or over 30 years of age. The diaries were kept for varying numbers of consecutive days and resumed at sporadic intervals.[11]

The earliest study of much comparative interest was carried out by Lundberg *et al.*[12] between 1931 and 1933 for an "opportunity sample" of some twenty-five hundred respondents in affluent Westchester County, New York. Here again, multiple-day time budgets were collected for various participants. Although some form of diary method was used, Lundberg *et al.* fail to provide important details about their procedures. Far more of this crucial detail is provided by Sorokin and Berger in their extended criticism of the Lundberg *et al.* study. Thus, while Lundberg *et al.* report that "the bulk of [diaries] are for three consecutive days," Sorokin and Berger add that the schedules were for the three days prior to the day the individual was contacted (thus being more vulnerable to memory problems) and that "specific directions were issued to the subjects to select typical weekdays, Saturdays, and Sundays for the listing of activities,"[13] thus leaving in limbo how much relative weight Saturdays and Sundays received in the final tabulations.

In short, although we can draw some few estimates from other narrower studies, we are largely limited to "readings" from 1931 to 1933, 1935, 1954, and 1965 to 1966 for any reasonably precise time allocations of comparative value. However, we have not as yet plumbed some of the other methodological ambiguities even of this set of studies.

Heterogeneity of Activities over Time. Most people have systematic cycles of activity not only in a daily sense, but in terms of weekly and annual rhythms as well. Time budgets covering a full day exhaust the diurnal variation so that it poses no problem; when, as in the J. A. Ward study, some portion of the day is systematically excluded, adequate comparisons might be drawn with the SRC 1965–66 study simply by analytically removing the same slice of time from the 24-hour records.[14]

[11] P. Sorokin and C. Berger, *Time-Budgets of Human Behavior*. Harvard University Press, Cambridge, Mass., 1939. Only individuals who kept records for at least four weeks were included in the published tabulations.

[12] George Lundberg, Mirra Komarovski, and Mary McInerny, *Leisure: A Suburban Study*. Columbia University Press, New York, 1934.

[13] Sorokin and Berger, *op. cit.*, p. 12.

[14] The residual danger, which we shall unfortunately see is a real one, is that change inferences may be biased by systematic shifts in the time of day when the population is engaging in certain activities.

There are, moreover, extreme differences in the way most people spend weekdays as opposed to Saturdays and Sundays, not to mention the smaller (and perhaps declining) differences between various days of the working week. If any attention be given to this part of the problem, it is more of an annoyance than a major methodological barrier. That is, in recent studies care has been taken to stratify the sampling across days of the week; and where these differences are not explicitly controlled in analytic work, any residual variation in the representation of particular days is removed by appropriate weighting of the data. The main inconvenience lies in the fact that for certain detailed purposes the sample must be split into sevenths, rapidly shrinking sample sizes within the control groups.

Unfortunately, a study like Lundberg's shows no cognizance whatever of the problem, and we remain uninformed as to what mix of weekdays and weekends is finally bundled into the published tables. This ambiguity thoroughly undermines any confident interpretation of the data. For example, we will soon note (see Appendix Table A) that the Lundberg materials taken at face value as unbiased representation of days of the week would suggest that sleep occupied almost an hour more per person-day than it did in our urban national sample of 1965–66. Yet our national data also make clear that all groups, particularly the employed, catch up on sleep over the weekend. The national increment for the employed on Sundays is between one and one-and-a-half hours of sleep relative to the weekday average, with Saturday sleep lying between the two. At this point, Sorokin and Berger's criticism of Lundberg *et al.*'s selection of days of the week becomes highly relevant. It is true that the apparent differences in sleep results would only disappear completely if it were assumed that almost all of the Lundberg data were drawn on weekends, and there is internal evidence that this cannot have been the case (e.g., the presence of work durations). The important point is, however, we have no way of knowing what true weights to assign. The figures for leisure and paid work are of course even more closely dependent on the weekday-weekend proportions.

Similar rhythmic variations can be expected by season. These are considerably less strong, however (at least in urban samples), and tend to center in the area of leisure, particularly indoor vs. outdoor forms. Other kinds of variation, such as an upsurge of shopping before Christmas, could readily be anticipated. Only one limited American study has attempted to ascertain the nature of these effects,[15] however, so seasonal factors remain another set of imponder-

[15] Sarah Manning, *Time Use in Household Tasks by Indiana Families.* Purdue University Agricultural Experiment Station Research Bulletin 837, Lafayette, January, 1968. Manning's sample consisted of 111 Indiana families in which the wife was not employed more than 15 hours a week. As implied in the title, the survey devoted its attention to time spent on household tasks by these housewives, a large number of whom belonged to homemakers' clubs. Despite these sampling biases, the focus of the report on seasonal variation

ables in attempting to compare studies from different years. The two national samples that recommend themselves for our closest comparative attention on other grounds (those of 1954 and 1965–66) were interviewed in some of the same months (March and April), but the bulk of 1965–66 interviews were taken between November 15 and December 15. While the monthly distribution of diary days is unknown for the Sorokin-Berger 1935 study, almost half of the period of data collection lay in the summer months. Summer is likely to be the most errant of the four seasons in terms of time use, and none of the other time-budget studies under consideration did field work in that period. With this fact known, such an apparent contrast between the 1935 and the 1965–66 tabulations as a 50 percent diminution in the Sorokin-Berger category "pleasurable activities" must be taken with some grains of salt.

Population Sampling. Although differences in gross patterns of time use between occupational strata are generally less than those within strata between weekdays and weekends, the composition of the respective samples requires scrutiny if one hopes to make any comparative inferences at all. The two studies of the 1930's do not rest on what we would now consider "samples" at all, even with respect to the narrow geographic areas in which they were conducted. This would be of some concern even if the social composition of respondents in each case bore some resemblance to their parent community population. But this is nowhere near the case.

We have already noted that the Sorokin-Berger diaries were largely kept by young women, who were either workers under the Works Progress Administration or were unemployed white-collar workers. The investigators conceived of themselves as addressing certain generic features of human behavior, rather than supplying parameter estimates representative of the period. Thus, the oddity of the "sample" was not considered any notable embarrassment.

Lundberg *et al.* appear far more aware of sampling problems than Sorokin and Berger, apologizing in many places for their haphazard sampling and low response rates. Their materials therefore have a less esoteric base, a universe consisting of Westchester County,[16] just north of New York City. If one wished to think of Westchester County as representative of the nation, it would be a "sample" enormously biased toward education and wealth. In fact, Lundberg

---

constitutes an important breakthrough. Manning generally found little seasonal variation in time devoted to 15 household tasks, except for a large increase in food preservation during the summer months. Washing and meal preparation were also somewhat higher in summer, while marketing, sewing, and mending decreased. Marketing, a term we shall use to differentiate shopping for food as opposed to other forms of shopping, showed dramatic peaks prior to the holidays of Thanksgiving, Christmas, and Easter.

[16] Two-thirds of Lundberg *et al.*'s respondents were high school students, but fortunately their schedules were tabulated separately and hence have been disregarded for the purposes of this paper.

et al. refer to Westchester as "the richest suburb in the world," and also note the unusually high proportion of professionals and business executives residing in the county. There are numerous features of the Lundberg time-use patterns that undoubtedly should be understood in these terms. For example, despite the fact that in 1930 only 40 percent of family units in the United States owned radios, 70 percent of the residents of Westchester did. While ownership rates among their respondents are not given, Lundberg *et al.* note that 60 percent of their diaries include radio-listening entries, a figure about the same as the 1965–66 sample which boasted 99 percent radio ownership. Television has obviously cut into radio use significantly in the interim, but the average time spent listening to the radio, six times as great as in the 1965–66 data, must be adjusted for the extremely unrepresentative ease of access to sets before any comparisons between 1931–33 and 1965–66 become valid.

The 1954 Ward study and our 1965–66 SRC study both rest on probability samples of clearly defined universes. The 1954 work was, to the best of our knowledge, a national probability sample of the adult population, or at least those adults between the ages of 20 and 59.[17] The 1965–66 study, while national in scope, rests on a more restricted universe. In effect, the more rural 36 percent of the national population was excluded from the universe; the sample was drawn by probability methods from those primary sampling units of the national sample frame which contained cities of 50,000 population or greater. Thus, it is deliberately an urban national sample. Furthermore, within these urban areas, an additional 22 percent of households was considered ineligible: to yield an eligible interview, a household had to contain some member between the ages of 18 and 65 (age limits quite similar to those that pertain for the data available from the Ward study), who was at the time a member of the active nonagricultural labor force.[18] Because of the urban base of the sample, very few households remained to be excluded as purely farm units and the proportion of urban households containing no employed members was likewise limited. The main effect of the exclusion, therefore, was the dropping of households containing only aged persons. It is therefore only slightly incorrect to

[17] The data presented by de Grazia from the Ward Study are limited to respondents between the ages of 20 and 59. It is not clear whether respondents over 59 were considered ineligible, or whether they were interviewed but deleted for analytic reasons from the tabulations presented.

[18] These eligibility requirements pertained to the household; when a household was qualified by the fact that it had one person of appropriate age in the labor force, this person was not automatically designated as the respondent. Rather, once the household qualified, sampling proceeded by the Kish method to determine a respondent within the set of household members between ages 18 and 65, regardless of their labor force status. Thus the wife of a worker who had served to qualify the household had an equal chance of being designated the respondent. In this fashion, an occasional farmer was interviewed, by virtue of living in a household qualified by some other member.

think of the study as a national sample of the urbanized population between the ages of 18 and 65.

Given the interests in the 1965–66 study as a bench-mark survey for future comparative work, the elaborate restrictions of the universe may seem unfortunate, as indeed they are. Of course, future "pure" national samples can be readily related to this sample by excluding from data analysis the same fringes as were excluded in the 1965–66 sample design, and as time passes, population growth and increased urbanization will mean that the proportion of cases being discarded for comparative purposes is less and less. Furthermore, if the small rural-urban differences from the Opinion Research Corporation survey of things done "yesterday" are at all indicative, our restricted sampling frame may be less of a handicap than one would initially fear.

The sole motivation for the restrictions arose from the fact that the study was also serving as the United States portion of a very ambitious cross-national research project being carried out under a rigorously standardized design including these particular sampling specifications. Comparable data were collected in single small industrial cities in the Soviet Union, Poland, Hungary, Bulgaria, Czechoslovakia, East Germany, and West Germany, two cities of conforming specifications in Yugoslavia, and six conforming cities in France. For this reason, in addition to the national urban sample in the United States, a smaller sample of almost eight hundred cases was interviewed in the conforming city of Jackson, Michigan. Parallel data were also collected on a national sample in West Germany and a national sample of Belgium.[19]

It is useful at this point to introduce one display of gross national comparisons from the Multination Time-Budget Research Project of which the 1965–66 SRC study is a part, because the synchronic cross-national comparisons have some relevance for the methodological problems we are encountering in attempting longitudinal comparisons within the United States. Indeed, by this point in the argument it would not be surprising if there were some question about why we continue to deal with the Lundberg and Sorokin-Berger studies at all, since their sample bases, both in terms of the sampling of time and in terms of population sampling, bear so little resemblance to the later national samples. In point of fact, we shall not place great weight on such comparisons, and have been motivated to deal with these two earlier studies in part to dramatize the kinds of defects that make recourse to studies of an earlier vintage rather thankless. Nonetheless, the distinction should be kept in mind between incomparabilities that are mechanically remediable, at least to a reasonable

---

[19] Studies in other countries conforming to the same design specifications have since been carried out or are being planned. Procedural details and basic data of this project are contained in the December, 1966, issue of the *American Behavioral Scientist* and its special Appendix. A much more extensive report will be published by Mouton (The Hague, Netherlands) in early 1972.

approximation, and those which are not. Thus, for example, the Lundberg data have a very sharp bias toward higher-status respondents. This incomparability with the later national samples can, however, be considerably reduced by taking similarly high-status respondents from the 1965–66 study for comparison, keeping in mind that any apparent historical changes that emerge might not have been mirrored, if the truth were known, in low-status groups. On the other hand, the distribution of weekdays and weekends in the Lundberg materials is not remediable in this sense, because that distribution is unknown and cannot be simulated for the 1965–66 study. By the same token, the fact that the studies from the 1930's are only local studies is nothing that is easily remedied if we wish to talk about the United States of that era as a whole. It is on this point, however, that the cross-national comparisons have some bearing.

In Table 1 we display the average time expenditures for a summarized activity code of some 27 categories, across the various national survey sites. Even casual inspection of the table suggests the degree to which societies have characteristic and identifiable patterns of time allocation. Whether we look at the Jackson data or the American national sample, for example, we see that life in the United States is distinguished in this period by relatively large amounts of time devoted to visiting, organizational activity (largely in the form of attendance at church services), moonlighting, and watching television. Comparable data from Pskov in the Soviet Union show larger figures for adult education, reading, and going to places of entertainment (sports events, movies, etc.).

By applying the generalized Euclidean distance formula between columns of Table 1, it is possible to arrive at a quantitative expression for the degree of multidimensional similarity between any pair of these profiles. When all possible pairs are assessed in this manner, a full triangular similarity-dissimilarity matrix is generated. By far the smallest entry in this matrix, tokening highest similarity, is that between the Jackson, Michigan, profile and the United States profile. The next smallest entry is that between Osnabruck, West Germany, and the full West German national sample. Hence, for purposes of cross-national comparison, these cities are much more nearly "representative" of the time allocations in their nations taken as wholes than anyone would have dared to claim without some more substantial proof.[20] To these relatively "hard" findings, we may add informal comments from East European participants concerning the close

[20] Subsequent reduction of the similarity-dissimilarity matrix to its two primary dimensions by means of a Guttman-Lingoes Smallest Space Analysis produces a rather remarkable facsimile of a map of the Western world, with the country sites located in generally appropriate positions. Thus the time-profile differentials capture North-South and East-West cultural gradients with great fidelity. See Philip Converse, "Gross Similarities and Differences in Time Allocations: A Progress Report," a discussion paper prepared for the Round Table on Time-Budgets of the Sixth World Congress of Sociology in Evian, France, September, 1966.

Table 1. Time Expenditures for 27 Activity Categories across the 13 Survey Sites in the Multination Time-Budget Research Project

(*In Hours per Day*)

	U.S. (Cities 50,000)	U.S. (Jackson, Mich.)	France (6 Cities)	Belgium (425 Cities)	West Germany (100 Districts)	West Germany (Osnabruck)	Hungary (Gyor)	Poland (Torun)	Yugoslavia (Maribor)	Yugoslavia (Kragujevac)	Bulgaria (Kazanlik)	Russia (Pskov)	Czechoslovakia (Olomouc)
1. Regular work	3.8	4.1	4.2	4.3	3.7	3.7	5.4	4.9	4.3	4.0	5.6	5.4	4.9
2. Second job	.1	a	.1	.1	a	a	a	a	.2	a	a	a	a
3. Nonwork	.4	.4	.2	.1	.3	.2	.5	.3	.3	.4	.6	.6	.1
4. Trip to/from work	.4	.3	.4	.4	.3	.3	.7	.6	.5	.5	.7	.5	.5
5. Prepare food	.7	.7	.7	.8	1.0	.8	1.0	1.0	1.3	1.1	.8	.9	1.1
6. Clean house	1.0	.8	1.2	1.1	1.2	1.2	.9	.8	.9	.8	.7	.6	.9
7. Laundry, mending	.4	.4	.5	.3	.4	.4	.6	.6	.7	.5	.3	.4	.6
8. Other upkeep	.3	.3	.3	.2	.3	.3	.3	.3	.4	.4	.2	.3	.4
9. Pets/garden	.1	a	.2	.1	.5	.3	.6	a	.8	.1	.4	.1	.1
10. Sleep	7.8	7.9	8.2	8.3	8.3	8.1	7.7	7.5	7.8	7.6	7.8	7.7	7.8
11. Personal care	1.1	1.0	.9	.7	.9	1.0	.9	.9	.8	1.0	.8	.8	1.2
12. Eating	1.2	1.1	1.7	1.6	1.5	1.6	1.0	1.1	1.1	1.1	1.2	1.0	1.0
13. Resting	.3	.4	.6	.5	.5	.6	.4	.6	.4	.7	.7	.3	.4

14. Child care	.4	.4	.6	.3	.4	.3	.4	.4	.4	.3	.3	.5	.4
15. Shopping	.5	.6	.4	.3	.4	.5	.3	.5	.3	.4	.4	.4	.6
16. Nonwork trips	.8	.9	.5	.5	.3	.4	.5	.6	.6	.8	.6	.9	.4
17. Education	.2	.1	.2	.3	.1	.2	.3	.3	.3	.3	.2	.6	.2
18. Organizations	.3	.3	.1	.2	.1	.1	.1	.2	.1	.1	.1	.1	.1
19. Radio	.1	a	.1	.1	.1	.1	.2	.2	.1	.3	.3	.1	.2
20. Television	1.5	1.7	.9	1.4	1.0	1.2	.7	1.2	.7	.6	.3	.7	1.1
21. Reading	.6	.6	.4	.6	.4	.5	.4	.6	.5	.5	.5	.8	.6
22. Social life	1.2	1.2	.6	.7	.8	.9	.4	.6	.6	1.1	.2	.3	.4
23. Conversation	.3	.3	.3	.2	.3	.3	.2	.2	.2	.5	.2	.2	.2
24. Walking	a	a	.2	.2	.6	.5	.2	.2	.3	.2	.4	.2	.3
25. Sports	.1	.1	a	a	.2	.1	.1	a	.1	a	.1	.1	a
26. Various leisure	.3	.3	.4	.5	.2	.3	.1	.2	.2	.6	.3	.2	.3
27. Amusements	.1	.1	.1	.2	.1	.1	.1	.1	.1	.2	.3	.3	.1
Total[b]	24.0	24.0	24.0	24.1	23.9	24.1	24.0	23.9	24.0	24.1	24.0	24.0	23.9
Free time (13, 17–27)	5.0	5.1	3.9	5.0	4.4	4.9	3.2	4.4	3.6	5.1	3.6	4.1	3.9

[a] Average time less than three minutes.
[b] Entries do not always add to 24 hours because of rounding.

match between time-use patterns from the city site examined for the multination project and quite different cities within the same country for which earlier studies are available. It might be emphasized that these part-whole similarities arise without any correction for some of the known sociological idiosyncracies of Jackson among American cities. Presumably adjustment of this kind would bring even stronger convergence of the profiles.[21]

Quite obviously, these data offer no proof that the large majority of cities within national societies would show comparable degrees of similarity with data from their parent nations. Nonetheless, they do suggest that, once known peculiarities are corrected for, data based on Westchester County or Boston may be much more nearly representative of time allocation patterns in the nation as a whole of that period than one would have believed on a purely intuitive basis. It is in this spirit that we are willing to consider these early materials as being at least suggestive.

The presentation of cross-national comparisons raises one other possibility. Since these data have been standardized to a remarkable degree, and since countries at a variety of levels of economic development are represented, might we not take variations associated with level of development as some indication of what time allocations might have been at an earlier period in the United States? Such information is indeed suggestive, particularly when a specific type of time use is closely tied to an area of technological innovation, in the sense that travel durations are logically linked to modes of transport. Substitution of such synchronic findings for diachronic conclusions is extremely risky, however, as the cross-national data attest at several points. Thus, for example, a striking gradient exists from West to East in the proportions of women working in the active (nonhousehold) labor force, with France, Britain, and Germany falling in the 30 to 40 percent range, and the percentage climbing steeply across Eastern Europe to highs in the 80 to 90 percent range for the Bulgarian and Soviet Union sites. When not controlled, these differences exert considerable impact on time allocation patterns, and the gradient represented coincides rather closely with level of national economic development. If we did not have much better information to the direct contrary, we would find ourselves inferring that with increased economic development, American women must have been disappearing progressively from the labor force! For reasons such as this, we seem well advised not to place undue faith in the cross-national evidence for the purpose of American historical reconstructions.

A final set of sampling factors to be considered involves the response rates

---

[21] The wary reader might protest with some justification that these data merely show that the Jackson and United States profiles are similar *relative to cross-national differences,* which themselves may be huge. However, the national differences in profiles are demonstrably very much smaller than within-nation differences in time allocations by social role or between weekends and weekday. Hence, relative to other sources of variation in the data, the Jackson–U.S. differences become truly miniscule.

achieved among persons approached for participation. Obviously, however excellent the sample design, a study securing cooperation among only 40 percent of its designated respondents needs evaluation in a much different light from one with a 90 percent response rate. Indeed, the problem is more pressing in work on time use than in many other areas, where the reasons for nonresponse may be relatively uncorrelated with the subject matter of the study. In the degree that some people refuse cooperation on genuine grounds of "being too busy," and others are simply hard to locate, one can well imagine major nonresponse biases developing in the results.

Generally speaking, high response rates are easier to attain with "captive populations"—ones over which the investigator has some degree of control, such as classes of students or work groups in an industrial setting—than with cross-sectional samples of larger and more historically significant populations, although the latter are of greater interest for the study of social change. Moreover, as we have seen, reliability is improved as data-elicitation procedures are elaborated, yet this very development places heavier demands on prospective respondents, and other things equal, inevitably reduces cooperation.

Given the relatively onerous requirements of the 1965–66 SRC study, we were quite pleased with a national response rate of 74 percent of the designated respondents. Moreover, the figure rose to a very respectable 84 percent of our Jackson sample. The national response rate is about 6 percent lower than one would expect from a less demanding interview of typical length, but still lies within a respectable range. Furthermore, detailed comparative analyses of the fractions of the sample who broke off the interview or who would not have been successfully contacted but for the considerable persistence of the interviewing staff, against those more readily accessible, reported to our surprise no higher or lower participation in various free-time activities. Where the 1954 Ward study is concerned, information is lacking as to the actual response rate. Considering that the demands of that study would appear as annoying as ours (two days of diaries, although without an extensive subsequent interview), along with the likelihood that less effort was made to coax respondents into cooperation, the effective response rate was probably visibly lower. Where the two studies of the 1930's are concerned, the lack of a fixed sample reduces the meaningfulness of the concept of response rate. Nonetheless, its rough analogue is the proportion of actual participants to persons approached, and Lundberg *et al.* note that this figure never rose above 50 percent for the various groups of interest to us. The Sorokin-Berger study has an even less satisfactory response rate, their tabulations being based on well under a 10 percent return.

At this point the Lundberg data become far more useful than those of Sorokin-Berger because separate figures are given for each occupational group in the Lundberg study (and for men and women within each occupation) so that variation due to these sources can be placed in some perspective.

The Categorization of Activities. One frequently cited advantage of time-budget work involves the convenient measurement properties of time as a variable. Unlike most of the other theoretically critical dimensions with which sociologists must suffer, time can be measured to infinite degrees of precision as a unitary dimension. Temporal durations are unquestionably "ratio scales." More important still for comparisons across space and time is the simple fact that time as an objective resource—at least the 24 hours of a day—is distributed with perfect equality across all members of the species at all periods and places.

Yet time in itself is meaningless. It must be subdivided and the resulting time slices paired up with bounded, categorizable activities in order for time-budget work to proceed. And however delectable time may be as a working currency, the infinite facets and blurred boundaries of human "activities" are not. While many of the difficulties of comparability we have surveyed up to this point are technical problems with clear solutions given adequate sophistication and resources, the reliable sorting of behaviors into meaningful equivalence classes remains an Achilles heel of the whole procedure.

In fact, the many noble efforts to gauge long-term trends in the balance of work and leisure have run aground not only for lack of solid historical information, but also on this basic definitional question itself. Industrialization helps to provide sharper boundaries than were displayed by agrarian pursuits and cottage industries. Nonetheless, formal definitions of the length of the workweek fail to take into account the amounts of time spent on the job in irrelevant "leisure" activities (like reading the paper), or the amount of time spent off the job on "do-it-yourself" efforts of an economically productive nature.[22] From one man's point of view, some of the latter activities may be necessary drudgery to avoid paying for outside services; for another, they may be a delightful hobby that he would pursue even if it cost rather than saved him money. The border between work and leisure in some professions approaches the truly seamless.

Just as behaviorally similar activities may have radically different subjective meaning, so activities that are easy to discriminate, such as watching television as opposed to reading the newspaper, may at points be perfect functional equivalents (e.g., information seeking, or idle entertainment). Some activities plead for multiple classification: "dining out with friends" needs to be considered a form of social visiting, but anyone who does it with great frequency may then appear to be in danger of malnutrition in the coded time budgets. Double entries are not welcome as they spoil the neatness of the 24-hour totals; dividing the diner's time by guesswork as to actual ingestion needs vs. a residual for chatting seems both complex and arbitrary.

[22] James Morgan and associates have recently completed an extensive assessment of time spent on unpaid productive activities in the United States, although respondents gave annual estimates instead of reports for more specific periods of time. Their results have important implications for the measurement of the gross national product. See James N. Morgan, Ismail Sirageldin, and Nancy Baerwaldt, *Productive Americans*. Survey Research Center, Institute for Social Research, University of Michigan, Ann Arbor, 1966.

These are but a few examples of a pervasive problem. Quite apart from ambiguities surrounding the psychological or functional meaning of a behavior for the actor (a consideration we shall postpone), few categories of overt activity are not rimmed with marginal instances. Some of these are of such rare incidence that they would have negligible effect on an aggregate of time budgets. But this is often not the case, particularly with coarse coding schemes, and it is futile to draw elegant quantitative comparisons of time allocations between studies that have sorted the same activities into different bins.

Some progress is being made on the problem by a combination of routes. Increasing the number and specificity of activity categories not only helps to reduce errors of inference as to what actual behaviors a rubric subsumes, but also adds great flexibility of recombination for various conceptual purposes, including comparison with other studies. The 1965–66 SRC study employed the 96–activity code standard for the Multination Project, and added another six to ten differentiations within certain global categories (e.g., types of shopping, types of content followed in the mass media, etc.). The Lundberg study employed 14 categories and the Ward study only 13. Sorokin and Berger's development of a 55-category code was one of the few strong features of this study.

The capturing of secondary and even tertiary concurrent activities (ironing while watching television and keeping an eye on the baby, or listening to the radio while driving to work) represents a further advance, one that was little more than verbally acknowledged prior to our survey. Not only are these intersections interesting to analyze in themselves, but they enrich considerably the realism of the record. Comparing those activities registered as "primary" within the multinational study, for example, the impression is created that in the United States television has all but wiped out radio listening, in contrast to the European situation where visible amounts of radio time continue to register as a primary activity. Actually, about nine-tenths of radio listening occurs as a secondary activity in the United States, and would have been obscured but for the effort to capture multiple activities.

While it is without question valuable to ascertain such secondary activities, the effort has some methodological limitations, particularly when data are being compared across studies. Both interviewer variation and interstudy variation are likely in the degree to which a probe such as "Were you doing anything else at the same time?" is "pushed," as well as variation in the range of concurrent events that the respondent will take to be meaningful additions to the record. Such sources of variation can be difficult to control. Finally, of course, since for many purposes the 24-hour time base is an important convenience in comparisons, only "primary activities" are taken into account and the question arises as to which of two concurrent activities is to be seen as primary. This problem is somewhat less severe than might appear, since it is quite natural to let the respondent's own implication as to the primacy of two activities define the situation for subsequent analytic work. Occasionally, however, the stated criteria of primary attention fit a concrete situation so poorly that the choice remains arbitrary.

A last advance worthy of note is the coding of verbal activity descriptions by computer.[23] Such procedures do not, of course, escape the difficult and often controversial decisions as to the proper location of specific activities in some more summary classification represented by the "code." Such decisions must be made and entered into the computer memory. The important point, particularly for comparative studies, is that once such decisions are made, they can be repeated with perfect reliability in the face of long-time lapses between studies and total disjuncture with respect to supervisory personnel. Moreover, by maintaining a detailed record of all specific variants assigned to a particular category, they could be updated at a later time in a way which should maintain higher intraclass homogeneity. Thus, the compilation of such records, while no panacea for coding problems, holds promise of solving rather definitively one crucial aspect of those problems, the lack of standardization in the coding process.

It is important to forewarn, therefore, that in the subsequent historical comparisons we draw, we have simply made the best common-sense judgments we can muster as to how our 96-activity code would have been distributed across the 15 categories of the Lundberg study or the 13 categories of the Ward study. Many of these decisions are entirely straightforward, but several remain ambiguous. Perhaps the most dramatic illustration of the difficulty is the fact that, whereas urban Americans in the 1965–66 study spent a weekly average of three and one-half hours shopping, this category is never mentioned in the Lundberg study. Moreover, the very few categories where shopping might conceivably have been placed ("care of self," "transportation," "household and children," "miscellaneous") all show average durations only about three-quarters as long as their 1965–66 parallels, even assuming that they do not conceal a half-hour's shopping as well. Therefore, some activity class must have shown a remarkable discrepancy over this period, but it is impossible to say just what it is without further information as to the disposition of the shopping totals.

Up to this point we have limited ourselves to the difficulties in making reliable assessments as to the way a population distributes its time across simple types of overt behavior, and the compound difficulties of arriving at "historical" comparisons across uncoordinated studies attempting such assessments.[24] Much

---

[23] Peter Kranz, Connecticut Research Institute, Darien, Conn. (informal communication).

[24] One facet of measurement of which we are just beginning to become aware concerns the completeness of activity reporting, the major index of which is the simple number of activities reported. This piece of information is entirely omitted in the earlier time-budget studies of Table 2. In our own study, respondents' diaries averaged about 29 entries (ranging from 11 to over 60). We regard this number as close to the lower bound of acceptable detail. We are aware of the unpublished studies in which the number of reported

more would need to be said about measurement and standardization were we to undertake a close examination of some of the more psychological and functional ways of treating time allocation as well. However, since even the simplest facts about activity change in the past few decades can only be seen as through a glass darkly, let us turn to a discussion of the glimpses available from the major studies under consideration. For reader convenience, Table 2 summarizes the methodological assets and liabilities of these studies that are useful to keep in mind as we proceed.

Recent Shifts in Time Use in the United States

If one were asked to imagine the way in which daily life in the United States has changed most dramatically since the 1930's, the introduction of television after the Second World War would seem an obvious choice. And indeed, our 1965–66 data show that, by that period, television viewing was occupying a figure approaching two hours a day, averaged over seven days a week, for the urban national sample. This figure is the more impressive when it is recognized as something on the order of one-third to one-half of all leisure or discretionary time available to the adult population.

Since television did not exist in popular form in the 1930's, there is no possibility whatever that this radical displacement of time is any methodological artifact. On the other hand, of course, the sheer viewing times themselves say very little about the human significance of this change. Has television simply replaced radio listening of the 1930's by the addition of its visual accompaniment, or has it cut more deeply into other areas of life? Although it is notoriously difficult to estimate the ultimate impact of an invention such as television on subtle psychological responses in a population, time budgets should minimally be able to suggest what "trade-offs" in daily activities the diffusion of the invention has occasioned.

Meanwhile, of course, other smaller changes in the structure of time use beside those associated with television appear to have occurred since the 1930's. Some of these changes are surprising, but seem reliably consistent in the data available. Our latest figures for time spent working are all larger than any reported in the three major previous studies. This is also true of time spent shopping. The comparisons for transportation and for housework or child care are not consistent enough to assure any clear trend, but the 1965–66 figures show

---

activities was approximately three times this number. Furthermore, in their exhaustive studies of daily activities of eight children, Barker and Wright recorded just under a thousand "behavior episodes" per child per day (R. Barker and H. Wright, *Midwest and Its Children*. Row, Peterson, Evanston, Ill., 1954). Only an unforeseen methodological breakthrough would allow us to obtain records of this detail from representative adult samples.

Table 2. Major Time Use Studies Compared on Various Characteristics

Study	Sample	Time Budgets	Interviewing Period	Coding Categories	Special Features	Major Shortcomings
Lundberg et al. (1934)	2,460 residents of Westchester County, New York (of these almost 1,600 were students)	3–7/person; total = 4,460	November–May 1931–32 and 1932–33	15 (but no code for shopping)	1. "Good time patterns" i.e., enjoyable parts of day	1. No day of week differences (possible over-sample of weekends) 2. Low response rate 3. Affluent community with no illiterates and few working-class respondents 4. No summer months 5. Respondents reconstruct days from memory 6. Possible restriction to activities over 30 minutes
Sorokin and Berger (1939)	176 adults in Boston	At least 28/person; total = 3,476	May–November 1935	55 (reduced to 8 general categories)	1. Predictability of budgets 2. Motivations for activities 3. Social contacts for activities	1. Oversampling of unemployed, young women 2. Summer months only 3. Low response rates 4. Differences due to sex, employment, marital status, etc. not available

J. A. Ward–Mutual Broadcasting (de Grazia, 1962)	Nationwide sample of all individuals over 5 years of age in 7,000 households	2/person; total = 17,000 for ages 20–59	March–April 1954	13 (no separate code for TV)	1. Nationwide probability sample 2. Day of week variations accounted for	1. Only 17 hours period covered 2. No summer months 3. Breakdowns by age, education, etc. not available
Opinion Research Corporation (de Grazia, 1962)	Nationwide sample of 5,021 persons aged 15 and over	1/person total = 5,021	June–July 1957	20 (only certain leisure activities)	1. Participation only	1. Actual time spent not ascertained
Converse and Robinson (1966)	Urban probability sample of 1,244 adults in employed households + 788 adults in Jackson, Michigan	1/person total = 1,802 budgets 2/person total = 440 budgets	November–December 1965; March–April 1966	96 (reduced to 27 activities)	1. Part of 10 nation study 2. Activities most easily given up 3. Most enjoyable part of the day 4. Yearly participation figures	1. No data for rural areas or unemployed households 2. No summer months

more time spent on each of these activities than in two of the three earlier sets of data.[25]

At this point we propose to examine all of these more consistent or impressive changes in greater detail, supplementing the discussion liberally with information drawn from specialized studies that are often helpful either in substantiating the fact of a change, or in illuminating its likely significance.

Television. Even a casual inspection of the tables in the Appendix make clear that the large swath of time now occupied by television viewing in American homes has come principally from activities that could be seen as its most direct "functional equivalents": listening to the radio, reading fiction, and going to the movies or other places of entertainment, such as sporting events or the theater.[26] Even within this set of activities, it is the most complete equivalent, radio listening, which has suffered the largest proportional losses. At the same time, there is some reason to suspect that the awesome amounts of time now spent before a television set have been drawn at some expense to a wider range of less related leisure activities, including dancing, card playing, social visiting, and pleasure driving.

The literature is unusually rich in more specialized studies providing a chronicle of time displacements associated with the introduction of television. These studies taken as a whole strongly confirm the above generalizations and help to fill in further detail. For example, the figures in Table 3 were reported by Coffin from a study of 2,500 respondents in Fort Wayne, Indiana, in the early 1950's.[27] Consistent with our data, radio listening is much more sharply affected here by the arrival of television than is reading, with newspapers being

[25] To avoid distracting the reader with the myriad details and complications that surround comparisons of the four major studies, the basic data reflecting changes in time use are presented in an Appendix to this chapter, along with some explanatory text.

[26] One "mass" medium, long-playing phonograph records, financially prospered at the same time as the introduction of television, although the technology itself was going through its innovative stages and could not have been directly affected by television. However, we actually have no data indicating that people actually listened more to phonograph records than they did previously, although it is hard to imagine that the increased sales of records does not reflect time listening.

[27] The data include time spent on these forms as either primary or secondary activities. Data from control groups rule out the possibility of other factors affecting these results. The "after TV" figures were consistent with media usage time of other people who already had a set in their home, while those who did not purchase a set during the same period showed little or no change in their media habits. Furthermore, with the exception of television, which shows 30 more minutes in the Coffin figures, the radio and reading times "after TV" continue to match up well with our national and Jackson figures for 1965 and 1966. See Thomas Coffin, "Television's Impact on Society," *American Psychologist,* vol. 10, October, 1955, pp. 630–641.

the published form most resistant to displacement.[28] Coffin also reviews other data showing decreases in the reading of books with the advent of television that are intermediate between those for magazines and newspapers, as well as declining time spent at movies or sporting events (also noticeable in Tables A and B of the Appendix).

Table 3. Time Spent before and after Introduction of TV

Time Spent on	Minutes per Day before TV Was Available	Minutes per Day after Purchase of TV Set
Magazines	17	10
Newspapers	39	32
Radio	122	52
Television	12[a]	173

[a] Guest viewing.

The most ambitious study of the impact of television was conducted by the market research firm of Cunningham and Walsh in "Videotown" over the ten years from 1948 to 1958.[29] Although the study included some time-budget data, it was unfortunately confined to the evening hours, and most activities other than radio and television were measured in terms of the percent participating rather than the duration of time spent. Nevertheless, the conclusions were nicely congruent with other work. There were large declines in radio listening (down by 50 percent), magazine reading (down about 53 percent), and moviegoing (down 35 percent).[30] Entertaining and visiting friends also slumped off (down about 30 percent), although in the very earliest days of set ownership there was a large surge in entertaining which involved "guest viewing," either invited or uninvited. Newspaper reading was again relatively unaffected, and if anything showed slight increases between 1948 and 1958. Several other studies reviewed

[28] Davis, however, found that national probability samples in 1947 (before TV) and 1957 (85 percent set ownership) reported the same *number* of magazines read. Robert Davis, *The Public Impact of Science in the Mass Media*. Survey Research Center, Institute for Social Research, University of Michigan, Ann Arbor, 1958.

[29] Videotown was actually New Brunswick, New Jersey, a community within adequate reception range of New York City television transmitters although more typical a community than the city itself. We are indebted to Anders Krall of Cunningham and Walsh for making the Videotown reports available to us.

[30] Average weekly attendance at motion picture theaters dropped from 2.2 times per household in 1948 nationally to just under once per household in 1955. See M. DeFleur, *Theories of Mass Communication*. McKay, New York, 1966.

by Bogart, as well as Belson's panel study of television impact in London in the early 1950's, lead to similar conclusions.[31]

When the introduction of television is examined across the 13 sites of the multinational study, where there were at the time vastly different rates of set ownership, certain intriguing constancies appear. The rate of television viewing was much lower in Eastern European countries than in the West, but TV ownership rates were much lower as well (Table 1). When one graphs viewing times against ownership rates, the results show a striking tendency toward uniform amounts of watching per set owner.[32] Numerous diachronic studies have again produced analogous results.[33] It appears that the appetite for television is rather constant in a population of any size once sets are available, and that the aggregate time spent viewing in a society is readily predictable once rates of set ownership are known.

Nevertheless, more subtle cross-national differences in television viewing arise that remain suggestive of variations in impact from country to country. Thus, despite the basic similarities in viewing time per owner, the underlying correlation between educational background and television viewing varies quite widely across the multinational survey sites. In the United States, France, Germany, and Belgium, the less-educated tended to spend longer times viewing television, while exactly the opposite pattern occurred in a number of East European sites, most notably Bulgaria, Yugoslavia, and Hungary. Although it would be tempting to conclude that early in the diffusion process the more educated portions of a population tend to buy sets and therefore to spend more time viewing, whereas in later periods lower strata attain sets and surpass the well-

---

[31] Leo Bogart, *The Age of Television*. Ungar, New York, 1958; and William Belson, *The Impact of Television*. Archon, Hamden, Conn., 1967. Belson found that attendance at sports events was *increased* (especially for horse racing), as was attendance at art galleries. Greatest reductions were again in movie attendance and book reading (radio was not covered), but also in theater-going and the visiting of historical monuments. Smaller decreases were registered for card playing, keeping up with politics and science, visiting, and strolling. Gardening, participation in organizations, and playing phonograph records were hardly affected at all.

[32] John P. Robinson, "Television and Leisure Time: Yesterday, Today and (Maybe) Tomorrow," *Public Opinion Quarterly,* vol. 33, Summer, 1969, pp. 210–222.

[33] In Videotown, television viewing per set owner varied sporadically over the years but showed no tendency toward any long-term increase or decline. Readings on Nielsen's audimeters also remain rather stable from year to year. In *Television and the Child* (Oxford University Press, New York, 1958), Himmelweit, Oppenheim, and Vince found that the introduction of a second television channel in Great Britain, offering more popular programming, did not increase the amount of time children were spending with television. An early study of an Iowa community, which added a commercial station after a period of operation with an educational channel, noted the same phenomenon. See Lucinda Crile, *Some Findings from Television Studies*. Department of Agriculture Extension Service, Washington, D.C., 1953 (Circular 490).

educated in time spent with them, this pattern cannot be demonstrated for the United States. Although the relevant data are sketchy, there does not appear to have been a time when American college graduates had higher rates of ownership than high school graduates, nor is there any evidence of a positive correlation between education and viewing time in the United States of the early 1950's.[34]

Patterns of this kind help to alert us to the possibility of sharp qualitative variation that may underlie gross quantitative regularities. For example, differences in viewing time by education from country to country may need to be understood in terms of systematic variations in television content at the societal level. There is a strong interest in the didactic possibilities of television in Eastern Europe, and programming tends to resemble American educational television more closely than it does our commercial television. What will happen in these countries if and when the less-educated segment of the audience begins to influence television content, as it has so clearly in the West, forms an interesting subject for conjecture.

Similarly, while newspaper reading has been the form of media use that has suffered the least inroads from television in public attention, some students of the mass media argue that newspapers have felt obliged to change the format of their product to adjust to the challenge from television, with shifts toward greater use of pictures, shorter and simpler stories, and more sensational content. If true, this constellation of observations would illustrate a type of change in the mass media that simply does not register in popular time allocations, despite its likely significance.

Nevertheless, the shifts in time use that have accompanied the advent of television remain thoroughly impressive. While a substantial portion of the change has come from the more direct functional equivalents of television, as we have seen, the medium is so seductive that it has clearly usurped time from a broader range of activities as well. Coffin's Fort Wayne data show a 41 percent increase in time devoted to the mass media after the introduction of television.[35] Almost identical figures are quoted in two relevant studies in Bogart's review.[36] Other forms of more parochial leisure, such as the playing of games and socializing with friends, have certainly undergone shrinkage as well. Although television is used more as an entertainment medium in this country than

---

[34] John P. Robinson and Philip E. Converse, "The Impact of Television on Mass Media Usage," in *Transactions of the Sixth World Congress of Sociology* (Milan, Italy: International Sociological Association, 1970).

[35] Coffin, *op. cit.*

[36] Bogart, *op. cit.* Data from the multinational study show a great deal of variation in increased media time from country to country. The average gain is 30 percent for all time spent with the media, but for primary activities alone the gain is much more dramatic, on the order of 80 percent.

as an information medium, there is a sense in which a more nationally oriented and homogeneous culture is being forged.

Moreover, it is not absolutely certain that television has made inroads only on leisure time. Our cross-national data show an intriguing tendency for owners of television sets to have more "free time" available to them. Whether this is a matter of persons with more free time being more likely to avail themselves of sets, or whether access to television has increased the degree to which other duties (particularly household ones) are shunted aside, cannot of course be answered at this point. It is a question worth pursuing in a future longitudinal study, however, particularly in those many societies where television is in the pioneering stage and the large-scale shifts in time budgeting that characterized America's adjustment to television have not yet occurred.

In sum, the impact of television on daily life has been of major magnitude. Indeed, we shall see that not even the automobile has had the major effect on time spent traveling that television has had on time spent with the mass media. It seems fair to conclude that, although the automobile has revolutionized American life *spatially,* television has revolutionized its *temporal* dimensions.

Work. In common parlance, the most important subdivision of the waking day is made between work and leisure. It therefore verges on the absurd that endless difficulties seem to encumber efforts to determine just how much time is spent working by a heterogeneous population, not to mention whether this time is on the increase or decrease. Nevertheless, the blurred boundaries of work itself, along with problems in defining any stable or meaningful population of reference, sharply limit the interpretability of most figures that are cited.

In point of fact, almost all comparisons from our 1965–66 data show longer work times than were registered in previous surveys (see Appendix). Nevertheless, the fact that two of the three earlier studies were conducted in depression years and failed to report any proportions of employment largely destroys the interest this pattern might otherwise hold.

In one sense it is pointless to struggle with small samples in view of the 100 years of quantitative information on the length of the workweek that have been accumulated on the basis of much larger samples by government agencies such as the Census Bureau and the Bureau of Labor Statistics. Their relevant averages, computed for nonagricultural employees at selected years over the past half-century, show a dramatic decline in the workweek between 1920 and 1950, with little change since (see Table 4).

One prime virtue of these figures[37] lies in the fact that they are at least re-

---

[37] The first series of figures is drawn from de Grazia, *op. cit.,* p. 41, whose data stop at 1960. They are based on reports collected from industries and refer only to formal jobs of production workers. Thus, white-collar workers and numerous groups showing long work hours, such as the self-employed, are excluded. Similarly, individuals holding multiple jobs are ignored. The figures in parentheses are estimates (developed from household

Table 4. Decline in Workweek, Selected Years, 1920–1950
(*In Hours per Week*)

Year	Production Workers	All Workers
1920	45.5	
1930	43.2	
1940	41.1	
1945	43.1	
1950	38.8	(40.7)
1955	38.9	(40.9)
1960	38.0	(40.0)
1965		(40.2)

stricted to nonagricultural workers. Of course if one is contemplating the human condition more generally, such a restriction conceals one kind of decline in the work burden of the population. Farm workers appear to put in significantly longer workweeks (6 hours longer in 1960, and 15 hours longer in 1920), and they have comprised a progressively smaller proportion of the labor force.[38] Nonetheless, it is useful to get a glimpse of what has been happening within the labor force apart from such a major source of heterogeneity.

Beyond this point, however, such government figures are less satisfying than they may appear. First and foremost, it should be clear that the data presented only pretend to cover "hours worked for pay." Thus, the toil of housewives as well as employed persons around the home makes no contribution to these estimates. If it is true that the management of a home in the 1960's requires more time than it did in the 1930's—and we shall shortly consider some suggestive evidence in this regard—then such figures ignore an important countervailing trend.

Even with this important caveat stated, the full human significance of the government figures remains shrouded. This is particularly true if, as is inevitable, we tend to read into a declining workweek visions of an individual or comparable individuals whose workload is less now than it once was. We should keep in mind at least the following considerations:[39]

interviews) kindly provided us by John Bregger of the Bureau of Labor Statistics. Thus, they enjoy a broader occupational base and appropriately reflect moonlighting. Since they often rest on second-party reports (*viz.* from housewives), they are probably less reliable than our first-person time diaries.

[38] As de Grazia contends, however, farm workers needed much less time for the "trip to work" than characterized the urban labor force. In the degree that one is interested in any secular trends in discretionary time, the significant number of hours per week spent commuting needs to be added to urban work figures (de Grazia, *op. cit.*, pp. 70–71).

[39] Many of these points are raised in Morgan *et al.*, *op. cit.*, p. 39, and de Grazia, *op. cit.*, p. 69.

1. The government figures refer to a population that has been shifting in its composition. In recent times there has been a decided increase in the proportion of part-time workers in the labor force, including especially women and teen-agers. The 10- and 20-hour workweeks of these employees exert a marked influence toward the apparent "shortening" of the average workweek. De Grazia presents purified figures for full-time employees (people working over 35 hours a week) that showed almost no decline at all in the workweek during the 1950's: 45.3 hours in 1950, 45.1 in 1955, and 45.2 in 1960.[40] If anything, this statistic appears to have increased slightly in 1965.

2. There is some ambiguity as to how people who are laid off from work should be handled. Apparently persons in this situation were excluded in the government figures during the years of the Great Depression.[41] The figures for such a period would thus conceal a large-scale diminution in collective work output.

3. The government figures developed from industry report as work time all paid hours, including those in which persons are not working as a result of illness, bad weather, or vacation time. Since there has been a sharp increase in the tendency toward such forms of paid "nonwork," there is an artificial inflation of the time spent at work in recent estimates. A complementary problem arose during the depression, when some employees were paid their full week's wages despite the fact that they did not have enough work to cover the entire week.[42] Such angularities due to the "pay" definition are less damaging in the household interview data.

4. Periods of full employment are marked by larger percentages of the work force engaging in overtime hours for pay. Indeed, in the current period these broad swings in the economy may account for more of the apparent trends in the average workweek than do social programs toward shorter workweeks. This kind of variation is especially marked under wartime conditions, the latest example being the increase in the workweek spurred by the Vietnam War. Not only does the war demand higher production, but those going into military service are often persons with skills that are hard to replace. This increases demand for moonlighting and overtime among remaining persons of the labor force with comparable skills.

5. "Average" workweek figures can conceal significant variations in the proportions of the population working extremely long or extremely short workweeks. This has become particularly true over the past 20 years. Between 1948 and 1965 the proportion of full-time workers putting in more than 60 hours a week increased by 50 percent (from 4.9 percent to 7.4 percent), while the proportion working less than 40 hours rose by 69 percent (from 4.8 percent to 8.2 percent). Of course these intriguing trends in the dis-

[40] de Grazia, *op. cit.,* p. 443.

[41] This fact makes it the more difficult to verify the representativeness of the work data contained in the studies by Lundberg *et al.* and Sorokin and Berger, both of which were conducted during this period.

[42] These factors are discussed in *Historical Statistics of the United States.* Bureau of the Census, Washington, D.C., 1960.

position of the labor force are thoroughly obscured in extracting mean workweek durations.[43]

6. While there is an honest effort to include hours spent on second jobs in the workweek totals, de Grazia presents a number of reasons—taxes, difficulties with primary employers, etc.—why the extent of moonlighting is likely to be systematically underestimated.[44]

Perhaps these are the major considerations to be remembered in evaluating the government workweek figures, but they do not exhaust all the difficulties in defining what worktime really is. Calculating the 1965–66 estimates for our Appendix comparisons alerted us to the question whether other activities related to work (beyond commuting time) should be considered as work. These include such variegated items as coffee breaks, lunch breaks, changing clothes at work, and work delays, and they amount to a full 10 percent of all time comprised under the category "work for pay" assembled for purposes of comparison with Lundberg in Table A (see Appendix).[45] Since it is only in relatively recent years that formal breaks from labor have been legitimated in work contracts, it is likely that these nonwork activities at the work place are more prevalent today than they were 20 or 30 years ago, further blurring the human significance of long-term workweek comparisons.

Whatever reductions do occur in the time spent working over the next few decades may be expected to come from longer paid vacations and more paid holidays. Indeed, these two factors alone may well account for most of any reduction in working time that can be documented for the period since the Second World War. There even appears to be some resistance to shorter workdays or four-day workweek among employees who are often not captivated by the thought of free time during periods when children are in school or when the worker will be in some degree out of step with other meaningful activity in the society around him.[46] Moreover, in the degree the economy permits, there is

[43] The basic data are presented in Peter Henle, "Leisure and the Long Workweek," *Monthly Labor Review,* July, 1966, pp. 721–727. Henle notes that there are three groups working long hours: (1) people who enjoy their work, mainly professionals; (2) people who must work long hours, mainly managers; and (3) people who need additional income, mainly those in low-paying trade and service occupations. Henle also indicates that the 7.4 percent of the labor force that put in more than 60 hours of work a week actually worked the amazing average of 69 hours per week.

[44] de Grazia, *op. cit.,* pp. 70–71.

[45] These activities were included as part of "work for pay" simply because this seemed to be the only conceivable place that the Lundberg team could have located them. The trip to work is not, however, included in this gross category.

[46] The American worker may find reason to be jealous of his Western European counterpart who has a longer standard workweek but also a greater number of days off in terms of vacations and holidays. See Ewan Clague, "Hours of Work," a paper prepared for the Select Subcommittee on Labor, House Education and Labor Committee, Washington, D.C., June, 1963.

a marked tendency for workers with shortened hours on their primary job to turn to moonlighting as a means of increasing family income and standard of living, thereby introducing an intriguing degree of inelasticity in the duration of the workweek. Since this occurs frequently among workers who are in no sense struggling to keep above a bare subsistence threshold, it is suggestive of some rather basic human preference structures.

Housework. The time spent on chores associated with the upkeep and management of a home and family, including care of children and shopping for food ("marketing"), is remarkably higher in our 1965–66 data than in the two studies from the 1930's. This seems peculiar at first glance, given the tremendous advances that have occurred in the diffusion of time- and labor-saving facilities in American homes during roughly the same period (see Table 5).[47] The amounts of electricity consumed by private dwelling units, much of it associated with a wide assortment of labor-saving devices, has increased many fold since 1930.

Table 5. Trends in Labor-Saving Devices, U.S. Homes
(*In Percent*)

Facility	1940	1960
Bathtub or shower	61	88
Wood, coal, or oil stoves	45	5
Wood or coal for heating	78	16
Electricity	79	99

It is, of course, simply inconceivable that these technological changes have failed to remove substantial amounts of drudgery, once a normal and accepted part of the housework routine. Automatic furnaces alone have wiped away one staple wintertime chore of the past, and important activities such as the fetching of water have substantially disappeared from the daily round. Yet there is a difference between these known reductions in drudgery and any facile conclusion that time thereby freed has passed over into an increased leisure. This does not appear to have been the case.

In view of the esoteric nature of the samples involved in the two time-budget studies of the 1930's, a factor which is likely to exert particular influence on the housework category because of maids in affluent homes of the period, it is wise not to place too much weight on contrasts between their figures and data from the 1960's. Nevertheless, other studies which provide points of comparison, while yielding somewhat more complex patterns, tend to suggest the same surprising results.

[47] The data are drawn from Ben Wattenberg and Richard Scammon, *This U.S.A.* Doubleday, Garden City, N.Y., 1965.

The gap between the 1954 Ward-Mutual study and our 1965–66 investigation considerably foreshortens the time period within which change might occur, but the comparisons are somewhat more reliable. They show a slight decline in time spent working around the house on the part of men, although one which is offset by an increase in time spent shopping. For women, they show a more substantial decrease (from 5.3 to 4.8 hours), although again increases in shopping times of 0.3 hours daily wipes away much of this reduction.[48] However, evidence from all countries shows that working women spend much less time on housework than do housewives—in our 1965–66 data, only about half as much—and the proportion of working women has increased significantly between 1954 and 1966. When this latter factor is appropriately taken into account, the implication is strong that, whereas some women have escaped the home in favor of outside employment, those remaining housewives are spending more time at such chores than the housewife in 1954.

There is an expansive literature on the disposition of homemakers' time that we could hardly hope to review here. One set of these studies, conducted by Kathryn Walker at Cornell, recommends itself particularly because it has inquired into changes in housework time over a period of more than a decade.[49] Professor Walker has drawn comparisons between data collected on homemakers' time allocations in 1967 in the Syracuse, New York, area with data collected from the nearby community of Auburn in 1952. These studies are of unusual interest not only because of the time span covered, but also because they have been purposely comparative in design, implying a stronger degree of equivalence in coding decisions than can be assumed for comparisons between the Ward-Mutual study and our 1965–66 data.

The Walker materials are largely consistent, however, with our efforts at national comparisons. They show significant decreases in time spent on food preparation and ironing, much as one would expect with the advent of prepared foods and no-iron fabrics. These "gains" are more than offset, however, by marked increases in time spent shopping and in travel, particularly travel associated with household errands and the chauffeuring of children. The net effect is that greater amounts of time are being spent on home management.

Finally, corresponding results are reported from the cross-section study by

[48] See Table C of the Appendix. The statements above are made after eating times for men and women have been removed from the Table C category "eating and preparing food."

[49] Marketing time was found to contribute one of the most dramatic increases in the activities performed by rural New York housewives between 1936 and 1952. Food preparation and household chores were greatly decreased. Information from the Walker studies has been drawn from Kathryn Walker, "Time Use for Home-making Work," a paper presented to the 14th Congress of CIOSTA in Helsinki, Finland, July, 1968; *Idem,* "Homemaking Still Takes Time," *Journal of Home Economics,* vol. 61, October, 1969, 621–624; and from personal communication with Professor Walker.

Morgan *et al.* which show that the possession of "labor-saving" home appliances is simply unrelated to the amount of time spent on housework. By far the most crucial determinant of housework time is the obvious variable: the employment status of the woman in the household.[50] Such patterns of findings probably help to explain why housework figures are not much higher in Eastern European countries (Table 1) where ownership of most appliances is rare, but where the vast majority of women work.[51]

All told, the conventional assumption that the advent of home appliances and other conveniences would divert large amounts of time from home management chores to leisure and recreation seems purely wrong. Naturally, labor-saving devices *do* save both time and drudgery. In fact, they probably make a major contribution in permitting women the "luxury" of outside employment while maintaining a household at a tolerable level. Nevertheless, for the woman who stays in the home, it seems that expectations concerning the level of household care have risen significantly in the past 30 years and that, in an affluent society, there is a good deal more at home to take care *of*. The household with three or four dozen appliances undoubtedly accomplishes a great deal of "work output." But with such an array, a breakdown every week or two would not be surprising. And in a society where it is rumored that even plumbers are on the verge of refusing to make house calls, the fuss and erranding associated with such breakdowns is substantial.

By far the most important consideration, however, lies in the simple fact that the number of individual purchases of items per household per week must have soared astonishingly in the past 50 years. While the introduction of appliances and conveniences has reduced their related activity times either not at all or somewhat less than might have been assumed, those travel times associated with shopping have by all studies shown substantial increases in the past 15 to 30 years, and have been primarily responsible for increasing the absolute times required for home management. The most noteworthy difference between the time-budget figures of the Ward-Mutual study and our 1965–66 study was a .3 hour increase in time spent shopping.[52] While the figure in this form seems insignificant, it is worth remembering that if taken at face value it represents an *increase* of more than 2 billion man-hours per year for the adult population of the United States in over little more than a decade. Our latest figure is somewhat inflated by the fact that some of the 1965–66 data were collected as late as two

[50] Morgan *et al., op. cit.,* pp. 111–112.
[51] Some "trade-off" of activities is suggested, however, by the larger housecleaning times in Western Europe conceivably "replacing" the longer food preparation times that seem required in Eastern Europe.
[52] Data in Appendix Table B also show larger figures for shopping in 1965–66 than in the Sorokin-Berger study. As already noted, Lundberg *et al.* did not mention shopping at all in their study.

weeks before Christmas. Nevertheless, the fact that other studies imply in their fragmentary way that an increase of this rough magnitude in shopping times has been occurring for the American population leads us to credit it as a real trend of major significance.[53] We live in a consumption society, as numerous observers have remarked. But while consumption has increased, so have the time costs of hunting and gathering.

Transportation and Travel Time. Numerous empirical studies bearing on individual transportation have been undertaken in the United States, but none to our knowledge has successfully delved into the totality of trips that individuals take on a given day (particularly those that involve walking or public transportation). Transportation specialists tend to turn their primary attention to other parameters such as the distance of trips and their geographical origins and destinations. Moreover, those studies that give time durations any major focus tend to be quite recent and hence of very limited use in the assessment of long-term change. As a result, this literature, while voluminous, is less germane to our purposes than might be imagined at first glance.

Table 6. Hours Spent in Person-Trips Per Day Per Household

Trip Purpose	1953	1965
Work	2.8	2.5
School	.3	.5
Social-recreational-meals	1.6	2.0
Shopping-personal business	1.5	2.6

The sole study with much temporal depth was the Detroit Transportation and Land Use Study (TALUS), which demonstrated a 23 percent increase in person-trips per day per household over the period between 1953 and 1965. A breakdown of these data by trip purpose is shown in Table 6.[54] If it can be assumed that travel times per trip have not changed radically in this 12-year period, the increase in trips for shopping and personal errands is simply part of the trend discussed above.[55]

[53] Not only do the Walker studies confirm the direction and magnitude of this trend, but also two transportation studies covering the Detroit area, the first conducted in 1953 and the other in 1965, showed that the greatest increase in types of trip within that period was for "shopping" and "personal business." We shall examine these latter studies in more detail in following paragraphs.

[54] These figures are calculated from *A Profile of Southeastern Michigan*, Detroit Transportation and Land Use Study, 1248 Washington Boulevard, Detroit, Mich.

[55] Shopping trips tend, however, to be somewhat shorter than other types of trips, according to data in Allan Voorhees and Associates, *Factors and Trends in Trip Lengths*. Highway Research Board, Washington, D.C., 1968.

Our 1965–66 data show a parallel increase in time spent traveling by comparison with the Ward-Mutual study over almost exactly the same period. Pushing comparisons back to the two studies of the 1930's reveals somewhat lower travel times in the Lundberg data, although the Sorokin-Berger travel times, in perplexing fashion, exceed those currently found. However, two forms of leisure transportation—pleasure drives and walking—appear to have declined rather unequivocally as the automobile has become a standard way of life during the last 30 years.

More detailed analyses of the changes chronicled in the TALUS data have demonstrated rather conclusively that the prime factor lying behind the increase in person-trips is the addition of second and third automobiles to the more affluent households in this period. That is, there was some sign of increase in trips even for households with the same number of cars across the two periods studied. But these differences were minor compared to differences in trips between households with one car and those with more; and the proportion of multiple-car households increased impressively between 1953 and 1965.[56] Thus, the implication is clear that, as second cars are added to a household's possessions, the wife becomes freed for travel ventures despite the immobilization of the first family car during the day at the husband's place of work. Such an interpretation is directly corroborated by the national-level data, since we find a proportionately greater increase in travel time for women than for men between 1954 and 1965–66. As second cars come within economic reach of more and more households, it is therefore likely that aggregate numbers of trips will continue to rise.

At the same time, it is rather remarkable that the automobile per se does not affect total travel *times* (as opposed to numbers of trips) more radically than appears to be the case. The automobile owner has greater mobility and might be expected to use it for increased travel. On the other hand, he is likely to achieve any given destination more rapidly than the non-owner. Our data indicate that automobile owners in the United States do not spend appreciably more time on travel than non-owners. In some of the countries of the multinational study, they actually were spending less time. Of course automobile users cover much greater expanses of ground in a given time, and the true impact of the private car has been registered dramatically in the outward explosion of the suburbs. Nonetheless, the near-constancy of travel times (including the trip to work) in the face of such a basic technological revolution is remarkable. It seems to have taken the addition of second and third cars to produce more than trivial changes in per capita travel times.

The changes discussed above do not exhaust interesting trends in time allocations that may be found in the Appendix tables, although they do form the

---

[56] William Ladd, *The Generation of Travel in the Detroit Region.* Center for Urban Studies, University of Michigan, Dearborn, 1968.

bulk of comparisons that entail major shifts in time use. Furthermore, they appear consistently in those data, and are not subject to unusual methodological doubt. The reader convinced that the pace of American life has become increasingly hectic in the past generation will naturally be intrigued by the fact that both the Lundberg and the Sorokin-Berger respondents averaged almost an hour per day more sleep than did our respondents in 1965–66.[57] His suspicions might be further fortified by the observation that all relevant comparisons in the Appendix show less time now spent in eating meals. Regrettably, any excitement over these differences must be suspended in view of exogenous discrepancies in the samples, such as the upper-middle-class nature of the Lundberg respondents as well as a possible overrepresentation of weekend days, and the fact that the Sorokin-Berger sample had an undue number of persons in the involuntary leisure of unemployment.

It should not be forgotten that we have mentioned certain important changes in passing while discussing other changes with which they appear associated. Thus, for example, data in our Appendix tables show a decreasing amount of time spent visiting and entertaining. We associated this decline with the advent of television, and the links do indeed appear quite clear in more specialized studies of the problem.[58] On the other hand, it is hard to believe that television alone has been responsible for the observed decline in this type of social interaction. Moreover, there are other forms of social interaction that reflect fascinating aspects of American life. Correspondence, religious participation, the playing of sports, and activities connected with formal organizations may also consume declining amounts of time since the 1930's, as our Appendix tables hint at a number of points. Unfortunately, activities of this kind are engaged in by such small minorities of a cross-section population on any given day that average durations are miniscule and difficult to use as a basis for detecting solid trends.

Whereas television has intruded dramatically on time allocations in daily life over the past 20 years, we have some right to be impressed at what seems to be a rather strong measure of inelasticity in common time use in the face of major and continuing technological change. As increased productivity and other factors permit a shorter working week, many people use the time freed to engage in second jobs. As new inventions are diffused that make various facets of home management easier and more efficient, expectations about home care rise and other problems seem to intervene that minimize changes in time allocations. People capitalize on the private automobile to extend their ranges of geographic

---

[57] Unfortunately, the Ward-Mutual data exclude the prime hours of the day for sleeping.

[58] The Videotown study in particular attests to the strength of this link (see Videotown, *op. cit.*).

mobility and reshape the urban areas, but the amount of time spent traveling seems fixed within a remarkably narrow range.

From this point of view, average time durations for grossly categorized activities yield an insensitive reflection of social change. These constancies are not without interest in their own right as they hint at some of the relatively fixed properties of the species. They are magnificently displayed in the multinational data where populations on three continents, living in a variety of climates under sharply differing political systems and at various levels of economic development, show overwhelming similarities in their gross time allocations.

At the same time, some of this sense of constancy clearly arises from the grossness of the categorization of activities. The shell or frame constituted by gross activity divisions refers largely to basic functional requisites and may have less latitude for change than is commonly supposed. Specification of the more detailed content and modes of activity could be expected to show a considerably more lively picture of change. Time spent in "travel" has changed very little in the past generation, and time spent in "attention to the mass media" only somewhat more. However, "travel by private car" and "watching television" have changed a great deal. Some of these more detailed changes may turn out, on closer inspection, to be relatively superficial in their significance, but others will not be.

The important point is that we have limited our historical comparisons to sets of grossly categorized activities simply because this is the only form in which time-use data from the past are available. Our 1965–66 data are much richer in detail than those we have so far observed, and it is our assumption that in coming decades they will be of much greater utility as "baseline" information than any earlier work has been for our comparisons here. As we look to the future, however, our 1965–66 data might well have been further enriched in a large number of dimensions, any of which might help to clarify the human significance of time use changes.

Let us turn therefore to some of the further activity delineations that have already been carried out even though we lack much historical perspective on them. Ultimately we will examine other data specifications concerning time use that would be important to implement in the future.

Supplementary Parameters of Time Use

An effort was made in connection with the multinational study of time use to enrich the description of events catalogued for the respondent's day in several systematic directions. First, data were collected on secondary activities that may have simultaneously accompanied the primary activity, such as listening to the radio while driving to work. Second, some broad information was collected as to where each activity took place, such as at home, at the work place, on the streets, and the like. Third, for each activity catalogued, data were recorded as to what other persons, if any, were present or partners in the activity. Finally, the data were assembled in such a fashion that it is possible to reconstruct the sequence of events for individuals over the course of their day, including the precise time of day at which each activity took place.

While these may seem almost minimal further specifications of events in daily life, few if any earlier studies have tried to capture information in anything like this detail. Indeed, most published studies of this genre provide information only on average durations of activity types totaled across a day, and it is clear that even such data on primary activities can be cast in a much greater variety of forms.

Thus, although a fair range of supplementary information is available in the 1965–66 study, there is rarely any basis for historical comparisons. The existence of parallel information from the various countries in the multinational study provides some external frame of reference for assessing the American results, but we continue to be wary of forcing synchronic data toward diachronic conclusions.

Our purpose in this section, then, is less to speak of long-term change than to convey a brief glimpse of the utility of some of these supplementary descriptors or statistical formulations of the basic time information, as well as some of the methodological hazards in their collection. We assume that future studies monitoring time use in the United States will wish to collect these types of supplementary information at the very least.

Secondary Activities. No person's activities are neatly divisible into packets of time that total to the 1,440 minutes of the day. The performance of two or more activities simultaneously creates conceptual and methodological problems that all investigators have been obliged at least to acknowledge. Unfortunately, none of the three major American studies of historical interest to us offered the problem more than lip service: in each case, coding conventions were employed to limit activity records to the appropriate fixed total of minutes in the span of time covered, thereby capturing only activities deemed primary.

For the multinational study, cognizance was taken for each activity noted as to whether any second activity was accompanying it, and if so, what that activity was. Respondents were encouraged to record such entries in their time diary under a heading "Doing anything else?" and were further probed by the interviewers who went over the diaries with the respondents.[59]

---

[59] Numerous "secondary activities" were reported originally as a part of two primary activities, such as "eating and watching television." The convention adopted for such entries was to divide the time allocated to this entry into two halves, one with eating as a primary activity and television as secondary, and the other segment with the positions reversed. More typically, however, the respondent himself defined what activity was secondary in response to the probe: "Doing anything else?"

There is reason to believe that the registration of secondary activities is much more sensitive to variations in interviewer thoroughness and verbal skills of the respondent than is the case for primary activities. This fact sets some stringent limits on the kinds of inference that seem warranted from the second-ary-activity data. Thus, for example, it is tempting to imagine that people with greater education engage in more complex activity patterns and, indeed, in al-most every site of the multinational survey, more secondary activities are re-corded by respondents of higher education. But the higher verbal facility of these respondents, along with their greater probable compulsiveness in keeping such records, makes it wise to leave such a hypothesis a moot point.[60]

Nevertheless, collection of secondary-activity information even in some-what unreliable form serves to deepen the historical record in useful ways. For example, first glances at data on primary activities across the multinational sites made it appear that Americans, unlike respondents at European sites, had almost completely deserted the radio in favor of television. Nevertheless, sub-stantial radio listening times reported as secondary activities in the United States help to clarify the continuing importance of the medium.

Table 7 provides a summary glimpse at the patterns of secondary activities at the United States sites in the 1965–66 study and should be a useful bench mark for future work. It can be seen that conversation and mass media usage accounted for about 80 percent of all secondary activities reported.[61]

Location of Activities. Sociologists and city planners have a strong in-terest in the locus of activities in daily life, although their more specific informa-tion needs diverge somewhat. Sociologists are likely to focus on rather gross typological data indicating the pattern of activities centered at home, at work, in various public settings, and the like. One would expect the "other-directed" man to spend more time away from home, and the "organization man" or the "marketing personality" to frequent locations that are distinctive from each other and from their predecessors. On the other hand, this gross information is of limited utility to planners and transportation specialists who need to know precise geographic locations and travel routes as well as durations and time of

[60] No parallel relationship emerges at a societal level, however. That is, survey sites with high aggregate education levels did not produce any marked increment in incidence of secondary-activity reports over those with low educational backgrounds. There is strong internal evidence that the thoroughness of interviewer training at various sites, uncorre-lated with the educational level of the sites, made a major contribution to variations in such mentions.

[61] Table 7 helps to dramatize the sensitivity of secondary-activity data to variations in field methods. Whereas Jackson, Michigan, falls below the national urban mean in levels of education, and might, therefore, be expected to have generated sparser reports of sec-ondary activities, more than an extra hour, largely in "conversation," was recorded there. The difference can be traced to personal instruction and closer supervision of the Jackson field work, as opposed to mailed instructions for the national study.

Table 7. Secondary Activity Time Expenditures for 27 Activity Categories for the U.S. Survey Sites

(*In Hours per Day*)

	National Sample	Jackson, Michigan
1. Regular work	a	a
2. Second job	a	a
3. Nonwork	a	a
4. Trip to/from work	a	a
5. Prepare food	a	a
6. Clean house	a	a
7. Laundry, mending	a	a
8. Other upkeep	a	a
9. Pets/garden	a	a
10. Sleep	a	a
11. Personal care	a	a
12. Eating	.1	.2
13. Resting	.1	.1
14. Child care	.1	.2
15. Shopping	a	a
16. Nonwork trips	a	a
17. Education	a	a
18. Organizations	a	a
19. Radio	.9	.8
20. Television	.6	.6
21. Reading	.3	.2
22. Social life	.2	.2
23. Conversation	2.6	4.0
24. Walking	a	a
25. Sports	a	a
26. Various leisure	.2	.2
27. Amusements	a	a
Total	5.3	6.7
Free time (13, 17–27)	4.9	6.1

a Average time less than three minutes.

day, in order to decide upon optimal locations of homes, offices, and shops within a particular community. One useful effort to bridge this gap is provided by the research of Stuart Chapin, Jr., who has begun investigations into the patterns of two-dimensional spatial movement in a clearly formulated community context.[62] It is, of course, much more costly to maintain data on precise move-

[62] See Stuart Chapin, Jr., and Henry Hightower, *Household Activity Systems—A Pilot Investigation*. Institute for Research in Social Science, Chapel Hill, N.C., 1966.

ments when dealing with a national sample, and our 1965–66 data only contain data on gross locations of sociological interest.

Probably the most extensive analyses of the relation between time and location is the research on "behavior settings" produced by the Barkers at Kansas University. One particularly commendable phase of this research is the development of advanced indexes of the interplay between individuals and social locations. In one cross-cultural study, for example, it was found that total percentages of time spent in "community behavior settings" were practically the same in two small towns, one in Kansas and the other in England. However, sharp differences existed in the manner in which children were allowed to participate in events in these settings, with children much more restricted in England.[63]

Our 1965–66 national urban figures indicate that Americans were spending just over two-thirds of their *weekly* time fund at home, with almost half of this figure being absorbed of course by sleep. Another sixth of their week is spent at their place of work, and the remainder in streets (5 percent), other people's homes (3 percent), stores (3 percent), restaurants and bars (1 percent), churches (1 percent), and all other places (1 percent).

As always, such figures taken alone do not vibrate with meaning, but could be expected to take on increased meaning as measurements might be repeated in future decades, laying bare the development of trends. Two external points of reference are available, however. Compared to other survey sites in the multinational study, Americans spend average amounts of time at home, but larger than average amounts of time at places of business, in other persons' homes, and at restaurants and places of entertainment. Some fragmentary diachronic comparisons are possible as well, since partial data on locations can be drawn from the 1954 Ward-Mutual study. These latter comparisons (Appendix Tables C and D) show shifts toward increased total time away from home, especially at work, in stores, in transit, and at places of leisure. These increases are particularly clear for women and are corollaries of trends mentioned earlier, such as increased proportions of women working, increased access to second cars permitting travel and shopping during the day, along with some additional recreation. These increases in time spent away from home have been accompanied by a decrease in time spent visiting in other people's homes, despite the fact that, in a cross-national sense, such visitations remain high for Americans even in 1965–66.

Social Contacts. Information on time spent with various types of social partners or in solitude are of more interest to social scientists than to planners

---

[63] Roger Barker and Louise Barker, "Behavior Units for the Comparative Study of Cultures," in Bert Kaplan, ed., *Studying Personality Cross-Culturally*. Row, Peterson, Evanston, Ill., 1961.

but can illuminate an equal range of significant hypotheses. If the appropriate data had been collected over the past century, for example, one would expect them to document quite clearly a growing break with the extended family, with increasing leisure time being passed in the nuclear family or with friends and work colleagues, rather than in the company of relatives.

In perhaps the most comprehensive earlier study of time spent in various types of social contact, however, Reiss failed to confirm a number of stereotypic expectations concerning differences along urban-rural or class lines. He did find urban males spending more time with close associates and "pure clients" than was true of rural males, and less time alone; but only minor differences emerged for six other categories of interpersonal contact. Moreover, he found even fewer significant social-class differences.[64]

The categories of social contact for the multinational study were less detailed and cannot be closely matched to the Reiss findings. Moreover, our respondents were unexpectedly lax in their reporting of partners, leaving unusual blocs of missing data (Table 8). Nevertheless, entries for the American data in Table 8 show at least two notable departures from the foreign data that cannot be written off as artifacts of methodological difficulties. Over the multinational set, Americans spent: (1) the largest amounts of time alone, and (2) some of the smallest amounts of time with children—despite such factors as relatively large numbers of children in American families, high proportions of housewives to working women, and relatively small proportions of children in day-care centers. Americans were also spending relatively small amounts of time with their spouses and other adults living in the same households (because, of course, so few Americans live in extended families) and, conversely, higher amounts of time with friends and relatives living outside the household.

The amount of time Americans spend out of contact with other household members and, more particularly, alone brings to mind visions of American individualism or, for that matter, the "lonely crowd." We are currently investigating some more mundane likelihoods that might, however, continue to have significant relationships with some of these "national character" hypotheses. In dealing with the multinational data, one is impressed by a gradient of increasing density of the "social life space" as one progresses eastward from the United States through Western Europe to Eastern Europe. Representing the small American industrial city is Jackson, Michigan, where a wide swath of the city center is given over almost exclusively to nonresidential buildings, surrounded by a very extended concentric zone of private, one-family dwelling units surrounded by what are, at least in cross-national perspective, very large yards. All told, the set of persons depending on Jackson in a direct and personal eco-

---

[64] Albert J. Reiss, Jr., "Rural-Urban and Status Differences in Interpersonal Contacts," *American Journal of Sociology,* vol. 75, September, 1959, pp. 182–195.

Table 8. Time Expenditures on Various Types of Social Contact[a]
(*In Hours*)

Social Contact	U.S. National Sample	Jackson, Michigan
Alone (including all "sleep")	14.1	13.6
With one's spouse (but not children)	1.7	1.7
With one's children (but not spouse)	1.1	1.4
With one's spouse and children	1.5	1.6
(Total with nuclear family)	(4.3)	(4.7)
Other household adults	.5	.3
Other friends and relatives	1.6	1.7
Work colleagues	2.2	2.5
Organization members	.2	.2
Neighbors or their children	.5	.3
Other combinations	.9	.9
No report	1.2	1.0
Total	25.5	25.2

[a] Categories are not mutually exclusive and hence figures add to more than 24 hours.

nomic way extends to a circle 50 kilometers or more in radius. In the Eastern European cities of comparable population and industrial function included in the multinational study, large apartment buildings are tightly packed even in the center of the city, and the same functional population may occupy as little a circle as 3 to 5 kilometers in radius. Not only do distinct dwelling units occur with much greater geographic density, but it is likely that the number of persons per household room is much larger than in the United States, even though the differences in family size are not noteworthy.

The interdependence between the density of the social space, factors such as the prevalence of private cars and, for that matter, affluence more generally on the one hand, and the simple parameter of time spent alone on the other seems rather compelling. It is unfortunate that the social contact data do not distinguish between intensities of social interaction, so that we would know whether an evening spent by a man, wife, and children in the same living room is marked by a continuous series of three-way interactions, or whether the several parties are engaged in private pursuits and the presence of others is a consequence, perhaps annoying, of the lack of anywhere else to be.

None of this is to say, of course, that such differences in the spatial density of living arrangements may not have tight, more subtle, interactive links, both cause and consequence, with significant national differences in modal value systems. The interest of such hypotheses, including mundane spatial characteristics in an intervening role, is of self-evident interest to both the sociologist and the historian.

Daily Rhythms of Activities. Another way of casting time-budget data involves the examination of flows of activity by varying proportions of the population over the sequence of 24 hours of the day.

One of the more prominent contrasts that arises in the multinational data assembled in this form, for example, is the fact that at the stroke of midnight, a far higher proportion of Americans are awake than in any other country.[65] Some of this idiosyncracy may have roots in the rapid diffusion of electric lighting, along with cheaper electricity, which clearly reduced the ancient premium on fitting waking hours to daylight earlier in the United States than in Europe. Nevertheless, there is reason to believe that late television has made a signal contribution in this direction as well. Such appears to have been the case in Japan between 1960 and 1965, a period when television ownership moved from 28 percent to 85 percent. During this period, time-budget studies showed average times for retiring and rising set back about half an hour.[66]

The same general trend emerges in Figures 1 and 2, where we have graphed the cycles of daily activities for employed men on weekdays across the daily analysis periods of the 1954 Ward-Mutual study and the 1965–66 study.[67] Again, there are some methodological inconveniences due to the failure of the 1954 study to capture a full 24-hour cycle of activity, and certain coding ambiguities.[68] Thus, we are barred from calculating average hours of retiring or rising and obliged to shape some coding adjustments, but these are minor difficulties compared to some of the other ambiguities we have encountered, and the trends in hours for sleeping over this period remain obvious.

Figures 1 and 2 suggest little change in the flows of daily activity over the 11-year period, although leisure activities have decreased in the evening hours in favor of increased participation in home and family obligations, eating, traveling, and semi-leisure activities. Despite a noteworthy increase in set ownership in the intervening time period, television's effect on the evening round of activities has been confined to the late evening hours.

---

[65] A recent survey of television usage in Spain indicates that these earlier retiring times do not characterize all European societies. At 12:30 A.M. on an average weekday 12 percent of the Spanish population is still up and around; moreover, on Saturday the figure rises to 30 percent (*Variety*, April 8, 1970, p. 92).

[66] N. Nakanishi, *A Report on the How-Do-People-Spend-Their-Time Survey*. NHK Public Opinion Research Institute, Tokyo, 1966.

[67] We are indebted to Sebastian de Grazia for making these data available to us.

[68] In the Ward-Mutual data, percentages for "eating" meals include small amounts of time preparing meals, and percentages for "other media" do not include radio listening. Furthermore, the figures for "semi-leisure," "other leisure," and television could only be arbitrarily derived from the closest parallel categories used in the Ward-Mutual study. "Semi-leisure" in Figures 1 and 2 includes such diverse activities as washing and dressing, going to school, and attending meetings. "Home and family" includes household chores, child care, and shopping.

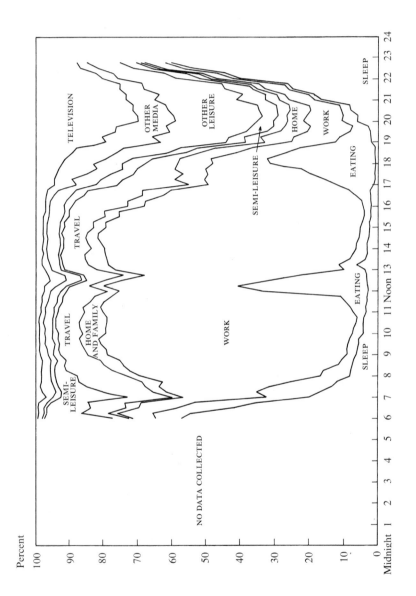

Percent

Figure 1. Cumulative Percentages of Employed Men Engaged in Nine Activities across Twenty-Four Hours of an Average Weekday, 1954

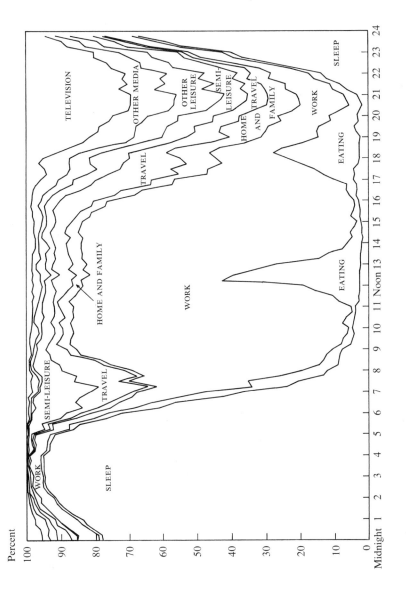

63

Figure 2. Cumulative Percentages of Employed Men Engaged in Nine Activities across Twenty-Four Hours of an Average Weekday, 1965–66

While space has permitted only a "once-over-lightly" survey of the role which supplementary parameters of time use and different ways of assembling time-duration data can have in enriching time-budget materials, we hope to have conveyed some of the sheer variety of illuminations that such additional information can provide. Perhaps our earlier comment, that time-budget information constitutes substrate data pointing in a wild profusion of directions of substantive interest but never carrying very far in any one of them, has been sufficiently exemplified. We would argue that even data of this limited depth, if regularly monitored for populations over long periods of time, would be of intense social interest. Although a skeletal view of human behavior has been captured up to this point, our final section, calling for future elaborations of time-use data, will try to put more flesh on the bones.

Descriptors of the Meaning of Time Use

Attempts to plumb the human significance of time as a resource divide broadly into two currents. One is concerned with the meaning of time uses; the other is concerned with the meaning of time itself. Let us follow the second stream first.

The Meaning of Time. From the major theoretical works of observers such as Simmel and Sorokin through the recent studies of Inkeles, students of social evolution and economic development have been intrigued by what appears to be a profound reorientation of human attitudes toward time that accompanies the passage from traditional society to modern industrialism. The change posited is less a matter of revised feelings about the nature of time than it is a progression from a state in which time has so little significance that it is simply not an attitude object, to a state in which time is vividly salient as a criterion or yardstick for many facets of social behavior. It becomes a precious resource, to be valued, husbanded, and guarded against loss. Such a view is epitomized by the famous dictum of Ben Franklin, written as early as 1748: "Time is money."

While the multinational study largely ignored orientations toward time in favor of chronicles of behavior, some of the participating studies developed relevant measurements on the side. One of the most interesting of these involved the "leg" of the study conducted in Peru by Professor Rudolf Rezsohazy of Louvain. The Peruvian study originated independently of the time-budget investigation and was aimed at exploring links between social notions of time and economic development. The design involved comparative surveys in a traditional Peruvian village, in modern Lima, and in more and less modernized areas in Belgium. Because of the obvious compatibility, time-budget measurements conforming to specifications of the multinational project were subsequently added.

The Rezsohazy data are fascinating but can only be highlighted here. One cluster of findings is of particular note. When a behavioral measure of leisurely attitudes toward time was employed—the length of siesta or rest times during the day—the Peruvian data showed longer rest times by a factor from two to five, depending on the comparison groups. The Belgian data showed little differentiation in rest times from traditional milieux to inhabitants of the most modern and industrialized areas: in Peru, however, there were impressive differences in siesta times in the expected direction between the traditional village and the metropolis. On the other hand, key *attitudes* toward time showed a somewhat different distribution. A central measure here assessed the respondents' sensitivity toward the possibility of "losing" time. In Belgium, less than one person in five showed insensitivity to time loss; in Peru, almost two-thirds of persons interviewed gave insensitive responses. Within-country differentiation by areas of economic development, however, reversed its pattern. Indifference to time as a valued resource was a norm broadly shared in Peru across both traditional and modern sectors, despite the fact that members of the metropolis were behaviorally observing "modern" expectations. In Belgium, there were marked attitudinal variations by economic development: in traditional milieux, there was much less concern about time than in the modernized environments. One apparent implication is that behavioral adjustment to the time requisites of modern life comes first, and attitudes are only brought into adjustment after some lag.

In the social-psychological portions of the 1965–66 U.S. study, we placed more emphasis on the psychological meaning of various time uses than on general attitudes toward time as a resource. Nevertheless, an attempt was undertaken to measure differences in individual senses of "time pressure," with items quite similar to those used by Rezsohazy. We probed to learn how often the respondent felt "rushed," as opposed to the frequency with which he felt that he had "time on his hands." While analytic work with the measure is not complete, it shows a good deal of apparent validity. Thus, for example, employed women, who seem from a number of behavioral aspects of their time budgets to be the most harried major segment of the population, give highest time-pressure responses, with employed men second, and unemployed women most likely to have a sense of time on their hands. Despite the interest of internal analysis with this measure, we are convinced that its greatest value is as a bench-mark measure for future decades, to register changes in the "felt pace of life."[69]

The Meaning of Time Uses. Although it would not be hard to add other important aspects of attitudes toward time worth monitoring on a national base in the future, perhaps the most important frontier involves the development of

[69] It is perhaps noteworthy that a crude measure of life satisfaction contained in the 1965–66 study moves in a curvilinear relation to the time-pressure variable, much as we would like to expect. The harried on one end and the unoccupied on the other give less satisfied responses than are made by individuals lying between.

more incisive measures of the relative significance—social as well as individual —of the alternate ways in which time can be used. However important in the history of ideas Ben Franklin's model of man "spending" or "saving" time as he does money, such a perspective risks implying that units of time are equally experienced, perceived, or appreciated. Time budgets themselves are largely imprisoned in such an implication. De Grazia has put the matter clearly:

> . . . by using a strictly quantitative, assembly-belt conception of time—time as a moving belt of equal units—one ignores the significance of most activity. A moment of awe in religion or ecstasy in love or orgasm in intercourse, a decisive blow to an enemy, relief in a sneeze, or death in a fall is treated as equal to a moment of riding on the bus, shovelling coal, or eating beans.[70]

The point is easy to grant, but any desire to deal with something as vague as the differential "meaning" of various activities opens a very wide gate. We sense immediately that the possible approaches, if not perhaps infinite, are incredibly numerous. On the other hand, most approaches that have been suggested can be roughly divided into three broad classes according to three differential properties of activities: (1) the energy expended in the activity; (2) the motivation underlying its selection; and (3) the gratification drawn from engaging in it.

The second and third of these properties are tightly locked to perceptions of the actor himself. The first is somewhat more "objective," and lends itself as well to more collective definitions of "output" and "efficiency." Depending on the researcher's interest, "energy expended" might encompass anything from physiological measurement of heart rate or blood pressure[71] to ratings by trained observers[72] of effort required, or similar ratings by respondents themselves.[73] A combination of the latter two methods was successfully employed by Havighurst who asked psychiatrists to rate respondents' levels of "role performance" on the basis of lengthy open-ended interviews. The ratings of involvement moved from perfunctory (or solely self-centered) through "sporadic," to full ego involvement in each of eight role areas, such as parent, spouse, and citizen. Four basic syndromes of role performance emerged from these ratings that are surely intriguing enough to warrant verification on more representative samples

[70] de Grazia, *op. cit.,* p. 142.

[71] Work is currently underway at the Research Center for Group Dynamics of the University of Michigan's Institute for Social Research using medical instrumentation to detect physiological reactions to an individual's everyday work situation. See Robert Caplan and John R. P. French, Jr., "Physiological Responses to Work Load: An Exploratory Field Study," a paper available from the Center.

[72] Observations on a full day's activity, although not rated as to energy expenditure, are presented in R. Barker and H. Wright, *One Boy's Day.* Harper, New York, 1951.

[73] R. Meier, "Human Time-Allocation—a Basis for Social Accounts," *Journal of the American Institute of Planners,* vol. 25, February, 1959, p. 27.

.n Havighurst was able to study. Two of the syndromes were constituted simply by high or low involvement in all eight roles. The other two syndromes—both labeled "home-centered"—showed somewhat high ratings in all areas related to the nuclear family but not for the role areas of friend, citizen, and club member. The pattern of these ratings suggests that there is a significant carryover from one role to another, so that we may expect positive correlations between a person's energy expenditures in one area and the vigor of his involvement in other areas.[74]

The economic interest in energy definitions lies less in individual involvement in activity than in the collective significance of any output. Heirich has argued as follows:

> To be conceptually useful, however, allocation of time (an input) must be linked to output from time use. An activity may not have diminished in importance if less time is spent on it but the same output is maintained. Rather, other activities will have gained in relative importance.[75]

Heirich's concern clearly extends beyond the area of work where much effort has been put into the measurement of output. However, adequate modes of "output" measurement that are universal enough to encompass activities as divergent as attending church services, playing golf, and sleeping do not readily come to mind. It would probably be necessary to provide a restrictive answer to the question: "Output with respect to what?" before much progress could be made in this direction.

A second broad approach involves assessment of the actor's *underlying motivation* for engaging in a particular activity. Is the viewer of television simply whiling away the hours, escaping from the problems of his day, or is he intensely challenged by the telecast he has found? It is apparent that answers to questions of this sort would illuminate many time-budget entries, although a wide range of qualitatively different responses are possible, in equally various intellectual currencies, from the respondent's own explanation to interpretations that might be made by a psychoanalyst or a sociologist.

Attempts to categorize the differential motivation for activities was perhaps the major innovative feature of the Sorokin-Berger study, as is obvious from the headings used to characterize activities (see Table B of the Appendix). An earlier and more psychoanalytically-oriented study of motivations underlying time expenditures was undertaken by Thorndike, who had diary entries rated by a jury of psychologists. Except for a few curious exceptions—6 percent of church activities brought sexual entertainment and 4 percent protection from

---

[74] Robert Havighurst, "The Nature and Value of Meaningful Free-Time Activity, in R. Kleemeier, ed., *Aging and Leisure*. Oxford University Press, New York, 1961.

[75] Heirich, *op. cit.*, p. 387.

hunger and cold—the results were obvious enough to produce little excitement.[76]

A narrow but rather critical dimension associated with the motivation underlying activities involves the degree of discretion represented by the selection of an activity. It is not of great interest to discuss the motivation underlying sleep or evacuation for although there are some variations, these are, by and large, biological imperatives. The question of motivation becomes most interesting when behavior is least constrained by biology, economy, or even, to some degree, strict social expectations, as in the central concept of "free time." There is no point, however, in trying to force activities into a dichotomy of "free time" and time which is constrained: there is obviously some continuum along which activities fall for different people, representing "degree of constraint." A closely related notion involves the relative "elasticity" of various activities in a population.

Where time is truly open to short-term discretion—and only small proportions of the 24-hour day are likely to be—interest in activity motivation is likely to turn to hierarchies of preferences for alternate optional activities. One approach toward measurement of such hierarchies is to ask the respondent hypothetically what he would do if suddenly awarded some extra hours in his day. There is reason to believe, however, that such an approach tends to draw highly idealized answers. The father imagines that he would capitalize on such good fortune to spend more time with his children, although internal evidence suggests strongly that he would find other things to do.[77]

We attempted in the 1965–66 study to get some rough assessment of differing degrees of felt constraint about various types of activities, as well as some notion of hierarchy of motivations across activities actually engaged in, by a rather different approach which involved the relative "replaceability" of activities. After the respondent had completely accounted for his activities "yesterday," the interviewer took this non-hypothetical record and asked which of the activities would have been given up if an unexpected problem had suddenly arisen that had to be taken care at some time before the 24 hours was completed. The respondent was obliged first to free two hours of "yesterday's" record, then two further pairs of hours, helping to indicate the order with which activities were replaced.

Television viewing stood head and shoulders over all other activity types in its felt dispensability, whether measured in terms of absolute numbers of hours replaced or in terms of the proportion of time given to the activity that would have been discarded. Evidence that such a finding is not simply hypothetical may lie in the fact that our time-pressure variable shows a much higher correla-

[76] D. Thorndike, "How We Spend Our Time and What We Spend It For," *Scientific Monthly,* vol. 44, May, 1937, pp. 464–469.

[77] Informal communication with Stuart Chapin, Jr.

tion with television viewing than with any other activity. That is, large amounts of television viewing are concentrated among people with most "time on their hands"; people under strong time pressures watch relatively little. Such data do not tell us much about the varying types of motivation that bring people to their television set, but they give some indication of the casual level of those motivations relative to other demands of the day. Watching television is truly a "pastime" in the primitive sense of the term.

The degree of *psychological satisfaction* that people draw from various of their daily activities can of course be seen as an aspect of motivation, broadly construed. It constitutes a related dimension which is not too difficult to treat systematically, however, and is central enough to warrant separate discussion in its own right. We would naturally expect a substantial correlation between expected satisfaction from various discretionary activities and participation in those activities. Nevertheless, certain "reality" factors of an economic or social sort can intervene to limit access to some highly gratifying activities. Moreover, it is fortunate that people can find strong gratification in some kinds of activities that are not open to much discretion in any event. Hence it remains of interest to learn what relative satisfaction people attach to various types of activity.

Several scholars, including Foote[78] and Lough,[79] have attempted to explore the satisfaction dimension associated with time budgets, by asking the respondent to rate each activity performed during a day in terms of its gratification. Little in the way of systematic findings has been publicized from such work, although we know that they have tended to show a rather small proportion of daily activities that occasion strong satisfaction or dissatisfaction for anybody, suggesting the degree to which most of daily life is experienced in a routine way.

Other work has gone forward estimating satisfaction in a more general way, less tightly linked to specific activities of a time budget. Inkeles focused on one expression of satisfaction that he found useful for aggregative purposes: whether or not a person had laughed on a particular day. The replies showed the expected higher incidence of happiness among the more affluent, a result confirmed across societies.[80] Bradburn and Caplovitz extended the observation period to a full week, asking whether during such a period respondents had felt particularly proud or happy, or lonely or depressed.[81]

We used two different approaches in attempting to associate satisfaction

[78] Nelson Foote, "Methods for the Study of Meaning in Use of Time," in R. Kleemeier, ed., *Aging and Leisure.* Oxford University Press, New York, 1961.

[79] Thomas Lough, "An Equilibrium Model of a Relationship Between Feelings and Behavior," unpublished doctoral dissertation, University of Michigan, 1960.

[80] Alex Inkeles, "Industrial Man," *American Journal of Sociology,* vol. 66, July, 1960, pp. 1–31.

[81] Norman Bradburn and David Caplovitz, *Reports on Happiness: A Pilot Study of Behavior Related to Mental Health.* Aldine, Chicago, 1965.

with varying forms of time use in the 1965–66 study. Since it seemed prohibitively time-consuming to obtain ratings for all activities, we merely asked respondents to indicate which of "yesterday's" activities had brought them greatest satisfaction, and which had been least satisfying. As might be expected, the range of activities noted as most satisfying varied widely. Work-related activities were singled out by 25 percent of the employed segment of the sample, but at the same time 35 percent of employed men said that work was the part of the day they enjoyed least. The high frequency of work mentions is a straightforward indication of its centrality in the lives of employed persons. Nonetheless, the polarization of feelings it occasions is of considerable interest.

Next in frequency of mention as most satisfying of the preceding day's events was a cluster of forms of social interaction, including family activities, visiting, and conversation. Eating and sleeping were singled out with somewhat surprising frequency, and despite the casual reactions of the sample as a whole to television, it also was mentioned with some frequency as most satisfying. Each of these more prominent "free-time" uses was mentioned only by 10 to 20 percent of the sample, however. Housework was by far the least satisfying activity for women, with over half the housewives noting their particular displeasure with it. Over-all, there seemed to be a margin of positive feeling about daily activities: over 90 percent of the sample indicated some part of the day enjoyed most, while less than 80 percent identified activities they enjoyed least.

We also sought to evaluate some of the more generic sources of satisfaction by means of a simple rating scale that respondents were asked to apply to a large variety of items including central objects (house, car) and role relations (marriage, family) as well as many broad types of activity. If the proportions giving ratings of "great satisfaction" to such items can be used as a loose yardstick, work pales by comparison with children and marriage as a source of gratification, for each of the latter drew the most extreme positive responses from over three-quarters of the sample. The next most frequent source of great satisfaction (40 percent) was registered by living quarters. Stimulating least enthusiasm (falling well behind "sports," "relaxing," one's car) were organizational memberships and following politics, pursuits which have little visibility in time-budget diaries.

It is not surprising, of course, that there are positive correlations that run consistently at levels which are rather strong by normal social science standards between satisfaction gained from particular activities and the amounts of time the individual devotes to them, or the frequency with which he engages in them. Yet such correlations are far from perfect and invite analysis of constraints that intervene to weaken them.[82] Nevertheless, here as elsewhere, it is likely that

---

[82] Some of these considerations, as well as a closer examination of variations and subtleties shown by the satisfaction dimension in various segments of the population, lie beyond the scope of this paper. They are being treated in the monograph on American time use under preparation by the current authors.

such information will take on its richest meaning as component measurements are repeated over the decades and secular trends in satisfaction from various kinds of activities can be detected.

It would not be difficult to extend the list of directions in which efforts might run, all seeking to probe more deeply the meaning of time use. It is also clear that measurement experimentation in these domains is in its infancy. The important point, in addition to providing the reader with some sense of what has been tried, is that elaborated information of this sort must be added to traditional time-budget material if the latter is to make any extensive contribution beyond mechanical and pedestrian forms of social planning, such as where to locate stores or how to time traffic lights.

We have already emphasized that raw time budgets themselves cry out for more thorough specification of the sheer content of activities. While our 96-category activity code is the most detailed to have been attempted in a major national study, it remains cursory enough to risk missing much that is important about life styles.[83] Even with the detail that would bring life styles into sharpest resolution, however, a further layer of information would remain necessary. It is not enough to know how different segments of the population organize their lives. It is important to know as well what meaning the various facets of these life styles have for their participants, from some of the points of view we have most recently described above.

At the same time, no demand for a richer texture of information would be very responsible if left without some sobering recognition of collection costs involved. Our 1965–66 study involved people in what was typically almost two hours of personal interviewing in a three-day period, with the onerous chore of filling out a time diary in the intervening day. There was widespread feeling that we had pushed a cross-section sample to the outer limits of its patience, and that attempts at much further information from it would have produced disastrous

---

[83] A variety of obvious social-class differences are concealed. Under "playing cards," for example, poker and bridge become equivalent, although the social distribution of their incidence is probably very different. The same is true of "playing sports," where a separate coding of bowling, a sport engaged in rather homogeneously across social strata, would probably reveal much higher participation in remaining sports activity by members of the middle class. Any more detailed monitoring of the content of communicative behavior, whether "reading," "watching television," or informal conversation, would probably show sharp class differences as well. An interesting differentiation of attendance at drinking establishments which would escape the gross categorization of activity is provided in N. Gottlieb, "Neighborhood Taverns and Cocktail Lounges: A Study of Class Differences," *American Journal of Sociology,* vol. 62, May, 1957, pp. 559–562. Some fascinating and unexpected functions of television viewing which would be equally ignored are contained in A. Blum, "Lower-Class Negro Television Spectators: The Concept of Pseudo-Jovial Skepticism," in Arthur Shostak and William Gomberg, eds., *Blue-Collar World.* Prentice-Hall, Englewood Cliffs, N.J., 1964, pp. 429–435.

rates of refusal.[84] Turning to captive populations for more extensive information is one recourse that is of little interest because of the loss of representativeness involved. The only other obvious recourse is to specialize studies satellited in more or less direct ways to a time-budget core, each of which could explore one or two domains of daily life in far more extensive detail.

However all this may be, there seems to be some fairly obvious utility in an occasional over-all assessment of how the national population is spending its time, even in rather bare-bones, time-budget form. Since the completion of the 1965–66 study, we have been approached for a bewildering assortment of specific parameters that can be uniquely estimated from the study, each of which serves as some critical point of departure or frame of reference in more specialized theoretical or practical discussion. Moreover, while we have done little to emphasize the fact in passing, the data have broader relevance for social policy. For example, any sensitive contact with these materials rapidly creates an appreciation for the hectic lives imposed on women who desire to work while maintaining a family and household. Even small changes in institutional forms, such as day-care centers, could produce marked increments in the "quality of life" for a substantial and growing proportion of the population. Similarly, while the West has for some time congratulated itself on escaping the affliction of a retail distribution system so inefficient as to require the long shopping queues notorious in Eastern Europe, it may not be too early to cast about for new innovations that would keep its own shopping times within bounds, dedicated to the society of extremely high consumption levels.

Whereas one would be loath to hinge some of these more sweeping aspects of social planning and policy on a single time-budget study without detailed supporting information from more specialized studies, such bare-bones work repeated at infrequent intervals (15 years would probably suffice for most purposes) can serve as something of a distant early-warning system of unforeseen trends, as well as a monitor of trends expected from technological change that for one or another set of reasons has failed to materialize.[85]

---

[84] Although the problem is more readily solved, samples for time-budget studies ideally should be much larger than is necessary in many types of investigation. This is so simply because there are a number of basic lines of sharp heterogeneity so obvious as to be trivial, which must be controlled at the start. Thus, the vast majority of analyses with the time budgets themselves make limited sense except as the sample is initially divided into men, employed women, and housewives, crosscut at the very least by a division into weekdays and weekends. This means that a national sample of normal size is reduced at the outset to six subgroups averaging less than three hundred cases in size. The addition of one further complex variable with strong bearing on time use—"life cycle," involving multiple categories reflecting marital status, presence of children in the household, and age, provides an excellent example—and case numbers in many cells have already become so small that any estimates are subject to distressing sampling error. All this, so to speak, before the interesting part of an analysis has begun.

[85] The numerous difficulties we have had drawing firm temporal comparisons in time

Small displacements of time use averaging to a few minutes per day per capita may seem at first glance to be of such limited magnitude as to be no more than intellectual curiosities. Writ large against the national population, however, they refer to billions of man-hours per year, and in this mode have a much more obvious collective interest. Although time displacements do not begin to capture all that is important about structural, institutional, and technological change, and capture what they do only in rather muffled form, they at least reflect those "trickle-down" effects at a rather ultimate point: the daily lives of human beings.

APPENDIX

Contrast of Time-Budget Figures from Different Eras

This Appendix provides the detailed contrasts between time-budget figures from our 1965–66 study and each of the first three studies outlined in Table 2. The limitations of the earlier time-budget studies have been heavily stressed in the text, but can also be considered in greater detail here. Indeed, it is to this facet of the data in these tables and the intricate problems of subsequent interpretation that we draw the reader's attention.

The comparison between 1965–66 national data and those from the earliest study by Lundberg and his associates in Westchester County is presented in Table A in terms of the original Lundberg categories.[86] Since these authors provided figures separately by occupational groups, a major barrier to the comparability of the two sets of data is removed. However, it raises further problems as well, for Lundberg *et al.* do not provide enough detail on the respondents' occupational backgrounds to assure precise equivalences to be established with groups from our sample. Thus, the Lundberg "labor" category, which contains only 10 men, might have been comprised of 10 unskilled workers (e.g., construction workers) or 10 highly skilled workers (e.g., carpenters); and we have found certain reliable time-budget differences between such categories of blue-

---

allocations will not characterize work in the future. Virtually all the difficulties spring from the simple fact that no earlier studies were conducted with later work in mind. In the case of the 1954 national study, this meant that the data were thrown away, eliminating any secondary analysis and leaving us with the limited tabulations run with other goals in mind. Not only are the data from the 1965–66 study "banked," but the raw records and detailed documentation of coding conventions are all being carefully preserved. Aside from the limited size of the national sample and its urban universe, future comparisons with it should be extremely straightforward and incisive.

[86] The 1965–66 figures are drawn from data in John P. Robinson and Philip E. Converse, *66 Basic Tables of Time-Budget Data for the United States.* Survey Research Center, Institute for Social Research, University of Michigan, Ann Arbor, June, 1966.

Table A. Comparison of Average Time Expenditures for Various Groups in Lundberg et al. (1934) with Similar Groups of the 1965–66 Study (in Parentheses)

	Men			Employed Women		Housewives
	Executives Professional	White Collar	Labor	White Collar	Labor	
(N =)	97 (126)	268 (97)	10 (283)	276 (182)	60 (112)	107 (176)
Nonleisure:[a]						
Sleep	8.2 (7.7)	8.3 (7.6)	9.0 (7.5)	8.2 (7.6)	8.3 (7.6)	8.6 (7.5)
Work for pay	6.2 (6.8)	6.4 (7.2)	5.9 (6.8)	5.9 (5.4)	6.7 (4.5)	0.1 (0.2)
Care of self	0.7 (0.7)	0.7 (0.8)	0.8 (1.0)	1.0 (1.1)	1.0 (1.1)	1.0 (1.0)
Transportation	1.2 (1.6)	0.8 (1.5)	0.9 (1.4)	1.1 (1.3)	1.0 (1.2)	0.8 (1.0)
Household and children	0.9 (0.7)	0.5 (0.6)	0.6 (0.6)	1.2 (2.9)	1.4 (3.4)	4.2 (6.2)
Total nonleisure hours	17.2 (17.5)	16.7 (17.7)	17.2 (17.3)	17.4 (18.3)	18.4 (17.8)	14.7 (15.9)
Shopping	(0.4)	(0.3)	(0.4)	(0.5)	(0.7)	(0.7)
Undisclosed, private	(0.2)	(0.2)	(0.2)	(0.3)	(0.3)	(0.3)

Leisure:[b]

Eating	106	(78)	114	(73)	101	(70)	116	(59)	109	(59)	106	(79)
Visiting	79	(68)	81	(74)	94	(80)	94	(74)	74	(90)	151	(138)
Reading	74	(50)	61	(36)	95	(37)	43	(29)	38	(21)	84	(40)
Entertainment	15	(11)	45	(13)	35	(6)	48	(14)	29	(14)	44	(10)
Sports	40	(11)	34	(13)	35	(13)	19	(7)	20	(4)	16	(4)
Radio	22	(5)	34	(4)	32	(5)	18	(5)	45	(3)	29	(2)
Motoring	15	(2)	20	(2)	12	(1)	25	(4)	13	(1)	10	(3)
Clubs	10	(17)	8	(10)	0	(7)	3	(8)	0	(4)	61	(19)
Television		(80)		(75)		(120)		(58)		(85)		(75)
Miscellaneous	40	(38)	35	(54)	5	(39)	33	(48)	8	(53)	50	(56)
Total leisure minutes	401	(360)	438	(354)	409	(378)	399	(306)	336	(324)	551	(426)
Total leisure hours	6.7	(6.0)	7.3	(5.9)	6.8	(6.3)	6.6	(5.1)	5.6	(5.4)	9.2	(7.1)
Total hours	23.9	(24.1)	24.0	(24.1)	24.0	(24.2)	24.0	(24.2)	24.0	(24.2)	23.9	(24.0)

[a] Hours per day.
[b] Minutes per day.

collar workers in our own sample. In lieu of any better criteria, the figures in Table A represent our complete blue-collar sample, consisting mainly of skilled workers. Similar problems arise in finding a suitable comparison group for Lundberg's white-collar sample, all of whom worked for a large utility company, their "executive-professional" category, and housewives, the latter two groups having been contacted directly or indirectly through a women's club.[87] Nevertheless, most of the differences between the 1931–33 data and the 1965–66 data are so consistent across all occupational groupings that these definitional problems probably are not critical.

The data in Table A indicate substantial differences in almost every one of the 14 activity categories employed by Lundberg *et al.* Examining differences on an activity-by-activity basis, one finds the following:

1. *Sleep* in the 1965–66 data is anywhere from 30 to 66 minutes less than in the early 1930's. The questions of day-of-the-week weighting and sampling of unemployed in the Lundberg *et al.* data are confounding factors, but the differences seem too large for this explanation alone.

2. *Work for pay,* in contrast, is almost an hour *longer* for men in our sample, again running counter to any assumption of a decreasing workweek. However, Lundberg *et al.* fail to mention the percentage of their respondents who were unemployed in these depression years, and this vital information could easily account for the surprising differences for men in Table A.

   Two further unknowns that confound interpretation of these figures: (a) the recurrent question of how sampling days of the week was accomplished,[88] and (b) how eating at work was coded by Lundberg *et al.* The latter activity occupied an average of 15 minutes for employed people in our 1965–66 sample, and one of the largest changes in the leisure-time expenditures in Table A lies in the category of eating. Note, however, that eating times for housewives show the same pattern as for employed people —although the differences are smaller where housewives are concerned than they are for employed persons. Interestingly enough, time at work for employed women in Table A does show a decrease, which may accurately reflect the increasing proportion of women with part-time (vs. full-time) employment.

3. *Care of self* is the activity that reasonably enough shows the smallest change over the 34-year interval, with the 1965–66 figures being slightly larger than the 1931–33 figures for most occupational groups. The major

[87] Against these groups in Table A, we have matched the 1965–66 data from all our white-collar workers (separately for men and women), all our male respondents in professional occupations, and all our housewives in households where the husband was in a professional occupation.

[88] Lundberg *et al.* mention that their respondents worked a five and one-half day week, with almost everyone starting work at nine A.M. and finishing at five P.M. during weekdays. This information squares with their time-estimate figures in Table A and would indicate that day-of-the-week differences were controlled.

coding problem here centers around how these investigators classified activities that respondents failed to disclose for personal reasons or because of oversight. It may be that a substantial portion of such undisclosed activities[89] (averaging close to 14 minutes per day in our study) should be classified under care of self, but how Lundberg's group handled such missing diary entries is unknown.

4. *Transportation* figures show a considerable increase in the 1965–66 data, especially for men. There is a leisure category in Lundberg *et al.*—"motoring"—that may account for part of this difference. Lundberg *et al.* report that "motoring" included only what we would now call "pleasure driving," when a trip has no particular destination. Our 1965–66 diaries contained almost no entries of this sort, indicating that such unstructured activity has given way to more purposive traveling.

5. Time spent on *household and children* shows little difference for men, but a very surprising increase of almost two hours for women. We might suspect that the figures for housewives would be low because the higher-status housewives in the Lundberg study would have been relatively able to afford housemaids. However, the figures for the employed women are almost of the same magnitude. Moreover, the differences between the two time periods grow even larger if the figures for shopping are included.[90] We have already noted that shopping is mysteriously overlooked in the Lundberg code categories, probably because the authors' major focus was on leisure time.

6. *Eating* is the first major "leisure" category listed by Lundberg *et al.*, who do comment upon the arbitrary nature of assigning all eating to "leisure." We noted in the text that the 1931–33 figures for eating are at least a half an hour longer than they are today. However, there are three subcategories of eating which need to be distinguished in the estimation of times spent eating: (a) *meals at work* (we have already concluded that this does not entirely explain the observed differences); (b) *meals while visiting* (in both our data and Lundberg's these meals are coded as "visiting"); and (c) *less formal meals at restaurants,* such as taking the children out to dinner or eating alone at the drugstore. Lundberg *et al.* do not mention how these latter activities were coded, but they are included in our figures and take up about 11 minutes per day. Judging from the recent rapid increase in restaurants (especially the drive-in type), it is not unexpected for this 11-minute figure to be far larger than it would have been 34 years previ-

---

[89] As might be expected, not one of our 1,244 respondents explicitly reported any bodily elimination or sexual activity during their diary day, although other "care-of-self" items like washing and dressing were mentioned with regularity. These two activities are thus the ones likely to be grossly underestimated in our respondent diaries. Such activity, if it had to be coded into one of Lundberg's categories, would still fall under "care of self" and would result in substantially larger portions of time spent on this activity than is reported in Table A.

[90] It is possible that affluent suburban households of the period depended on telephone and delivery for much common shopping.

ously. The greatest decreases in eating time are for employed women, quite conceivably reflecting the elasticity of eating time for a group which has least free time available.

7 *Visiting,* along with care of self, represents an activity that has shown relatively little change over the years, with the 1931–33 figures tending to be slightly larger. Within the category of visiting, Lundberg *et al.* isolate two activities which most certainly suffered sharp declines in popularity—playing cards (58 minutes in 1931–33 vs. 8 minutes in 1965–66 for housewives) and dancing (10 to 20 minutes in 1931–33 to less than 2 minutes today). The decreases in these two activities may mean that social visiting in a conversational sense is actually more prevalent today than in the 1930's. In both surveys, housewives spent by far the most time visiting.

8. A considerable drop in *reading* is apparent in Table A, but it is well to keep in mind here the sophisticated composition of Lundberg's sample and the fact that no illiterate respondents were included.[91] As noted in our text discussion, reading times have certainly diminished as a result of television, but the decline is not as steep as the rate implied in Table A. It is unfortunate that Lundberg *et al.* do not provide separate estimates of book, magazine, and newspaper reading so that more precise comparisons could be made. However, they do note that 75 percent of the books and most of the magazines dealt with fiction, the type of material that was to become more impressively conveyed to the mass audience by television.

9. *Entertainment,* consisting of attendance at movies, sports events, etc., is markedly lower in the more recent data. While Lundberg *et al.* report that adults in their sample went to see a motion picture at least once a week, less than 10 percent of our national sample said they attended a movie almost every week. To the extent that such changes have occurred, television again is the likely culprit. In this connection, it is worth noting that Lundberg *et al.* describe typical movie fare in those days much as we would describe television today—unimaginative and predictable.

10. *Sports* also show a tremendous decline since 1931–33. Moreover, most of our sports entries in 1965–66 were bowling, one of the least active of all sports. On the other hand, most of the 1965–66 diaries were collected between November 15 and December 15, hardly the ideal time for engaging in sports. Lundberg *et al.'s* diaries were spread across the non-summer months, affording a little more opportunity for sports participation.

11. *Radio* listening, the activity most directly affected by television, shows the expected large decline. Since residents of Westchester were far more likely than other Americans in those depression years to own a radio receiver, the Lundberg figures cannot be considered representative for the early 1930's. Moreover, as they did not indicate what proportion of their respondents owned sets, it is not possible to correct the figures for this factor properly. It is known that under 60 percent of their respondents listened to the radio in an average diary, so that times per respondent listening at all

[91] The authors also note that many of their respondents rode a commuter train to New York City, affording them an ideal opportunity to catch up on their reading.

totaled over an hour per day. About 8 percent of our respondents said they listened to the radio on an average day, which averages out to 46 minutes per listener—not greatly different from the Lundberg figures except that these times represent listening only as a *primary* activity.

Lundberg *et al.* note a considerable amount of listening as background or as a secondary activity and quote one contemporaneous study showing radio taking up almost three hours a day as either a primary or a secondary activity. Our more recent survey shows radio today is almost entirely used as a secondary activity, but our estimated duration is now down to just under an hour of total radio usage as a primary or secondary activity. It is also interesting to find that today about a quarter of television time is also as a secondary activity.

12. The only dramatic change in *club* activity is a tremendous drop for housewives. The reader is immediately reminded that Lundberg's housewives (and their executive and professional men as well) were all drawn from membership lists of formal organizations, so that this difference cannot be lent much meaning.

13. The *miscellaneous* category for Lundberg *et al.* consisted mainly of church attendance, artistic hobbies, personal communication, and being idle. (Our miscellaneous category, in addition, includes three activities not mentioned by Lundberg *et al.:* adult education, gardening, and care of pets.) Of the four main activities in the miscellaneous category, Lundberg provides no data on personal communication and relaxing, and in both studies time spent on artistic hobbies is too small to detect any trend. Furthermore, only two subgroup estimates are given for time spent at church services, although both are consistent in showing a moderate decline: in the 1931–33 figures professional-executive men averaged 11 minutes per day (vs. 7 minutes in 1965–66) and housewives gave 17 minutes (vs. 10 minutes in 1965–66).

To summarize the results of Table A, we could conclude that if the Lundberg data are not drastically distorted by uncontrolled day-of-week differences, Americans are now spending noticeably less time sleeping, eating, reading, frequenting places of entertainment (especially movies), playing sports, listening to the radio, motoring, playing cards, dancing, and going to church services. Many of these decreases seem attributable directly to the arrival of television. On the other hand, Americans are spending much more time traveling, taking care of home and family (especially true of American women), and perhaps working. Contrary to stereotypes, the largest increases have occurred in the nonleisure areas with the result that Americans in the national sample of 1965–66 had up to two hours less leisure time than the selected residents of Westchester County in 1931–33.

The data in Table B come from the next time-budget study, that of Sorokin and Berger, conducted four years after that of Lundberg began. Because the proportion of unemployed in the Sorokin-Berger materials is unknown, only the grossest comparisons are possible with the laudably detailed code of 55 activi-

Table B. Comparison of Figures from Sorokin and Berger (1939) with Those in the 20–29 Age Bracket in the 1965–66 Study

	1935	1965–66
Physical needs	11.2 hrs.	9.9 hrs.
Sleeping	505 min.	448 min.
Eating	89	76
Health	3	0.3
Exercise	0.2	0.5
Personal care	76	69
Economic activities	7.1 hrs.	8.2 hrs.
Work	207 min.	272 min.
Transportation	62	69
Walking	46	6
Shopping	16 ⎫	
Errands	6 ⎭	31
Household (phys.)	77	110
Men's household	3	2
Women's household	5	5
Miscellaneous	2	a
Societal activities	1.4 hrs.	1.8 hrs.
Altruistic	5 min.	5 min.
Staying with children	1	20
With family	1	a
Ceremonies	1	a
Visiting	21 ⎫	
Entertainment	5 ⎭	45
Cards	9	3
Correspondence	3	6
Talking	31 ⎫	
Phoning	1 ⎭	18
Political and civic	0.1	1
Social (clubs)	3.3	6
Religious activities	.1 hrs.	.1 hrs.
Intellectual activities	1.4 hrs.	.8 hrs.
Attending lectures	4 min. ⎫	
School	0.1 ⎭	8

ties devised by these authors. As indicated in Table B, moreover, we cannot find even reasonably close comparative categories for nine of the Sorokin-Berger codes, and most of the other comparisons are advanced with utmost caution.

Confining ourselves to those comparisons which seem most reliable, we note decided decreases consistent with Table A in sleeping, eating, card playing, reading, radio listening, attending theaters and movies, dancing, automobile riding (for pleasure), and attending sports events. In addition we find decreases

Table B (cont.)

	1935	1965–66
Study	3	8
Reading books	14	4
Reading magazines and papers	29	18
Reading, unspecified	8	3
Radio	26	6
Artistic activities	*.4 hrs.*	*.2 hrs.*
Active arts and crafts	2 min.	3 min.
Theatre, movies	22 ⎱	10
Musical	2 ⎰	
Love and courting	*.1 hrs.*	a
Courting	2	a
Dancing	7	3
Pleasurable activities	*1.5 hrs.*	*.7 hrs.*
Amusements	1	a
Auto riding	22	3
Idling	18	16
Smoking	2	a
Play	2	a
Observing games	7	2
Walking	22	1
Picnics	2	a
Refreshments	5	a
Hobbies	1	2
Gardening	2	1
Indoor games	1	2
Indoor sports	0.2 ⎱	
Outdoor sports	5 ⎰	9
Outdoor play	2 ⎰	
Television	a	1.7 hrs.
All other activities	.8 hrs.	.6 hrs.

a No comparable categories.

in walking (both for transportation and for exercise)[92] and in talking. Contrary to Table A, we here find decreases also in the time spent traveling.

Unfortunately, the unknown proportions of Sorokin-Berger respondents

[92] Sorokin and Berger take pains to point out (presumably to their more nostalgic readers) that people still received much exercise from walking, whereas today we must report that Sorokin and Berger's worst fears have been realized: we have truly become a nation of "riders" rather than "walkers."

who were either employed or married preclude further speculation on whether the increases in work time and time with home and family can be used legitimately to confirm parallel increases relative to the Lundberg activity categories. The same factors furthermore confound any interpretation of the greater proportions of time spent shopping and visiting found in the 1965–66 data relative to the 1935 data. As in Table A, more activities show a decline than an increase, with television probably the major factor in this rearrangement.

By 1954, the date of the next time-budget study, television had already begun to make its presence felt: about one-half of American households had a set. In fact, there is good reason to suspect that the sponsor of this study—the Mutual Broadcasting Company, a radio network—was interested in estimating the inroads television had made on its potential audience. The Mutual study, carried out by the market research firm of J. A. Ward, Inc., appears to be the first nationwide study of time use in America. We have already commented on the misfortune that the original data are no longer available for further analysis, so that variations by education, employment status (especially crucial for women, as we shall see), marital status, etc., can be examined. This is particularly unfortunate for the variable of community size, since our 1965–66 study was confined to metropolitan regions. Fortunately, the age limits of our study (18 to 65) and their study (20 to 59) are similar enough to remove age as a major source of ambiguity (remembering that most of our 60-and-over sample were employed).

One further difficulty impedes straightforward comparison of Ward-Mutual data and our data in Table C. The Ward-Mutual data, being confined to the most active daily period between 6 A.M. and 11 P.M., neglected a seven-hour period of the day during which a significant minority of the population was still active. The 1965–66 data in Table C are given for the restricted 17-hour period examined in the Ward-Mutual study. There were noticeable shifts (see Figures 1 and 2 in the main text) in the 11-year interim in the times of day when people retired for the day,[93] so that the common 17-hour time period still does not completely ensure the desired degree of comparability.

Nevertheless, there are changes in Table C that should remain unaffected by these extraneous factors.[94] For example, significantly less time is now spent

---

[93] At 6:00 A.M. on an average weekday, 57 percent of the men in the 1954 study were asleep; at 7:00 A.M., 20 percent, and at 8:00 A.M., 7 percent. In 1965–66, the comparable figures were 72 percent, 36 percent, and 12 percent. At 10:00 P.M. in 1954, 40 percent were asleep and at 10:45 P.M., 60 percent. In 1965–66, the figures were 14 percent and 37 percent. These data are presented in de Grazia, *op. cit.*, p. 475.

[94] The reader may be interested in how the remaining time (between 11:00 P.M. and 6:00 A.M.) was spent by our 1965–66 respondents. Men used this seven-hour period as follows: work, .3 hours; traveling, .1; restaurant, .1; other's home, .1; leisure away from home, .1; leisure at home, .3; dressing, .3; and asleep, 5.8 hours. The extra seven hours for women was divided among work, .1; other's home, .1; leisure at home, .4; reading, .1; miscellaneous work, .1; and asleep, 5.

Table C. Comparison of 1954 J. A. Ward–Mutual Broadcasting Company Estimates with Those of the 1965–66 Study (in Parentheses)[a]

	Hours per Day			
	Men		Women	
Away from home:				
At work	6.0	(5.9)	1.5	(2.2)
Traveling	1.4	(1.5)	0.7	(1.1)
Shopping	0.1	(0.4)	0.4	(0.7)
Restaurant, bar, etc.	0.2	(0.3)	0.1	(0.1)
Friend/relative's home	0.7	(0.5)	1.0	(0.7)
Leisure (church, sports, etc.)	0.5	(0.9)	0.5	(0.7)
	8.9	(9.5)	4.2	(5.5)
At home:				
Leisure (except reading)	2.4	(2.4)	2.8	(2.5)
Reading	0.9	(0.6)	0.8	(0.4)
Miscellaneous work at home	0.7	(0.6)	1.1	(1.3)
Household chores	0.2	(0.2)	2.7	(2.3)
Eating or preparing food	1.2	(1.1)	2.5	(2.2)
Dressing, bathing, etc.	0.6	(0.7)	0.9	(1.0)
Asleep	2.1	(2.0)	1.9	(2.0)
	8.1	(7.6)	12.7	(11.7)
Total	17.0	(17.1)	16.9	(17.2)
All leisure activities	4.7	(4.7)	5.2	(4.4)

[a] In both sets of data the period between 11 P.M. and 6 A.M. was not included.

at home than was true in 1954. The amount of extra time away from home (5.5 — 4.2 = 1.3 hours) is truly dramatic for women, mainly a result of the expanded entry of women into the labor force, reflected in almost a 50 percent increase in time at work for women.[95] Both men and women also show some increase in traveling and a significant increase in time spent shopping, both increases corroborated by recent transportation studies reviewed in the main body of this chapter. Time spent visiting friends and relatives has gone down somewhat; conversely, time attending restaurants and places of "leisure"— churches, schools, organizations, bowling alleys, theaters, and nightclubs— shows a substantial rise, especially for men.

[95] Wattenberg and Scammon, *op. cit.*, refer to this phenomenon as "the most stunning statistic in recent labor force studies." However, the changes in Table C probably exaggerate those that have occurred, mainly because of our sampling restrictions on city size and employment status. Wattenberg and Scammon note an increase from only 35 percent to 41 percent in the number of women aged 18 to 64 in the labor force between 1950 and 1960. The figures for married women, on the other hand, jumped from 22 percent to 31 percent, which is roughly the proportionate jump for the work entry in Table C.

Needless to say, certain at-home activities have suffered decreases as a consequence. The most noteworthy decline is for the activity that was a prime casualty of television: reading (not differentiated into books, magazines, and newspapers in the Ward-Mutual data). Women spend less time on household chores or eating and preparing food, perhaps as a result of the introduction of wash-and-wear clothing and convenience foods, together with the pressure of their increased time at work. They also have less time available for leisure activities (mainly television), although we have no idea how much television viewing itself has been altered in these figures. Time spent viewing television has increased with set ownership, as discussed in the text. The remaining at-home figures in Table C are quite constant across the two surveys.

Because day-of-week differences were published for the Ward-Mutual data, we can further investigate how the above changes were distributed across the week, and this result is portrayed in Table D. In terms of away-from-home activities, the greatest changes for women have come on weekdays, while Saturdays display the greatest changes for men. Among some of the trends in Table D:

1. Women's increased work participation has been during the week rather than on weekends. While we might have expected the increased Saturday shopping to require more female sales personnel, Saturday work for women has actually declined. Associated with this change on weekdays is a decrease in visiting and increases in traveling and, surprisingly, shopping and leisure outside the home. That women sleep longer on weekends can be seen as compensation for the sleep they have to give up during the week because of work.
2. Men show more shopping on weekdays (and on Sunday), but the largest change in Table D is their increased shopping on Saturday. Similarly, going to restaurants and places of leisure have become much more popular for men on Saturday, while visiting has become a less popular weekend activity.
3. Home leisure, mainly television viewing, has decreased for men on Saturdays but increased for men on Sundays (perhaps as a result of increased professional football coverage by 1965–66). Women's decreased home leisure is more evenly spread across the week.
4. The dramatic decreases in reading are least pronounced on Sundays for both men and women, indicating perhaps the stability of the Sunday newspaper in their lives.

The pattern of changes in other home activities is generally too complicated to be reducible to a single theme, however.

The data in Table E, while dealing only with housework, are of great help in decoding some of the Ward-Mutual data regarding differences between employed women and housewives. The data come from Walker,[96] who in 1968

---

[96] Walker, *op. cit.*, pp. 621–624.

Table D. Comparison of 1954 Ward-Mutual Estimates with Those of 1965–66 Study (in Parentheses) by Day of Week[a]

	Men			Women		
	Average Weekday	Saturday	Sunday	Average Weekday	Saturday	Sunday
Away from home:						
At work	7.2 (7.3)	4.3 (3.1)	1.2 (1.1)	1.0 (2.8)	.9 (.6)	.3 (.4)
Traveling	1.4 (1.5)	1.4 (1.7)	1.3 (1.4)	.6 (1.1)	.7 (1.1)	1.0 (1.0)
Shopping	.1 (.4)	.3 (1.0)	.1 (.3)	.4 (.7)	.8 (.9)	.0 (.1)
Restaurant, bar	.3 (.3)	.3 (.6)	.1 (.2)	.1 (.1)	.2 (.2)	.1 (.1)
Friend/relatives	.4 (.3)	1.2 (.8)	1.4 (1.0)	.8 (.5)	1.2 (1.3)	1.4 (1.3)
Leisure (church, etc.)	.3 (.3)	.6 (1.2)	1.4 (1.2)	.4 (.6)	.4 (.8)	1.1 (1.1)
At home:						
Leisure (except reading)	2.1 (2.0)	2.8 (2.3)	4.0 (4.3)	2.7 (2.4)	2.8 (2.6)	3.5 (3.1)
Reading	.8 (.5)	.9 (.6)	1.1 (.9)	.8 (.4)	.9 (.3)	1.1 (.7)
Miscellaneous work at home	.6 (.6)	1.0 (.7)	.8 (1.0)	1.1 (1.5)	1.1 (1.0)	.7 (1.1)
Household chores	.2 (.1)	.2 (.2)	.2 (.5)	3.0 (2.4)	2.6 (2.5)	1.7 (1.5)
Eating or preparing food	1.2 (1.0)	1.2 (1.2)	1.3 (1.4)	2.5 (2.2)	2.5 (2.1)	2.5 (2.2)
Dressing, bathing	.6 (.7)	.7 (.9)	.7 (.7)	.9 (1.0)	.9 (1.1)	.9 (1.2)
Asleep	1.8 (1.6)	2.1 (2.6)	3.4 (3.0)	1.8 (1.6)	2.1 (2.5)	2.7 (3.4)
Total leisure hours	3.6 (3.1)	5.5 (4.9)	7.9 (7.4)	4.7 (3.9)	5.3 (5.0)	7.1 (6.2)

[a] In both sets of data the period between 11 P.M. and 6 A.M. was not included.

Table E. Comparison of Time Spent Daily on Household Work between 1952 and 1967–68 (from Walker, 1969)

(*In Hours*)

	Employed Women		Housewives	
	1952	*1967–68*	*1952*	*1967–68*
All food activities	1.9	1.6	2.6	2.3
Care of house	.8	1.2	1.6	1.6
Care of clothes	.8	.9	1.6	1.3
Care of family members	.3	.8	1.1	1.8
Marketing and recordkeeping	.3	.8	.5	1.0
Total	4.1	5.3	7.4	8.0

replicated a study of homemaking activity done 16 years earlier. Both studies were focused on women in urban areas in and near Syracuse, New York.

Consistent with the data in Table C (which covers roughly the same temporal span between the Ward-Mutual and Converse-Robinson studies), Table E shows a marked increase in shopping and a slight reduction in food preparation. Both trends hold equally for employed women and housewives. The trend for household chores (care of house and clothes) is more complicated, a slight decline appearing for housewives, some increase being detectable for employed women. Nevertheless, since employed women spent one-third less time on these activities than housewives, and since there has been a greatly increased proportion of them relative to housewives, the slight reduction found in Table C would be consistent with the Table E data.[97]

[97] The one activity that is not compatible between Tables C and E is "care of family members." This activity has shown the largest increase in Table E, but cannot be identified in the Ward-Mutual data.

3

Community Social Indicators

Peter H. Rossi

The world has become increasingly cosmopolitan, but the daily lives of most people are contained within local communities. Europe is only a few hours from the East Coast by fast jet, yet only a very small proportion of Americans have visited Europe. Indeed, the majority of Americans have still to take their first airplane trip within the United States. One in five Americans changes residence each year, but the typical move covers but a few miles.[1] One out of three Americans have never traveled more than two hundred miles from their birthplaces, and a majority are still living in the states in which they were born.

Even for those proportionately few who have migrated from one part of the country to another, or who travel often and far, daily life is acted out within rather narrowly circumscribed areal limits. The daily comings and goings of individuals ordinarily do not take them far from their residences. Places of work, schools, shopping, recreation, and even the residences of most friends and kin are ordinarily located within easy reaching distance. Although it is true that these distances have increased as transportation has improved, the daily lives of most Americans are still lived within a 50-mile radius of their homes.

More than anything else, these areal characteristics of daily life account for the persistence of local communities as centers of public attention and societal

This paper arose out of the work of Program II, "Social Accounts," of the Center for the Study of the Social Organization of Schools, Johns Hopkins University. A number of my colleagues have contributed their ideas to this paper. It is a pleasure to acknowledge the help of James S. Coleman, Mark S. Granovetter, Richard Berk, W. Eugene Groves, Bettye K. Eidson, and David Boesel, all of whom took the time to read the original version of the paper and to criticize its shortcomings.

[1] Peter H. Rossi, *Why Families Move*. Free Press, Glencoe, Ill., 1955.

concern. In the final analysis, social trends and social policy have their direct impacts upon individuals in the form of *local* manifestations. Fluctuations in the rate of employment are experienced directly in the hiring and firing behaviors of specific plants and businesses in localities throughout the country. The decline of an industry means empty plants in specific places. Consumer price changes are reflected in the price tags and markings in specific *local* stores. The administration of justice and law enforcement is largely in the hands of *local* police forces and local courts. Federal policy in education ultimately affects school children and their parents through the impact of such policy on *local* school systems and neighborhood schools.

Perhaps the most dramatic contemporary example of the localized character of larger social changes are the events associated with the changing status of American Negroes. Although much of the drive for movement toward equality has been directed at the national government, most of the action has taken place on the local scene. In the early stages of the civil rights movement, it was *local* public accommodations which were the targets of sit-ins. City halls have been picketed far more frequently than state legislatures or Congress. Desegregation in either schools or in housing has taken place in *local* school systems and *local* neighborhoods.

The civil disorders since 1964 have been *local* disturbances in which the antagonists have been ghetto residents, *local* police, and *local* institutions. The manifestations are parochial, although it is not at all clear that the underlying problems are mainly local. The problems of race relations press most heavily on local institutions, but are significant powers to affect relevant outcomes clearly at the command of mayors, city councils, police chiefs, or other local officials? Local officials frequently are not able to provide effective remedies for grievances. Many of the root causes lie in the national economy and national institutions, and certainly the major amounts of legal power and resources are in the hands of national, not local, officials. Thus, while city hall and municipal agencies are on the receiving end of complaints and demands, they are relatively impotent to meet those demands effectively. To be sure, a sensitive and charismatic mayor can help to mitigate conflict (e.g., John Lindsay of New York), but the half-life of charm and concern, unaccompanied by power and resources, is getting shorter as demands for equality and equal treatment grow.

In one sense the local community clearly is an important link in national policy: national policies have to be implemented on the local level, and effective municipal officials can either make efficient use of the resources given to them or they can transform a national policy into a local farce.[2] Much of local civil

---

[2] Indeed, one of the major problems in the evaluation of social action programs is what has come to be called the "nonprogram problem"; that is, a local school system or other local institution has often accepted funds to run a local program, has turned in regular progress reports, but investigators sent from Washington or regional offices can find no sign that the program has ever existed.

rights conflict stems around this point although, without clear measures of program effectiveness, much of the struggle turns around symbolic (as opposed to "real") issues. Thus the local community is important at least as the point at which the outputs of our national society and its international relations are delivered to citizens.

The local community is also the setting for the major events in the life cycles of individuals. It supplies to its individual citizen the medical facilities in which he is born, the schools in which he is taught, the housing in which he lives, the social milieu in which he finds his mate and sets up his household, the factories and businesses in which he finds employment, and finally the cemetery in which he is buried. Individuals and households live mainly and almost entirely within local communities. The local community plays a significant role in the shaping of those experiences.

Even the minimal role of backdrop can be important, at least as forming part of childhood memories and perhaps conditioning one's sense of space and tolerance for density of structures and people. To grow up in a rural neighborhood may mean no more than a preference for more space and a lower tolerance for high levels of interpersonal contacts, but this is an important effect.

If we accord a more important position to the local community, then it may be viewed as a factor of considerable weight in a wide range of outcomes. For example, some educators accord an important role to the average level of support for intellectual achievement in a community in motivating students to learn. If this view is correct, then a child's achievement in school can be related to the characteristic climate of opinion in the residential community in which he lives.

Thus, one of the main empirical issues in the social-psychological study of local communities is to ascertain whether the roles played by the local community in the lives of individuals are more in the way of a backdrop, providing a setting in which autochthonous processes are going on, or whether local community characteristics are a significant input to the levels of well-being within areas above and beyond the characteristics of individuals and households living in such areas. Furthermore, assuming that there are such community effects, another critical issue concerns unraveling the causal links between community characteristics and effects manifested in individuals and households.

Still another role that the local community can play in the lives of individual residents is as a link to the larger society. For example, the fact that one lives in a community whose industry suffers a general decline in demand for its products on the national market conditions the ability of the individual to obtain employment. The source of the employment difficulty lies in the national market for the product in question, and the community plays a role as a mediating link between national processes and local events. Similarly, changes in national policies concerning support for local school systems, procurement policies vis-à-vis defense material, and the like can all have their impact on individuals and households through the way in which community characteristics interact with those national processes.

So far we have emphasized the locality as a causal factor in affecting outcomes in individual or household behaviors. Another way of looking at locality is as a consummatory goal. Thus, a locality would be regarded in the same manner as any other consumer good, a source of gratification or annoyance but not as a conditioner of behavior in other respects. From this viewpoint we may regard localities in much the same way that we regard automobiles: as a means of transportation, it matters very little whether a car is a Ford or Chevrolet, but this brand distinction may be important as far as some types of gratification are concerned. In the same way, where one lives—within a broad range of differences in neighborhood composition, housing types, etc.—may not make much of a difference, for example, in opinions on foreign policy, but it may make a difference in individuals' satisfaction with their housing and neighborhood.

In other words, people may care whether they live in one or another locality because living in one place or another affects their levels of satisfaction and not because they are profoundly affected by one or another community.[3] Under this last interpretation, local communities are market phenomena created by the price structure of housing, differential distribution of income, and the varying schedules of preferences held by individuals and households concerning the priorities they are willing to allocate to expenditures on housing and location as opposed to other types of goods or investments.

This paper will not be able to distinguish to what extent it is proper to think of local communities as major inputs into individuals and households or to what extent residential location is mainly a matter of individuals' and households' ability and willingness to compete on the housing market. The ability to make that analysis (or at least to get closer to doing so) would be the outcome of a program on research on local communities.

Concept of Community

The term "community" carries with it such a freight of meanings from vernacular usage that sociologists might be much better off to drop the term and invent new ones to cover the phenomena in question. We all "know what we mean" by community when we use the term in the contexts of everyday con-

---

[3] Similar phenomena can be seen in other areas of life. Thus, virtually no studies of classroom size have found class size related to measures of learning achievement, yet students, teachers, and parents all express strong preference for small classes. (Cf. James S. Coleman *et al., Equality of Educational Opportunity.* Government Printing Office, Washington, D.C., 1966.)

versation, but these meanings interfere with the comprehension of the term when it is used with more precise intentions.[4]

Much of the difficulty with the use of the term community stems from its use to cover two quite different classes of phenomena. On the one hand, a community designates a *commensalistic* social group, in which each member shares an important common characteristic and in which each member of the group is significantly conscious of being a member of the group. Thus, we speak of the "scientific community" composed of scientists who share in common an occupational activity and who view themselves as sharing common interests and even a common fate. Or, we may think in terms of the "Jewish," "Catholic," or "Negro" communities, in which members share religious beliefs or common ancestral origins. Very often such communities also have a spatial location, or members may sufficiently concentrate in space to be able to add a modifying phrase incorporating a geographic location. Thus, we may speak of the "Hasidic Community of Williamsburg," an area of Brooklyn, New York, which contains an unusual concentration of members of this particular Jewish sect.

A community may also refer to a social group held together by the complementarity of its differences. Thus, Muncie, Indiana, as a community, refers to a *symbiotic* social group whose members inhabit and, on a diurnal cycle, circulate within a circumscribed geographic area but who also have a rather wide diversity of socioeconomic, ethnic, and political backgrounds. The ties that bind individuals and households together in such a symbiotic community are ones of exchange in which the units specialize in activities that produce products used largely by others.

"Community" in a symbiotic sense usually refers to larger groupings than the use of the term in a commensalistic sense. Thus, a metropolitan area plus its surrounding dependent hinterland may be viewed as a community engaged in intensive intra-area exchange of sociability, goods and services, but hardly as a community in the sense of sharing a common identity. For the latter type of community, we generally look to smaller areas characterized by socioeconomic and/or ethnic homogeneity, areas that are primarily residential in character.

Neither the commensalistic nor the symbiotic versions of the concept of community are readily translated into operational forms. It is not easy to determine areas that can be marked off characterizing either places in which residents engage in interchange of sufficient density or which are inhabited by relatively homogeneous populations. Sharply delineated boundaries ordinarily cannot be found, and a sharply delineated boundary when found usually turns

[4] For example, at the present time, the term "community" is used as a shorthand to mean the black ghettos of our large cities. There have been several conferences in which black militant leaders and sociologists have been completely talking past each other because the former used the term to mean blacks and the latter used the term to cover a much wider group, usually the central city or the metropolitan area.

out to be trivial, e.g., water fronts, mountain ranges, etc.[5] In the usual case, boundaries have to be drawn somewhat arbitrarily, leaving the researcher with a feeling of dissatisfaction over not having done adequate justice to the richness of the concept of community he had in mind. In the end we are reduced, *faute de mieux,* to drawing the areal boundaries of communities using the seemingly arbitrarily drawn boundaries of political units (cities, counties, wards, etc.) or the equally arbitrarily drawn boundaries of census small areas (census tracts, enumeration districts, blocks, etc.). The areal aggregation of small units is ordinarily to be preferred over the use of larger units, although greater operational discretion is given to the researcher and hence greater anxiety results.[6]

From the viewpoint of developing a social psychology of local communities it is not clear whether the commensalistic version or the symbiotic version of the concept of community is to be preferred. It would appear at first thought that the commensalistic view which stresses solidarity and consciousness of kind would be preferred by social psychologists, but it turns out that whether or not (and why) a particular areal aggregation of individuals and households manifest consciousness of kind or solidarity is a major question raised by the social psychologist who looks at local communities. Hence, the relationships between the phenomena underlying the two alternative definitions of community constitute one of the major problems for sociologists and social psychologists intertested in the study of local communities.[7] If we view the process of modernization as involving an increase in the complexity of the division of labor along with a corresponding increase in the densities of human settlements, then a major problem arises: What are the conditions in which the sense of community as a commensalistic collectivity can be maintained in populations characterized by increasing differentiation?

This general question is also an important one politically, the problem being the conditions under which the differentiation within a population leads to a breakdown in widespread commitment to the political structure governing an area. How to define the public interest in such a fashion as to attain the support

[5] They are trivial in that such physical features become boundaries because they are barriers to human habitation. Homes, factories, and office buildings cannot be built on water, on the side of steep mountains, etc., except at prohibitive costs.

[6] A number of schemes have been proposed and used as rules for aggregating small areas into relatively homogeneous larger areas or into noncontiguous strata of similar areas. For example, Shevky and Williams (Eshref Shevky and Marilyn Williams, *The Social Areas of Los Angeles,* University of California Press, Berkeley, 1949.) have proposed a method of aggregating census tracts into homogeneous strata by using factor analysis of census tract characteristics. Despite considerable criticism, the methods proposed have been widely used, largely because reasonable alternatives are equally arbitrary.

[7] Maurice A. Stein, *The Eclipse of Community.* Princeton University Press, Princeton, 1960. Stein, reviewing major community studies undertaken by sociologists and anthropologists, finds that the central problem in each of the studies is the disappearance of the sense of community as a positive shared membership on the part of the community residents.

of most of the city's residents is the prime question facing the local public officials of our time.

The search for *an* adequate definition of the term community is in all likelihood another search for the Holy Grail. There are too many diverse connotations to the term for any definition to encompass all. Much more fruitful conceptual advances can be made by differentiating specific aspects of the global term and devising new concepts, each constructed with a view to problems of operationalization.

I have found it useful to employ the definitions which follow:

A *residential locality* consists of the population (individuals and households) who make their residences in an arbitrarily defined area along with those organizations and institutions which are also "resident" in that area.[8] Thus, a municipality is a residential locality, defined by political boundaries (more or less arbitrary), consisting of the persons, business firms, municipal agencies, churches, voluntary organizations, etc., that have addresses in the area defined by the boundaries. A census tract or ward or enumeration district may similarly be regarded as residential localities, with only the minimum requirement that some persons and/or some organizations have addresses within that area. Thus, a park is not ordinarily a residential locality, nor is a tract of vacant land.

The concept "residential locality" is useful to designate the basic units of inquiry in the study of local communities, being flexible enough to cover a variety of specific types of units (e.g., regions, municipalities, counties, census tracts, blocks, etc.) and easily translated into operational form. It should also be obvious that one would be interested more in some types of residential localities than others: for example, residential localities that are also municipal corporations would be of greater interest to the student of local politics than residential localities that cut across a number of municipal boundaries. Thus, a research worker would define residential localities differently depending on his problem, seeking boundaries that are more likely to be relevant to the problem under study.

Notice that the concept of residential locality completely sidesteps the issue of what are optimum areal boundaries for the definition of areas of interest to

[8] By social convention each individual and household is characterized by an *address*, designating a place in space, in which personal possessions are usually stored and to which other persons seeking to contact the unit in question can go with the knowledge of a relatively high probability of finding the unit in question. For many organizations and institutions, an address can be defined in the same way, although the unit to be contacted would often have to be defined as some individual authorized to receive messages on behalf of the organization or institution in question. Thus, a school has an address, and the administrators, clerks, and teachers are persons who can receive messages on behalf of the school. For some aggregated units, addresses would not be easy to define; e.g., a friendship group may not have a unique address but be defined by the addresses of each of its members. Or a police detachment that services the residents of an area may have no specific address within that area because the police are on mobile patrol.

social scientists. It proposes as a methodological device that arbitrary boundaries around areas be set, guided by convenience (as, for example, in the picking of census tracts, wards, or other administratively defined areal units as residential localities) or by some substantive interest (e.g., residential localities that are also areas governed by significant political structures).

Once the boundaries or localities are set, then it becomes a question whether the areas so set have other properties of interest derivative from the general concept of community discussed earlier. The remainder of the terms listed below are concerned with the properties of residential localities, expressed in terms of variables:

The *solidarity* of a residential locality designates the extent to which residents in the locality identify themselves as similar in some significant way to other residents. In this connection we can distinguish between *total solidarity,* designating the extent and strength of bonds of identification with all of the residents of a locality, and *segmental solidarity,* the extent and strength of bonds of identification with subgroups of residents in a locality. Note that *solidarity* is at least a large part of the global concept of community, especially when the commensalistic aspects of community are stressed. Thus when the Lynds, in their studies of Muncie, Indiana, remark on the changes in that city's sense of community which accompanied industrialization, they are referring to a change in the total solidarity of the residential locality formed by the political boundaries of Muncie.[9] In contrast, Elin Anderson's study of Manchester, New Hampshire, stressed the extent of segmental solidarity in Manchester, the main segments being those formed by class, religion, and ethnicity.[10]

Rather obviously, total solidarity and segmental solidarity might tend to be negatively related. Thus, a residential locality in which the residents consider themselves mainly as members of ethnic or religious groups would probably not have much identification with the total community. But this is a point that can be answered by empirical evidence. Residential localities may well fall into a typological scheme as shown below with significant numbers of localities to be found in each of the cells of the typological scheme:

Total Solidarity

		High	Low
Segmental Solidarity	High	Type A: E.g., New York City or other major metro	Type B: Community in conflict
	Low	Type C: Homogeneous dormitory suburb	Type D: Transient neighborhood

[9] Robert S. Lynd and Helen M. Lynd, *Middletown.* Harcourt, New York, 1929; *idem, Middletown in Transition.* Harcourt, New York, 1937.

[10] Elin Anderson, *We Americans.* Harvard University Press, Cambridge, Mass., 1937.

Type A would represent a locality with both high segmental solidarity and high total solidarity. This may be best represented by our great metropolitan areas, e.g., New York and Chicago, which are characterized by a widespread sense of identification of residents with the total community, and at the same time, a high sense of ethnic, racial, and religious identities.

Type B would represent a locality in which the population is divided into solidarity subgroups with little sense of collective identity, as, for example, Gary, Indiana, shortly after the election of Richard Hatcher, a Negro, as Mayor, when some of the white residential neighborhoods made moves toward seceding from the city. Perhaps some of the cities in the Deep South might also be characterized as falling into this group.

Type C might best be represented by small homogeneous towns or one-social-class dormitory suburbs. Finally, Type D is best represented by a locality with no particular sense of identity as, for example, a transient apartment hotel area.

The *integration* of a residential locality designates the extent to which the residents of the locality are linked by ties of exchange, ranging from relatively intangible transactions involving sociability through participation in formally structured organizations to the more tangible exchanges involved in the labor, services, and consumer markets. Again, one may distinguish between *total integration,* the extent to which *all* the significant ties of exchange entered into by residents are with other residents, and *segmental integration,* the extent to which ties of particular types are formed among residents of a locality. Obviously, a given residential locality may be highly integrated as far as sociability is concerned, with many friendship and visiting ties among residents, but may be rated very low as far as segmental integration in a labor market sense, with most residents working in some other locality. Indeed, this is the stereotype of the upper-middle-class suburb, most of whose residents are reputed to commute to work to the central city.

One may also find it useful to distinguish between *vertical* and *horizontal* segmental integration, the former characterizing the density of ties of specific types in a residential locality (e.g., purchasing heavy durable consumer goods, membership in community improvement associations, friendships, etc.) and the latter singling out the types of individuals and households among whom ties are developed (e.g., race, ethnicity, socioeconomic level, etc.). Thus, a residential locality may be characterized as having a high degree of horizontal segmental integration, meaning that there are high densities of some ties within delineated social groups but few ties across group lines, as, for example, kinship or friendship ties in relation to race.

Important differences exist between the concepts of solidarity and integration. By solidarity we mean the extent to which residents of a locality consider themselves to be members of some social group either identical with the locality in extent or some subgroup within that locality. Thus, the extent to which residents of New York City identify themselves as New Yorkers is an expression of the solidarity of New York City as a residential locality. Expressions of solidarity may range from mere identification with place names, e.g., New Yorkers, Chicagoans, etc., to willingness to make personal sacrifices in the name of the locality, e.g., service in the locality's armed forces, payment of local taxes, etc.

In contrast, the concept of integration covers transactions among individuals and groups. Thus, a residential locality may be integrated in a soft-goods market sense if the residents purchase most of their soft goods from others in the locality. Or, a locality may be integrated in a social sense if most of the interpersonal contacts of the residents take place with other residents. Integration is defined by transactions of any sort and hence would ordinarily appear with a modifier indicating the type of transaction involved; for example, consumer-market integration would refer to transactions involving individual and household purchases, sociability integration refers to ties of friendship, visiting, and so on.

Note, too, that the concept of integration is much more complex than the concept of solidarity. There are more specific ways in which a locality can be integrated than there are ways in which its residents can express their solidarity. In the end, the measurement of the solidarity of a locality is some variant of the extent to which residents identify themselves in some essential sense as sharing the same social characteristics. The term integration has a much larger set of operational forms, each covering transactions of a different sort. In this connection one may distinguish between several broad types of transactions: *sociability transactions,* involving exchanges among residents in the form of friendship ties, visiting relationships, informal talk, etc.; *political transactions,* involving the exchange of support and benefits in the process of wielding legitimate political authority; and *economic transactions,* involving the exchange of goods and services using money as the medium of exchange.[11]

It is also useful to consider the degree to which a residential locality is *politically autonomous* as a third variable. A residential locality is politically autonomous to the extent that it may legitimately make collective decisions which are binding on the residents of that locality. To attain political autonomy, a residential area would have to have a set of legitimate rules for making collective decisions, a set of officials designated as having the authority to enforce

[11] Other writers have used the term integration to cover somewhat different phenomena. For example, Robert C. Angell, "The Social Integration of Selected American Cities," *American Journal of Sociology,* vol. 57, 1951, pp. 575–592, has defined integration as the extent to which elites in cities demonstrate a commitment to social welfare action. An early attempt to differentiate among types of integration is represented by Werner S. Landecker, "Types of Integration and Their Measurement," *American Journal of Sociology,* vol. 56, 1950, pp. 332–340. Both attempts center around the use of integration to designate the extent to which various aspects of a society are consistent with each other.

compliance with those decisions, and a set of sanctions available to be applied in the case of noncompliance: in short, it must have a government. Governments vary widely in the extent to which their decisions are binding and over which types of human behavior the decisions can be legitimately made. Hence residential localities may be viewed as spanning a range from those completely lacking any separate government and political autonomy, to those which have so much autonomy that they may be regarded as separate national states, as in the city-states of late medieval Europe. For our purposes, however, we would be mainly concerned with the lower end of the autonomy continuum dealing with varying degrees of autonomy within the range occupied by most American local government units.

The concepts of solidarity, integration, and political autonomy offered in this paper are a set of terms which cover the main meanings of the term community, yet which have the important properties of being able to differentiate among residential localities in important ways. Thus, when we ask whether a particular residential locality is a "community," we need now to describe the locality along a minimum of three dimensions. Thus, at the one extreme, the folk societies described by Robert Redfield are residential localities characterized by high solidarity, high total integration, and high political autonomy.[12] The residential localities to be found in industrialized urbanized societies can be expected to vary along all three dimensions. We can anticipate, however, that the empirical correlations among the dimensions place some restrictions on their free play; for example, we hypothesize that there are few highly integrated localities that are not also politically autonomous.

Of course, there are many aspects of residential localities that are not dealt with within the context of these three concepts. For example, among the more important dimensions are those of size and density, viewed either in terms of space or population. Size of place, roughly indexed by the number of people inhabiting a politically autonomous locality, has been found time and time again to condition strongly important characteristics of cities. Nor have we dealt with stratification phenomena. This does not mean that we do not believe them to be important; it only means that we do not consider them to be relevant to the *definition* of the class of phenomena that are part of the over-all concept of community. Obviously, in any empirical analysis of a given class of phenomena, e.g., achievement in learning within a school system, such variables would come to play an important role.[13]

[12] Robert Redfield, *Peasant Society and Culture.* University of Chicago Press, Chicago, 1956.

[13] Indeed, given existing politically defined local communities as the subjects of inquiry and relying mainly on census-derived data, one would be well advised to devise classification systems that used primarily size of place and socioeconomic variables. See Otis Dudley Duncan and Albert J. Reiss, *Social Characteristics of Urban and Rural Communi-*

Some Social-Psychological Problems in the Measurement of Community

The preceding section of this chapter has developed a frame of reference for the elaboration of a set of operational definitions of community which are centered around geographical areas as basic units. It is concerned with developing measures which could place such units within a multi-dimensional property space expressing basic ideas underlying the global concept of community. In very specific terms, the framework developed is concerned with measuring the extent to which an area (e.g., New York City) can be likened to another area (e.g., Chicago) with respect to characteristics that are at the heart of the concept of community.

The global concept of community, however, is one which is very much in popular usage and hence carries with it a bundle of meanings for individuals in our society. For example, the question: "How do you like this community?" is a meaningful one to most individuals, and is frequently asked of persons newly arrived in a residential locality. Similarly, the term "neighborhood" has some meaning to individuals, at least in the sense that everyday conversations apparently contain the term without so much ambiguity that meaningful interaction is impossible.

The apparent meaningfulness of such terms as community and neighborhood has led to their use in empirical studies. Respondents have been asked to rate their neighborhoods and communities according to a variety of criteria ranging from friendliness to shopping convenience. Respondents have also been asked to assess the social composition of their communities, to list community organizations and indicate whom they consider to be influential and powerful.

The precise referent of neighborhood or community as used in such research is left to the respondent to supply. Without further specification, it is obviously not at all clear whether respondents have in mind any clearly delineated residential locality, or whether a set of respondents who reside in a given residential locality have the same spatial referents in mind. Thus the aggregation of such responses over the residents of a specific residential locality in order to characterize the residential locality by some aggregated measure is fraught with some danger. Of course, in the case of political or other types of areas to which definite and well-known boundaries are given, it is possible to specify the residential locality in strongly enough delineated terms that there is less question whether respondents in such localities are using the same frame of reference. For example, questions that ask who is influential in Atlanta, Georgia, or in

---

ties, 1950. Wiley, New York, 1956; Brian J. L. Berry and Elaine Neils, "Location, Size and Shape of Cities as Influenced by Environmental Factors: The Urban Environment Writ Large," in Harvey S. Perloff, ed., *The Quality of the Urban Environment.* Resources for the Future, Inc., Johns Hopkins University Press, Baltimore, 1969.

Peoria, Illinois, are more likely to evoke a common residential locality as a frame of reference than questions that ask who is influential in "this neighborhood."[14] Only those residential localities that have definite and well-known boundaries are amenable to such treatment, however. Smaller residential localities, such as named neighborhoods whose boundaries are not either formally fixed or well known, do not lend themselves easily to such treatment.

Some research has been conducted on how individuals conceive of their neighborhoods. However, these researches have not been able to show that there are definite principles which govern how individuals define their neighborhoods.[15] Indeed, in some cases there is considerable disagreement among residents over the name "commonly" used to designate their neighborhoods. There are some hints that salient physical boundaries, e.g., a main thoroughfare, an elevated line, or a stream or river, are likely to be chosen as boundaries, but in the more usual case, individuals define their neighborhoods in what seems to be almost idiosyncratic ways.

In a pioneering and very fascinating attempt to get at how people view their cities, Kevin Lynch asked small samples of persons living in the Boston, Los Angeles, and Jersey City metropolitan areas to draw maps of their cities in which those features significant to the subjects were marked.[16] Subjects tended to draw maps which exaggerated prominences in the downtown areas and accented the lines of daily travel of the subjects. The downtown prominences (tall buildings, art museums, city halls, etc.) tended to be the objects marked in common by the subjects, with idiosyncratic elements in each map conditioned by the special diurnal motility of the drawer. As might be expected, the three cities studied varied in the extent to which the subjects' maps had features in common. Los Angeles, in particular, stood out as a city with few prominent features that all subjects would place on their maps, reflecting the fact that in Los Angeles, a central business district never developed to the same extent as in older East Coast cities.

Even the fragments of researches cited in the last few pages should demonstrate that the operational definition of a particular residential locality is

[14] Even such questions may have a false sense of specificity since some respondents may answer in terms of the political boundaries of Peoria, for example, and others in terms of the city and its adjoining suburbs.

[15] S. Reimer, "Villagers in Metropolis," *British Journal of Sociology,* vol. 2, March, 1951; R. L. Wilson, "Liveability of the City," in F. S. Chapin and S. F. Weiss, eds., *Urban Growth Dynamics in a Regional Cluster of Cities.* Wiley, New York, 1962; H. L. Ross, "The Local Community: A Survey Approach," *American Sociological Review,* vol. 27, February, 1962, pp. 75–84. The present author (in an unpublished research) asked respondents in four census tracts in the city of Philadelphia to name the four boundaries of their neighborhoods. Only in one census tract, which was bounded by railroad tracks running in deep cuts, was there any significant agreement on neighborhood boundaries.

[16] Kevin Lynch, *The Image of the City.* MIT Press, Cambridge, Mass., 1960.

not likely to match the general conceptions of either "community" or "neigh-. borhood" which individual residents form in their minds, or the specific referents of those terms in the immediate life experiences of individuals. Indeed, precisely because it would be difficult, if not impossible, to define neighborhoods and communities in such a fashion that residents would agree on common boundaries and membership criteria a concept of residential locality was developed independent of the existence of consensus among residents.

There are, however, types of residential localities that are useful for research purposes and are also likely to have some meaning to many individual residents as social-psychological entities. Major political subdivisions such as cities, towns, counties, and states are quite likely to be quite meaningful as frames of reference to individual residents. Thus, it is possible to frame attitude items concerning specific political entities such as New York City, Peoria, Illinois, or Baltimore County. Indeed, precisely because such politically defined residential localities are the focus of political decision-making—ranging from electoral battles to the passing of ordinances by local legislatures—political subdivisions are residential localities that have some meaning to all of their residents. Note that not all political subdivisions have this characteristic: special-purpose subdivisions that are purely administrative in character (e.g., mosquito-abatement districts, the catchment area of a general hospital, and so on) and that do not define a political decision-making institution and accompanying electoral contest are not likely to have very much meaning to persons who are resident within such areas.[17]

Hence the residential localities that are of special interest turn out to be relatively autonomous political subdivisions. Their residents tend to be aware of them as such and perceive themselves as members. They are also of interest from a social policy point of view since, as relatively autonomous political entities, they are capable of formulating policy within certain constitutional limitations as defined by states and the federal government, in the case of American cities.

The most useful operational definition of community is that of relatively autonomous political subdivisions. Sub-areas within such political subdivisions which are also residential localities are close to the idea of neighborhood, although they are necessarily vaguely defined in social-psychological terms and can only be given any precise definition by assuming arbitrary boundaries.

---

[17] Milton Kotler in his recent book, *Neighborhood Government* (Bobbs-Merrill, Indianapolis, Ind., 1969), makes the point that when we find sub-areas within larger political subdivisions that have established and well-recognized names (e.g., Brooklyn, Kensington, Philadelphia, Hyde Park in Chicago, etc.), they tend to have been areas that were once autonomous political subdivisions. His point is that political autonomy and electoral systems are the institutions around which the sense of "community" (solidarity, in our terms) is built.

Appropriate Research Design Strategies

There are two broad classes of usage to which indicators of some of the social-psychological aspects of life in residential localities may be put. First, such indicators may be used to assess the state of residential living in the country as a whole or in broad regions or other areas composed of aggregates of many specific residential localities. Thus, in this connection one might be concerned with changes in levels of satisfaction with police protection in the United States as a whole, or in contrasting levels according to cities of varying sizes in the several regions of the United States. Indeed, some times series (although of a primitive nature) can be constructed at present from repeated questions asked by the national polling organizations over the past two or three decades. Special surveys can be repeated again to establish trends over time. In this last connection it may be worthwhile to repeat the special surveys[18] conducted for some of the recent national commissions on crime or violence or on general life satisfactions.

The second way of proceeding would be to relate such social indicators to specific residential localities. Although establishing national, regional, or even place-size differences on a variety of measures would certainly be an important aim of a program of social-psychological indicators, more important substantive and policy-related series could be constructed using specific residential localities as the units of analysis. The advantages of this mode of proceeding would be twofold: First, it would be possible to determine the characteristics of residential localities that are related to such social-psychological indicators. For example, localities containing homogeneous populations in socioeconomic terms might be more likely to evidence high levels of total solidarity, especially under the condition of relative political autonomy, than communities with opposite characteristics. Second, there is enough interest in specific localities, especially the major metropolitan areas, to be able to make comparisons between, for example, Chicago and Detroit, or New York and Los Angeles, especially as trends in those cities are related to differences in policies pursued by local municipal administrations. Finally, a program of social-psychological indicators which could make statements about specific communities could also be designed to provide generalizations about the nation as a whole, about regions, and about places of various sizes.

The strategy suggested here is that of large-scale comparative community studies. A much more convincing case could be made for this strategy if there

---

[18] President's Commission on Law Enforcement and the Administration of Justice, *The Challenge of Crime in a Free Society.* Government Printing Office, Washington, D.C., 1967. National Commission on the Causes and Prevention of Violence, *To Establish Justice, To Insure Domestic Tranquility.* Government Printing Office, Washington, D.C., 1969.

were a large and distinguished body of empirical research to which one could refer for evidence on its utility. Despite the fact that local communities have been a favorite research subject for sociologists from the beginnings of empirical social research, it is not possible to point to many precedents. The tradition of research on local communities has tended to focus on particular local communities. Although such case studies tended to be implicitly comparative, the comparisons involved have ordinarily been either very restricted (as, for example, in the case of the Lynds' 1937 study of Muncie, Indiana, in which Muncie at a particular point in time is compared with itself at another point in time) or with some other unspecified communities (as, for example, in Vidich and Bensman's 1958 study of a small upstate New York community which is compared with an "image" of a metropolis).[19] Systematic comparative community studies covering a large enough number of cases to permit the establishment on a firm basis of the existence of significant intercommunity differences in these respects are almost nonexistent.[20]

The major factor impeding the development of comparative community studies along the lines necessary has been the high cost of conducting such studies. Since most of the measures to be developed below would require sampling residents of communities to develop aggregate measures of social-psychological dimensions of residential localities, each such locality to be studied would require a sample of sufficient size to establish a fairly firm reading on each locality. If one is to study localities of appreciable size assuming a given fixed level of accuracy in estimation, the sample size required for each locality is, for all practical purposes, the same as that required for a sample of the nation as a whole.[21] Hence, a study of 50 localities requires a total sample size that is 50 times the sample size required to study the nation as a whole. Few research plans have been able to enjoy the level of support to be able to study a large enough number of localities to provide some hard empirical basis for evaluating the utility of the measures suggested below.[22] Note, too, that a sample size of 50

[19] Lynd and Lynd, *op. cit.*; A. Vidich and W. Bensman, *Small Town in a Mass Society*. Princeton University Press, Princeton, 1958.

[20] Comparative community studies based upon data collected in the decennial censuses and ranging across a relatively large number of cities have been the major type of large-scale comparative studies. However, the decennial census contains no data on the issues raised either in the definitions given in the previous section of this chapter or on related social-psychological dimensions of residential localities.

[21] This is so because the fiduciary limits of a sample measure are much more affected by the size of the sample than by the size of the universe sampled, especially if that universe contains more than a hundred units.

[22] For example, two studies of 15 major American cities conducted on behalf of the Kerner Commission by the University of Michigan's Survey Research Center, one involving small samples of blacks and whites in general population samples and the other, by James S. Coleman and the present author, involving members of selected occupational

is by no means a fully adequate sample size. Since residential localities that are also major political subdivisions vary widely in population size and density, and it can also be anticipated that both will have important impacts on most of the social-psychological indicators proposed here, a sample size of 50 would be quite inadequate for all but the most primitive analyses.[23]

Of course, one may ease the requirement that the same level of accuracy is desired for each residential locality that one would desire for the nation as a whole. Thus, although any one individual city may not be measured very well with intracity samples of 50 respondents, the relationships across cities may be just as accurately represented for a relatively large number of cities, than if intracity samples of 500 were used.[24]

Comparative community studies employing large samples of communities can be accomplished relatively inexpensively if the topics to be studied are those for which probability samples of the general population are not required or are inappropriate. Thus, a study of the formal characteristics of school systems as related to the method of selection of school board members can be accomplished by interviewing a small number of people in each school system. A plan for setting up a data-gathering apparatus for the purpose of conducting such studies and for archiving data on a large sample of American cities is presently in the early stages of organization and testing.[25] Within the next few years it

---

groups (policemen, social workers, educators, merchants, employers, and political party workers), cost almost $400,000 initially for data collection for the first round of analysis and will probably cost an additional $100,000 to carry the analysis through to completion (National Advisory Commission on Civil Disorders, *Supplemental Studies*. Government Printing Office, Washington, D.C., 1968).

[23] The issues involved in studying localities on a comparative basis have been extremely well stated in a plan to provide a long-range evaluation of the Model Cities program planned jointly by the Urban Institute and the Survey Research Center of the University of Michigan. (See J. S. Wholey *et al., Survey Research Related to Evaluation of the Model Cities Program: Second Quarterly Progress Report*. Urban Institute, Washington, D.C., 1969; mimeographed.)

[24] Perhaps the easiest way to bolster this strategy is to consider that, in a regression analysis in which the units are cities, the degrees of freedom and hence the statistical significance of correlation coefficients and associated regression coefficients are dependent on the number of units used, i.e., number of cities, and not on the number of observations that go into each of the values for each city. Somewhat the same reasoning can be derived from considering an analysis of variance model in which one is trying to estimate the unique contributions of intercity variance and intracity variance to the total variance among individuals. In the analysis of variance model, more is gained by increasing the number of cities than by increasing the number of individual observations within cities.

[25] Peter H. Rossi and R. Crain, "The NORC Permanent Community Sample," *Public Opinion Quarterly*, vol. 32, Summer, 1968, pp. 261–272. For an example of the kinds of studies that can be conducted using the Permanent Community Sample, see R. Crain and P. H. Rossi, "Comparative Community Studies with Large N's," *Proceedings of the American Statistical Association*, Social Statistics Section, 1968.

should be possible to undertake continuing studies of the political and institutional structures of a large sample (150) of American municipalities in the size ranges of 25,000 and above. Note, however, that the social-psychological indicators suggested in this chapter mainly require the use of adequate samples of the general populations of residential localities and hence would not be appropriately served by the community-sampling strategy proposed by Crain and Rossi.

Lying behind the argument of this section is the assumption that most social-psychological indicators would be based on sample surveys of individuals in which the answers to survey questionnaires would be aggregated over residential localities in order to obtain summary measures that would characterize the social-psychological characteristics of those areas. In an intriguing volume, Webb and his associates have proposed that for many variables of the sort considered here, a more valid approach would be to define indicators that were not dependent upon verbal responses to personal interviews or written questionnaires.[26] Thus, a measure of interracial tensions might rely on samples of conversations overheard by observers riding public transportation, or on the sales records of firms that sell firearms. Webb and his associates assert that such "unobtrusive" measures reflect more nearly the "true" state of affairs than the responses made to questions posed by interviewers, or written on questionnaires. Many of the measures suggested are ingenious and intriguing, and may well be adapted for use as social-psychological indicators. Whether obtrusive or unobtrusive measures are employed, the same general problems of research design will be encountered, and thus the discussion in this section applies regardless of specific data-collection techniques employed.

Social-Psychological Community Indicators

The issues discussed in the previous sections of this chapter set forth a general framework for the development of a set of specific social-psychological indicators. The task of this section is to suggest what forms such indicators might take and the specific topics to be covered. In some cases it has been possible to cite concrete researches that have developed measures which might be used directly or with slight modifications as working definitions. In the main, however, the suggestions made below require additional development and some experimentation before workable operational measures exist.

The general framework suggested in the earlier part of this chapter provides only part of the impetus for the set of indicators of this section. There are aspects of life in communities of traditional concern not encompassed in that

---

[26] E. J. Webb *et al., Unobtrusive Measures: Nonreactive Research in the Social Sciences.* Rand McNally, Chicago, 1966.

framework; only the more important of such concerns are covered in this section. For example, since residential localities, by definition, are made up of housing units and are very heavily influenced by housing market considerations, attitudes toward housing, neighborhood amenities, cost-time factors in travel, and so on are important aspects of life in localities. Measures of attitudes toward such matters are considered part of the set of social-psychological indicators outlined in this section.

The strategy of this section is to suggest the variables that should be tapped by the set of social-psychological indicators. Specific forms for the indicators (e.g., interview schedule items, existing statistical series, etc.), when available, have been described in footnotes, indicating the tentative status of such suggested operational forms. For the most part, well-established social-psychological indicators for the variables listed below have not yet been constructed and/or tested extensively enough for me to be comfortable in suggesting their adoption.

No distinction has been made in this section between those indicators that could be applied to very large residential localities (e.g., central cities of major metropolitan areas) and those to small localities and neighborhoods that are sub-areas within larger political subdivisions. In principle, the indicators are applicable to any arbitrarily defined area, whether a part of a city block or a large municipality. In practice, areas that are also political subdivisions will be the localities in which one mainly would be interested, at least for the purpose of establishing a set of social indicators.

A. Orientations to Localities as Collectivities

The main issue in the set of variables to be considered under this rubric is whether or not (or the extent to which) the members of a particular residential locality consider the population and institutions of that area to constitute a significant collectivity. The literature of community studies has been much concerned with this issue, although it cannot be said that measures of the orientations of residents to their localities as collectivities have been developed beyond the most primitive level.

In terms of the definitions presented earlier in this chapter, *solidarity* is the quality of residential communities that is to be measured by the indicators suggested here. For a residential locality to exhibit relatively high solidarity, two conditions have to be obtained: First, a relatively large proportion of the residents have to conceive of the locality as having the characteristics of a collectivity, i.e., be perceived as an identifiable group with some ability to act as a group. Second, a relatively large proportion of the residents have to feel that their well-being is significantly affected by the fate of the collectivity involved.

Some specific indicators follow:

1. Perception of Locality as Collectivity.[27] Measures of the extent to which residents in a particular residential locality see their fellow residents as members of a collectivity, relatively distinct from members of other localities.

   a. Existence of place names over which there is consensus among residents as applying to the locality.
   b. Recognition that residents are different in some critical respect from residents of other localities.
   c. Use of place names as terms of self-description; extent to which residents consider themselves as New Yorkers, Chicagoans, Baltimoreans, etc.
   d. Recognition of sharing with other residents of some significant set of interests, that their fates are tied together.

2. Affective Involvement in Residential Locality as Collectivity.[28]

   a. Feelings of pride in self-identification as a resident of the locality.
   b. Depth of anticipation of sense of loss if resident were to move from locality.
   c. Readiness to define fellow residents as potential friends, mates, persons with whom one should make common cause.

3. Interest and Involvement in Local Events.[29]

   a. Existence of locality-oriented media, e.g., local newspapers, magazines, separate radio or TV stations, sections or editions of metropolitan or regional media.
   b. Existence of locality-oriented and based voluntary associations, i.e., asso-

[27] Operational forms of these variables depend heavily on the existence of place names for the localities involved. Hence, the critical first question is whether there is some degree of consensus among residents over a commonplace name. This is particularly critical for areas that are not political subdivisions and therefore do not ordinarily have place names as part of post office addresses. For political subdivisions, b, c, and d become of critical importance.

[28] Some examples of survey items which might tap these variables are as follows: "How proud are you to be a [Chicagoan, etc.]? Very proud, Somewhat proud, Indifferent, . . . etc." "Suppose for some reason or other you had to move from [locality]. Assuming that you would not suffer economically from the move, how sorry would you be about moving from [locality]?" "Compared to people from other places, do you think it more likely, less likely, or doesn't make any difference that someone in [locality] would make the sort of friend you would want to have?" See Marc Fried, "Grieving for a Lost Home," in Leonard Duhl, ed., *The Urban Condition*. Basic Books, New York, 1963, a study of reactions of low-income families on being forced to relocate when their "slum" neighborhood was demolished in an urban renewal program.

[29] Morris Janowitz, *The Community Press in an Urban Setting*. Free Press, Glencoe, Ill., 1952. Presented is the thesis that the local neighborhood weekly newspapers in Chicago help residents of those neighborhoods in defining the limits of their neighborhoods and in developing a sense of identification with those neighborhoods.

The measurement of attention paid to media of various types has been worked out very well by commercial social researchers intent on measuring the audiences of various media and media messages.

ciations whose goals are to affect the course of events within the locality, e.g., political clubs, civic associations, neighborhood protective associations, etc.

c. Attention paid by individuals to local events as reported in mass media.

d. Membership in and participation in locality-oriented voluntary associations.[30]

4. "Social Climate" Measures of Residential Localities. Certain aspects of residential localities are perceived by residents as establishing a "social climate," general conditions of the locality generated by its social characteristics. Some of the more commonly expressed "climatological" factors are:

a. Friendliness of locality: extent to which other residents are seen as open to the formation of friendship.

b. Mutual aid and responsibility: extent to which residents see each other as likely to help each other out in the event of need, e.g., borrowing small items, looking in on a neighbor to see if he is well, and so on.

c. Sense of personal safety: extent to which the residents see themselves as free to travel through the locality without fear of robbery or assault, safety of possessions in one's house or on the grounds of the homesite, etc.

d. Tolerant-intolerant: extent to which residents see each other as accepting of a wide range of personal behavior or as disapproving of behavior that is outside a narrow range.

5. Residential Localities as Reference Groups.[31] Although "reference group" is one of the social psychologist's favorite ideas, it is not at all clear that

---

A number of social scientists have tried to work out measurements of what has come to be called "local-cosmopolitan" orientations. R. K. Merton, "Patterns of Influence," in P. F. Lazersfeld and F. N. Stanton, eds., *Communications Research 1948–1949*. Harper, New York, 1949, found that he could classify persons regarded to be highly influential in a small New Jersey city according to whether they were oriented to local events (locals) or events occurring on the national or international scene (cosmopolitans). Although Merton did not develop an attitudinal scale devised to measure these orientations (indeed they were inferred mainly from the communications media exposure rates of individuals), several subsequent researchers attempted to do so, notably T. R. Dye, "The Local-Cosmopolitan Dimension and the Study of Urban Politics," *Social Forces,* vol. 41, 1966; and W. M. Dobriner, "Local and Cosmopolitan as Contemporary Suburban Types," in Dobriner, ed., *The Suburban Community.* Putnam, New York, 1958. Although in these scales the attempt has been made to place "local" and "cosmopolitan" on opposite ends of the same continuum, it might make more sense to consider these not as polar concepts but as existing separately.

[30] This variable is discussed in greater detail later in this chapter.

[31] A collection of examples of how researchers have employed the concept of reference group in empirical research is contained in H. Hyman and E. Singer, *Readings in Reference Group Theory and Research.* Free Press, New York, 1968. No examples are given, however, of the use of community, neighborhood, or other types of residential localities as reference groups.

Rossi, *op. cit.,* used correlations between residents' own class identifications and the

great success has been experienced in giving the concept operational definition. In essence, the concept of reference group is designed to cover those individuals, groups, or social categories with which an individual compares himself in order to establish a conception of his relative standing with respect to some evaluative dimension. Thus, in order for an individual to establish whether he is well off or not, e.g., with respect to his ability to use standard English, he has to have some sort of standard against which he compares himself, e.g., TV announcers.

In this connection, the concept of reference group raises the question whether residential localities define significant reference groups for their residents. It is uncertain whether the use of reference group in this sense is a measure of the solidarity or a measure of the lack of cohesion of a residential locality. One may argue that, if the residents compare themselves with each other, they are showing the extent to which the locality is important to them and represents a positive bond. The opposite argument is that, in localities whose residents are continually making invidious comparisons among themselves, the resulting status competition reduces solidarity. In either event, a measure of the salience of the locality is whether or not a locality is a reference group to its inhabitants.

These considerations suggest that it would be important to distinguish among the following states:

> Residential Localities as *Positive Reference Groups:* The extent to which residents see the residents of an area positively as persons they would like to be similar to or are in fact similar to.
>
> Residential Localities as *Negative Reference Groups:* The extent to which residents aspire to be different from or surpass other residents in the locality.

Thus, it should make quite a difference if the residents in an area say that they are very much like each other in social class and, furthermore, that they like this equality (as compared with a situation where they do not wish to be like their neighbors).

There are many ways in which residents of a locality can compare themselves with each other. Among them:

---

imputed class placement of other residents in their neighborhoods as measures of the extent to which the residents in each of four census tracts in Philadelphia identified with their fellow residents. The correlation coefficients for each census tract were used to characterize the tract according to the extent to which residents identified with each other in a social-class sense. The higher the correlation, the more stable were the residents in the tract.

Social-class identification has been measured in a number of ways ranging from presenting the respondent with a set of fixed class names from among which to choose essentially patterned along the lines of R. Centers, *The Psychology of Social Class*. Princeton University Press, Princeton, 1949, to the relatively open-ended method employed by W. Lloyd Warner, *Social Class in America*. Science Research Associates, Chicago, 1949.

a. Socioeconomic status:
   (i) Residential localities as reference groups in social-class placement (e.g., of which social-class residents think they are members).
   (ii) Reference groups with regard to economic well-being (e.g., how well off the residents think they are).
b. Race and ethnicity: Extent to which residents see themselves as members of the same race and/or ethnic groups.[32]
c. Life-cycle stage: Extent to which residents see each other as the same or different with respect to age, family status, household composition, etc.[33]
d. Other comparative judgments: Residential locality as reference group with respect to other areas of life—health, job satisfaction, progress of children in school, and so on. Almost any area of life satisfaction might be used in this connection, even though some may appear to be very remote from residential considerations.

It can be anticipated that residential localities would serve as significant reference groups to their residents in life areas closely related to activities that go on either within a household or within the area itself. Thus, for young children, the "neighborhood" is more important in a number of respects than the larger political subdivision. We can also anticipate that the residential locality will serve as an important reference group with respect to consumer goods: in "keeping up with the Joneses," the Joneses are supposed to be living nearby.[34]

   6. Segmental Solidarity: Intra-Locality Differences and Conflict. Even in the most homogeneous housing areas, such as mass-produced tract housing or public housing, residents will see some degree of heterogeneity among their fellow residents. Especially where residential localities are also political subdivisions, perceived lines of cleavage ranging from the neutral perception of differences to preparations for armed conflict can be expected to exist. Indeed, the

---

[32] Despite the considerable attention American sociologists have given to ethnicity, it is difficult to find a large number of empirical studies of either ethnic self-identification or the importance of such identifications in important areas of behavior and activity. See Andrew M. Greeley, *Why Can't They Be Like Us?* American Jewish Committee, New York, 1969, for a review of studies of ethnicity. For a good review of the general problem of ethnicity see Milton M. Gordon, *Assimilation in American Life.* Oxford University Press, New York, 1964. Perhaps the best-known study of contemporary ethnic groups is Nathan Glazer and Daniel P. Moynihan, *Beyond the Melting Pot: The Negroes, Puerto Ricans, Italians, Jews and Irish of New York City.* MIT Press, Cambridge, Mass., 1963.

[33] Some attention has been given to life-cycle homogeneity of residential localities, particularly in connection with planning retirement communities. Here the question has been whether retired persons would be more satisfied to live in communities composed of retired persons or in communities with a more heterogeneous life-cycle composition. See Irving Rosow, *The Social Integration of the Aged.* Free Press of Glencoe, New York, 1967. Studies of other life-cycle stages, e.g., young childless couples, are less frequently encountered.

[34] W. H. Whyte, *The Organization Man.* Simon & Schuster, New York, 1956.

lines of cleavage, expressing segmental solidarity, may in many cases exceed in strength the sense of total solidarity for most residential localities of any appreciable size.

Although in principle any population characteristic that is relatively visible and marks off a sizable group of individuals or households could serve as a fault line along which intra-locality cleavages could arise, in fact the lines of cleavage tend to be generated by the following intra-locality differences:[35]

    a. Socioeconomic: Income, formal education, and related characteristics, including housing style and price.

    b. Ethnic, racial, and religious.

    c. Life-cycle stages: Differences among residents according to age, composition of household, and accompanying demands for different mixes of local services.

    d. Time of arrival: Cleavages among "newcomers" and "old-timers."

These characteristics are ordinarily not independent of each other and tend to reinforce the perception of intra-locality differences and enhance the possibility of conflict being generated along such lines. Thus, because housing in a sub-area tends to be relatively homogeneous in price, socioeconomic differences tend to be structured along sub-areal lines. Similarly, racial groups tend to be relatively homogeneous internally with respect to religion, socioeconomic level, and sometimes with respect to life cycle and time of arrival.

In the present historical context, the major fault line in our large metropolitan areas is that of race. Blacks and whites in many localities are vying for political power, with the mayor's office often the focus of political contest. Indeed, some writers have seen the relations between whites and blacks as the major problem of our major metropolitan areas.[36]

There are two directions in which indicators of differences and cleavages may go. On the one hand, one might be concerned with the extent to which socioeconomic levels coincide with differences in political loyalties or with opinions on particular issues. Employing this approach, a residential locality is characterized by relatively high segmental solidarity if the correlations are high be-

[35] James S. Coleman, *Community Conflict*. Free Press, Glencoe, Ill., 1957. R. L. Crain, E. Katz, and D. B. Rosenthal, *The Fluoridation Decision*. Bobbs-Merrill, Indianapolis, Ind., 1968. W. A. Gamson, "Rancorous Conflict in Community Politics," in T. N. Clark, ed., *Community Structure and Decision-Making*. Chandler, San Francisco, 1968. K. Underwood, *Protestant and Catholic*. Beacon Press, Boston, 1957. The above are but a few of the references to a very large literature on conflicts that have arisen within politically defined residential localities. They are presented here as examples of the kinds of studies which have been made and which illustrate the variety of intra-locality differences which have formed the basis of conflict.

[36] M. Grodzins, *The Metropolitan Area as a Racial Problem*. University of Pittsburgh Press, Pittsburgh, 1958. C. E. Silberman, *Crisis in Black and White*. Random House, New York, 1964.

tween the lines of cleavage and measures of attitudes on relevant issues. For example, if there is a stronger correlation between race and voting in a mayoralty election in Cleveland as compared with Los Angeles, then the former city is characterized as having higher segmental solidarity than the latter.

On the other hand, one may proceed to study the extent to which potential fault lines are perceived as lines of cleavage. Thus, one would ask residents of a locality whether they perceive blacks and whites as essentially in agreement or in disagreement on relevant issues.

These two modes of approaching the operational definition of intra-locality cleavage are not mutually exclusive and, indeed, both directions may be pursued in the development of social-psychological indicators. Because the mode of perceived differences is somehow more social-psychological, it will be elaborated here:

a. Social distance: Among the earliest attempts (circa 1925) to develop social-psychological measures was Bogardus' "Social Distance Scale."[37] Variations and refinements on his original measures have been used to measure the extent to which individuals would admit various ethnic groups into varying degrees of intimacy, ranging from marrying to allowing into the country as an immigrant. Adaptations of this scale have been used to establish trends in intergroup relations and in measuring the perceived distances among socioeconomic groups.

The application suggested here is to establish the extent to which groups in a residential locality would admit members of other groups into different levels of intimacy.

b. Perceived group cleavages: Measures of the extent to which the various groups in the community are seen as agreeing or disagreeing on a variety of issues.[38]

[37] E. S. Bogardus, *Immigration and Race Attitudes*. Heath, New York, 1928. Adaptations of the original scale have been used by Mildred I. Schwartz, *Trends in White Attitudes Toward Negroes*. National Opinion Research Center, Chicago, 1967; E. O. Laumann, *Prestige and Association in an Urban Community*. Bobbs-Merrill, Indianapolis, Ind., 1966, in a study of social distance among occupational levels.

[38] For an example of one way of measuring such perceived differences see P. H. Rossi *et al.,* "Between White and Black," in National Advisory Commission on Civil Disorders, *Supplemental Studies*. Government Printing Office, Washington, D.C., 1968. An abortive attempt was made in the period immediately following World War II to develop tension indexes for the state of race relations either in neighborhoods or among larger politically defined subdivisions. For a suggested neighborhood set of measures see S. A. Star, "An Approach to the Measurement of Interracial Tension," in E. W. Burgess and D. J. Bogue, eds., *Contributions to Urban Sociology*. University of Chicago Press, Chicago, 1964. A rather elaborate attempt to measure roughly the same phenomena on a cross-community basis was made by a group of researchers at Cornell University, reported in Robin Williams, *Strangers Next Door*. Prentice-Hall, Englewood Cliffs, N.J., 1964. Some ingenious suggestions for the measurement of intergroup tensions through unobtrusive measures have been suggested by Webb *et al., op. cit.*

7. Attachment to Residential Locality: Residential Mobility and Migration. One might suppose that the ultimate test of the solidarity of a residential locality would be the rate of turnover of residents, an index which would seem to measure the extent to which residents are attached to their locality. Indeed, such measures are easily generated—e.g., counting the proportion of billing changes in public utility household accounts for an area—and it is relatively easy to construct reliable measures of potential for moving using survey interviews with household members.

Yet it would be an error to use mobility or migration rates as a direct measure of attachment to an area. Many moves are occasioned by events that are beyond the control of individuals or households (e.g., the destruction of a dwelling unit through fire or conversion to other use, or because death has broken the primary household marital bond). Many moves are necessary consequences of other decisions that an individual or household has made, for example, new household formation or the voluntary dissolution of a household in separation or divorce. Still other moves are the side effects of labor market decisions: The most migratory of all occupational groups are young persons in the professions and technical occupations whose jobs are ordinarily sought on a national or regional labor market. Thus, for an engineer to seek a position means often enough that he must also consider moving. The migratory middle manager in a large business enterprise or an aspiring young assistant professor are other examples of occupational groups whose labor market decisions may often involve long-distance moves.

One of the more important sources of short-distance moves lies in the shifting housing needs of households accompanying increases or decreases in household size. Thus, the birth of children or their subsequent marriage and removal from the household can radically alter the housing needs of a household and produce a strong desire to move on those grounds alone.

Indeed, the proper measure of attachment to a locality would be some indicator of "what it would take" in the way of income, cramped living quarters, etc. to produce a decision to move from a locality. Low levels of residents' attachments to locality might be measured by the extent to which residential mobility is highly sensitive to shifts in household composition, or, how much an increment in income would make it attractive to an individual to consider migrating from one place to another.

Comparisons across localities in migration or mobility rates should be undertaken with some caution, keeping in mind that both rates are sensitive to differences in life-cycle and socioeconomic compositions of localities as well as residents' attachments to the areas in question.[39] Residential turnover rates are only partially a reflection of attachment to a locality and can be used as an in-

[39] John B. Lansing and Eva Mueller, *The Geographic Mobility of Labor.* Survey Research Center, Institute for Social Research, University of Michigan, Ann Arbor, 1967; Rossi, *op. cit.*

dicator of attachment only when corrected for life-cycle and socioeconomic composition differences among areas.

The measurement of residential turnover can be accomplished fairly easily. To begin with, decennial censuses routinely collect information on whether residents were living in the dwelling unit the previous year. The Current Population Survey also asks the same information once a year and can provide a breakdown for large political subdivisions (e.g., major metropolitan areas). Turnover measures can sometimes be assembled through city directories, voter registration lists, and records of utilities companies. The measures suggested relate to past turnover and tend to overestimate turnover in areas in which there is new construction or extensive demolition of dwelling units.

Prospective measures of anticipated residential turnover can be constructed using sample survey data. Several studies have shown that mobility intentions are rather good indicators of future behavior, sufficiently predictive to be used as forecasts of future turnover rates for localities.[40]

The measures suggested below assume some sort of standardization for life-cycle and socioeconomic composition:

    a. Past mobility rates: Census measures, directory turnover, etc.

    b. Prospective mobility rates: Based on reported intentions of moving.

    c. Measurement of incentives necessary to induce movement: Essentially measures of how much in the way of better housing, additional income, reduced housing costs, etc., it would take to induce moving intentions on the part of locality residents.

B. Interaction and Exchange: The Measurement of Integration

The integration of a residential locality has been defined earlier as the extent to which the residents of that locality have developed relatively enduring relationships in either formal or informal organizational contexts. Residential localities with dense networks of friendship in this sense are more integrated than those whose friendship networks cover the area in question sparsely. Similarly, residential localities in which most of the residents use the locality for their buying of goods, selling of labor or services, procuring essential services, and so on are more integrated than those which do not.

The variables listed in this subsection are designed to measure integration in this sense; they lend themselves to two broad types of measures:

Absolute density measures: Extent to which social relationships of a given type cover an area, e.g., the average number of relatives of residents living in the locality in question.

---

[40] Rossi, *op. cit.* The measures used have been simply to ask whether the household has any intention to move, what steps have been taken to search for an alternative dwelling unit, etc.

Relative concentration measures: Proportion of all relationships of a given type that are with other residents of the locality in question, e.g., the proportion of all relatives of residents in an area who live in that area.

Although absolute density measures would seem to come closer to the general concept of integration, indicating the extent to which a locality is covered by relationships of a given type, such measures are affected by the extent to which persons enter into such relationships regardless of the locations of the partners in the relationship. Thus, membership in voluntary organizations of all sorts tends to vary positively with socioeconomic level.[41] A locality may be classified as having a dense network of voluntary associations, not because memberships of the residents are especially clustered in the area, but because upper-middle-class residents tend to join more organizations. If attention is to be focused on the extent to which residents' activities are centered in the locality, the relative density measures are to be preferred.

Obviously, whether the one form or the other is to be used in a particular research depends on the purposes of the research and on whether or not there are real differences between the alternative definitions in practice. Rank orderings of localities may well not be substantially changed by shifting from one definition to another.

Listed below are the main forms of integrative ties which researchers might profitably employ:

1. Market Relationships. Measures of the extent to which the procurement of goods and services (including labor) are concentrated within residential localities.

    a. Individual employment: Measures of the extent to which the jobs held by residents are at places within the locality in question.

    b. Firm employment: Measures of the extent to which firms within the locality draw upon the locality for their labor forces.

    c. Small-purchase consumer goods: Local purchases of low-priced items, e.g., gasoline, food articles, drugs, newspapers.

    d. Major-purchase consumer goods: Local purchases of high-priced articles, appliances, automobiles, furniture, jewelry.

    e. Professional services: Medical, legal, and other professional services.

    f. Other services: Repairs to appliances, goods, cleaning services, etc.

The variables listed above have been primarily concerned with the market relationships involving individuals. A similar classification could be centered around relationships among firms, mercantile establishments, and other types of economic organizations. Indeed, a functionally autonomous residential locality has been defined as one in which the vast bulk of the market relationships involving

---

[41] M. Hausknecht, *The Joiners.* Bedminster, New York, 1962. See also D. P. Foley, "The Use of Local Facilities in a Metropolis," in J. P. Gibbs, ed., *Urban Research Methods.* Van Nostrand, Princeton, N.J., 1961.

individuals and firms are among persons and firms located within the boundaries of the unit.[42]

2. Voluntary Formal Associations. This form of social organization in which individuals join together for special purposes without explicit monetary return (i.e., almost all members are not employees) has been touched upon earlier in the form of voluntary associations that are community-oriented in their goals. Voluntary associations can have a very wide range of goals from revolution to philately, providing a context in which individuals and households can be in close contact with one another and contribute to the exchange of interaction in a residential locality.

A useful classification of voluntary associations for a wide variety of purposes and acceptable to all social researchers has yet to be worked out. The one listed below is designed to be particularly relevant for the study of residential localities:

a. Professional associations and unions: Associations designed to protect and advance the interests of a particular occupational group, including bargaining with employers and other users of services offered by the occupation. Sometimes borders on the "involuntary," as when membership in a union is required for all workers on particular levels in a plant or when access to important facilities (e.g., hospital privileges for doctors) is contingent on membership.

b. Religious associations: Churches, chapels, fellowships, and the like, voluntary associations whose purpose it is to express solidarity with others professing the same views concerning God and the Universe.

c. Political and parapolitical associations: Political clubs, political parties, civic associations, and so on, voluntary associations whose major goal it is to propose and elect public officials, and/or influence the course of decision-making in a political jurisdiction.

d. Restricted-purpose "leisure" activity associations: Country clubs, bowling clubs, etc. Voluntary associations whose purpose it is to indulge in a restricted band of nonwork-connected, nonpolitical, and nonreligious activities.

e. Other voluntary associations: Associations not covered in the classification proposed above.

The classification offered above has been phrased in terms of the major purposes of voluntary associations. However, every voluntary association, whatever its expressed purposes may be, also fulfills other needs for its members. A political club designed to influence the selection of candidates for political office also serves the sociability needs of its members, and the country club can also be the scene in which major political transactions take place.

3. Kinship Relationships. The American kinship system is a simple and loose one as far as the total range of kinship systems that men have invented.

[42] T. N. Clark, "Community or Communities," in Clark, ed., *op. cit.*

We recognize descent in two lines, one stemming from the maternal and the other from the paternal line. Newly formed nuclear families are supposed to set themselves up in separate households and most do so within a year or two of marriage. Our legal system prescribes strong financial and legal responsibilities of parents toward minor children and some states require children to provide financial support for their parents in the case of the latters' disability. We also permit divorce and have moved in the past few decades to make the obtaining of divorces somewhat easier.

Beyond this very general outline the system appears to be vague and variable, however. The reciprocal obligations of spouses and parents and children have been spelled out in some detail in domestic law but the obligations among kin of different degrees of relationship have not been elaborated either in custom or in law. Whether one owes any obligations (for example, visits) to one's second cousin is not clear, or is it clear whether one's mother's brother's wife is a relative at all. Primary kinship ties are clear within the two nuclear families to which the individual belongs at one time or another in his life: ties to his parents, his siblings, and his children. Other degrees of kinship are more or less optional ties.[43]

Despite the loose cultural definition of kin, kinship ties are still of considerable importance. For example, social researchers in the Bell Telephone System estimate that the more frequent private telephone calls are between kin, with mother-daughter telephone calls probably the most frequent.

Ties of kinship could conceivably produce a considerable set of strong bonds among the residents of a residential locality if such residents are composed of sets of kin who recognize kinship as imposing mutual obligations. In this connection, we would be concerned with two main variables:

a. Density of kin relationships within residential locality: The extent to which residents in the locality have persons they recognize as relatives living in the area.
b. Viability of kinship relationships: Extent to which kinship ties imply communication, visiting, participation in ritual occasions (marriage, funerals, confirmations, christenings, etc.) and mutual aid obligations.

4. Friendship. If, in our culture, we judge that kinship is vaguely defined, then how should we judge the clarity of our conceptions of friendship? The term stretches to cover a range of intimacy from the exchange of greetings on chance meetings to the sharing of the most private thoughts and wishes. The English language and its vernacular versions contains only a few terms to designate degrees of friendship and virtually no terms to designate friendships of different sorts, i.e., cross-sex as opposed to same-sex friendships, long-standing friend-

---

[43] A more detailed description of the American kinship system and an empirical study of kinship ties among whites in Greensboro, N.C., is contained in Bert N. Adams, *Kinship in an Urban Setting*. Markham Publishing, Chicago, 1968.

ships from those of relatively recent duration, friendships between age and status peers as opposed to those which span a generation or different social statuses, and so on.

Despite the ambiguity of the term, the phenomena covered by our loose concept of friendship is of considerable importance to residential localities.[44] We judge communities according to their friendliness, meaning that localities vary according to the ease with which it is possible to establish friendship ties with residents. A locality with dense friendship networks may be expected to be more likely to have a rich and varied set of voluntary associations.

Friendship ties lend themselves to complicated measurement possibilities. The very notion of network involves connections among more than pairs of individuals, possibly in the form of cliques or other groupings. Communities can be characterized not only by how probable it is that any two individuals will form friendship ties, but also by the extensiveness of ties among larger numbers of individuals, the extent to which such groupings are themselves connected to each other, and so on. It seems doubtful, however, that one would be concerned in the present connection with more than the crudest measures of levels of friendship formation in residential localities, leaving to rather specialized studies the graphing and mapping of more complicated networks of such ties. For present purposes then, the measuring problem can stop at the point of calculating the probabilities that friendship ties of various sorts will be formed between pairs of residents.

Following common usage we can distinguish among three different levels of friendship.[45]

a. Persons "known": The average number of persons that residents in a residential locality recognize by face and name.

b. Acquaintances: The average number of persons with whom residents have had some communication, and whose addresses or other regular spatial locations is known (e.g., place of work).

c. Friendship: The average number of persons with whom residents share some degree of intimacy, e.g., receive visits from, know about details of personal life, etc.

These averages are obviously strongly affected by the size of the population in a residential locality. Thus, the number of unique pairs of individuals

---

[44] Joel Smith, William H. Form, and Gregory P. Stone, "Local Intimacy in a Middle-Sized City," *American Journal of Sociology*, vol. 60, November, 1954, pp. 270–284.

[45] Mark Granovetter (Johns Hopkins University) suggested the strength of such friendship (and kinship) ties be measured, using as indexes the time spent in the relationship, the emotional intensity of the tie, and the amount of mutual confiding. The categories listed are more or less close to common usage in which Granovetter's suggested measures are involved to some unknown and possibly variable degree. Obviously, if one were to make an intense investment in measuring friendship and kinship ties, one would want to go in the directions suggested by Granovetter. For a superficial, but not necessarily irrelevant approach, the suggested categories are probably sufficient.

that can be formed out of a population of Size N is $N(N-1)/2$, a figure which soon reaches astronomical proportions even in relatively small-size communities. Perhaps a more realistic way to compare localities is to consider the average number of local residents with whom individual residents have friendship relations. Furthermore, as indicated earlier, one may distinguish between the absolute level of friendship relationships in a locality (i.e., the average number of friendships entered into by individual residents) and the relative concentration of friendships in the locality, the proportion of all friendships entered into by residents which are with other residents. This last measure may be regarded as one which indicates the relative importance of the residential locality as a source of friendships for its members.

C. Relationships to Central Local Institutions

A central local institution is an institution that is recognized in law or custom as having the right to act on behalf of the locality and/or to regulate the behavior of other institutions and individuals in the locality. In this sense, all politically autonomous localities by definition have central local institutions, a set of social positions with the powers to make decisions within constitutional limitations which are binding on the residents of the locality. Politically dependent localities may also have institutions that act in political ways on behalf of the locality—for example, the local press and mass media, neighborhood improvement associations, civic clubs, political party clubs, and the like.

Such institutions are central in two important senses: First, the existence of such institutions serves an important symbolic function, providing the residents with a focus for their feelings about the locality as a collectivity. In an important sense, a mayor represents his city vis-à-vis the rest of the society; it is the mayor who tenders the key to the city to visiting dignitaries. Second, these central institutions are important sources of critical services and amenities to residents—police protection, street maintenance, elementary and secondary education, and the like.

One of the critical questions concerning a residential locality is whether the residents view its institutions as representing the locality as a whole. Of course, for politically autonomous units, the question may be trivial if most residents view the mayor and other major public officials as serving that function for them. But for politically dependent units, this may be of critical importance in determining whether or not the locality is seen to be a collectivity.[46]

---

[46] In a Chicago neighborhood, Hyde Park-Kenwood, the critical appearance of a parapolitical association, the Hyde Park–Kenwood Community Conference, which attempted to enlist as members all residents of the area and acted to represent the area in its attempts to obtain urban renewal assistance, made it possible for the area's residents to act almost as a politically autonomous unit in obtaining special services from Chicago city government and special consideration from federal officials. See P. H. Rossi and R. Dentler, *The Politics of Urban Renewal*. Free Press, Glencoe, Ill., 1961.

What are the institutions which typically can serve as central local institutions? The list which follows contains some of the more frequently cited "community" institutions:

1. Decision-Making Institutions.
   a. Politically defined decision-making institutions: Mayor, City Council, Commission, School Board, other major public officials.
   b. Locality-oriented voluntary associations: Associations whose avowed goals are to act on behalf of the locality and in the "public interest": civic associations, improvement associations, political clubs, chambers of commerce, etc.
   c. Local media: newspapers, radio, TV, magazines.

2. Service-Providing Institutions.
   a. Law enforcement and regulatory agencies: Police, courts, health department, assessment agency, zoning board, other licensing boards.
   b. Elementary and secondary education.
   c. Public and quasi-public medical services.
   d. Other local government services: Sanitation, water supply, street maintenance, public works, etc.

The first three categories in the above list may be viewed as those institutions in a locality that are either making binding decisions or attempting to influence the content of such decisions. These three form the decision-making machinery (although not the total group of decision-makers) of a locality. The remaining categories may be viewed as institutions designed to provide essential collective services to the residents of a locality. Social-psychological indicators concerned with the first sector are necessarily different from those directed at the second sector as the list below suggests:

1. Concerning the Decision-Making Sector.[47]
   a. Trust in decision-makers: Extent to which residents feel that decision-makers are making decisions with their best interests in mind.
   b. Access: Extent to which residents feel that they have access to decision-makers, are able to bring their views and ideas before them.
   c. Efficacy: Extent to which residents feel that they can affect the outcome of decisions.

2. Concerning Services.
   a. Adequacy of supply: Are there enough services being rendered? Do the police come when they are wanted? Are the schools overcrowded?
   b. Quality of supply: Are the services rendered efficient for the ends being served? Is public education of high quality? Is police protection efficacious?

[47] Considerable research has been undertaken at least with respect to national political leaders that can be adapted to the decision-making structures of local communities. See J. B. Robinson, J. G. Rusk, and Kendra B. Head, *Measures of Political Attitudes.* Survey Research Center, Institute for Social Research, University of Michigan, Ann Arbor, 1968, for a useful and comprehensive collection of attitudinal scales bearing on these areas.

The measurement of attitudes toward services may be extended considerably beyond the brief outlines given above. For example, the activities of the police may be separated into several types of services—emergency services rendered in the case of accidents, enforcement of traffic regulations, handling of suspected criminals, investigation of crime, relationship to criminals, crime prevention, etc. Similarly, the list of services provided by welfare departments, sanitation departments, etc., may be extended to cover all of those services rendered to individuals and households.

It should be remembered that the average ratings given by recipients to the services rendered by the central institutions of a locality are only loosely related to the quantity of such services as judged by perhaps professional standards. For example, a survey of Roman Catholics' attitudes toward their parochial schools found that most parents were very satisfied with the schooling received by their children although, at the same period of time, Catholic periodicals were full of criticisms directed at the Catholic schools.[48] Similarly, national sample studies of Americans' attitudes toward public schools show them to be satisfied with public education with only a small minority feeling that the schools are not doing well in general or doing well with respect to their own children.[49]

Another critical issue in the understanding of the social psychology of "community" life is the relationship that can be found between consumer satisfaction with municipal services and the professional appraisal of such services. It may well be that for services rendered directly and those which require apparently little professional expertise (e.g., police treatment of traffic offenders, removal of garbage and waste, maintenance of streets, etc.) both professional and lay opinions of services rendered would tend to coincide, while for indirect services (e.g., sewage treatment) or highly professional services (medical care), expert judgments and popular appraisals would tend to diverge.

D. Social-Psychological Aspects of Housing

At the heart of the concept of a residential locality is that one of its main functions is to provide homes for its inhabitants. We spend more time in our homes than in any other place, and although a good proportion of that time is spent in sleeping, some of the more important human activities are carried on

[48] A. M. Greeley and P. H. Rossi, *The Education of Catholic Americans*. Aldine, Chicago, 1966.

[49] Because these studies have focused on national samples, considerable school-system-to-school-system variation may have been glossed over that is related to the quality of schools as judged by professional opinion. For example, Howard Schuman finds significant community-to-community variation in ratings of police treatment of citizens. He finds, furthermore, that blacks and whites tend to agree in their rating of police treatment. (H. Schuman and B. Gruenberg, "The Impact of City on Racial Attitudes," *American Journal of Sociology,* vol. 76, September, 1970, pp. 213–261.

there: eating, making love, raising children, talking intimately with our families and friends, and doing most of our nonwork reading, listening, and viewing. The house is a many-purpose envelope surrounding the space in which much that is the heart of human activity is carried out. For minor children and housewives, the home looms even larger in importance.

Stressing the importance of the home in the lives of its inhabitants may be belaboring the obvious. Yet these "obvious" statements are easy to lose sight of in the study of residential localities. They imply that the main reason why individuals and households are residents is because of the housing involved. In a study of "communities" and the attachments individuals and households have to residential localities, it is easy to stress the nonhousing aspects at the expense of paying attention to housing as a major factor in forming the social characteristics of such areas.

Despite the importance of the housing industry to our economy and the importance of the house to the daily lives of humans, remarkably little research has been devoted to either the housing-choice behavior of individuals or to the impact of housing on people. In large part, this lack of research stems from the structural characteristics of the housing industry. There are few large producers, most of the market transactions in housing are not in new housing units but in the sale or rental of old units, and housing is remarkably unstandardized. In short, competition on the housing market is not among large industrial firms producing branded products, but among households attempting to sell one unit and small firms attempting to sell or rent a very small (compared to total market) proportion of housing units.

As for research on the impact of housing upon individuals and households, the house turns out to be such a complicated bundle of factors that it has proved almost impossible to discern any appreciable effect of housing.[50] People have shown themselves to be remarkably able to adjust to the particular features of a dwelling so as to minimize the impact which such features may have upon their lives.

This is not to say that housing is unimportant to individuals or households —the experience of everyday existence would belie such a statement. It is merely to state that the importance of housing does not lie in the way in which homes shape the lives of their inhabitants. Housing is an important source of gratification. A home may provide aesthetic pleasure or offend one's aesthetic sensibilities; it may make it easy to prepare and serve meals, provide enough

---

[50] Perhaps the most careful of all studies in this area was conducted by D. Wilner *et al.*, *The Housing Environment and Family Life.* Johns Hopkins University Press, Baltimore, 1962, in which a sample of families entering public housing was compared with a set of families who had applied for such housing but were not admitted. The two sets of families were studied over a number of years, only to find that the end differences between the two groups were minimal.

heat in the winter or be uncomfortable; provide enough privacy for solitary activities or make it hard to do anything alone; and so on. Individuals and households choose their housing from among the alternatives they know and within the price ranges they can afford with a view toward maximizing those aspects that are important to them.[51] Nevertheless, whether or not their choices enable them to maximize the desirable enabling characteristics of their housing, people have shown themselves to be remarkably flexible in adapting to their housing environments.

It is easy to overemphasize the importance of nonhousing factors in the locational choices of households. A great deal has been made of the trend toward the suburbs in terms of the kinds of life styles that households are seeking in making such choices. The cry arises that our cities are being deserted and that the middle class is running away from the dangerous central cities to seek a more tranquil existence in the suburbs. Yet the fact of the matter is that, regardless of choice, given the increases in our population and the lack of land available for residential development within central cities, most of the expansion of the stock of housing had to occur in suburban areas. Furthermore, national policy toward aiding American families to purchase homes had made it financially less burdensome to "own" rather than rent.[52] Federal home mortgage policy has fostered the development of the suburbs and of the single-family detached home. The development and continued expansion of the suburbs can be largely accounted for on the basis of housing choices in relation to the way in which the housing markets of metropolitan areas have been structured by public policy and the economics of the housing industry.

From the point of view of this chapter, the social-psychological issues are those involved in establishing what are the housing preferences of different segments of the population and the roles played by such preferences in selecting a residential locality. One would also be interested in charting whatever changes in such preferences occur over time. Several alternative approaches to the measurement of such preferences suggest themselves:

> *Housing behavior as the expression of preferences:* This is an approach that seeks to understand housing preferences by examining the characteristics of housing that is purchased (or rented) by households. Using this approach, one would be mainly concerned with describing the characteristics of housing that is presently being occupied by households and using such character-

---

[51] Nelson N. Foote *et al., Housing Choices and Housing Constraints.* McGraw-Hill, New York, 1960.

[52] In a study of mass-produced tract housing in Levittown, Pennsylvania, Herbert J. Gans concludes that the main motivation of the residents in locating in that community was to take advantage of what they saw to be a housing bargain. (*The Levittowners.* Pantheon, New York, 1967.) In short, Levittown offered more house for what they could afford than was available to them in alternative choices.

istics as expressions of their preferences as mediated by their ability to indulge such preferences in the housing market.

Housing satisfactions and dissatisfactions as the expression of preferences: Under this approach one would be concerned with measuring the extent to which the housing occupied by households meets their needs and desires. Using this approach, one would be concerned with measuring degrees of satisfaction with various aspects of housing occupied.

Housing choice behavior as the expression of preferences: This approach seeks to understand preferences by studying the choices made by households and individuals as they seek to purchase (or rent) housing. By contrasting the differences among alternatives actually considered and observing those housing characteristics present in the housing actually chosen and absent in those which were rejected, one could construct a schedule of preferences.

Direct measurement of preferences: This approach would ask households and individuals to state directly their preferences in housing characteristics. A variety of scaling techniques could be employed to develop a hierarchy of preferences in such characteristics for individual households and for aggregates of households.

I lean toward the measurement of satisfaction with housing as an indicator of housing preferences. Previously research has shown such measures to be strongly related to choices actually made in subsequent housing market behavior and to be highly predictive of whether households would move or not.[53]

The specific aspects of housing with which such social-psychological indicators should be concerned are outlined below. For the present purposes I have made distinctions between housing as a "bundle of utilities" and housing as a location in social and physical space. Although these may be important analytical distinctions, in fact, the characteristics of dwellings are closely related to their location, and in the empirical world it is hard to separate out these dimensions.

1. Interior Characteristics of Dwelling Units.

a. Space: Volume of space and floor area in dwelling unit.

b. Space configurations: The most important aspect of interior space is the number of rooms into which the space is divided and the uses to which these rooms may be put. In this connection the number of bedrooms, the existence of a dining room, storage space, etc. are all important with the number of bedrooms being perhaps of overriding importance.

c. Heating and cooling: Facilities for heating and cooling interior of dwelling unit. Here one would be concerned with the adequacy of the facilities and the ability of the dweller to control.

[53] Rossi, *op. cit.* Subsequent researches conducted in later periods when the housing market was not as tight or in other areas of the country have confirmed these findings. See, for example, Barrie B. Greenbie, "New House or New Neighborhood?" *Land Economics,* vol. 45, August, 1969.

d. Food preparation: Adequacy and convenience of facilities for preparation, . storage, and serving of food for meals.

e. Noise insulation: Degree to which noise is transmitted through the dwelling unit.

f. Other amenities: Light, air, adequacy of electrical supply, maintenance of multiple dwellings, etc.

2. Exterior Characteristics of Dwelling Unit.

a. Space: Closeness to other dwellings.

b. Appearance of exterior: Style of housing, maintenance of exterior.

3. Location in Physical Space.

a. Location in reference to work: Travel time to work, cost of journey to work.

b. Location in reference to shopping.

c. Location in reference to other activities: Recreation, cultural centers, schools.

d. Location in reference to significant others: Kin, friends, desirability of neighbors.

e. Other external physical features arising from location: Noise from other people, traffic; quality of air; physical appearance of neighborhood; etc.

4. Location in Social Space. Most of the elements that would be considered under this heading have been previously discussed in this chapter. Here one would be concerned with the social meaning of the location, the social status indicated by the neighborhood, the kinds of sociability opportunities presented by neighbors, attachment to the locality as a collectivity, etc.

A Strategy for Community Social Indicators

The purpose of a set of social indicators is to provide periodic readings of important and critical social trends. The choice of a particular set of indicators for a specific area of social life should be guided by a number of considerations, among which the following might be considered important: (1) a set of social indicators should be based upon a model of how the area of social life in question "works"; (2) the number of indicators ought to be small in number so that it becomes easy to observe trends; and (3) the indicators ought to be related to potential social policy.

Given these considerations, it should be immediately apparent that the catalogue of indicators presented in this paper do not fit any of the criteria listed above. To begin with, the model underlying the catalogue is scarcely to be dignified with that name. The indicators were chosen in an attempt to be exhaustive rather than to pick the small number of critical indicators that existing theory indicates would be worthwhile. Finally, because social policy in the community area is not clearly defined, except with respect to the newest legislation of the War on Poverty, it is difficult to indicate which of the community characteristics would be most relevant to social policy.

The major obstacle to developing a model of residential localities that would enable one to pick and choose in a more decisive way the social indicators of prime interest lies in the all-inclusive nature of the phenomenon involved. After all, a residential locality is where we mainly live and the adequacy of the locality may be indexed in a wide variety of ways, depending on how strong a role one's implicit theory imputes to community effects. As yet, social scientists know too little to impute a reasonable degree of strength to community characteristics as conditions or as causes of any set of outcomes. Indeed, it is not at all clear which are outcomes and which are inputs among the characteristics listed in this chapter.[54]

In the absence of such models that appear to be reasonable, it may be best to adopt a strategy which states that, at minimum, the residents of localities ought to be satisfied with what the localities in question provide to their residents. Hence, one might pare down the catalogue presented in this paper into the following set of satisfaction measures:

1. *Satisfaction with dwelling unit:* Space, interior amenities, exterior styling, cost.
2. *Satisfaction with access to major markets:* Employment opportunities, retail outlets, transportation.
3. *Satisfaction with central institutions of locality:* Local government, public officials, public and quasi-public services, etc.
4. *Satisfaction with sociability opportunities:* Friendliness of neighborhood, number of friends, number of kin in neighborhood, personal safety.
5. *Satisfaction with locality as gratification:* Pride in residence, positive attachment to fellow residents as reference groups, solidarity, desires, intentions, willingness to move.

While measures along the lines suggested above may provide a sense of whether our residential localities are satisfying their residents, they do not provide a good understanding of why residents are satisfied or not. This means that research leading to a working model for residential localities still has to be undertaken. We need to know, for example, whether sociability satisfactions are

[54] If one makes some crude assumptions, it is possible to construct a model of some restricted phenomenon, as Jay Forester has done (*Urban Dynamics.* MIT Press, Cambridge, Mass., 1969). However, most urban economists and sociologists would agree that there is little reason to start with the basic model that Forester lays out and hence that his projected workings out of various social policies in the housing area are at best sterile exercises and at worst highly misleading.

higher in life-cycle homogeneous or heterogeneous neighborhoods, or whether communities that are integrated with respect to retail markets are more solidaristic than those which are not.

In short, while it may be possible to monitor how well our residential localities are doing in the eyes of their residents, it is still an open question as to the processes that generate satisfaction or its opposite.

4

Family, Kinship, and Bureaucracy

Marvin B. Sussman

This chapter is both pragmatic and descriptive in its approach. Some of the current institutional and structural changes that have taken place in modern society are examined, along with their concomitant effects upon family and kinship structure and behavior. Out of a vast array of ideas, a number have been selected that are compatible with this view and relevant to the social psychology of the family as it has been affected by social and institutional change. In making this selection, I eliminated those ideas and thoughts that I felt were commonplace, noncontroversial, or productive of little excitement, or those which could easily be verified with a substantial body of empirical evidence. What is left are the perceptions of one social scientist concerning what is disputable, speculative, exciting, and generative of the most promising areas of research for understanding the nature of changes in family and kinship relations.

Certain assumptions and givens are stated in this chapter. They include the family's basic responsibility and opportunity to socialize its members for competence in handling the normative demands of bureaucracies, the most central task for the individual in modern society;[1] the existence and functioning

The author expresses his deep appreciation for the assistance received from Vivian Anne Joynes, one-time research assistant, for her aid in the preparation of this chapter.

[1] For an analysis of this issue see Marvin B. Sussman, "Some Conceptual Issues in Family-Organizational Linkages," and Marvin B. Sussman and Margaret P. Brooks, "The Competence Concept," working papers of the Cross-National Research Studies on the Family, sponsored by the Committee on Family Research of the International Sociological Association and financially supported by the Institute of Child Health and Human Development. For copies, write to the author.

of an active urban kin network as an optional voluntary system based upon exchange and reciprocity;[2] increasing education and gainful employment of women and the emergence of the dual-career family with "two heads of the household" as a 1970's reality;[3] the expansion of heterosexual relationships and liaisons in various life sectors as women become "professionalized" and enter the labor force;[4] and the emergence in the 1960's of anti-traditional nuclear family structures which resemble the classic extended family of the eighteenth and nineteenth centuries in certain rural regions of the United States and which incorporate some of the ideological postures and socialization practices of the kibbutz, Gandhi's ashrams, and Communist communes.[5]

The problem of social adaptation, omnipresent in social relations, is focused on throughout this overview. Social adaptation refers to the vital process through which individuals and systems meet the reality demands of the social milieu and retain their power and viability in the face of social change. It is a process in which power differentials play a critical role.

The paradoxical consequences of power and influence in social transactions are most dramatically exemplified in the shifting patterns of kinship and marriage in contemporary American society. Lacking an institutional organization through which to resist change, the family has been a mediator between its members and the bureaucratic organizations with which they must deal, and a rival with these and other primary groups and voluntary associations.

Social change will provide the context for our study of process to sharpen our analyses of family interaction, the character of units, and the available strategies they use for responding to new demands and challenges.

The Family in a Complex Society

Societal complexity in the modern era is characterized by the interrelations of bureaucratic organizations and primary groups within a network marked by

[2] Reviews of kin network research will be found in Marvin B. Sussman and Lee G. Burchinal, "Kin Family Network: Unheralded Structure in Current Conceptualizations of Family Functioning," *Marriage and Family Living,* vol. 24, August, 1962, pp. 231–240; *idem,* "Relationships of Adult Children with Their Parents in the United States," in Ethel Shanas and Gordon Streib, eds., *Family Intergenerational Relationships and Social Structure.* Prentice-Hall, Englewood Cliffs, N.J., 1965, pp. 62–92.

[3] This thesis is elaborated in Rhona Rapoport and Robert N. Rapoport, "The Dual Career Family," *Human Relations,* vol. 22, February, 1969, pp. 3–30; M. Fogarty, R. N. Rapoport, and Rhona Rapoport, *Women and Top Jobs.* Political and Economic Planning, London, 1967.

[4] See John Cuber and Peggy B. Harroff, *The Significant Americans.* Appleton-Century, New York, 1965; Gerhard Neubeck, ed., *Extra-Marital Relations.* Prentice-Hall, Englewood Cliffs, N.J., 1969.

[5] The main sources for descriptions of these new family forms are *Time, Life, Look,* and *Newsweek* magazines.

a coincidence of interdependence and conflict. Each organization has specialized functions, an ethos, norms, and values which command the loyalty and identification of its members. Students of bureaucracy have extensively developed the theme of the incompatibility between the bureaucratic organization and the primary group as exemplified by the family.[6] In line with Max Weber's classic theory of the nature of bureaucracy, it has been repeatedly stressed that the primary group, because of its particular structural properties, goals, and functions, is antithetical to the purposes, needs, and functions of the bureaucratic organization. For this reason, social distance between these two organizational forms has appeared to be a prerequisite for their mutual survival in a society.

The high level of differentiation of function in industrial society places extraordinary pressure on the nuclear family and collateral members of the kinship network to capitulate to the normative demands of bureaucratic organizations. The more extensive, permanent, and powerful system (the bureaucracy) may logically be expected to dominate the lesser and weaker one (the family) if there are necessary changes in relationship which require role modifications. Yet, some families develop a *modus operandi* for handling the demands of bureaucratic organizations while maintaining their own internal structure and function, and under certain conditions and situations, may surpass the bureaucratic organization in the extent of their influence.

The structural characteristics of these two types of institutions have been cited to lend support to the position of family subordination. The bureaucratic organization is based on efficiency and rationality and functions instrumentally and in a scientific and objective manner to achieve its goal, an orientation which is necessary for the continued survival of complex societies. The family, on the other hand, is an affective structure in which behavior is a response to emotional feelings and sentiments with little regard for objective analysis. As the social sphere of bureaucratic institutions has extended, their greater power presumably has allowed them to pre-empt the more important of the adaptive functions once performed by the family. The latter structure has been left with only such tasks as socialization into generalized roles and identities and tension management of family members, chores which more rationally ordered organizational systems cannot perform or find unacceptable because these objectives lack specificity.

[6] Eugene Litwak and Henry J. Meyer, "Administrative Styles and Community Linkages of Public Schools," in Albert J. Reiss, Jr., ed., *Schools in a Changing Society*. Free Press, New York, 1965, pp. 49–97; *idem,* "The School and the Family: Linking Organizations and External Primary Groups," in P. Lazarsfeld, W. Sewell, and H. Wilensky, *The Uses of Sociology*. Basic Books, New York, 1967, pp. 522–543; "A Balance Theory of Coordination Between Bureaucratic Organizations and Community Primary Groups," *Administrative Science Quarterly,* vol. 11, June, 1966, pp. 31–58.

Accommodation is an alternative concept through which to view primary group–bureaucratic relations and to analyze the structural basis of the division of labor which exists between family and organization. Note that certain purposes and goals are vital to the persistence of the society itself and all of its institutions. Sherif aptly described this situation as one of superordinate goals where each of two groups requires the aid of the other to obtain a desired objective which both partly or completely share.[7] For example, family and bureaucracy both share the valued goal of individual survival and development and support it with the means and resources available to them. The functions of a family and a bureaucratic organization are complementary in this respect, a complementarity which has been achieved by means of accommodating behavior on the part of each of the participating structures. This is possible principally because these interaction systems have developed expertise in performing specialized functions and, therefore, need each other. Although accommodation is a better concept to invoke in this context, contest is also involved since a jockeying for position has taken place which aims to reinforce or maintain discreteness in established spheres. A give-and-take process is implied in which the hostilities of each party are mitigated and the structures become linked.

A contemporary efficiency model which is based on differentiation of functions supports the argument that primary groups and bureaucratic organizations accept the expertise of each other. Each has its own specialists who socialize novitiates for competence in the performance of specific and diffuse roles, and effectiveness determines which of these structures will assume paramountcy in a particular area. In addition to this toleration of role expertise, structural interdependence enhances the need for the entire network to sustain each link so that it may perform its unique function, since structures and functions are interrelated.

The bureaucracy possesses characteristics which make it a durable and powerful instrument in the hands of its administrators. As Weber first pointed out, the hierarchical, differentiated structure of this type of organization is suited to rational, purposive action.[8] It depends in its functioning upon specialization and the use of experts and provides opportunities for individuals who strive for personal achievement.

Among the social roles available which rest upon achievement, those designated as professional provide a more complete linkage between service and

---

[7] Muzafer Sherif and Carolyn Sherif, *Groups in Harmony and Tension.* Harper, New York, 1953. The testing of the superordinate goal concept in a field situation occurred in 1954 and is reported in Muzafer Sherif, *The Robber Caves Experiment.* Group Relations Laboratory, Norman, Okla., 1956.

[8] Max Weber, *The Theory of Social and Economic Organization,* ed. by Talcott Parsons and trans. by A. M. Henderson. Oxford University Press, New York, 1947.

status. The professional has been granted his status and autonomy on the basis of his theoretical preparation and orientation toward service to the general public. In actuality, this often turns out to be the specific public served by the bureaucratic organization with which he is affiliated. These institutions make extensive use of his knowledge and expertise, seek his advice and opinion in policy development, and utilize his services in dealing with their clients.

The purposive rationality of the bureaucratic setting, which is best actualized in the professional expert, serves to complement and support the affective and expressive functions of the family in which roles of another character predominate. Although its sphere and membership may be considerably less extensive than that of the bureaucratic organization, the family has intrinsic features which are invaluable in affording sustenance and personal identity to its members. It is an institution that has long experience in handling affective matters and responding to them in an intuitive fashion. Because of its limited range, ample opportunity is provided for individual emotional expression and gratification, and the individual enjoys a sustained orientation toward group belongingness, which may support him even in the face of the most shattering crises.

Litwak and Meyer[9] identify three categories of tasks in which primary group members are most efficient and most effective: (1) those which require sufficiently simple knowledge, permitting nearly anyone to perform them or to instruct others in their performance; (2) those which raise problems which neither the family nor experts have enough knowledge or consensus to analyze and solve; and (3) those related to idiosyncratic events.

Tasks of the first category would include taking care of one's own or another's physical needs, such as those associated with rising, bathing, eating, dressing appropriately, and going to school. Instruction in these chores is well left to socialization agents such as parents or siblings.

Although expert advice would help the performance of the tasks of the second category, they remain in the primary-group sphere because experts are not prepared to deal with them. Many important individual and social matters must be decided by untrained persons. These include such questions as: What is the "best practice" in child rearing? What does one have to do to attain marital happiness? What types and forms of communication and interaction enable one to achieve fullness of expression of one's sexuality? What criteria should one employ in selecting a mate? Whom should one vote for as the next President of the United States? The contribution of an expert is of limited value in deciding such issues and problems; their resolution relies heavily on the experience and folk wisdom of persons in primary or reference groups.

Category three includes those infrequent happenings for which special

[9] Litwak and Meyer, "The School and the Family," pp. 528–532.

preparation would be wasteful. Floods, fires, and earthquakes provide illustrations. These events are unique, and responses to them cannot be predicted or patterned; their anticipation must be limited to considerations of community survival. Preparing individuals for definite roles in connection with events of this unusual character would constitute a squandering of talent. Furthermore, observation and experience reveal that individuals involved in disasters turn nearly exclusively to family members to provide succor and comfort. Survivors of disasters are generally unable to function effectively in rescue and help roles until they are apprised of the fate of members of their own families. Rescue or service agencies are not sought out at such times to satisfy emotional needs, even when they are prepared to extend this type of help.

We may view these functional adaptations among structurally different organizations as illustrations of the manner in which two parties, having identified areas of common concern, might mitigate their hostilities and accommodate their differences. This should not be permitted to overshadow awareness that both cooperation and contest are operative and perceptible. Areas in which bureaucratic-familial relations are mutually supportive coexist with others in which relations are not so well adjusted. This fact concerns us here because conditions of widespread social change are likely to affect the direction of inter-institutional relations so that new points of conflict and cooperation emerge. I will focus on this issue when exploring the context of value change and its implications for American family life.

Linkage

Despite these bases for the structural efficiency and functionality of family-bureaucratic organizational relationships, a division of labor and complementarity of functions does not exist universally in the real world in the behavior of structures with disparate goals, means, and roles. Actually, there are over-lapping areas of ambiguity and ambivalence in the functions and activities of the family and bureaucracies, and competition often borders on conflict over control of their interactions.

One important reason for the persistence of the family in modern society is its role in the linkage process; it counteracts domination by bureaucratic or-ganizations through using interstitial groups and socializing its members for competence in linking roles. Consequently, it is appropriate to analyze the social-psychological bases of linkage for the family.

The linkage phenomenon is based on a number of assumptions. First, it is both a process and a condition interrelating groups, organizations, and individ-uals. The particular pattern is the linkage condition, and how it is formed in the process. A second assumption is that in any linkage, especially between struc-tures, it is possible for one participant to be or become subordinate or superordinate to the other, even after institutionalization of the relationship has occurred. Consequently, in any relationship, the family can be in a superordinate position wielding influence and affecting the policy, structure, and activities of bureaucratic organizations. Or it can be subordinate, accommodating the normative demands of the formal structures.

Another assumption is that the family can optimize its possibilities of survival and sustain intact its interactional system and territory if members develop handling, manipulating, and mediating skills in linkage activity. Competence in interpersonal relationships, use of options, and problem-solving are prerequisite and appropriate activities of a family socialization system.[10] Still another assumption is that linkage operates within some system of reciprocity based on bargaining. Specific exchanges are of unequal value, and reciprocates are maintained when each bargaining part receives sufficient payoff to maintain the relationship rather than accept the alternative of breaking off.[11]

Figure 1 illustrates the linkage system of the family with bureaucratic organizations.[12] Family objectives and needs include achieving a livelihood, thus meeting basic and derived needs for shelter, clothing, satisfaction of hunger, conditions under which procreation and sexual gratification can occur and socialization take place. Social interaction implies relationships with others in order to satisfy the need for emotional response, warmth, and affection. The shelter that houses the family unit, the food provided for its members, the clothing that protects individual members from the elements, and protection of family members against outside aggressors are necessary to meet physical maintenance objectives and needs.

Mental well-being has been an increasingly recognized need in societies of high complexity. Here the objectives of family socialization include the development of capabilities to handle frustrations that emanate from conflicting demands within and outside the family, competition over scarce rewards, and

---

[10] Important discussions of competence are found in M. Brewster Smith, "Competence and Socialization," in John A. Clausen, ed., *Socialization and Society.* Little, Brown, Boston, 1968; Robert W. White, "Motivation Reconsidered: The Concept of Competence," *Psychological Review,* vol. 66, September, 1959, pp. 297–333; Nelson Foote and Leonard S. Cottrell, Jr., *Identity and Interpersonal Competence.* University of Chicago Press, Chicago, 1965.

[11] T. Schelling, *The Strategy of Conflict.* Harvard University Press, Cambridge, Mass., 1960; *idem,* "An Essay on Bargaining," *American Economic Review,* vol. 46, June, 1956, pp. 281–306; John W. Thibault and Harold H. Kelley, *The Social Psychology of Groups.* Wiley, New York, 1959, especially Chap. 3, "Rewards and Costs," for bases of exchange between dyads; Marcel Mauss, *The Gift, Forms and Functions of Exchange in Archaic Societies,* trans. by Ian Gunnison. Cohen & West Ltd., London, 1954; C. Levi-Strauss, "The Principle of Reciprocity," in L. A. Coser and B. Rosenberg, eds., *Sociological Theory.* Macmillan, New York, 1957, pp. 204–294.

[12] Taken from Sussman, "Family Organizational Linkages."

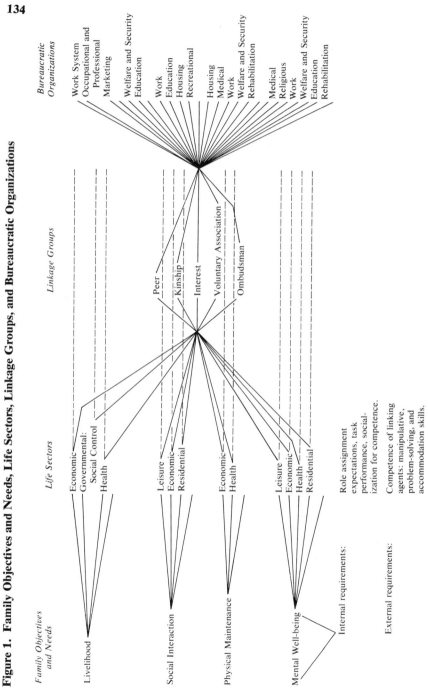

Figure 1. Family Objectives and Needs, Life Sectors, Linkage Groups, and Bureaucratic Organizations

Family Objectives and Needs

Livelihood

Social Interaction

Physical Maintenance

Mental Well-being

Internal requirements:

External requirements:

Life Sectors

Economic
Governmental:
  Social Control
Health

Leisure
Economic
Residential

Economic
Health

Leisure
Economic
Health
Residential

Role assignment expectations, task performance, socialization for competence.

Competence of linking agents: manipulative, problem-solving, and accommodation skills.

Linkage Groups

Peer

Kinship

Interest

Voluntary Association

Ombudsman

Bureaucratic Organizations

Work System
Occupational and
  Professional
Marketing

Welfare and Security
Education

Work
Education
Housing
Recreational

Housing
Medical
Work
Welfare and Security
Rehabilitation

Medical
Religious
Work
Welfare and Security
Education
Rehabilitation

SOURCE: Marvin B. Sussman, "Some Conceptual Issues in Family-Organizational Linkages." Working paper of the Cross-National

134

frustrations stemming from failure of reciprocal expectations in interpersonal relationships. The family provides the psychological and physical territory in which one can be emotional, express one's feelings, and give and receive affective response. These relationships are relatively free of status position restraints and are essentially the characteristics of a primary group. Relationships based upon mutual trust and reciprocal expectations enable the family to serve as a safety valve system, i.e., a haven for its frustrated members. The family serves the bureaucratic organization in handling the consequences of frustration, although the family as a social system can also create frustrated members. Nevertheless, our concern is how it nurtures and succors its mentally ill and prepares its members for handling frustration and defeat effectively.

These objectives and needs of the family are related to internal and external requirements for its survival over time. Internal requirements of the family are similar to those of any social system. They include role assignment of its members and development of reciprocal role expectations; the performance of tasks; development of a system of norms and socialization into appropriate roles, especially socialization for competence in handling internal and external relationships, identity, and a concept of self. The external requirements include socialization for competence in linking the family with outside interstitial groups and bureaucratic organizations. Essential to such socialization is development of knowledge of options and skills to manipulate these perceived alternatives, solve problems and, under certain conditions, accommodate to the power of bureaucratic organizations.

Life Sectors

In highly complex industrial societies such as the United States, where diverse services are performed by rapidly expanding bureaucratic organizations with elaborate administrative mechanisms, individuals in primary groups such as the family are thrust into a bewildering maze of interrelationships. Modern man has so many options that it has become analytically useful to create the concept of life-sector categories of major activities. A life sector is an area of activity usually occurring in a defined territory and which can be observed to have a beginning, duration, and an end in time. Life-sector categories include economic, governmental, health, leisure, residential, and family activities. It is presumed that individuals and groups function within these areas to meet their needs and achieve their objectives. Further, within each of these areas, bureaucratic organizations and linkage groups have come into existence to help man and his primary group achieve their objectives and needs.

Linkage groups may also be devised by bureaucracies in order to "create" needs or to socialize family members into roles consonant with their objectives and norms. In the course of time, linkage groups, which were originally created to help primary groups achieve their objectives and needs, may develop bureaucratically their own rules and objectives and must continue to link as many families as possible in order to achieve a higher status. In this process, their own rules, objectives, and needs may take priority over those of the primary group and those of the original bureaucracy with which they were supposed to be linking.

Linkage Groups

Presented in Figure 1 are five types of groups that link the family with bureaucratic organizations in the various life sectors. The principal function of these linkage groups is to reduce the social distance between the family and bureaucratic organizations through establishing effective communication and interaction networks. In reality, these networks developed by the linkage group can act to bring the primary group and bureaucratic organization closer together or can keep them at greater distances. Potentially, the mechanisms of bringing them together or separating them can be operated from both sides of the bridge, or, in other words, from either of these two subsystems.

Our concern is not to examine all the functions of linking groups. Our focus is on linkage points, those occasions when family representatives, i.e., linkage agents, opt to use a linkage group (or are required to, as in the case of union membership) in dealing with a bureaucratic organization in order to achieve a family objective or satisfy a family need. The vital point of contact with a bureaucratic organization is made to develop some form of exchange; the strategic role at this time is the linking one of the family member.

The listing of linkage groups is by no means all-inclusive. An extensive discussion of the kin network as a mediating, decision-making, and socializing system takes place in the next section of the chapter. Peer and kinship groups are structural forms found in every society. The functions they perform in linkage behavior are only now being established through empirical inquiry. Interest groups are those found in the leisure sector, e.g., hobbyists, or groups that represent an occupational calling or economic interest such as lobbying and trade associations, labor unions, credit unions, burial societies, and so forth.

"Voluntary association" in Figure 1 is a misnomer, because some associations are not completely voluntary. When it is voluntary, the family member opts for the association if it is particularly advantageous to do so. In contrast is an ascriptive association; the family member belongs because he is expected to and such membership may determine his identity and position in society and may influence his activities in many other life sectors through group norms and values, discriminatory practices, and preferred relationships.[13]

---

[13] W. T. Morrill, "Immigrants and Associations: The Ibo in Twentieth-Century Calabar," *Comparative Studies in Society and History*, vol. 5, 1963, pp. 424–428.

The ombudsman group and derivations of this form are emerging in societies of high complexity.[14] A nonnegotiable superordinate goal, so defined by objecting clients, seeds the genesis of an organizational structure which uses collective strength to counteract the oppressive actions of bureaucracies. Lower-class families in ghetto areas are the most recent users of this group form, although it has functioned effectively for many years in other societies. The head of the organization, the ombudsman, is a grievance presenter. He defends members against official wrongs and carries out negotiating, educating, and linking roles.

Given the four components: family objectives and needs, life sectors, linkage groups, and bureaucratic organizations, the possible number of linkage combinations increases geometrically. In addition, more than one bureaucratic organization may be functioning to meet specific family objectives and needs in a given life sector, a condition which is not recorded on Figure 1 and adds to the possible number of combinations. Not all families will use linkage groups in given situations; for a variety of reasons, many will deal directly with bureaucratic organizations. One general hypothesis is that the conditions of feasibility, utility, knowledge, and competence determine the use of linkage groups or their circumvention. Once the usefulness and feasibility are established on the basis of need and knowledge, the extent to which the family receives a "payoff" depends upon the competence of its representative. Can one use a linkage group without reprisals from the bureaucracy or disturbance to other relationships in various life sectors? Is the payoff derived from linkage group participation equal or better than that received from dealing directly with the bureaucracy? Knowledge of linkage group options and skills in handling bureaucratic demands are two additional factors in the use of linkage groups.

Options and Linkage

A description of the family interstitial group bureaucratic organization linkage process requires some analysis of the concept of options. Options are opportunities available to a family member or a family for role participation in different life sectors. The availability, knowledge, use, and successful outcome of an option sequence depend upon cultural, structural, experiential, situational, and personality factors. The elaboration and documentation of this concept and its applicability are reported elsewhere.[15] The option sequence begins with availability and hopefully ends with a successful outcome. Steps after option

[14] "The Ombudsman or Citizen's Defender: A Modern Institution," *The Annals,* vol. 377, May, 1968, entire issue.

[15] See the "San Juan Document: Cross-National Research Studies on the Family, Theoretical Problems and Approaches," prepared by Marvin B. Sussman, January, 1969. For copies write to Mrs. Margaret Brooks, Institute on the Family and Bureaucratic Society, Department of Sociology, Case Western Reserve University, Cleveland, Ohio 44106.

availability include: *awareness of all possible options; knowledge of routes to option use; selection of one or more options; training or socialization into role behavior requisite for appropriate utilization of the option;* and finally *option outcome,* the goal of the option sequence. An example of the connectedness of the option sequence with the linkage process follows.

One linkage point is the family's initial contact with bureaucratic organizations concerned with housing in the residential life sector. The availability of housing options for an in-migrant family depends upon the supply and demand for houses in the market; discrimination practices; the financial position of the family; the size of the family; location of kin, friends, and peer group members; legislation and the special efforts of interest groups such as those which advocate open and fair housing.

Awareness of options may come from a number of sources, including linkage groups and bureaucratic organizations. At this stage of the option sequence the member's personal resources, motivation, needs, and objectives are determinants of the type and extensity of the linking role to be performed in behalf of the family. In addition to the information on housing options provided by linkage groups and bureaucratic organizations, kin, peers, friends, and work colleagues may be sources of knowledge. In addition, the individual may obtain knowledge of housing from the mass media and other communication and education sources.

Commencing with awareness of the routes to achieve the option, family members and representatives of linkage groups activate linkage roles until an option outcome is achieved. Here is a strategic point in the linkage sequence. Awareness of options and awareness of routes to option achievement are two distinctively different phenomena. Option awareness implies knowledge of theoretical possibilities of housing for the family while awareness of routes involves a realistic appraisal of available housing given the variety of constraints already enumerated. A decision regarding the selection of one or more options depends initially upon an appraisal of realistic possibilities of achieving the option outcome. It is at this stage of the option sequence that the individual is very likely to select a particular service. If options for housing are restricted because of discrimination, he may seek a special interest group or voluntary association to assist him in increasing the options in housing selection. In some instances, the family may become the target of selection for betterment because a particular community action group feels that increasing his options in housing is in the best interests of the larger society. If his options in housing are limited because of economic considerations, he may join with linking institutions which are part of the marketing system through a credit union, consumer's organization, mutual benefit society, or kinship group which can assist him with information, money, and other services connected with the purchase of a home or determining an adequate rent, lease, and other legal matters. This selection process does not preclude the joining of a linkage group for more general reasons, e.g., promote harmonious relationships, effective communication, improve living conditions, etc.

Training in the role of homeowner or tenant to meet the standards of other families in the residential area and the norms of financial and social control organizations may be facilitated through neighborhood peer groups and other linkage structures which serve as sponsors. Socialization through linking agents may focus more on training the individual family member for the option sequence, especially skills for wending one's way through the maze of bureaucratic rules and procedures.

All members of families take on linking roles at some time during the family life cycle; some of these roles are initiated by the family and others by outside groups and organizations. Circumstances, situations, age and sex of members, family needs and objectives, the presence or absence of linking groups, and policies and programs of bureaucratic organizations regarding linkage are among the factors that determine whether the individual family member takes the initiative in linking with bureaucratic organizations or with some interstitial group, or whether he is linked as a consequence of the efforts of socialization agents of already existent groups and bureaucratic organizations. The extent to which a member will take on linking roles on behalf of the family depends upon the skill of the particular individual, level of need, motivation for achieving specific family objectives, and interaction patterns within the family.

The efforts of family members to link with groups and organizations in a society are an ongoing process. The intensity of such efforts and the direction they take depend upon circumstances, situations, needs, desirability of objectives, and so forth. Powerlessness may be a condition which initiates linkage roles of families, especially with interstitial organizations. Families that function at a level higher than deprivation may find participation in linkage groups less profitable and may link directly with bureaucratic organizations.

Members function as representatives of the family unit in linkage activities in which family concerns are paramount. Agents in linking roles also carry out socialization activities and a frequent outcome is reallocation of roles and tasks within the family. For example, some adolescent children of single-parent ADC families in St. Louis reportedly take on linking roles with welfare and education bureaucracies. They develop their expertise in handling teachers and social workers from exchanges of experience and mutual aid among adolescent peers. These teen-agers assume the representational role for the family and reduce the mother in status and power because they take over major responsibility for the socialization of younger children.[16]

---

[16] Alvin Wolfe, anthropologist, reported this event to the author after completing a study among a small group of families living in the Pruit-Igoe Housing Project in St. Louis, Missouri, 1965.

If migrants move into urban areas where there are active voluntary associations and other types of linkage groups carrying on economic, political, and social activities, the linking agent may initially be the same person who represented the family in dealings with the major social structures of the rural or tribal community. This is the situation in West Africa where voluntary associations in newly developed cities are extensions of tribal associations or syncretist cults found in the rural or tribal lands.[17] These African associations provide immigrants with economic aid such as sickness and death benefits, capital loans, insurance against theft and other losses, family allowances, and educational support for children. Their major functions are to facilitate the adaptation and integration of immigrants to values, attitudes, and practices of bureaucratic organizations in the major life sectors of the urban culture.

Families that obtain urban experience and those which come in later migration waves may undergo a rapid transformation in role structure. As women begin to participate more in the economic, leisure, and residential sectors, they become the major linking agents with bureaucratic organizations in these sectors. They also facilitate the development of new linkage groups in a number of life sectors. Korean women, for example, are becoming the financial managers and developers of the family through the creation of loan and borrowing groups, informal systems of financial exchange which parallel the traditional banking systems of Korea where interest rates are 27 percent inside the bank and 50 percent on the curb. These types of activities have resulted in a decided shift in the power structure and decision-making processes within the Korean family.

These illustrations indicate that family members are not passively acted upon by the needs or demands of bureaucratic organizations. Linking activities are endemic to the family. Taking on linking roles provides opportunities for changing one's status and power position within the family. Linking roles are essentially socializing ones. The family representative or linker develops skills and knowledge for handling bureaucratic organizations and uses these to meet family needs and objectives in a particular life sector. He may teach other family members or hide his expertise in an assumed aura of ignorance in order to maintain position within the family. A more sanguine view is that the linker acts in the family's best interest and socializes other members for competence sufficiently for them to function in behalf of the family without necessarily jeopardizing his or her status as an expert in this particular linking role.

Although some family members are expert linkers, possess generalized competencies, and can initiate linking activities in a variety of life sectors, they

[17] Kenneth Little, *West African Urbanization*. Cambridge University Press, Cambridge, 1965. There is a prolific literature on voluntary associations. Among the most recent and extensive analyses of the nature of these structures is a collection of articles edited by J. Roland Pennock and John W. Chapman, *Voluntary Associations*. Atherton, New York, 1969.

tend to work in particular sectors with a set number of linkage groups and bureaucratic organizations. In consonance with our conceptualization of differentiation into the life sectors of contemporary urban life, a single family member is not likely to be *the* linker for the entire family. In traditional or transitional societies in early stages of development, one family member may link the family to organizations in all life sectors. Rural in-migrants to urban areas may also have one family member function as the linker until other members become acculturated and socialized into modern roles which involve linkage activity.

Mediation and the Kinship Network

The challenge faced by the American family of adapting to the demands of a bureaucratic society seems to have been most vividly apparent to early students of this social structure. The problem of family mobility became a central issue because full adult participation in the larger society often entails geographic or social movement. Since the nuclear family was viewed as best suited for participating in a bureaucratic society, this unit tended to be treated as conterminous with the entire institution of the family as it existed in the American milieu. Talcott Parsons considered it to be a completely integrated unit which survived by virtue of its superior adaptability.[18] This view was further supported by the fact that, in the United States, only the nuclear family has legal or corporate responsibility for its affiliated members.

For a considerable time, however, social scientists have been aware that social process is not exhausted by contractual arrangements between bureaucratic organizations and discrete nuclear families. Studies make it necessary to recognize that a greater degree of structural complexity is extant. Even in urban settings, nuclear families living in separate households are functionally related so as to form kin family networks. These extensions of the nuclear family remain viable through a system of unequal exchanges which in goals, norms, and values vie with other primary and bureaucratic systems for the loyalty of those who are participants. In this section of the chapter, the kin network is examined as a linking structure and one with objectives, processes, and means for commanding the attention and support of its members.

Studies of middle- and working-class urban families reveal visitation among members of nuclear family units with financial aid, advice, and child care as primary modalities. These studies reveal many dynamic aspects of intra- and interfamily relationships. These are processes in which linkages are forged or rendered inoperative on the basis of intra-network values. On all levels, conflict as well as cooperation exist. As they attempt to meet their own needs and

[18] Talcott Parsons and Robert F. Bales, *Family, Socialization and Interaction Process.* Free Press, Glencoe, Ill., 1955.

to achieve desired rewards, there is an ongoing struggle among lesser units in each larger system for the achievement of in-group goals. When shared goals cannot be identified among component units, disintegration of the kin network may result. A study of nuclear family units at differing generational levels revealed cultural factors to be highly influential in assuring family continuity.[19] Notable among these were differences in the socioeconomic cultural background of marriage mates, the types of courtship and wedding ceremony that preceded the formation of a family unit, differences in child-rearing philosophy and practice, and the extent to which a help pattern was developed between parents and their married children. Proximity of residence, as it was utilized by the family to forge closer links or, alternatively, to lessen tensions was also found to be a factor which influenced family continuity.

Within the kin family network, the struggle to reach an agreement in order to achieve organizational goals is once more juxtaposed with organizational in-group efforts to obtain an advantage. In particular instances, the outcome is by no means assured, so that self-interest and mutual interest may or may not be simultaneously realized. "Payoff" may be too crass a term to describe the preferred objective of a particular organization such as a family, school, or business. Nevertheless, it conveys the same meaning as frequently used expressions such as "meeting maintenance needs of the system," "satisfying the needs of its members," or "obtaining rewards according to normative means."

By definition, the family lacks the institutional type of organization that is most resistant to outside influences and change. As a consequence, it and its larger kin network must function as a mediator between its members and bureaucratic organizations as it provides socialization and competence in coping with the normative demands of bureaucratic systems. Mediation, if it is to be perceived as successful, must involve action which results in compromise without an undue loss of position, integrity, or power by participants. It must also involve being able to influence as well as to be influenced. A party to any transaction that is shorn of its strength and power to act on behalf of its members cannot remain viable. Every system must provide sufficient support and success in transactions so that its members believe that it is worthwhile for the group or organization to persist over time.

The kin network and its member families may assist in individual adaptation to the larger society and, in some instances, influence organizational policy and practices. The educational sphere will provide an illustration of these processes. Education implies learning new roles as well as new knowledge. The former task is usually achieved in the family setting, and although the latter

[19] Marvin B. Sussman, "The Help Pattern in the Middle-Class Family," *American Sociological Review,* vol. 18, February, 1953, pp. 22–28; *idem,* "Family Continuity: Selective Factors Which Affect Relationships Between Families at Generational Levels," *Marriage and Family Living,* vol. 16, May, 1954, pp. 112–120.

takes place in the school, the family often exercises influence over its performance. The educational program of the school takes cognizance of the social class of the families it serves, their patterns of socialization, and their home environmental conditions. It must cater to these as well as to the needs and demands expressed by their clients.[20]

All families are not equally prepared to perform this mediating function. Research reveals that the extent to which they are able to perform depends upon their location and activity in the kin network, life-cycle stage, and experience with organizations. The community status of a nuclear family is affected by its kin connections. The stance and attitudes of member units of the kin group also affect family planning and size, and sponsorship in achieving educational and occupational objectives. This network can be an opportunity structure if it accepts the priorities of the bureaucratic society and has the socio-economic resources to deal with it. Middle- and upper-class families are most competent in using the network to achieve individual and nuclear family goals. Lower-class families, however, may consider that the intrinsic advantages of familism take precedence over those of increased mobility. The unskilled enjoy little security in the larger social sphere, a condition that encourages dependency on kin for services which support economic as well as emotional ends.[21] Thus, family cohesiveness, persistence, and continuity are not necessarily coincident with family-unit effectiveness in coping with the larger society.

Obviously, the resources of some families leave them at a disadvantage in those transactions that take place outside of primary groups. In the mediation process, the bureaucracy may rely on the professional expert as its representative. He has been formally socialized into assuming this role and is permitted, through his mandate for public service, to go beyond organizational goals and to concern himself in part with public or primary group needs. Nevertheless, he primarily supports the more extensive concerns of the bureaucratic institutions with which he is associated. He is likely to possess more resources to be used in the bargaining transaction than are available to the representative of the primary groups, and he is under structural requisites to mediate in the best interests of his employing organization.

Functionaries of bureaucratic organizations often co-opt primary-group

[20] Marvin B. Sussman, "Adaptive, Directive and Integrative Behavior of Today's Family," *Family Process,* vol. 7, September, 1968, pp. 239–250; *idem,* "The Family in the 1960's: Facts, Fictions, Problems, Prospects, and Institutional Linkages," in William Bassett, ed., *The Bond of Matrimony.* University of Notre Dame Press, South Bend, 1968, pp. 223–246.

[21] Marvin B. Sussman, "The Urban Kin Network in the Formulation of Family Theory," Ninth International Seminar on Family Research, Tokyo, Japan, in Reuben Hill and René Konig, eds., *Families in East and West: Socialization Processes and Kinship Ties.* Mouton, Paris, 1970; *idem,* "Adaptive, Directive and Integrative Behavior," pp. 244–249.

members in the mediation process. Even when families or their representatives are given a "piece of the action" through mediation, the degree of shift in their superordinate-subordinate power relationship is determined by the linkers from the bureaucratic organization. The experiences of black families on AFDC provide examples.

If primary groups are going to influence the mediating process, have any effect on the policies and programs of organizations, and maintain the integrity of their own internal structure, then they must socialize their members into the means for coping with mediating relations of this character. The goals and functions of primary groups and bureaucratic organizations must be understood and a competence developed in dealing with the complexities of their inter-action.

The kin network may be a veritable gold mine for linkers with mediating skills and connections in different life sectors. Initial findings from a pilot study of a barrio in Puerto Rico indicate that members of the kin network and *compadre* system take on "specialist linker roles." If a family member needs a loan of money, is in trouble with the police, requires a social security number, wants a job, needs to obtain a driver's license, or wants to make a trip to the main-land, he goes to an "expert" kin or *compadre* family member if one is not present in his household. This individual links the family with the appropriate bureaucratic organization. He frequently may educate the help seeker into the use of options and skills and socialize him into mediating and handling new roles required by the bureaucratic structure.[22]

The Issue of Value Change

The discussion so far has focused on the processes of conflict and coopera-tion which render social relations paradoxical as well as patterned. Particular attention was given to family-organizational linkages which may increase or reduce conflict and cooperation in social relationships. The reference to the values which sustain group interaction has relied upon an intuitive or common-sense use of the term which might well be given more specific references at this point. The implications of value change for social process and social change as they relate to kinship and marriage in the United States today must now be explored.

F. Ivan Nye suggests that the term "value" implies an abstraction which encompasses a whole category of objects, feelings, and/or experiences.[23] Harold Christensen tells us that values are "the mental and emotional sets which aid

[22] Observations from pilot study in Caguas, Puerto Rico, on Family–Bureaucratic Organizational Linkages.

[23] Ivan Nye, "Values, Family and a Changing Society," *Journal of Marriage and the Family*, vol. 29, May, 1967, pp. 241–248.

persons in judging the relative worth of importance of things, the criteria one uses in choosing among alternatives. Norms are value systems at the societal level—backed by rules, rewards, and penalties to enforce conformity. Values are a part of the personality, norms a part of the culture."[24]

If we accept these views, we see that values provide the context for the behavioral transactions dealt with above and may be expected to influence their character. Values provide a context in which the individual and the social coincide as efforts are made to actualize them in human relations.

As we explore the evidence for, and implications of, the emergence of new values within the family, we must introduce important caveats before proceeding. Even if the social theorist could be aware of all the values potentially present among interacting parties in a specific situation, he might not be able to predict their operation. Sometimes the presence of contradictory values causes little or no conflict in social transactions since these may coexist without conflict within the psyche of the actors involved. Thus, a person who believes in loyalty to one's primary group, emotional identification with and support for even its most inefficient member, and other similar orientations internalized in childhood, may not necessarily feel the inconsistency of performing according to a model of rationality and efficiency demanded by bureaucratic organizations.

In the case of the kin network, we have seen that the social dialogue sometimes serves to limit the extent and persistence of a system; its mediating and linking functions at times serve to extend it beyond sociocultural and generational barriers. These are natural processes of social system adaptation. The continuity and change of particular systems need not imply that parallel continuity or change is occurring in the realm of institutions or values. The most accurate description of ongoing relations may be misleading when applied to these more abstract levels of analysis. This may be illustrated in the domain of the familiar. It is recognized that intrafamily relationships must undergo change in the patterning of role relationships if the family is to accommodate developmental changes on the part of its members and still survive. Thus, over-all values are being sustained as lesser ones undergo transformation. A parallel may be made in the context of a global society. An inordinate degree of continuity and resistance to change in the relations and the values that animate a society may herald its cultural collapse should it be exposed to drastic alteration in its social or physical environment. Therefore, change and reorganization of existing social relations within a system may not necessarily be a sign that the system itself is being undermined.

Individuals, systems, and institutions all differ in the patterning of their social existence and in their extent and duration. We also expect actual social

[24] Harold Christensen, "Normative Theory Derived from Cross-Cultural Research," *Journal of Marriage and the Family,* vol. 31, May, 1969, pp. 209–222.

systems to be different in these respects from the concepts we abstract from them such as "marriage," "kinship," "bureaucracy," as they exist in a setting under study. On all levels, however, the vicissitudes of the social dialogue concerning values are operative, affecting the persistence of structures through the processes sketched above. When a new rhythm becomes perceptible in ongoing social cycles, the notion must be entertained that it is being stimulated by shifts in prevailing value orientations. The student of society is therefore inevitably led to contemplate the influence that values have in determining the social dimensions and the continued viability of each of these units.

What may we expect to find under conditions of value change? Values and norms evolve throughout history and, over time, undergo metamorphosis. Many of our dominant values are today undergoing processes of change, with some persons adapting the new while others retain the traditional. What are the mechanisms by which this occurs, and what implications does change have for the systems which incorporate new cultural features? Do values in primary familial systems tend to keep pace with those of the larger society?

Apparently they do, because new cultural inputs become incorporated in the value system through being actualized in new behaviors in ongoing social systems. Behavior change often proceeds in advance of value change, but it cannot be assumed to herald basic shifts in and of itself. Criteria for determining value dominance are relevant here. Williams differentiates values according to their extensiveness, duration, intensity, and the prestige of their carriers.[25] Studies indicate that systemic behavior change does not automatically follow new cultural inputs.[26]

When change does take place, as in the case of the modernization that accompanies widespread technological change, we may assume that the form and persistence of the social relations that new practices generate may be expected to rest on the same dynamics that operate under conditions of stability. Once more, one may expect to find the same ongoing processes of cooperation, contest, and mediation as human beings seek to meet the requirements of their social condition and gain the best advantage for themselves and for the systems in which they participate. We may expect, however, to find discernible but subtle alterations in adaptive style which will better support the over-all persistence of the social group in its changed circumstances.

Personal Happiness as an Emerging Ethic

The speed and extent of value change are difficult to measure from an examination of specific behaviors. Nevertheless, we may analyze the processes

---

[25] Robin Williams, "Individual and Group Values" (in Social Goals and Indicators for American Society), *The Annals,* vol. 371, May, 1967, pp. 20–37.

[26] Marvin B. Sussman and Marie R. Haug, "The Vicissitudes of Change," *Social Science and Medicine,* vol. 3, April, 1969, pp. 57–64.

and assess their direction and valence through examining some of the trends associated with the emergence of the value of personal happiness which now coexists in societal and family life with values of survival and personal development. The essence of the personal happiness value is that self-fulfillment is a continuous quest and that extensive self-denial or sacrifice is unnecessary. It recognizes that the achievement of important life goals may rest upon the pursuit of personal happiness, while disregard of this value may contribute to the development of personality distortion. Further, parent-child relationships, which even under "normal" circumstances are fraught with tension and conflict, may be exascerbated in its absence.

As the dimensions of this new value are explored, we are led to speculate on its implications for new directions in inter-institutional relations, kinship and marriage. The concept of personal happiness is an invitation to human relationships of an achieved character which are unspecified in regard to duration, content, and sphere. A premium is placed on a type of transaction which combines the features of bureaucratic and familial social systems; it is rational in that it implies a free contract, and expressive in that it rests upon personal definitions of goals. Actualization of this value may identify new areas of social relations which, in many instances, crosscut more formal systems of payoff and opportunity and have a temporal and spatial reference which may be limited to the individual life space and life span. Its individual reference sets it apart from either the familial or the bureaucratic spheres. The individual is given increased options and invited to link and socialize himself with existing systems, or to create new ones.

At the outset, roles within such systems are relatively indefinite. This ambiguity of role content can be interpreted as a chance to create or to contract for a role which has been adapted to meet individual needs. It is a social condition frequently faced by persons who are aged or those who are at leisure, and it may constitute a problem as well as an opportunity. Personal happiness is the value behind the effort to increase the options of persons who are retired or who voluntarily remove themselves from gainful employment. The objective is to permit the individual to "do his own thing," which will make him satisfied with himself, whether taking an unambitious "career" line or moving into a new second or third work career in the labor force.[27]

The new value placed on happiness is likely to introduce this challenge into other spheres as well. In this regard, recognition of a new sort of expertise becomes possible—one which is egalitarian and is based on human relations skills. Everyone is invited to exploit his abilities as a mediator or linker as he pursues his own goals. This orientation is one with a great potential for generat-

[27] Marie R. Haug and Marvin B. Sussman, "The Second Career—Variant of a Sociological Concept," *Journal of Gerontology,* vol. 22, October, 1967, pp. 439–444; Marvin B. Sussman, "An Analytical Model for the Sociological Study of the Retirement Process," in Frances M. Carp, ed., *Retirement.* Behavioral Publications, New York, 1971.

ing change in behavior and in relationships throughout those systems that embrace it.

The spheres of kinship and marriage may be sensitive to this new value just as they were responsive to the trends toward secularization and liberalization which have emerged since about 1860, the beginning of the urban period in this society. Marriage and divorce practices altered during this period, gathering momentum during two world wars. These changes were associated with changes in the social roles open to women as they took on employment outside of the home and worked toward professional status.

Marriage today tends to function under a mandate which regards it as a civil rather than a sacramental contract, so that it is amenable to dissolution. Consequently, there is a rather widespread acceptance of divorce. This alteration in the conditions of the marriage contract has not lessened its attractiveness. The United States today surpasses all other Western nations in the proportion of married citizens—almost 90 percent of Americans marry at least once during their lifetimes. The difference in age between spouses is being lessened, which improves the length of joint survivorship of couples.[28]

Estimates and statistics support the assertion that the 1960 divorce rate was eight times that of 1860.[29] Nevertheless, this rate has not increased over the past 20 years, except for a brief rise during the war followed by a decline. Once more, socioeconomic differences emerge which affect the relationship between the expected and the potential duration of marriage. Research indicates that the highest divorce rate is found among working-class families and the poor, with the higher professional and business groups having the lowest rates.[30] These findings do not support the popular myth that the wealthy and prominent have the highest rates. Differences between the stability of marriage of white and nonwhite men decline as income, schooling, and job levels rise among the latter.[31]

Although divorce has become more acceptable as an alternative to marital unhappiness, this process does not appear to be linked to a deterioration of child-rearing and socialization practices. Children of unhappy parents who stay together tend to have more adjustment difficulties than those whose parents divorce. Unhappy families that remain together for intactness sake are generally recognized as nonfunctional, since it appears that it is the emotional

[28] Robert Parke, Jr., and Paul Glick, "Prospective Changes in Marriage and the Family," *Journal of Marriage and the Family,* vol. 29, May, 1967, pp. 249–256.

[29] Paul C. Glick, *American Families.* Wiley, New York, 1957, pp. 120–145; Paul H. Jacobson, *American Marriage and Divorce.* Reinhart, New York, 1959, pp. 60–83; "Population: Marriage and Divorce Rates with Percent Changes from Preceding Years: United States, 1920–1959," *Vital Statistics of the United States,* 1959, Part 2, pp. 2–17.

[30] *Ibid.,* p. 251.

[31] *Ibid.,* pp. 254–255.

divorce preceding the actual one which causes the damage to the children. From the point of view of the socialization function, maintenance of an unhappy union tends to distort the conception of marriage held by the children and to engender guilt on their part since they sense their responsibility for binding their unhappy parents together.

As increasing numbers of women work outside of the home, they have more opportunity to express their intellectual interests, their strivings toward independence, and their gratification of material and personal needs and desires that cannot be achieved in marriage. Furthermore, in regard to satisfying the needs of spouses, marriage itself tends to have less of a renunciatory sacrificial character. Cuber and Haroff indicate that many marriages that are sustained over time are utilitarian in character, and express purposes other than intimate personal need fulfillment, particularly among the middle-aged.[32] These purposes may or may not have been associated with the marital context at an earlier time.

Thus, circumstances support a freer contract within marriage, accompanied by more opportunities outside of the marriage bond for adults of both sexes to actualize their interpersonal strivings. Men and women have increased opportunities to develop liaisons on a continuum from mild to serious involvement because of the participation of women in institutional areas outside of the home. These heterosexual relationships may range from colleagueship to love affairs, and although they are not entirely condoned, neither are they strongly condemned.

Sexuality appears to be undergoing autonomous institutionalization in its nonprocreative, extra-familial aspects, developing its own bases of reciprocity and exchange.[33] This seems due, in part, to the rise of interest in autotelic pursuits (those activities engaged in for their intrinsic value). As in other areas of sociability, however, sexuality has its exploitative relationships as well.

These new patterns of heterosexual relationships outside marriage reflect a greater degree of sexual development arising out of the changed status of women. The lessened dominance of the male may be expected to have an effect upon the relations between the sexes in this and other spheres. This alteration in the relations between the sexes constitutes a fertile area for future research.

This permissiveness and absence of sacrifice that exists between marital partners may also be perceived in the attitudes of parents toward their offspring. The new happiness mandate states that parents as well as children have rights. Children are no less important or esteemed than before this new orientation; the move toward limited sacrifice and increasing self-orientedness is not

---

[32] Cuber and Harroff, *op. cit.,* pp. 43–65.
[33] Jetse Sprey, "On the Institutionalization of Sexuality," *Journal of Marriage and the Family,* vol. 31, August, 1969, pp. 432–440.

a complete denial of parental responsibility. "Doing what is best for a child" occurs within the context of what is best for the parent and for the family as a total unit.

Children are encouraged to explore their environment voluntarily. This serves to increase their awareness of their own desires and the flexibility of parent-child relations. Parents feel less compelled to sacrifice to achieve goals for their children. The parental attitude that young people who wish to go to college should seek a scholarship has become a more acceptable one in middle-class homes. New opportunities present themselves for young people to realize their own goals more autonomously.

It has become apparent that the phenomenon of the working mother in itself has not eroded the socialization of the young.[34] Education of women for occupational careers has accelerated in the past 30 years and, since the Second World War, the expectation has been that married women should continue their careers in some fashion soon after children are in school. There is evidence that women who return to the work force as employed mothers may be better prepared for an easier adjustment when their children are old enough to leave home.[35] There is also ample evidence that mothers who are employed outside the home may have a "stretching effect" on the formation of a child's perceptions and social concepts, may afford adolescent children the opportunity to develop responsibility for their own behavior and a chance to assume adult roles.[36]

It would be a mistake to conclude that the participation of women in the work force simply means that women are taking on work as an additional role to marriage and that their major problem is to reconcile the incompatibilities of these roles, creating an appropriate stability between them so that they can be successful mothers, wives, and careerists.[37] It is more complicated than reaching role compatibility; it is a family problem and represents a shift in the role structure, interaction patterns, and value stance of the family. The Rapoports suggest a dual-career family with two heads who both have careers and share activities related to familial roles, with the exception of pregnancy and childbirth.[38]

This new dual-career family operates on principles of efficiency and bargaining and, consequently, the activities performed by marital partners are not

---

[34] Marvin B. Sussman, "Needed Research on the Employed Mother," *Marriage and Family Living,* vol. 23, November, 1961, pp. 368–373.

[35] *Ibid.,* p. 370.

[36] Urie Bronfenbrenner, "The Split-Level American Family," *Saturday Review,* vol. 50, October 7, 1967, pp. 60–66; Sussman, "Needed Research on the Employed Mother," p. 371.

[37] A. Myrdal and V. Klein, *Woman's Two Roles: Home and Work.* Routledge & Kegan Paul, London, 1956.

[38] Rapoport and Rapoport, *op. cit.,* pp. 3–30.

necessarily sex-linked.[39] Time is a scarce commodity in this type of family, time to perform marital, parental, and career roles. Consequently, to make the best use of available time, household and child-care tasks tend to be allocated according to competence rather than in relation to traditions regarding sex-linked roles. Bargaining over real and alleged competencies of partners and for a share of the "dirty" tasks is a common phenomenon. Even in this age, early socialization training in the family is in reference to perceptions of the traditional roles of men and women in marriage, e.g., women are most effective in nurturance roles and men in instrumental ones. More formal socialization systems, such as the school, counteract this role routing and use egalitarian norms, common experience, and a single evaluative procedure to provide some bases for equality in the work-family relationships of married couples.

The shift to this new family form in a post-industrial society is not without strain. A major question concerns the costs vs. the benefits in personal satisfaction for members of a dual-career family. The Rapoports indicate that role overloads, normative dilemmas, maintenance of personal identity, reconciling obligations of the social network, harmonizing the demands of each role system and the separate work system of each spouse and family system ("role cycling") are sources of strain endemic to this family system.[40] The mechanisms and processes used by couples to sort out these costs and benefits in each of these areas and achieve a *modus operandi* which optimizes personal satisfaction, and the institutional support programs which are needed to sustain this emergent family structure are research issues of the 1970's.[41]

One development accompanying these value changes regarding personal happiness in marriage and expressions of sexuality both within and outside matrimony is a growing concern about the roles, interactions, and mental health of the marital dyad. Clark Vincent, an advocate of "divorcing marriage from the family," forcefully argues that the exaggerated concern over child rearing has led to neglect of the needs and aspirations of the marital dyad. Yet this unit lasts longer and is more intimate than any other of the nuclear family. In suggesting that marital partners are human beings with rights and privileges, he calls for a new posture in family research " . . . to develop concepts and methods for studying marital health, marital roles, and dyadic dynamics as distinct from parental roles, parent-child dynamics, child development, and child socialization."[42]

---

[39] See William J. Goode, "Theory of Role Strain," *American Sociological Review*, vol. 25, August, 1960, pp. 483–496, for an interesting analysis of "role bargains" as a means of reducing strain in interpersonal relationships.

[40] Rapoport and Rapoport, *op. cit.*, pp. 24–25.

[41] *Ibid.*, pp. 26–27, for a discussion of the "built environments," housing developments with shared child- and household-care facilities.

[42] Clark E. Vincent, "Mental Health and the Family," *Journal of Marriage and the Family*, vol. 29, February, 1967, p. 34.

In the 1960 census, 5.7 million Americans were not counted. Bureau of the Census officials believe that the largest number of "no-counts" are urban slum dwellers, mostly black, Puerto Rican, Appalachian white, and other minorities. Difficulties in making complete counts of households were caused by the reluctance of census takers to remain in such units long enough to get the necessary information, a high census taker turnover, as well as an inadequate callback system.[43] One inference is that many of these 5.7 million U.S. citizens, "unknowns" to the Bureau of the Census, were members of nontraditional nuclear units, experiencing communal living in a common household, sharing available resources, and having a role structure adaptive to this non-orthodox form.

The anti-establishment movement of the 1960's has bolstered the genesis of variant family structures which are anti-traditional in philosophy, practice, and structure. The most widely publicized of these are the hippie communes of California: Strawberry Hills, Big Sur, Morningstar Ranch in Sonoma County, Haight-Ashbury in San Francisco, Holiday Lodge near Santa Cruz—and New York City's East Village.[44] The pervading ideology of these communal families involves living in the present, absorbing what occurs, feeling what is happening, rejecting the past, and being ambivalent about the future. The quality of life is found in the details of everyday existence, living spontaneously and openly with other family members. Intimacy is not experienced in the usual one-to-one relationship but in "being with," i.e., absorbing, the group. The individual's identity is constantly being discovered in "scenes," situations, and interactions; identity is ever-changing, and the member is more likely to have a group (family) rather than an individual identity.

The structural characteristics of this emergent family system and its functions, such as providing socialization, role options, and status for its members, are still to be established. The stress on group-oriented behavior, "doing one's own thing" within the group, suggests a structure similar to a classic extended family with one head organizing the interaction of its members. Another possible structure resembles the kibbutz communes with marital partners, shared tasks, and separate facilities for child rearing and education. Still another communal structure is composed of sub-units fashioned after the traditional nuclear family system but sharing a common shelter and organizing a role system that will permit expression of quality group living.

Despite the current persecution of these variant family groups and the terror they are now experiencing, every indication is that tolerance and compassion may counteract institutionalized oppression against these families and force

---

[43] A Staff Report, "The Census—What's Wrong with It, What Can Be Done," *Transaction,* vol. 5, May, 1968, pp. 49–56.

[44] Wide publicity has been given to the flower children by *Newsweek, Time, Life, Look,* NBC, ABC, and CBS. See also Lewis Yablonsky, *The Hippie Trip.* Pegasus-Western, New York, 1968, for a participant observer's account of these colonies.

removal of the current label of heresy. The inability of the current traditional family structure to meet the needs and expectations of its members may induce acceptance, or at least toleration, of these variant family structures. The nuclear family and its kinship structure will not be replaced by any of these new forms but their coexistence can be anticipated. It is difficult to predict the future distribution of individuals according to types of family structures or the staying power of such marriages. One hypothesis relates to life-cycle changes. It holds that a greater proportion of young adult and aged persons than the middle-aged will be members of these variant structures. The tendency will be for persons to move from the classic extended family structure to the nuclear structure and back to the classic extended as they proceed over the route of the family life cycle.[45]

Equally important to the social-psychological issues of socialization, authority, power, and identity are the variant family's relationships with bureaucratic organizations. Our social, economic, welfare, education, and health policies and programs are organized to deal with the nuclear family unit, the legally bona fide and culturally recognized family. What changes in legislation, program, and structure of the ADC program, for example, will be required to handle the needs of poor children of a variant family structure? This is only one of the many problems which coexistent family structures will present to the society.

New Patterns and Their Social Implications

What effect will these trends have upon existing organizational structures? In general, the transactional aspect of social relations is likely to be given support through increased stress upon the process of mediation between systems. New developments that are most apparent will, of course, occur on the level of behavior. The changes we have considered do not augur disintegration of the family and kinship networks. As individual family members pursue interests that are intrinsically rewarding, they may serve to link the family more firmly than ever to the other social networks available to it at every level. Furthermore, its viability as a social sphere may increase as it becomes more responsive to concerns that are genuinely shared by its members. A family that is more rationally based may still be a unit of solidarity, becoming less brittle due to freer definition of relationships. These trends may lead to reintegration of the family on the level of increased interpersonal gratifications.

Both familial and bureaucratic social systems will be permitted or en-

[45] Brown, Michael E., "The Condemnation and Persecution of Hippies," *Transaction*, vol. 6, 1969, pp. 33–46. Brown cites the current oppression of the hippies by the establishment. There are indications, however, that these initial efforts to destroy the hippie family commune are abating because of middle-class tolerance and support (their children are the principal members of these communes) and the moral integrity, ethical values, and ideals which characterize the more "honest" hippie communities.

couraged to assume roles and activities characteristic of the other. The increasingly client-centered approach of public and private agencies and their adoption of primary-grouplike structures, such as foster grandparent plans, are evidence for this expectation.[46]

These changes also appear to have favorable implications for the persistence of structures on the institutional level. The increased flexibility that surrounds divorce and marriage provides a case in point. Flexibility implies variability in the content and form of individual marriages; it also suggests an increased resiliency which gives support to marriage as a contract. We may also expect the proliferation of available options, arising from the stress placed on creative linkages among systems, to provide additional support to institutional structures insofar as such transactions facilitate intercommunication among systems.

These assertions have yet to be tested in the context of research. It may be noted that many of them lead us to contemplate the phenomenon of social boundaries as they respond to a changing environment. The processes described above presuppose a greater degree of interpenetration among differing organizations and structures in their purposes and functions. We may not expect that all spheres of social interaction will react similarly, however. New bases of system discreteness are likely to arise, and in some areas, greater emphasis will be placed upon those already in existence. The increased stress being placed on face-to-face community relations in the delivery of health and education services may indicate the directions in which major boundary definition is proceeding.

The growing awareness of the importance of demographic and geographic factors seems to be part of the process of adapting to the demands for new types of services, and it exemplifies boundary maintenance for the purpose of facilitating in-group interaction. It appears to coincide with increased efforts to improve articulation between service agencies and those families that are most marginal to the prevailing culture. The role of the indigenous nonprofessional is emerging as a linker in this context. As efforts are being made to improve the quality of transactions between systems at different cultural and socioeconomic levels, subprofessionals and indigenous persons are serving as agents in numerous spheres. This is particularly true of services related to the welfare and legal status of poor persons and to their rehabilitation.

Many of these changes appear to support existing family networks by integrating them more firmly into the larger milieu. As the community focus intensifies, however, it may be expected to further the development of subcultural systems and introduce new boundaries into the societal sphere.

---

[46] Marie Haug and Marvin B. Sussman, "Professional Autonomy and the Revolt of the Client," *Social Problems,* vol. 17, Fall, 1969, pp. 153–161.

In other areas as well, system relations appear to be emerging. Many individuals recognize that a community of interests exists among them, and they are seeking means of self-help and mutual aid. They include widows, persons who are overweight, those who have had heart attacks, former mental patients, and others. Although these processes and their social implications have received less attention than they deserve from social scientists, a superficial impression would be that there is a strong trend toward facilitating communication among social aggregates which are utilizing new bases for solidarity.

Summary

One major thesis in this chapter is that the family is still a viable social system. In societies of high complexity such as the United States, the overwhelming majority of urbanized nuclear units voluntarily choose to participate within a kin network, based on exchange and reciprocity, which is composed of other nuclear units living in separate households. The positive and negative consequences of such participation are only now being studied.

Considering the need of the family to represent strongly its position in dealings with bureaucratic organizations, the kin network can assist in socialization for competence in linkage roles. Some kin members may be deputized to handle the problems associated with family-bureaucratic organizational relationships. Others may provide knowledge, support, and entry into the option sequence in various life sectors.

Socialization into roles and identities has long been one of the central activities of the family system. Initiating the child into socially approved roles is in itself no easy task for family socialization agents, but an even greater requirement in today's society is the development of competence in family members for handling the normative demands of bureaucratic organizations. Consequently, socialization training requires providing the individual with options and skills in their usage, and developing interactional and political sensitivities for dealing with bureaucracies. Training in manipulation must be countermanded with an ideology and experiences which enable the individual to feel a sense of accomplishment and fulfillment in performing his social roles.[47] If this is not accomplished, there is the danger that the individual will be unable to live with himself and with others. Thus, the task of family socialization—and other socialization systems for that matter—is to develop appropriate mechanisms for regulating these apparent inconsistencies. On the one hand, for survival the family must train its members to manage successfully nonfamily group and or-

---

[47] Barbara Solomon indicates that social psychologists are suggesting that the other side of developing competence in social role performance is the individual's need to obtain a sense of accomplishment and fulfillment. See "Social Functioning of Economically Dependent Aged," unpublished doctoral dissertation, University of California, 1966.

ganizational relationships; on the other hand, the family must provide a sense of fulfillment for participating members and sustain their identification with the primary group. The requisites for maintenance may make a person less than human. Nevertheless, the needs of the group and of the society are for socialization into "humaneness." Harmonizing these incongruities with appropriate mechanisms and procedures is one task of social-psychological research.

Family-organizational linkage is a largely uninvestigated arena of interaction. The usual approach to this type of problem is to examine the family member's relationship with bureaucratic organizations; little attention is given to the representational role he may be performing for the family in such linkages. Largely ignored is the relationship of marital, parent-child, and other interactions of family members to role behavior related to nonfamily systems. The omission of family interaction patterns, value postures, and ideologies in studies of influence and behavior in family-organizational linkage is caused by faulty conceptualization; namely, that bureaucratic organizations dominate primary groups and individuals in all their relationships. Consequently, problems are formulated so that the question asked usually is: How does the organization do this or that? Or: Why is the organization not working effectively? Establishing the reciprocal power and influence of organization-family associations requires that the family system be conceptualized both as an independent and dependent variable.

It is necessary to develop linkage models in which interactional systems of family and nonfamily groups and organizations are the basic elements, and models which describe the relevant actors, the arena of interaction, orientations of participants, and relationships to other systems. These can provide (1) the bases for descriptive and analytic analysis and (2) an understanding of the "value-relevance" of the observer's statement, i.e., the value bases of his analysis.[48] In this sense, models check the grounds upon which an observation is made and the degree to which it is biased by the individual's particular value position. Obviously, the need for development of theoretical models in the family field is a high priority in efforts to disavow current misconceptions of the family as a social system and to provide the means for accurate description and analysis of empirical reality.

The payoffs, liabilities, and symbolic significance of family members' participation in kin-related activities are problems for the social-psychological study of the family. A recently completed study on family inheritance suggests that property transfers are valued not so much for their economic worth but for the conveyance of feelings which may characterize the relationships between the

---

[48] For a discussion of models see Daniel Bell, "Twelve Modes of Prediction—A Preliminary Sorting of Approaches in the Social Sciences," in Warren G. Bennis, Kenneth D. Benne, and Robert Chin, *The Planning of Change,* 2nd ed. Holt, New York, 1968, pp. 532–551.

testator and his children.[49] Inheritance, in the usual sense, signifies a straightforward economic transfer usually required in most societies for the orderly shift of generational power and authority. Family transfers from one generation to the next complement those society-wide ones that come about in modern nations because of legislation and programs which supply across-the-board care for the young and the aged. Social security, education, and welfare programs are illustrations of society-wide transfers whereby the middle generation of gainfully employed support themselves and, in addition, create sufficient surplus to take care of the very young and the very old. With increasing complexity, such programs dominate a society, and the transfers that occur between families take on more symbolic meaning than economic importance. One significant research question is: How are family transfers used to enhance or destroy emotional-affective, intergenerational, and bilateral kin relationships?

The increasing incidence of dual-career families in complex societies raises important social-psychological issues regarding allocation of roles, handling of stress, changed interaction patterns, and the reorganization of physical and social space to conform to the emotional needs and socialization objectives of family members. To date, the research has concentrated largely on the professional family and very little attention has been given to the dual-career patterns of nonprofessional and lower-class families. Only passing notice has been given to the potential role of the kin network members in providing caretaking services, affection, counsel, and instruction in the child's own residence while parents pursue their careers in society's work systems. One desirable research study would be to obtain analytic descriptions of marital interaction and the mechanisms used by marital partners of dual-career families in role and task allocations and expectations. Do shifts away from traditional role patterns affect retention of masculine and feminine identities? Another research area would be studies of the best uses of physical and social space for monitoring and socializing children of dual-career parents. How can one build environments for the family that will utilize the most salient architectural designs and research knowledge on group processes, learning, motivation, and socialization?

In this age of Aquarius, the anti-traditional nuclear family structure increasingly will become attractive to larger groups of younger marriageable persons. Emergent family structures will resemble a variety of types such as the classic extended family in eighteenth-century United States or the stem family of India. Even if these family structures are declared illegal and are outlawed, as were the polygamous families of the Mormons in the nineteenth century, this event will not negate the impact upon the traditional nuclear family's role structure, social and physical space needs, socialization patterns, value systems, and

[49] Marvin B. Sussman, Judith N. Cates, and David T. Smith, *The Family and Inheritance*. Russell Sage Foundation, New York, 1970.

ideology. Family sociologists should undertake immediately historical case studies of these variant family structures for comparative analysis with traditional nuclear forms in order to discover similarities and differences in the organization of marital role systems, socialization patterns, uses of social and physical space, linkages with bureaucratic organizations, decision-making, task assignment, and so forth. It would also be important to document whether such family systems are time-limited and attract the very young who, after a period of communal living, leave the "family," shift into a "modified" traditional nuclear form, and perhaps return in old age to the communal form. Will life-cycle changes be related to shifts in membership in different types of family structures? One reason for this hypothesis is the extreme difficulty anti-establishment family systems have in working out their relationships with other bureaucratic organizations, especially those concerned with social, welfare, and health care. Most of our society-wide support systems are based upon the recognized legality of the nuclear family. Whether such society-wide caretaking systems can modify their policies and programs and create new legislation to accommodate new, emergent, variant forms is questionable.

There are social-psychological bases for the formation of communal-type family systems. Among the poor, underclassed, and aged, organization along communal lines may provide the structure for survival, use of options, and available talent for dealing with bureaucracies. Among the middle class whose children make up the largest number of members of the hippie families, this extended family structure provides insulation from the outside world, expression of self through others, approval and acceptance by "doing one's own thing" through the group, and the luxury of living with nonmaterialistic values. The openness of this type of family system may provide the individual with an answer to the question: Who am I? without necessarily insisting upon a commitment to this identity. Experience gained in such communal families in handling interpersonal situations may provide the best competence training for the individual if he ever moves out of the communal family and has to deal with the organizational systems of society. For the imaginative investigator, this is one of the more fascinating variant family systems for social-psychological research.

5

The Meaning of Work: Interpretation and Proposals for Measurement

Robert L. Kahn

There is a current surge of interest in social measurement, and a number of catchwords have already been proposed to identify it. Whatever its name, the purposes of this new effort are reasonably clear: to develop a set of procedures that will monitor the quality of life in a society, record over time the various gains and losses in that quality, and contribute to its improvement.

The last of these purposes is the most problematical in the consideration and advocacy of social indicators. Any datum that is to be taken as an indicator is presumably to be taken also as a guide to action—to response in terms of policy and administrative practice. The linkage from social indicator to social policy and administration, however, is by no means obvious. It involves at least four elements: the *indicators* themselves; a set of demonstrated *relationships* that explain and define the underlying social processes and conditions that are signaled by the indicators; a set of social *values or goals* that define preferred states on the dimensions identified as or underlying the indicators; and an apparatus or *technology for bringing about change* on one or more of the relevant dimensions. These can be labeled more briefly in terms of the functions they serve: *description, explanation, evaluation,* and *implementation.*

Let us consider each of these functions in relation to the substantive area of work and the conditions of work. In this field the decennial census provides the most venerable example of descriptive statistics that can be taken as social indicators for the United States. Many kinds of occupational data can be compared over periods up to 100 years, if one accepts various adjustments for altered definitions and techniques, and for the last 30 years the Current Population Survey has provided monthly estimates of employment and unemployment for the country as a whole.

As with almost all descriptive data, they have become tremendously more useful because they are collected repeatedly. Descriptive data in themselves simply tell us the state of some system, with respect to some characteristic, at some point in time. If the descriptive process is repeated regularly, it is still only descriptive, but the description has become dynamic rather than static; we are told the direction and rate of change in the system with respect to the measured characteristics.

The theoretical and pragmatic implications of dynamic description as compared to static, one-time description are very great. The development of astronomy as a science provides a good example of the dependence of theory on accurate description over time, but the pragmatic power of trend data can be illustrated with data closer to the topic of this chapter. If we learn that the average hours worked per week in factories are 41, we may take that as causal and slightly obvious confirmation of the fact that the 40-hour workweek is the norm in the United States, sanctioned by union contracts, by law, and by apparent usage. If we are given the additional descriptive datum that the factory workweek in 1900 was 59 hours, we can draw additional conclusions about the trend toward increased leisure and the tendency to take productivity gains in free time as well as increased goods. But what if we are told that the workweek was already reduced to 44 hours in 1929, and that in 1940 it was only 38 hours? Now new questions arise: Is there something particularly appropriate about the work routine of the eight-hour day and the five-day week? Have we seen the end of the downward trend? Will the new leisure, if there is to be such, be taken in terms of new alterations in the pattern of work—long vacations, nonacademic sabbaticals, and the like? The point is not that the answers to such complex questions can be generated from such meager data, but that the questions themselves emerge only because of the existence of trend data—description over time. And the example is modest enough—one descriptive statistic repeated at four points in time.[1]

The second kind of information needed to guide policy-making I have called *explanatory,* which in its most elementary form means relational. Explanation consists in demonstrating that one thing is related to another, and then elaborating the set of things so related. As the elaboration continues, we are able to speak of causal sequences, of predictions and consequences, of models and theories.

In his presidential address to the American Statistical Association, Rensis Likert emphasized the distinction between descriptive and explanatory data, and insisted on their joint indispensability for the construction and implementa-

---

[1] Albert Rees, *Real Wages in Manufacturing 1890–1914.* National Bureau of Economic Research, Princeton University Press, Princeton, 1961, p. 33.

tion of social policy.[2] To illustrate these points, he used the example of the practicing physician. To diagnose and treat his patients, the doctor must have both descriptive and explanatory information. The descriptive data in a particular case may begin with the familiar measures of temperature, blood pressure, and pulse rate, supplemented by qualitative signs of various kinds. These the physician obtains directly and immediately from the patient, and he may then decide on more complex measures—blood chemistry, radiology, and innumerable other procedures.

But to interpret these descriptive data, and to have chosen in the first place which data should be obtained for the patient, the doctor requires information of a different kind, the kind I have called explanatory. He must know, for example, what state of health or illness, what other characteristics of the patient are indicated by different degrees of body temperature or blood pressure or pulse rate; he must know the properties to which his descriptive measures are related. The more of such relationships he knows, the more he possesses, in Likert's terms, information about the nature of the system (patient) and its present state. Such information is not developed quickly, or is it likely to be developed from the particular case being described. On the contrary, explanatory relationships are developed from extensive research and long accumulation relating symptoms to causes, building gradually from discrete sets of such relationships to large explanatory networks of the nature of human life, health, and illness. The doctor, in other words, is the beneficiary and the user of explanatory information that has been accumulated and winnowed over many centuries of practice and fewer centuries of systematic research. Increasingly, he knows what his indicators indicate.

Likert argues that the situation is very different with respect to social data, and that we do a far better job of collecting information about the *state* of the social system (description) than in producing information about the *nature* of the social system (explanation), that is, valid relationships, generalizations, and theories. For example, we count and categorize delinquent acts, but we know very little about the nature and causes of juvenile delinquency. We measure with some accuracy the level of employment and unemployment, prices, and gross national product, but we are reduced quickly to partisan argument when questions of prediction and control are raised; we know more about the state of the economy than about its nature.

The same point can be made, perhaps with even greater force, with respect to the area of work. We know the numbers of employed and unemployed, the number of strikes and the man-hours lost from them, and we esti-

[2] Rensis Likert, "The Dual Function of Statistics," *Journal of the American Statistical Association,* vol. 55, March, 1960, pp. 1–7.

mate with somewhat larger error the productivity of labor in certain occupations and industries. We know less about the causes and consequences of such facts, and we rely on folklore and judgment as well as research when we attempt to explain *why* unemployment rises or falls, what kinds of management lead to greater or lesser productivity, or what the causes and cures may be for strikes.

To continue the example of hours of work, we might want to know whether the number of hours worked per week is related to job satisfaction, frequency of accidents, quality of performance, and total amount produced. We might also want to know the relationship, if any, between the number of hours spent at work and the effectiveness with which the worker fulfills the other major life roles as husband, father, friend, citizen. Data about such relationships are not available on a representative and recurring basis, although one can find studies that bear on these issues.[3] We know a little better some of the antecedents of unusual hours of work, at least to the extent of being able to identify occupations and industries in which demands for overtime and part-time labor are most common. But we cannot claim to have in hand an explanation of how hours of work are determined. Yet without such explanatory information, information which takes the form of relationships rather than univariate statistics, we cannot choose wisely what social indicators to create, or successfully interpret the meaning of those chosen.

There is an additional advantage conferred by knowing the explanatory chain of causes and effects that leads to and from a particular social indicator—the advantage of time. As patients, we submit to the doctor's diagnostic procedures not only to discover what may already have gone wrong, but also to anticipate problems of health before they become serious. We want blood pressure readings (and appropriate action) before an unmanageable hypertension has developed; we want to prevent or avoid the possibility of stroke, not merely record it. Causal sequences are temporal sequences as well; by choosing an indicator early in the sequence, once we have discovered it, we increase the possibility of influencing its course.

In the universe of social events, unfortunately, our understanding of such sequences is so limited that we tend to collect data only about the terminal or crisis event in some unidentified sequence. We are doing this when we count strikes without any index of worker attitudes toward job and company, or when we count violent crimes without any measure of the attitudes, tendencies, or values that precede such crimes. Prediction and control call for indicators and for understanding, for explanation as well as description.

The third element in linking social indicators to social policy is *values*. In

---

[3] Paul E. Mott, *et al.*, *Shift Work: The Social, Psychological, and Physical Consequences.* University of Michigan Press, Ann Arbor, 1965.

this connection one need not think of lofty sentiments or abstractions. It is easy to get agreement about the desirability of such remote notions as the welfare of mankind, but the agreement is only apparent and dissolves when the conversation becomes more specific. I would propose instead that the issues of value be treated in exactly the same terms as the social indicators themselves; in other words, that value choices be made explicit with respect to each dimension proposed as a social indicator.

At least two kinds of value judgments are implicated for each indicator dimension, however simple. As example, let us take again the measurement of hours worked per week by employed men, a statistic collected in the decennial census, in the Current Population Surveys of the Census Bureau, and by the establishment-reporting procedures of the Department of Labor. It is obvious that this investment of resources in hours of work as a social indicator expresses a value judgment about its importance. It has been judged worth measuring and, by implication, more valuable than a number of unspecified alternative data that could have been assembled with the same expenditure of resources.

It is perhaps less obvious that, in order to act on data about hours worked, one must invoke a second scale, a scale of values—ranging perhaps from very bad to very good—coordinated to the scale of actual behavior (hours worked). Suppose, for example, that we think it is better for men to work 40 hours per week than 60 or 20, that they *ought* to work 40 hours, and that they ought to have the opportunity of doing so. This is a value judgment, and it can be expressed as shown in the accompanying illustration.[4]

Evaluative Judgments Associated with Hours of Work

Hours of work per week	Evaluative ordering of hours of work
80	Bad
60	Good
40	Very good
20	Bad
0	Very bad

The scale of hours worked ranges in the illustration form 0 to 80. The scale of value-rankings about hours worked ranges from "very bad" to "very good" and includes two intermediate points, "bad" and "good"; it is a four-point scale. To order the value judgments from "very good" to "very bad," we would, in effect, fold the scale as if we were picking it up physically at the point marked "very good," and then let the other alternatives fall in the order of

[4] John R. P. French, Jr., and Robert L. Kahn, "A Programmatic Approach to Studying the Industrial Environment and Mental Health," *Journal of Social Issues,* vol. 28, July, 1962, pp. 1–47.

their positive evaluation. In this order, we find that it is very good to work 40 hours per week; it is good to work 60, equally bad to work either 20 or 80, and very bad not to work at all.

Such value judgments are in some respects unavoidably relative. They are, in the first place, specific to some judge, some person or persons whose values are being expressed. In the above example, the values expressed are probably more slanted toward long hours than many people would wish. Many might prefer 20 hours of work to 40.

Values are also relative to the persons and situations to which they are being applied. Few if any values are held to be universally applicable. If we assert that working 40 hours per week is very good, we probably do not mean to include children, or the aged, or the ill, for example.

Moreover, value preferences involve beliefs or hypotheses about the consequences of choice; a course of action may be advocated because it is valued for itself or because it is seen as instrumental to some value, or for both reasons. For example, if one believes that work is virtuous in itself and nonwork is sinful, the value preference is obvious. But one may value work not for itself but because it is the source of goods and services that satisfy human needs. If work were negatively valued in that intrinsic sense but positively valued for its product, then the value choice with respect to hours, kinds and speeds of work would involve the weighing of these positive and negative aspects. Galbraith makes such assumptions and concludes that "a reduction in the work week is an exceedingly plausible reaction to the declining marginal urgency of product. . . ."[5]

All these value conflicts and qualifications are relevant when we move from description of social facts to social action, the utilization of facts. If we are attempting to propose policies that reflect the value choices of the population at large, we will want to measure the evaluative preferences that correspond to the range of possible alternatives offered. We will want to know, in the present example, to what extent the value preference for 40 hours of work per week is common, and perhaps also to what extent it is shared, that is, known to be common. This is what we mean by a social norm—a value that is both common and shared.

A minimum guide for social action, however, is that some value differentiation be made among alternative behaviors or behavior opportunities. If it is equally good to work 80 or 40 hours or none at all, then description of the present facts leads to no action whatsoever. Action implies goals, a preference for some states rather than others, and requires an expression of values.

Even these three elements—description, relationship, and evaluation—do not suffice for bringing about change. Although they tell us the present state

[5] John K. Galbraith, *The Affluent Society*. Houghton Mifflin, Boston, 1958, p. 335.

of things, some antecedents and consequences of that state, and some state that would be preferred, they leave us with the most difficult question in the linkage from description to utilization: how to bring about desired changes. How can one induce change from a present state of affairs, as indicated by one's descriptive measures and their trend, to the state deemed preferable in terms of one's values?

The answers to this question lie comfortably outside the subject of this chapter. It is relevant to point out, however, that they are many and include the whole range of influence attempts, from individual persuasion to institutional change. The means of achieving such changes have been the preoccupation of governors and would-be governors from the beginning of history; in one form or another they are among the core problems of the social sciences, especially psychology and political science. Moreover, in recent years they have become the core of a new discipline, not yet properly named, but identifiable by key words and phrases such as research utilization, long-range planning, and the like.

In short, the idea of *social indicators* implies social action as well, and the elements of static and dynamic description, explanation, value choice, and technology for implementation are the requirements for appropriate social action. On each dimension we deem sufficiently important, we must know our position, our present rate and direction of movement, the causes and consequences associated with these facts, the attainable state we consider preferable, and the approaches that can be taken at different points in the causal linkage in order to bring about desired change. With this framework in mind, let us turn to a more specific assessment and set of proposals regarding the meaning of work.

The four categories of *description, explanation, evaluation, and implementation* will serve to organize our review of present research on the meaning of work and our proposals for future research on this broad topic. We must begin that review by noting the confusion and diversity that marks the concept of work itself.

General usage of the term is imprecise and the multiplicity of meanings has expert sanction—definitions of work are given nine pages in the *Oxford English Dictionary* and more than a dozen entries in Webster's unabridged. In physics, work is defined precisely as the product of force and distance, and Maxwell's conceptual definition of work as the transference of energy from one system to another continues in modern physics.

Social science has no satisfactory analogue, and would not be well served by using the physical concept unmodified. The broadest meaning of work in social sciences is at least reminiscent of the physicist's terms of force (magnitude and direction) and distance; in social terms, work involves the exercise of effort toward some defined end. But many forms of play would satisfy that meaning equally well.

I propose, therefore, a more restrictive definition that includes the terms of *effort* or activity (physical or intellectual) and direction or *purpose,* and adds the qualification that the effort be *cyclical* or recurring, and that it involve *economic gain.* To distinguish this concept from other uses of the term work, let us speak of the *work role.* The concept of role refers to any set of purposeful recurring activities (i.e., expected behavior) associated with a particular social position. When such activities are undertaken for economic gain, we shall say that the person is working, or is in the work role. As Vroom points out in a discussion of the same issues, the concept *work role* fits closely the colloquial term *job.*[6]

This is a convenient definition and relatively unambiguous in application. Admittedly, it suffers from some conspicuous inadequacies in its application to "fringe" roles—housewives, unpaid family laborers, volunteer workers in civic organizations, and amateurs of all sorts. It is also conspicuously culture-bound. It fits the mode of production of goods and services in "developed" societies, that is, societies that have an institutionalized division of labor, a monetary system in which exchange takes place, and an explicit linkage of consumption rights to productive obligations (with various exclusions for reasons of age, sex, physical condition, inherited wealth, or dire need).

Moreover, it may be an eroding definition. Such authors as Galbraith, Piel, and Theobald have predicted or urged that the tight linkage of individual productive effort and consumption be loosened.[7] They argue that for reasons of automation, affluence, and social values, the old decision rule for deprivation—they who do not work shall not eat—is already modified more than we usually recognize and is destined for further change. Although this trend may be desirable, it is well to define the work role in terms that do not reflect it. We will thereby be reminded that a society which no longer requires purposeful recurring effort in exchange for access to goods and services will have abolished the work role as we know it.

Descriptive Measurement

The present state of descriptive measurement of work roles in the United States can be quickly summarized. Certain aggregative statistics about jobs have been collected by the federal government for a long time. These have to do almost exclusively with labor-force economics and with occupational classifica-

[6] Victor H. Vroom, *Work and Motivation.* Wiley, New York, 1964, p. 6.

[7] Galbraith, *op. cit.;* John K. Galbraith, *The New Industrial State.* Houghton Mifflin, Boston, 1967; Gerard Piel, "An End to Toil," *Nation,* June 17, 1961; Robert Theobald, *Abundance: Threat or Promise. Free Men and Free Markets.* Clarkson N. Potter, New York, 1963.

tion. They are purposely non-psychological, and tell us nothing directly about the meaning of work to the worker and his family. They are, however, collected on a relatively ambitious scale—in the decennial censuses or by large samples of persons or establishments.

Characteristics of the Labor Force

Some occupational statistics were inherited from colonial times, as Hauser points out.[8] Data on the wage levels of workmen were collected on some systematic basis from the year 1621, and on the slave trade from 1619. The beginning of occupational and industrial classification was made in the census of 1820. The three categories—agriculture, commerce, and manufacture—were expanded to seven categories of work in 1840 and to an occupational inquiry of some detail in 1850. In 1880, questions were added about the duration of unemployment during the census year. Major additions to the work-related inquiries of the census appear next in 1940, and the concepts of "gainful worker" and "usual occupation" were abandoned at that time, made obsolete by the depression years. The alternative concept of the labor force, defined in terms of all persons actually employed or seeking employment during some defined period (e.g., a census week) has been in active use from 1940. It is used currently in decennial censuses and in the monthly sample surveys that are jointly produced by the Bureau of the Census and the Department of Labor. In 1960, the questions relating to work were again expanded, mainly to provide data to deal with the emerging crises of transportation and movement out of central urban areas.[9]

Other descriptive series of statistics relating to work are produced in the federal establishment, particularly in the Departments of Labor, Agriculture, and Health, Education, and Welfare, and in private associations such as the National Industrial Conference Board. For the most part, these series have been developed to serve the executive functions of the several agencies and institutions by providing information on conditions such as hours of work, employment of women and children, and exposure to work hazards.

In combination, these data tell us a great deal about the economic, demographic, occupational, and industrial characteristics of work and very little about social-psychological conditions or the meaning of work. We can sketch

[8] Philip M. Hauser, "Social Accounting," in Paul F. Lazarsfeld, William H. Sewell, and Harold L. Wilensky, eds., *The Uses of Sociology.* Basic Books, New York, 1967.

[9] Hauser, *op. cit.;* Nathan Keyfitz, "Government Statistics," in *Encyclopedia of the Social Sciences.* Crowell-Collier, New York, 1969; Alba M. Edwards, *Comparative Occupation Statistics for the United States.* Government Printing Office, Washington, D.C., 1943; Philip M. Hauser, "The Labor Force and Gainful Workers—Concept, Measurement, and Comparability," *American Journal of Sociology,* vol. 54, January, 1949, pp. 338–355.

quickly the profile of work which emerges from these official data and some of the major changes that have been recorded over the years.[10]

Labor Force Composition

The labor force of the United States currently includes more than eighty million people; more than four out of five are wage and salary workers. The major long-term trend in the labor force has been its growth which, for the most part, reflects the growth and changing age composition of the population as a whole. The labor force, however, has grown more rapidly than the population and its composition has changed in several ways. Child labor, after increasing from 1870 to 1900, began a continuous decline to virtual elimination by 1940. Retirement from work has become increasingly institutionalized and occurs at earlier ages. Most striking of all, the proportion of the labor force made up of women has increased markedly and steadily for almost a hundred years. The census of 1870 showed that women workers numbered only one out of seven; the census of 1970 is likely to show a figure close to one out of three.

The occupational and industrial composition of the labor force has changed as well and the changes show a persistent and accelerating trend away from unskilled and physically heavy labor, toward white-collar, skilled manual, and intellectual work roles. The magnitude of these occupational changes since 1900 is shown clearly in Table 1 and indicates that the percentage of white-collar workers more than tripled, the percentage of laborers was reduced by more than half, and the percentage of farmers and farm workers was cut by more than two-thirds.

The industrial allocation of work roles has changed concomitantly and perhaps even more dramatically. In 1870, more than half the labor force was in agriculture; in 1970, it was about one-tenth. The major industrial shift has been away from agriculture and toward trade, finance, government, and professional activities. The major changes *within* industrial categories have occurred in manufacturing, where the over-all stability in recent decades and the significant increases during the past century result from diverse occupational trends already noted, gross reductions in the proportion of laborers and more than compensating increases in the proportion of machine operatives and craftsmen.

This review of aspects of work measured on a representative and continuing basis could be extended to show the past reductions and recent stability in hours of work, major gains in earned income, fluctuations in unemployment, and changes in the "nonworker" population as well as trends in the labor force.

[10] This summary has been compiled from various sources, as indicated. It is based primarily on Thomas C. Fichandler, "The American Labor Force," in Sigmund Nosow and William H. Form, eds., *Man, Work, and Society*. Basic Books, New York, 1962.

Social-Psychological Attributes of Work

No aspect of work as it is experienced and responded to by the worker is measured on a representative and recurring basis. This is not to say that social scientists have ignored such questions; many studies have been done on the meaning and experience of work. Psychologists and sociologists share an interest and, to some extent, a research vocabulary in this area. They speak of satisfaction, involvement, meaning, variety and monotony, energic and psychic demand, machine-pacing, alienation, cohesiveness and isolation, communication, openness, and other characteristics of work roles and work experiences. But while many measures of such concepts have been devised, few have been applied to representative population samples, and still fewer have been applied more than once.

Job Satisfaction

A partial exception to this inefficient and unnecessary state of research affairs is provided by the research on job satisfaction. Studies of job satisfaction have been reviewed in some depth by Hoppock, Herzberg, Blauner, and Robinson and his associates.[11] Blauner and Robinson were particularly interested in identifying serious efforts at descriptive measurement and found 10 that qualified. Five of these were based on national samples and five on samples limited to a particular city. Measurement approaches varied; in only one instance (Converse and Robinson) is there a purposeful replication of the measures used in an earlier nationwide survey (Gurin, Veroff, and Feld). When one considers that some two thousand studies of job satisfaction have been done, the low priority of repeated measurement on representative samples is obvious.[12]

In spite of such differences in technique, time, and coverage, there is a certain consistency in the response patterns: few people call themselves extremely satisfied with their jobs, but still fewer report extreme dissatisfaction. The modal response is on the positive side of neutrality—"pretty satisfied." The proportion dissatisfied ranges from 10 to 21 percent. Table 2 incorporates and extends Blauner's summary.[13]

[11] Robert Hoppock, *Job Satisfaction*. Harper, New York, 1935; Frederick Herzberg *et al.*, *Job Attitudes: Review of Research and Opinion*. Psychological Service of Pittsburgh, Pittsburgh, 1957; Robert Blauner, "Work Satisfaction and Industrial Trends in Modern Society," in W. Galenson and S. M. Lipset, eds., *Labor and Trade Unionism*. Wiley, New York, 1960; John P. Robinson, Robert Athanasiou, and Kendra B. Head, *Measures of Occupational Attitudes and Occupational Characteristics*. Survey Research Center, Institute for Social Research, University of Michigan, Ann Arbor, 1967, especially Chap. 3.

[12] Herzberg *et al.*, *op. cit.*, recorded 1,500 such studies in 1957.

[13] Blauner, *op. cit.*; Harold Wilensky, "Varieties of Work Experience," in Henry

Table 1. Percent Distribution by Major Occupation Group for the Economically Active Civilian Population, by Sex, for the United States, 1900 to 1950[a]

Major Occupation Group and Sex	1960	1950	1940	1930	1920	1910	1900
Both sexes:							
White-collar workers	43.3	36.6	31.1	29.4	24.9	21.3	17.6
Professional, technical, and kindred workers	11.8	8.6	7.5	6.8	5.4	4.7	4.3
Managers, officials, and proprietors, exc. farm	8.8	8.7	7.3	7.4	6.6	6.6	5.8
Clerical and kindred workers	15.1	12.3	9.6	8.9	8.0	5.3	3.0
Sales workers	7.6	7.0	6.7	6.3	4.9	4.7	4.5
Manual and service workers	50.2	51.6	51.5	49.4	48.1	47.7	44.9
Manual workers	38.6	41.1	39.8	39.5	40.2	38.2	35.8
Craftsmen, foremen, and kindred workers	14.2	14.1	12.0	12.8	13.0	11.6	10.5
Operatives and kindred workers	19.3	20.4	18.4	15.8	15.6	14.6	12.8
Laborers, except farm and mine	5.1	6.6	9.4	11.0	11.6	12.0	12.5
Service workers	11.6	10.5	11.7	9.8	7.8	9.6	9.0
Private household workers	2.8	2.6	4.7	4.1	3.3	5.0	5.4
Service workers, except private household	8.8	7.9	7.1	5.7	4.5	4.6	3.6
Farm workers	6.4	11.8	17.4	21.2	27.0	30.9	37.5
Farmers and farm managers	4.1	7.4	10.4	12.4	15.3	16.5	19.9
Farm laborers and foremen	2.3	4.4	7.0	8.8	11.7	14.4	17.7
Male:							
White-collar workers	36.4	30.5	26.6	25.2	21.4	20.2	17.6
Professional, technical, and kindred workers	10.8	7.2	5.8	4.8	3.8	3.5	3.4
Managers, officials, and proprietors, exc. farm	11.2	10.5	8.6	8.8	7.8	7.7	6.8
Clerical and kindred workers	7.2	6.4	5.8	5.5	5.3	4.4	2.8
Sales workers	7.2	6.4	6.4	6.1	4.5	4.6	4.6
Manual and service workers	54.9	54.6	51.7	50.0	48.2	45.1	40.8

Manual workers	48.5	48.4	45.6	45.2	44.5	41.3	37.6
Craftsmen, foremen, and kindred workers	20.4	19.0	15.5	16.2	16.0	14.1	12.6
Operatives and kindred workers	20.9	20.5	18.0	15.3	14.4	12.5	10.4
Laborers, except farm and mine	7.2	8.8	12.1	13.6	14.0	14.6	14.7
Service workers	6.4	6.2	6.1	4.8	3.7	3.8	3.1
Private household workers	0.1	0.2	0.3	0.2	0.2	0.2	0.2
Service workers, except private household	6.3	6.0	5.7	4.6	3.6	3.6	2.9
Farm workers	8.7	14.9	21.7	24.8	30.4	34.7	41.7
Farmers and farm managers	5.8	10.0	13.3	15.2	18.4	19.7	23.0
Farm laborers and foremen	2.9	4.9	8.4	9.6	12.1	15.0	18.7
Female:							
White-collar workers	57.5	52.5	44.9	44.2	38.8	26.1	17.8
Professional, technical, and kindred workers	13.8	12.2	12.8	13.8	11.7	9.8	8.2
Managers, officials, and proprietors, exc. farm	3.9	4.3	3.3	2.7	2.2	2.0	1.4
Clerical and kindred workers	31.5	27.4	21.5	20.9	18.7	9.2	4.0
Sales workers	8.3	8.6	7.4	6.8	6.3	5.1	4.3
Manual and service workers	40.7	43.9	51.0	47.3	47.6	58.1	63.2
Manual workers	18.1	22.4	21.6	19.8	23.7	25.7	27.8
Craftsmen, foremen, and kindred workers	1.3	1.5	1.1	1.0	1.2	1.4	1.4
Operatives and kindred workers	16.3	20.0	19.5	17.4	20.2	22.9	23.8
Laborers, except farm and mine	0.5	0.8	1.1	1.5	2.3	1.4	2.6
Service workers	22.6	21.5	29.4	27.5	23.9	32.4	35.4
Private household workers	8.4	8.9	18.1	17.8	15.8	24.0	28.7
Service workers, except private household	14.2	12.6	11.3	9.7	8.1	8.5	6.8
Farm workers	1.8	3.7	4.0	8.4	13.5	15.8	18.9
Farmers and farm managers	.6	0.7	1.2	2.4	3.2	3.8	5.9
Farm laborers and foremen	1.2	2.9	2.8	6.0	10.3	12.0	13.1

[a] David L. Kaplan and M. Claire Casey, *Occupational Trends in the United States, 1900 to 1950*. Bureau of the Census Working Paper, No. 5, Washington, D.C., 1958. Data for 1960 are quoted from the 1960 decennial census, Vol. I, *Characteristics of the Population*, Part 1, pp. 1-216–1-219.

Table 2. Methodological Characteristics and Proportion of Dissatisfied Workers in Ten Major Population Studies of Job Satisfaction

Researchers	Year	Scope of Sample	Sample Size and Composition	Percentage Dissatisfied	Measurement Approach			
					Direct Questions	Preference for Other Jobs	Work/ Nonwork Preference	Discrepancies: Job-Self; Actual-Ideal
Hoppock	1935	New Hope, Pa.	309 labor force members	15	√	√		
Shister and Reynolds	1949	New England City	800 manual workers (two samples)	12 21	√			
Centers	1949	Representative national	811 men	17	√			
Kornhauser	1952	Detroit, Mich.	324 employed persons	11	√			

Study	Year	Sample	N	%				
Morse and Weiss	1955	Probability national	401 employed men	20			✓	✓
Palmer	1957	Norristown, Pa.	517 labor force members	10	✓		✓	
Gurin, Veroff, and Feld	1960	Probability national	2,460 persons	23[a]		✓	✓	✓
Wilensky	1964	Detroit, Mich.	1,156 employed men	15			✓	✓
Kilpatrick, Cummings, and Jennings	1964	Representative national	1,142 employed persons (approximately 4,000 occupational supplement)	[b] minority			✓	
Converse and Robinson	1967	Probability national (urban)	1,244 persons	11[c]		✓	✓	

[a] Includes neutral and ambivalent responses; based on men only.
[b] Self-anchoring scales and reported means make comparison with other studies difficult, but responses are heavily positive. Mean is approximately 7.0 on a scale of 1–10.
[c] Percentage for men is 12.

Studies of single plants and other small undefined populations have produced results in the same range. In 1946, Hoppock began the practice of summarizing in the *Personnel and Guidance Journal* results of all published studies of job satisfaction; 12 years and 406 studies later, the median percentage of dissatisfied workers was 13.[14] Commercial polls, especially those of the Roper organization, asked direct questions about job satisfaction in hundreds of samples and seldom found the proportion of dissatisfied responses exceeding 20 percent.[15]

The interpretations that can be made from these data are discouragingly modest in relation to the number of researches and the years of work. There is relatively little active expressed dissatisfaction, although we must remind ourselves that each percentage point represents many hundreds of thousands. Neither is there much expression of great satisfaction; "pretty satisfied" is the mood. Whether that mood is changing cannot be determined from these data. The differences over time are confounded beyond resolution with differences in sample populations, procedures of data collection, and statistical treatment. Some authors regard the data as persistently biased toward overreporting satisfaction and understating dissatisfaction. Blauner attributes such biases to ego defense, Wilensky to a general cultural tendency to give socially approved responses, and Kornhauser to other adjustive processes.[16] But these are speculations in the course of substantive research, rather than methodological research findings in their own right.

The convergence of the satisfaction data is the most impressive characteristic in the above studies. In other respects, however, the satisfaction research is disappointing, and its disappointments are not all susceptible to remedy. Certainly we could have more systematic use of the same measures, repeated in time and for populations of known and representative characteristics. We could also gain from an insistence on accompanying data regarding the reliability and

---

Borow, ed., *Man in a World of Work.* Houghton Mifflin, Boston, 1964; Robinson, Athanasiou, and Head, *op. cit.;* Nancy C. Morse and Robert S. Weiss, "The Function and Meaning of Work and the Job," *American Sociological Review,* vol. 20, April, 1955, pp. 191–198; Gladys L. Palmer, "Attitudes Toward Work in an Industrial Community," *American Journal of Sociology,* vol. 63, July, 1957, pp. 17–26; Joseph L. Shister and L. G. Reynolds, *Job Horizons: A Study of Job Satisfaction and Labor Mobility.* Harper, New York, 1949; Hoppock, *op. cit.;* Arthur Kornhauser, *Detroit as the People See It.* Wayne University Press, Detroit, 1952; Richard Centers, *The Psychology of Social Classes.* Princeton University Press, Princeton, 1949; Gerald Gurin, Joseph L. Veroff, and Sheila Feld, *Americans View Their Mental Health.* Basic Books, New York, 1960.

[14] Blauner, *op. cit.*

[15] Wilensky, *op. cit.*

[16] Robert Blauner, *Alienation and Freedom.* University of Chicago Press, Chicago, 1964; Wilensky, *op. cit.;* Arthur Kornhauser, *Mental Health of the Industrial Worker.* Wiley, New York, 1965.

validity of such measures. But there are two inherent deficiencies in the concept of over-all job satisfaction in the above cited studies: (1) there is ample evidence that job satisfaction is not unitary, and (2) satisfaction, by any definition, is an interactive product of the person and his environment. These limitations do not, in my opinion, eliminate the concept of job satisfaction from serious research. They do, however, require that the thermometer readings on job satisfaction be accompanied by data showing responses to such specific job components as the work itself, co-workers, supervisors, and rewards, including mobility and security. A further requirement for interpreting responses of satisfaction and dissatisfaction is that they be shown in relation to the relevant properties of the person (e.g., needs and expectations). Such views are becoming increasingly common among researchers on the meaning of work.[17]

Robinson, Athanasiou, and Head have assessed 12 scales of job satisfaction in terms of methodological characteristics, including data on reliability and validity.[18] Table 3, which summarizes their assessment, is reprinted here for the convenience of research workers and for its relevance to the above criticisms.[19]

Occupational Status

The status of occupations, variously defined, is second to job satisfaction as a favored topic of research in the area of work. From a social-psychological view, the most interesting descriptive research on occupational status is based

[17] Raymond A. Katzell, "Personal Values, Job Satisfaction, and Job Behavior," in Henry Borow, ed., *Man in a World of Work*. Houghton Mifflin, Boston, 1964; William A. Faunce, "Job Satisfaction and the Meaning of Work," Michigan State University, Lansing, 1968, mimeographed.

[18] Robinson, Athanasiou, and Head, *op. cit.*

[19] Patricia C. Smith *et al.*, "Cornell Studies of Job Satisfaction: I–VI, Scale Characteristics of the Job Descriptive Index," Cornell University, Ithaca, 1965 ff., mimeographed; Kornhauser, *Mental Health of the Industrial Worker*; Marvin D. Dunnette *et al.*, "Factors Contributing to Job Satisfaction and Dissatisfaction in Sex Occupational Groups," University of Minnesota, Minneapolis, 1966, mimeographed; SRA Attitude Survey, Science Research Associates, Chicago; Robert Carlson *et al.*, *Minnesota Studies in Vocational Rehabilitation: XIII The Measurement of Employee Satisfaction*. Industrial Relations Center, University of Minnesota, 1962, Bulletin 35; Nancy C. Morse, *Satisfactions in the White-Collar Job*. Survey Research Center, Institute for Social Research, University of Michigan, Ann Arbor, 1953; George H. Johnson, "An Instrument for the Measurement of Job Satisfaction," *Personnel Psychology,* vol. 8, Spring, 1955, pp. 27–37; V. Schletzer, "A Study of the Predictive Effectiveness of the Strong Vocational Interest Blank for Job Satisfaction," unpublished doctoral dissertation, University of Minnesota, 1965; A. H. Brayfield and H. F. Rothe, "An Index of Job Satisfaction," *Journal of Applied Psychology,* vol. 35, 1951, pp. 307–311; Hoppock, *op. cit.;* W. A. Kerr, "On the Validity and Reliability of the Tear Ballot," *Journal of Applied Psychology,* vol. 32, June, 1948, pp. 275–281; A. Woods, "Employee Attitudes and Their Relation to Morale," *Journal of Applied Psychology,* vol. 28, August, 1944, pp. 285–301.

Table 3. Twelve Scales of Job Satisfaction: Methodological Characteristics

Feature of the Scale	Smith et al.	Kornhauser	Dunnette et al.	SRA[a]	IRC (Carlson et al.)	Morse	Johnson	Schletzer	Brayfield and Rothe	Hoppock	Kerr	Wood
Items:												
Sampling of content	+	+	+++	+	+	+	+	+	0	+	+	+
Item wording and simplicity	++	++	++	++	++	++	++	0	++	+	−	−
Item analysis	++	0	++	++	+++	++	++	0	++	0	0	+
Freedom from response set:												
Acquiescence	++	0	+	0	0	0	0	0	+	0	0	0
Social desirability	0	0	++	0	0	0	0	0	0	+	0	0
Statistical procedures:												
Sample	++	+	+	++	++	+	−	+	+	0	+	−
Norms presented	0	0	0	+++	++	+	+	++	+	+	++	+
Reliability: test-retest	++	0	++	++	0	0	+	0	0	0	0	0
Homogeneity	+	0	+	++	+	+	+	0	+	+	+	0
Discrimination of known groups	++	++	0	0	0	+	0	0	+	+	+	0
Cross validation	++	0	++	0	0	0	0	0	0	0	0	0
Other procedures	++	+	++	+	+	+	0	0	+	0	+	0
Scale itself over-all rating	++	++	++	++	++	+	+	+	+	+	0	0

Note: The above are scored according to the following scheme:

+++ Excellent and exemplary
++ Competent
+ Adequate
− Inadequate
−− Incompetent
0 No information or not enough information (or too conflicting) to make a final judgment
[a] Being revised.

on an ambitious survey and related work carried out at the National Opinion Research Center (NORC).[20] In the initial nationwide study in 1947, about three thousand respondents were asked to rate each of 90 occupations in terms of their *"own personal opinion* of the *general standing* that such a job has." The rating scale offered five alternatives, ranging from *"excellent* standing" to *"poor* standing." Converting the responses to a scale of 100 points, pooling responses, and reducing the 90 occupations to 11 major categories produced Table 4.

Table 4. Prestige Ratings of Occupations

Classification	Average Score
Government officials	90.8
Professional and semi-professional workers	80.6
Proprietors, managers, and official (except farm)	74.9
Clerical, sales, and kindred workers	68.2
Craftsmen, foremen, and kindred workers	68.0
Farmers and farm managers	61.3
Protective service workers	58.0
Operatives and kindred workers	52.8
Farm laborers	50.0
Service workers (except domestic and protective)	46.7
Laborers (except farm workers)	45.8

SOURCE: Paul K. Hatt and C. C. North, "Prestige Ratings of Occupations," in Sigmund Nosow and William H. Form, eds., *Man, Work, and Society.* Basic Books, New York, 1962.

The procedure was repeated in 1963 with a much smaller sample, and the over-all ratings showed remarkable stability ($r = .99$). They are stable also across cultures.[21]

The ratings are not "objective" if objectivity implies expertise and a kind of emotional neutrality. They have been criticized directly on these grounds, and in my opinion inappropriately.[22] The concept of status is by definition

[20] Paul K. Hatt and C. C. North, "Prestige Ratings of Occupations," in Sigmund Nosow and William H. Form, eds., *Man, Work, and Society.* Basic Books, New York, 1962.

[21] R. Hodge, P. Siegel, and P. Rossi, "Occupational Prestige in the United States: 1925–1963," in R. Bendix and S. M. Lipset, eds., *Class, Status, and Power.* Free Press, New York, 1965; R. Hodge, D. Treiman, and P. Rossi, "A Comparative Study of Occupational Prestige," in R. Bendix and S. M. Lipset, eds., *Class, Status, and Power.* Free Press, New York, 1965.

[22] J. Gusfield and Mildred Schwartz, "The Meanings of Occupational Prestige: Reconsideration of the NORC Scale," *American Sociological Review,* vol. 28, April, 1963, pp. 265–270.

evaluative; it is the combined judgments of the relevant public concerning how good (or not good) it is to occupy a particular social position. The NORC scale was generated by procedures that seem to correspond almost exactly to this conceptual definition. A society in which such consensual judgments were not made in daily life would be literally without status, although occupations could of course be differentiated on specific dimensions of skill, physical demand, hazardousness, variety, and the like.

The NORC ratings have been compared with the socioeconomic scores of the 1960 census which are based on the average of the percentiles of income and education for each occupation. The NORC ratings have been compared also with those of the Duncan *Socio-economic Status Scale,* which is based on 1950 census data for occupations, income, and education. The weighting of income and education in the Duncan scale was determined by regression equations relating the census data to the NORC ratings.[23]

These three scales are in close agreement, partly for artifactual reasons, partly because people apparently evaluate jobs according to the income they provide and the education they require. The latter point is of course researchable, and our understanding of status would be deepened by research on the bases of social evaluation of occupations.

Alienation and Connectedness

Explorations into the meaning of work beyond expression of satisfaction and dissatisfaction have been made by various authors, but by methods too diverse to permit the sort of summary comparisons we have attempted for job satisfaction and status. In such studies, there is a recurrent pattern of ambivalence, however, that I consider to be deep-rooted and important.

It is well exemplified by the results of two sample surveys—one on the meaning of work and one on the definition of work.[24] In the first of these studies, which was based on a nationwide sample, 80 percent of employed men said that they would go on working even if they inherited enough money to live comfortably without working. This response, although it was considerably higher than the authors expected, is consistent with the relatively high ratio of satisfied to dissatisfied workers based on more direct questions. The reasons for continuing to work, however, suggest a qualified kind of satisfaction, to say the least. Almost 40 percent of employed men gave obviously negative reasons for continuing to work—that is, reasons having to do with the fear and uncertainty of not working. Men said they "would feel lost, would go crazy, wouldn't

[23] A. J. Reiss, Jr., O. D. Duncan, P. K. Hatt, and C. C. North, *Occupations and Social Status.* Free Press, New York, 1961.

[24] Morse and Weiss, *op. cit.;* Robert S. Weiss and Robert L. Kahn, "Definitions of Work and Occupation," *Social Problems,* vol. 8, Fall, 1960, pp. 142–151.

know what to do with the time." And more than another 30 percent stated in more positive terms what seems to be a similar view; they said they would continue working in order "to keep occupied."

These respondents sound unable to think of any other activity as "occupying" as work, rather than work-involved and fulfilled. This clearly implies an attachment to work, but not necessarily to one's present occupation or work status. Indeed, the majority of men expressed a preference for continuing work at a different occupation—typically higher in status and autonomy. The definition of work, in the words of employed men, further reveals their ambivalence. In response to the question: "What makes the difference between something you would call work and something you would not call work?" almost 60 percent of the definitions could be summarized by the phrase: Work is necessary but not enjoyed. Typical definitions: Work is something you have to do whether you like doing it or not. If it's something you can do or not as you wish, it's not work. You have to do one (work), and don't have to do the other (hobby).

The descriptive data support the common assertion that the work role is perhaps the major linkage of individual to society, at least for the adult man. But the questions of theory and of social policy do not turn only on the choice of being so linked or cast adrift; they have to do also with the nature of the connectedness. For most workers it is a choice between no work connection (usually with severe attendant economic penalties and a conspicuous lack of meaningful alternative activities) and a work connection burdened with negative qualities (routine, compulsory scheduling, dependency, etc.). In the circumstances, the individual has no difficulty with the choice; he chooses work, pronounces himself moderately satisfied, and tells us more only if the questions become more searching. Then we learn that he can order jobs clearly in terms of their status or desirability, wants his son to be employed differently from himself, and if given a choice, would seek a different occupation.

Relationships and Explanations

I introduced this chapter on the meaning of work by asserting that the choice of statistics for social indicators in this area, as in any other, should be made in the context of what is known about relationships among variables. An indicator, to be literal about it, is of interest only for the significance of what it indicates, and that significance is defined by the network of causes, effects, and associations of which the indicated variable is an element.

To the extent that we know that network, we can choose more wisely what variables to measure as social indicators. We can, for example, choose a variable that allows us to intervene early in some causal sequence, rather than being forced to deal with more costly and difficult social outcomes. If it were established that monotonous and repetitive work led to feelings of alienation, which in turn led to poor functioning in the life roles of husband and father, with consequent problems of personality and performance on the part of the children—if all this, which has been more asserted than demonstrated—were known, it would be a great social gain to choose as indicators the changing content of jobs and the emotional state of alienation among workers.

A second reason for introducing the idea of relationships into a discussion of social indicators, however, is the possibility of treating a relationship itself as a social indicator. The relationships between some variables may be beyond our power to change; in other cases, the relationship may properly be made a matter of social policy and intervention. For example, a strong positive relationship exists between occupation and satisfaction. Since over-all satisfaction is a complex outcome of the attributes of a job—content, pay, supervision, and others—the differences among occupations could be made larger or smaller as a matter of social policy. The practice of giving premium pay for particularly hazardous or unpleasant work would presumably reduce occupational differences in over-all satisfaction, if that were deemed desirable.

The relationships among variables that might be included as relevant to the meaning of work are almost beyond count. Our discussion of some of them is organized around the concept of *job satisfaction,* its determinants and its consequences. We do this partly because job satisfaction, while by no means an ideal social indicator, is the most researched variable in the area of work. It is significant in its own right, if we make the value assumption that human satisfaction and dissatisfaction are outcomes of importance for social theory and practice. Moreover, for a generation or more, much of the research and theorizing about work has involved satisfaction, either as a cause or as an outcome. We will consider it in both ways.

Determinants of Job Satisfaction

There are many studies dealing with hypothesized causes of satisfaction and dissatisfaction at work, and there have been many interpretations of such studies. There have also been bits of theory and speculation on the subject, unencumbered by data. Fortunately, several excellent summaries of research on satisfaction have been made in recent years. The most useful for our present purposes are Vroom's *Work and Motivation* and Robinson's *Measures of Occupational Attitudes and Occupational Characteristics.*[25] I have relied heavily on these two works for coverage of the research literature and occasionally for interpretation.

In reviewing studies of determinants of job satisfaction, it may be useful to keep in mind three different approaches. The first infers the causes of satis-

---

[25] Vroom, *op. cit.;* Robinson, Athanasiou, and Head, *op. cit.*

faction from its components. If factor analysis, for example, indicates that satisfaction with supervision is distinct from satisfaction with pay or job content, the inference is made that changes in any of these conditions would cause corresponding changes in its component of satisfaction. There is a sort of naive realism inherent in this approach and, unfortunately, it is not often put to the test.

A second approach attempts to establish the causes of satisfaction by means of correlations (or other measures of association) between descriptive characteristics of jobs and the affective responses of job holders. This is certainly preferable to the first approach, especially if the job descriptions are not based only on statements of the same person who attests to his own satisfaction or dissatisfaction.

The third approach is experimental; it involves the introduction or observation of changes in the work role, and subsequent determination of changes occurring in level of satisfaction. Such evidence, given reasonable attention to other aspects of research design, would be more compelling than that produced by the other approaches.

There is, however, room for more than one approach; experimental and quasi-experimental designs typically suffer from lack of representativeness, survey designs from uncertainties about temporal order. The two can complement each other, but unfortunately the research on job satisfaction offers few studies that are either representative or experimental. Rather, the field is filled with studies that are done on unrepresentative populations, that omit any mention of negative findings, and that neither replicate nor are replicated. This state of methodological affairs is almost ideal for the production of false positives, and they must be many.

With these risks in mind, we can still claim the following factors to be highly probable causes of satisfaction and dissatisfaction at work: occupation, status, supervision, peer relationships, job content, wages and other extrinsic rewards, promotion, and physical conditions of work. In addition, we can mention organizational structure as a separate contextual factor. All these, however, are categorical descriptions rather than specific determinants of satisfaction and dissatisfaction; we will consider the pattern of evidence within each category, citing specific studies for illustrative purposes. At the end of the discussion, we will present schematically the major studies bearing on each determinant of satisfaction at work.

Occupation

Almost everyone who has studied job satisfaction across any considerable array of occupations has found significant differences among occupations. Moreover, these differences bear a strong linear relationship to status, whether defined in terms of pooled evaluations (NORC) or in terms of socioeconomic data alone (census). Table 5 illustrates the magnitude of the status-satisfaction relationship; it is synthesized from several different studies, each of which used as a measure of satisfaction the proportion of persons in an occupation who said they would try to get into the same kind of work if they were to begin their careers again.[26]

Table 5. Proportions in Occupational Groups Who Would Choose Similar Work Again[a]

Professional and Lower White-Collar Occupations	Percent	Working-Class Occupations	Percent
Urban university professor[b]	93	Skilled printers	52
Mathematicians	91	Paper workers	42
Physicists	89	Skilled auto workers	41
Biologists	89	Skilled steelworkers	41
Chemists	86	Textile workers	31
Firm lawyers[b]	85	Blue-collar workers[b]	24
School superintendents[c]	85	Unskilled steelworkers	21
Lawyers	83	Unskilled auto workers	16
Journalists (Washington correspondents)	82		
Church university professors[b]	77		
Solo lawyers[b]	75		
White-collar workers[b]	43		

[a] Data in this table are based on responses to the question: "What type of work would you try to get into if you could start all over again?" Entries are primarily from a study of 3,000 workers in 16 industries, conducted by the Roper organization.

[b] Probability samples or universes of six professional groups and a cross section of the "middle class" (lower middle class and upper working class) in the Detroit area, stratified for comparability with respect to age, income, occupational stratum, and other characteristics. From Harold Wilensky, "Varieties of Work Experience," in Henry Borow, *Man in a World of Work*. Houghton Mifflin, Boston, 1964.

[c] From a 1952–53 Massachusetts sample taken from Neal Gross, Ward Mason, and W. A. McEachern, *Explorations in Role Analysis: Studies of the School Superintendency Role*. Wiley, New York, 1958.

The table is remarkable for the range of response—from 93 percent of university professors to 16 percent of unskilled auto workers say they would seek the same type of work again. The sharpest break comes between professional and nonprofessional jobs, although there is an additional difference between white-collar and blue-collar jobs in favor of the former. But that differ-

---

[26] For related versions of this table and further description of the samples, see Robinson, Athanasiou, and Head, *op. cit.;* Wilensky, *op. cit.;* Blauner, *Alienation and Freedom*.

ence is not so great as the differences within these categories which correspond to skill and status levels in the blue-collar jobs and to clerical and sales vs. professional work in the white-collar jobs. Indeed, there is some overlap between blue-collar and white-collar jobs, with the skilled trades showing a larger proportion of satisfied workers than the sales and clerical jobs.

Studies that compare occupations in terms of responses to more direct questions about satisfaction show a similar but less sharp relationship. It seems likely that this reflects the combination of wish and realism that is evoked by such questions. The researcher asks the worker if he is satisfied with his job, and leaves him to provide his own frame of reference—his own reference group, his own range of accessible occupations, his own assessment of his talents and the opportunities of the labor market. To the extent that he has made a "successful adjustment," he reports some degree of satisfaction.

The occupation-status-satisfaction pattern is not limited to the United States. Inkeles reports it for six other nations high in industrial development; Hodge and his colleagues for 23 countries in different stages of industrial development; and Zdravomyslov and Iadov for a random sample of Leningrad workers under the age of 30.[27]

There are few findings so consistent as these, and it is interesting to speculate on the reasons for the consistency. Many authors have done so and propose explanations in terms of prestige, control over conditions of one's own work, cohesiveness of one's work group (if any), ego gratification from the challenge and variety of the work itself, and many others.

A somewhat different, although not incompatible, explanation would begin by regarding an occupation as a role that is defined in terms of certain expected activities and certain rewards for their performance. Each occupation comprises a unique cluster of satisfaction-giving and dissatisfaction-imposing activities, and a unique set of extrinsic rewards (and penalties). When occupations are ordered according to status (in the NORC sense of the term), we are simply asking people to tell which occupation-defined sets of activities and rewards are best and which are least attractive. If we subsequently find that these rankings correspond to expressions of satisfaction or dissatisfaction on the part of individuals actually performing these different occupational roles, we have only demonstrated that the norms about what makes jobs good or bad are widely shared, irrespective of one's own occupation.

If we find, as we do, that these rankings correspond well to less subjective measures of status, such as the socioeconomic measures of the Census Bureau, we have demonstrated that, in the particular culture under study, the financial

[27] Alex Inkeles, "Industrial Man: The Relation of Status to Experience, Perception, and Value," *American Journal of Sociology*, vol. 66, July, 1960, pp. 1–31; Hodge, Treiman, and Rossi, *op. cit.;* A. Zdravomyslov and V. Iadov, "An Attempt at a Concrete Study of Attitude Toward Work," *Soviet Sociology*, vol. 3, 1964, pp. 3–15.

rewards of jobs and the education required for access to them generally follow and thus intensify the pattern of other rewarding characteristics.

The importance of status as a determinant of job satisfaction can be overstated of course. There is variability in satisfaction within occupations, and there is variability as well in the various aspects of jobs that make them good or bad in the eyes of men. These points are well illustrated in Tables 6 and 7, the first from a nationwide study of the Survey Research Center which investigated time use and the meaning of time to the individual. Directed by Converse and Robinson, this survey included 1,244 adults (aged 19 to 65) resident in urban areas throughout the United States (see Table 6).[28]

Table 7 presents schematically an interpretation of the research results on occupation, status, and satisfaction.[29] Since it is a composite of many unrepresentative and incompatible studies, it is best regarded as a set of hypotheses.

Job Content

It is difficult to separate the content of a job from its status, prestige, and the constellation of other characteristics included in a real-life occupation or job-in-organization. If one risks interpretation in spite of such confounding, it appears that the intrinsic characteristics of the work have substantial effects on satisfaction and dissatisfaction. Direct questions to workers about sources of satisfaction and dissatisfaction, or about elements that make jobs good or bad, show job content among the several most important aspects of work.[30]

Fractionation, Repetition, Specialization

Most observers of industrial development would agree that jobs tend to become more atomized and repetitive as technology becomes more sophisticated, in the current sense of that term. The doctrines of Taylor, the Gilbreths, and the succeeding generations of time-study engineers have been explicit about the productive advantages of simplicity and repetitiveness and specialization in industry.[31] This view has been supported and implemented actively by industrial management, and it has been largely unchallenged by organized labor.

[28] This study of time use, directed by Philip E. Converse and John P. Robinson, was deliberately planned as a bench-mark study for comparative use in future decades.

[29] Tables 6 and 7 are reprinted from Robinson, Athanasiou, and Head, *op. cit.*

[30] F. Herzberg, B. Mausner, and Barbara Snyderman, *The Motivation to Work,* 2nd ed. Wiley, New York, 1959; Gurin, Veroff, and Feld, *op. cit.;* F. Kilpatrick, M. Cummings, and M. K. Jennings, *The Image of the Federal Service.* Brookings Institution, Washington, D.C., 1964.

[31] F. W. Taylor, *The Principles of Scientific Management.* Harper, New York, 1911; F. B. Gilbreth and Lillian M. Gilbreth, *Fatigue Study.* Macmillan, New York, 1919.

The critics of extreme specialization have, for the most part, been social scientists. From the British studies of 40 years ago to the present, they have provided a consistent and substantial body of evidence that highly fractionated and repetitive tasks are performed by dissatisfied workers.[32]

Job rotation and job enlargement are counterproposals to conventional time study and work simplification; definitive evidence of their effects is not yet available. Whether automation reduces or eliminates dissatisfying repetitiveness in factory jobs is also unsettled, although it may tend in this direction.[33]

We badly need a set of objective measures to characterize job content in commensurate terms across a wide range of occupations. These could then be used to establish base lines and trends within job categories, to make comparisons between jobs, and to determine experimentally the effects of changing job content.

Autonomy and Control

The assembly line, which has come to be regarded as the epitome of industrial work, not only defines jobs in simplified and repetitive terms, it stipulates the exact method by which the job shall be done and the pace at which it must be performed. Fewer studies have been made of the effects of these characteristics on satisfaction, but those that have been made show negative relationships, especially between control of work pace and satisfaction. Workers on assembly lines express dissatisfaction about the mechanical pacing;[34] comparisons of factory-worker satisfaction under mechanically controlled and self-controlled conditions show substantial differences in favor of the latter;[35] and workers in all occupations rate self-determination highest among the elements that define an ideal job.[36]

Supervision

That the characteristics of supervisory behavior are related to worker satisfaction is undeniable; many studies attest to the relationship and none present contrary evidence. Many theoretical schemes and many measures have been proposed to describe the relevant behaviors. Most of the research depends

[32] S. Wyatt, J. A. Fraser, and F. G. L. Stock, *The Effects of Monotony in Work*. Her Majesty's Stationery Office, London, 1929 (Industrial Fatigue Research Board Report 56).

[33] F. C. Mann and L. R. Hoffman, *Automation and the Worker*. Holt, New York, 1960.

[34] C. R. Walker and R. H. Guest, *The Man on the Assembly Line*. Harvard University Press, Cambridge, Mass., 1952.

[35] J. Walker and R. Marriott, "A Study of Some Attitudes to Factory Work," *Occupational Psychology*, vol. 25, July, 1951, pp. 181–191.

[36] Kilpatrick, Cummings, and Jennings, *op. cit.*

Table 6. Average Ratings of Various Aspects of Job, by Occupation[a]

	Pay	Job Security	Kind of Work Place	Chance to Use Skills	Kind of People	Freedom to Plan	Chance to Learn
Professional, people-oriented:							
Artist, musician	3.40	3.80	1.80	2.00	1.25	1.80	3.00
Professor, librarian	2.75	1.57	1.75	1.25	1.13	1.63	1.63
Advising profession	2.08	1.63	1.60	1.20	1.37	1.26	1.43
School teachers	2.59	1.74	1.94	1.15	1.65	1.50	1.35
Other medical	2.53	1.73	1.67	1.47	1.71	1.73	2.00
Professional, data-oriented:							
Scientist, physician	1.75	2.06	1.25	1.56	1.50	1.69	1.56
Accountant, auditor	1.94	1.31	2.25	1.62	1.85	1.62	1.69
Engineer	1.97	1.58	1.84	1.72	1.58	1.58	1.79
Technician	2.73	2.12	1.91	1.79	1.82	2.03	2.09
Managerial:							
Self-employed (large firm)	2.52	1.83	1.95	1.43	1.64	1.26	1.65
Self-employed (other)	2.91	2.47	2.00	1.62	2.03	1.47	1.91
Salaried	2.14	1.57	1.72	1.46	1.68	1.62	1.87
Clerical:							
Bookkeeper	3.06	2.06	2.17	1.56	1.56	1.94	2.06
Secretary, typist	2.59	1.87	2.04	1.90	1.66	2.14	2.57
Other clerical	2.61	2.18	2.00	2.46	1.74	2.43	2.78

Sales:						
High status (goods)	2.91	1.91	1.78	1.64	1.36	1.64	1.45
High status (services)	2.55	1.82	1.73	1.18	1.73	1.27	2.00
Sales clerk	3.33	2.43	1.93	2.25	1.71	2.64	3.04
Other sales	2.86	2.59	2.50	1.95	1.58	1.59	2.49
Skilled:						
Self-employed	3.13	3.38	2.50	1.88	1.86	2.25	2.50
Foreman	2.18	2.15	2.28	2.05	2.24	2.13	2.34
Other	2.54	2.41	2.22	1.93	1.95	2.67	2.60
Semiskilled:						
Operatives	2.72	2.49	2.32	2.71	1.93	3.34	3.34
Service:						
Protective	3.14	1.29	2.19	2.33	1.52	2.85	2.76
Armed forces	3.00	1.33	1.78	2.67	1.89	2.33	2.67
Household	3.50	2.79	2.09	2.75	1.81	1.83	3.50
Other service	3.16	2.12	1.91	2.44	1.83	2.35	3.13
Unskilled:						
Laborer	3.10	2.31	2.27	2.72	1.83	2.97	2.93
Over-all average:						
Men	2.63	2.19	2.12	1.53	1.79	2.30	2.51
Women	2.73	2.13	1.91	2.11	1.63	2.27	2.72
Standard Deviation	1.33	1.34	1.17	1.36	.90	1.48	1.58

[a] Scores run from 1 = very good to 5 = poor.

Table 7. Hypothesized Differences between Occupations in Job Satisfaction

Occupational Category	Most Satisfied	Very Satisfied	Satisfied	Ambivalent	Slightly Dissatisfied	Somewhat Dissatisfied
Professional-Technical	Professors Librarians Schoolteachers (female)	Public Advisers Other people-oriented Nurses Artists	Scientists Accountants	Engineers Schoolteachers (male)	Technicians	
Managerial	Salaried (upper mgmt.)	Salaried (other)	Self-employed (large firm)		Self-employed (other)	
Sales			High-status	Salesclerks (women)		Salesclerks (men)
Clerical			Secretaries Bookkeepers	Misc. clerical		clerical Repetitive
Skilled			Foremen	Craftsmen	Skilled	
Semiskilled				Higher	Middle	Repetitive
Unskilled						Laborers
Service		Protective	Armed	Household Other (women)		Other (men)
Farmer		Owner (large)		Owner (small)		Laborer

upon reports of individual workers both for satisfaction and for the supervisory behavior that satisfies or dissatisfies—a weak basis for inference. There are conspicuous exceptions, however: studies that measure supervisory behavior independent of worker satisfaction and studies that measure changes in satisfaction after changes have been induced in supervision.[37]

The effects of the supervisor's interpersonal behavior are better documented than his planning, execution, or technical skills. High worker satisfaction is associated with behaviors that are considerate of employees and that are employee-centered.[38] It is associated also with supervisory behavior that shares decision-making power and accepts influence from subordinates. Evidence for the effects of such behavior, sometimes described as delegation and sometimes as participative or consultative management, extends from the experiments of of Lewin, Lippitt, and White to the current summary of Tannenbaum.[39]

Peer Relationships

Most people are more satisfied to work as members of a group than in isolation. This statement must be qualified by other factors, particularly those of personality and those referring to the quality of interaction in the group. Nevertheless, most research has not taken such "third factors" into account but has sought and found direct relationships between interaction and satisfaction. Workers prefer jobs that permit interaction, are more likely to quit jobs that prevent peer interaction, and cite congenial peer relationships as among the major characteristics of good jobs.

In addition to the studies showing positive effects of peer interaction, peer accessibility, and limited physical distance, a number of studies in the laboratory and a few in the field show the importance of acceptance by the group. It is likely that the consistent pattern of research on peer interaction alone reflects a general norm of acceptance within work groups. Little work has been done on the conditions under which such a norm develops, but Newcomb's work has emphasized similarity of attitudes and Deutsch's the existence of

[37] Morse, *op. cit.;* Nancy C. Morse and E. Reimer, "The Experimental Change of a Major Organizational Variable," *Journal of Abnormal and Social Psychology,* vol. 52, 1956, pp. 120–129; Alfred J. Marrow, David G. Bowers, and Stanley E. Seashore, *Management by Participation, Creating a Climate for Personal and Organizational Development.* Harper, New York, 1967.

[38] J. K. Hemphill and A. E. Coons, "Development of the Leader Behavior Description Questionnaire," in R. M. Stogdill and A. E. Coons, eds., *Leader Behavior: Its Description and Measurement.* Bureau of Business Research, Ohio State University, Columbus, 1957, pp. 6–38 (Research Monograph 88); Rensis Likert, *New Patterns of Management.* McGraw-Hill, New York, 1961.

[39] Arnold S. Tannenbaum, ed., *Control in Organizations.* McGraw-Hill, New York, 1968.

shared goals under conditions in which cooperation is rewarded.[40] Sherif and Jones and Vroom have demonstrated the same effect as Deutsch.[41]

Wages and Promotion

The importance of pay to work satisfaction, and the nature of the relationship is not clear. Income level is often found positively associated with satisfaction but in most studies other factors are varying as well. Lawler and Porter have found that wage level was related to wage satisfaction among 2,000 managers, even when managerial level was held constant.[42] Other recent studies have suggested that the effect of wage level on satisfaction depends on frame of reference, on perceptions of equity, or on cognitive dissonance.[43]

It seems likely that the over-all pay-satisfaction relationship will hold.[44] In any monetary culture in which wages and salaries constitute for most people the major or only source of income and the means of access to almost all goods and services, it is difficult to imagine that wages will not be a determinant of job satisfaction. About the variations and qualifications of that statement, however, we still have much to learn.

Promotional opportunities are considered by some authors as distinct from wages and other extrinsic rewards, although some factor analyses do not support the distinction.[45] Studies of promotional opportunities are not numerous and those that have been done are limited to the individual's perception of his own opportunities. Such studies show the perceived likelihood of promotion to be positively related to satisfaction. One attempt to test this relationship

[40] T. M. Newcomb, "The Prediction of Interpersonal Attraction," *American Psychologist*, vol. 11, November, 1956, pp. 575–586; *idem, The Acquaintance Process.* Holt, New York, 1961; M. Deutsch, "An Experimental Study of the Effects of Co-operation and Competition Upon Group Process," *Human Relations*, vol. 2, no. 3, 1949, pp. 199–231.

[41] M. Sherif and Carolyn W. Sherif, *Groups in Harmony and Tension: An Integration of Studies on Intergroup Relations.* Harper, New York, 1953; S. C. Jones and V. H. Vroom, "Division of Labor and Performance Under Cooperative and Competitive Conditions," *Journal of Abnormal and Social Psychology*, vol. 68, March, 1964, pp. 313–320.

[42] E. E. Lawler and L. W. Porter, "Perceptions Regarding Management Compensation," *Industrial Relations*, vol. 3, October, 1963, pp. 41–49.

[43] M. Patchen, *The Choice of Wage Comparisons.* Prentice-Hall, Englewood Cliffs, N.J., 1961; J. S. Adams, "Toward an Understanding of Inequity," *Journal of Abnormal and Social Psychology*, vol. 67, November, 1963, pp. 422–436; E. Jaques, *Equitable Payment.* Wiley, New York, 1961; J. S. Adams, *Wage Inequities, Productivity, and Work Quality.* Institute of Industrial Relations, University of California, Berkeley, 1964; Robert B. Athanasiou, "Opinion Formation Through Dissonance Reduction," unpublished thesis, Rensselaer Polytechnic Institute, Troy, 1965.

[44] Lawler and Porter, *op. cit.*

[45] Robert P. Quinn, and Robert L. Kahn, Survey Research Center, Institute for Social Research, University of Michigan, 1969, unpublished manuscript.

in the laboratory produced an opposite and unexpected result.[46] Vroom proposes an ingenious reconciliation of the data, but the issue remains unsettled.[47]

The inherent difficulty in interpreting the promotion-satisfaction relationships is the complexity and variety of promotion as a concept. It is, by definition, a change of job, a change of status, and not infrequently a change in occupation. On this basis alone, the concept of promotion is subject to all the confounding and merging of variables already discussed in considering problems of status and occupation. But in addition, promotion constitutes a major means of recognition for work done, a means of showing approval and acceptance. It also introduces variety (as in job rotation) and, by presumption, the challenge of expanded or more difficult activities. It would require a major effort to isolate the effects of these components of promotion on satisfaction, and there is no present sign that such an effort is being made.

Certainly one would predict a strong positive relationship between promotional opportunities and job satisfaction, given the obtained relationship between status and satisfaction. Since status ranking is an ordering of jobs according to their desirability, and promotion is by definition an increase in status (and, therefore, satisfaction), promotional opportunity becomes an instrumental value in a job and a source of satisfaction itself.

Working Conditions

The physical conditions of work and the hours required are difficult to assess in terms of over-all job satisfaction. Certainly, extremely bad working conditions (hours, temperature, ventilation, and the like) can make any job literally unbearable. In the range ordinarily encountered, however, such conditions are prevented by law, by union contract, and by the norms of the larger society. As a result, working conditions emerge as a separate and identifiable factor, but as affecting satisfaction less than the other factors we have considered.[48] Herzberg considers working conditions incapable of satisfying, although quite capable of dissatisfying.[49] Kilpatrick *et al.* find them very low on the list of things that make a job either ideal or "worst possible."[50]

Shift work appears as an exception to the preceding pattern. Studies of shift work typically (but not always) show significantly lower levels of satisfaction among employees who must work at night, and still lower satisfaction levels for those who must change from one shift to another. A large and in-

[46] A. J. Spector, "Expectations, Fulfillment, and Morale," *Journal of Abnormal and Social Psychology,* vol. 52, January, 1956, pp. 51–56.

[47] Vroom, *op. cit.*

[48] Quinn and Kahn, *op. cit.*

[49] Herzberg, Mausner, and Snyderman, *op. cit.*

[50] Kilpatrick, Cummings, and Jennings, *op. cit.*

tensive study of shift workers by Mott *et al.* explains this effect in terms of the individual's pattern of other valued activities and the extent to which shift work interferes with these.[51]

Organizational Structure and Context

Most studies of job characteristics and job satisfaction have ignored the larger structure in which particular jobs are located. Within the past few years, however, there has been an increasing emphasis on the systemic properties of organizations.[52] This implies the study of jobs in the context of organizational characteristics. Kahn *et al.* found that job-related tensions increased with organizational size.[53] Porter and Lawler summarize the evidence for relationships between satisfaction and a number of organizational and sub-organizational properties.[54] They find that satisfaction decreases with organizational size, although the issue is complicated by the size of the total organization and the relevant sub-unit. They find the evidence unclear with respect to tall vs. flat organizational structures: satisfaction is greatest in small, flat organizations, but in large organizations the relationship does not hold. It also seems plausible that large organizations differ from small ones in the dimensions on which they provide greatest satisfaction, with small organizations providing more opportunity for self-actualization and large organizations more security and social gratification. Porter and Lawler find the evidence ambiguous with respect to a third organizational characteristic—degree of centralization or decentralization.

Within organizations, they report higher satisfaction at upper managerial levels than at lower, in line positions than in staff, and in small sub-units than in large ones. Whether span of control has any effect on satisfaction independent of these factors is unclear.

Consequences of Satisfaction

The consequences of job satisfaction have been much less researched than its causes, with the signal exception of the long-hypothesized relationship between satisfaction and performance. The evidence on the latter point, in my

[51] Mott *et al., op. cit.*

[52] Daniel Katz and Robert L. Kahn, *The Social Psychology of Organizations.* Wiley, New York, 1966; Paul R. Lawrence and Jay W. Lorsch, *Organization and Environment.* Harvard University, Cambridge, 1967.

[53] Robert L. Kahn *et al., Organizational Stress: Studies in Role Conflict and Ambiguity.* Wiley, New York, 1964.

[54] L. W. Porter and E. E. Lawler, III, "Properties of Organization Structure in Relation to Job Attitudes and Job Behavior," *Psychological Bulletin*, vol. 64, July, 1965, pp. 23–31.

view, is that satisfaction is related to productivity in some circumstances and not in others, and that these circumstances have yet to be defined. In ordinary industrial situations the relationship seems on the average to be negligible. Brayfield and Crockett in an extensive review come to a decision of no relationship.[55] Herzberg *et al.* reviewed 26 studies, including some of those assessed by Brayfield and Crockett, and found evidence for a positive satisfaction-productivity link in 14 studies, none whatsoever in 9 studies, and a negative relationship in 3 studies.[56] Vroom reviewed 20 studies in which the magnitude of the satisfaction-productivity relationship was given, and found a correlational range from —.21 to +.86, with an excessively modest mean of +.21.[57]

Likert proposes that there is an inherent tendency for low satisfaction to be expressed in low productivity, but that several factors obscure or counteract this tendency.[58] One such factor is the pace-determining constraints and demands which in many jobs, particularly on the assembly line, determine the rate of production regardless of the affective and motivational state of the worker. Another is the inadequacy of productivity criteria—for example, their failure to take account of the costs of conflict, retraining, and the like. A third is the neglect of time; Likert argues that the effects of low satisfaction are often not immediately manifest.

Evidence is consistent, if not rich, with respect to the association of satisfaction with other behavioral measures, including absence, turnover, and accidents.

Least in quantity but impressive in their implications are those studies that show a relationship between job satisfaction and the success with which the individual functions in other life roles.[59] Problems of causality are extremely difficult in this connection, and we badly need studies that resolve them.

Outlined below are the major sources for our discussion of the determinants and consequences of job satisfaction. The names of authors are grouped to show the research findings on which I have relied.

I. Some hypothesized determinants of job satisfaction, by author
  A. Job content
    1. General
      Herzberg, Mausner, and Synderman, 1959; Schwartz, Jenusaitis, and Stark, 1963; Walker and Guest, 1952; Gurin, Veroff, and Feld, 1960; Kilpatrick, Cummings, and Jennings, 1964.
    2. Fractionization—Repetition—Specialization

[55] A. H. Brayfield and W. H. Crockett, "Employee, Attitudes and Employee Performance," *Psychological Bulletin*, vol. 52, September, 1955, pp. 396–424.
[56] Herzberg *et al., op. cit.*
[57] Vroom, *op. cit.*
[58] Likert, "Dual Function of Statistics" and *New Patterns of Management.*
[59] Mott *et al., op. cit.;* Gurin, Veroff, and Feld, *op. cit.*

Brown and Ghiselli, 1953; Kephart, 1948; Wyatt, Fraser, and Stock, 1929; Walker and Guest, 1952; Walker, 1950, 1954; Guest, 1957; Elliott, 1953; Trist and Bamforth, 1951; Baldamus, 1951; Mann and Hoffman, 1960; Kornhauser, 1922; Viteles, 1924; Kriedt and Gadel, 1953; Bills, 1923; Karsten, 1928; Kornhauser, 1965.

3. Autonomy, control over methods

Viteles, 1932; Coch and French, 1948; Walker and Guest, 1952; Walker and Marriott, 1951; Marriott and Denerley, 1955; Kilpatrick, Cummings, and Jennings, 1964.

4. Status and level

Uhrbrock, 1934; Hoppock, 1935; Thorndike, 1935; Super, 1939; Miller, 1941; Paterson and Stone, 1942; Heron, 1948; Centers, 1948; Katz, 1949; Mann, 1953; Morse, 1953; Gurin, Veroff, and Feld, 1960; Kornhauser, 1964; Baldamus, 1951; Reynolds, 1951; Porter, 1962.

B. Supervision

1. General

Robinson, Athanasiou, and Head, 1967; Jackson, 1953; Bell and French, 1950; Robinson, Athanasiou, and Head, 1967; Vroom and Mann, 1960.

2. Human relations skills

Kahn and Katz, 1960; Halpin and Winer, 1957; Fleishman, 1957 a, b; Likert, 1958; Katz, Maccoby, and Morse, 1950; Katz, Maccoby, Gurin, and Floor, 1951; Hemphill and Coons, 1957; Halpin, 1957; Fleishman, Harris, and Burtt, 1955; Likert, 1961; Fleishman and Harris, 1962; Morse, 1953; Kahn, 1958.

3. Delegation, sharing of influence

Baumgartel, 1956; Lewin, Lippitt, and White, 1939; Jacobson, 1951; Wickert, 1951; Ross and Zander, 1957; Morse, 1953; Morse and Reimer, 1956; French, Israel, and Aas, 1960; Kay, French, and Meyer, 1962; Tannenbaum and Kahn, 1958; Tannenbaum, 1962, 1968.

C. Peer relationships

1. Interaction, accessibility, distance

Homans, 1950; Festinger, Schachter, and Back, 1950; Newcomb, 1956, 1961; Strodtbeck and Hook, 1961; Kipnis, 1957; Walker and Guest, 1952; Kerr, Koppelmeir, and Sullivan, 1951; Sawatsky, 1951; Richards and Dobryns, 1957; Robinson, Athanasiou, and Head, 1967.

2. Acceptance by group

Van Zelst, 1951; Zaleznik, Christenson, and Roethlisberger, 1958; Jackson, 1959; Kelley, 1956; Dittes, 1959; Kelley and Shapiro, 1954; Zander and Cohen, 1955; Sagi, Olmstead, and Atelsek, 1955.

3. Goal commonality

Deutsch, 1949; Jones and Vroom, 1964; Sherif and Sherif, 1956.

D. Wages and rewards

1. Reward structure

Herzberg, Mausner, Peterson, and Capwell, 1957; Thompson, 1939; Miller, 1941; Bennett, Handelman, Stewart, and Super, 1952; Marriott and Denerley, 1955; Centers and Cantril, 1946; Terman and Oden, 1959; Lawler and Porter, 1963; Smith and Kendall, 1963; Helson, 1947; Patchen, 1961.

2. Wage payments

Robinson, Athanasiou, and Head, 1967; Kornhauser, 1965; Haire, Ghiselli, and Porter, 1963; Adams, 1963; Nealey, 1963; Andrews and Henry, 1963.

3. Expectation and aspiration

Crespi, 1942; Zeaman, 1949; Bevan and Adamson, 1960; Black, Adamson, and Bevan, 1961; Lewin, Dembo, Festinger, and Sears, 1944; Spector, 1956; Jaques, 1956, 1961; Patchen, 1961; Homans, 1961; Adams, 1963; Stouffer *et al.*, 1949; Zaleznik, Christiansen, and Roethlisberger, 1958.

E. Promotional opportunities

Morse, 1953; Sirota, 1959; Patchen, 1960; Spector, 1956.

F. Working conditions

Mann and Hoffman, 1960; Mott, Mann, McLoughlin, and Warwick, 1965; Robinson, Athanasiou, and Head, 1967.

G. Organizational structure

Porter and Lawler, 1965; Porter, 1962; Haire, Ghiselli, and Porter, 1963; Kahn, Wolfe, Quinn, and Snoek, 1964.

II. Some hypothesized consequences of job satisfaction, by author

A. Performance

Herzberg, Mausner, Peterson, and Capwell, 1967; Brayfield and Crockett, 1955; Herzberg, Mausner, and Synderman, 1959; Likert, 1961.

B. Absence

Vroom, 1964; Metzner and Mann, 1953.

C. Turnover

Vroom, 1964; Hulin, 1966; Herzberg, Mausner, Synderman, and Capwell, 1957.

D. Nonwork activities

Mott, Mann, McLoughlin, and Warwick, 1965.

Work and Values

Any social indicator involves questions of value, both in its initial choice and in its subsequent use, and the answers to such questions are seldom obvious. By questions of value, I mean literally the evaluation of some thing or some state as good or bad, relatively or absolutely.

Social scientists who have had the experience of taking their descriptive research findings into some sector of the world of affairs have been confronted by such questions in very pragmatic forms. For example, imagine an industrial psychologist telling the management of a company that half the employees are satisfied with their jobs and half are not. The general manager listens politely and then asks: "Is that good or bad?"

The question can be answered in many frames of reference—in comparison to last year's data, in comparison to other companies, in terms of demonstrated relationships between satisfaction and turnover, or undemonstrated relationships between satisfaction and productivity. Sooner or later, however, both the management and their research associates must answer the question in terms of their values, some variable or variables that they believe should be maximized.

To acknowledge the inevitability of such choices is a beginning, but not more. The act of choosing will be made more difficult by the interconnectedness of the world to the extent that we know it, and more dangerous to the extent that we do not. Do we, for example, want more industrial productive efficiency even if the required methods make work less satisfying intrinsically? Can an increase in other rewards compensate for such changes in work content? And so on, through a series of questions that will always provoke provisional answers subject to new discoveries and new societal contexts.

This chapter cannot contain a thorough discourse on value nor exploration of the terminological forest of beliefs, needs, motives, attitudes, and other value-related concepts. We can point to two kinds of evaluative or preferential statements that are important for the creation and use of social indicators: (1) a person's preferred states for himself, and (2) a person's preferred states for others.

These may or may not coincide, of course. A person may feel that it is most important that his own work be full of interest and variety, but that it is not important that this be true for all jobs and all people. Regardless of how we define our concepts, these are different ideas and they have different implications for the use of social indicators. Social policy might be defined to maximize individual preferences, or to conform to individual prescriptions for others, or neither. In any case, however, the implementation of policy will have to deal both with what people want for themselves and with what they think "ought" to be for others as well.

Ideally, therefore, social indicators having to do with the meaning of work should include measures of both kinds, and should do so in terms commensurate with the conceptualization and description of the job itself. To continue the example of variety and monotony, we would utilize that dimension to describe existing jobs, individual needs or wants, and preferences for others. Currently, available scales do not meet all these requirements, but some could be made to do so without great difficulty.

Of the available scales of occupational values, those of Kilpatrick *et al.*, Rosenberg, and the related scales of Marvick and Slesinger best illustrate this potentiality.[60]

Kilpatrick and his colleagues have developed an instrument of 30 statements, each of which the respondent answers on a 10-point scale of agreement to disagreement. The statements are concerned with the factors listed in our earlier reference to this work—financial reward, occupational mobility, status and recognition, interpersonal relations, self-development, opportunity-security, and others. In its present form, the instrument mingles personal preferences and general expressions of value. For example: "It is satisfying to direct the work of others. . . . A person has a right to expect his work to be fun. . . . To me, a very important part of work is the opportunity to make friends." We would propose to develop two forms of the scale, one with the self and one with others as the referent. The self-anchoring procedure could be used as Kilpatrick has done, to describe the job presently held in comparison to these "ideals."[61]

Rosenberg's scale of occupational values consists of 10 statements, each of which the respondent classifies as high, medium, or low, according to its importance for him.[62] Each statement reiterates the individual basis of the requested evaluation: "The ideal job for me would have to provide an opportunity to use my special abilities or aptitudes . . . enable me to look forward to a secure, stable future . . . leave me relatively free of supervision by others . . . etc." Rosenberg was concerned with discriminating among three orientations—self-expression-orientation, people-orientation, and extrinsic-reward-orientation. These he used to predict occupational choice. His scale, however, could be readily adapted to describe existing jobs and to ask for evaluation of jobs in relation to preference for others as well as self.

Marvick's scale of career-oriented values consists of 16 statements about "factors important in a job."[63] They include such items as "opportunity to learn . . . getting ahead in the organization . . . enjoying the work itself." His purpose was to distinguish among different "career types" in government. Each

---

[60] Kilpatrick, Cummings, and Jennings, *op. cit.* M. Rosenberg, *Occupations and Values.* Free Press, Glencoe, Ill., 1957; D. Marvick, *Career Perspectives in a Bureaucratic Setting.* University of Michigan Press, Ann Arbor, 1954; Jonathan A. Slesinger, *Personnel Adaptations in the Federal Junior Management Assistant Program.* Institute of Public Administration, University of Michigan, Ann Arbor, 1961.

[61] H. Cantril, *The Pattern of Human Concerns.* Rutgers University Press, New Brunswick, 1965.

[62] Rosenberg, *op. cit.*

[63] Marvick, *op. cit.*

respondent rated each statement as very important, fairly important, or not important to himself. At the same time Marvick's scale asks: "Does your job actually provide this?" Responses were again made on a three-point scale.

Several more recent studies illustrate the use of commensurate scales for assessing individual needs (preferred states for self) and actual characteristics of a present job, although none of these studies has extended the approach to measure values of job characteristics advocated for others. Bachman, Kahn, *et al.,* and Long apply scales of preferred states (needs) and environmental requirements (roles) to a population of adolescent boys in a study of the student role.[64] Quinn and Kahn do so in a current study of the work role, based on a national sample of adults.[65]

We look forward to the extension of such approaches to include the characteristics of the job as it actually exists; of the individual's needs, abilities, and preferences for himself; and of his expressed value for others.

Social Indicators in Use: The Technology of Social Change

The achievement of planned change is a monstrous subject in more than one sense of that word, and its theory and practice are not the subject of this chapter. We should not leave the topic of social indicators about work, however, without mentioning the implications of such research for planned change.

I believe that the interest in and commitment to social indicators is no less a commitment to planned social change (including, of course, acts of conservation as well as alteration). No one really imagines otherwise; the data are collected for use, not for aesthetic reasons. When the three broad questions proposed in the introduction to this volume have been answered—when we know where we stand on certain chosen dimensions (description), what that standing means in terms of other causes and consequences (explanation), and how that standing compares to where we want to be (need and value preferences)—at that point we confront the fourth broad question of how to achieve the desired changes, how to move from an existing situation to a preferable one.

The social actions undertaken in answer to that question close the circle. They create a new state or standing on the dimensions chosen for social indicators, which is in turn assessed in relation to goals defined by needs and values, and the cycle continues. The process, however, is not so simple and orderly as global description makes it seem. Individuals and organizations differ in values, interests, access to and perception of the facts. Efforts to communicate and utilize data encounter resistances and distortions to prevent their use.

[64] Jerald G. Bachman *et al., Youth in Transition,* Vol. I. Survey Research Center, Institute for Social Research, University of Michigan, Ann Arbor, 1967; Judith A. Long, "Self-Actualization in a Sample of High School Boys: A Test of Some Propositions from Self-Identity Theory," unpublished doctoral dissertation, University of Michigan, 1968.

[65] Quinn and Kahn, *op. cit.*

There is a growing conviction that the transition from unplanned to planned change is the major task of our time. Daniel Bell describes it as the transition from crescive to contrived change and asserts that "perhaps the most important social change of our time is a process of direct and deliberate contrivance.[66] Men seek now to anticipate change, measure the course of its direction and impact, control it, and even shape it for predetermined ends. The transformation of society is no longer an abstract phrase but a process in which governments are engaged on a highly conscious basis." Similar views of the need for such planning are expressed by Merton and by March and Simon in their emphasis on intended vs. unintended consequences; by Michael in terms of the transition to long-range planning; by Gross and many others in the language of systems analysis, which aims to provide a framework in which the ratio of anticipated to unanticipated consequences is increased.[67]

Research on and demonstration of data-based social change has become the subject of major conferences, for example, the Conference on Scientific Progress and Human Values at the California Institute of Technology and many books.[68] Perhaps more significant is the establishment of new organizations with the mission of research on, and in some cases demonstration and facilitation of, planned change. The Center for Research on the Utilization of Scientific Knowledge (CRUSK) of the University of Michigan is one example; the Organization for Social and Technological Innovation in Cambridge (OSTI) is another; the Institute for the Future is a third, and the list is growing.

Developments of this kind, as encouraging as they are to people already persuaded of the importance of planned, data-based change, are inadequate to the present task in an important respect. With very few exceptions, the models, experiences, and organizations are on too modest a scale. They are at the individual level (counseling, therapy), at the group level (laboratory experiments, sensitivity training), or at the organizational level (survey research and feedback, organizational development).

In all these cases, the context is that of a relationship between a client who presents a problem and an expert who offers help through data collection, advice, or both. Although writers speak of "client systems," perhaps to emphasize

[66] Daniel Bell, *The End of Ideology*. Free Press, New York, 1967.

[67] Robert F. Merton *et al., Reader in Bureaucracy*. Free Press, Glencoe, Ill., 1952; J. G. March and H. A. Simon, *Organizations*. Wiley, New York, 1958; Donald N. Michael, *The Unprepared Society*. Basic Books, New York, 1968; Bertram M. Gross, *The Management of Organizations*. Free Press, New York, 1964.

[68] Edward Hutchings and Elizabeth Hutchings, eds., *Scientific Progress and Human Values*. Elsevier, New York, 1967; R. Lippitt, Jeanne Watson, and B. Westley, *The Dynamics of Planned Change: A Comparative Study of Principles and Techniques*. Harcourt, New York, 1958; Warren G. Bennis, Kenneth D. Benne, and Robert Chin, eds., *The Planning of Change*. Holt, New York, 1962; Raymond A. Bauer and Kenneth J. Gergen, *The Study of Policy Formation*. Free Press, New York, 1968.

the fact that the presenter of problems and potential user of data may be a community or a government as well as an individual or organization, the accumulation of research and experience has been at the level of the single organization, usually an industrial company. Usually the attempt at planned change has occurred when formal authorities (officers, managers) in such an organization asked for assistance in carrying out more efficient organizational operations, using their own criteria, in support of goals they had already established. Approaches and research experience at this level have been categorized in various ways by different authors. Katz and Kahn distinguish among information and exhortation, individual counseling and therapy (as a means of organizational change), the influence of the peer group, sensitivity training, group therapy, survey and feedback, and systemic (structural) change.[69]

Data of the social-indicator kind—for example, continuing data on the meaning of work—can be thought of as informational feedback to the society. We need better theory and more carefully evaluated practice at the level of multiple and interacting organizations, however. Many agencies of the federal government would be interested and active in response to data on the meaning of work, and this interest and felt responsibility would also be found at state and local levels, particularly if data pertaining to those levels were available.

Outside the public sector, the major employers and associations of employers should be involved in any proposals to redefine jobs or compensation for jobs on the basis of data on the meaning of work. Examples are obvious: the U.S. Chamber of Commerce, the National Industrial Conference Board, the National Association of Manufacturers, and others. Trade unions, separately and in federation, should develop their own responses and demands on employers, individual corporations and their own policies.

The outcomes with respect to new norms, new practices, perhaps new laws with respect to work and the compensation for work, are not predictable in terms of informational feedback alone. Bauer and Gergen, in a recent book on the study of policy formation, have brought together the attempts of nine authors to deal with some of the processes of conflict and coalition that emerge in the transition from data to policy.[70] Bauer summarizes some of the characteristic complications: incompatibilities between the over-all interest (e.g., national) and internal inequities, lack of unity of any policy problem (interconnectedness, changes over time), uncertainty as to the relevant actors (individuals, organizations), tautology and vagueness of the concept of "self-interest," involvements of actors in issues, and obligations other than the ones under consideration.

Some of the great national issues of recent times provide examples of these complications. Perhaps the examples of relative success in linking social indica-

---

[69] Katz and Kahn, *op. cit.*
[70] Bauer and Gergen, *op. cit.*

tors to social policy are in the economic sphere, in the management of interest rates and currency flow by the Federal Reserve Board or in the policy recommendations of the Council of Economic Advisers to the President. The example that shows most completely and painfully the conflicts of interest and the collisions of value that are not resolved by the presence of social indicators alone is, of course, the current effort to achieve racial equality in education, housing, and employment. Certainly, the accumulation of data on the facts and effects of discrimination played a part in the development of national policy (in the 1954 Supreme Court Decision and the 1964 and 1968 Civil Rights Acts, for example). And it may be hoped that continuing data on the racial distribution of employment and school attendance will strengthen the implementation of present policies. Nevertheless, this problem area will remind us for a long time of the limitations of present theory and practice of social change, data-based or not.

A Summary and Some Proposals

In this chapter we discussed four activities related to social indicators of work—description, explanation, the enunciation of values and goals, and implementation. We emphasized the first and second of these, and introduced the others primarily to provide perspective. It remains to conclude, partly by summary, partly by advocacy.

1. Our society is changing rapidly, deeply, and dramatically. Some of those changes are generally seen as desirable: increased longevity, physical convenience, increased education, gains in productive efficiency. Some are of uncertain or at least debated value: more television sets, expanded cosmetic lines, more advertising through all media. And some changes are unarguably bad: increases in violent crime, pollution of the air and water, and crowding in areas already densely populated.

2. The nature of work and the work force is one of the areas of great change. Bell[71] has provided a useful summary of changes that have already taken place: Employment in manufacturing is now less than in service, if we include trade, professional, and government activities in the latter category. Indeed, the service sector so defined includes more than half of the employed labor force and accounts for more than half of the gross national product. This fact is unique in our national history and in the history of all nations.

A related fact, or perhaps another indicator of the same underlying trend, is that the number of white-collar workers is larger than that of blue-collar workers, has been so for more than a decade, and continues to grow proportionately. A concentrated part of this growth is in professional and technical employment, where the rate is twice that for the labor force as a whole. And

[71] Bell, *op. cit.*

within that category the rate is in turn, concentrated among scientists and engineers, who are increasing in numbers at about three times the rate of the total labor force.

3. These changes, and the increased productivity that they reflect and cause, not only describe alterations in the nature and distribution of work; they create the possibility of still greater choices with respect to work. Galbraith[72] has summarized these well: We can attempt to maintain the present ideology and practice with respect to work (40 hours or more per week with no other activity as an acceptable substitute, at least for able-bodied men), and we can rely on advertising and other devices to counteract the diminishing marginal utility of goods to the affluent.

We can reduce the workweek further, or introduce other variations on the 40-hour theme (longer or more frequent vacations, nonacademic sabbatical years, and the like). As Galbraith[73] reminds us, "Over the span of man's history, although a phenomenal amount of education, persuasion, indoctrination, and incantation have been devoted to the effort, ordinary people have never been quite persuaded that toil is as agreeable as its alternatives."

We can arrange for fewer people to work. At present, several different trends are operative—earlier retirement, more education and later entry into the labor market, but also more women in the labor force.

Or we can do the thing that is, if not unmentionable, at least very seldom mentioned—we can make work easier or more pleasant.[74] Variety, choice of work methods, self-pacing, accessibility to congenial colleagues or work mates, job enlargement have been considered and evaluated in terms of their ability to demonstrate an increment of production. We are in a position as a nation to consider the definition of work in broader terms, to reduce its damages and increase its benefits to the worker even if he is not thereby made more productive on the job. The development of trend measures on work satisfaction would be important to such choices, as would research designed to explain further the causes and consequences of satisfaction and dissatisfaction with work.

The following concrete proposals are made to suggest the scope and direction of a program of social indicators on the meaning of work:

1. Initiate a nationwide annual measurement of over-all work satisfaction. This should be based on a sample sufficient to provide occupational data of some detail, perhaps comparable to the Current Population Survey (Bureau of the Census). Such an index could be based on a limited number of questions including direct expression of satisfaction or dissatisfaction, hypotheti-

---

[72] Galbraith, *The Affluent Society; idem, The New Industrial State.*
[73] Galbraith, *The Affluent Society.*
[74] Katz and Kahn, *op. cit.*

cal advice to a friend, own occupational choice if beginning career again, wish to continue work in the absence of economic need, etc.[75]

2. Develop a set of measures to describe the major characteristics of jobs (demands and opportunities), and of individuals (need-value preferences and abilities) in commensurate terms. Components are likely to include the nature of the work itself (challenge, visibility of results, opportunity to use valued skills and abilities, etc.), supervision, rewards, relationships with co-workers, and working conditions. The comparison of these measures for individuals will provide an indication of "goodness of fit" between the person and his work role. A derivative problem of importance is to distinguish between subjective (from the person himself) and objective (independently derived) measures of job characteristics and characteristics of the individual.[76]

3. Conduct pilot studies on experimental changes in the definition, conditions, time requirements, and rewards of work. These should be field trials with full evaluative research to determine effects not only on job satisfaction but on the functioning of the individual and family in their major life roles. Such experimental studies should routinely precede and provide the basis for proposed changes in national policy and employment norms.

In proposing to measure anything, we must keep in mind the likelihood that "the very effort to measure . . . as well as the nature of the yardstick used, tends to determine organizational procedures."[77] But this is a truth that applies to present approaches to the measurement of work and its outcomes, as well as those proposed in this paper. With few exceptions, the present measures of work and its consequences are those of conventional accounting and engineering: profit and loss, productivity and scrap, absence and turnover. They are necessary measures, but in the absence of comparably comprehensive and valid data about satisfaction and dissatisfaction, positive mental health and stultification or outright illness, the measures of economic and engineering outcomes urge one-sided and limited social policies. The initiation of social indicators of work satisfaction and meaning would provide an antidote, a source of balance. It can be objected that such measures are presently crude and of limited validity. That is true, but it is also true that the present state of measurement justifies beginning the process, and that there is a healthy tendency for good measures to drive out bad ones. The initiation and use of trend data on the meaning of work will create a demand for improved measurement as well as practice.

[75] Robinson, Athanasiou, and Head, *op. cit.;* Quinn and Kahn, *op. cit.*

[76] For a discussion of this issue see the paper by John R. P. French, Jr., Willard Rodgers, and Sidney Cobb, "Adjustment as Person-Environment Fit," in G. V. Coelho, ed., forthcoming.

[77] Peter M. Blau, *The Dynamics of Bureaucracy.* University of Chicago Press, Chicago, 1955; Bernard Berelson and Gary A. Steiner, *Human Behaviour.* Harcourt, New York, 1964.

6

Leisure

Rolf Meyersohn

This chapter concerns itself with leisure.[1] Because leisure is compared with work yet consists of a series of activities that can be more or less "leisureful," I have divided the discussion into several sections that represent different approaches. The first section analyzes the relationship between leisure and work and attempts to locate the structural shifts in society that provide the framework for an expansion of leisure.

The second section deals with the very loosely organized difference between free time and leisure, a difference that stems largely from the question of the subjective meaning of free-time experiences: if they meet certain criteria they constitute leisure; if not, they are "merely" free-time activities. Particularly important in this delineation is the concept of play which has been successfully analyzed for specific subgroups in the population but treated only speculatively for the population as a whole.

[1] Because work in the area of leisure is scattered through various disciplines, ranging from philosophy to the behavioral sciences, bibliographic material is necessarily scattered and incomplete. Several collections have appeared recently, and the reader is urged to consult these for a more comprehensive view of the state of the field at this time. See, for example, Fred W. Martin, "Bibliography of Leisure: 1965–1970." Program in Leisure Education, Recreation and Related Community Services, Teachers College, Columbia University, New York, January, 1971 (mimeographed); Joffre Dumazedier *et al.*, "La Sociologie du Loisir," *Current Sociology,* vol. 16, no. 1 (special issue), 1968; Rolf Meyersohn, "The Sociology of Leisure in the United States: Introduction and Bibliography, 1945–1965," *Journal of Leisure Research,* vol. 1, Winter, 1969, pp. 53–69; Rolf Meyersohn and Erwin K. Scheuch, eds., *Soziologie der Freizeit,* Verlag Kiepenheuer & Witsch, Cologne, in press, Part VI. An earlier, comprehensive bibliography may be found in Eric Larrabee and Rolf Meyersohn, eds., *Mass Leisure.* Free Press, Glencoe, Ill., 1958.

The third section considers a variety of leisure activities for which suggestive findings have been gathered that are relevant to future monitoring of human change. They encompass a wide range of activities which may have very little in common beyond the fact that they occur during leisure time. The fourth section highlights some of the issues in the interplay between the environment and the individual in the area of leisure. There is no single monitoring device or concept which can trace this interplay, although the variety of problems generated by the demands and opportunities in contemporary society suggests a series of questions worthy of systematic, synchronic monitoring.

Work and Leisure

A discussion of leisure must begin with consideration of the concept of work. Beginning with the Industrial Revolution and perhaps preceding it, work has constituted the one value around which other values scattered. The issues involved in the concept of work are epitomized by the following two statements, the first by Russell Sage, the second by Karl Marx which appears to contradict it:

> Work has been the chief, and, you might say, the only source of pleasure in my life; it has become the strongest habit that I have and the only habit that I would find it impossible to break.[2]

> The worker feels himself at home only outside his work and feels absent from himself in his work. He feels at home when he is not working, and not at home when he is working. His work is not freely consented to but is a constrained, forced labor. Work is thus not a satisfaction of a need, but only a means to satisfy needs outside work.[3]

Yet we cannot be sure of the extent to which the value of work was ever taken seriously by the "working classes" or their predecessors. A report from a recent conference on pre-industrial work and leisure notes that

> belief in the value of work as such (as distinct from and opposed to labour as a commodity) was prevalent in pre-industrial society, even among unskilled labourers though always rejected by anti-social or marginal minority groups like gypsies. Even under capitalism, workers failed for a long time to accept that aspect of the commodity view of labour which might have favoured them, the logic of working as little as possible for the highest possible wage, but worked "a fair day's" work for a fair day's pay.[4]

[2] Quotation appears in Irvin G. Wyllie, *The Self-Made Man in America*. Rutgers University Press, New Brunswick, N.J., 1954, p. 43.

[3] Karl Marx, "Die Entfremdete Arbeit," *Economic and Philosophic Manuscripts*. Progress Publishers, Moscow, 1959, p. 69.

[4] "Work and Leisure in Industrial Society," *Proceedings of Seventh Past and Present Conference* (summarized in *Past and Present*, no. 30, April, 1965, p. 100).

In England, the concept of the value of work was one force in the process of industrialization which came earlier than in the United States. E. P. Thompson describes the process as a violent imposition from above, with the lower classes serving as unwilling victims. Industrialization, he writes,

> was unrelieved by any sense of national participation in communal effort, such as is found in countries undergoing a national revolution. Its ideology was that of the masters alone. Its messianic prophet was Dr. Andrew Ure, who saw the factory system as "the great minister of civilization to the terrageous globe," diffusing "the life-blood of science and religion to myriads . . . still lying in the region and shadow of death." But those who served it did not feel things to be so, any more than those "myriads" who were served. The experience of immiseration came upon them in a hundred different forms; for the field labourer, the loss of his common rights and the vestiges of village democracy; for the artisan, the loss of his craftsman's status; for the weaver, the loss of livelihood and of independence; for the child, the loss of work and play in the home; for many groups of workers whose real earnings improved, the loss of security, leisure, and the deterioration of the urban environment.[5]

During this same time, the United States came to be seen as the land of opportunity for work and for success without such oppressiveness, although some critics questioned the total commitment to work and wondered whether the "impoverishment of leisure" might lead to a "dull and stultified national character."[6] The seriousness of work remained a leitmotiv of the American experience for the remainder of the century. By then, the question could at least be raised what it was all for, and why a man would persist in working even after he had become rich.

If the Industrial Revolution began by attempting to convert reluctant peasants toward accepting the value of work, it resulted in developing an emphasis on the value of leisure. One of the major social goals since the height of the Industrial Revolution has been the liberation of man from toil and the striving toward ever-increased periods of free time. However, whether or not leisure is an ideal which can be attained through the industrialization is not at all clear. Judging from the recent past, in which Americans have opted for additional work rather than leisure when the choice was presented, there is some reason to believe that the goal-structure is probably more complicated than the simple choice between work and leisure can suggest.

The nature of work appears to dictate the nature of leisure. The value of work has apparently always been bifurcated, resulting in a complex value for leisure as well. Insofar as work is carried on beyond the practical and neces-

[5] E. P. Thompson, *The Making of the English Working Class*. Pelican, Middlesex, England, 1968, pp. 486–487.

[6] R. Richard Wohl, "The 'Country Boy' Myth and Its Place in American Urban Culture: The Nineteenth Century Contribution," *Perspectives in American History*, vol. 3, 1969, p. 99.

sary purpose of earning one's daily bread, symbolic meaning is attached to it which is culturally derived and culturally sanctioned.

This shift in attitude toward work has so far not been accompanied by a clear-cut shift in attitude toward leisure. The expansion of professionalism has provided superficial analogies for avocational careers, and energies that are applied to paid work are also applied to leisure. But as yet there is no indication that the preference for leisure over work is increasing.

Research in work motivation and work satisfaction has provided evidence to demonstrate that meaningful work is more likely to be found among professionals and executives than among factory workers (see Chapter 5). Studies have indicated that factory workers would not, however, want to stop working altogether and that, for most adults, the solution to dissatisfaction with work is another kind of job rather than leisure.

The fact that leisure is not chosen as an alternative to dissatisfaction with work does not suggest that leisure is therefore not desired. As Herbert Gans has recently suggested:

> The real threat is not more leisure but feelings of social uselessness brought about by unemployment; and these feelings cannot be dealt with by leisure education, for leisure cannot really help people feel useful.[7]

The contrast must be made between leisure as a desired period of time and set of activities, and leisure as a replacement for work. The former is probably on the increase, whereas the latter is not likely ever to predominate.

The important differentiation and the one that appears likely to become more critical in the future is between professional and low-level service workers, and between executives and blue-collar workers. The nature of work provides the basis of the individual "life-satisfaction," in Harold Wilensky's terms, and leisure does not appear to provide a compensation for meaninglessness in work.[8] Robert Blauner answers the suggestion that the lost opportunities for self-expression and creativity in work can be regained in leisure:

> The problem with the leisure solution is that it underestimates the fact that work remains the single most important life activity for most people, in terms of time and energy, and ignores the subtle ways in which the quality of one's work life affects the quality of one's leisure, family relations, and basic self-feelings. . . . The implicit policy of emphasizing leisure as a solution to the problems of unfree work [would] involve a basic inequity—a division of society into one segment of consumers who are creative in their leisure time but have meaningless work and a second segment capable of self-realization in both spheres of life.[9]

[7] Herbert J. Gans, "Popular Culture in America," in Howard S. Becker, ed., *Social Problems: A Modern Approach.* Wiley, New York, 1966, pp. 605–606.

[8] Harold Wilensky, "Work as a Social Problem," in Becker, *op. cit.,* pp. 136 ff.

[9] Robert Blauner, *Alienation and Freedom.* University of Chicago Press, Chicago 1964, pp. 183–184.

The basic self-feelings that Blauner alludes to are treated more systematically by Robert S. Weiss and David Riesman, who are equally skeptical about a leisure solution to the problems of work:

> Americans tend to look to their performance on a job, even if it is a repetitive one, as a basis for recognition of their worth. . . . Few Americans would want to do without work even if they were not forced by economic necessity to stay at a job.[10]

Experience with workers who are unemployed or who are intermittently employed has shown quite clearly that

> work [regardless of] whether it is becoming more or less central as a source of personal identity and social solidarity, still remains a necessary condition for drawing the individual into the mainstream of social life.[11]

Once the patterns of relationships between different occupational groups and their work satisfactions are better understood, it will be possible to establish links between these patterns and patterns of leisure preference. A monitoring over time of the extent to which various occupational groups consider work central, and in what ways, will help provide synchronic material that can be used as one basis for the comprehension of changes in leisure attitudes. Until now, sociologists and social psychologists have had to rely on small and selective studies, done at a single point in time with populations that are not easily comparable. Although they reinforce the finding that work as a central life interest is far more likely to occur among professionals or among special communities of workers than among industrial workers at large, there are few systematic studies of workers and their relationship to work; hence, there is little comprehensive knowledge of the role of leisure.[12]

Free Time and Leisure[13]

Not all free time is leisure, although all leisure occurs during free time. If the changes in the nature and conditions of work have provided for an in-

[10] Robert S. Weiss and David Riesman, "Work and Automation," in Robert K. Merton and Robert A. Nisbet, eds., *Contemporary Social Problems,* 2nd ed. Harcourt, New York, 1966, pp. 579–580.

[11] Wilensky, "Work as a Social Problem," p. 130.

[12] See especially Robert Dubin, "Industrial Workers' Worlds: A Study of the 'Central Life Interests' of Industrial Workers," *Social Problems,* vol. 3, January, 1956, pp. 131–142; L. H. Orzack, "Work as a 'Central Life Interest' of Professionals," *Social Problems,* vol. 7, Fall, 1959, pp. 125–132; and Walter S. Corrie, Jr., "Work as a 'Central Life Interest': A Comparison of the Amana Colony Worker with the Non-Amana Colony Worker in a Given Industrial Setting," unpublished doctoral dissertation, State University of Iowa, August, 1957.

[13] Several ideas in this section are discussed in Rolf Meyersohn, "Freizeit in den westlichen Industrieländern," in C. D. Kernig, ed., *Sowjetsystem und demokratische Gesellschaft.* Verlag Herder, Freiburg, Germany, 1969, pp. 694–702.

crease of free time, it yet remains to be established whether this has also resulted in an increase in leisure. The answer to this question depends to some extent on the way in which leisure is defined and on the extent to which subjective qualities and experiences are taken into account in the definition. The subjective qualities which the participant must bring to his free time in order that it be leisure have not been well elaborated in empirical work, although some efforts have been made. (See the discussion below of leisure as rest, entertainment, self-realization, and spiritual renewal.)

The result of such efforts to deal with leisure as an entity occurring during some but not all free time has led to a direct focus on the meaning of leisure activities and hence on the "functional substitutability" of activities which share common meanings. Meaning is seen in terms of satisfactions, uses, and gratifications. In a 1959 study conducted by Robert Havighurst and his collaborators, an effort was made to get at the meanings attributed by a sample of adults in New Zealand and in Kansas City to their favorite two leisure activities.[14] A set of 12 meaning statements were given to respondents which they could apply to the leisure activities they mentioned. Table 1 lists the meaning statements and indicates the frequency of mention. Havighurst concluded that "the differences in the meanings or values people find in their leisure seem to depend more upon their personalities than upon their age, sex, or social-class characteristics."[15]

Had the study asked respondents to describe the meanings of activities

Table 1. Relative Frequencies of Mention of Meanings of Leisure Expressed in Percent of Respondents Choosing a Given Meaning

Meaning	Kansas City		New Zealand	
	Male	Female	Male	Female
O—Just for the pleasure of it	71	65	58	69
Q—Welcome change from work	55	41	65	64
V—Gives new experience	38	46	40	43
P—Contact with friends	32	26	53	46
Y—Chance to achieve something	18	27	30	33
W—Makes time pass	20	26	22	25
Z—To be creative	6	24	16	18
R—Benefit to society	12	15	19	15
T—Helps financially	11	7	16	11
S—Self-respect for doing it	7	6	13	17
X—Gives me more standing with others	6	2	7	9
U—Makes me popular	2	0	6	6

[14] Marjorie N. Donald and Robert J. Havighurst, "The Meanings of Leisure," *Social Forces,* vol. 37, May, 1959, pp. 355–360.

[15] *Ibid.,* p. 360.

pursued in free time that are *not* considered "favorite leisure activities," it would have produced a more general statement on the difference between leisure and free time; presumably some activities carried out during leisure time that are identified as "leisure activities" are not, in fact, perceived as pleasurable or in any other way endowed with any of the 12 meanings that Havighurst isolated for favorite leisure activities.

That is to say, if the question is raised to what extent people enjoy what they do during their leisure time, then the rate of enjoyment is dependent not only on the dispositional elements (e.g., the euphoric personality) or on the general level of contentment which persons in various subgroups in the population experience, but is dependent also on the nature of the relationship that is established between different persons and their free-time experience.

We do not know much about these relationships. We do know the variations that exist in the more general human states such as *well-being, happiness,* and *concern.* It has been found that, by and large, despite minor cultural differences

> the well-to-do are more likely to state that they are satisfied with life. The relationship derives from the nature of the socio-economic position, particularly the level of education and economic security.[16]

American society is moving very clearly toward the greater enhancement of styles of life that permit an increasingly wide expression of the choice of such styles.[17] At the same time, the essential aspects of leisure might not be realized according to some critics, and problems arise based on the way in which leisure is defined and separated from free time.

Four distinct meanings are allotted to the concept of leisure: (1) leisure as rest, respite, restoration; (2) leisure as entertainment; (3) leisure as self-realization; and (4) leisure as spiritual renewal.

All four meanings distinguish between leisure and free time.[18] According to the assumptions behind each of these meanings, leisure does not occur during free time unless some kind of subjective meaning and a particular quality is experienced. This is in contrast to the conceptualization of leisure as a set of activities commonly considered "leisure activities." (The latter will be discussed in a later section.)

Rest, Respite, Restoration. Rest and its various aspects have always been a component of leisure. This meaning comes closest to the conceptualization

[16] Alex Inkeles, "Industrial Man: The Relation of Status to Experience, Perception, and Value," *American Journal of Sociology,* vol. 66, July, 1960, p. 13.

[17] See, for example, Norman M. Bradburn and David Caplovitz, *Reports on Happiness.* Aldine, Chicago, 1965, pp. 8 ff.

[18] Leopold Rosenmayr, "Leisure: Illusion and Reality," Report on European Seminar on The Leisure of Workers in Modern Industrial Societies. United Nations, Geneva, 1968 (unpublished), pp. 8 ff.

of leisure as a necessary interlude between work. In societies and settings where work is strenuous, the moment of leisure is necessarily different and less autonomous than at times and in places where work is not physically hard. In post-industrial society, however, it is suggested that work is still strenuous in a more diffuse mental and moral sense. Because work exhausts the spirit, not the body, leisure also suffers. In such a state, the argument runs, leisure becomes meaningless and unrestful:

> . . . under modern technology free time can be used only as an escape from the oppressiveness of the industrial system . . . free time is itself "industrialized."[19]

Although such critiques are widespread, they are rarely substantiated. Whether rest and respite during leisure occur more frequently among workers who are not alienated is not clear. One study, carried out among Swiss workers, found that the contented workers sleep better and go to the movies less frequently, but it found few other differences in their free-time use. Even these differences might be due to other facts correlated with being contented and sleeping better; for example, married workers are on the whole more contented; they also tend to sleep better and to go to the movies less frequently than unmarried workers.[20] To be sure, subjective reports by workers that they are contented in their work does not constitute an undisputed measure of an absence of alienation. As Blauner has noted:

> The absence of opportunities to develop inner potential, to express idiosyncratic abilities, and to assume responsibility and decision-making functions, may not be a source of serious discontent to most workers today. For this reason, empirical studies show that the majority of industrial workers are satisfied with their work and with their jobs.[21]

Regardless of whether alienation is high or low and whether it has been possible to measure satisfaction, the Seligman argument that, because society is growing increasingly oppressive as a result of the industrial system, leisure is also increasingly unsatisfactory, constitutes only one possible alternative. The other, expressed by Joffre Dumazedier, suggests that the "production tempo, the complexity of the industrial setting, the long distances in the urban centers to and from work—all have increased the worker's need for rest and quiet, for idleness, and the aimless small pastimes."[22]

[19] Ben B. Seligman, "On Work, Alienation, and Leisure," *American Journal of Economics and Sociology,* vol. 24, October, 1965, p. 354.

[20] Dieter Hanhart, *Arbeiter in der Freizeit.* Verlag Hans Huber, Bern, 1964, pp. 215–216.

[21] Blauner, *op. cit.,* p. 183.

[22] Joffre Dumazedier, *Toward a Society of Leisure.* Free Press, New York, 1967, p. 15.

Paradoxically, there is some suggestion that the time reserved for such recuperation, the weekend, appears to have negative consequences for returning to work. V. W. Bladen has suggested that Monday might have to be considered as a day in which people can recuperate from the weekend.[23] W. Baldamus has recently discovered strong indications that not only absenteeism but also industrial accidents occurred at a significantly higher rate on Mondays than on other days of the week, suggesting that workers might have some difficulty in returning to work on "Blue Monday."[24] Recent years have seen increased interest in standardizing American holidays so that they are celebrated on Mondays; one of the arguments in support of this revision has been the greater possibility for workers to have at least one day of rest out of a three-day weekend.[25]

The actual activities or inactivities likely to provide rest have not been formalized. They might be considered "voluntarily chosen idleness," a phenomenon that is on the decline in a society which appears to be characterized by increased shortage of time for all the activities that are available for expenditure.[26]

Entertainment. Rest and relaxation are meanings of leisure that are tied to work; they express recovery from fatigue. Entertainment, according to Dumazedier, "spells deliverance from boredom."[27] The concept "entertainment" refers both to activities as well as a set of meanings, sensations, or gratifications.[28] There has been some confusion in the historical development of entertainment in the first meaning. It is widely believed that entertainment activities are a new phenomenon, more or less growing out of the mass media. Harold Mendelsohn writes:

[23] Quoted in Staffan B. Linder, *The Harried Leisure Class.* Columbia University Press, New York, 1970, p. 46.

[24] Unpublished research on relation between industrial accidents, absence, and labor turnover, University of Birmingham, England.

[25] Unless three-day weekends are sufficiently widespread, they can be self-defeating. If workers in selected plants or industries are given an extra day off, they are likely to find the extra day burdensome. See Rolf Meyersohn, "Changing Work and Leisure Routines," in Erwin O. Smigel, ed., *Work and Leisure.* College & University Press, New Haven, 1963, pp. 97–106; also see David Riesman, "Leisure and Work in Post-Industrial Society," in Eric Larrabee and Rolf Meyersohn, eds., *Mass Leisure.* Free Press, Glencoe, Ill., 1958, pp. 368–370. For other arguments in support of standardized Monday holidays see U.S. Congress, House, Committee on the Judiciary, *Providing Monday Holidays: Hearings on H.B. 1292 and H.B. 11679,* 90th Cong., 1st Sess., August 16–17, 1967.

[26] See Linder, *op. cit.,* especially pp. 24–26.

[27] Joffre Dumazedier, "Sociological Aspects of Leisure," *International Social Science Journal,* vol. 12, no. 4, 1960, p. 523.

[28] Rolf Meyersohn, "A Critical Examination of Commercial Entertainment," in Robert W. Kleemeier, ed., *Aging and Leisure.* Oxford University Press, New York, 1961, pp. 243 ff.

The motion picture, radio, the phonograph, the mass-produced newspaper, magazine, and popular book, and television have wrested the realm of entertainment from that of the private and semi-private domains of exclusive patronage by kings, princes, and commercial elitists of former centuries.[29]

In fact, of course, the amusement-providing machinery of Western civilization has had a very long history, including such diverse entertainments as circuses, public hangings, festivals, passion plays, bull fighting, burlesques, bear baitings, and so forth.

What distinguishes contemporary entertainment activities is their enormously diverse public. In the past, entertainment was restricted to particular geographic communities and, no doubt, greater separation existed between public and private entertainments. Perhaps most striking in this respect is television where relatively similar television viewing patterns are found among Americans of highly diverse backgrounds. As Harold Wilensky has noted, "Even those with opportunity to develop highbrow tastes are becoming full participants in mass culture."[30] Entertainment is also a form of experience and a kind of gratification not bound to any particular activity. Martha Wolfenstein has suggested that entertainment, or "fun," is becoming a new form of morality, a sensation that is becoming obligatory in leisure as well as work. "Fun has become not only permissible but required, and this requirement has a special quality different from the obligations of the older morality [the morality of goodness]."[31] It is not known whether this tendency, which Wolfenstein observed 20 years ago, continues to prevail.

Entertainment is associated with less active forms of leisure; according to Nels Anderson, "play is one way of using leisure, amusement is a somewhat opposite way. One participates in play, but for amusement, he may watch others play."[32] The mass media are most frequently associated with this kind of gratification, although a priori assumptions about the "passivity" of audiences as compared with the activity of participants do not do justice to the great range of ways in which the mass media are in fact utilized.

Self-Realization. This use of leisure is taken over from the world of work, placing a value on achievements of various kinds. Capacities which are not utilized by work—creative talents, intellectual and physical interests, social and organizational abilities—are all capable of being utilized during leisure.

The movement from amateur to professional in leisure activities ranging

[29] Harold Mendelsohn, *Mass Entertainment.* College & University Press, New Haven, 1966, p. 57.

[30] Harold L. Wilensky, "Mass Society and Mass Culture: Interdependence or Independence?" *American Sociological Review,* vol. 29, April, 1964, p. 173.

[31] Martha Wolfenstein, "The Emergence of Fun Morality," in Larrabee and Meyersohn, eds., *op. cit.,* p. 46.

[32] Nels Anderson, *Work and Leisure.* Free Press, New York, 1961, p. 46.

from golf to photography suggests that the expansion of self is a process very similar to the development of a career.[33] David Riesman has described this phenomenon as "leisure competence":

> It is . . . largely through competence in leisure that most other-directed people can develop autonomy and political imagination. For while . . . the inner-directed man even if he could not play could feel, qualitatively, that he was a participating member of his society by virtue of his work alone, the other-directed man if he cannot play is apt to feel disqualified from participation in a society which is governed increasingly by a leisure ideology. And even apart from such cultural pressures and definitions, I believe play is of basic human importance for achieving autonomy.[34]

Riesman groups the leisure competences into two categories of skills: *craftsmanship,* a concept from the world of work where it has been under suspicion ever since the turn of the century when Veblen suggested that craftsmanship has meaning only if the product resulting from it has some use; and *consumership.*

Craftsmanship is most clearly demonstrated in the activities classed under "do-it-yourself" and hobbies. To some extent and for some people, this form of activity can result in self-realization; it is equally likely that do-it-yourself remains a way to avoid costly services of one kind or another or that it represents, as Jürgen Habermas has suggested, merely the illusion of pre-industrial craftsmanship while, in fact, it has been reduced to the fitting together of industrially prefabricated parts according to detailed instructions for the non-expert.[35]

Consumership is usually regarded as reflecting interest in material goods rather than an interest that can express self-realization. It is not known whether the fit between the goods and services that are acquired and the satisfaction that is derived from the acquisition can ever be regarded as self-realization. In the case of labor-saving devices, there is clearly a potentiality for liberating time spent with chores (even though several studies have shown that the amount of time saved is often negligible).[36] Time-spending goods and services, ranging from television sets to theater tickets, can reflect the consumer's interest in obtaining the gratifications offered by the activities engendered in the product or service, but only if the item constitutes what the con-

---

[33] Cf. Rolf Meyersohn, "Commercialism and Complexity in Popular Culture," in Meyersohn and Scheuch, eds., *op. cit.,* in press.

[34] David Riesman in collaboration with Reuel Denney and Nathan Glazer, *The Lonely Crowd.* Yale University Press, New Haven, 1950, p. 347.

[35] Jürgen Habermas, "Soziologische Notizen zum Verhältnis von Arbeit und Freizeit," in G. Funke, ed., *Konkrete Vernunft.* Bouvier, Bonn, 1958, pp. 219–231.

[36] See, for example, James N. Morgan *et al., Productive Americans.* Institute for Social Research, Ann Arbor, 1966, pp. 111–112.

sumer had in fact desired. This requires not only considerable information concerning the alternative products and services available, but also the ability on the part of the purchaser to project himself into the role of the consumer of that particular product or service. Consumership implies both of these traits and, to the degree that it exists, it provides the possibility of self-realization through the utilization of available leisure goods and services.

It has recently been suggested that the eventual limit on consumption is time rather than money, which in no way reduces the expertise required for proper decision-making concerning purchases, but adds the dimension of allocation of time to allocation of money. In a prediction of what life will be like with continued affluence, Staffan B. Linder raised the following prospects:

1. There will be an increasingly hectic tempo of life, marked by careful attempts to economize on increasingly scarce time.
2. There will be an expanding mass of goods which will make great demands on time in the form of such maintenance and service tasks that cannot very well be mechanized. This will happen in spite of a decline in maintenance per item.
3. Since affluence is only partial, there will be increasing hardships for those whose welfare does not primarily require abundant goods but the scarce time of their fellow creatures. While the aged, in the beginning of the initial growth period, lacked bed and bread, they will, toward the end of the period of growth mania, lack a nurse.
4. There will be a curious combination of an increasing attachment to goods in general and, owing to a low degree of utilization and rapid turnover, an increasing indifference to them in particular.
5. There will be a declining competitive position for time devoted to the cultivation of mind and spirit and for the time spent on certain bodily pleasures (love, for example). *Dolce far niente.*
6. There will be a declining utility of income but not an exhaustion of wants; in order to achieve some addition to material well-being, increasing attention will therefore be given to further economic advances.
7. In the name of economic progress, there will be increasing emphasis on rational economic policies and behavior, but for this very reason also . . . there will be a growing number of ill-considered decisions.
8. There will be a new form of economic "unfreedom" marked, not by a fight for economic survival, but by an obsession with growth that sometimes forces us, in the name of registered increases in economic growth, to allocate our economic resources, including time itself, in destructive ways—to destroy God-given bases for life, i.e., air, water, earth, natural beauty, and our own heredity.[37]

Self-realization becomes more possible in terms of the readier access to the various means of consumption that make it more possible; at the same

[37] Linder, *op. cit.*, pp. 143, 144.

time, according to Linder, it will be more difficult to sustain because of the increasing competing demands on time and, by implication, the more rapid jading process.

Spiritual Renewal. Some believe that this is the true pursuit of leisure. Pieper, for example, has written that man should have "something to do which is neither simply rest nor simply entertainment, play, amusement."[38] Drawing on Aristotle's statement that "leisure is the cardinal point around which everything turns," Pieper argues that contemplation is the highest form of leisure. Paralleling this argument is de Grazia's view that modern man has very little leisure because the exaggerated emphasis on activity removes him from the possibility.[39]

Very little empirical work can be carried out on the basis of such value statements. They can, however, be translated into a series of propositions that approximate some of the aspects of *play,* as it has been treated by Huizinga, Caillois, and more recent philosophers.[40]

Elsewhere I have compared *play* with *charisma* in terms of common elements that are shared by both.[41] These elements are relevant for the aspect of leisure that is sometimes called "spiritual renewal." These elements are:

1. The non-specificity of the concept, referring to a quality or an orientation rather than to behavior as such
2. The mysterious nature whereby only some persons are considered capable of playing or of possessing the gift (talent) for leisure
3. The transcendence of play and its extraordinariness
4. The contrast of play with routine free-time activities
5. The separation of play from the everyday world
6. The transformation of play into style

Particularly important among these elements are those that concern themselves with separation from the routine. Play is regarded as central to vital processes.

Huizinga, particularly, distinguished play from ordinary activities. "Not being 'ordinary' life, it stands outside the immediate satisfaction of wants and appetites, indeed it interrupts the appetitive process." Play consists of activities that are an end in themselves. "Play begins, and then at a certain

[38] Josef Pieper, "The Social Meaning of Leisure in the Modern World," *Review of Politics,* vol. 12, October, 1950, p. 415; *idem, Leisure: The Basis of Culture,* trans. by Alexander Dru. Random House, New York, 1952.

[39] Sebastian de Grazia, *Of Time, Work, and Leisure.* Twentieth Century Fund, New York, 1962.

[40] For a recent discussion see articles by Fink, Ehrmann, and others in *Yale French Studies,* no. 41, September, 1968.

[41] Rolf Meyersohn, "The Charismatic and the Playful in Outdoor Recreation," *The Annals of the Academy of Political and Social Science,* no. 389, May, 1970, pp. 35–45.

moment it is 'over.' . . . While it is in progress, all is movement, change, alternation, succession, association, separation."[42] It is removed from the ordinary, and has "only internal purposes, unrelated to anything external to itself.[43]

No empirical research has been carried out that has attempted to gauge the incidence of extraordinariness, of transcendence, of withdrawal and isolation from everyday life, as it occurs in the leisure-time lives of Americans. Such a measure would approach the rigorous definition that is often applied to leisure, and would contribute to a more penetrating description of the quality of life. Along with measures of the extent to which rest, entertainment, and self-realization occur during leisure, they would provide some clue to the nature of the leisure experience.

The discussion so far has not concerned itself with any activities in particular. Some of the problems and prospects of analysis in more specific areas are discussed in the following section.

Leisure Activities

Because leisure activities differ in the extent to which they can provide various human satisfactions, it is important to consider them singly or in functional groups. In other words, it would be a mistake to extend too far the idea that there is nothing meaningful in leisure activities per se and that because meaning is provided by the user, it can be derived equally from all activities.

Some leisure activities are *developmental,* others are not. Continued practice leads to advancement, much as in work. Tennis, violin playing, music listening, are examples of developmental activities. Television viewing has no such cumulative value, and after a decade of viewing commercial television, the viewer is no more adept at the activity than he was when he started (though he may be more able to turn the set off when he thinks nothing of interest will be on the air).[44]

More importantly, different leisure activities have different ranges of rewards or gratifications and are endowed with activity-specific meanings that cannot be directly transferred to another activity. Although there may be functional substitutes, such as photography for hunting, television viewing for moviegoing, viewing televised baseball for attending the ball game, there are losses (and gains) in each of these substitutions.

Characteristic of post-industrial society is the expanding rate of partici-

[42] Johan Huizinga, *Homo Ludens: A Study of the Play Element in Culture.* Beacon Press, Boston, 1955, p. 9.

[43] Eugen Fink, "The Oasis of Happiness: Toward an Ontology of Play," *Yale French Studies,* no. 41, September, 1968, p. 21.

[44] Cf. Rolf Meyersohn, "Commercialism and Complexity in Popular Culture," in Meyersohn and Scheuch, eds., *op. cit.*

pation in a variety of leisure activities, that is, activities pursued during leisure time. The reasons for the expansion have been discussed in various publications, usually under the context of increased affluence.[45] Increases in such varied activities as boating, concert-going, amateur painting, skiing, have been attributed largely to the fact that Americans can afford to pursue these diverse activities. Less importance has been given to the intervening variable of the opportunity structure which must provide not only the necessary financial opportunity but also the necessary informational facilities enabling interested individuals to find out where to go to obtain instruction.

It can be argued only from hindsight that the informational opportunities have apparently expanded sufficiently to permit nonusers to "switch" to beginner status. From studies of particular leisure activities it is apparent that considerable momentum is required culturally and social-psychologically in order that a nonuser be "persuaded" to try a leisure activity. This momentum has been provided by a number of elements in society, including schools and colleges, but probably more importantly, commercial facilities that have been established in postwar years to cater to the beginner in various fields of leisure pursuits.[46]

In other words, the combination of increases in discretionary income plus the increases in persuasive apparatus for overcoming the natural resistance on the part of nonusers against trying new leisure activities, has played an important role in the oft-noted expansion of leisure in postwar United States and Western Europe.

Because of the heavy reliance on particular inventions and technological innovations, it has always been impossible to make exact predictions about the particular leisure activities that might become prevalent at some future time. Thus, no one could possibly have predicted the current interest in snowmobiles, for example, or in eight-track stereophonic tape decks. By extension, future predictions in such specificities are also impossible. Yet the more general class of activities into which these two interests fall, winter sports and music listening, is quite manageable in terms of prediction of growing interest. In other words, the extent of knowledge and accuracy of prediction concerning leisure is susceptible to fairly accurate determination if the level of generality is high enough.

What is of interest in determining indicators for leisure, however, is less the particular leisure activity or even the more general class of leisure activity, and more the kinds of interests that underlie such pursuits. These remain rather more constant, and even though they have not been studied in great

---

[45] See, for example, Alvin Toffler, *The Culture Consumers,* St. Martin's Press, New York, 1964; also his "The Art of Measuring the Arts," in Bertram M. Gross, ed., Allyn and Bacon, Boston, 1969, pp. 262–280; and Clemens A. Andreae, *Oekonomik der Freizeit,* Rowohlt, Hamburg, 1970, pp. 146 ff.

[46] See Meyersohn, "Commercialism and Complexity in Popular Culture."

detail, it is possible to examine some leisure activities to isolate their commonalities.

In the analysis of leisure activities and their engagement, social scientists commonly separate the *intrinsic* from the *extrinsic* motivation. Neither intrinsic nor extrinsic motivations operate on a single dimension for any particular leisure activity. Hence, although the distinction is useful as a rough separation of attribute inherent in the activity and its use from aspects that are related to the social setting in which the activity takes place, each of the two dimensions must be explicated before a leisure activity can be said to have been described.

At least three questions appear relevant in the study of leisure activities in the context of motivation: (1) What are the predominant intrinsic and extrinsic motivations for the leisure activity? (2) How are they distributed in the population? and (3) Are these distributions likely to change?

For different activities and different population groups the answers to these questions are, of course, very different. In the case of television viewing, to take one extreme, many persons report not being interested in watching the particular program they have turned to but wanting to be with the rest of the family.[47] In activities which involve other people, the involvement itself is often given as the main reason for the participation. For example, in a survey of motivations for going dancing, "to meet or be with the opposite sex" was the single most frequent response among boys; interest in dancing as such took second place.[48]

The absence of intrinsic motivation has been used as an indictment against leisure as, for example, by Thorstein Veblen who considered leisure activities as they were pursued by middle-class Americans the result of "conspicuous consumption," a mode of display of wealth and power which had no intrinsic motivation. The intrinsic enjoyment of activities was not thought to be an important factor in the pursuit of leisure activities.

Yet leisure activities are often defined by virtue of their intrinsic motivation. *Play* is only intrinsically motivated since there are no extrinsic elements inherent in it. Indeed, the extensiveness of intrinsic motivation has led D. E. Berlyne, in his recent review of the literature on the psychology of play, to conclude that play is not a useful category for psychology.

> The chief element common to the infant shaking his rattle, the little girl holding a doll's tea party, the adolescent football player, and the aged rake at the roulette table is that they are all under the sway of intrinsic motivation. Yet intrinsic motivation predominates also in exploratory behavior, epistemic be-

[47] Gary Steiner, *The People Look at Television*. Knopf, New York, 1963, p. 69.
[48] Frances Rust, *Dance in Society*. Routledge & Kegan Paul, London, 1969, pp. 167–169.

havior (including scientific research and philosophical thought), hobbies of all sorts, and the enjoyment of works of art.[49]

From the point of view of the observer of an activity, the intrinsic/ extrinsic dichotomy can be readily made; in the area of leisure, great value is placed on the pursuit of the activity for intrinsic motivation. The authentic participant is the one who expresses or implies commitment to the activity itself. The committed person, as Howard Becker has stated, acts "in such a way to involve other interests of his, originally extraneous to the action he is engaged in, directly in that action."[50] This commitment can be measured in a variety of ways, such as time and money spent, amount of interest expressed, and degree of talent exhibited.

The inauthentic participant is one who does not express commitment to the activity itself but to some external or extrinsic aspect. In the study of gardening, persons who did not enjoy the activity but spent considerable time and money gardening were considered uncommitted.[51] Similarly, in a study of residents in a middle-class suburb, Benjamin B. Ringer found a number of persons who pursued sports but expressed no interest in them. He explained: "The intrinsic character of the activity may seem less rewarding than certain extrinsic functions such activities perform. . . . Such activities bring people together."[52]

The intrinsic/extrinsic dichotomy was recently used by Bruce Watson to differentiate different types of publics for an art show (see Table 2).[53]

Table 2. A Typology of Art Publics

	Attitude Dimension	
Value Dimension	*Positive*	*Negative*
Intrinsic	Art for art's sake	Pseudo-critical
Intrinsic-extrinsic	Educational	Didactic
Extrinsic	Recreational	Status seekers

[49] D. E. Berlyne, "Laughter, Humor, and Play," in Gardner Lindzey and Elliot Aronson, eds., *The Handbook of Social Psychology,* vol. III, 2nd ed. Addison-Wesley, Reading, Pa., 1969, p. 843.

[50] Howard S. Becker, "Notes on Commitment," *American Journal of Sociology,* vol. 66, July, 1960, p. 34.

[51] Rolf Meyersohn and Robin Jackson, "Gardening in Suburbia," in William Dobriner, ed., *The Suburban Community.* Putnam's, New York, 1958.

[52] Benjamin B. Ringer, *The Edge of Friendliness.* Basic Books, New York, 1967, p. 113.

[53] Bruce Watson, "On the Nature of Art Publics," *International Social Science Journal,* vol. 20, no. 4, 1968, pp. 667–680.

Watson's distinction between intrinsic and extrinsic motivations (or values) comes close to separating the organizers of an art exhibit from those who attend it. The *intrinsic value–positive attitude* category is exemplified by the art-for-art's-sake public which is composed of artists, collectors, patrons, and connoisseurs; this public, according to Watson, "comes closest to the creative act."[54] The *intrinsic value–negative attitude* category is found most readily among those who are "conservative in their opinions . . . stemming from a high commitment to a particular kind of art. . . . It is accompanied by a negative attitude, however, because any work that deviates from this mode of art is considered to be bad or not art at all."[55]

The *extrinsic value–positive attitude* category represents the use of an art show to enhance sociability. "Visits are simply a means of using time in a socially approved manner."[56] The *extrinsic value–negative attitude* category applies to those members of the public who are not interested in art, are not committtted to art, but use art in Veblen's sense, as conspicuous consumption, in order to enhance their social position.

Watson reflects very distinct value preferences. It serves art far more to have a public that maintains an intrinsic value–positive attitude, inasmuch as such a public comes closest to the artistic experience and the creative act. It also makes less possible a functional substitution of some other leisure activity for art. Thus, the larger the following for art for its own sake, the less likely there is to be a decline in interest. What is true of art, it might be noted, is equally true of all other activities. Those who are intrinsically motivated are closest to the experience and importance of the activity, regardless of whether it be art, music, sailing, or the taking of drugs.

Authenticity might best be related not to intrinsic motivation, but to the extent to which, as Etzioni recently defined it, "its appearance and underlying reality are responsive to basic human needs."[57] Leisure activities are human constructions in which rules for their proper pursuit are made and remade according to the ways in which they best fit circumstances. From a sociological view, an individual using an art show to enhance his social position might be far more authentic—in the sense that he serves his ambition and desires without inflicting pain on anyone—than the "intrinsic value–positive attitude" public which is experiencing a creative act.

Regardless of the values placed on the pursuit of leisure for extrinsic vs. intrinsic motivations, there is compelling reason for social scientists to obtain

---

[54] *Ibid.,* p. 675; see also, Bernard Rosenberg and Norris Fliegel, *The Vanguard Artist.* Quadrangle, Chicago, 1965, Chap. 6.

[55] Watson, *op. cit.,* p. 676.

[56] *Ibid.,* p. 676.

[57] Amatai Etzioni, *The Active Society.* Free Press, New York, 1968, p. 667.

information on the extent to which the one or the other motivation prevails for various activities.

Perhaps the most elaborately developed typology for a public was provided by Theodor W. Adorno in his discussion of music listeners.[58] Like Watson, Adorno issues the typology from the point of view of one who is intrinsically motivated himself. Again like Watson, the ideal participant is one whose motivation is clearly intrinsic, and who also comes closest to the creative act itself. Adorno's typology consists of the following kinds of music listeners:

1. *The expert* has a fully crystallized ability to comprehend what he hears and exhibits compatibility between his listening activity and what he listens to. He is a fully conscious listener, very often a professional musician. The type is very rare and is declining in relation to the growth of total music listening.

2. *The good listener* is not fully conscious of the technical and structural implications of what he hears, although he can go beyond listening to the individual musical phrases and can make connections spontaneously based on judgment and not merely prestige categories or the arbitrariness of what is fashionable.

3. *The culture consumer* (*Bildungskonsument*) listens to music very frequently, is well informed on details of musical biography and other external details which replace his knowledge of the structure of music; his interest approaches fetishism. This type is likely to be found in the "upper bourgeoisie," which dominates the musical life of Western society.

4. *The emotional listener* does not want to know anything about music but listens merely to "feel." Music becomes sheer projection of internal states.

5. *The ressentiment listener* constitutes the counterpart to the emotional listener; his ideal is one of static musical listening, denying the official musical life; he is likely to escape into a *period* such as the Baroque. The ressentiment listener tends to be a purist. Concerned with the quality of performance as measured by its fidelity with the original, the ressentiment listener takes into the goal of music the bourgeois ideal of musical showmanship.

6. *The jazz expert* is close to the ressentiment listener in his aversion to the romantic music ideal, though he is free of the ascetic concern with faithful rendering of the original.

7. *The entertainment seeker* (*Unterhaltung*) includes the largest number of music listeners. These are listeners who play music all day while they work and engage in other activities. The purpose of listening is distraction and the mode of listening is one of distraction and lack of concentration.

8. *The indifferent*, unmusical, and antimusical listeners are social types that cannot be explained by an absence of natural gifts, but more likely early childhood experiences. What it means to be musical has not been studied in relation to society.

[58] Theodor W. Adorno, "Typen musikalischen Verhaltens," in his *Einleitung in die Musiksoziologie*. Suhrkamp Verlag, Frankfurt, 1962, Chap. 1.

The wide range of music listening as suggested by the Adorno typology is illustrative of the multi-dimensionality of human activities. Participation in any activity provides a very crude and frequently misleading measure of involvement; the typology suggested above, which has not been confronted with empirical materials (although Adorno pleads for further research and makes some useful suggestions), provides merely one of many frameworks in which particular leisure activities can be cast. Clearly, the more closely the typology is related to substantive and substantial differences, the more meaningful it becomes to trace changes over time. To be sure, culture-critical arguments, which are frequently based on a series of very subtle nuances, usually imply distinct value judgments; these values have not been fully exposed although, by and large, they represent what in its ideal-typical form has been called the "Great Tradition."[59]

For most leisure activities, great traditions do not exist since, by definition, these refer to works of art and literature, to creative masterpieces in the various arts. There are, however, minor traditions such as rules in games, historically-shaped customs in hobbies, conventions in all leisure activities. Little is known about the rates in changes for different leisure activities. When the change is rapid, it is identified as "fad behavior," itself an important component in leisure.[60]

In essence, the study of leisure activities divides into two modes of evaluation. One is based on criteria external to participants but deriving from the society directly, as in the case of the Great Tradition. The other involves the subjective perception and attitudes of members of society who engage in the activity. The depth and breadth of perception, rather than the choice of activities as such, becomes the evaluated behavior.

The distinction between different kinds of purposes, performances, and pleasures derived from an analysis of any leisure activity creates problems for the construction of meaningful measures or indicators concerning the quality of life. Most of the existing typologies have avoided this question by presenting types of participants in terms of the frequency of their participation, their stated gratifications or some other fairly superficial response. To evaluate the relationship between a participant and his activity in more demanding ways, such as those outlined by Adorno for music, means to begin with a model of society and the relationship of that activity to it. Further, it means that the social scientist must himself comprehend the leisure activity as a coherent and unique cluster of stimuli whose perception by the participant can vary in profundity, attentiveness, concern, understanding, appreciation, technical skill, and the other dimensions suggested by Adorno. Such penetration of leisure

---

[59] This tradition is most clearly elaborated in F. R. Leavis, *The Great Tradition*. New York University Press, New York, 1964.

[60] For a further discussion see Rolf Meyersohn and Elihu Katz, "Notes on a Natural History of Fads," *American Journal of Sociology,* vol. 62, May, 1957, pp. 594–601.

activities has not been carried out in any empirical work perhaps, in part, because few leisure activities have been considered "coherent" in the sense in which Adorno describes music.[61]

A promising line of inquiry which can be applied to leisure activities, in which the *time* dimension is a significant aspect, is found in "phase analysis." This has been used in the 1966 study of outdoor recreation by Marion Clawson and Jack Knetsch.[62] The phases are identified as follows:

1. Anticipation, planning, preparation
2. Travel to the destination
3. On-site experience and activities (which can include travel or might even consist largely of travel)
4. The return trip
5. Recollection

The amount of time spent in the first and last phase is difficult to assess and, indeed, both of these activity classes are likely to be lost in most time-budget studies. Yet they constitute an integral part of all leisure activities, although for many they might be relatively insignificant. Likewise, for different classes and groups in the society, the amount of attention paid to the preparation for and the recapitulation of particular leisure experiences doubtless varies considerably. The mechanisms of information gathering (phase 1) and information sorting (phase 5) that are relied on by different kinds of persons at different stages in the life cycle are not understood. It is becoming apparent, however, that for certain kinds of leisure activities, such as tourism, the first and last phase are closely linked to institutionalized and more or less commercialized sectors within the leisure "industry." The apparatus of travel, such as travel agencies and the variety of tourist and transportation services, play an important role in the information supply available;[63] the apparatus of the photography industry and related services are connected in important ways with the last phase, recollection. Yet how the five phases are linked is only dimly understood.

[61] To be sure, a typology of music listening does not provide direct application to any other activity since music constitutes a unique activity and consists of a special language. "But that music is a language by whose means messages are elaborated, that such messages can be understood by the many but sent out only by the few, and that it alone among all the languages unites the contradictory character of being at once intelligible and untranslatable—these facts make the creator of music a being like the gods and make music itself the supreme mystery of human knowledge." Claude Lévi-Strauss, *The Raw and the Cooked*, trans. by John Weightman and Doreen Weightman. Harper, New York, 1969, p. 18. See also Edmund Leach, *Lévi-Strauss*. Wm. Collins & Co., London, 1970, pp. 115–116.

[62] Marion Clawson and Jack L. Knetsch, *Economics of Outdoor Recreation*. Johns Hopkins Press, Baltimore, 1966, pp. 33–36.

[63] Fritz Machlup, *The Production and Distribution of Knowledge in the United States*. Princeton University Press, Princeton, 1962.

Conclusion

The possibility of meaningful monitoring of leisure is enhanced by the ability of social scientists to develop frameworks within which leisure can be placed. Even if a social bookkeeping operation could be defended and a recommendation made for such "sheer" descriptions as time budgets or participation rates, these statistics would do little to furnish an account of the quality of post-industrial life. And since it is precisely the quality of life and the expansion of attention paid to the nature of experience which are deemed the important aspects of post-industrial life, bookkeeping can do no more than to provide guidelines.

Table 3 indicates the kinds of research activities that can be carried out in the area of leisure, distinguishing between data that are gathered at the level of the individual from data gathered in the aggregate.

Table 3. Research Modes According to Types of Information and Units of Analysis for Leisure Research

	Unit of Analysis	
Type of Information	*Individual*	*Aggregate*
Time expenditure	Observation Interview Diary	Attendance figures Membership figures
Money expenditure	Budgets	Sales figures
Attitude studies	Activity-based interviews Individual-based interviews	
Performance studies	Individual evaluation studies	Product analysis Content analysis

Not all of the modes of research indicated have, in fact, been employed. Lundberg in his study of leisure in Westchester County during the 1930's has pointed out what the ideal research would consist of:

> The ideal method of securing a detailed record of activity would presumably be to assign an investigator (preferably unseen) with a stop watch and a motion picture camera to follow an individual during every minute of the twenty-four hours, or at least during his waking hours.[64]

[64] George A. Lundberg *et al.*, *Leisure: A Suburban Study*. Columbia University Press, New York, 1934, p. 88.

Yet even with such detailed recordings, no data would be obtained on the quality of experience and attitudes toward leisure.[65] Monitoring and time-budget analysis have inherent limitations which cannot be circumvented even with the finest instruments.

What then are ways in which meaningful monitoring of social-psychological changes in leisure can be carried out? To answer such a question requires the establishment of a conceptualization of leisure which goes beyond the abstraction and disembodied conceptualization of leisure as a particular unit of time or a particular set of activities; recording of changes in the amount of time available for leisure or the kinds of things that people will do in their leisure time is useful for many purposes, but not for a measure of social-psychological change. A record of *what* people do and *when* provides only a measure of choice of what is available and ignores the element of *concealed choice,* of activities that people would like to do if the opportunity existed. Further, time and activities are unclear indicators of those aspects of leisure that are most significant, namely, the quality of experience. Unless monitoring can include the meaning behind choice, the social construction of reality, it remains empty statistical reckoning.

The social intelligence for America's future needs to concern itself with the relationship of time and activities to their underlying meaning. The incidence of euphoria, of transcendent experience, of awe and insight would give us a better indication of the state of leisure in America than the varieties of leisure experience that are more commonly recorded.

If the *subject* of leisure studies should shift from duration (time) and content (activities) to process and meaning, the *unit of analysis* should shift from the disembodied individual, randomly selected, to the various communities which provide the relevant context for leisure activities. Above all, leisure is a social phenomenon; the meaning and importance of leisure activities are provided by the groups in which activities are shared. These groups are systematically ignored in random samplings of individuals and can only be captured in research designs which treat as their unit of analysis the groups in which particular leisure interests occur.

The recent rediscovery of "social circles" provides one wedge into such a mode of analysis. Charles Kadushin has shown how social circles are employed by individuals and affect them in the pursuit of several activities.[66] The interplay between the individual and his social circles provides one signifi-

[65] For one such effort see Nelson N. Foote, "Methods of Study of Meaning in Use of Time," in Kleemeier, ed., *op. cit.,* pp. 155–176.

[66] Charles Kadushin, "The Friends and Supporters of Psychotherapy: On Social Circles in Urban Life," *American Sociological Review,* vol. 31, December, 1966, pp. 786–802; *idem,* "Power, Influence and Social Circles: A New Methodology for Studying Opinion Makers," *American Sociological Review,* vol. 33, October, 1968, pp. 685–699.

cant variable that must be taken into account in leisure research. Within such contexts, the expression of meaning and reaction to various leisure activities can then be studied and understood.

It is at this level that one can begin to ask questions about changes in American society. The changes—in labor force distribution, in the nature and meaning of work, in the distribution of income and wealth, in the degree of urbanization—are mediated and realized not by individuals acting as single "players" in the various arenas of choice that are presented, but as a series of "coalitions" and interdependencies, that is, as a series of social circles radiating outward.

Because leisure behavior is more voluntaristic than other kinds of behavior, there is greater need to examine the forms of social life within which leisure takes place. To some extent, these are set by tradition and prior commitment. Yet they are also emergent, growing out of the tastes and preferences that different humans select and develop. A social circle may seem as fixed and rigidly established as a kinship group; in reality, it is permeable and shifting. Hence, the study of activities within such a setting is a study of change.

To be sure, it is the individual in whom we are ultimately interested. But the setting in which we study the individual and the ways in which we relate what we find out about him to what we know about the context of his life, that is, the others for whom his leisure experiences are also meaningful, provide the insights needed to understand the quality and meaning of his leisure.

7

The Human Factor in Economic Affairs

George Katona

Changes in the American Economy

The American economy at the beginning of the 1970's differs greatly from that before the Second World War. The major forms of change are well known and are amply documented by aggregate statistical data compiled by governmental agencies. Although economists would emphasize different aspects of change and thus would differ in how they formulate the essence of the new developments, most would probably agree that the list given below describes some major differences between the American economy in the second half of the 1960's and the period prior to the Second World War.

Major Aspects of Change:

1. Considerable improvement in the standard of living of very broad groups of the population ("affluence").
2. Relatively high rate of economic growth, interrupted by short and mild recessions only.
3. Wants- and aspirations-economy, rather than needs-economy.
4. Inflation; slow but continuous price increases.

In our new mass-consumption economy the majority of families make substantial discretionary expenditures and constantly replace and enlarge their stock of consumer goods. Affluence in the sense of more for the many, rather than much for a few, is a new phenomenon. In the past, rich societies were characterized by relatively few individuals or a thin upper class living in abundance, while the great majority struggled for subsistence. The well-documented fact that today the majority of American families have a higher stand-

229

ard of living than their parents had (point 1 in the list above) does not suffice, however, to characterize affluence. The income received by the majority of families has become large enough so that the common man has funds at his disposal not only for what he must have to satisfy minimum needs, but also to pay for many things he would like to have. Satisfaction of wants (point 3) means much more than the occasional purchase of luxuries or splurging. What is wanted and what is thought to be needed for an acceptable standard of living have grown greatly.

Poverty is no longer a condition shared by people from many walks of life. The poor have become a special group. Those handicapped by old age, lack of education and training, physical disability, absence of male earner, and racial prejudice represent the overwhelming majority of the poor. For those outside the poverty segment, subsistence is taken for granted. For many of them the problem is not one of getting a job, but getting a better job. During the late 1960's, practically full employment prevailed. Not only has the proportion of those who are unemployed at a given time declined greatly, but so has the proportion of the labor force that has ever experienced unemployment. Diverse areas of the economy are characterized by a shortage of labor rather than by a shortage of work opportunities.

Has the business cycle become obsolete? This is a question widely discussed by economists. The mere fact that this question has been raised points to a substantial change, indicated in point 2. In the 25 years after the Second World War, good times were interrupted by short and mild recessions and in the 1960's the rate of economic growth was unusually high. Most Americans believe that alternations of periods of boom or bust are no longer in the cards.

Although in some postwar years prices rose very little, even before the acceleration of inflation in the late 1960's experts as well as consumers agreed that we are living in an age of inflation. But what history taught us about runaway inflations is not applicable to the American situation. Our creeping inflation consists of slow and gradual increases in the price level rather than of rapid depreciation of money (point 4).

Postwar American economy is a consumer economy. Although it was traditional in introductory chapters of economic textbooks to stress that the end of all production is consumption and the often-repeated expression that the consumer is king is at least a hundred years old, in earlier economic analysis the consumer was usually shoved off the stage. Fluctuations in the economic activity and in the rate of economic growth were explained primarily by changes in the rate of business investment and by government activities. In the private economy, the business sector was viewed as the one and only major autonomous force. Yet, in the postwar period consumer expenditures on durable goods, which represent consumer investment, fluctuated more than business investment. From 1956 to 1965, consumer expenditures on durables increased by 62 percent (on nondurables by 31 percent and on services by 45 percent), while business investment increased by 37 percent.[1]

Nowadays, good years in the automobile industry mean an upturn in the economy, while bad years imply stagnation or recession. Good or bad years depend primarily on consumer demand, which thus influences the economy greatly (point 1 in the list below).

Consumer Economy:

1. Consumer expenditures on durable goods exert a great influence on the economy.
2. Rise of consumer debt is more rapid than that of government or business debt.
3. Nonbusiness wealth, in owner-occupied houses and in human capital, represents a very large share of national wealth.
4. The majority of consumers have discretion in spending and saving.

It should be noted, however, that our statistical data are incomplete, and although data on expenditures on durable goods are available, there are no data on the sum total of discretionary expenditures made by consumers which include expenditures on additions and improvements to homes, on vacations and travel, and on hobbies and leisure-time pursuits.

Since 1945, consumer debt increased at a much sharper rate than government or business debt. One might go as far as to divide the history of the American economy into three periods. From the early days of the Industrial Revolution until 1914, business debt grew rapidly and made it possible to build industry, railroads, utilities, mines, etc. From 1914 to 1945, government debt increased much more than the debt of the other sectors, which is hardly surprising because these years encompassed two world wars, the Great Depression, and the New Deal. After 1945, the rate of increase in business debt and in government debt was smaller than that of consumer debt. (The increase was particularly small in federal debt held by the public.)

In bygone days, national wealth consisted primarily of the productive facilities of the nation, that is, of business assets. However, a gradual change has taken place in business ownership over many decades; corporations have become predominant and business firms owned by their managers are relatively unimportant. But stock ownership remained highly concentrated among institutions and very rich individuals in the period before the Second World War as well as in the postwar years when there was a great increase in the number of stock owners who are, for the most part, small stockholders.

Beyond the fact that the common stock held by many institutions (e.g.,

---

[1] The data are from compilations by the Department of Commerce, expressed in constant prices.

life insurance companies, pension funds) represents consumer wealth, the great increase in home ownership should be pointed out. Early in this century approximately 40 percent of 20 million family units lived in one-family houses they owned; in 1946, close to 50 percent of 38 million families and in 1967, 67 percent of 60 million families lived in their own homes. The total value of owner-occupied one-family houses was estimated in the early 1960's at $400 billion. This is about the same amount as the estimate of all business investment in plant and machinery. Both estimates are gross; businesses owe money on their assets as do consumers on their mortgages.

Wealth or capital can no longer be defined as fixed assets. Human capital —the sum total of the value of skills, education, and training, and also of the health of the people—is the most important productive asset in our time.[2] Although no exact estimates are available, it is clear that there are now two major forms of nonbusiness wealth—owner-occupied houses and human capital—in which not 5 or 10 percent of the people but the majority hold a sizable share.

Affluence enhances consumer choice and discretion. Having some discretionary purchasing power, more and more people have become free to program the gratification of their wants and to speed up or postpone their purchases. Consumers exercise their discretion in a manner which makes them an autonomous factor in the economy. If consumers were just transmitters of income, received overwhelmingly from business and government, by increasing their spending as their income increases and reducing it as their income decreases, then the study of consumer psychology could be excluded from economics. (Such a study might still be important for marketing because of consumers' discretion to choose among different makes, brands, and stores.) If, however, as will be amply discussed in this paper, attitudes and expectations may make consumer expenditures grow or decline independently of the change in their income, economics must be concerned with the socio-psychological determinants of decision-making and choice as well.

Factors Contributing to Economic Changes

Little insight is gained when recent changes in the economy are catalogued without a discussion of the developments which caused or made possible the changes. The two considerations are so closely related that in describing economic changes in the previous section, we needed to refer to some of their probable causes. Yet an analysis of the causal factors is in order and is outlined in the list below.

[2] Human resources represent a very important asset of business firms as well, as Likert emphasizes. See Rensis Likert, *The Human Organization*. McGraw-Hill, New York, 1967.

Causal Factors:

1. Change in the size distribution of income.
2. Technological changes: consumer durable goods; rapid accumulation of knowledge brings forth innovations and increased productivity.
3. Institutional changes: use of credit by consumers; improvements in business and governmental policy.
4. Psychological changes: change in motives, attitudes, and expectations.

The distribution of income among American families has undergone a substantial change. The change is hardly noticeable in the position of the "rich": the top 1 to 5 percent of income receivers still receive a disproportionately large share of total income.[3] Nor is the change a major one when the situation of the "poor" is analyzed, although the proportion of the poor has declined over the last few decades. The proportion of the well-to-do, those not wealthy but in a position to have a good and comfortable life, has grown so that in the late 1960's it consisted of one-half or more of all families, who controlled an even larger share of total personal income.

In Table 1 those with more than $20,000 income are classified as "rich" and those with $6,000 to $20,000 income as well-to-do or as having some discretionary purchasing power. The limits chosen are fairly arbitrary, but the picture would not change much if the well-to-do group were defined somewhat differently. (For instance, in 1968 those with $7,500 to $25,000 income com-

Table 1. Size Distribution of Income in 1968

Income before Taxes	Percent of Family Units	Percent of Total Personal Income
Under $3,000	17	3
$3,000–$6,000	20	10
$6,000–$20,000	58	67
Over $20,000	5	20
Total	100	100

SOURCE: Survey Research Center's Survey of Consumer Finances.

prised 50 percent of the family units and obtained 66 percent of total income.) Over the last 50 years, and also over the last 20 years, there were three significant increases in (1) the number of families, (2) personal income in constant prices, and (3) the proportion of families with discretionary in-

[3] Income inequality, as measured by the share of top income receivers, was reduced during the depression of the 1930's and during the Second World War, but not in the postwar period.

come. The third increase was larger than the second, and the second larger than the first.

Among technological changes, the most relevant for consumer behavior is the invention and marketing of consumer durable goods, beginning with the automobile early in this century and spreading later to a great variety of household appliances. When consumers spent most of their income on perishable goods and short-run services (rent), their discretion for speeding up or postponing their purchases was limited. Today in America, only a very small proportion of new cars is bought by people who must have a car because they have none, or because their old car needs to be replaced. Most buyers of new cars trade in a car which, they believe, is in good or fair condition. Nevertheless, they want a new car because of advantages they see in owning it. In buying durable goods, consumers are motivated in the same manner as business firms are when they make capital investments in new plants and machinery. The new purchase is no longer a simple function of the age and condition of the product to be replaced.

Technological changes extend, of course, far beyond consumer durables. New industries have developed in the postwar period—plastics, electronics, and the computer industry—making for substantial changes in the composition of production and distribution. Furthermore, productivity has grown greatly as a result of improved technology and improved management practices.

Change in management practices is related to the growing role of research and development. The last few decades saw a rapid accumulation of scientific and technological knowledge. The newly acquired knowledge made for increased productivity, and also brought forth institutional changes. Business and governmental policies have acquired some scientific basis thanks to vast accumulations of statistical data, improved forecasts, and new theoretical insights. Sophisticated use of fiscal and monetary policy in conjunction with "automatic stabilizers" or built-in stabilizing features of government budgets is a development of the last 20 years.

A specific and highly relevant institutional change for consumer behavior consists of the ready availability, as well as acceptance, of consumer credit. Mortgage credit had been widely used for buying houses, and installment credit for car purchases was popular even in the 1920's. Yet consumers' use of credit grew greatly in the last 20 years when commercial banks took up this form of lending. At the same time, the acceptance of buying on credit spread to broad groups of consumers.

Point 4 in our list of causal factors of economic change, change in motives, attitudes, and expectations, had a different function. To some extent, it represents the underlying change because acceptance of technological or institutional innovations depends on psychological factors. Mass production of automobiles was not implicit in the invention of the horseless carriage. Availability of credit did not ensure the blossoming of installment credit as an important feature of American economy. The causation goes in both directions. Demand for products as well as for credit promotes technological, institutional, and economic changes. Income sufficient to cover more than necessities opens the way for choice and discretion. At the same time, the exercise of discretionary behavior yields new perspectives by changing people's aspirations and strivings. Although consumption in the past was thought to be a function of income, in recent years income has become a function of consumer needs and wants. Because of their great needs and wants, many consumers work hard to increase their incomes, and wives return to the labor force.

It does not follow that income does not influence consumption. Consumer expenditures, and especially discretionary expenditures, have become a function of ability to buy and willingness to buy. Ability to buy depends primarily on income, on financial and other assets, and on access to credit. Willingness to buy reflects, and can be measured by, changes in attitudes and expectations. How the American people's economic attitudes and expectations differed in the postwar period from those before the Second World War, and how they changed during the postwar period, thus becomes a crucial question for the understanding of changes in the economy.

Major Features of Consumer Psychology

The discussion of the relation of changes in personal variables to economic changes is far from complete; in at least two respects the available data are insufficient. First, when we focus exclusively on the relation of consumer behavior to consumer psychology, we necessarily neglect personal factors underlying the economic behavior of businessmen and of government decision-makers. Second, although it is true that extensive data are available on consumer motives, attitudes, and expectations in the postwar period, there are no comparable quantitative data for the prewar period. There is, of course, ample justification for the assumption that the postwar psychological features of consumers differ in many respects from those before the war, but the point cannot be demonstrated in an exact manner. Clearly, an understanding of current consumer psychology and its relation to current behavior has pronounced implications for the future.

Some major psychological features underlying present consumer behavior are listed below. An analysis of these features will occupy us first; their relation to spending and saving will be taken up later.

Consumer Psychology in the 1960's:

1. Optimism about personal financial prospects.
2. Levels of aspiration raised with success and lowered with failure.
3. Similarity of change in economic attitudes among very many people, promoted by group-belonging.
4. Thing-mindedness and security-mindedness prevail at the same time.

Optimism and Rising Levels of Aspiration. The first crucial finding is that in the 1950's and 1960's consumers, on the whole, were optimistic and confident about their personal financial prospects. Just one of numerous available measures will be cited here, taken from the 1967 Survey of Consumer Finances which was conducted at a time when uncertainty was rather pronounced, thus, the data do not represent peak findings. Early in 1967, of all heads of family units,

51% said that 4 years from now their income would be higher than now,
25% said that 4 years from now their income would be the same as now,
8% said that 4 years from now their income would be lower than now,
16% said that they are uncertain about their income 4 years from now.

100% (all heads of family units).

Among respondents with a family income of $10,000 or over, more than 60 percent expressed optimistic income expectations, and among respondents under 35 years of age, the proportion expecting income increases was larger than two-thirds.

What kind of developments contributed to this high rate of optimism? We may recall that early in this century, the majority of Americans in the labor force were unskilled workers and farmers. People in these occupations reach a peak lifetime income at a fairly early age. Today, white-collar workers exceed blue-collar workers in number, and the educational attainments of the American people have grown tremendously. The proportion going to college is now larger than the proportion going to high school 50 years ago. When "brain" rather than "brawn" is the major determinant of income, young men start with a relatively low salary which is expected to increase over a career lasting several decades. Survey data indicate that, in the early 1960's, the average American family head estimated that he would receive his peak lifetime income at age 50 to 55 years, with unskilled workers and farmers giving earlier estimates and managers and professionals later ones. Surveys also revealed that the majority of Americans were aware of the fact that income increases with age and also with education.[4]

Optimistic income expectations are a function not only of age, education, and income level, but also of past progress. Not fewer than 63 percent of a representative sample of family heads reported in 1967 that they then made more than they had four years earlier. The proportion with optimistic income expectations in this group was found to be very much higher than among people with stagnant or declining past income trends. Moreover, people who experienced substantial and subjectively satisfactory income trends in the past were found to be much more optimistic than people who reported small income gains. Table 2 indicates that these relationships cannot be explained by

[4] For additional data on consumer optimism regarding income prospects, see George Katona, *The Mass Consumption Society*. McGraw-Hill, New York, 1964, Chap. 12.

Table 2. Relation of Past to Expected Income Trends
(*In Percent*)

Change in Income as against 4 Years Ago	Expect Higher Income 4 Years from Now	
	Unadjusted Frequency	*Adjusted Frequency*[a]
A large increase	73	59
A small increase	51	51
No change in income	20	37
A decrease	35	45
Over-all mean	51	

[a] Adjusted for the influence of age, income level, self-employment, and race.

SOURCE: 1967 Survey of Consumer Finances (Survey Research Center, Ann Arbor, Mich., 1968). Number of cases, 3,026.

differences in socioeconomic conditions, even though the adjusted frequencies taken from multivariate studies show smaller differences than the unadjusted frequencies.

It appears that income increases often evoke the expectation of further income increases. The relation of satisfaction with past personal financial trends to the expectation of further improvement is still more pronounced. The proportion of Americans reporting that they were better off than a year earlier, or than four years earlier, has been much smaller than the proportion reporting income increases, and has fluctuated with changing conditions. Nevertheless, a high degree of satisfaction with income increases is indicated by the finding that in most postwar years many more respondents said they were better off than said they were worse off. The relation of expecting to be better off to expecting to be worse off was even more lopsided. In fact, answers to questions about future well-being or the expected standard of living differed little from income expectations expressed at the same time.

The last finding helps to contradict the notion that optimistic income expectations should be given little weight because rising incomes would reflect inflation rather than gains in real income. It is true that, in the late 1960's, most Americans expected the prices of consumer goods to advance over the next few months and the next several years. Nevertheless, on the whole, the expected changes in income appear to reflect notions about real income gains rather than gains in money receipts that would be dissipated by rising prices. The two questions, about expected income trends and expected price trends, are answered in rather different contexts.

When the many survey respondents who reported that their income had increased over the last few years were asked: "How come you are making more now than four years ago?" the question appeared to be puzzling and the answers were given after hesitation. Although many respondents could not give any answer beyond saying that they received raises, a substantial proportion said: "I do a better job now" or "I deserved more" or "I've advanced in my job," and thus pointed out that they had made progress in their careers. Ego-involvement and a feeling of personal contribution are reflected in these responses, while references to inflation were made by a small proportion only.[5] Studies of attitudes toward inflation, to which we shall return in the next section, indicate that (1) inflation is considered as something bad, (2) inflation is believed to result from circumstances which cannot be influenced by an individual, and (3) in the opinion of the great majority of Americans, nothing can be done to safeguard oneself against inflation. Some people blame the government, business, or labor unions for inflation; it is always "they" and not "we" who make prices go up. Gains in income, on the other hand, are very often related to what the individual has done rather than to what others have done. Inflation is seen as an outside influence which detracts from the enjoyment of well-deserved fruits of one's labor.

Optimism about personal finances is one major feature of consumer thinking and feeling. A second related feature was already mentioned when it was shown that satisfaction with income gains makes for optimistic income expectations. This dynamic feature of stepping up aspirations following accomplishment applies not only to income, but to wants and desires for consumer goods and amounts saved as well.

Economic wants are not static. Levels of aspiration are not given once and for all time. As shown in many psychological studies, they are raised with success and lowered with failure. Success and failure are subjective concepts indicating the individual's perception of his accomplishments or disappointments. They are group-determined by being viewed in relation to the success or failure of others in one's group. Usually aspirations are reality-oriented and are slightly higher or slightly lower, rather than substantially higher or lower, than the level of accomplishment.

The change in levels of aspiration will be studied in the next section in relation to the presence or absence of saturation with consumer goods following the gratification of wants.

Similarity in the Evaluation of Economic Trends. The first two features of consumer psychology, which relate to personal financial trends, give a one-sided view of consumers' life space. A third major psychological feature of present-day consumers derives from the fact that group-belonging influences individual behavior.[6]

Individuals (and families) function as parts of broader groups. The

---

[5] More extensive data along the same lines are presented in George Katona, Burkhard Strumpel, and Ernest Zahn, *Aspirations and Affluence: Comparative Studies in the United States and Western Europe.* McGraw-Hill, New York, 1971.

[6] Some of the following discussion is based on Katona, *op. cit.,* Part IV.

groups to which people feel they belong, those with which they identify and share a common fate, may be constituted by face-to-face groups (friends, neighbors, colleagues), by the firm or corporation for which they work, or by such broad groups as all those in similar occupations, or the community, or the entire country. Attitudes and expectations, and especially their changes, tend to be similar among members of the same group. Not only what happens to oneself, but also the perception of general economic trends, and of political and international developments as well, influence consumer behavior and even the appraisal of personal financial prospects. Favorable or adverse news about general trends, even if the news is not expected to alter the personal financial situation, has an affective connotation which may influence aspirations and promote or impede the gratification of wants.

If at any given time some people turn optimistic while a similar proportion turn pessimistic, depending, for instance, on their personality, the impact of expectations would cancel out. Then the change in expectations would not influence aggregate consumer demand. But the influence of enduring personality traits of optimism or pessimism appears minor in view of the finding that individual attitudes such as confidence or distrust, optimism or pessimism, change rather frequently and sometimes fairly suddenly. As a rule, the direction of the change appears fairly uniform among very many people. Two considerations explain the similarity of change. First, the same economic news is transmitted by mass media from coast to coast. Television, radio, newspapers, and periodicals all report and feature the same trend at the same time—higher or lower retail sales, governmental expenditures, taxes, etc.—representing either an improvement or a deterioration in the economic situation. Information constitutes the stimulus, the apprehension and salience of which depends on intervening variables. A second factor that makes for similarity of changes in expectations results from the similarity of the intervening variables among members of the same groups. Union members, for instance, learn about a substantial wage settlement arrived at in a labor conflict and tend to view it as improving the prospects for their own wages. Businessmen learn about increased profits or investment outlays in certain industries and tend to evaluate the news in a similar manner. Surely word of mouth reinforces the interpretations of such news.

Differences in group membership may make for differences in attitudes and expectations. Among groups there will be significant differences in attitudes and expectations. The influence of group differences on economic attitudes should not be overestimated, however. For instance, solutions desired for protracted strikes in the steel or automobile industries showed much variation, especially between businessmen and union members. Yet both groups viewed the strikes with concern and both feared that economic prospects might be impaired by the outcome of the strike: Should labor win, inflation may threaten; should management win, business investment may be lowered. Similarly, large differences appeared from group to group in their attitudes toward the acceleration of the Vietnam War. Yet, although they differed greatly about how to bring the war to an end, hawks and doves held similar opinions about the impact of the war on the domestic economy; the notion that more "guns" meant less "butter" was widely shared.

Response to ever-changing news represents one aspect of the influence of developments other than personal financial ones. In addition, the response to the economic environment in the postwar years depended on certain broad stereotypes that were found to have prevailed among many people and constituted the frame of reference for spending and saving decisions. Although some of these stereotypes appear to have been stable over long periods, others did undergo changes during the last 10 or 20 years, and these changes again appear to have been rather uniform among most people. Here is a brief description of some widely prevailing economic beliefs.

1. It was found in the early 1950's, and was repeatedly confirmed later, that the great majority of Americans believed a depression such as that experienced in the 1930's was no longer possible. Most people thought that alternations of periods of upswing and of mild recessions would continue to occur, but not long-lasting, severe depressions. We have learned how to deal with depressions, most people believed, usually without being able to say whom they meant by "we." Yet, in the opinion of the same people, we still did not know how to avoid recessions and occasional increases in unemployment. The optimistic bias noted regarding personal financial expectations prevailed also about business expectations. The answers to a survey question: "Regarding business conditions in the country as a whole, do you think that during the next 12 months we'll have good times, or bad times, or what?" varied in the 1950's and 1960's between 55 percent "good times" when a recession threatened and 85 percent "good times" when prosperous times seemed assured. Nevertheless, those saying "good times" always constituted the majority of respondents in representative samples.

The continued belief in the persistence of relatively mild economic fluctuations appears to be related to variations in the salience of favorable and unfavorable news. Toward the beginning of a period of upswing, favorable news was reported much more frequently than after a year or even longer periods of prosperous times. The Survey Research Center regularly asks: "Have you heard of any favorable or unfavorable changes in business conditions during the past few months?" and in the case of an affirmative answer, probes: "What did you hear?" The answers have indicated habituation to good news: references to improved business, growing incomes and profits, etc., became less frequent as prosperity progressed, even though sales, incomes, and profits continued to gain. After long periods of good times many people, thinking that "trees don't grow to heaven," were found to be receptive to occasional unfavorable news. Habituation to bad news was also observed occasionally.

2. To what do people attribute fluctuations in business conditions? Two kinds of influences were revealed in studies conducted in good as well as bad times: Survey respondents referred primarily to changes in purchasing power (e.g., "People have more money to spend") and to the power of the government to influence economic conditions. Most Americans believed in the 1950's and 1960's, under Democratic as well as Republican administrations, that the government was in a position to improve economic conditions and was intent on doing so. To be sure, information about how the government could or would proceed was restricted to a small proportion of people, and relatively few people were able to explain how recessions occurred in spite of the power of the government. The majority of Americans have also been continuously in favor of the major domestic economic programs of the government: the war against poverty, expanded social security, slum clearance, highway construction, Medicare, and most recently, pollution control.

3. At the same time that expensive social programs were supported, people believed that deficits were bad. The understanding of modern fiscal policy is impaired by the belief that private and public budgets are analogous. Very many people, knowing that the expenditures of a family or a business firm may exceed its income only for short periods, were amazed about substantial federal deficits persisting over several years, and considered this trend dangerous. Nevertheless, in 1964 and 1965, many people learned to understand, and to approve, some basic ideas of modern fiscal policy. In these years people learned that a tax cut raises purchasing power and higher purchasing power stimulates the economy. From 1966 to 1968, when an increase in income taxes was discussed and finally enacted, the reverse effects were widely understood.

4. Knowledge of the function of interest rates and of monetary policy is rather limited, although in certain years when interest rates rose substantially, the majority of people had heard of that development. Such increases were viewed overwhelmingly as having an unfavorable impact on the economy, primarily because of the old-established association of easy money with good times. In addition, many people considered interest rates as business costs, and rising business costs were thought to result in higher prices. These notions did not change much during the 1960's, even though the proportion of people profiting from high interest rates increased with growing savings deposits and high interest rates were advocated as a weapon against inflation.

5. Among the fairly stable stereotypes that characterize the thinking of American consumers in the postwar period, the belief that inflation is bad is prominent. As described before, Americans as a whole are convinced that rising prices hurt them and hurt the economy, even though many people re-

ceived income increases far exceeding the rate of price increases. For these . people, years with rising prices were, in fact, good years. The general adverse evaluation of inflation serves to explain consumers' reactions to rising prices. Only rarely did a few people buy in advance to beat inflation. Most commonly, people decided to abstain from, or to postpone, discretionary purchases because they thought that, with rising prices, they would need to spend a larger share of their income on necessities. Consistently in the 1960's, fewer persons who expected large price increases expressed the intention of buying a car in contrast to those who did not have that expectation. At the same time, savings deposits remained the most favored form of saving. Thus, people differentiate between a runaway and a creeping inflation without necessarily knowing these terms.

6. Not only deficits, tight money, and inflation, but also international conflict and the Cold War were viewed as having unfavorable effects on the economy. There were some short periods during the 1950's and 1960's when a substantial number of people thought that large defense budgets (specifically, war expenditures for Korea and Vietnam) tended to make wheels turn and thus to stimulate business. Nevertheless, whenever international tensions heightened or military expenditures increased, the majority of people thought that their own financial situation and the economic situation of the country had been influenced adversely. Good times are identified with an improvement of the people's standard of living; they are endangered by higher taxes that may be required because of large military expenditures. A "generalization of affect" prevails both for bad news and for good news. As early as 1945–46, very many consumers expressed doubts about the probability of a postwar depression by thinking that the very good news—the end of war and the unconditional surrender of the enemy—could not have unfavorable economic consequences. Similarly, prospects of rapprochement with Russia, occasionally noted in the 1950's and early 1960's, were responded to with rising optimism in economic matters.

Our listing of prevailing economic opinions consists primarily of a description of fairly specific notions about depressions, deficits, and the like. To be sure, by emphasizing habituation with news or the generalization of affects, we have pointed to nonspecific attitudes. On this somewhat higher level of abstraction, one might note the disrupting effect of uncertainty, associated with a wait-and-see attitude, and the reassuring function of being able to predict what will come. Acceptance of change and the belief that change commonly leads to improvement were also often noticeable among respondents in our surveys, especially in personal financial matters, while no evidence was found for many people believing that a change would tend to be a change for the worse. A further broad generalization about the psychological features of the postwar American consumer is suggested, although the evidence for it is fragmentary: improvement in income and in the standard of living leads many people to believe that they have the power to influence their own fate.

Desire to Spend and to Save. Achievement-orientation prevails not only among businessmen or entrepreneurs but also among very many people in their roles as employees and consumers. Striving for higher income and preference for a job with good chances for advancement represent one aspect of achievement-orientation. Stepping up the level of aspiration following accomplishment rather than being satisfied with past success has already been mentioned as a major feature of this orientation. The desire to get ahead prevails strongly in consumption aspirations as well. People who have many things are those who purchase new products and adapt their behavior promptly to changes in market conditions rather than sticking to the same way of living as in the "good old days."

Specifically, the fourth feature of consumer psychology in the 1960's (see the list above) says, first, that there is great concern with consumer goods ("thing-mindedness"). Improvement in the standard of living is seen as consisting primarily of having more and better goods and services that provide comfort, fun, and leisure. The emphasis placed on more leisure and on large expenditures for leisure-time pursuits has been rising to a pronounced extent. Social critics have frequently described the American consumer as gadget-minded. Consumers were said to purchase, often on credit, a great variety of goods which they did not really need. I shall postpone the discussion of this argument to the last section of this paper. At this point, I must emphasize that preoccupation with the standard of living and with consumer goods represents only one of two broad economic strivings of the American people.

The finding that the middle-class American, i.e., the great majority of the American people, is not only achievement-minded but also security-minded is neither new nor surprising. The more one has, the more one has to lose, many people think. The prevailing standard of living is felt to represent a minimum; its worsening is thought to be intolerable, and inconceivable. Yet, the standard of living is maintained only through a continuous fulfillment of large contractual obligations (repayment of mortgage and installment debt, etc.). At the same time people feel that the future is uncertain—rainy days might come and illness or accidents might cause great expense or might reduce earning power. Therefore, the need for accumulating financial reserves is felt keenly.

Evidence for security-mindedness and saving-mindedness has been collected through a variety of inquiries, of which three may be mentioned:

1. A consistent finding over the postwar period was that, when asked whether they expected to save money during the next twelve months, a much larger proportion answered "Yes, we will save money" than actually saved money (as determined by reinterviews conducted a year later). Questions

about intentions to buy cars and other durable goods yielded the opposite result: fewer people expressed intentions to buy than actually bought. The latter result could be explained by finding that the planning period even for large purchases has often been much shorter than twelve months. While most expressed purchase plans are realized, expressed saving plans are often not carried out. Plans to save must be viewed primarily as reflections of desires and "good intentions."

2. When asked whether they are satisfied with the amount of their financial reserves (in banks, saving and loan associations, and securities), a large proportion of people say that they are dissatisfied. Even people with sizable savings often say that they do not have enough. On the other hand, the majority of Americans express satisfaction with their income as well as with their standard of living.

3. Panel studies in which a representative sample was interviewed at three-month intervals indicate that the increment from income increases is promptly used by a large proportion of people for two purposes: the purchase of durable goods, often done on credit, and additions to liquid savings. It could be shown that improvement in the standard of living and higher financial reserves represent highly valued goals to broad groups of people.[7]

It is frequently thought that liquid saving (net additions to deposits and securities) would be higher in "bad times" (periods of stagnation or recession) than in "good times" (periods of growing prosperity). True, in prosperous years liquid savings are reduced by some people who draw on their assets to finance their unusually large expenditures. On the other hand, income increases stimulate saving and they are more frequent in good than in bad years. Therefore, no general statement may be made about the fluctuations of the rate of liquid saving over the business cycle, and the relatively high saving rate in the prosperous mid-1960's should not have come as a surprise.

Attitudes and Action

We have reviewed the psychological characteristics of American consumers in the 1960's; now these characteristics must be shown to influence consumers' behavior. Such an analysis should serve to indicate how psychological factors have contributed to bringing about the changes in the American economy described in the first section of this paper. Various forms of discretionary spending and saving, such as purchases of durable goods, borrowing, and adding to liquid reserves, represent the major candidates for a demonstration of the relation between change in attitudes and change in actions. Findings obtained in two areas of investigation will be summarized:

[7] George Katona and Eva Mueller, *Consumer Response to Income Increases*. Brookings Institution, Washington, D.C., 1968.

1. The relation of changes in willingness to buy to subsequent purchases of durable goods, indicating the predictive value of attitude change in the short run.
2. The relation of the subjective evaluation of personal financial trends, and especially of rising levels of aspiration, to stimulating new wants and the trend of consumer purchases over the postwar period.

Predictive Value of Willingness to Buy. Development of a measure of change in willingness to buy constituted the first necessary step for investigating the influence of consumer attitudes on demand. Beginning immediately after the Second World War, the Survey Research Center, in surveys with representative samples of American consumers, asked numerous questions about their motives, attitudes, and expectations. In 1951, a summary measure of change in optimism or pessimism was constructed in the form of an Index of Consumer Sentiment.[8] The Index consists of attitudes toward personal finances, the general economic outlook, and market conditions of durable goods (especially their prices). The usefulness of the Index over the entire period for which it is available was investigated by calculating predictive regression equations. In the simplest equations, two explanatory variables were used, the Index (or change in the Index), representing willingness to buy, and disposable income, representing ability to buy. Three forms of consumer action for which government statistics provide continuous data were used as the major variables to be explained, each for the period of six months *following* the quarter in which the Index and income were determined. (Thus the lead time is six to eight months.) The amount of expenditures on durable goods, the number of new cars sold, and the amount of installment debt incurred, as dependent variables, yielded a correlation coefficient of approximately . 90 over the 1952–67 period (40 observations). Both income and the Index proved to be highly significant.

In these calculations, data obtained in various periods are summarized and all periods are treated alike. One may differentiate, however, between

[8] Since 1960 the Index values have been determined and published at quarterly intervals. Annual monographs entitled *1960 Survey of Consumer Finances, 1961 Survey of Consumer Finances,* etc. (published by the Institute for Social Research, University of Michigan, Ann Arbor) reproduce, in addition to the Index values, the reports issued each quarter. These reports include data on attitudinal questions not included in the Index, an analysis of the reasons for changes in sentiment, as well as forecasts for the next six to nine months. For a statistical analysis of the predictive value of the Index of Consumer Sentiment, see Eva Mueller, "Ten Years of Consumer Attitude Surveys: Their Forecasting Record, *Journal of the American Statistical Association,* vol. 58, December, 1963, pp. 899–917; George Katona, "Anticipations Statistics and Consumer Behavior," *American Statistician,* vol. 21, April, 1967, pp. 12–13; and E. Scott Maynes, "An Appraisal of Consumer Anticipations Approaches to Forecasting," *1967 Proceedings of Business and Economic Statistics Section,* American Statistical Association, pp. 114 ff.

(1) periods in which no major new developments occurred and the prevailing trend continued, and (2) crucial periods characterized by turning points. In the first kind of period, a "naive model," postulating that "tomorrow's weather will be the same as today's weather," would have yielded correct predictions. Even then, scientific forecasting has an important function because it is known only *post hoc* that there would be no change in the economic trend. Nevertheless, it can be demonstrated only for periods of substantial change, and especially for periods in which the direction of consumer activity underwent a change, that attitudinal data did foreshadow large changes in the economy and were indispensable for that purpose (because the changes could not have been predicted from an analysis of such traditional economic variables as income, inventories, past purchases, or liquid assets).

The relevant data are shown for two periods: for 1958, when the most severe postwar recession occurred (Figure 1); and for 1969–70, the most recent economic slowdown (Figure 2). Both charts demonstrate that consumer sentiment deteriorated much earlier than consumers' discretionary activities declined. The same was true during the "minirecession" of 1966 which interrupted a five-year-long continuous growth of durable expenditures. In 1958 and in 1967, consumer sentiment improved before consumer activities increased again, indicating in advance that the recessions would be of short duration.

Consumers' disposable income grew prior to each of these recessions. From 1955 to 1959, the rate of increase was small and there were quarters of income stability; from 1965 to 1967, the advance in incomes was uninterrupted and substantial. In 1969 and 1970, real income continued to grow but to a smaller extent than in the previous years because of an acceleration in the rate of price increases. Thus it was not a reduction in consumers' ability to buy which ushered in the slowdown in consumers' expenditures. The Index of Consumer Sentiment declined steadily and substantially in 1957, also in 1966, although to a lesser extent, and again in 1969. The Figures present a composite measure obtained by multiplying the Index with disposable income for each quarter so as to take account of both ability and willingness to buy.[9] The decline of the line "Index Times Income" was less steep than the decline of the Index alone.

It can be seen from Figure 1 that purchases of durable goods remained very large during the entire year 1957. The amount of durable expenditures and the number of new cars sold were about the same in the fourth quarter of 1957 as in the fourth quarter of 1956, while the amount of installment debt

---

[9] The construction of the measure "Index Times Income" is explained in the note to Figure 2. Predictions of the extent of forthcoming changes in discretionary consumer expenditures are much more difficult than predictions of the direction of these changes.

incurred was even higher. Consumer sentiment, however, began to deteriorate during the first half of 1957. The usefulness of the attitudinal data is enhanced because the Index values are published immediately after the conclusion of each survey, that is, in the same quarter in which the survey is conducted. The recession of 1958 and the end of the recession were foreshadowed by the movements of the Index, although the lead time was much shorter in the second instance.

Figure 1. Consumer Attitudes and Behavior: Recession of 1958

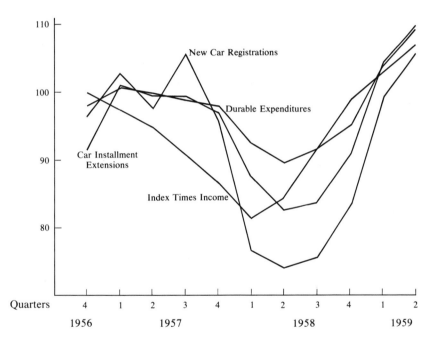

NOTE: Income, expenditures, and debt in constant dollars, seasonally adjusted. Index and income: fourth quarter 1956 = 100; other data: first half 1957 = 100.

Similarly, consumer purchases of durable goods and their debt incurrence were substantially stable in 1966 when the Index fell sharply and the measure "Index Times Income" declined moderately but steadily. The low rate of consumer activity in the first quarter of 1967 coincided with a substantial improvement in the predictor. The need for advance information may have hardly been smaller in 1966–67 than in 1957–58. That car demand did not continue to rise with incomes, as it did during five previous good automobile years, was indicated in advance by attitudinal data, and exclusively by these data.

There was no recession and hardly a slowdown in any economic activity in 1969. The Index began to decline in May 1969 and reached much lower values in August and November of that year. Figure 2 shows that personal consumption expenditures for cars and extensions of installment credit for car purchases declined substantially in the first quarter of 1970. Had the data been presented in percent of income, rather than in absolute amounts, the decline would have been larger still. In addition to automobile demand and other discretionary expenditures by consumers, the recession was indicated by a substantial increase in unemployment and in the amounts of personal saving in 1970. The Index of Consumer Sentiment continued to decline in the first and second quarters of 1970, but at a much slower rate than in 1969, indicating a lengthy though mild recession. In the third quarter of 1970 the Index registered a slight improvement.

The quarterly surveys conducted by the Survey Research Center have a dual purpose: to indicate changes in consumers' willingness to buy and to point to the factors responsible for these changes. In addition to the questions included in the Index, survey respondents are asked to explain their opinions (e.g., why do they think that business conditions will improve or worsen) and to tell what they think of various new developments and their impact on economic conditions. In the light of the answers received to such questions, it was possible to relate the deterioration of sentiment in 1966 to the impact of widely noted price increases, rising interest rates, the possibility of tax increases and, first of all, the uncertainty created by the war in Vietnam. In 1967–68, surveys disclosed some habituation to the adverse news of the preceding year. Consumers were pushed toward larger spending by rising incomes and satisfaction with the trend of their incomes. At the same time, the uncertainty about Vietnam grew, and people were increasingly dissatisfied with being dependent on developments in a faraway country. Therefore, many people adopted a wait-and-see attitude rather than proceeding to gratify their wants and desires.

In 1968, consumer sentiment improved somewhat because the prospects for peace were thought to have increased by the halting of bombing in North Vietman, the start of negotiations in Paris, and the election of a new President. (The elections of new Presidents increased consumer optimism in 1952 and 1960 as well, even to a larger extent than in 1968.) But in 1969, people were disappointed; an end to the war was not in sight and the new President was not seen as strengthening the economy. Consumer apprehension grew substantially because of rapid price increases, sharply rising interest rates and, later in 1969, anxiety about a recession and unemployment which were

Figure 2. Consumer Attitudes and Behavior: Recession of 1970

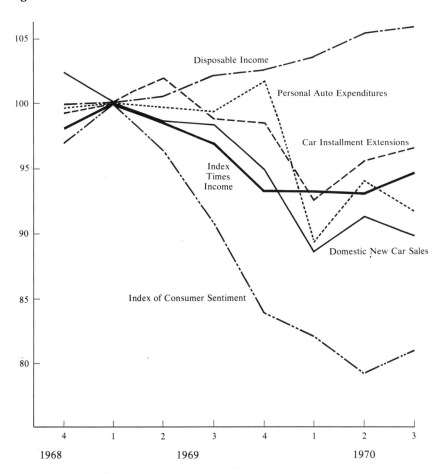

NOTE: Income, personal automobile expenditures, and debt in constant dollars seasonally adjusted. Number of domestic new car sales, from *Survey of Current Business,* seasonally adjusted. Because of the automobile strike, the average data for July and August,
1970, are shown as the third quarter of 1970 data. All data: first quarter 1969 = 100.

In order to construct the measure "Index Times Income," relative weights were assigned to the quarterly values of the "Index of Consumer Sentiment" and to disposable income before multiplying the two series. This was necessary because quarterly percentage
changes in the index are substantial in comparison to the changes in disposable income.
(The percentage changes in income would be much larger if measured against supernu-
merary or discretionary income, which constitutes only one-fourth or one-third of total
income.) That relative weight was determined which achieves the optimum fit, in terms of
a minimum sum of absolute deviations, in a bivariate equation over the period from 1966
through the third quarter of 1970. "Index Times Income" was the independent variable
and "Personal Automobile Expenditures" the dependent variable in that equation.

thought to threaten as a consequence of the fight against inflation. Instead of believing in an end to inflation, many people feared both inflation and lower incomes (due to layoffs and less overtime).

The possibility of making conditional forecasts—e.g., "If war expenditures are reduced, then . . ." or "If interest rates go up, then . . ."—is of great importance. Fulfillment of economic forecasts is subject to developments unforeseen at the time the forecasts are made. The standard forecasts computed from econometric models through solving numerous regression equations yield definite forecasts (e.g., GNP will be so many billion dollars next year) predicated, however, on the persistence of past relationships (e.g., on the extent to which consumption has been a function of income). The introduction of "ex ante variables"—business investment plans, consumer buying intentions, or changes in consumer sentiment—adds substantially to the standard forecasts by reflecting the economic actors' probable response to recent developments. Nevertheless, new developments unknown to those whose plans and attitudes are studied may occur during the periods for which forecasts are made. Behavioral economics may contribute to an understanding of the probable response to such developments on the international scene, or in prices and taxes. Indeed, economic policy must make use of the possibility of ascertaining the probable response of consumers, because economic behavior depends not only on the fiscal or monetary policy introduced, but also on the expectations aroused by it.

The studies that have been described briefly in the preceding pages indicate that consumers are capable of influencing economic trends and that psychological changes underlie the changes in the rate of discretionary spending and saving. It is also apparent that the relevant psychological changes are not exhausted by the evaluation of personal financial developments. People's evaluation of economic trends, the impact of the government's economic policy and international developments strongly influence economic behavior. Yet, much remains to be done both for the practical purpose of improving the forecasting methods and in the interest of basic research on the psychological foundations of economic behavior. Some unsolved problems are apparent in the figures presented above, for instance, regarding the length of the lead time of attitude change and the extent rather than the direction of change in action in response to attitude change. More generally, short-run economic fluctuations are influenced by recurring developments as well as by those unique at a given time. Far too little is known of the interaction of these two kinds of changes and, therefore, the dependence of the future on what happened in the past. What happens a second time, be it an increase in taxes or interest rates, for instance, need not influence behavior in the same way as it has the first time.

Influence of Personal Financial Progress on Purchases. The two most fundamental objections to assigning great influence on economic behavior to psychological factors may be stated as follows: (1) While attitudes and expectations are relevant for a study of individual behavior, the influence for all individuals would cancel out and, therefore, need not be considered in an analysis of market trends. (2) The influence of attitudes and expectations is restricted to fluctuations in behavior over short periods; in the long run, however, such "basic" factors as income and assets alone would determine the course of the economy.

The analysis just presented serves to disprove the first assertion; we now turn to a report on findings that contradict the second statement. The discussion will be restricted to the impact of the subjective evaluation of personal financial trends on consumers' discretionary activities.

During the postwar decades, the great majority of Americans experienced continuous and substantial income gains. As reported in the previous section, satisfaction with past income changes and optimism regarding forthcoming changes were major characteristics of consumers in that period. At any given time a substantial proportion of consumers evaluated their income trend in a favorable manner.

We classify representative samples of consumers according to their evaluation of past personal trends into three groups, improvement $(+)$, stability $(=)$ and deterioration $(-)$. We proceed in the same way regarding expected trends. By combining the two distributions, we divide all consumers into nine groups. In order to simplify the analysis, we then recombine the nine groupings into five, as shown in Table 3.

Table 3. Consumer Groupings, Based on Personal Trends

	Percent in 1968
Cumulative gain: $++$	31
Intermittent gain: $+=$, $=+$	15
Reversal: $+-$ and $-+$	9
Stagnation: $==$	10
Deterioration: $--$, $-=$ and $=-$	11

NOTE: The first sign denotes change in the evaluation of the past trend and the second sign change in the expected trend. The frequencies in the various groups do not add to 100 percent because a sizable group expressing uncertainty about future trends is omitted.

This classification can, of course, be carried out regarding income changes alone. In that case, however, the classification becomes confounded and the differences in the behavior of the five groups are less pronounced. An income increase may be unsatisfactory because it is smaller than the increase in the cost of living; or because other people (reference groups) have obtained larger increases; or because it is a one-time transitory gain. The data presented in Table 3 relate to being better or worse off than four years ago and to expecting to be better or worse four years hence, as obtained in a survey conducted in 1968.[10]

Progress in financial trends is not always perceived by people to be necessarily continuous. There are people who expect no change following an improvement or who expect improvement following no change; reversals—improvement followed by deterioration or vice versa—also occur. But the majority of those who feel that they have made progress expect further progress.

Which consumer activities should be chosen in order to be related to the perception of personal financial trends? Conceptually, it is not difficult to define discretionary expenditures, but it is not possible to devise a satisfactory operational definition that would be applicable to large groups of consumers. Many leisure-time expenditures and especially luxury expenditures are sporadic or restricted to small proportions of the population. For some people, vacation expenditures are habitual rather than discretionary. Purchases of automobiles may likewise be nondiscretionary; well-to-do people may buy a car even when they are not optimistic, and the same may hold true for the purchase of cheap used cars on the part of low-income people. The car purchases of the "rich" and the "poor," however, are usually cash purchases. Therefore, incurrence of installment debt in the 12 months prior to the determination of attitudes was selected as the first kind of activity considered. This debt is incurred primarily for the sake of buying a new car or other large durable goods.

Expressed intentions to buy durable goods represent the second set of variables related to perceived financial trends in Table 4 and Figure 3. Three variants were chosen, intending to buy at least one large durable good, two or more large durable goods, and a new car during the next 12 months. Both intentions and personal financial expectations are expressed at the same time. While actual purchases include many nondiscretionary purchases made necessary by breakdown or damage of goods owned, this is much less true of purchase plans.

Finally, automobile turnover rates were calculated by relating the year in which each family last purchased a car to the year in which it expected to purchase a car again. Thus, for instance, those who last bought a car in 1966 and said in January, 1967, that they planned to buy one in 1967 or 1968, or who last bought in 1965 and said they would buy in 1967, were classified as having a turnover rate of two years or less.

[10] Katona, Strumpel; and Zahn, *op. cit.;* also see Survey Research Center, *1967 Survey of Consumer Finances.* Institute for Social Research, University of Michigan, Ann Arbor, 1968.

The relation of the five trend groups to the selected consumer activities is shown in two ways in Table 4. First, the frequencies of incurring debt, intending to buy, etc., are presented for each group. These unadjusted data do not suffice, however. The influence of at least two important factors must be eliminated before the assertion may be made that certain personal financial trends stimulate economic activity. Families at a higher income level purchase and intend to purchase more frequently than families at a lower income level, and younger families do so more frequently than older families. At the same time, income level and age are also associated with an improvement in the financial trend. Therefore, a multivariate analysis has been carried out which yields adjusted deviations indicating the contribution of income trends net of the influence of income level and age. By adding these deviations to the mean frequencies, adjusted frequencies are calculated and presented in Table 4.

It can be seen from the table that 52 percent of families with a cumulative gain incurred installment debt in 1966, while only 37 percent of all families did so. Among families with an intermittent gain and a reversal, the frequencies were 41 and 48 percent, respectively. Families with stagnation or deterioration show still smaller frequencies (26 and 29 percent). As expected, the differences among the five groups are much smaller when the data are adjusted for the influence of income and age. Yet sizable differences in the same direction still appear; the group with a cumulative gain shows the highest adjusted frequencies among the five groups.

Similar results are apparent in each of the four other activities presented in the table. In each case families with a cumulative gain are conspicuous by having the highest unadjusted as well as adjusted frequencies. Families with either stagnation or deterioration have the lowest frequencies. The extent of the influence of financial trends on the different activities can also be evaluated from the table. Regarding intentions to buy we find a progression in the relative size of the difference between the groups when we proceed from planning to buy any durable good to planning to buy two or more durables and, further, to planning to buy a new car. The more discretionary an activity, the greater the influence of the perceived financial trend.

Visual evidence for the conclusion that perceived financial trends make a difference in the frequency of discretionary activities is provided by presenting a few of the data of Table 4 in Table 5 and Figure 3.[11]

Improvement in the standard of living, a continuous process for many

[11] Further data along similar lines, both for the United States and Western European countries are presented in Katona, Strumpel, and Zahn, *op. cit.* The relation of perceived financial trends to discretionary behavior was found to be similar on both sides of the Atlantic, but the proportion of families with perceived cumulative gains was by far the greatest in the United States.

Table 4. Relation of Perceived Financial Trend to Discretionary Activities
(*In Percent*)

Activities	All Families	Past and Expected Financial Situation[a]				
		Cumulative Gain	Intermittent Gain	Reversal	Stagnation	Deterioration
Incurred installment debt:						
Unadjusted	37	52	41	48	26	29
Adjusted[b]		43	37	40	34	34
Intend to buy:						
Any durable goods:						
Unadjusted	44	64	53	46	32	34
Adjusted[b]		55	50	43	38	40
Two or more durable goods:						
Unadjusted	14	26	17	15	8	8
Adjusted[b]		21	16	14	11	11
New car:						
Unadjusted	7	14	8	4	5	4
Adjusted[b]		12	7	4	6	6
Car turnover 3 years or less:						
Unadjusted	33	45	35	35	29	19
Adjusted[b]		39	33	33	34	24

[a] Compared to one year ago and one year hence.
[b] Adjusted for the influence of income level and age.
SOURCE: *1967 Survey of Consumer Finances.* Number of cases, 3,165 family units (for car turnover, 2,031 family units).

Table 5. Intentions to Buy, All Groups vs. Families with Cumulative Gains
(*In Percent*)

Intentions to Buy	All Groups (1)	Families with Cumulative Gains (Adjusted) (2)	Excess of Col. 2 over Col. 1 (3)	Col. 3 in Percent of Col. 1 (4)
A durable good	44	55	11	25
Two or more durable goods	14	21	7	50
A new car	7	12	5	71

Figure 3. Relation of Personal Financial Trends to Buying Intentions

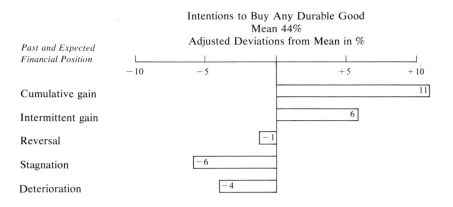

Intentions to Buy Any Durable Good
Mean 44%
Adjusted Deviations from Mean in %

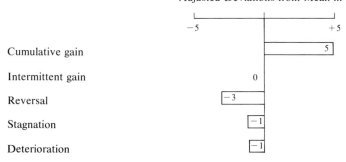

Intentions to Buy a New Car
Mean 7%
Adjusted Deviations from Mean in %

NOTE: See footnotes to Table 4.

American families during the postwar period, manifests itself in the upgrading of possessions and the acquisition of kinds of goods not previously owned. Upgrading also prevails regarding some expenditures on food, clothing, and home furnishings; kinds of expenditures not previously made were also taken up regarding many forms of services. Yet, in the United States, durables and expenditures connected with leisure-time pursuits constitute the prime indication of a family's way of living. The transition from a rented apartment to home ownership, equipping the home with more and better appliances and furniture, and ownership of a better car or a second car are major aspects of an improved standard of living. Although leisure-time expenditures also consist of spending money on nondurables and services, they are closely connected with the purchase of durables. By far the most frequent form of vacation travel is by means of the family car, and the car is frequently replaced in order to have a better one before starting on a trip. When survey respondents are queried about how they spend their free time (evenings, weekends), driving around and sight-seeing by car are mentioned most frequently, in addition to viewing television, and represent highly cherished pursuits. Fishing, boating, and many other leisure-time activities require durable equipment and, first of all, a car in order to reach the place of activity. The desire for a "second home" (often a place in the woods or at a lake), widely noted recently, involves the purchase of a durable good and increases the need for a car (a better car or a second car).

Therefore, the rate of car turnover is a good indication of improvement in the standard of living. The useful life of an automobile is now close to 10 years. Yet the time span between two successive car purchases by the same family is usually much shorter. Data collected in 1967—earlier data were rather similar—revealed that among all car-owning families, 19 percent set the time span between their last purchase and the planned next purchase at two years or less. An additional 14 percent had a time span of three years. Compared with the average frequency of 33 percent for a time span of three years or less, those with a cumulative gain had a frequency of 45 percent (the adjusted frequency was 39 percent—see Table 4). Among those with a deterioration, the frequency was only 19 percent (adjusted frequency, 24 percent). Thus, this important form of upgrading is strongly influenced by the perceived trend in the personal financial situation.

When survey respondents were asked in the late 1940's about their wishes and desires—specifically, about things they would like to spend money on—only such basic items as better housing, a car, and a few appliances were mentioned frequently. The list of items mentioned by at least 5 or 10 percent of representative samples lengthened during the 1950's and grew further in the 1960's. Although in the intervening years millions of consumers gratified many of their wishes, the proportion of those who said "we have most of the things we need," and who did not mention a desire for specific things, did not grow. Such answers were restricted, in the main, to the old and the poor. (Poverty appears to impede not only ability to buy, but also desires and aspirations.) In addition to desires for more and better traditional durables, new wants arose as incomes increased and the standard set of consumer goods was acquired. A large proportion of the new wants centered around leisure-time pursuits, vacation, and travel.

A priori it could be argued that prosperity is its own gravedigger because, after several good years in which many people satisfied their wants, "people run out of things they can't do without." But the price of affluence is not saturation and the lack of incentives. Saturation is not a function of the number and quality of consumer goods possessed. Progress and accomplishment evoked optimistic expectations in the 1950's and 1960's, so that many people had great incentives to continue to strive toward their goals. The closer a person comes to his goals, the greater is his incentive to work hard because concrete and attainable rewards stimulate activity.

Credit plays an important role in this respect. Buying on the installment plan is thought to be justified by many consumers who believe it is right to use goods while paying for them. But the function of credit goes beyond this simple consideration. Accumulation of funds which would make it possible to pay cash for desired goods is a slow process. Being deprived of greatly desired possessions for a long time, and thus getting accustomed to a lower standard of living, is avoided by buying on credit. By stepping up their living standard early in life—by having children as well as the things deemed necessary—satisfactions and aspirations of American families are enhanced.

Thus, it is understandable that consumer debt grows most in prosperous years, and increase in debt is associated with rising incomes as well as optimistic income expectations. Debt is a sign of prosperity and contributes to it. The importance of distress credit has declined.

Consumer behavior in the postwar era would have been rather different if satisfaction with personal financial progress and the expectation of further progress had not prevailed among very many people. Receipt of increased income alone would have had an impact, but a much smaller one than in the actual situation when many wage and salary increases aroused optimistic expectations. Rising levels of aspiration have contributed to shaping postwar economic trends.

Social Learning and Social Change

If economic changes are to be explained in terms of human behavior, changes in motives, attitudes, and expectations must contribute to bringing about economic changes. Yet the notion that changes in psychological variables alone may change economic trends is as little justified as the other much more prevalent extreme notion that changes in money supply, income, interest rates, etc. alone determine those trends. Motives, attitudes, and expectations are intervening variables which shape the perception of stimuli as well as the response to stimuli. We disregard what may be called purely psychological causation (for instance, price increases resulting exclusively from the notion that prices will go up) as we disregard purely economic causation (e.g., price increases resulting exclusively from incomes exceeding supplies). Economic changes originate both in market forces and in motives, attitudes, and expectations.[12]

The typical stimulus to which human beings respond by changing their spending, saving, investing, or pricing is information about economic matters. How information about one's own or other people's income, about prices, interest rates, taxes, or business trends is apprehended, and how people respond to that information, is a function of personal intervening variables. Direction and extent of change in economic trends in a given country at a given time are influenced by those psychological variables which change among very many people in a similar manner at approximately the same time. For an understanding of international differences and historical trends, sociocultural norms and the distribution of personality types also matter.

Behavioral economics can, therefore, make a substantial contribution. One of its crucial problems is the understanding of social learning which consists of the acquisition of new or changed motives, attitudes, and expectations by masses of people. Contradictory notions may be maintained about the learning process. The first one, expressed most pointedly by Galbraith in two brilliantly argued books, relegates the consumer to a minor role by assigning all power to the giant corporations and their marketing and advertising activities. According to Galbraith, the consumer is managed or controlled by the producer and the seller;[13] according to Vance Packard, he is a pawn in the hands of "hidden persuaders." Galbraith, no doubt intentionally, overstates his case so as to contradict the opposite extreme notion proposed a long time ago by economists who coined the thesis of consumers' sovereignty which argued that the sovereign consumer determines what is produced and sold.

[12] It is hardly necessary to say that the argument about dual causation also holds if the origin of economic changes is traced farther back. People's expectation of inflationary price increases originates not only in their personal experience, but also in new economic stimuli (e.g., news about large war expenditures or sharply increased wage rates).

[13] See, for instance, "The producing firm reaches forward to control its markets and on beyond to . . . shape the social attitudes of those, ostensibly, that it serves." John K. Galbraith, *The New Industrial State.* Houghton Mifflin, Boston, 1967, p. 212; *idem, The Affluent Society.* Houghton Mifflin, Boston, 1958. Galbraith's views of consumers have been discussed in greater detail by the author in Chaps. 7, 8, and 9 of *The Mass Consumption Society* and in the *American Economic Review,* vol. 58, May, 1968, p. 29.

Yet, except under extreme circumstances of conditioning and compulsion, learning is characterized by interaction between the learner and stimuli originating in others—the teacher, information received by word of mouth, the printed page, radio and television, including advertisements. The unidirectional flow of influence, which characterizes both Galbraith's "revised sequence" and what he calls "accepted sequence," is an exception least applicable to the acquisition of social attitudes. This is not to deny the importance of outside influence and even of advertising, especially regarding choices that do not matter much to the consumer (for instance, choices among certain brands and stores). Thus, although the consumer is not sovereign because the environment sets limits on his choices, he does retain some discretion of action. Business, including the giant corporations, is not sovereign either. It watches consumers' notions and attitudes carefully and adapts its policies to the consumer. Most commonly, business firms' endeavors to influence the consumer consist of their trying to reinforce and make use of prevailing consumer attitudes.

In the sense economists use the term, consumers are "autonomous." As has been shown in the preceding section, at certain times, which are often of great importance for economic trends, changes in consumer attitudes and action do not correspond to what would result from, and could be predicted by, changes in incomes, prices, supply conditions, and the like. In a more general sense, neither consumers nor business are autonomous because they are interdependent.

Yet, an understanding of the spread of economic news and generally of the process of influence requires extensive further studies. The widely accepted notion about the paramount influence of word of mouth and peer groups, rather than of the printed word originating in opinion leaders, does not suffice. It needs elaboration regarding the rapid diffusion of news that causes waves of confidence and surges in spending, or waves of uncertainty and widespread postponement of expenditures. There is a great deal not known about the process of diffusion of attitudes and the relation of opinion leaders to followers. The same is true of the influence of news transmitted by television and of advertising.

In studying consumer influence, or the joint influence of consumers and business firms on economic trends, the question is: In which direction does this influence lead our society? This broad question is closely related to a study of what may be called the seamy side of affluence. Our society disposes of greater resources than ever before. What use does it make of its resources and to what extent does it waste them? This problem may be discussed under several headings.

Clearly, the major goal of our society is not abundance of material goods. Release of human potential is not achieved by greater material well-being, greater comfort, and more fun. Does interest in the possession of more and better consumer goods forestall the gratification of spiritual and cultural aspirations? Does an improved standard of living impede self-fulfillment? No doubt, not necessarily. If under certain conditions gratification of wants results in rising levels of aspiration, the newly arising wants may not be concentrated exclusively on material goods but may spread to cultural and spiritual matters as well. Absence of preoccupation with subsistence needs may open up the possibility of spending more time and money on acquiring additional skills and education, on art and culture and, generally, on achieving a better life. Even though many people, having improved their standard of living, have increased the time and money spent on education, reading, music, and performing arts, far too little is known of the extent of interest in and aspirations regarding cultural pursuits. The relation of increased material affluence to the emergence and growth of spiritual and cultural values is no doubt susceptible to empirical studies.

Similar considerations apply to the relation between the public sector and the private sector. In this respect, Galbraith again emphasized most strongly the discrepancy between the extent to which personal ownership of consumer goods has increased and the insufficient progress in the improvement of such public facilities as schools, hospitals, and outlets for recreation. But desire to satisfy what I want for myself need not exclude desire for more and better public goods. The realm of egotistic interests may be extended to wanting better schools and hospitals, as well as to desiring clean water and fresh air, and readiness to make sacrifices to achieve these goals. Understanding of the interrelatedness of personal well-being with that of neighbors and many other people may lead to an extension of the realm of "I" into a more comprehensive "We."

On the other hand, it is doubtful whether an expansion of public goods could be achieved by restricting the gratification of personal desires (for example, by making buying on credit difficult, or by raising taxes). Since improvement of the standard of living represents a major reason for working hard, clamping down on the private sector might impede the growth of the entire economy. Deficiencies are best remedied by increasing the total output, and not by redistributing the available resources.

America has become rich compared to bygone times and to most other countries of the world. But few Americans feel rich; they still feel that most of the money they spend serves to satisfy urgent needs—even though what they feel they need far exceeds what they have needed at earlier times. The struggle to obtain what people feel they should have has remained intense. Finally, a mass-consumption society in which most people consume similar goods has been achieved, but not a mass-saving society. The distribution of wealth is much more highly concentrated among a small proportion of people than the distribution of income. The rate of saving, and level of the accumulated savings or wealth, are very low among the great majority of Americans.

There also exist the threat that the rich are getting richer. In the second half of the 1960's, the proportion of families with more than $15,000 to $25,000 income has grown disproportionately. Furthermore, only those with substantial assets are in a position to reap great profits from capital gains. The appreciation of stock and real estate values in the mid-1960's as well as some of its underlying causes, inflation and also increased payoff of research and development, have made for greater inequality rather than for spreading well-being among all people.

Turning to basic problems connected with affluence, we must note first that social learning is usually slow and gradual. Barring major disturbances such as full-scale war or revolution, the acquisition of new attitudes and aspirations by masses of people does not occur suddenly or rapidly. This has been found true of general attitudes toward inflation, recession, and the government, as well as of specific attitudes such as the change in the evaluation of investment in common stocks or of buying on the installment plan. In contrast, scientific and technological progress takes place at a rapid pace and often occurs fairly suddenly. Moreover, in certain areas, for instance in race relations, social change has also been fairly rapid in recent years. To what extent the slowness of the learning process and the frequent maintenance of established stereotypes make for difficulties in economic adjustment represents a challenging question for which few answers are available.

How to improve the economic position of the lower middle classes and the poor are urgent problems of the day. Affluence may make it possible to increase welfare payments and even to provide a guaranteed annual income to the poor. But these measures may not suffice to satisfy the aspirations of poor people and to allay their dissatisfaction and alienation.

The "malaise of affluence" extends to many people beyond those in the poverty sector. Even though most Americans take economic survival for granted, the constant struggle for advancement has not become easier. Our competitive society makes for stress, frustration, nervous tension, and anxiety. It is commonplace to say that material affluence is not identical with happiness.

We live in a dynamic society. In the past several thousand years, the static society was the rule. Human beings still desire stable, safe, and predictable conditions which are no longer common. It is therefore hardly surprising that adaptation to dynamic change is incomplete and fraught with difficulties. The current problem is not lack of challenge and absence of incentives. The opposite problem of being unable to tackle the many problems that confront us may be of greater import.

Possibly even the prevailing economic incentives and the extent of aspirations toward an improvement of material well-being are undergoing some change. The United States has not only been the land of opportunity, but also the country in which a far greater proportion of the population than, for instance, in Western Europe welcome and adapt to change and aspire to have more goods and services, as well as education. Such findings were obtained through surveys with representative samples of family heads. Recently, however, there are indications of young people rejecting business careers, saying "No" to the consumer economy, and denying that hard work leads to progress and success. Sometimes doubts are expressed about the beneficial nature of rising production and even of improved standards of living. There is great need for reliable data on changes in satisfactions with material well-being as well as on changes in incentives and aspirations in the economic sphere.

Social indicators must extend beyond much-needed data on changes in mental health, race relations, and other forms of social interaction. They must include data on changes in economic attitudes, expectations, and aspirations, because the quality of life has economic determinants. It was the purpose of this chapter to indicate that some personal socio-psychological data on economic beliefs, satisfactions, and aspirations are available. Nevertheless, the variety of data collected should be expanded, the methods of data collection improved, and data on economic attitudes and aspirations integrated with other social indicators.

Comparative international studies may be expected to add to an understanding of economic change. Developments in other affluent societies show both similarities and differences when compared with American trends. Studies that my colleagues and I conducted recently, in which the economic attitudes and aspirations in Western Europe were compared with those in the United States, suggest that some substantial differences in the behavior of consumers on the two sides of the Atlantic result from personal rather than from environmental factors.[14]

Analysis of the role of human factors in economic affairs has made some progress during the last 20 years. Recent changes in the American economy and American society call for additional intense effort not only along the lines developed in this chapter, but also in a manner which will shed light on the impact of personal factors on economic and social matters at the same time.

[14] See Katona, Strumpel, and Zahn, *op. cit.*

8

Change in the American Electorate

Philip E. Converse

By its very nature, mass political participation has left an historical record of almost unparalleled density, geographic extent, and time depth in the United States. Thus, it stands in sharpest contrast to most of the substantive areas treated in these volumes, where exactly the right data have almost never been collected, and where surrogate data of an "indicator" sort are fragmentary and subject to fierce admixtures of known or suspected measurement bias. Although there certainly are difficulties akin to "measurement problems" in the development and interpretation of historical voting statistics, as we shall see, there remains a very real sense in which such statistics, as formally reported, constitute "exactly the right data." For however poorly the voting system may be operating at some point in time as a means of gauging mass opinion, it is the votes as counted that determine, with limited further refractions through the Congress or the electoral college, the winners and losers for elective office. Recorded votes are the key output of the system, and here the extant historical record in the United States is massive.

At the same time, no single or unidimensional time series, be it ever so long and conceptually relevant, can carry inquiry very far. This fact may be a bitter pill for specializations faced with decades of work in order to reconstruct so much as one theoretically pregnant series over a significant stretch of history, and I would not wish to imply that such effort is misguided. A number of statistical techniques of varying elegance can, after all, be brought to bear on such a single series to elucidate crude properties of change. Disjunctures in trends can be loosely related, for example, to other historical "events" in ways that are often of suggestive theoretical importance. Nevertheless, most single time series of broad societal interest represent little more

263

than the movement of superficial "symptoms" whose true causes and genuine human significance remain quite unspecified. A trend of any given directionality and rate can have totally different implications, according to the nature of the microprocesses that happen to be generating the change. For the student of national economic development, evidence in price series of even severe inflation may be evaluated in almost perfectly contradistinct ways, according to whether or not the spiral is a product of one or another type of capital formation. The symptom alone remains at least ambiguous and often in the early stages of inquiry, downright misleading.

Yet, even in these terms, the historical study of mass American political participation is richly informed, at least in a relative sense. This is true in two important ways. First, the historical voting record necessarily bears the imprint of many large changes in the distribution, social composition, and technological environment of the American electorate: the waves of migration westward to the frontier; the depositing of new pockets of ethnic groupings across the land; the persistent upgrading of the national-level communication system are but a few of these. What is important is that, despite variations in data quality and occasional lacunae in the record, the correlative time series are usually available in great historical depth either through the decennial censuses or less directly from other sources. The additional fact that, unlike many key national economic series, voting records as well as correlative series are available in highly disaggregated geographic form adds further enrichment to the collection, since causative agents have acted at different rates and at different times across the national domain, and inferences as to effects can be put on much firmer footing by disaggregated and essentially anachronistic comparative study. From the point of view of sheer data availability, then, a remarkable variety of key features in the political development of what S. M. Lipset has aptly called "the first new nation" are in principle "knowable."

There is, moreover, a second source of information, differing from the first less in qualitative terms than in a very foreshortened time depth, compensated for by an extreme density and extensiveness of information. This is the national sample survey. Here again, relative to other substantive specialties, the study of electoral process is remarkably well endowed. Public attitudes and the voting system were among the first targets of large-scale sample survey techniques in the 1930's and 1940's.[1] Since 1948, the Survey Research Center of the University of Michigan has conducted a major national

---

[1] Most noteworthy here from a theoretical point of view are the major studies by Lazarsfeld and his associates of Erie County, Ohio, during the 1940 presidential election (Paul F. Lazarsfeld, B. Berelson, and Hazel Gaudet, *The People's Choice*. Columbia University Press, New York, 1944). Commercial surveys on a national-sample base were conducted in 1936 and 1940 with a variety of interim measurements, and the National Opinion Research Center conducted an excellent national study of the 1944 election which, although never reported in major monograph form, is available in full detail in data archives.

survey in each presidential election and in most of the off-year congressional elections as well.[2] Given the programmatic nature of these studies, they yield up literally dozens of conceptually interlocked time series measures at an individual level, and these are increasingly coming to be exploited in just this vein. Indeed, where public decision-making on a national scale is concerned, the only comparable programmatic monitoring of this detailed infrastructural information has been developed in areas of consumer behavior.[3]

The sheer expanse of the information base presents something of an embarrassment of riches for the purposes of a single orderly essay. Much is known in the area, and the advent of the computer means that very much more is about to be known. Hence, we need spend little or no time on consideration of what key data are absent, although legitimate items could certainly be cited. Instead we may turn our attention in more substantive directions, attempting at the very least to illustrate some of the theoretical interests that may be satisfied when a sufficient depth and breadth of temporal data are available. Even here, however, the range of choice is vast.

I plan to focus in the first instance on types of longitudinal change in the American public and its electoral response that are (1) long-term and (2) apparently "secular" or even irreversible in character. Of course, judgments as to the irreversibility of trends must remain inferential, even in astrophysics, and highly dependent *inter alia* on the time scale chosen. That which is an enduring secular trend within one time scope may turn out to be merely part of an oscillation if the temporal reference is greatly expanded. But enough work has been done in the area to know that certain types of electoral change, however important they may be politically, are best treated as at least nonsecular, and sometimes roughly oscillatory, in any short term (say, five to thirty years); these we will exclude from consideration.[4] Thus we discard, with some regret, any historical discussion of what Key and others have called "critical" or "realigning" elections—those points in history such as 1896 or 1932, when the balance of partisanship in the electorate appears to have shifted dramatically, to settle into new and relatively enduring patterns.[5]

---

[2] Major monographs from these surveys include Angus Campbell *et al., The American Voter*. Wiley, New York, 1960; *idem, Elections and the Political Order*. Wiley, New York, 1965.

[3] George Katona, "The Human Factor in Economic Affairs," Chap. 7 of this volume.

[4] This exclusion is scarcely intended to cast doubt as to the theoretical interest of short-term changes. Examination of their properties, including attention to equilibrium values and boundary conditions, as well as the analysis of the correlates, is of course, central to any dynamic analysis.

[5] V. O. Key, Jr., "A Theory of Critical Elections," *Journal of Politics,* vol. 17, February, 1955, pp. 3–18. The best recent treatment of the full historical sweep of realigning elections is presented in W. Dean Burnham, "Critical Elections and the Dynamics of American Electoral Politics," a paper presented at the meetings of the American Political Science Association, New York, September, 1969.

Among long-term secular changes, I shall focus largely (although not exclusively) on those which have to do with "the nature and quality of electoral response" in the United States. The American electorate in 1968 is vastly different, both in key compositional features and important elements of the relevant environment, from the American electorate of 1824. Moreover, short of thermonuclear cataclysm, the American electorate of the year 2000 will differ from that of 1968 in a variety of highly predictable ways.

Of course, one of the most striking and truly secular trends affecting the electorate and its political responses over these two centuries has been the progressive intensification of mass education. This putative upgrading of the mass public is of particular interest where the American experiment in popular democracy is concerned, for of course the two were causally intertwined in the historical sense. Indeed, on the world stage, the venture of our fledgling republic into extended mass education was as radical a sequence of measures as its earlier experimentation with a constitution. And against the traditional view that instruction of the indolent classes would be futile, dangerous, or both, stood the conviction articulated so well by Jefferson that popular democracy would not be viable in the long run without a literate and informed mass public. This piece of the "liberal tradition," assisted at later times by alarm over the difficulties of assimilating a polyglot population, played a critical role in developing this remarkable national commitment. The question remains, however, what if any difference such policies have made in the common workings of popular voting, and what differences may be expected in the future when by sheer population replacement, if by no other mechanism, the mean levels of formal education of the adult electorate must continue to forge forward.

The Long View: Trends in American Voting Statistics

Since election statistics have been published for as long as popular voting has existed, they have attracted scholarly perusal for over a century, and the resulting analytic literature is vast. Nevertheless, only a small and rather recent portion of this literature is of any direct relevance to our present purposes. The bulk of earlier work involved examination of specific election contests in order to elucidate the particular outcome, and has limited dynamic or theoretical interest. Where there has been interest in the dynamics of voting over more extended periods of time, work until recently has been seriously hampered by the impossibility of manipulating by hand any large masses of data. Some scholars coped with the problem of data mass by restricting their attention primarily to very gross levels of aggregation such as returns by states.[6] Others have delved with profit to more disaggregated data by fore-

---

[6] A good example is Louis Bean, *How to Predict Elections*. Knopf, New York, 1948.

shortening the time perspective and/or restricting the focus to a region or, more often, a particular state.[7] The latter tactic, of course, always left doubts as to the generality of the propositions illustrated by the analysis.

As the development of computer technology has proceeded, however, the old limitations on data handling have rapidly evaporated. At first, access to voting statistics over broad stretches of time and space remained a bottleneck, especially since centralized collections of such data were partial at best. More recently, however, the Interuniversity Consortium for Political Research (Ann Arbor) has been assembling in machine-readable form all voting data for major offices in all elections since 1824, at the level of the county.[8] While occasional sets of returns, especially at lower levels of office, seem to have been lost, the total collection is over 90 percent complete and is beginning to be used. It seems likely that our knowledge of long-term trends in American voting behavior will expand rapidly in the near future as computer exploitation of these materials is brought to fruition.

A good example of ingenious use of materials of this kind for unearthing long-term secular trends in voting patterns is provided in a recent article by Stokes.[9] He has partitioned the temporal variance associated with sequences of votes—where the key statistic can be alternatively either the partisan vote division or turnout—in American congressional districts into components reflecting relative influence arising at the national, state, and local (constituency) levels. At one logical pole would be the case in which turnout or the vote division would move in perfect parallel within all constituencies across the nation from election to election. The variance components model would then allocate all of the variation to "national forces." If, at the other extreme, there was no more than chance similarity in the movements of vote or turnout across congressional districts in the nation, the variation would be totally idiosyncratic to the particular districts, or assumed to be entirely the product of constituency influences. Obviously the truth lies somewhere in be-

---

[7] Important studies in this category would include many of the works of V. O. Key, Jr., such as *Southern Politics*. Knopf, New York, 1949; or V. O. Key, Jr. and Frank Munger, "Social Determinism and Electoral Decision: The Case of Indiana," in E. Burdick and A. Brodbeck, eds., *American Voting Behavior*. Free Press, New York, 1959. Other examples are provided by L. Benson, *The Concept of Jacksonian Democracy: New York as a Test Case*. Princeton University Press, Princeton, 1961; D. McRae and J. Meldrum, "Critical Elections in Illinois, 1888–1958," *American Political Science Review*, vol. 54, September, 1960, pp. 669–683; and S. M. Lipset's use of more localized referenda in *Political Man: The Social Bases of Politics*. Heinemann, London, 1960.

[8] This effort has been successively directed by W. Dean Burnham, Howard Allen, and Jerome Clubb at the Survey Research Center, Institute for Social Research, University of Michigan.

[9] Donald E. Stokes, "Parties and the Nationalization of Electoral Forces," in W. Chambers and W. D. Burnham, *The American Party Systems*. Oxford University Press, New York, 1967, pp. 182–202.

tween, with both national-level and constituency-level influences affecting the voting, along with the reasonable possibility of intermediary state-level influences as well. The point of the Stokes model is to assign precise values to these relative influences.

Applied to *turnout* data for the five congressional elections from 1952 to 1960, the model indicates that virtually all the temporal variance (86 percent) can be allocated to influences at the national level, with the negligible remainder split between state and district influences. Applied to the *partisan division of the vote* in the same period, however, about half the variance is shown to be allocated to local district influences and only one-third to shifts common to the national level. Thus, swings in turnout—largely the alternation between presidential and off-year elections—follow national rhythms, but shifts in the vote division, despite some fair national commonalities, tend more to reflect factors peculiar to local congressional districts.

The most striking findings arise, however, as the same model is applied to successive decades of congressional voting back to 1870. For the 1870's, the local-district component influencing turnout was much stronger than in the 1950's (40 percent, as against 5 percent), and the intervening period has been marked by a steep and almost perfectly monotonic decline in the relative strength of factors peculiar to the district, with a roughly corresponding increase in the weight of the national component. While the data for the partisan division of the vote move somewhat less regularly, they also show an overall decline in the influence of district factors over the same period.

Hence, such patterns testify to the progressive "nationalization" of influences bearing on voting changes over the past century. Presumably this growing national homogeneity of electoral response reflects, among other things, the progressive nationalization or centralization of the mass media, which creates within the realm of politics the same kind of "common culture" assumed with less crisp evidence to be developing in other spheres of life.[10]

Another whole cluster of dramatic changes in the global character of aggregate election returns over much the same post-Civil war period have been summarized and discussed in a major and seminal essay by Walter Dean Burnham, one of the prime movers in the effort to establish a central archive for voting statistics.[11] Burnham has assembled lengthy time series, either at the level of selected states or on a national base, for five relatively accessible

---

[10] A comparative analysis performed on data for British constituencies suggests not only a similar increase in nationalization of forces, but indicates as well that the nationalization of partisan variation there considerably exceeds that in the United States at present, and matched current American levels as early as the turn of the century (*ibid.*, pp. 187–192).

[11] W. D. Burnham, "The Changing Shape of the American Political Universe," *American Political Science Review*, vol. 54, March, 1965, pp. 7–28.

statistical properties of aggregate voting statistics, all of which intuitively bear on the nature and quality of the American electoral response. Each of these indicators has shown a striking shift in characteristic levels since the late nineteenth century, and the direction in which each shift has occurred seems to tell the same conceptual tale concerning the evolution of the electorate. Since these changes represent the most impressive secular ones to be found in the pre-survey voting record, it seems worthwhile to devote an extended discussion to them.

The first of the five Burnham indicators is voting turnout, the most direct measure of active political participation on the part of the public. The proportion of eligible voters coming to the polls in national presidential elections, after running a high and steady 80 percent in the closing decades of the nineteenth century, dropped precipitously around the turn of the century, plunging progressively to a nadir achieved in the middle of the 1920's, from which the recovery even in the 1960's has been modest indeed. Such gross change had not of course gone undetected by earlier observers,[12] and at least some of the contributing factors were obvious to the most casual glance. Thus, for example the later portions of the downturn, roughly between 1912 and 1924, were strongly influenced by the enfranchisement of women, a rapid change in legal definitions of the "electorate" that more than doubled the denominator of the turnout ratio in a short space of time. It is unquestionably true that women took up their new privileges somewhat slowly, and even in the 1960's turn out to vote at lower rates (by 5 to 10 percent) than males. Indeed, resurgent rates of turnout in the intervening period certainly reflect in part the progressive acculturation of women into habitual voting. A conceptually independent set of events clarifies some of the earlier portion of the decline (1900 to 1908). This was the period in which the disfranchisement of the Negro in the South became complete and, in view of the massive partisan consensus among whites, all political significance shifted back to the "white primary" of the Democratic Party.[13] Between the presidential elections of 1896 and 1904, turnout in the eleven states of the Confederacy was cut in half, from nearly 60 percent to less than 30 percent.

As Burnham points out, however, even these major events do not account in any full way for the known historical deterioration in national turnout. For example, with the Confederacy set aside, a still remarkable decline in presidential turnout began elsewhere in the nation after the election of 1896, and a noteworthy change had already been registered before female suffrage became a significant factor. In the several elections prior to 1900, turnout in

---

[12] The change is carefully plotted and discussed in R. E. Lane, *Political Life*. Free Press, Glencoe, Ill., 1959, pp. 18–26.

[13] Key, *Southern Politics*, Chap. 29.

non-Southern states had been running 85 percent or more. By 1912 it had fallen close to a 70 percent figure. If, as is congenial with modern survey data,[14] one thinks of the American electorate as divided roughly into a set of faithful, active voters, another set of peripheral voters whose participation is weak and sporadic, and a final set of chronic nonvoters, then it seems clear that the fraction of the electorate that was peripheral or utterly indifferent had at least doubled in a short time *outside the South* and *before* women entered to confuse the picture further.

The only major line of explanation recently adduced for this portion of the turnout phenomenon has to do with the waves of foreign immigration which were descending on American shores around the turn of the century. Since, in most cases, such immigrants became part of the "eligible electorate" only after becoming naturalized citizens, and since enumerations of citizens and noncitizens are spotty at best for this period, comparable turnout figures are more difficult to estimate reliably during this era than at virtually any other time in American history.[15] This leaves room for the suspicion that turnout proportions based on broader census enumerations of adult males are artificially depressed by inclusion of many new arrivals formally ineligible to vote, and that even where naturalization went on rapidly or was not required, immigrants (then largely from Southern and Eastern Europe) would have become acclimated only at a slow rate into popular democratic participation. Undoubtedly, this state of affairs must have contributed to some decay of turnout. Nonetheless, Burnham goes on to show (at least within certain selected non-Southern states) a marked and progressive decline in turnout after the 1896 election, even in hinterland counties that were by census records almost exclusively of native white stock. Thus, some fundamental puzzle remains.

The Burnham case is considerably strengthened, moreover, by the curious and less-often-noted behavior of the other four indicators over the same period. For example, "roll-off," defined as the tendency of voters to express themselves with respect to the most important offices on a ballot but to ignore the lesser contests, was almost nonexistent until the 1890's, and then grew visibly up to 1930 in all of the states examined. "Drop-off" refers to persons voting in presidential elections but not bothering with participation in off-year congressional elections, thus leaving a sawtooth pattern to turnout over the series of biennial national elections. This was a very modest phenomenon

---

[14] See Angus Campbell, "Surge and Decline: A Study of Electoral Change," *Public Opinion Quarterly,* vol. 24, Fall, 1960, pp. 397–418.

[15] At the time of earlier waves of immigration, the citizenship requirement was frequently nonexistent or unenforced, so that the eligible electorate continued to approximate census figures on adult males (or, in the earliest periods, those fulfilling various other qualifications).

prior to the turn of the century but then grew sharply in tandem with the other changes, and remains at high levels today. Indeed, if turnout estimates were based not on presidential elections taken alone, but on braces of presidential and adjoining off-year elections, the verdict of increasing public apathy would be dramatically underscored.

The other two indicators capture a slightly different aspect of voting process, but one which modern survey research has come to link conceptually with levels of political interest. Split-ticket voting, crudely measured though it must be with aggregate data,[16] appears to have been almost nonexistent before the 1890's, much like roll-off, and to have grown rapidly thereafter. In some of the states examined, it has simply continued to trend upward to the current period; in others, it reached a peak about 1930 in parallel with some of the earlier indicators and remained constant or sloped off mildly thereafter. And the fifth indicator, the average percentage swing of the partisan vote division from one election to the next within the same voting jurisdiction, similarly showed a tendency to increase its amplitude between 1896 and 1930, with more mixed evidence across particular states subsequently. Both of these trends may be taken to imply some kind of deterioration in the strength of party loyalties over this period.

Within sample-survey data from the modern period, a weak but not insignificant individual-level correlation exists between forms of political participation or expressions of psychological involvement in politics on one hand, and expressed intensity of party loyalty on the other. Indeed, Campbell's analysis of the drop-off phenomenon in current survey data shows that citizens who contribute most directly by voting in presidential elections but failing to take part in off-year congressional voting are disproportionately people of low political interest *and* weak sense of party allegiance.[17] They are also people who would be expected to float back and forth between the parties with more abandon from one presidential election to another, thereby adding to aggregate measures of "partisan swing." They would probably show a higher propensity for ticket-splitting as well.

Thus, if we dare extrapolate current knowledge of the "infrastructure" of voter behavior backward to 1890 or 1910, assuming these modern relationships to have been valid under earlier conditions (and there is no obvious rea-

---

[16] In lieu of individual testimony, the incidence of split-ticket voting must be inferred from discrepancies between the greatest and least proportions of the vote garnered by a given party at different levels of office on the same ticket. Any pair of individuals who split their tickets in diametric opposition remain concealed from such a calculation, much as compensating "gross changes" go unrepresented in statements of "net change." Thus such an index of ticket-splitting tends to constitute a minimal estimate of the incidence of such behavior.

[17] Campbell, *op. cit.*

son to challenge this assumption), then the common movement of Burnham's five indicators seems not surprising, for they are of a single piece, however independent statistically they may be. Moreover, the general deduction that some deterioration in democratic participation occurred after the 1890's is vividly underscored, for it certainly seems reasonable to suppose that whatever historical forces led to a progressive reduction of public interest in voting and hence a dramatic shrinkage of the core electorate, were also responsible for the further signs of partisan indifference—drop-off, ticket-splitting, and party vacillation from election to election—that were registering dramatic upturns even among the residue of citizens continuing to vote with some fidelity. By way of summary, Burnham observes:

> In the United States these transformations over the past century have involved devolution, a dissociation from politics as such among a growing segment of the eligible electorate and an apparent deterioration of the bonds of party linkage between electorate and government. . . . Such a pattern of development is pronouncedly retrograde compared with those which have obtained almost everywhere else in the Western world during the past century.[18]

In one sense important for the general aims of this essay, the Burnham observations from aggregate voting statistics are even more impressive than he paints them. This is certainly true if one is willing to imagine that static correlations ubiquitously characteristic of modern survey data have also a dynamic significance for the movement of key variables over time,[19] and are also likely to have underlain aggregate voting data in the nineteenth century every bit as clearly as they underlie it today. For in current survey data, two of the stronger demographic correlates of political interest are education and age. Interest is greater with more advanced education, and quickens with age over most of the life cycle. Strength of party loyalty increases quite sharply with age as well, although not notably with education.

Now if one were to consider in what common demographic respects the American electorate of 1870 differed from that of the 1960's, two of the major "compositional" differences would be in terms of formal education and age. The difference in education is obvious. While rates of pure illiteracy were not particularly high save in the South and, indeed, they were very low by world

[18] Burnham, "The Changing Shape of the American Political Universe," p. 10.

[19] Simon Kuznets has discussed the possibility of erroneous dynamic conclusions stemming from static correlations. The paradigm is one in which a is positively related to b in a static sense within time-1 and within time-2. Moreover, the mean value of a is known to have increased between times 1 and 2. Hence it would seem obvious that the mean value of b would also have increased over the same period. A little thought may show that this conclusion does not follow in any strict sense, and requires independent confirmation. See Simon Kuznets, *Shares of Upper Income Groups in Income and Savings*. National Bureau of Economic Research, New York, 1953.

standards of the time, much of the "three R's" education of the 1870 electorate had been achieved before 1850 and was rudimentary by comparison even with educational practice of 1910. Unfortunately, good data on the most relevant variable, functional literacy, are lacking for any of these periods. Nevertheless, if we assume that prolonged exposure to the printed word past the time when it becomes possible to read to the time when it becomes effortless to do so is important for functional literacy, then it seems significant that only a tiny proportion—certainly less than 5 percent—of the 1870 electorate had received as much as a high school education, whereas the figure today is around 40 percent and climbing rapidly.[20] At the same time, the differences in age composition are noteworthy as well. In 1870, nearly one-third of the electorate was under 30 years of age, or in that decade of life when the limits on political interest are currently most striking. The comparable figure for the electorate of 1960 was 18 percent.[21]

What this means is that, if we were to extrapolate backward in time, simulating terms such as political interest and strength of party loyalty on the basis of current levels witnessed among age and education classes of the electorate, both terms would decline progressively. In the late nineteenth century, political interest and, to a lesser degree, partisan feeling, should have been somewhat weaker than they are today.[22] This in turn means that Burnham's evidence of higher political interest and partisanship before the turn of the century is all the more astonishing. For one is forced to conclude that any absolute decline in interest has occurred in the face of strong shifts in demographic composition of the electorate that should have been exerting considerable upward pressure on any aggregate index of such interest. Hence, "other factors" sapping interest over this period must be seen as all the more powerful, at least if it is legitimate to extrapolate backward from modern survey correlations.

[20] Both figures would require upward adjustment if the South were set aside.

[21] This figure is, of course, turning upward again in the late 1960's in view of the increased birth rate of the late 1940's. However, the dramatic increases in life expectation since 1870 virtually preclude any approach to the contours of the earlier life table.

[22] That such simulations are not totally improbable is suggested by comparative analyses of political interest in France and the United States, completed with sample surveys in the late 1950's. In response to parallel items eliciting degree of subjective involvement in politics, the distributions in France were significantly lower than those in the United States. However, responses within groupings equated for number of years of formal education were nearly identical. Thus it seemed clear that lesser political interest in the French mass public was a direct reflection of lower levels of education in the electorate. Indeed, the education distribution among French adults in 1958 was roughly equivalent to that of the United States electorate in 1920 at the latest. See P. Converse and G. Dupeux, "Politicization of the Electorate in France and the United States," *Public Opinion Quarterly,* vol. 26, Spring, 1962.

Burnham is not, however, totally happy with this latter assumption. While he is willing to accept the implication of some functional relationship in modern data between partisanship and political interest which in turn illuminates the parallel movement of his indicators in an earlier period, he encounters several other patterns in the historical statistics that are anomalous in the light of current findings. Perhaps the clearest of these involves the relationship between turnout and rural-urban residence. Sample surveys have consistently shown lower political interest and more irregular voting turnout as one moves from the city to the peripheral hinterland. These patterns have customarily been interpreted as indicative of rural populations less firmly bound into the mainstream of mass political life through up-to-date education and access to national-level communications on public affairs.[23] Burnham notes that ecological data from the late nineteenth century show exactly the opposite situation, however, with voting turnout in rural areas outside the South typically exceeding that of urban centers! And once again, the shift to modern patterns was going on in just those years after 1900 when the other indicators were showing their most dramatic movement. Indeed, while urban turnout undoubtedly declined over this period, the decline registered in rural areas was all the more massive. On grounds such as this, Burnham calls into question any assumption of the historical generalizability of modern survey findings, however compelling these relationships may seem to be at an intuitive level.

The mystery, then, is clear. What was going on around the turn of the century that could in Burnham's terms have changed so violently the "shape of the American political universe"? More precisely, perhaps, we might ask what *happened* at that time, speaking in a less durative mode, for the standing evidence smacks more of some particular event than of the slow accumulation of demographic trends leading to change. Although their trend lines are not perfectly synchronous, the Burnham indicators generally move along a flat plateau throughout the late nineteenth century and then break suddenly downward at the outset of the new century, continuing this devolution through several elections, as though the electorate were progressively adjusting to some initial impact that struck in the vicinity of 1900.

Burnham himself comes to focus largely on the presidential election of 1896 and its immediate aftermaths. This election has long attracted scholarly attention as one of the few realignments in American political history, when stable patterns of partisanship across the land were brusquely shifted and locked into the molds of potent new coalitions.[24] In brief, the period from the Civil War until 1896 had persistently shown a rather even balance in popular support between the two major parties at a national level. After the depression of 1893 occurred under a Democratic administration, however, the Republi-

---

[23] See, for example, Campbell *et al., The American Voter,* Chap. 15.
[24] See Key, "A Theory of Critical Elections."

cans under McKinley in 1896 defeated the Democratic and Populist coalition of William Jennings Bryan by a margin that was, for its period, moderately convincing, and proceeded to consolidate a period of Republican dominance until 1932, broken only by the Taft-Roosevelt split in 1912 that permitted the Wilson intrusion for two administrations. Roughly speaking, the features of American voting statistics to which Burnham addressed himself "deteriorated" rapidly after this pivotal election.

Following hypotheses advanced by Schattschneider concerning the significance of the 1896 election,[25] Burnham suggests that partisanship fell away and voter apathy grew after the election of that year because through it the barons of the Industrial Revolution, which was then moving to its initial climax, succeeded in stealing the electoral system from the people as a necessary step in consolidating that revolution. He points out that historical experience under a variety of regimes has shown the take-off phase of industrialization to be a "brutal and exploitative process," demanding adequate insulation of the critical elites from mass pressures. While in most developed European countries this phase was encountered before full-scale mass democracy was established, the sequence was reversed in the United States. Democratic institutions with universal (male) suffrage had taken root before the great trajectory into industrialization was achieved. The full crisis between growing corporate power and the strong democratic and pluralistic elements in the political structure came to a head in the 1890's. A series of fortuitous events produced an election victory in 1896 for the Mark Hannas and other captains of industry, however. These included the happenstance that the depression of 1893 struck during a Democratic administration, promoting antipathies among industrial workers who might otherwise have resisted the Republican-business alliance, and the fact that, under the banner of William Jennings Bryan in 1896, the Democratic-Populist coalition tailored its appeals toward the rural South and West rather than toward the new and restive urban proletariat of the Northeast and Middle West. The resulting realignment of that year "brought victory beyond expectation" to those elites involved in giving business interests their necessary way without formal disruption of democratic traditions. Subsequent consolidation of the new Northern coalition led to further routs of the demoralized Democratic Party, a slackening of meaningful party competition at the national level, and an alienation of the mass public from that democratic process which had been such a vigorous popular battleground in preceding years. The sharp changes in the cast of election statistics after 1896 are manifest symptoms of this fundamental deterioration of the American electoral response.[26]

However cogent and attractive the Burnham thesis may be, there are

---

[25] E. E. Schattschneider, *The Semi-Sovereign People*. Holt, New York, 1960.
[26] Burnham, "The Changing Shape of the American Political Universe," pp. 24–25.

numerous counter-hypotheses that deserve investigation. None of them calls into question the dramatic nature of the changes in aggregate voting statistics which occurred between the 1890's and the 1930's. These changes are certainly real, and Burnham has done a major service not only to bring attention to them, but also to point out how internally coherent they seem to be in the light of modern survey findings. It is rather to suggest that the reasons for these changes may lie closer to the surface than Burnham implies, and hence the statistical trends may say relatively little about any growing popular disaffection with democratic alternatives.

First, it is worth keeping in mind that not all the recorded changes in the 1890–1930 period are in any sense "unexplained," even for the area outside the old Confederacy. That is, the size of the national electorate was more than doubled within a decade as a result of female suffrage, and there is no question whatever but that over-all statements of turnout were drastically affected as a result. Moreover, it seems likely on the basis of current survey evidence from the United States and from other countries with different electoral histories, that the behavior of some of the other Burnham indicators is about what one would expect, given the temporary but massive dilution of the over-all "political socialization" of the electorate represented by the opening of the system to participation by women. Thus, while definitive research on the precise effects of female suffrage remains to be done, it is not clear that much mystery remains to be explained for the latter half of the Burnham period.

The perplexing data are those from 1890 to roughly 1915, outside of the South. Of course, some modest contribution to the change even over these years must have come from the new waves of foreign immigrants arriving for the first time in American history from countries remote from anything resembling popular democratic traditions or systems of mass education. The effect of incorporating these newcomers progressively into the eligible electorate would have been similar to those registered at the time of female suffrage. Nevertheless, Burnham has shown convincingly that immigrants alone cannot have accounted for all the change, much of which occurred in rural areas not settled by the new visitors.

What the Burnham account treats inadequately, however, is the fact that the three decades prior to 1915 were highlighted by a succession of sweeping changes in the sheer mechanics of the conduct of popular elections.[27]

---

[27] As this manuscript awaited press, a new Burnham discussion of the period appeared which does explicitly recognize the likely impact of the various changes in voting regulations on the indicators he noted earlier (see Burnham, "Critical Elections and the Dynamics of American Electoral Politics"). A highly abridged version of this excellent manuscript was published as "The End of Party Politics," *Trans-action*, vol. 7, December, 1969, pp. 12–22. I have chosen to leave my text largely as it was originally written, however, for several reasons beyond the obvious one of time pressure: (1) a certain amount of the exposition would have to be included in any event, despite overlap with the new Burnham manuscript; (2) a number of elements had been woven into this exposition

And the direct and intuitively obvious effects of these multifarious changes should have been exactly in the kinds of directions registered by the several Burnham indicators. Without much more painstaking research it would be unwise to claim that there is "nothing left to explain" once these rather mundane bits of history are taken into account. Perhaps after the dust of this work has cleared, it will remain worth entertaining the Burnham hypothesis to explain residual trends. But it would seem useful to pursue the more routine sources of variation in a systematic manner before putting too much weight on the type of explanation Burnham has proffered.

The changes in electoral procedures of this epoch were of two broad types, although roughly the same "reform" and "good government" forces played important roles in their propagation. And it is worth keeping the two types distinct in our minds because their establishment occurred in slightly different parts of this period, and their likely effects on the Burnham indicators would have been quite distinct.

The earlier of these two changes involved the form of the ballot available to the citizen and, indirectly but of capital importance, the whole atmosphere in which the voting act was carried out. The several states of the new republic had moved rather rapidly at the beginning of the nineteenth century from ancient methods of voice voting ("viva-voce" voting) to paper ballots. Originally, these ballots were to be prepared in the privacy of the citizen's home. Very rapidly, however, the political parties began to print their own slates on pieces of paper and distribute them for the "convenience" of the citizen who then had only to drop the slip of paper from the party of his choice into the ballot box. The practice spread like wildfire, and its constitutionality was upheld by a key Massachusetts decision of 1829. Not at all incidentally, in addition to printing the ballots, the parties took extraordinary measures to differentiate their ballots—in color of paper, flamboyant designs, and the like —to assure that the voter's choice would be apparent to anybody witnessing his submission to the ballot box and, indeed, would typically be visible from across the street. Sporadically here and there, legislative efforts were made to oblige the parties to print more "similar-appearing" ballots. Means were quickly found, however, to circumvent these regulations, and they were generally ineffective. The upshot was that, as a practical matter, the "secret ballot" did not exist in the United States for nearly the entire nineteenth century.

---

which have little counterpart in the new Burnham treatment, such as concern for the fit of earlier events with modern survey data or interest in voting fraud; (3) the new Burnham document does not answer the call for an exhaustive empirical examination of the impact of registration rules across all states; (4) most important, my ultimate interpretations of this chapter of history are almost diametrically opposed, despite common recognition now of some of the contributing factors. In addition to this and a few other footnotes added to take cognizance of new Burnham work, I have inserted one major revision in the body of the text concerning final interpretations to address that work.

The eagerness with which competing parties of the period colluded to differentiate their ballots and maintain a "visible" voting system, as well as the extremely limited enthusiasm of other nonparty elites to take those simple steps necessary to protect the privacy of the vote, attest to a political culture vastly different in its key assumptions from that which we have now taken for granted for some decades. Indeed, the party ballot system constituted a logical if informal extension of the primary feature of viva-voce voting, which was the provision for elite control and influence over how the masses voted. Election days throughout this period were everywhere described as confused and disorderly affairs, with the dispensers of the competing party ballots besieging citizens as they approached the polls, well equipped to enhance their bargaining power with side payments for the acceptance of the proper piece of paper. Perhaps the most orderly balloting occurred where the organization and control were most blatant, yielding ". . . the common spectacle of lines of persons being marched to the polls holding their colored ballots above their heads to show that they were observing orders or fulfilling promises. . . ."[28]

General recognition of the prevalence of corruption and intimidation in the voting process finally led, at the end of the century, to a drastic reform in these mechanical procedures. Australia, bedeviled with comparable travesties on popular democracy, developed in the 1850's a single consolidated ballot, printed at public expense and distributed only under carefully controlled conditions at the polling place itself, which contained the names of all the legal candidates. The voter's choices were to be checked in the privacy of the polling booth, guaranteeing secrecy. This "Australian ballot"—now commonplace but in its day a rather radical social innovation—began to diffuse with some rapidity to the limited set of other democratic states in Europe and Canada, and was generally adopted before 1880. The United States, as the most experienced democracy, moved somewhat more slowly, however. The earliest serious attention to the innovation was given in the middle 1880's, partly through the polemic efforts of Henry George. The first actual adoption came in 1888 in Louisville, covering municipal elections. After this point, things moved rapidly. By the election of 1890, 11 states had accepted the Australian ballot as official procedure, and three-quarters of the states had done so in time for the election of 1892, with another half-dozen entering the field before 1896. The last holdouts, largely in the noncompetitive South, were not converted until the second decade of the twentieth century.[29]

[28] Wayne Andrews, "Voting," in Andrews, ed., *Concise Dictionary of American History*. Scribner's, New York, 1962, p. 989.
[29] Two of the more useful histories of the evolution of voting forms are Spencer D. Albright, *The American Ballot*. American Council on Public Affairs, Washington, D.C., 1942; and Eldon C. Evans, *A History of the Australian Ballot System in the United States*. University of Chicago Press, Chicago, 1917.

What effect would we expect the shift from party ballots to the consolidated Australian ballot to have had on voting habits in general, and on the Burnham indicators in particular? As Rusk has pointed out in an excellent analysis,[30] certain intuitive expectations are obvious. Under the old system, the primary choice for voters was between parties, or perhaps more accurately, between slates of candidates put up by those parties. The situation defined for the voter was focused on the several party offerings taken as wholes. The situation did not invite him, as did the Australian ballot, to make separate choices between competing candidates for each level of office. Given what is now known about voting behavior, it is likely that a simple choice as to preferred party would have seemed quite natural and satisfying for a substantial majority of the citizenry.

What is interesting, of course, is the residue of voters sufficiently informed and motivated to make man-for-man comparisons down a pair of tickets. In particular, take the case of a voter who wants to split his ticket either because he has a specific dislike of one candidate put up by his own party or is eager for whatever reason to support one man of the opposing party. States varied rather widely in their relevant provisions. Enough states made no legal provision whatever for such a case to suggest that this was either seen as a very esoteric approach to voting, or there were positive motives to discourage such practice. Other states did make some provision, permitting the voter to "scratch" a particular name on a party strip and write in a replacement in some cases, and in others requiring him to collect two or more strips, marking separate offices and submitting the several ballots attached together. In these latter cases, ballots were voided if the concordance between strips was not exact. When legal provisions existed, they seem to have been little publicized. Instructions for ticket-splitting were not printed on the party strips, and it is unlikely that the hawkers of strips for the several parties would have been anxious to encourage their clientele with informal help. In short, ticket-splitting was a rather obscure and awkward act, where it was defined as an option at all. The general practice among voters discriminating enough to collect tickets from different hawkers and size up specific pairings of candidates must have been to make an over-all evaluation of ticket worth, much as one might assess, position by position, the relative superiority of two fixed baseball rosters.

By grouping the contestants for each office together in blocs on its consolidated form, the pure Australian ballot required office-by-office selection. It did not prohibit "straight-party" voting or, as adopted in the United States, discourage such a pattern of choice by removing the party label from the can-

---

[30] Jerrold G. Rusk, "The Effect of the Australian Ballot Reform on Split Ticket Voting: 1876–1908." Unpublished doctoral dissertation, University of Michigan, 1967.

didate's name, as was true in some countries. The voter could readily find the candidate offered by his party within each office bloc and check the proper box. But it would have been remarkable indeed if such a redefinition of the voting alternatives failed to produce an increase in split-ticket voting, relative to practice under the party ballot system of voting.

Some states were unenthusiastic enough about making old-style straight-ticket voting difficult that they devised an intermediary form, preserving the consolidated form with its virtues of secrecy, but organizing the candidates in party columns so that the faithful partisan need only check one clear column of boxes down the ballot, rather than search for his party's candidates in office groupings. This "Indiana ballot" therefore was little more than a set of the old party strips pasted together side by side. It did expose the voter visually to all of the alternatives, unlike the earlier system in which the relatively partisan citizen need not even have seen an opposing slate to cast his vote, and its organization made the ticket-splitting alternative more obvious. But it was designed to facilitate straight-ticket voting, and many states carried these measures further by providing a single box to be checked at the head of a column to signify acceptance of the total slate proffered by the party.

Since the initial acceptance of the Australian ballot, diverse states have shifted both ways between the Indiana party-column ballot and the office-bloc, or Massachusetts ballot. However, the general pattern of relative popularity of the two forms over time suggests that the goal of adoption was primarily the preservation of secrecy, and that the erosion of straight-ticket voting was an unintended consequence often seen as undesirable. The Massachusetts ballot was the more direct borrowing from the Australian example, and was the dominant form accepted initially in 1890. Some states made no adoption at all until awareness of the Indiana ballot had spread; others, which had initially accepted the Massachusetts form, soon switched to the Indiana variant, which, by a modest margin, has been the more popular in the subsequent period.

Rusk has provided a detailed analysis of the behavior of the Burnham indicator of split-ticket voting as a function of the timing of shift from the old system of voting to the Australian ballot. Split-ticket voting consistently increases in the first election after the ballot reform took effect locally, whether this was 1890, 1892, 1894 or later. Lesser increments appear in subsequent elections, as though voters were becoming progressively habituated to the new freedom, or young voters operating with less of a "party-team" assumption were replacing an older generation that had taken this single-decision approach to voting for granted. As expected, the increase in split-ticket voting is much more substantial in states adopting the Massachusetts form than in those adopting the Indiana form. Thus, it seems very clear that the increase in split-ticket voting at a national level in the period between 1888 and 1908 was closely associated with the Australian ballot reform, and had little to do with the specific political conjuncture of 1896, having largely antedated it. Moreover, Rusk develops actuarial norms for the increases in split-ticket voting to be "expected" upon enactment of one or another type of reform based on the experience of all states at whatever time they made the change, and shows that the increases in split-ticket voting noted by Burnham in a small selection of states is essentially what would have been expected from the ballot reform taken alone. No additional explanatory hypothesis need be introduced.[31]

While Rusk has confined his attention to split-ticket voting, the behavior of at least one of the other four Burnham indicators is readily understood in terms of the Australian ballot form as well. Roll-off, the tendency of some small proportion of the voters not to finish making office-by-office choices after they get down to minor political levels, would generally be interpreted as a symptom of restricted information and a feeling of pointlessness in making further choices among names that are, for the voter, meaningless. On a priori grounds one would expect such interrupted voting to be unlikely to occur for the strong partisan pleased with the party label, even if the candidate name is unknown to him. But for the nonpartisan voter of limited political interest, the behavior seems intelligible as a way of avoiding meaningless cogitation. And indeed, Walker has shown with the office-bloc ballot, as compared with the more simplified party-column form, that the effect is more marked among people of limited education and political interest. He also suggests that the Burnham interpretation of roll-off as symptomatic of alienation may need reconsideration, in view of the ease with which mere ballot form affects it.[32] I concur heartily, for under the preceding party-strip system of voting, it would have cost the faintly interested voter much more effort to stop and cancel out unfamiliar names on the slate of his chosen party than simply to drop the given slate directly into the ballot box. And in many states such canceling, if carried out, would have succeeded in voiding the ballot in any event. Therefore, it does not seem surprising that roll-off was essentially nonexistent before the Australian ballot, and emerged progressively as it was adopted, just as in the case of split-ticket voting.

There is, however, no obvious connection between the Australian ballot reform and the remaining three Burnham indicators. Least imaginable, perhaps, would be any effect of the reform on turnout. Yet the zeal of reformers around the turn of the century was hardly exhausted by the introduction of the new ballot form. The advocates of clean democratic process were not only concerned about the possibilities of intimidation that nonsecret balloting en-

---

[31] *Ibid.*

[32] Jack L. Walker, "Ballot Forms and Voter Fatigue: An Analysis of the Office Bloc and Party Column Ballots," *Midwest Journal of Political Science*, vol. 10, November, 1966, pp. 448–463.

tailed. If anything, they were more alarmed by the fraudulence that ran rampant in the voting process due to lack of control over the identity of individuals arriving at the polling place on Election Day. In the earliest days of popular voting, the only eligible citizens were people of substance residing in what were, by today's standards, small communities. Being readily identifiable to their peers, the assumption of "one man, one vote" could be realized without elaborate precautions.

As the franchise was extended to all adult males and cities grew in size, however, control over voting that depended purely on visual recognition of the prospective voter at the local polling place became increasingly absurd. By mid-century, there was widespread recognition of the prevalence of voting fraud. The literature on the subject, while everywhere anecdotal, is large and colorful over the whole latter portion of the nineteenth century. The variety of mechanisms employed to swell the vote of a candidate artificially compel admiration. Within the cities, the most common method, however, involved the use of "repeaters," or swarms of men recruited for a day's drink or pay either from the transient districts of the city center or from surrounding towns in the rural hinterland, who walked or were carted from one polling place to another, casting and recasting the appropriate votes from dawn till dusk. There was often little or no attempt to disguise the nature of the operation. Men moving along recognizable trails between polling stations "in droves of 50 or more" were part of the familiar carnival of Election Day in some areas and, in a degree hard to comprehend by modern standards, the bystander reaction emerging in contemporary accounts was often as much amusement as indignation. Nor were such incursions on honest voting limited to the polling stations of large cities. Instances of rural authorities reporting vote tallies for their jurisdictions exceeding the number of adult males shown by the census appear on the public historical record. Cases were even reported of unknown men riding up to hinterland polling places and admixing wads of votes at gunpoint. All told, accounts of malpractice were sufficiently dense and colorful for this period that the oblivion into which they seem to have fallen from the point of view of modern scholars working on nineteenth-century voting data is remarkable in itself.

Unlike the Australian ballot reform, which consisted of a well-defined cluster of measures adopted in the vast majority of states within a short space of time, efforts toward more stringent controls over the voting process were quite various in nature and arose (and not infrequently, suffered later repeal) in very scattered fashion in time and space. However, from Harris's excellent set of case studies,[33] it is possible to piece together a reliable view of the gen-

[33] Joseph P. Harris, *Registration of Voters in the United States*. Brookings Institution, Washington, D.C., 1929.

eral trends of the chronology. The state of Massachusetts distinguished itself with the first voter registration law in the United States as early as 1800. The statute was subjected to much experimentation over subsequent years to increase its effectiveness while minimizing the burden of administration it entailed. In 1832, the constitutionality of compulsory prior registration in Massachusetts was upheld.

While features of the Massachusetts model enjoyed some diffusion within the New England states over the first six decades of the century, there was almost no legislative acceptance elsewhere in the country until around 1860.[34] Indeed, Harris brackets the primary period of the spread of registration laws with the dates 1860–1910. However, a more detailed description of trends within that general time span is of high relevance for the Burnham theses. It is important first to differentiate roughly between what might be labeled "weak" and "strong" registration control systems. The weak systems, characterizing the earlier part of the period almost exclusively, involved legislation commissioning certain election officials to draw up lists of the names of residents eligible to vote within their districts, either on the basis of their personal familiarity with their precincts or on the basis of door-to-door canvass. Voting was to be restricted to citizens claiming those names on Election Day.

Whereas the institution of such weak systems temporarily silenced clamor for the reduction of voting fraud, their frequent ineffectuality soon became apparent. The construction of the electoral registers rapidly fell into the hands of those ward heelers who had helped organize the earlier uncontrolled voting sprees, as part of the spoils of successful past performance. Under these circumstances, fraud was only slightly more laborious. "Repeaters" were still imported to make their rounds, although, where surveillance made it necessary, they were simply convened between stops and assigned new names, known to be on the registers at the next precinct, but representing either fictitious additions or the genuine names of the dead and the departed. Wherever possible, of course, it was easiest for the election official simply to begin, late on Election Day, to cast votes for people who had not turned out, as well as for the names that represented more forthright padding.

Recognition that weak registration systems were only modestly effective at best led to pressure for more stringent control measures, a movement that reached the crescendo of its success in legislative enactments between 1890 and 1910, the period of most critical interest to us. Such strong systems were characterized by provision for more frequent and supervised "purges" of the rolls to validate them and keep them up to date, with the typical requirement that the citizen himself appear before the election to get his name en-

---

[34] The one noteworthy exception was the registration law passed for the county of Philadelphia in 1836 on the heels of a series of gross election frauds in that city.

tered on the registry upon satisfactory proof of identity and eligibility, leaving behind him a signature that could be used for verification on Election Day.[35] Although the most enthusiastic proponents would not have imagined that fraud was impossible under such a system, it was expected to reduce its incidence dramatically, and there is every subsequent reason to believe that it has, although again with some unintended side effects on the voting process. Despite persistent rumors of a specific fraud or two perpetrated in almost every modern national election, the running expectation of gross and endemic fraud has largely vanished from the American political culture.

One other aspect of the registration chronology is of vital importance to our account. While there were two gross phases in the registration movement (from weak to strong systems of provisions), it would be quite inaccurate to imagine that weak systems first came to blanket the country and then were replaced by strong systems. The diffusion of weak systems before 1890 was extremely spotty from a geographic point of view, and some few states outside the South failed to institute any registration laws whatever until after 1910.

From a *post hoc* analytic point of view, the irregular adoption of variant laws scattered over a long period of time offers the scholar superb leverage for determining the general effects of these laws on voting practice and the cast of aggregate statistics, much as Rusk has done for the Australian ballot reform. Such a synchronized analysis might be clouded by the likelihood that fraud would have declined in this period even when registration laws failed to be passed. That is, the blatant practices of the late nineteenth century seem to have rested on a surprising degree of public indulgence. The growth of a hue and cry among progressive forces around the turn of the century turned this atmosphere of indulgence into one of moral indignation. Nor was mere "atmosphere" all that was involved. For areas not yet placed under strong registration control, there was a crescendo of litigation across the land based on suspicions of fraud. Under these circumstances, it would be reasonable to expect a marked toning down of vote padding even in those districts, usually rural, that did escape formal state registration laws.[36]

Nevertheless, even a broad-scale examination of the synchronization of turnout decrements with full registration laws is currently lacking. Yet, the

[35] We should recognize that important variants on personal registration requirements —annual registration vs. permanent registration and the like—have been subjects of controversy to the present day. For the purposes of this brief sketch, these subsequent distinctions are not crucial.

[36] Indeed, the most recent Burnham paper cites instances of modest depression in turnout occurring in the 1896–1910 period in some districts exempted from the new wave of registration laws. See Burnham, "Critical Elections and the Dynamics of American Electoral Politics."

gross concordance between the Harris account of the geographical evolution of registration laws and the areas selected by Burnham to illustrate his empirical case are sufficiently impressive to suggest that closer examination of the relationship between registration reform and the other Burnham indicators (turnout in particular) would be richly rewarding.

Thus, as we have noted, registration reforms occurred remarkably early in the New England states, where the 1860–1910 dates are quite irrelevant. No New England instances of the deterioration of the political universe around the turn of the century figure in the Burnham account, although other subregions outside the old Confederacy are amply represented. Burnham's most striking case of what he calls "the awesome rates of turnout" that can be found for relatively rural states in the decades before 1900 is Indiana, also singled out by Harris as a case history of a state that had remarkable difficulty getting any kind of registration control instituted whatever. Although Indiana governors were complaining of the prevalence of voting fraud in the state (particularly multiple voting) and begging their legislatures for the institution of controls as early as the 1860's, the state waited until 1911 before it succeeded in enacting a registration law that was not promptly struck down by the courts.[37] Philadelphia County, one of Burnham's most dramatic examples of turnout that plummeted astonishingly around 1900 on a more localized base, comes through with great prominence in the Harris account as an example of how sharply registration lists could shrink upon the enforcement (in 1906) of a new personal registration law (a strong control system) in an area which for decades had been among the most notorious in the country for the scale of its voting frauds, despite the long-term presence of a registration law, however weak.

More generally, the rural-urban axis, which Burnham uses to suggest that the collapse of turnout was not confined to the metropolitan havens of the new waves of immigrants, also plays a critical role in the Harris chronology, although it is one which (while consonant with the Burnham observations) puts quite a different light on the matter. Outside New England and the Confederate South, the institution of weak registration systems early in the 1860–1910 period was primarily aimed at the voting situation in large urban centers, and may even have been enhanced by some nativistic animus. This is to say, states adopting registration controls in the 1860's and 1870's tended to be those containing the largest urban metropolises and, more important still, the statutes were very often geared to have effect (by law) only on cities above a certain size level or, in some places and periods, only within the major city of the state (Philadelphia or New York City, for example).

[37] Harris, *op. cit.,* p. 85. The polar roles played by Massachusetts and Indiana in both the ballot reform and the registration movement would provide interesting raw material for a study in state-level political cultures.

Thus, the whole registration issue in states that had instituted any early controls represented a heated political controversy along very direct urban-rural cleavage lines in the period from 1860 to 1900. Minority groups in the largest urban centers typically used the Democratic Party as a vehicle to challenge the constitutionality of laws that forced them into an elaborate registration procedure but required nothing of their small-town and rural compatriots. Meanwhile, of course, the Republicans were painfully and often explicitly aware of how sharply their rural vote base might shrink with the extension of controls on voting to the countryside, and fought tooth and nail to preserve their artificial legal advantage. Many of the wanderings into and out of statewide registration laws that occurred in some states were a simple reflection of the momentary ascendancy of one or the other of these competing powers.[38]

After the rapid success in regaining the secrecy of the individual vote through the Australian ballot, the idealistic forces of reform, bent on cleaning up the fraud continuing to haunt voting process in the United States, lent their weight to the demands of the cities for broader registration control. Thus the years from 1890 to 1910 were principally marked by a shift from weak registration systems to strong systems for a much wider portion of the hinterland.[39]

The standard forms of vote fraud before 1900 involved the addition of illegitimate votes to the pile of legitimate ones by one or another mechanism, rather than the subtraction of legitimate but undesired votes from the stock cast. This is not to say that the latter form of skulduggery never occurred: familiarity with the period suggests anything would be possible. But it is virtually never mentioned and, without doubt, vote injections were the predominant style for helping elections along. Thus, any fraud is calculated to inflate turnout estimates artificially, and legislation progressively reducing fraud should progressively reduce apparent turnout at the same time. Although more painstaking correlational analysis is begging to be done in this area, the general behavior of turnout over this period noted by Burnham, and most particularly the differential urban-rural patterns (turnout soaring ahead peculiarly in many rural areas in the late nineteenth century, but then collapsing even more dramatically than it did in most cities over the 1890–1910 period), fit so astonishingly well with what is known of the spread of registration laws in exactly this same era that the counter-hypothesis surely deserves systematic investigation.

---

[38] Philadelphia, where the urban political machine was Republican rather than Democratic, forms a classic exception to the partisan patterns described here.

[39] Not all of the new laws had total state-wide applicability, although the size criteria exempting localities from bothering with registration procedures were typically shaved back in progressive fashion over time, so that ultimately only the most rural hamlets escaped the requirement.

One unpleasant implication of this construction has to do with the character of small-town and rural political life in the late nineteenth century. The Burnham data on turnout, as the author points out, seem to support the view familiar from C. Wright Mills and others of the cracker-barrel society deeply committed to democracy and intensely involved in the political issues of the day. Given this view, the sudden decline of rural turnout around the turn of the century would appear to token a wave of alienation among the honest yeomanry as the rural scene became shunted off into a position as a subordinate element in an urbanizing mass society.[40] Yet, if the behavior of turnout patterns in rural areas were more nearly associated with the stiffening of controls on voting, it would suggest that not only was political involvement unexceptional in these settings, but honesty as well. For a culture that has long held dear the conviction that sin is mainly enjoyed in large cities, such a conclusion may be disturbing.

In point of fact, electoral systems around the world differ rather widely with respect to rates of turnout between city and country in national elections; and the same nation may show a different pattern at different stages in its development, as has the United States. Although these foreign experiences are often of limited relevance to the American case, they make abundantly clear how risky it is to draw simple equations between turnout levels and public involvement or alienation from the affairs of state. For example, voting turnout in national elections in traditional rural villages in Turkey has been higher than that in the larger cities, including the national capital, despite the fact that villagers have extremely little education and virtually no contact with the mainstream of national political communications. This case is of interest because it is one for which survey data are available through the efforts of Hyman, Frey, and others. These data show that the normal villager has only the dimmest cognition of even the existence of the nation-state around him, and no understanding of the national-level political issues at stake in these elections. Why, then, such enthusiasm to vote? Frey believes that most voting occurs to comply with the wishes of the headman of the village, or some other influential person with whom the voter may be linked in the traditional village social structure. He concludes that the villagers are "more vot*ed* than vot*ing*."[41] Such traditional or deference voting calls to mind the alarm with which Virginia and Carolina gentlemen viewed the possible replacement of viva-voce voting with some more potentially secret device.

Similar patterns seem present in countries where literacy rates are much closer to those of nineteenth-century America than is true of Turkey. Turnout in the Philippines tends to run higher in rural than urban areas. Anthropologists have concluded that rural voting is largely a response to obligations

---

[40] Burnham, "The Changing Shape of the American Political Universe," p. 16.
[41] Frederick Frey, personal communication.

felt toward local leaders through kin ties or some economic dependence relation (landlord-tenant), and this view has received support from what survey
data exist.[42] In general, movement to the city appears to free voters from
debts to local notables which can be subjected to surveillance at the polls in
the more rural setting. Or again, Canton has shown that, in Argentina, the
electoral reform of 1912 patterned after those of the period in the United
States and Europe and designed to increase the secrecy of the ballot and
tighten voter registration, had the effect of immediately wiping out a long-
standing tendency for rural areas to outvote urban ones, as well as to change
the correlation between literacy and turnout from strongly negative to strongly
positive.[43] In this case, fraud in rural areas away from the eyes of urban officialdom seems to have been more important than deference voting.

What is known of rural life in the northern parts of the United States in
the nineteenth century would not lead one to expect extremes of deference
voting, although there is good reason to believe that such patterns pertained
over major areas of the South. It is far less certain, however, that the rural
North escaped the artificial turnouts of voting fraud. Although the dramatic
and persistent signs of corruption were mainly associated with the great urban
machines, many contemporary accounts felt that rural fraud was frequent
also. At the very least, our far-flung examples help remind us that urban-rural
differences in turnout, whatever their direction, do not necessarily reflect differences in political enthusiasm and knowledgeability across the broad electorate.[44] They also make clear how stricter guarantees of secrecy or greater
control over fraud could operate to turn surprising historical voting patterns
into more familiar ones.

[42] A 1963 survey study cited by Ando showed more than 20 percent of rural respondents indicating that their main reason for voting was to fulfill a social obligation deriving
from personal or kinship ties, whereas only about 5 percent of respondents in urban areas
gave such a response. Hirofumi Ando, "A Study of Electoral Behavior in the Philippines,"
Working Paper No. 17, Center for South and Southeast Asian Studies, University of
Michigan, 1968.

[43] Dario Canton, "Universal Suffrage as an Agent of Mobilization," Documento de
Trabajo No. 19, Instituto Torcuato Di Tella, Centro de Investigaciones Sociales, 1966.

[44] The point is, of course, a very general one. Turnout data are susceptible to a wide
range of influences, many of which have little or nothing to do with those variations in
voter apathy, involvement or "system alienation" that naive observers take for granted
they reflect. For example, Mather, working on data from 40 years of voting in Iowa, has
shown that an artificial decrement in turnout of about 5 percent was associated with the
use of first-generation voting machines in that state, because of voter misunderstanding of
the proper manipulation of the levers. The decrement disappeared as appropriate instructions were posted on the machines, or as improved voting machines were installed. However, several decades elapsed in the process. See George B. Mather, *Effects of the Use of
Voting Machines on Total Votes Cast: Iowa—1920–1960.* Institute of Public Affairs, University of Iowa, Iowa City, 1964.

Similar dramatic illustrations of the same general principle may be drawn from the United States experience. Some of the more illuminating involve sudden shifts in the ecological patterns of turnout within large cities before and after the tightening of voter registration laws. In general, it can be expected that, just as is true today, there was some upward progression of average education of the population as one moved from the transient districts of the city center outward toward the suburbs. The standard survey correlation would thus lead one to expect mounting turnout as one traverses the same route. This expectation is often not fulfilled in metropolitan data during the period of weak voter-control systems, however. The transient districts tended to show turnout proportions at least equal to those being registered in "silk-stocking" districts, and very frequently went significantly higher. (There is an amusing incidence of cases in which exactly 100 percent of registered voters succeeded in voting in such districts and, of course, some that strayed higher still.) Indeed, in a passage that would be quite bewildering to the modern reader, Harris, writing as late as 1929, refers to "the *common belief* that the lowest strata of society, the criminal element, prostitutes, gamblers and saloon keepers always register and vote. . . ."[45] (Italics added.)

Yet, when a well-conceived and impartially administered control system is applied to such a metropolis, results in all cases examined show the immediate emergence of turnout differentials running in the expected direction. In some instances, the "controlled" pattern does not last for more than an election or two, because the machine survived, developed new ways to circumvent the law, and occasionally even moved to new heydays of vote production. Over the nation as a whole, however, the pressure of the stricter measures and associated litigation did progressively reduce the rate of fraud. And whether in a given case the change in metropolitan voting patterns was temporary or permanent, the typical effect after strict controls are levied is for turnout in transient city center districts to fall from original figures in the 80 to 100 percent range to figures in the 30 to 50 percent range, with turnout in the better residential districts staying in the 75 to 85 percent range. Not only the direction, but even the relative magnitudes of such figures seem very familiar from current survey research.

It would be rash to claim that the relationships known from modern surveys—even those that remain constant across a wide variety of countries—have any immutable status. Nonetheless, it is well known that early social bookkeeping methods in a variety of domains have been plagued by both willful and more innocent inaccuracies. When extrapolations of these modern relationships are found to clash with the historical record, therefore, it is certainly worth entertaining the possibility that the "hard" record distorts what

---

[45] Harris, *op. cit.,* p. 302.

earlier social reality was like. Modern survey data may often be the better guide.

Although it seems likely that there was some meaningful relationship between the decline of turnout noted by Burnham after 1896 and the spread of stringent registration systems in the same period, there remain important questions of magnitude. Turnout in presidential elections outside the South fell off by more than 10 percent between 1896 and 1912, and the old high has never been recaptured despite some resurgence since the 1920's. If all of this decline represented names on registers being fraudulently "voted" in the 1890's but no longer viable in 1910, we would be talking about the fabrication of close to 2 million votes within an eligible electorate of about 17 million citizens. And this figure seems wondrously large, even when we keep in mind the many thousands of individual polling places across the land, many of which could well have been making small contributions to the total.

The true rate of fraud in that epoch can probably never be reconstructed, although interesting steps might be taken in that direction with the aid of evidence present and a few further assumptions of an extremely plausible character. The main issue, of course, is the relationship of the dramatically visible instances of fraud to the much more widespread residue that remained invisible because it was carried out on a more modest scale. The literature of the period providing any quantitative estimates at all naturally runs to the flagrant cases, such as the hireling in Denver who confessed in court at the turn of the century that by rapid circulation among polling places he had managed to contribute 125 votes on Election Day. Obviously such an athletic achievement would have been grandly abnormal whatever the system of payoff or the general state of corruption. Harris cites a number of investigations in which people listed as having voted in a suspect election were personally canvassed very shortly after the election, in order to discover what proportion of names were spurious, and what others had been generously voted without the bother of going to the polls. These investigations typically show anywhere from 30 to 75 percent of the votes cast to have been fraudulent.[46] The investigators naturally selected districts where they thought fraud was concentrated, however. What we would need to know are the comparable figures over a more representative sample of districts and, for that matter, elections. Certainly one element that would have reduced the over-all prevalence of fraud is the fact that manipulation even under weak control systems must have been costly in terms of time, money, and organizational effort, resources that would not have been expended even in potentially corrupt districts when victory was in clear view without artificial aid.[47] In any event, it remains true

[46] *Ibid.,* pp. 350 ff.

[47] This consideration would affect many fewer elections than might appear on the surface, however. In the first place, doubt as to the outcome of one important race on a

that most observers of the period were convinced that documented election fraud represented no more than the top of an iceberg.

It is important to emphasize, however, that the advent of stringent personal registration systems was very much a double-edged sword where "apparent turnout" is concerned and, instead of needing to imagine the sheer fabrication of nearly 2 million votes in the 1890's, we need only imagine some fraction of that, such as a million votes or less across the land. It seems beyond question that the new registration requirements put a burden on the citizen that constituted a significant deterrent to what had earlier been "honest votes." This was particularly true at the outset of the period, when the first strong control systems made it positively difficult to "stay registered," and these were only gradually replaced by more reasonable variants whereby only modest effort, such as fairly consistent voting, would suffice to remain on the registers. Many marginally interested citizens who would have managed to get to the polls on the day when election excitement was at its highest pitch (especially if let out of work for that express purpose) were unable to vote under the new system because they had not planned ahead and taken the necessary and often confusing steps to get registered before the deadline.[48] Thus, any drop in turnout that accompanies the establishment of a strong control system is not only a matter of purged names, but also of weakly motivated persons deterred from voting.

Indeed, election fraud aside, it has come to be widely thought in recent years that, apart from the unique problems of the South, much of the notorious disparity in voting turnout between the United States and countries of Western Europe with noncompulsory electoral systems lies in the relatively cumbersome nature of our registration procedures.[49] The case here is rather obvious, since turnout levels compared quite favorably with those of Europe

---

ticket would probably have been sufficient to spur such efforts, even though other contestants would thereby be gaining entirely superfluous votes. More important is the fact of higher levels of vote aggregation. Certainly the small jurisdiction that would give a clear majority to an important state-wide candidate was under extreme pressure to build the margin to as extreme a point as possible, in order to offset less pleasing results from other areas.

[48] For a most impressive empirical confirmation of the way in which these prior registration costs vitally affect subsequent turnout even in the current period, see Stanley Kelley, Jr., R. E. Ayres, and William G. Bowen, "Registration and Voting: Putting First Things First," *American Political Science Review*, vol. 61, June, 1967, pp. 359–377.

[49] The point has been made, *inter alia,* by Harold Gosnell, *Why Europe Votes.* University of Chicago Press, Chicago, 1930; S. M. Lipset, *Political Man.* Doubleday, New York, 1960; and Kelley, Ayres, and Bowen, *op. cit.* See also the excellent effort by William G. Andrews to estimate the major sources of error or incomparability in apparent turnout percentages for the United States. W. G. Andrews, "American Voting Participation," *Western Political Quarterly,* vol. 19, December, 1966, pp. 639–652.

when there was no registration or when the extra burden of registration lay on the side of public officials and record-keepers (as is more or less the rule abroad). The temporal coincidence between the erection of these hurdles and the drop in turnout seems quite compelling as evidence of effect, although for some time it was assumed that low turnout in the United States had causes of a more "romantic" nature, such as public dissatisfaction with, or alienation from, the "system."

Some estimation of the relative magnitudes of fictitious names to deterred voters over a total city area can be gleaned from figures such as those surrounding the establishment of a strict personal registration law between 1904 and 1906 in Philadelphia. The Philadelphia case is one of Burnham's examples, but notorious in its day for the scale of its corruption. The assessor's lists showed 385,036 names in 1904, but the figure dropped to 341,825 after the rolls were examined and purged in connection with the application of the law in 1906, instead of the near 400,000 that would have been expected by that year through population growth, had the original lists been correct. In point of fact, only 250,950 persons actually registered themselves to vote in 1906, however.[50] Thus, about 40 percent of the decrement seems to have been associated with spurious names, and the remainder with deterred voters. The sheer number of fictitious names on the registers does not of course pose any outside limit on earlier fraud, for it was standard practice also to "vote" legitimate names of people unlikely to get to the polls, particularly as this probability increased late on Election Day. In one of the more careful studies, Woodruff estimates that in Philadelphia alone some 30,000 to 80,000 fraudulent votes were cast in each election in the 1890's.[51] Taking all of these figures into account and assuming that every available latitude for fraud was used up at 100 percent rates in each election prior to 1906, the drop in turnout of the kind noted for the area by Burnham is "overexplained": it should have dropped more precipitously than the empirical data show between the general periods surrounding 1906 and preceding the entry of women into the electorate. It is easy, however, to relax the 100 percent assumption to a more moderate and realistic point that would fit the observed data exactly.[52]

I shall treat the final two Burnham indicators, drop-off and mean partisan swing, more summarily. Both involve temporal variability in voting statistics, the former referring to turnout (at least in the alternation between presidential and off-year elections) and the latter to the partisan division of

---

[50] Harris, *op. cit.* (cf. pp. 79 and 363).

[51] Clinton R. Woodruff, "Election Methods and Reforms in Philadelphia," *The Annals,* vol. 27, March, 1901, pp. 181–204.

[52] It may be useful to note that Philadelphia was one of the cities where the strict registration law was rapidly circumvented. The Republican machine soon succeeded in re-establishing a useful overproduction of votes.

the vote. Although we lack knowledge about the characteristic longitudinal properties of fraudulent votes in corrupt political settings, we can make the reasonable assumption that such fabricated votes would show at least in a middle term a rather strong constancy. Certainly such votes would, error aside, be cast 100 percent for the controlling party, and would be made as numerous as possible within the limits of probable detection in elections involving statewide contests that could be in reasonable party competition. A further variable involves the stability of control of the election apparatus in a jurisdiction by a specific party. If there were perfect alternation of control between two major parties from one election to the next, then any admixtures of fraudulent votes, first by one party and then the other, would add an element of the most extreme instability to the over-all vote returns, bulking larger or smaller according to the proportion of such votes. However, this example itself communicates the absurdity of such an assumption of alternation. In situations where fraud is unlikely, party control over specific election jurisdictions is already known to show high constancy. The one certain effect of fraud would be to increase the unbroken character of control by a specific party over time. With all these considerations in mind, then, it seems likely that persistent latitude for fraudulence would tend to exert a stabilizing influence on both turnout and the vote division, thus limiting both drop-off and mean partisan swing.[53]

Indeed, in the measure that detectability must have been a prime consideration in limiting the surfeit of artificial votes added to the totals of a jurisdiction, there may have been a built-in set of reference points that would contribute to leveling out the sawtooth pattern of turnout called drop-off. Thus, within a specific election, for example, the vote manipulator would feel relatively safe if he kept his turnout within 100 percent, and safer still if it was no higher than that of other nearby jurisdictions, such as the silk-stocking districts, subject to less manipulation. Similarly, over time, "safe" reference points might well have been votes cast in the next preceding comparable (here, national) election. If, in the off-year election, significantly more marginally involved voters failed to come to the polls, the manipulator may have simply felt more latitude in "voting" the stay-at-homes as long as he did no more than approach the turnout registered in the preceding presidential election.

[53] One important amendment consists of those cases in which periodic reform "squeezes" were placed on corrupt practices. Assuming these movements temporarily reduced the brazenness of the controlling party, they should act to "destabilize" the behavior of turnout longitudinally. However, drop-off as used by Burnham is figured on a two-year period, and waves of major reform within political jurisdictions certainly occurred on a very much slower "cycle" than this. Hence, the instability they would add to drop-off would be rather limited.

While all of the above is purest inference about the way vote manipulators would be likely to behave, somewhat clearer evidence shows that the new voting systems would have had influences in the opposite direction, i.e., toward increasing both drop-off and mean partisan swing. I have already discussed the demonstrated effect of the advent of the Australian ballot on split-ticket voting. Following the vote for any particular office over time, as mean partisan swing is calculated, swing is likely to increase as latitude for split-ticket voting increases. A simple example can make this clear. Under the old party strip ballots, a party could afford to insert some rather unpopular party hack on its ballot and trust that basic party loyalty, along with other attractive names on the slate, would bring the ticket through with very little damage. Under the new ballot, voters could simply split away from a less desirable candidate, without compromising in any significant way their sense of party fidelity. Indeed, the dictum "vote the man, not the party," which must have been next to meaningless under the old voting system, now could be implemented, and its effect on partisan swing over time at a given office level would be rather obvious.

Modern survey research findings suggest that had appropriate measurements been taken in the 1880–1920 period, the intensity of party loyalty expressed through now-standard measures would have shown at least some slight decrease. For there is a visible, if modest, relationship between the degree of partisan identification and variations in the degree to which electoral laws and ballot forms presume partisanship from state to state. These variations in the modern period have to do with relatively minor features of the election process. Thus, for example, some states require that the voter define himself in a relatively permanent sense as a sympathizer of one party or the other in order to participate in primary elections. Other states permit him to vote in the primary of whichever party he requests the day of the voting. Some states facilitate the expression of pure partisanship by providing for easy straight-ticket voting; states using the Massachusetts ballot make it more difficult. Residents of states whose electoral laws presume partisanship in these ways tend to show higher partisanship than residents of states whose laws convey more nonpartisan assumptions.[54] Since relatively minor features of the electoral process are involved here, the more major shift to the Australian ballot probably had some depressing effect on the intensity of partisanship, lending increased amplitude to partisan swing.

It seems likely as well that the addition of new registration hurdles would tend to accentuate drop-off, particularly where these hurdles required repetitive registration over time. Harris emphasizes the marked sawtooth pattern that begins to characterize registration figures as soon as a tight annual registration system was implemented in an area. He is addressing himself in this

[54] Campbell *et al., The American Voter,* Chap. 11.

instance to registration figures compared between even years and odd-numbered years not typically involving elections to national office, and the sawtooth pattern is with respect to registration, not voting turnout. The differences cited are rather substantial, however, and suggest the dampening effect of the extra hurdle of registration when interest declines for less important elections. Moreover, a few data are presented permitting an assessment of the way in which registration behaves between presidential and congressional elections as cities move from loose to tight registration procedures. In New York City, for example, the biennial *registration* drop-off before the enactment of statutes requiring personal identification for registration was 3 percent; it averaged 14 percent over four subsequent braces of elections.[55] Pending further work, it is not unreasonable to suppose that the accentuation of drop-off may have been largely due once again to the combined effects of increased control over fraud and the multiplication of registration hurdles.

We have now seen that two types of change in electoral laws may well account for much of the dramatic shift noted by Burnham in aggregate voting statistics between 1890 and the time of female suffrage. This hypothesis would leave a number of Burnham's original substantive contentions intact. For example, he deduced that party loyalties in the mass electorate had lost some of their intensity in this period, and our analysis of the Australian ballot reform would lead to a similar conclusion. Or again, he was interested in signs of shrinkage in the truly active fraction of the American electorate, and at least that portion of declining turnout attributable to citizens deterred from voting by the new hurdles of more stringent registration requirements is exactly of this order.

Nevertheless, a focus on two sets of changes in electoral procedures, rather than the pivotal election of 1896, makes for vast differences in interpretation of the phenomenon, and shifts considerably our sense of its significance as a symptom of some more fundamental deterioration in the American electoral response. The Burnham interpretation suggested that the ascendance of a powerful coalition of business elites and the Republican Party permitted the development of a degree of control over the electoral system which, facilitated by the collusion or sheer defaulting of the Democratic Party, alienated the electorate, leading to disaffection with the major parties and declining interest in democratic participation.

A more recent Burnham paper indeed recognizes the likely impact of intrusions such as the Australian ballot and registration systems on the behavior of the five indicators drawn from aggregate election statistics.[56] Never-

---

[55] Harris, *op. cit.,* pp. 107–108 and 266.
[56] See note 27. The text which follows has been revised to address the new Burnham work.

theless, there is a tendency to hew to the original historical interpretation of elite capture and control of the voting system in 1896, while incorporating the new considerations to fit such a thesis. In effect, it is argued at various points that the reform movement and consequent voting provisions cannot entirely explain the observed behavior, and that, in any event, the new voting system can be seen as simply the mechanical vehicle whereby the business-Republican elite coalition wrested control of the polity from democratic uncertainty, so that no revision of the original thesis is required.

I do not find this interpretation at all convincing. Indeed, I feel it suffers from numerous internal contradictions. Thus, for example, Burnham notes repeatedly that the shift from the old to the new voting system unleashed a "floating vote" that was no longer anchored to partisan loyalties. He concurs with a paper by Jensen that reconstructs in delightful and admirable detail a shift in the atmosphere of political campaigns around the turn of the century from a "militarist" style in which fixed party forces were subjected to drill and brought to combat at the polls, to a "mercantilist" style characterized by advertising appeals to a now-significant bloc of "independent" voters.[57] At the same time, harking to his original interpretation, Burnham argues that the new voting regulations were merely an effect, and not a cause, and represented a tightening of the elite control systems: "[Such regulations] were, in the main, devices by which a large and possibly fickle mass electorate could be brought to heel, could be subjected to management and control within the political system of 'capitalist democracy.' "[58] How one escapes fickleness and increases the certainty of control through measures which detach a large floating vote from older partisan anchors is not made clear. The historical record from the nineteenth century indicates that whenever reformers passed new measures to enforce the secrecy of the ballot, even competing party elites colluded with speed and high ingenuity to circumvent the laws and return to the certainties of the fixed-battalion voting culture. It was the reformed system which finally was pressed "over the top" on a broad scale at the turn of the century that invited uncertainty and decline of control.

Most important, perhaps, is to sort out as clearly as possible who was doing what to whom with these reforms. This is no easy task, for the situation was complex. Certainly the electoral measures under discussion were only a small part of a very large array of "progressive" proposals of the period, which included the direct primary, nonpartisan elections, extensions of civil service, and various regulations on business. Different power centers in the

---

[57] Richard Jensen, "American Election Campaigns: A Theoretical and Historical Typology," a paper presented at the meetings of the Midwest Political Science Association, April, 1968.

[58] Burnham, "Critical Elections and the Dynamics of American Electoral Politics," p. 67.

society reacted in varying ways to specific proposals in this broader array, and supported or resisted them in differing degrees at different times. Historians have, for example, begun to explore some rather surprising roles that business interests may have played in facilitating certain aspects of progressive legislation.[59] While such work remains controversial, it would certainly fit most congenially with the Burnham interpretation.

A number of the measures being pushed under the "good government" banner, including our electoral ones, had the potential to curb the power of the great urban machines and, as the matter was seen at the time, to protect the white Anglo-Saxon Protestant culture from further subversion by the hordes of new immigrants from Southern and Eastern Europe. While "morality" made a much finer platform than "our culture is better than yours," the nativist implications of the reforms were widely perceived and rallied many strange bedfellows, from Protestant workingmen to middle-class evangels of temperance, to their support. Given their deep roots in "Wasp" America, it would be surprising if numerous businessmen of nativist sensibilities had not appeared in their ranks as well, although such a fact taken alone would say little about the Burnham thesis, since the motives he attributes to the business elite are hinged much more on a Marxian power struggle between capitalists and the masses than on any nativist-immigrant culture clash. Nevertheless, the "business elite" as a more corporate interest group would naturally have been attracted to measures that might undermine the Democratic urban machines as a competing center of power, and might be expected to have supported proposals in the degree that they were perceived in this light. There is evidence that, at various times and places, such support was given and sometimes it was critical for adoption. But where the electoral reforms were concerned, the spottiness of business involvement suggests that such measures were only sporadically construed in this way.[60]

The spottiness of business involvement and support may be intelligible in a somewhat different light. Up to now we have focused on groups that simply came along in support of reforms that had already gained some initial visibility as proposals. If we consider where these proposals came from, then the Burnham picture of electoral reforms mapped out by a corporate elite to steal control of the election system sits even more poorly with the main lines of the historical record. The forces of good government who as "idea men" generated the proposals, struggled to publicize them, and remained their most energetic and reliable core of support through the process of adoption included mainly intellectuals, journalists, ministers, and other professionals. If

[59] See most notably Gabriel Kolko, *The Triumph of Conservatism*. Free Press, New York, 1963.

[60] We are grateful at this point for several helpful interpretive suggestions provided by Jack L. Walker.

anything, these people represented a counter-elite not only to the urban bosses, but to corporate management as well, and it is not surprising under such conditions that business involvement was spotty. In this regard, it is noteworthy that the piece of progressive legislation that bore most directly on the links between the business elite and the electoral system was that passed by Congress in 1907 specifically forbidding campaign contributions from corporations in federal elections.[61] If this was part of a grand design to consolidate corporate control over electoral politics, then the strategy is certainly obscure.

In short, then, whatever support the business elite may have lent to some pieces of progressive legislation, business per se was not in the steady vanguard of the reform movement. Of course, it is within the realm of the conceivable that those who *were* in that vanguard—social critics like Henry George or the muckrakers—developed reforms that willy-nilly aided an ascendant capitalist coalition to gain control over what was, in theory, a democratic system. What is inconceivable is that they did so with this purpose in mind.

Indeed, the effects that Burnham sees as evidence of deterioration appear almost prototypic of "unintended consequences." The Australian ballot was pushed through primarily to guarantee the secrecy of the vote; and upon discovery that one of its side effects was to weaken partisan fidelity in voting, steps were taken to provide at least a partial remedy in shifts to the Indiana ballot. Personal registration was advocated primarily as a means of eliminating gross overtones of fraud in American elections; most of its instigators were dismayed to find that measures sufficiently strong to prove effective in the fight against fraud had the side effect of discouraging significant numbers of legitimate voters from the polls. In fact, one of the main points of the 1929 treatise by Harris, surely a godson of the 1890–1910 movement, was to argue that it was possible to devise registration systems that would control fraud without shrinking the size of the active electorate, however insensitive earlier tacticians may have been to this problem. He points out that the proportion of eligible voters registered at any moment was running 15 percent higher in permanent registration systems than in those annual registration systems that placed such a heavy burden on the initiative of the citizen. He reports with satisfaction the substantial revisions of the first registration systems that were being accepted in state after state around the country in the latter half of the 1920's, a movement that undoubtedly contributed to the resurgence shown by Burnham's turnout figures in this period.[62]

Most important for the general themes of this essay, the likely associa-

---

[61] Edwin M. Epstein, *Corporations, Contribution and Political Campaigns.* Prentice-Hall, Englewood Cliffs, N.J., 1969, p. 29.

[62] Harris, *op. cit.,* pp. 91–92.

tion of aggregate voting shifts at the turn of the century with changes in electoral laws removes much of the sting one might feel at what otherwise seems to be a distinct and unique retrograde motion in the quality of the American electoral response, and also removes perplexity at why such regression should occur when other potent variables—education in particular—were moving sharply upward.

It is true that more stringent controls on the voting process had the side effect of "desocializing" a margin of the electorate from habitual political participation, and thus had retrograde consequences. Moreover; when an electoral system attempts through extension of the franchise to absorb new and relatively unsocialized categories of voters, as was the case with women, various signs of temporary regression can be expected to appear in voting statistics, although in this latter case it would generally be assumed that the costs are small relative to the closer approximation the extended system represents to "pure democracy." But it is worth keeping in mind the hidden ills, probably a good deal more serious, of the voting system in the decades prior to 1900. Rather than considering it a golden age, contemporaries not permissively amused by it saw it as an utter travesty on democratic process. And if abuses were as widespread as they appear to have been, this seems a reasonable judgment.

There may well be something of a natural history of development for early democratic systems of which the evolution of the United States has partaken in some degree. As democratic forms are imposed on traditionally stratified social structures involving unspecialized elites commanding very generalized deference from "subject" populations within a geographic domain, there is probably an initial period of voluntary deference voting in which the broad masses take for granted that the respected leader, so much better educated and in touch with the intricacies of national-level politics, is best equipped to judge what votes should be cast. Whenever there has been a history of antagonism toward the leader, or when the masses have come (in part through education) to see that his interests and theirs need not coincide, the deference voting would take on more of a coercive cast, and threats of reprisal on other fronts could be effectively exercised as long as the secrecy of the vote was compromised. This initial stage may well have been by-passed by those portions of the United States where education levels were already high by 1820; but it probably characterized the South until relatively late in the nineteenth century.

A second stage would involve the development, at least in more populous areas, of a specialized political elite anxious to maintain its position by winning elections at all costs, and in an excellent position to do so through control of a crude election machinery. Such cadres might work independently of the older, traditional elite, but the need for resources to aid in manipulation of elections would tend to influence toward collaboration. In such a period, although many of the formerly subservient classes would have become accustomed to exercising more independent political judgment, absolute levels of income and education would remain sufficiently low that there would be large reservoirs of manpower to help in defrauding the system: persons delighted with a day's pay to serve as repeaters, or willing to sell their votes to the highest bidder, and many others who saw limited enough stakes in the process not to take much umbrage at the "goings-on."

Perhaps it is too much to imagine that such manpower in sufficient quantity would exist today if proffered attractive opportunity by the officialdom concerned with the operation of elections. But in areas sufficiently backward and characterized by extremely ignorant populations very close to "subject" status, some of the old practices have not subsided even in the United States of the last 15 years. Mathews and Prothro, in their excellent 1961 sample survey study of Negro political participation in the South, encountered numerous communities allowing Negro voting where the main gesture of white politicians running for office was still to try to buy Negro ballots, either with direct payments of sums like $15 or $20 for a vote, or more indirectly with handouts of liquor and barbecues for the black community.[63] In our national election surveys, we occasionally pick up stray reports of vote-selling from benighted subpopulations in other regions as well, such as Spanish-American groupings of the Southwest. But the secrecy of the ballot makes such operations risky and, without doubt, their success depends as well on the presence of people living under sharp economic pressure, so cognitively vague about politics as to be indifferent to what vote they cast, and too inarticulate or subservient to create any public scandal if by chance the solicitation is resented. It seems likely that, whatever the situation today, the proportion of the population fitting these specifications in the latter half of the nineteenth century was very much larger.

Even assuming that many of the changes in the cast of electoral records were direct consequences of reformulations in electoral law over these stages of development, it should not be thought that the political implications of the reforms, intended or otherwise, were shallow. The mere encouragement of ticket-splitting, coupled with the relatively atypical American custom of voting for multiple officers at the same level of government in a particular election, has promoted a significant increase in the frequency with which branches of the same government (state, local, or national) find themselves internally divided along partisan lines, for example, with important consequences for

[63] Donald R. Mathews and James W. Prothro, *Negroes and the New Southern Politics.* Harcourt, New York, 1966, pp. 163–164. The report of a young black housewife in Texas is symptomatic of the situation: "They try to bribe you and give you $15 at the polls to vote for them. It would be hard for a hungry man to refuse."

the guidance of policy and the public assessment of party responsibility for the conduct of affairs. Nevertheless, while much more painstaking research is required on a variety of constituent points, there is nothing yet to convince us that the electorate of the twentieth century, despite its increased education and access to information concerning national affairs and policy controversy, is less politically involved, informed, or responsible than the electorate of the nineteenth century.

Recent Changes in the Complexion of the National Electorate

The American electorate has been monitored in sufficient depth by sample surveys over the past two or three decades that treatment of gross lines of change is much more straightforward than for earlier epochs. In addition, the infrastructure of information provided by surveys permits a much more detailed statement of the mechanisms underlying visible trends. Such information is obviously critical in predictions as to the extension of such trends into the future and are necessary building blocks for the construction of broader theories of political change in the mass public.

Where short-term political change is concerned, our understanding has advanced a good deal in the past 20 years. The election-to-election variations in vote division that shift party control of the White House and the complexion of Congress have been rather convincingly tied to a phenomenon of defection whereby voters, without significant revision of their sense of underlying partisanship, decide in some concert that in a particular election for a specified office they are going to cross party lines. The fact that short-term defection typically underlies such mundane shifts in the vote rather than more permanent party conversion is of capital importance. When, for example, the electorate rose up after 20 years of Democratic rule in Washington and "threw the rascals out" in decisive fashion in 1952, it appeared to many observers to mark the beginning of a new era of Republican dominance. Survey data, however, indicated that the critical Republican gains came from defecting voters who continued to report basic identification with the Democratic Party. These patterns suggested that, while Eisenhower enjoyed great personal magnetism with the voters, he would probably have difficulty keeping a Republican Congress (he lost it in the next election and failed to regain it in two further trials), and that the odds still favored the Democrats to control the White House as soon as Eisenhower withdrew from the scene.

More generally, these insights into the short-term dynamics of the electoral process suggest that, in most instances where the division of the vote swerves dramatically in a particular election, the worst prediction for the next election is an extrapolation of the trend, or even the expectation of its consolidation. Instead, the probabilities are very high that the vote in coming elections will revert back toward an underlying "normal division" represented by the distribution of basic party loyalties. Thus, a simple equilibrium system underlies most short-term electoral change. The statistical properties of this equilibrium have been subjected to close longitudinal study, and increasingly general statements as to the conditions under which defection takes place are now being pieced together. Work on other regularities in short-term change from the same general model has proved fruitful, for example, in explaining such old political riddles as why the party capturing the White House almost invariably loses seats in the next off-year congressional election.[64]

These lines of inquiry, while geared to cyclical changes on a short period or other kinds of transient perturbations rather than the long-term secular trends that are the main focus of this essay, have been extremely helpful in providing a first view as to which critical parameters show high sensitivity to immediate events and which are more stable over long periods of time. Work on shifts of longer-range significance, however, has been hampered by the fact that critical parameters of this type have displayed so little change during this period. Party identification, defining the equilibrium point of the party division and the amplitude of oscillations around it, has shown only the slightest of secular trends over the past 25 years at the aggregated national level. The Democratic Party in 1944 enjoyed nearly the same national majority that it does today in terms of these underlying loyalties, and the intensity of those loyalties has remained constant over virtually the same period. In theory at least, party identification defines a type of quasi-stationary equilibrium and at rare intervals is wrenched by events to a new level (the "critical" or "realigning" election) as citizens in great numbers shift their weight from one party to the other. Unfortunately, no such event has occurred on any large scale during the period of survey observation, although at the current writing there are signs that such a realignment may be imminent.[65]

Nevertheless, on a much more localized base, some shifts that bear a resemblance to realignments have been taking place, particularly in the 1960's. Moreover, other kinds of progressive change have been visible that leave the electoral map of the United States in 1968 quite different from that in 1944. Although these changes have not been exclusively located in the South, their focus has certainly been in that region, with changes elsewhere standing as "radiations" from this focus. I shall briefly describe the several major and intertwined facets of this change: (1) the re-enfranchisement of the Southern Negro, (2) changing patterns of partisanship that lie between high stability at the individual level and the stability of the aggregate national partisan division, and (3) an erosion of party fidelity in the late 1960's.

[64] Campbell *et al., Elections and the Political Order,* especially Chaps. 2, 3, 4, 7, and 10.

[65] Burnham, "The End of Party Politics."

Mobilization of the Southern Negro into Political Participation. One manifestation of the growth of egalitarianism on a world stage in recent centuries is represented by the advance of the democratic ethos and, more particularly, by the progressive acceptance of a larger and larger proportion of a nation's citizenry into voting on an equal basis. The extension of the suffrage has in most democracies now reached all but the relatively young. In the United States, in theory, this penultimate extension was achieved in 1920 as adult women were assured the right to vote. In practice, however, more or less strict limitations against black political participation were being implemented in the South in the first four decades of the century. Thus, the development of assurances of *de facto* suffrage which has been underway for the past 25 years represents in one sense the last "mobilization" of a significant population grouping into the national electorate, although of course Negroes had enjoyed some political participation in the South during Reconstruction.[66]

In the first four decades of this century, marked by a low level of legal sparring between the Supreme Court and inventive Southern legislatures, about 5 percent of Negroes in the 11 states of the old Confederacy succeeded in registering as voters, and even most of these were allowed to vote only in the now meaningless general elections. Against the national backdrop, the excluded population was rather small, representing about 6 percent of the potential United States electorate in 1940. Within the affected region, however, the black population amounted to more than a quarter of the adult citizenry. The disfranchisement signified that white politicians were under no temptation to curry favor with local Negroes, and public championing of the system of white supremacy became common campaign fare.

The death knell of "lily-white" Southern politics was finally sounded in 1944 when the Supreme Court in *Smith v. Allwright* arrived at a definitive outlawing of the "white primary." The decision was greeted almost immediately by more than a doubling of the size of the registered Negro electorate in the 11 core Southern states. The rate of increase remained vigorous until 1952, when it began to fall off markedly. Despite the fact that the latter half of the 1950's was marked by increased numbers of sit-ins, boycotts, and other forms of "extra-political" pressures in the region, the drive toward higher participation appeared to have arrived at a temporary level of saturation with little more than a quarter of the blacks registered. Momentarily it was thought that the extreme limits on education in the black community, along with a totally apolitical tradition, might represent severe limits on Negro participa-

[66] Karl W. Deutsch, "Social Mobilization and Political Development," *American Political Science Review,* vol. 55, September, 1961, p. 494; Stein Rokkan, "Mass Suffrage, Secret Voting and Political Participation, " *Archives of European Sociology,* vol. 2, 1961, pp. 132–152.

tion that could wear away only with the replacement of generations. The 1960's witnessed further abrupt change however (see Figure 1). Increasingly pointed civil rights legislation passed by the Congress in 1957, 1960, 1964, and 1965, the large-scale Voter Education Project conducted by the Southern Regional Council, and the turns taken by party competition in the region (especially with the Goldwater candidacy in 1964) all made facilitating or stimulating contributions to the upward trend. By 1968, the proportion of blacks registered in the old Confederacy was at least approaching the rough range that might be expected of a population with comparable rates of functional illiteracy under "normal" political circumstances. Given the extreme racial polarization in the area, however, political circumstances were far from normal, and with proper nurture, there was reason to expect that the participation figure might advance significantly higher.

Such an interpretation has been encouraged by several considerations, including the detailed picture of political interest among Southern Negroes compiled by Mathews and Prothro as of 1961, or the period between the two

Figure 1. Increase in Voter Registration of Negroes in the South 1940–68*

Percent of Negroes registered to vote in South

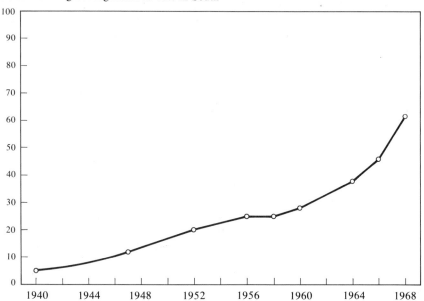

* This figure is based on data provided by Donald R. Mathews and James W. Prothro, *Negroes and the New Southern Politics.* Harcourt, New York, 1966, Table 1–1, p. 18. The observation for 1968 has been added on the basis of preliminary estimates provided by the Voter Education Project of the Southern Regional Council.

"take-off" phases in registration.[67] At that time, a broader index of political participation that included not only voting but reported informal discussions about politics, taking active part in election campaigns and belonging to political organizations (including the National Association for the Advancement of Colored People) or holding public office, showed a rather unique bimodal distribution across the black population in the region as a whole. This differentiation into a surprisingly active group and a larger but severely retarded *lumpenproletariat* can be understood in some degree by the abnormally skewed status structure of the Negro, with some small proportion of blacks having escaped to relatively middle-class occupations, income, and education, in the black side of the old segregated society, and the greater majority remaining imprisoned under extremely depressed economic and educational circumstances.

More important in accounting for the bimodality is the transitional phase in which the data were collected, and the uneven progress of "political liberation" across the South. Desperate local institutional pressures were exerted to offset the rising tide and its encouragement from the federal government in the Black Belt of the deepest South, within the states of Alabama, Georgia, Louisiana, Mississippi, and South Carolina. Thus, the dramatic gains in political participation of the first takeoff phase occurred largely in the more peripheral or bordering states, all except Florida being contiguous to the "North." Much more concerted pressure was required to make inroads on the institutional resistances of the Deep South but, as such pressure was applied in the 1960's, the proportionately greater gains in black mobilization were clearly taking place there. Everywhere, apart from the severe limits posed by education, Negro motivation to participate politically seemed high. Within groups equated by education, Southern blacks actually expressed higher interest in politics (although showed lower information levels) than their Southern white counterparts. It seemed likely that for a beleaguered minority, some long-lost political leverage was a matter of considerable attraction. Thus, while the black community would inevitably suffer in marked degree at its lower levels the disorganization of depressed circumstances and limited cognitive horizons, it remains plausible to suppose that, with increased freedom from reprisal and institutional restraint in the deepest South, levels of participation could increase further.

Sample interviews with the bulk of Southern Negroes in the 1950's, particularly when open-ended, free-answer material is used, provide a fascinating picture of a depressed, excluded population. Most protocols, especially from the deeper South, reflect high rates of functional illiteracy and utter insulation from national affairs or partisan controversy, along with a certain bewilder-

[67] Mathews and Prothro, *op. cit.,* Chap. 4; also pp. 169–172.

ment and disorientation when the interview required some attention be paid to it. At the lowest levels widespread confusion existed as to the identity of the two major parties and the presidential candidates. Where the social setting permitted, a certain amount of Negro voting was organized, particularly in the late 1950's, even in the face of such personal ignorance. Symbolic here might be the interview with the Florida woman who could not remember the names of either of the presidential candidates in 1960, or, when told, was she sure for which one she had voted. But she was pleased to have voted, and was secure in her confidence that she had voted for the "right" one because she and some friends had been driven to the minister's house for a session of practice on a ballot before proceeding to the polls.

Perhaps one of the best single indicators of psychological remoteness from the political process is the classification of "apolitical" given to the small fringe of our respondents who can make no meaningful affective response to either political party in connection with the standard item employed to measure party identification. The unusual nature of this nonresponse is witnessed by the fact that only about 1.5 percent of the total white electorate in the United States typically receives such a classification, and the majority of these are poor whites from the remote hinterlands of the South. But some 28 percent of Negroes in the "Census South" tended on the average to be classified as "apolitical" over the course of the 1950's.[68]

As Figure 2 suggests, the new surge of political awareness among Southern blacks in the 1960's was reflected most sharply in this population. In less than a decade, the proportion of apoliticals has fallen from 28 percent to about 3 percent. Although the Negro in the South makes up only 5 to 6 percent of the national electorate, during the 1950's he contributed the majority of the country's apoliticals. In that earlier period, apoliticals occupied 4 to 5 percent of the standard party identification distribution. The partisan mobilization of the Southern Negro has, by the late 1960's, reduced the expected figure to 2 percent or less. This is perhaps the sharpest trend of a clearly secular nature registered in that key distribution in 25 years.

Since the Southern Negro proffers a rare occasion to see new voting dispositions being formed, we are interested not only in the fact that partisan feelings have developed, but also the direction which that partisanship is taking. However, any meaningful discussion of such a topic requires a broader consideration of recent partisan trends in that region among whites as well.

[68] From this point on, data cited for the "South" refer not to the 11 states of the old Confederacy, but to the 15 states used by the Bureau of the Census for its regional definition. The states thus added are Maryland, West Virginia, Kentucky, and Oklahoma. Note that most regional peculiarities, including the proportion of Negroes classed as "apolitical," would stand out still more dramatically if data were available for the more restricted definition of the region.

Figure 2. Growth in Partisanship among Negroes in the South, 1952–68*

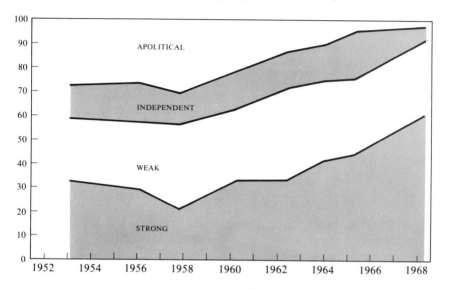

* Responses to the intensity portion of the standard party identification question permit a division into strong and weak identifiers with a major party, independents, and persons who are "apolitical" by virtue of inability to relate themselves to the question at all. Partisanship so measured has intensified markedly among Southern blacks during the 1960's. Because of small case numbers for Southern blacks, adjacent samples have been combined to yield this trend graph, with observations located at the mean point in time for each cluster of samples.

Patterns of Partisan Change in the South. The bitter reaction of Southern whites to the Civil War and Reconstruction under the aegis of the Republican Party forged the political phenomenon of the Solid South, a total region that could be counted on to cast its votes for the Democratic presidential candidate in election after election and one which kept almost purely Democratic delegations in both houses of the Congress in Washington as well. From 1880 through 1916, the Republicans managed to capture the electoral votes of exactly one border state in one of the ten presidential elections of the period. This was the true heyday of the Solid South.

The partisan homogeneity of the region had begun to erode enough by the 1920's so that, under favorable short-term influences visible across the nation, the Republicans were able to crack the Solid South around the edges. In the special case represented by the 1928 election, when the Democrats ran a Catholic for President, the devoutly Protestant South responded by giving the majority of its electoral votes to the Republicans. As the whole nation swung toward Roosevelt and the Democrats in the 1930's and early 1940's, the South appeared to resolidify as a Democratic region. However, as the strong

Democratic tides waned in the late 1940's and were replaced by a national-level Republican trend under Eisenhower in the 1950's, it became clear that the Democratic monopoly on Southern partisan loyalties had continued to decay to the point where, in favorable years at least, the Republicans could pick up numerous electoral votes in the South and had hopes for increasing harvests of successful candidates below the presidential level, particularly in the more progressive urban areas.

From most ideological points of view, the Democratic South was a complete anomaly in American politics, and an astonishing tribute to the inertia of history and human institutions. Partisan politics outside the South were characterized in the early middle portions of the twentieth century by a competition between the rural and small-town Protestant America represented in the conservatism of the Republican Party, and the liberal coalition of metropolitan minorities and industrial labor supporting the Democrats. Within the terms of this competition, there is no doubt where the South belonged, being the most nearly homogeneous rural, small-town, and Protestant section of the country, long known for its nativist antagonisms to religious minorities, Negroes, and "foreigners" in general. But the tides of history and the origins of the Republican Party had led in just the opposite direction.

As a result, patterns of partisan politics in the South at the dawn of the period monitored by survey research were in many respects the exact mirror image of those found elsewhere in the country. In the North, higher-status persons tended to be Republican. In the South, they tended to be Democratic. In the North, the more faithful Protestants tended to be, the more Republican they were. In the South, they were more Democratic. Outside the South, rural and small-town citizens tended to be Republican. In the South, however, they tended to be Democratic. Outside the South, Negroes were quite markedly more Democratic than whites. Within the South, those Negroes with some partisan feelings tended to be more Republican than whites, both out of memory for the "party of Lincoln" and, undoubtedly, because of the intense local association between the Democratic Party and white supremacy.

Where the South could operate as a self-contained political system, there was no problem. But whenever it was obliged to mesh with the national political system, the discomforts of the misalignment appeared almost continuously at both elite and mass levels. Democrats of more than nominal Protestant convictions, the majority of whom reside in the South, were twice offered a Catholic as their national party's presidential candidate. The more successful that local Democratic political figures might be in keeping the black man in his "proper place" out of the party, the more likely it was that their probity and credentials would be challenged at conventions of the national Democratic Party. And Southern Democrats in Congress honored their ideological affinities with non-Southern Republicans in such frequency that the coalition came to be taken for granted in much legislative maneuvering, despite its partisan peculiarity.

Any system-level analysis would label such a state of affairs as intrinsically unstable and ripe for reorganization. Indeed, for the past two decades or more, the impending partisan realignment of the South has been announced as imminent. Change has certainly occurred over this time: presidential contests have become quite meaningfully contested, and the admixture of Republicans winning at other levels of office has inched forward steadily. But by any means of accounting, the South remains a fundamentally Democratic region. While it seems unlikely to remain that way for very much longer, we have a right to be impressed with the extreme resistance to readjustment of the ongoing complex of relationships. It seems obvious that the severe ideological dissonance of the current alignment is more nearly tolerable than some of the disruptions that other change would entail.

Many of the resistances to change lie at the level of local political elites and involve very tangible flows of benefits such as patronage, seniority within a party system and the like, few of which could be maintained by the interested individuals and cliques in the face of a true partisan realignment. For such leadership, "States' rights Democratic" movements, although costly on some fronts, are generally more palatable than full-scale collusion with the Republican Party. But in situations where movements of this type do not develop, it is not clear why the tides of change do not impinge from other levels. Thus, for example, while the petty appointee or officeholder is unlikely to throw away his job simply to find a more congenial political party, the common voter has no such mundane interests to protect. Why does he not throw out the rascals obliged to collude from year to year with the civil rights firebrands of the North and replace them with local members of the party that has stood vigorously for States' rights over a number of decades and has shown little enthusiasm for revision of racial practices either nationally or in the South? Democratic change does not, after all, depend on the self-effacing behavior of the elected.

Sample surveys from the recent period give a good accounting of the resistances to partisan change at such a mass level in the South. This is scarcely to say that there has been no change in Democratic strength in that region. As Figure 3 amply attests, the over-all stability in the division of party loyalties in the nation as a whole over the past quarter-century is the composite result of a slow and steady erosion of Democratic strength in the South and a more muted but unquestionable secular gain in Democratic strength elsewhere in the country. This partisan shift in the South has now proceeded to a point where non-Democratic presidential candidates with special appeals to regional sensitivities can do very well in the electoral college, unlike the situation of 30 or 40 years ago.

Figure 3. Evolution of Partisanship, 1952–68, by Region and Race*

Percent Democratic, expected vote

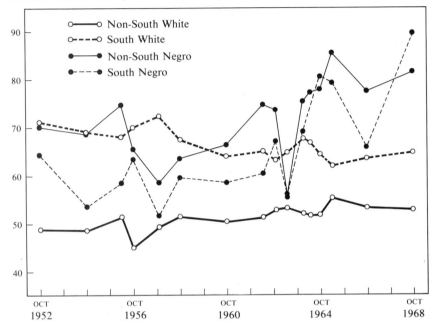

* The "expected" or "normal" vote is an expression of the central tendency of a party identification distribution. (See Angus Campbell *et al., Elections and the Political Order.* Wiley, New York, 1966, Chap. 2.) Small short-term oscillations at a national level reflecting reactions to particular candidacies have been analytically removed from the observations. The relative instability of trends for blacks largely reflects low case numbers and consequent sampling variability. Non-South white observations usually involve about 800 cases, with 400 for Southern whites. There are, however, rarely more than 100 cases for blacks of either region, and at points as few as 60.

At the same time, Figure 3 also suggests that the South remains "at heart" a Democratic region, and that partisan change among whites during this period bears little sign of the sharp discontinuity one would expect of a rapid realignment.[69] Indeed, there is a good deal more indication of this kind of sudden realigning change *in the opposing direction* among Negroes, a shift

[69] Although it might well be imagined that Southerners asked about their evaluations of or identifications with the "Democratic Party" would tend to think in terms of the state or local, rather than the national organization, direct research on the subject has suggested that virtually all Southern respondents, in the context of these interviews, assume that the referent is the national party and furthermore show remarkably little motivation to differentiate their statement of relative identification according to geographical level of organization. See Campbell *et al., Elections and the Political Order,* p. 219.

localized in the year or 18 months leading up to the 1964 presidential election. Let us consider what is known about these contrapuntal changes in partisanship between Negroes and whites during this period in the South.

First and foremost, partisan reactions of both whites and Negroes in the South have clearly been poised in this period to respond primarily to the racial issue. That has been the gripping day-to-day political issue in the region for over a century, and remains so today. This means in turn that, as the civil rights question moved into prominence after the Second World War, had the two major parties taken clear and diametrically opposed stands on the Negro problem per se, one would have expected the appropriate polarization of voting along racial lines in the South as a consequence. However, this is exactly what did *not* happen in the 1950's. Both national parties made some effort to maintain support in both white and black camps in the South.

As late as 1960, sample survey material from the Southern electorate show the results of such ambiguous cues. In effect, black and white sympathizers of both the major national parties were able to convince themselves quite readily that the party they preferred on other grounds or for historical reasons was either the better choice of the two where race was concerned as well, or at the very least posed no unusual threat. Many of course grumbled that the national parties offered them no clear-cut choice on the most important issue of the time. Over the 1950's, most outside observers would have seen the national-level Democratic Party as the more likely of the two parties to rally to the defense of the black man. If there was a modal perception in the South at the time, it was probably this view also. Nonetheless, this alignment of the parties ran so completely counter to "historical expectations" in the South that refusal to believe in the permanency of this state of affairs was widespread, aided of course by vehement efforts on the part of Southern Democratic politicians to dissociate themselves from, and do battle with, the national party on this score. Indeed, when Eisenhower sent federal troops into Little Rock in September, 1957, to protect school desegregation efforts just after a Republican administration had succeeded in passing the first civil rights act since Reconstruction over a Southern Democratic filibuster, there was considerable readiness in both black and white communities to believe that the battle had been joined between the party of Lincoln and the lily-white Democrats. A clear if transient polarizing motion of partisanship was registered in surveys in ensuing months (see Figure 3).

These events of 1957 were, however, the last noteworthy ones to associate the national Republican Party in the Southern mind with a pro-Negro or civil rights position. The rather vigorous efforts of the Kennedy Administration in the field of civil rights and perhaps more especially the emergence of Barry Goldwater as the standard-bearer of the Republican Party in the summer of 1964 courting Southern white conservatism, provided the mass public in the South for the first time with a sense of clear differentiation between the two national parties on the racial issue.[70] The sharp shift in a Democratic direction on the part of Negroes throughout the nation was the immediate consequence. In the South, for the first time in history, the black man had developed more solidly Democratic allegiances than his white antagonists.

But why does this realignment show itself so clearly and suddenly on the Negro side without a correspondingly sharp motion among Southern whites? The clarification of party differentiation on the race issue between 1962 and 1964 was not a perception limited to Negroes. Therefore, one might expect to have witnessed a comparable evaporation of Democratic partisanship among whites in the region.

To understand this asymmetry it is necessary to keep in mind the fact that, when crystallization of party loyalties was concerned, Southern whites and Negroes stood in almost polar opposition in the 1950's. Negro partisanship was weakly developed and remarkably labile. White partisanship was rigidly crystallized. With considerable regularity, Southern white respondents in the 1950's would treat the fact that they were Democrats almost as an immutable ascribed characteristic: "I was born a Democrat just as I was born a Baptist." Moreover, they would discard any possible defection from the faith —even a temporary one—as an inconceivable wrench from tradition. "My daddy would turn over in his grave if I ever voted Republican" was a frequently voiced sentiment. Southern Negroes in the 1950's were, as we have seen, frequently apolitical; and even among those who attempted to state some party preference, the choices were often rather haphazard. This fluidity of partisan preference at the individual level is handsomely summarized by the fact that, as late as 1960, two successive statements of party identification made by the same Southern Negro respondents across an interval of six to eight weeks shows only a correlation of .69, as compared to a figure of .90 for the remainder of the national electorate.[71]

In short, then, the very sharp impact of events of 1963 and 1964 on Negro partisanship as summarized in Figure 3 seems to stem in part from the fact that the Negro vote was only in the process of mobilization during this period, and hence was unusually malleable. It may be noted from Figure 2 that the enormous shrinkage of apoliticals occurred principally in this period.

---

[70] Mathews and Prothro have provided an excellent discussion of the rapid changes in detailed images of the major parties in the South between 1960 and 1964. See Mathews and Prothro, *op. cit.,* pp. 378 ff.

[71] In some degree, of course, the lability of Negro partisanship is reflected by the wider jumps and greater irregularity of the trend lines for Negroes as shown in Figure 3, when compared to the white trends in both regions. Much of the difference here, however, is a simple reflection of the greatly increased sampling error entailed by the more restricted case numbers available for the Negro estimates.

This makes clear in turn that, while some true partisan "conversion" must have occurred among Negroes both North and South during this period, a fair amount of the apparent realignment consisted of the mobilization of erstwhile apoliticals to the ranks of the Democratic Party. There was no such "slack" to be taken up where Southern whites were concerned.

As a matter of fact, more detailed analyses of the mechanisms underlying the partisan change among Southern whites captured in Figure 3 yield entirely surprising results. For although the Democratic ascendance among Southern whites appears to have withered by 5 to 10 percent over the 16 years portrayed in the graph, it turns out that only a small fraction of this change involves any partisan conversion of individuals. Whenever one sees change of the type being monitored in Figure 3, the assumption that individuals are "changing their minds" seems almost irresistible. Yet trends can also develop in open populations of this sort through two types of compositional change: the replacement of dying older generations with younger ones and population exchanges with other regions. Such compositional changes, while nicely cumulative, tend to be too slow to provide much explanation for a change of partisanship as rapid as that shown by Negroes all over the country between 1962 and 1964. However, the drift of partisanship among whites over this period has a form that might well reflect composition trends.

Indeed, much of the steady convergence in partisanship between whites in the South and those elsewhere that has occurred over the past 20 years has sprung from interchanges of population between the two regions. We have published some of the relevant data elsewhere,[72] and will merely add a few more recent figures to underscore the argument. If we partition the "Southern" whites of Figure 3 according to whether they are natives of the region or grew up outside the South, we discover that the expected partisanship of Southern *native* whites in 1952 was 73 percent Democratic, and in the 1964–66 period was 71 percent Democratic. About four-fifths of the decline in Democratic partisanship registering in the figure over the 1950's and 1960's springs directly from rather dramatic changes in the rate and nature of immigration to the region from other parts of the country. As of 1952, about 6 percent of the Southern white electorate had grown up in some region outside the South. By the mid-1960's, the proportion had nearly tripled. In 1952, the small admixture of non-Southerners living in the South had done relatively little to adulterate the homogeneous Democratic character of the region, since their own partisanship leaned in a Democratic direction (expected vote of 59 percent Democratic), perhaps through a lengthy acculturation. But the white migrants entering the region in such large numbers in the 1950's and 1960's were of a totally different partisan coloration and showed little signs of im-

[72] Campbell *et al., Elections and the Political Order,* Chap. 12.

mediate change. They typically came from high-status urban occupations in other regions, with a good 50 percent being business, professional, or technical personnel. Generally, they were either of two types: the junior executive transferred to a position in a Southern subsidiary, or the retired non-South-erner financially capable of taking advantage of the Southern climate in his old age. In view of these backgrounds, they tended to be much more homogen-eously Republican in their party identifications than the non-Southern popula-tions from which they were drawn. Indeed, migrants arriving in the South after 1952 have had an expected partisanship of not much more than 30 percent Democratic, and thus have been about as homogeneously Republican as South-ern whites have typically been Democratic.

Of course, this new generation of carpetbaggers has not settled in any even way across the region; in view of their motives for migration, they have tended to concentrate themselves in industrializing urban areas or in resort set-tings along the coast. Florida, combining both technical development and out-door sport, was prototypic of the attraction and showed the most rapid popu-lation growth of all of the states between 1950 and 1960. But this uneven distribution, while leaving hinterlands that remain Democratic bastions, has brought serious party competition relatively rapidly to many of the modern-izing host areas, and the concentration of entering Republicans probably re-duces the likelihood of long-term acculturation toward the Democratic Party.

In any event, this large influx of very disparate partisans accounts for a good four-fifths of the trend in Southern white political loyalties captured in Figure 3. Thus, at most one-fifth of the change could conceivably be attributed to individual conversion, and some of this undoubtedly is instead change as-sociated with the turnover of native generations within the region. Hence, the phenomenon here is very much different from the partisan change observed in the Negro case, where large-scale individual conversions have been present.

In a somewhat similar vein, the export of population from South to North over the same period has affected the trends in Figure 3. White migrants com-ing out of the South in the past 30 years have tended to be of relatively rural backgrounds and have entered Northern cities in search of urban employ-ment at levels of limited skill, the prototypes here being the arrivals for war industry work during the 1940's. In terms of partisanship, their departure from the South has done relatively little to affect the coloration of parent popu-lation, for the simple reason that the emigrants were of about the same par-tisanship as that population. Moreover, their impact on the host population outside the South has been somewhat limited by the fact that they have never bulked as large in the new setting as have the North-to-South migrants, nor has their partisanship been as remarkably disparate. However, they have been visibly more Democratic (by 20 to 25 percent) and thus, their entrance has contributed in a major way to the slow evolution of the non-Southern white electorate toward the Democrats.

When all these facts are recognized, the *national*-level stability of partisanship over this period becomes a little less wondrous. Observers have often been impressed at how major partisan change in presidential voting can occur —as it has during this period—when the national distributions have shown so little sign of movement, for the situation suggests internally compensating shifts which (if caused by individual conversions) must be in some remarkably delicate adjustment with one another. We see, however, that much—although by no means all—of the change is not at the level of the individual, and hence does not register as change within the nation taken as a whole. Rather, it hinges on exchanges of populations between regions; and since whatever partisans one region loses through migration another region must acquire, the over-all stability is a logical requirement rather than the result of some amazing but hidden forces of an equilibrating type.

Although it is true that much of the change among whites shown in Figure 3 can be traced to *apolitical* causes in population exchanges, this fact should not in any way obscure the *political* significance of these redistributions. In the first place, of course, it is worth stressing that a variety of key political changes would have been occurring in the South in this period even if the migrations had not been taking place. This is certainly true of crucial events like the emergence of the civil rights movement. It is also true of some changes in voting patterns. While the migrations have significantly changed the distribution of underlying loyalties in the region and helped stir meaningful party competition, native white antagonisms to harsh treatment of regional "sensitivities" by the national Democratic Party were already leading to more frequent short-term defections from the Democrats in 1948 and 1952, especially at the presidential level, before regional partisanship was much affected by migration; and the vote from the region has continued to be less Democratic at the presidential level than measures of party identification would lead one to expect for a number of presidential elections in a row (although *more* Democratic at other levels of office, partly but not completely because of uncontested seats). As long as national Democratic conventions continue to pick liberals on the racial question as presidential candidates, this asymmetric defection among whites is likely to continue, particularly when there is a vigorous States' rights Democratic alternative offered, or a Republican candidate that looks significantly more conservative on the race problem, as Goldwater did in 1964.[73] This is not to say, however, that party identification has lost ex-

[73] We do not know how long these party loyalties on the part of the native Southerners will resist change. It has been apparent all along that Southern white partisanship was much more deeply ingrained than among Southern Negroes. The continued Democratic

planatory significance in the Southern situation. It helps to explain why the Republican Party does not take the Southern popular vote by utter storm when it presents a candidate seen by the majority of Southern whites to be unequivocally preferable on the issue that virtually all would consider to be the overriding one of the period. Indeed, in such situations, the Republican Party to date has been lucky to seduce a third of white Democrats to defect. It helps explain also why it is that the white electorate of the Deep South, when offered a choice between a maverick third-party Democratic candidate with no hope of winning the presidency and a Republican who is quite palatable on the race issue and obviously courting the South, will pick the former. In such cases, survey evidence suggests that Southern voters do not even tend to think of themselves as having defected from the Democratic Party, as they would if obliged to vote for a Republican.[74] Finally, the continuing clear Democratic coloration among Southern white voters would lead to the prediction that if, in some upcoming presidential election, the National Democratic Convention were to nominate not a liberal on the race issue but some figure as encouraging to Southern whites as Goldwater, such a candidate would take the Southern popular vote by storm again, for he would be permitting these voters at last to "have their cake and eat it, too." This is, however, one of the points where the immigration of white Republicans to the region has long-range significance; for, in such an eventuality, we would also predict that the swing to the Democrats could never again match that of the Roosevelt period.

At the same time, the apolitical migration phenomenon has likely had

---

ascendance at state and local levels also helps to keep the Southern white thinking that basically he remains a Democrat. Moreover, it is *not* true, although the voting record is deceptive in this regard, that there is a bloc of white Southerners that consistently expects to vote Republican at the presidential level, while continuing to identify with the Democrats even nationally. This latter inference would be easy to make when, for example, the South gave about half of its popular vote to the Republicans in each of the Eisenhower elections and in the ensuing 1960 election, despite an "expected vote" of 65 to 70 percent Democratic. However, a sample survey panel made clear that the overlap between Southern white defectors from the Democrats in 1956 and 1960 for President was scarcely above the chance level, the reasons for defection in the Eisenhower elections having been quite different from those in the 1960 election, and neither having involved any consensus among Southern whites that one national party was clearly preferable to the other with respect to the race problem. See *ibid.,* Chap. 5. With the parties more clearly aligned on the race question in the 1964 and 1968 presidential campaigns, it remains to be seen how much longer Southern whites can maintain their Democratic allegiance.

[74] Note that, in 1968, preliminary survey data suggest that while Nixon won a plurality of votes from the South as defined by the census, he made no major inroads on the traditional Democratic vote. The 36 percent of the regional popular vote which he captured is about the "expected" Republican vote. Humphrey and Wallace divided the votes of the traditional Democratic majority between them.

other significant political consequences than simply these relatively durable effects on partisanship of the electorate in the region. Perhaps the most noteworthy may have to do with the rate at which the South has been adjusting its racial practices to cope with pressures from the rest of the country. This adjustment process has been slow, bitter, and painful across the South. But it seems plausible that it might have been even more difficult but for the wave of new migration into the region that was beginning to swell at just about the time the Supreme Court made its landmark desegregation decision in 1954. On most socioeconomic issues having to do with the role of the federal government and the extent of its power, the substantial contingent of white immigrants looked in the 1960's about as conservative as their native Southern colleagues. But on matters of racial policy, these immigrants displayed attitudes that were usually about as liberal as those of the non-Southern populations they left behind, and in some instances were even more liberal, in part because of the higher education of the migrants.

If some items of racial policy had been made the subject of regional referenda in the South, the admixture of non-Southerners in the electorate would not by any means have been large enough to have changed the political outcomes. Where school desegregation is concerned, for example, the migrants only serve to move the Southern attitudinal distribution five or six percentage points in a liberal direction, nowhere nearly enough to bring desegregation up to the point of being a majority preference. However, it is likely that this construction tends to minimize the true effect that the migrants may have had on moderation of racial policies, for several reasons. First, the migrants are on balance a well-educated group and have moved into a region where education is backward. Thus, while only about one in six white adults in the Southern electorate grew up in some other region, almost a quarter of college-educated people in the South in the mid-1960's grew up in some other part of the country and hence were relatively moderate in their racial views. Second, since few of these migrants settle in other than major urban areas of the region, their relative concentration is probably even greater in these key places. Finally, it is clear from the survey data that the migrants, having grown up in somewhat more actively "participant" political cultures than the traditional South represented, tend to be more interested in and articulate about political matters than their Southern counterparts. When all of these considerations are put together, it would be surprising if the immigrants had not exercised a disproportionate moderating influence on racial adjustment within the South since 1954.

The Erosion of Party Fidelity. With some regularity, journalists after each election seize upon some local instance of massive ticket-splitting to develop the thesis that partisanship has suddenly lost its meaning for the American voter. And the theme becomes particularly prevalent after such major "turning-point" elections as 1952, which broke 20 years of Democratic occupancy of the White House.

Most such accounts turn out to be exaggerated, to say the very least. With the benefit of hindsight, for example, the record shows nothing like a steady decline in the capacity of partisanship to predict voting choice at various levels of office in the period since the Second World War. The proportion of people calling themselves independents, rather than adherents of either party, was almost exactly the same in 1964 as it had been in 1944, with nothing more exciting than faint sampling variability in between. The other levels of partisan intensity registered in our measure have remained constant over the same period as well.

In 1966 and 1968, however, the proportion of self-styled "independents" increased rather markedly, from about 22 to 28 percent. If apoliticals are added in among independents to accumulate all persons who refuse any party allegiance, the change is much less impressive (from an earlier norm of 26 percent to about 29 percent). Yet we have already seen that the sharp decline of apoliticals in the 1960's can be traced exclusively to Southern blacks, and Figure 2 makes clear that these apoliticals have not merely begun to call themselves independents but rather have tended to become clear partisans. It follows that any decline in partisanship in the national aggregate in the late 1960's would simply be more dramatic among whites taken alone. This development will be assessed briefly here.

There are a variety of "indicators" in our surveys that might be taken as reflective of the levels of party fidelity in the land available for examination over nearly a 20-year period. These include such items as reports of ticket-splitting incidence and proportions of the electorate indicating they have voted for different parties for President within their citizen lives. Several of these indirect measures have moved in a direction suggestive of lowered partisan fidelity since 1952, and none that we have explored show any noteworthy counter trend. Nevertheless, the changes registered in these measures do not coincide particularly with the swelling of independents in the late 1960's, and it is relatively easy to see that, while each of these indirect indicators can be affected by changes in levels of partisanship, they can be powerfully influenced by other factors as well.

For example, reports of voting for different parties for President can be strongly affected by particular sequences of candidate pairings and events that throw up third-party intrusions. This index has in fact increased: setting aside blacks, who have been less likely to vary their presidential votes in recent years, we find that 30 percent of whites prior to the 1952 election reported having voted for different parties, a figure that had advanced to 45 percent in 1968. The lion's share of this change occurred between 1952 and 1954, however, and was centered in the South. After the long period of Democratic presidential dominance, many white Democrats voted Republican for the first time in 1952, and this large wave of defection to Eisenhower showed up first in the 1954 reports of past behavior. There was another smaller increase in the "different-party" proportion in 1966, after some relatively consistent Republicans had voted against Goldwater in 1964. It should increase again among whites in 1970, since all Wallace voters who have voted in at least one other election will now qualify. It might be argued that such increases are themselves evidence of declining party fidelity that is a mere extension of trends set in motion at the turn of the century. Yet, there is as much reason to believe that we happened upon a dramatic local minimum of this measure in 1952, and that event sequences have probably produced local maxima as great as 1966 or 1970 in the past. Consider, for example, the likely situation in 1934, after Roosevelt overturned an era of massive Republican dominance in 1932, in an electorate partially populated by voters who had also participated in the Wilson intrusion of 1916 or the La Follette intrusion of 1924 or (for the Solid Democratic South) the repudiation of Catholic Al Smith in 1928. It is hard to imagine that the proportion of "different-party" voters would have been much lower at such a conjuncture than in 1966–70. Obviously, these event sequences are of supreme political importance, and high proportions of different-party voters may well characterize realigning epochs. But the available data of this type do not provide very compelling evidence of a long-term, irreversible decline in the impact of partisanship.

Another measure that seems to hint at a secular erosion of party fidelity is an item that asks people whether they voted a straight party ticket for state and local offices. In 1952, 73 percent of the voting citizens claimed to have voted a straight ticket. Through 1960, the same figure hovered near 70 percent. In 1964, it fell suddenly to a point near 60 percent, and proceeded downward to 51 percent in both 1966 and 1968. Again, the case for diminishing partisanship seems straightforward. However, it is clear that other factors than individual feelings of party allegiance can affect such a measure. In particular, for an extended period prior to the 1950's, large areas of the country showed little partisan competition in general elections. Large numbers of Democrats could run unopposed at lower offices in the South, and Republicans could do so in the North. As partisan balance between regions began to increase after the Second World War, fueled largely by population redistribution, many districts both North and South began to be worth contesting by the minority party. Thus, the sheer possibility of ticket-splitting at lower levels of office must have increased in this period rather dramatically, quite independent of levels of partisan intensity. Moreover, the decline of straight-ticket reports for lower offices has been accompanied by a decline in proportions of persons claiming to have split their ticket fairly evenly, as opposed to a stray defecting vote or two. There have been coding and probing problems with this questionnaire item which militate against putting too much weight on such anomalies; nonetheless, they suggest ways in which straight-ticket voting might decrease while the incidence of crossing party lines might decrease as well.

It is in one sense pointless to deal with such indirect measures when much more direct measures are available, and we have done so only because of the hasty conclusions that have been drawn from some of these other indicators. Certainly the most direct measure is that which indexes the degree of felt partisan loyalty and, as we have seen, the relevant measure has shown no change in the period 1944–64, but indicates some loosening of partisanship in the late 1960's. However, some scholars are distinctly uncomfortable with such "soft" psychological measures and are apprehensive that people might routinely report normal identifications while progressively losing their inhibitions about crossing party lines. Perhaps the most direct behaviorally oriented measure, however, is also available in our data: the frequency with which partisans defect to cast ballots for the opposing party. For most of the biennial elections since 1952 we have been able to make such calculations covering most major offices, including votes cast for presidential, senatorial, gubernatorial and congressional candidates. We have set aside ballots cast in races not contested by major parties: thus, we focus here on individual propensities to cross party lines when proffered a genuine choice between party loyalty or defection. Between 1952 and 1964, this culling amounts to a sample of some 15,600 decisions over six elections, and it is of interest that in this period partisans defected on less than one vote in seven (13.5 percent of all ballots cast).[75] Our prime interest here is in how these defection rates have behaved over time, however, and the data are divided by election in Table 1. Unfortunately, such a refined estimate was not as yet available for 1968, although it will become so in the future, and we have filled in this critical observation on the basis of raw rates of defection, adjusted very slightly in the direction that more refined estimates typically deviate from raw estimates.

The data attest to a significant decline of party fidelity in the late 1960's, a judgment that would be further enhanced if figures were presented for whites alone and if increases in pure independents were taken into account as well. On the other hand, they provide no proof whatever that party allegiance has

[75] Note that another source of lability in party voting resides among pure independents, who refuse to indicate even a faint party "leaning," and whose ballots cannot therefore be judged as "loyal" or "defecting." While data cited earlier refer to a swelling of "independents" in the 1966–68 period which includes "leaners" who can be classed as loyal or defecting in above terms, much of the 1966–68 change in the party identification distribution has occurred in an expansion of the "pure" independents. This additional source of vote variability cannot be represented in Table 1, although it is a highly meaningful contribution to evidence for a recent decline in partisanship.

Table 1. Rates of Voluntary Defection among Partisans Voting at Higher Levels of Office, 1952–68[a]

Year	Percent Defecting
1952	18.0
1956	13.2
1958	11.1
1960	10.3
1962	11.1
1964	15.9
1966	19.3
1968[b]	19.8

[a] Ballots accumulated here cover congressional and senatorial votes in all years, presidential votes quadrennially, and gubernatorial votes in years when these were requested. Generally speaking, there is remarkable similarity in levels of defection for the three types of national office in any given year, and strong temporal covariation as well. Gubernatorial votes tend to show somewhat higher rates of defection, by 3 to 6 percent. Since the votes for governor were not canvassed in 1956, 1960 or 1962, it may be wise to think of these estimates as properly a percent or two greater.

[b] Estimated. The estimate presented here excludes the presidential vote, clouded by the Wallace candidacy. The Wallace candidacy poses problems in part because of the likelihood that many Southern Democrats would not have thought of themselves as defecting to vote for fellow Southern Democrat Wallace. If *all* Wallace votes are considered automatically as voluntary defections, the appropriate value would be about 21.7 percent defecting. If Wallace voters were simply dropped from consideration, but loyal and defecting votes for Humphrey and Nixon were considered in 1968, the estimate would be 19.0 percent defecting.

been steadily declining in salience since the turn of the century. Indeed, if anything, Table 1 appears to have tapped into some more cyclical phenomenon, in the vague sense that moments of electoral realignment seem to have shown a rough periodicity in the past.[76] It is extremely plausible to imagine that the loosening of partisanship in the current period renders the electorate fallow for such a major transition. Generational fault lines in the 1968 presidential vote were apparent, with older voters outside the South attending to standard "New Deal" issues of social welfare and choosing between Humphrey and Nixon on these issues in ways conventional in the 1950's, while younger voters were more attentive to issues of the 1960's, including Vietnam, the racial crisis, and campus disorder. This meant that one stream of younger voters, including many Democrats, supported Wallace, and another stream

[76] Burnham among others has argued that full realignments occur once every "long generation," and that some less permanent dislocation seems to appear at the midpoint of such epochs—putatively, in the data of Table 1, at the time of the 1952 election. See W. D. Burnham, *Critical Elections and the Mainsprings of American Politics*. Norton, New York, 1970, Chap. 1.

was disillusioned by nothing better than the Humphrey choice on the left. Whether a full realignment does occur depends to some degree on the policy directions pursued by the Republican Party in the next few years. Nevertheless, the "Southern strategy" and the prominence of the Agnew backlash philosophy seem calculated to appeal both to the South generally and to many working-class elements elsewhere, previously Democratic, while alienating liberal Republicans of the more cosmopolitan urban sectors of the country.

At the same time, one can predict with some confidence that partisanship will not re-solidify immediately, and is likely in the aggregate to show signs of further loosening well toward 1980. This expectation hinges on the simple fact, thoroughly documented, that as a pure life-cycle phenomenon, young voters come into the electorate with much weaker levels of partisanship than more habituated voters. Under normal circumstances, there are about twice as many "independents" among people aged 21 to 24 than among those over 70.[77] The 1968 election was the first to be affected at all by the massive postwar boom in the birth rate, and some small portion of the increase in independents can be traced to this fact. Still, the impact of the young moving into the electorate was slight in 1968 compared to what may be expected over the next decade. Extension of the vote to 18-year-olds nationwide would simply speed and strengthen these effects. Thus, quite independent of political discontent or the attractiveness of party fidelity, the evolution of the age table for the country will produce an electorate that shows higher partisan volatility in the next decade.

Nonetheless, it would seem quite inappropriate to imagine that we have witnessed in 1966 and 1968 an "end of party" in American electoral politics. For one thing, even with the loosened levels of partisanship of 1968, party allegiance remained far and away the strongest determinant of most political cognitions and behavioral choices in the electorate. It could wane many times as much again without losing its dominant role. The fact that the influx of young voters is about to lower levels of conventional partisanship further means that we will hear a good deal about the "end of party" in the 1970's. And indeed, it is possible that, overlaid on the realigning discontents of the late 1960's, there are some seeds of a more truly secular decline of party fidelity. There is, however, no very conclusive evidence of such a development at this time. If we wish to consider irreversible trends in the nature of the country's electorate, we must turn in other directions.

Education and the Upgrading of the Electorate

Perhaps the most massive social change that registers in our samples since the 1940's is not itself directly political, but seems calculated to have

---

[77] See Philip E. Converse, "Of Time and Partisan Stability," *Comparative Political Studies,* vol. 2, July, 1969, pp. 139–171.

political effects and is, to all intents and purposes, irreversible. This is the rapid increase in levels of formal education of the adult electorate. There is an inescapable tendency in thinking about educational levels in the population to work in terms of current levels of educational practice. Any current adult population reflects the educational practices of at least two earlier generations, however. Thus, for example, going to high school was becoming a commonplace expectation at the beginning of this century, and was widely established by 1920. Yet almost half of the electorate eligible for the 1948 election was made up of people who had not gone beyond grade school.

It is in this sense that the change in the educational background of the electorate is essentially irreversible under any plausible circumstances. Even were educational expectations to be frozen at current practice or trimmed back, the experience in formal education of the adult population would forge forward for a long time to come. Since expectations are likely to continue rising, the electorate of 1970 should look positively uninstructed by comparison with that of the year 2000.

The magnitude of the change often goes unrecognized. Much comment is directed at trends such as increasing urbanization, rising proportions of working women, shifting occupation distributions, changes in the age table, the increasing black population, and the like. All of these are important changes in their own right, with their own significant implications for various spheres of life. But as chartable movements in a percentage space, most of them are dwarfed by the shifts in education. In the electorate that participated in the 1952 election, for example, people whose education was limited to grade school outnumbered people exposed to any college education by almost 3 to 1. In 1968, just four presidential elections later, college persons outnumbered grade school persons by almost 5 to 4. Reflections of this change are charted, based on our election samples, in Figure 4.[78]

What political difference, if any, does this great advance in the educational composition of the electorate make? By most normative theories of democracy—although admittedly not all—it should have some degree of ameliorative effect with regard to the quality of electoral response, as noted earlier. An alert, informed electorate has been considered vital to popular government, and the main path to such an electorate has been considered to be the extension and intensification of formal public education. If man-years spent in classrooms is any indicator of sophistication, then the American electorate is the most sophisticated in the world, among the large set of countries enjoying universal suffrage.

---

[78] In evaluating this figure, remember that there is a modest tendency for some fraction of persons to edge above the truth in reporting their level of education. Compared with other data sources, the higher grades of education in Figure 4 are a bit fuller than they should be. However, *rates* of change over time fit the historical record quite well, and this is what is important for us here.

Figure 4. Increasing Levels of Education in the U.S. Electorate, 1948–68

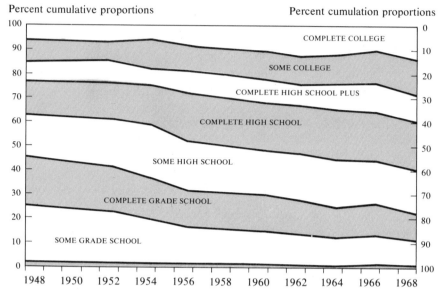

Percent cumulative proportions   Percent cumulation proportions

Moreover, there is strong empirical reason, built up from past survey research on political behavior, to imagine that advancing education should indeed have the potent impact commonly ascribed to it. There is probably no single variable in the survey repertoire that generates as substantial correlations in such a variety of directions in political behavior material as level of formal education. Some of these relationships turn up with respect to partisan differences, where education is likely to be thought of as one among several handy indicators of social status; and here, it is usually surprising how discriminating an independent variable it turns out to be, relative to other indicators of status such as occupation or income. But the true domain of education as a predictor has to do with the large class of indicators of popular involvement and participation in politics. Whether one is dealing with cognitive matters such as level of factual information about politics or conceptual sophistication in its assessment; or such motivational matters as degree of attention paid to politics and emotional involvement in political affairs; or questions of actual behavior, such as engagement in any of a variety of political activities from party work to vote turnout itself: education is everywhere the universal solvent, and the relationship is always in the same direction. The higher the education, the greater the "good" values of the variable. The educated citizen is attentive, knowledgeable, and participatory, and the uneducated citizen is not.

As social science relationships go, these links between education and political involvement are uncommonly strong. By way of illustration, let us consider what has come to be seen as a central variable of a mediating sort where political participation is concerned. We have treated this indicator under the name "sense of political efficacy." Others have called it "sense of political competence," and still others have turned the variable on its head and labeled it "political alienation" (absence of a sense of political efficacy). We have measured the notion with a small scale of four simple agree-disagree items, and this scale has been very widely borrowed.[79] Others have developed variant measures, or have split the concept into diverse components. What is important is that the general notion itself has attracted such high interest, and tends to be seen in rather common terms: people differ markedly in the degree to which they feel confident about participating in politics and getting some meaningful response from "the system." This variable became one of the central foci in the classic Almond-Verba "Five-Nation Study" of the quality of mass political participation, and it is of interest that this study rested very heavily on cross-national differences in levels of education as a prime explanatory term for cultural variation in citizen participation.[80]

Moreover, it is noteworthy that a more generic concept, but one which is closely related, has turned out to be something of a "sleeper" variable in a much wider range of social research. This indicator has been variously called "sense of personal competence," "ego strength," or, turned on its head, "fatalism." Thus, for example, the Coleman report on racial segregation of schooling discovered to the surprise of the investigators that a measure of personal sense of competence turned out to be the best predictor of child performance in schools, outstripping a very wide variety of other structural, relational, and psychological factors.[81] It is not surprising that political efficacy turns out to

---

[79] The four items surviving from the original five-item scale are: "I don't think public officials care much what people like me think"; "Voting is the only way that people like me can have any say about how the government runs things"; "People like me don't have any say about what the government does"; and "Sometimes politics and government are so complicated that a person like me can't really understand what's going on." The first formal description of the measure, along with some discussion of its initial measurement properties, was provided in Angus Campbell, Gerald Gurin, and Warren Miller, *The Voter Decides.* Row, Peterson, Evanston, Ill., 1954, pp. 187 ff. It might be said that long work with the measure has left us well aware of its shortcomings, particularly in its sensitivity to acquiescent response sets. See Campbell *et al., The American Voter,* especially pp. 515–519. We have, however, maintained the measure in its current form because of our strong interest in the kind of long-term trend analysis employed here.

[80] G. Almond and S. Verba, *The Civic Culture.* Princeton University Press, Princeton, 1963.

[81] James S. Coleman, *Equality of Educational Opportunity.* Government Printing Office, Washington, D.C., 1966. See also Brim's work on a measure of "fatalism" in O. G. Brim, Jr., *et al., American Beliefs and Attitudes about Intelligence.* Russell Sage Foundation, New York, 1969.

be strongly related to measures of personal competence, since it seems a specific manifestation of such a syndrome. And both of these entities are in turn closely related to level of education. Table 2 provides a glimpse at the strength of covariation that tends to pertain, drawing one of the component items of our scale from one of our studies quite haphazardly.

Table 2. Political Efficacy and Education (1966 Data)

Level of Education	Percent Agreeing[a]
None	77
Partial grade school	68
Completed grade school	53
Partial high school	48
Completed high school	32
Partial college	16
Completed college	10

[a] To statement: "I don't think public officials care much about what people like me think."

In short, then, all the ingredients are present for a demonstration that the level of political efficacy and, with it, the quality of electoral participation in the United States, is advancing on a mounting tide of educational advantage. People of college background are much more efficacious politically than others, and the proportion of people with college exposure in the electorate has about doubled in the last 16 years alone.

Yet, these are mere static correlations and cannot in themselves ensure that we are dealing with dynamic or causal ones. Even the Almond-Verba work rests on synchronic comparisons between societies rather than diachronic measurement. Counter-models in some variety can be imagined. Formal education may develop the capacity to read or some understanding of the calculus but is political efficacy dispensed by the educational system in anything like the same way? Let us argue for the moment that progress through an educational system contributes absolutely nothing to enhancement of an individual's sense of political efficacy. Instead, let us see this efficacy as some residue of the individual's interactions with other actors and institutions in the political domain over time, a summary expression, to be blunt, of how often he "wins" and "loses." There is a natural pecking order in societies, we might argue, which arises from a variety of individual traits and determines the ratio of wins to losses, including success at completing an education. The well-educated in modern societies are, on balance, the winners in such transactions, and the poorly-educated are the losers. Hence, there is naturally a strong static correlation between education and sense of political efficacy, although if there were no formal educational process at all, individuals would still differ in about the same degree in their felt capacity to participate effectively in the political system. If we accept this model, then we encompass the static fact that education relates strongly to efficacy, but we do not expect that increasing levels of education lead over time to any particular change in aggregate levels of efficacy.

On the face of it, most people would expect the truth to lie somewhere between the "education-driven" model and this latter model which rests on an assumption of a relative pecking order. That is, we would expect education to make some instrumental contribution to efficacy, in part because of demonstrations like the Almond-Verba cross-national comparisons, which belie any model of efficacy levels as a universal constant within societies across space and time. On the other hand, most would suspect that there is some adulteration of education effects as the upper levels of education recruit more and more widely in the population. What is attractive about these two simplistic models is that each produces an exact prediction as to how our efficacy data should behave over time. Although details vary somewhat by item, for example, the education-driven model would require that other things equal, our efficacy measures should have forged upward by about 5 or 6 percent nationally between 1952 and 1968, with efficacy levels within education classes resting constant over this time. The pecking-order model would predict constant levels of efficacy over this period, with declining levels of efficacy visible within specified education categories. Moreover, if other things could be taken as equal, one might be willing to see any intermediate level of gain in efficacy falling between 0 percent and 5 or 6 percent as a reflection of the relative weight of the two models, which would be an extremely interesting specification in itself and one which would be helpful in long-range predictions about efficacy change.

Other things rarely do remain equal, however, as a first inspection of the behavior of four efficacy items over 16 years (Figure 5) makes clear. Neither of our competing models receives any resounding confirmation here. It is not that the data are incoherent; indeed, they seem quite well-behaved, and warrant closer attention. Setting aside the one errant item ("voting only way"), each trend line moves smoothly through time. There is only one main reversal of direction in each line, and this coincides in time for all three measures, as one would expect if there was some underlying syndrome of efficacy for which these items are adequate indicators. But this common trend does not fit either model. The early observations do move as though education-driven, although it can be shown that they tend to outrun slightly what gains could be expected from education taken alone. In the 1960's, other forces of a rather potent sort were clearly intruding to contravene any gains associated with increases in education.

Figure 5. Trends in Responses to Political Efficacy Items, 1952–68

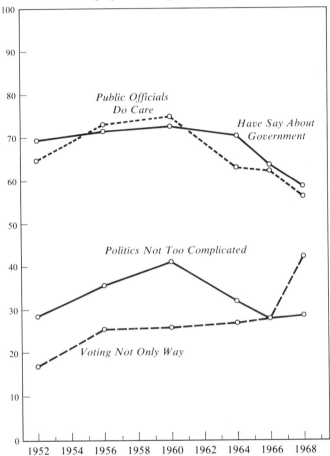

Percent efficacious (proportion disagreeing with the item)

The one item departing from this pattern by its persistent and uneven upward movement is the one which proposes that "voting is the only way" to have an impact on government. The performance of this item is not surprising in context. Developments of the 1960's were marked by a great expansion of forms of political participation associated primarily with the civil rights movement and resistance to the Vietnam War. Sit-ins, demonstrations, marches, and various more or less violent disruptions came to be a common recourse for dissent, as means of exerting grass-roots influence on government beyond voting alone. At first we assumed that, because of civil rights innovations, the upsurge in the belief that there are other ways of exerting influence than voting would be concentrated among blacks. But examination showed that, whereas blacks had contributed their share or more to the faint rise in these beliefs from 1952 to 1964, the bulk of the rapid upturn after that date came among whites both North and South. Further analysis has succeeded in clarifying what is going on here, however. The lowest educational levels have shown little or no gain in perceptions of other ways to influence government over the whole period from 1952 through 1968. At each higher educational category, however, the gain in these perceptions increases. Thus, for people who have not completed grade school, the gain has been on balance less than 1 percent in 16 years. For those who have completed grade school, the gain is nearly 5 percent. The progression continues quite regularly to those who have completed college, where the gain is of the order of 30 percent![82] Given the fact that many of the new forms of political participation have been spawned and most heavily practiced on college campuses, it is not surprising that cognizance of them should be most strongly registered among persons closer to college milieu, with a diminishing "trickle-down" effect to lower levels of education, where "people like me" have little participation in such affairs.

Several morals, both substantive and methodological, can be drawn from these simple materials. This is an interesting case, for example, of a scale deemed unidimensional by Guttman criteria in 1952, one component of which has pulled out of line rather markedly in response to phenotypic events in a subsequent period. Our analysis of these trends would have been greatly muddied if we had proceeded with the composite scale taken as a whole.

More important is the substantive message conveyed by the other three items. The fact that they move rather nicely in tandem suggests that it remains reasonable to think in terms of some generic sense of political efficacy which these items tap. This suspicion is reinforced by analyses showing that, unlike the situation with the voting item, the depression in efficacy of the 1960's was shared more or less across all categories of education. This is not to say that divergences from parallel trends between educational groups fail to appear on other items. There are some such divergences, of a minor but systematic sort. For example, the item suggesting that politics is too complicated to understand is the most purely cognitive of the efficacy items and reflects more on the person agreeing with it than it does upon flaws in the political system. When agreement with this item increases in the 1960's (declining efficacy), the upswing is somewhat stronger among people of lower education. In other words, when political events seem chaotic to the observer, he is more likely to attribute it to his own inferiorities if he is of limited educa-

---

[82] As this pattern logically requires, correlation coefficients linking this efficacy item and education have been increasing over time, despite the fact that comparable correlations for the other items have remained essentially constant. The gamma coefficient for 1952 was .33 on the voting item, substantially below the normal levels of relationship between efficacy terms and education. The same coefficient had advanced to .51 by 1968, at the high edge of the usual range.

tion; the well-educated observer tends instead to assign the difficulty to the responsiveness of the system. While styles vary mildly in these ways, the decline of "efficacy" registers in both groups, however, and in reaction to more or less common events.

It is not hard to imagine what some of these events were during the 1960's, although specific items on any list would produce somewhat different impact in various segments of the electorate. A list should undoubtedly include the three shocking political assassinations in 1962, 1967, and 1968; the perception in some small but articulate quarters early in 1965 that Lyndon Johnson, after winning a landslide vote for his campaign against Goldwater's proposals to escalate the war, immediately had turned himself to escalating that war; resentment in other larger sectors of the population concerning official pressures toward school desegregation, particularly after 1964; race riots and campus disorders from 1965 on; and throughout, the increasing weariness and frustration with the bleeding war in Vietnam that the government could not seem to win or otherwise terminate. This sequence of national catastrophes, disruptions, and blunders seems adequate to account for a considerable loss of confidence in the government and politics on the part of the public. Nor is there much doubt that the decline of efficacy is functionally related to the weakening in sense of partisanship after 1965, which was discussed earlier.

It is appropriate to call the efficacy change in the 1960's one of "disenchantment," both because there is a strong affective component in the items used as indicators (evaluation of government responsiveness), and because the aggregate drop in efficacy has been too large and rapid to be accounted for by any influx of young people alienated from government. It must have involved an actual constriction at the individual level of many persons' feelings of political efficacy. At the same time, efficacy, with its blend of affective and cognitive factors, is not the only manifestation of political involvement which is potentially "education-driven." More purely cognitive are such terms as levels of political information and sophistication, or attentiveness to what is going on in politics. It would be interesting if one could show that political information processing at the individual level, more obviously related to education in any event, has continued to increase in tempo with education advances despite situational setbacks to general feelings of political efficacy.

I cannot show such a pattern in any direct way, although I shall shortly provide some presumptive evidence that it may well exist. By and large, the most direct measures that might be useful to document such a trend are simply lacking. Up to now I have made few pleas for new measurement in the course of this article, in contrast to other pieces in this volume; its very length may attest to the fact that we are drowning in temporal data rather than starving for lack of it. However, there is a major lacuna where trend materials on information processing are concerned, and from a theoretical point of view, it is a serious deficiency. Stray items of an information-level variety appear here and there in our political surveys and those of others. What has not been developed, however, is a set of items that are (1) nontrivial (depend on political understanding, as opposed to rote memory for stray facts); and (2) well proofed against the obsolescing of its referents so that it could be meaningfully applied over a long period of time. Without such measures, we are likely to miss the most probable impact of rising education within the electorate.[83]

The only items collected in series back to 1952 that are relevant to levels of political attentiveness and information-seeking activities are (1) items which measure interest in the current campaign; and (2) questions about whether this campaign was followed in each of four major media (radio, television, newspapers, or magazines). Both types of measures, being focused on each campaign per se, are quite sensitive to variations in the intrinsic interest of particular presidential contests. Thus, for example, perhaps the dullest pairing in the 1952–68 series occurred in 1956, when Eisenhower faced Stevenson for the second time after having beaten him handily in 1952. Except in extremely partisan Democratic quarters, the outcome was a foregone conclusion, and all our measures of interest and media attention show marked lows for that year. On the other hand, 1952 was, on the face of it, an uncommonly absorbing election relative to those of 1944, 1948, and 1956, so that the high attentiveness values found for that year are scarcely surprising either. In the long run, it should be possible to detect more fundamental secular trends within such materials, but in the absence of independent measures of the "intrinsic interest" of specific election pairings, the effect of which could then be statistically removed, such judgments remain risky in any short term.[84]

[83] Some years ago we devised a measure intended to bear on the degree of sophistication with which our respondents made key political assessments, based on a delicate and elaborate evaluation of openended commentary captured in the interview protocols. (See the discussion of "levels of conceptualization" in Campbell *et al.*, *The American Voter*, Chap. 10.) Work is currently going forward to extend this coding over a wider span of studies and may show interesting education effects over time. However, even this measure is likely to be somewhat sensitive to various specific elements that are present in some elections and not in others, and in the broad sweep of history is rather timebound as well.

[84] Trends in data on mass-media attention to campaigns are further obscured by shifting patterns of general media use during this period, and in particular, the advent of television (see Chap. 2 of this volume). Thus, while all other media show marked drops in campaign attention between 1952 and 1956, reports of following the campaign by television moved from 51 percent to 74 percent of the electorate in that span. Moreover, correlations between education and use of radio or television to follow campaigns are quite low, and are only moderate where newspapers are concerned. There is a substantial correlation between education and magazine reading about the campaign, although it remains lower than that between education and efficacy or expressions of campaign interest. However, when we discover that 5 percent *less* of the electorate report having followed the campaign in magazine articles in 1968 than was the case in 1952, we are still without ground for concluding that there has been any meaningful decline in media attention to electoral politics, in view of the vast incursion of television over the same period.

With such caveats in mind, however, it is well worth mentioning that expressions of general interest in each succeeding presidential campaign clearly do *not* show the kind of temporal trajectory displayed by the efficacy measure (see Table 3). That is, there is no sign of a collapse of interest accompanying the decline in sense of efficacy or partisanship registered in mid-1960's. If anything, one would have to judge that interest in presidential elections was inching forward rather steadily over this period. The differences are slight and concentrated within the lower interest levels. Nevertheless, they are of magnitudes compatible with an "education-driven" model.[85] Most important conceptually is the juxtaposition of declining efficacy with aggregate levels of political interest that have at the very least been maintained, and probably have risen. I will comment on this pattern shortly.

First, however, it is equally significant to note that other measures of unusual political activity monitored over the full 1952–68 period have shown on balance the same faint upward trends as campaign interest. Differences are nowhere large, and for any given pair of temporal comparisons, lie within sampling error. However, the sequence of results over a span of five presidential studies leaves little doubt that we are witnessing real change. Moving from more to less prevalent forms of campaign participation, we find that 27 percent of the population reported having engaged in information influence attempts to sway another person's vote in the 1952 study; the figure was 28 percent in 1956, and has been in the 31 to 35 percent range during the 1960's. Seven percent of the electorate in both 1952 and 1956 reported having attended campaign rallies; the comparable figure moved to 8 percent, then 9 percent in the elections of the 1960's. Three percent of the electorate in both

---

[85] Rather exacting tests conducted on the two terminal distributions—1952 and 1968—fit the education-driven model quite nicely, with one exception that seems intelligible in other terms. If the three-category distribution of interest is converted to a mean value based on integer scoring (0, 1, 2), then the observed data show an advance of interest from 1.084 in 1952 to a value of 1.182 in 1968. If the distribution of interest within education categories for 1952 is referred to a 1968 distribution by education, then the predicted 1968 value under the terms of the education-driven model would be 1.216, or a modest degree higher than observed. Now there is much evidence that, phenotypically in 1968, a small proportion of "hard-core" supporters of Eugene McCarthy lost interest in the campaign after the primaries, refused to vote for President, etc. although under normal circumstances they would have been among those intensely interested. This group was, moreover, concentrated almost exclusively among the college educated. If we proceed to the second test required by the education-driven model, i.e., to see whether levels of interest have remained constant aside from nonsystematic sampling variation within parallel education categories between 1952 and 1968, we find that they have beyond much doubt *save for* a depression which occurs in 1968 among the college educated. In sum, then, the fit with the education-driven model is excellent apart from the McCarthy-based disenchantment; if that disenchantment had not occurred, the full interest distribution for 1968 would have fallen not at 1.182, but close to the predicted value of 1.216.

Table 3. Variations in Popular Interest in Presidential Campaigns, 1952–68[a]
(*In Percent*)

	1952	1956	1960	1964	1968
Very much interested	37	30	38	38	39
Somewhat interested	34	40	37	37	40
Not much interested	29	30	25	25	21
	100	100	100	100	100
Number of cases	(1,771)	(1,753)	(1,919)	(1,564)	(1,659)

[a] The question asked is: "Some people don't pay much attention to the political campaigns. How about you, would you say that you have been very much interested, somewhat interested, or not much interested in following the political campaigns so far this year?" The insertion of "so far" arises because the item is typically asked prior to the election, when the campaigns are in full swing. Analyses of the data by time of interview give little sign that individual responses are affected by the point in the campaign at which the interview was conducted. Posing of this question after the election leads to more contaminated results: losers tend to decide the campaigns were not very interesting, while winners attribute them high interest.

1952 and 1956 reported engaging in some kind of party work during the campaign; the figure ran between 5 and 6 percent during the 1960's. Less than 2.5 percent reported membership in political clubs or organizations in 1952; the figure was 2.9 percent in 1956, and has risen to the 3.2 to 4.0 percent range since. The actual maxima for these items in the 1960's falls once at 1960, twice at 1964, and once at 1968. The differences within the 1960's are, however, extremely slight in most cases (a few tenths of a percent). Of all the activities we have monitored since 1952, only one—the giving of campaign contributions—fails to show clearly higher levels in the 1960's than in the 1950's.[86]

Although some of these increases may seem rather paltry numerically, they are probably of major significance. Taken at face value, the estimates imply that the proportion of the electorate engaging in some kind of party work during presidential campaigns has nearly doubled over the past decade. This is a great deal of additional manpower. Similarly, the figures suggest an increase almost as large in formal political organization memberships in the same period. Moreover, although in the popular mind the prime indicator of mass political interest is taken to be voting turnout, it probably is a less significant political parameter than the types of activity catalogued above. Indeed, there is little reason to expect voting turnout to show anything like perfect co-variation across time with trends in more strenuous political activ-

[86] Even here, whatever trend there is must be seen as rising. The figures for the sequence of five presidential elections from 1952 to 1968 are 4 percent, 10 percent, 12 percent, 11 percent, and 9 percent.

ity, for the simple reason that the decision whether or not to bother voting in a particular presidential election is made in sectors of the population—the poorly educated, for example—that are socially and politically remote from the strata where current political conditions push people over the threshold into fuller activism or leave them "sitting on their hands." And from the point of view of political influence and outcomes, it is likely that the potential activists are a more important group than the sometime voters.

To summarize, then, indicators of political attentiveness and activism appear to have edged forward over the past two decades in something like the measure that advances in education, with which all are closely correlated, would lead one to expect. And these trends stand in rather marked contrast to the evolution of feelings of political efficacy in the population. Efficacy has been accorded central theoretical importance in the field and, in general, is more strongly correlated with education than any of the other terms, yet it has shown a marked regression during the middle 1960's.

As implied at several points, it is useful conceptually to partition gross feelings of political efficacy as we have measured them over the years into at least two components, which might be more precisely labeled "personal feelings of political competence" and "trust in system responsiveness." The first term refers to the individual's sense of his own fundamental capacities and experience in operating in a political domain. The second refers to perception of properties of the political system as it stands at a point in time. The distinction is essentially the same as one made by Gamson between "efficacy" and "trust."[87]

Although the distinction is easily made at a conceptual level, it is much more difficult to make empirically, for there are obvious causal interactions between the two terms. Moreover, the sheer definition of personal skills that are politically effective is to some degree dependent on the shape of the political system itself, and most specifically, the kind of influence attempts to which it is open, if any. Imagine the articulate and gregarious individual with great organizational expertise transplanted from a democratic setting where he has employed his capabilities in party organization with high success to a closed and heavy-handed authoritarian regime. The transplantation would not have affected his skills and, ideally, measurements should show a high sense of political competence but a low estimate of system responsiveness. However, most ways of assessing the individual's own sense of political competence would be inadvertently influenced in such a situation by limitations on skills that could plausibly achieve a political response in his immediate setting.

The political efficacy scale with which we have worked since 1952 in-

[87] William A. Gamson, *Power and Discontent.* Dorsey, Homewood, Ill., 1968, pp. 39–48. Others, such as Almond and Verba, have made somewhat parallel distinctions.

volves a considerable blend of these elements. The item most clearly directed at personal competence independent of system responsiveness is the one which suggests that politics and government seem too complicated to understand. Assuming that complexity is seen as a neutral property (i.e., is not concocted by official malice or obscurantism), then responses are focused on the individual's own capabilities alone. Items such as those dealing with the individual's "say in government" or how much "public officials care" are directed primarily at system responsiveness, although the recurrent phrase "people like me" invites a response which takes into account as well the individual's sense of location in a capability pecking order. The item "voting is the only way that people like me can have any say" rather straddles the two components: It is manifestly addressed to a system property, but individual tastes and capabilities are strongly drawn in. The individual who is aware of, and perhaps appalled by, the apparent influence of demonstrations and disruptions on governmental decision-making would still be likely to agree with the item, given a refusal to countenance any personal participation in such influence attempts.[88]

It is intuitively plausible that, as education advances, it could be expected to stimulate the personal competence term, but education has no necessary connection with the system responsiveness component. Now we have seen that the more personal item, "politics too complicated," has registered a declining level of efficacious responses in the 1960's, despite continuing increases of education. The decline is at least slightly less than for items directed more purely at system responsiveness, however, and the decline has also been heaviest among people of less than high school education.

Taking these patterns together, including those involving political interest and behavioral forms of political participation, it seems reasonable to imagine that "driven" by education, the personal competence component of political efficacy has been steadily advancing in this period within the ranks of the better-educated, however glacial the pace, and underlies the increases in attentiveness and participation in this period as well. But, in the middle 1960's, sequences of events occurred which sharply jarred the component of efficacy that bears on confidence in system responsiveness or integrity. For the less well-educated, this perceived souring of the system tended to draw a response of acquiescence and resignation which is probably age-old, and which surfaces partly in the increased belief that politics is simply beyond the

[88] It should be noted that we have also occasionally used a scale of "political cynicism" that is somewhat more purely addressed to estimates of system responsiveness and respectability. However, we lack any full portfolio of trend measures here. See D. E. Stokes, "Popular Evaluations of Government: An Empirical Assessment," in H. Cleveland and H. Lasswell, eds., *Ethics and Bigness: Scientific, Academic, Religious, Political, and Military*. Harper, New York, 1962.

grasp of "people like me." While the well-educated were not completely immune to such reactions, there is also a tendency among them toward a less passive response, witnessed most clearly perhaps in the increased interest and belief in other ways of influencing policy beside voting.

Gamson has given attention to the juxtaposition of high levels of felt political competence with low levels of confidence in the political system which seems to describe very well what has been new in American politics in the 1960's, or at least new in the period since the Second World War. He proposes that this disjunctive state of affairs is the prime setting for the effective mobilization of discontent. If trust is high, there is no problem; and if sense of personal competence is low, distrust is absorbed in resignation and apathy.[89] And, of course, it is this potential for mobilized discontent that has led some of the more heterodox commentators on democratic theory to suggest that a highly attentive, politically involved electorate may be well nigh beyond any coherent governance in a democratic mode: given the necessary inertias in policy formulation and implementation, as well as the toes which must be trod in any regulation of conflicts of interest, a major "leaven of apathy" among the governed is essential.

Extrapolations from this point are, however, extremely tricky. The Gamson treatment, sensitive to the inevitable interaction between personal efficacy and system response, assumes that efficacious influence attempts under conditions of declining trust, if unrequited, are merely stimulated further in the short term. But in the longer term, persistent nonresponse will act back to pinch out the original feelings of political competence and produce apathy. Applied to the current concrete situation, we would simply append the observation that, as education advances, it is likely that personal levels of efficacy can be reduced only at slower and slower rates. Yet, rather different scenarios for the concrete case can be imagined. Some would take account of the likelihood that severe inroads on the capacity to govern coherently would entail collective costs that would first be recognized by the well-educated, leading either to restraint or to necessity mothering the invention of new institutional forms.

All that is known with certainty is that the educational level of the electorate has been increasing rapidly and must continue to do so for decades into the future. Less completely certain, but highly probable, is that this increase will keep an upward pressure on at least the personal-competence component of political efficacy, along with manifestations of political attentiveness and citizen participation. There is no reason at this point to suppose that mobilized discontent is any inevitable accompaniment to these trends. All that rising efficacy produces is a heightened probability that, under certain conditions

---

[89] Gamson, *op. cit.,* especially p. 48.

of reversal and stress in the political system, mobilized discontent will occur. Only as one sees such conditions recurring with certainty over a specified period of time would the incidence of mobilized discontent be predicted to rise as well.

What is important in this final observation is yet another implied scenario whereby the sources of distrust are remedied in the fairly immediate future. Although problems such as Vietnam, which has certainly contributed in a major way to the current malaise, are susceptible to reasonably clear-cut terminations, it would be a mistake to imagine that all contributory problems are of this order. For example, in some sectors of the population, the decline in confidence that government is responsive has accelerated in the 1960's, with bitter perceptions that officialdom is trying to force a liberal racial policy down the throats of a white majority which, if given any "say" in the matter, would defeat it resoundingly on a direct vote. Problems of this order are not likely to be resolved cleanly.

Obviously, we know far too little at this point to choose between any of these scenarios. Useful predictions must await the development of a surer sense of causal dynamics as well as various kinds of thresholds for some of these key variables, not simply for the nation as a whole, but within critical subgroupings, often very small numerically, within the country. These developments will be aided, in turn, by stronger and more frequent measurement on larger samples, on the one hand, and upon a heavier investment in theoretical attention on the other. Nonetheless, the weak and infrequent measurements already made can stimulate such attention, and whatever else they lack, can provide baselines to help us know in the future if and when we return to "normal" with respect to popular orientations toward the political system. To paraphrase the appeal for cooperation in the 1970 census: In order to know where we are going, we have to know where we have been. Rudimentary steps have been made in this direction.

9

Dimensions of Social-Psychological Change in the Negro Population

Herbert H. Hyman

When two decades ago I labored with this book, I came increasingly to understand that I had happened to come to the study of the Negro problem in America at a time when big changes were pending and a new trend was at the point of asserting itself. As my study dragged me through all the serious imperfections of American life related to the Negro problem, I became ever more hopeful about the future. This sense of hopefulness, together with the complete identification I could feel with the moral force, which in this book I referred to as the American Creed, made it subjectively easier for me to carry out an assignment which, in fact, called upon me to become an expert . . . on almost everything that is wrong in America. . . . The most important conclusion of my study was, however, that: "Not since Reconstruction has there been more reason to anticipate fundamental changes in American race relations, changes which will involve a development towards American ideals." . . . A student who has often been wrong in his forecasts will be excused for pointing to a case when he was right.[1]

Gunnar Myrdal wrote these lines in 1962, in the Preface to the twentieth-anniversary edition of *An American Dilemma*. His words encourage those beginning similar, if smaller, endeavors in the 1970's, who try to penetrate the obscurities of Negro-white relations and chart the course of change in the United States. Indeed, he gives special encouragement to those who

The research assistance of John S. Reed and the editorial help of Eleanor Singer are gratefully acknowledged. A Fellowship at the Center for Advanced Studies, Wesleyan University, provided the opportunity and ideal milieu for completing the manuscript, and I express my appreciation to the Director, Philip Hallie, and staff at the Center.

[1] Gunnar Myrdal (with the assistance of Richard Sterner and Arnold Rose), *An American Dilemma,* Twentieth Anniversary ed., Harper, New York, 1962, p. xxiii.

would chart that future course along *social-psychological* coordinates, since his major theme, "The American Creed," and the dynamic principle underlying his prediction, its "moral force," fall within the domain of psychological concepts.

But Myrdal's example suggests that we blend caution with courage. If the republication had waited for a more eventful anniversary, for example, the twenty-fifth, coinciding with the riots of 1967 in many American cities, would the same Preface have been warranted? Some might answer, "No," but caution should not overwhelm us, since the question might be couched in many forms. Would that Preface have suited the occasion of the tenth anniversary in 1952? The fifteenth in 1957? Will it fit the thirtieth or even the fiftieth as we approach the year 2000? If "No" would be the correct reply part of the time, "Yes" would certainly be applicable to some of these questions. The only way to approach the *general* question is not to dwell on the occasion instant, but rather to adopt a longer time perspective. And the only way to obtain the answer is by collecting empirical evidence on trends. As Arnold Rose strikes this note in his Postscript to the twentieth-anniversary edition, he also conveys the importance of another psychological dimension in charting the future.

> While to the student of social change, who must have historical perspective . . . the changes in American race relations from 1940 to 1962 appear to be among the most rapid and dramatic in world history without violent revolution, to the participants themselves the changes did not appear to be so rapid. People generally live from day to day, and from month to month, without historical perspective, and hence tend not to perceive changes that occur over a period of years. The "social present" usually means much more to people than does social change. Young people who have come to awareness of the world around them during the latter part of the period under consideration see only the conditions of the last few years; for them the conditions of the pre-1940 period are "ancient history," and hence the changes of twenty years are not part of their image of the modern world.[2]

The trend in the *perception* of the speed of social change may itself be one change to be charted. This perception, as Rose suggests, may not reflect the actual pace of previous events, but it may influence the speed of subsequent social change if the participants demand that society move to their tempo. Direct psychological description again seems both necessary and important, but complicated. Different groups may perceive change as proceeding at different rates; the same group may perceive things moving fast at one point and slow at another, or may never waver in the view that things are standing still. The image of Alice comes to mind:

[2] *Ibid.,* p. 44.

> The Queen kept crying "Faster! Faster!" but Alice felt she *could not* go faster. . . . Just as Alice was getting quite exhausted, they stopped. . . . Alice looked round her in great surprise. "Why . . . everything's just as it was!" "Of course it is," said the Queen: "what would you have it?" "Well, in *our* country," said Alice, . . . "you'd generally get to somewhere else—if you ran very fast for a long time, as we've been doing." "A slow sort of country!" said the Queen. "Now, *here*, you see, it takes all the running you can do, to keep in the same place. If you want to get somewhere else, you must run at least twice as fast as that!"[3]

Lewis Carroll's fantasy provides one model to guide our empirical efforts and to haunt our thoughts. We return, however, to the scholarly literature and research findings of the past for more conventional guidance toward the systematic measurement of changes in race relations in American society.

As one scans that literature and ponders its utility, the need for long-term psychological modes of description becomes all the more evident and some of the dimensions to be charted are suggested. To be sure, no one can render a comprehensive judgment on this total body of material. By 1942, when Myrdal faced it, the bibliography already numbered "several hundred thousand titles" and he concluded that "nobody has ever mastered this material exhaustively, and probably nobody ever will."[4] By now, the growth of the literature makes his prediction all the more true,[5] and the problem seems also to grow in complexity. No single essay can encompass it.

I shall focus on the attitudes and characteristics of the Negro population, rather than on the white population. Race relations, of course, involve both groups, and other groups whose numbers are fewer, such as Indians, Mexicans, Japanese, and Chinese. Some of my suggestions for measurement apply equally well to such minorities, and the interpretation of some of the data will require statistical norms for the white population. Although white attitudes and behavior toward nonwhites have been antecedent conditions to the problems we face currently, a great deal is known about them, and we can rest assured that such essential research will continue. Much less is known about the social-psychological patterns within the Negro population. I shall treat this theme under the following major headings and subheadings, leaving the detailed aspects to unfold in the course of the paper.

1. *Deficiencies of current objective indicators,* with special reference to:
   Economic Status and Feelings of Deprivation: Some Missing Psychological Links

---

[3] Lewis Carroll, *Through the Looking Glass.* Macmillan, London, 1921, pp. 40–42.

[4] Myrdal, *op. cit.,* p. 27.

[5] One bibliographer estimates that 10,000 periodical articles on the Negro were published between 1945–65, and estimates recent book publication at "a current rate of more than one new title each day." See E. K. Welsch, *The Negro in the United States: A Research Guide.* Indiana University Press, Bloomington, 1965, p. 11.

Important Aspects of the Environment of Negroes: Some Missing Objective Indicators

2. *Specialized methods for the study of change,* with special reference to:
Comparisons between Age Cohorts
Studies of Influentials

3. *Dimensions for describing social-psychological changes in the Negro population*
Definition of the Universe for Study and Conceptions of Self
Feelings and Sentiments: Hate, Desperation, and Distrust

4. *Beliefs and attitudes about race relations*
Estimates of Past and Future Progress in Race Relations and Psychophysical Measures
Measures of Specific Grievances and Dissatisfactions
The Resolution of Grievances: Measurement of Ideological Positions

5. *A methodological note*

Deficiencies of Current Objective Indicators

Economic Status and Feelings of Deprivation: Some Missing Psychological Links. Of all the material on race relations available to an analyst, by far the richest source in its span of time and space is government statistics on the changing circumstances of life for Negroes and whites throughout the country. Statistics on health and welfare, educational attainment, residential location, occupation and income, and family structure yield all manner of refined indicators of the way Negroes are handicapped, segregated, and treated unequally and/or in a discriminatory manner. To construct indexes that are accurate in representing these changing circumstances, and unambiguous in their interpretation, is most important and exceedingly difficult.[6] But it is the meaning the participants themselves confer on their circumstances that is critical. That is lacking in the data, and the present-day analyst must confer that meaning by sheer speculation. For example, noting the circumstances of economic inequality, Duncan *"wonders* if we do not have here a good part of the explanation for the recent rise in effective agitation," and he hypothesizes that young Negroes are attaining sufficient education "to *understand their personal situation in social terms"* and thus, "it is *hardly surprising*

[6] An analyst as sophisticated as O. D. Duncan can reveal the potential wealth in such data, provided we are mindful of the methodological traps, but he also reveals the ultimate limitations of this avenue to understanding. His conceptual paradigm, the "socioeconomic life cycle," may need the companion paradigm which he labels but does not elaborate, "the socio-political life cycle," which includes variables that may well modify the future course of the socioeconomic trends. How essential therefore to explore that sphere. Among the time series needed, he lists such social-psychological variables as "social acceptance, morale, aspiration, and cultural assimilation." O. D. Duncan, "Discrimination against Negroes," *The Annals,* vol. 371, May, 1967, pp. 85–103.

that organized and intelligent forms of protest are increasingly in evidence."[7] His speculations, dating from 1961, now appear plausible and farsighted, but they remain unproved in the absence of measures of the intervening variables.

Brief reflection will suggest that "to understand their personal situation in social terms" can imply many ideas which may, in turn, be translated into many different forms of action. Those ways of thought ought certainly to be described. But obscurity surrounds the sheer judgment that individuals make of their personal situation, apart from understanding how it arose or can be improved. The very group that Duncan specified, young Negro adults, figured conspicuously in recent protests. Nevertheless, their behavior may well stem from factors other than the economic, since that situation, in the most fundamental sense, is indefinite. Like all the young, their situation is inchoate in contrast with that of the old. One would really like to know the situation in which they see themselves, when they think they will have arrived there.[8]

Negroes who are older may also arrive at a judgment of their present, personal situation in ways that are not obvious. The poverty that some are experiencing has absolute and compelling significance.[9] In evaluating their

---

[7] *Ibid.*, p. 102, italics added.

[8] Studies of the occupational aspirations and expectations of Negro vs. white children are obviously relevant to the problem and will be discussed later. Our treatment of "fraternalistic" reference group processes may also help explain the paradoxical patterns among young Negroes.

[9] There is considerable evidence that *absolute* deprivation does not explain Negro protest. Surveys comparing rioters and nonrioters in Newark and Detroit find no significant differences in income, when age is controlled. See N. S. Caplan and J. M. Paige, "A Study of Ghetto Rioters," *Scientific American,* vol. 219, August 1968, pp. 15–21. For more of these data, see the Report of the Kerner Commission, pp. 331–333. In a survey of a sample of Negroes living in metropolitan areas of the United States in 1964, scores on a scale of militancy were positively correlated with socioeconomic status. See Gary Marx, *Protest and Prejudice.* Harper, New York, 1967, pp. 62–63, 79, where he reports similar findings from at least five other studies. In a survey conducted in 1968 on a sample of Negroes in 15 cities, the investigators report that "advocacy of violence appears to be surprisingly unrelated to measures of current socioeconomic achievement." See Angus Campbell and Howard Schuman, *Racial Attitudes in Fifteen American Cities.* Survey Research Center, Institute for Social Research, University of Michigan, Ann Arbor, 1968, p. 57. Studies of the Watts riot also report that social class does not differentiate rioters and nonrioters. The finding that protest has increased with improvements in the status of Negroes argues against the predictive power of absolute deprivation and of indicators of absolute position. For such an analysis, see J. A. Geschwender, "Social Structure and the Negro Revolt: An Examination of Some Hypotheses," *Social Forces,* vol. 43, December, 1964, pp. 248–256. The implied importance of *relative* deprivation is thereby suggested. The evidence can be presented, but the findings are not really critical for such a theory in the absence of knowing what comparative reference group to employ in the computation of a relative-position index.

present position, however, Negroes may compare it with their own past or with the current position they *perceive* others to be in; or they can engage in a still more complicated judgment, comparing their rate of movement over time with the perceived movement of another person or group over time. Depending on the comparative reference groups or individuals they select, they will judge their own situation differently and their sense of relative deprivation will vary.

Rashi Fein, in a thorough analysis of socioeconomic indicators, remarks:

> Others may consider whether the most significant influence on the psychology and attitudes of the Negro is where he stands in relation to the white, where he stands in relation to his parents and grandparents, how his status relative to whites compares with the relative status of his parents and grandparents in an earlier period, or a mixture of these that takes account of relative progress as well as relative position. Surely, however, all have some measure of influence.[10]

He has pointed out the problem, but has not pointed toward a specific solution. The quandary becomes more severe as we realize that those huge *aggregate* groups, Negro or white, contain within them an endless number of smaller reference groups which can serve to determine the individual's sense of relative deprivation and thereby influence his behavior.[11]

Table 1 presents income data for white and Negro families grouped into smaller units for one Northern and one Southern state to illustrate how many different levels of relative deprivation might lie below the surface of the national figures. Obviously, the figures could be disaggregated even more, but this will serve to convey the argument.[12] Given the substantial migrations of Negroes from South to North and from rural to urban places, the cells tabled may actually represent points of origin or places of destination. An average Negro urban family in Michigan would feel itself advantaged compared to farmers, white or Negro, in Mississippi, and not disadvantaged com-

---

[10] Rashi Fein, "An Economic and Social Profile of the Negro American," *Daedalus,* vol. 94, Fall, 1965, p. 816.

[11] American Negroes may also be selecting comparative reference groups from within a third aggregate, other nonwhite groups, e.g., Indians, Chinese, Japanese. While there is a good deal of discussion of the mobility of Negroes vs. other *white* immigrant groups, there appears to be little discussion of this possibility, perhaps because nonwhites are often not further differentiated in statistical series, and Negroes comprise the overwhelming bulk of this aggregate.

[12] The fact that our data refer to 1959, and to nonwhites generally, should not obscure the point. The general point is exemplified by the inspired concept, *aggregatics,* defined by Bertram Gross as "a form of mental acrobatics in which nonspacial, macroguesstimates are juggled in the air without reaching the ground in any territorial entity smaller than the nation itself." Bertram Gross, "A New Orientation in American Government," *The Annals,* vol. 371, May, 1967, p. 3*n.*

pared to an average white farm family in Michigan.[13] It would feel disadvantaged compared to urban whites in the same state, however. Further, Negro farmers in Mississippi would feel more deprived if they compared themselves with urban Negroes in Michigan than if they compared themselves with white farmers nearby.

Table 1. Median Family Income in 1959
(In Hundreds of Dollars)

Type of Area	Michigan	Mississippi
Urban:		
White	60	45
Nonwhite	37	16
Rural nonfarm:		
White	52	32
Nonwhite	22	10
Rural:		
White	41	24
Nonwhite	21	9

SOURCE: *The Census of Population: 1960,* vol. I, pp. 24–206, 26–132.

The choice of some of these possible reference groups may seem highly unlikely to those who have assumed that the national white population has become the only salient reference group for Negroes. Certainly the mass media can bring the status of distant white groups vividly into the awareness of Negroes, and certainly Negro leadership can make such points of invidious comparison salient. But such trains of theory must somehow come to terms with the kind of empirical finding obtained in the recent studies of Detroit and Newark: "Rioters are particularly sensitive to where they stand economically in relation to other Negroes, not to whites,"[14] and the general evidence that individuals tend to choose reference groups in terms of similarity and pro-

---

[13] The ratio in the latter case is $3,700 to $4,100, and the assumption is that this objective difference is experienced as approximate equality of income. What difference is above the threshold of awareness, or what is a "just noticeable difference" remains problematical. See the discussion of Psychophysics below.

[14] Caplan and Paige, *op. cit.,* p. 20. If this comes as an implausible finding, note Martin Luther King's statement: "Every riot has carried strong overtones of hostility of lower-class Negroes toward the affluent Negro and vice versa." Martin Luther King, "The Role of the Behavioral Scientist in the Civil Rights Movement," *Journal of Social Issues,* vol. 24, January, 1968, p. 7. Another finding in this study is suggestive of a reference group process. Nonrioters were much more likely to be migrants who had been reared in the South. There may be many psychic accompaniments to Southern rearing, including the tendency to compare oneself with Negroes back home and, as the table suggests, to feel relatively advantaged.

pinquity.[15] As the mass media increase their portrayal of Negroes in middle-class life, the saliency of Negro reference groups may increase.

Enough has been said to suggest that the objective socioeconomic data constitute, at best, the raw materials for the measurement of the sense of personal deprivation Negroes experience. Only when we know the reference group processes employed can we construct indexes that will adequately represent the sense of deprivation and the course it is taking.

Recent writings in reference group theory suggest two other lines of psychological inquiry that may be essential to the construction of sensitive indexes of deprivation among Negroes. In a discussion of relative deprivation, Runciman proposes an important conceptual distinction which may have special relevance for Negroes.[16] An individual may engage in two processes of comparison, an "egoistic" one in which he locates himself relative to others; a "fraternalistic" one in which he locates his *group* relative to the larger society. As Pettigrew has noted, if the boundaries of the group were defined in the most extensive national way, fraternalistic comparisons on the part of Negroes would by definition involve white reference groups. A Negro might define the group in a more limited way, however, e.g., Southern Negroes, Negroes over 50, and could make a fraternalistic comparison of that subgroup with another subgroup of Negroes.[17] The indexes that have been used to describe the relative position of Negroes and whites in the aggregate are perhaps fairly good representations of the deprivation that Negroes would feel, if they engaged in *fraternalistic* comparisons. Obviously, it is important to know to what extent Negroes employ such comparisons, and to examine the effects of various patterns of egoistic and fraternalistic deprivation which the individual might jointly experience. How do the *vicariously* experienced deprivations or gratifications affect the behavior of those individuals who are themselves deprived or advantaged?[18]

[15] For a summary of many such findings see Herbert Hyman and Eleanor Singer, eds., *Readings in Reference Group Theory and Research*. Macmillan, New York, 1968, *passim*.

[16] W. G. Runciman, "Problems of Research on Relative Deprivation," *European Journal of Sociology*, vol. 2, 1961, pp. 315–323. *Idem., Relative Deprivation and Social Justice*. Routledge & Kegan Paul, London, 1966.

[17] T. F. Pettigrew, "Social Evaluation Theory: Convergences and Applications," in D. Levine, ed., *Nebraska Symposium on Motivation 1967*. University of Nebraska Press, Lincoln, 1967, especially p. 300.

[18] A recent article in the *Times* suggests one possible outcome: "With the new sense of community and collectivism among the Negro activists, the yardstick that measures progress is no longer calibrated to individual Negroes who have 'made it' but rather to the masses of Negroes who have not." *New York Times*, October 22, 1968, p. 33. If we juxtapose this pessimistic speculation about those who are themselves advantaged but vicariously experience the deprivation of other Negroes with the finding from Caplan and

Certainly the growth of many large-scale organizations among Negroes and the more recent emphasis on distinctive symbols of language, culture, dress, and style suggest a heightened sense of group identity. This may bespeak a trend toward fraternalistic comparisons, but one wishes for better evidence on whether Negroes think of their own ego, or of the group, when they weigh questions of relative position.

The contrast in responses to the question Marx asked of his sample: "Do you think that in general things are getting better or getting worse for Negroes in this country?" given by a retired cafeteria worker and by a fireman suggests how individuals may differ in the way they merge or separate the self and the group.[19] The cafeteria worker responded: "*They* are getting better jobs because they are getting more education, so there are more opportunities for the young people than *we* had." The fireman said: "*We* are getting better jobs and whites respect us more." Unfortunately, systematic data of this sort are not available, and these volunteered comments are but an occasion for serendipity.

In analyzing the dissatisfaction that may accompany comparative reference group processes, Patchen has introduced another valuable distinction that may have special application to the situation of Negroes. In comparing himself with another reference group or reference individual on some dimension, e.g., salary or job, an individual takes into account other secondary attributes which may or may not be consistent or "consonant" with their relative position. If the disadvantage the person then perceives is consistent with the divergence on other relevant attributes, dissatisfaction does not occur. Thus, one of Patchen's subjects, an industrial worker, compared himself with a higher salaried certified public accountant, but said that he was "satisfied," explaining, "he has more education; he is a college graduate; he should be

---

Paige mentioned earlier, that those who are themselves disadvantaged relative to other Negroes react negatively rather than experiencing vicarious gratification, the prospects are grim indeed. Clearly what is needed is more research based on a typological treatment of egoistic and fraternalistic reference group processes.

[19] Marx, *op. cit.*, p. 6, italics added. Through the courtesy of Gary Marx and the International Data Library at Berkeley, all the spontaneous comments to this question were examined. It is difficult to discern any modal pattern in the 150 such comments. Respondents make all varieties of distinctions between advances for the self or family members vs. advances for specified subgroups of Negroes, e.g., Southern, Northern, but not for other subgroups vs. advances for the general group, Negroes. By their usage of "we," the self and the group sometimes seem merged. Some who use "they" sharply distinguish between their own progress and that of the group. A few more answers will convey the variety. "I don't know how to answer that because *I myself* have never been mistreated." "*My children* have not been successful in getting jobs." "Perhaps for the upper one-third." "For some it's better; not for *me*." Italics added.

earning more."[20] By this line of reasoning, relative deprivation would be felt most keenly when an individual compares himself with a group enjoying superior rewards, but whose other relevant attributes provide no appropriate justification for the differential rewards.

The statistical data on the socioeconomic position of Negroes suggest that many Negroes in comparing themselves with whites should perceive the comparison as "dissonant" and feel dissatisfied and deprived. This should be the case for well-educated Negroes whose earnings or occupations are lower than whites of equivalent education.[21] Some data from the Newark survey by Caplan and Paige, presented in the Kerner Commission Report (p. 333), are relevant. Rioters, in contrast with "non-involved" young males, are significantly more likely to say that their job and income level are not commensurate with their educational attainment. This positive finding, in conjunction with the negative findings on absolute income, certainly supports a theory of dissonant, relative deprivation and its consequences. It should be stressed, however, that the indicator employed is the *perception* that education and occupation or income are discrepant, rather than an *objective* index of status inconsistency as defined by the analyst. In several recent studies the use of objective indexes of status inconsistency has not been found fruitful. Marx found *less* militancy among Negroes of college education in low occupations than among those who had attained high occupations.[22] Campbell and Schuman report tentatively that such modes of analysis are not promising in explaining Negro advocacy of violence, on the basis of similar tests comparing Negroes whose occupation is not up to their high level of education with Negroes whose occupation is consistent with it.[23]

Important Aspects of the Environment of Negroes: Some Missing Objective Indicators. The meaning that Negroes confer on their socioeconomic circumstances may, for the time being, remain obscure, but at least those particular circumstances are under continuing and comprehensive measurement. And future psychological research may guide us toward indexes that are more likely to capture and convey the various definitions they would give to that economic situation. But other important aspects of the objective situation are not even being measured regularly. To be sure, the varieties of response to these aspects must also be explored, but the changing stimulus to which the responses are linked is the obvious point at which to begin. A few illustrations will establish how uneven is the measurement and indexing of the environment.

[20] Martin Patchen, "A Conceptual Framework and Some Empirical Data Regarding Comparisons of Social Rewards," *Sociometry,* vol. 24, no. 2, June, 1961, pp. 136–156.

[21] See for example, Duncan, *op. cit.,* p. 102.

[22] Marx, *op. cit.,* pp. 57–59.

[23] Campbell and Schuman, *op. cit.,* p. 57.

On the basis of its studies of the 1967 riots, the Kerner Commission reported that, among "12 deeply held grievances," three were at the "first level of intensity." Two of these, housing and employment conditions, are certainly under continuing scrutiny via objective data, but the third grievance relates to a feature of the environment for which simple, objective indexes are not accessible. The *police,* by the conclusion of that report, are as important a condition as the houses and jobs that Negroes occupy.[24] The practices of the police and the perception of those practices are more subtle and difficult data to collect, but the racial composition of various ranks of the police force, a "dangerous irritant" to the Negro community when it is predominantly white, is certainly readily collected information.[25]

Such data are presented by the Kerner Commission but only for 26 cities and two state police forces as of 1967. By way of summary, it is noted that the median percent of nonwhite on these forces was 6 percent whereas the median percent of nonwhite in the general population was 24 percent.[26] The variability is quite staggering: the Michigan State Police have only one Negro officer on a force of 1,502; the Philadelphia Police Force is 20 percent Negro.[27] One may speculate as to the most appropriate forms of index construction and analysis. Perhaps discrimination in recruitment is better indexed by comparison not with general population, but with the percent of Negro males within a certain age and educational bracket, the eligible labor force from which policemen could be recruited. Perhaps absolute figures rather than percentages are a better index of the *visibility* of Negro police to the larger community: 1,485 Negro police in New York City may be a big enough number to produce high visibility even if it is only 5 percent of the force.

But these are secondary considerations, as all such refinements are dependent on having the comprehensive time series available. By 1968, the figures may have risen sharply as a result of vigorous attempts at recruitment. And the 1967 figures take on much clearer meaning in a historical context. Evaluate them in light of the picture presented in a buried footnote by

---

[24] Kerner Commission, *op. cit.,* p. 4. In a survey in the spring of 1968, Louis Harris finds that 84 percent of Negroes and 81 percent of whites agree that "there should be more Negro police officers in Negro ghetto areas." In another question on the major causes of riots, 51 percent of Negroes indicated that police brutality was a major cause; this ranked below lack of housing, jobs, and education, but close in magnitude. See Release of the Harris Survey, April 16, 1968.

[25] Again one senses the need for inquiry into what I shall call "social psychophysics." What is the perception or judgment of the number and proportion of Negro policemen held by the Negro populations of various cities, and the discrepancy between the perception and the objective fact?

[26] Kerner Commission, *op. cit.,* pp. 165–169.

[27] To be precise, the statistics are in terms of nonwhite.

Myrdal, and the change seems dramatic. He reports for 1940 that "Mississippi, South Carolina, Louisiana, Georgia, and Alabama . . . have not one Negro policeman in them"; that North Carolina had one and Florida five, and that in non-Southern states the ratio was one Negro policeman to every 41,000 Negroes.[28]

On an aspect of the environment that has been documented to be consequential, we should not have to be dependent on sporadic and incomplete data which at best provide gross characterization of a complex entity. Myrdal once described "the average Southern policeman [as] a promoted poor white with a legal sanction to use a weapon. His social heritage has taught him to despise the Negroes, and he has had little education which could have changed him."[29] Certainly the educational distribution as well as the racial composition of police forces can be enumerated.

The number of Negro policemen describes an aspect of the environment to which many Negroes respond strongly, but it is incidentally a characterization of the occupational status of a *few* Negroes. Although it is a trivial component of the general socioeconomic picture, an ironical fact is worthy of emphasis. In indexing this aspect of the environment, we are not dependent on the collection of official police statistics. The facts are contained within hundreds of sample surveys and in the census. Wherever occupation has been enumerated and can be classified by race, it is possible, in principle, to determine the racial composition and other characteristics of police, as well as their changing attitudes, and thus to construct the detailed time series.[30]

To be sure, this strategic area of inquiry must be pursued through deeper

[28] Myrdal, *op. cit.,* p. 534n. According to the Kerner Commission, in 1967 Atlanta had 98 nonwhite police; New Orleans 54, Tampa had 17. It is impossible to make more precise comparisons since the data are only for selected cities.

[29] *Ibid.,* pp. 540–541.

[30] The North Carolina Advisory Committee to the United States Commission on Civil Rights used census data to obtain estimates of the racial composition of the police and other governmental forces over time. The proportion of whites to nonwhites in the total labor force in 1950 was about 3 to 1, but the ratio among the police (plus sheriffs and marshals) as estimated from the census was 47 to 1. For 1960, the detailed occupational breakdowns were not available at the time of the state report, but for the gross category of police, sheriffs, marshalls, and protective workers the ratio was 16 to 1, suggesting a considerable improvement in the recruitment of Negroes. By the same procedure, estimates are presented for other categories of public service employees. For example, in 1950, among state and local officials and inspectors the ratio of whites to nonwhites was 99 to 1, but among schoolteachers the ratio was in parity with the composition of the labor force. See *Equal Protection of the Laws in North Carolina.* Government Printing Office, Washington, D.C., 1962, pp. 83–84. Judging from the reports of some other states, the North Carolina Committee seems to have been more ingenious in exploiting census materials. The racial composition of the police in particular areas within those states is described occasionally on the basis of testimony obtained from local officials. The U.S. Commission quotes interesting testimony for 1965 for areas of Mississippi where, with one exception, there were no Negro policemen. More interesting is the testimony of the

studies of policemen and the attitudes they bring to their encounters, through studies of the beliefs and attitudes about police held by the adult Negro population; through studies of the ideas about the police held by Negro children and the ways these are learned. Each time we explore an objective aspect of the problem, a vista of essential psychological studies appears before our eyes and evidences the general need for the social-psychological approach discussed in later sections of this paper.

Several major studies of this type can be briefly summarized here, however. Under the sponsorship of the Kerner Commission, Rossi and his associates completed about four hundred interviews with samples of policemen in about a dozen cities, stratified so as to include ones with varying histories and degrees of civil disorders. In the aggregate, only a minority of the police perceive Negroes as hostile, but almost half describe youth as hostile. The large majority of police report that they are personally acquainted with various types of individuals in their precincts, but such acquaintanceship is least likely to occur with teen-age and youth leaders. Negro policemen, who incidentally are found to have a higher level of education—50 percent having some college—are less likely to impute hostility to the residents of their areas, are more likely to feel that Negro residents are not being treated fairly by the police, and to have a more sympathetic outlook.[31]

In another study sponsored by the Kerner Commission, samples in 15 cities of white and Negro population down to age 16 were interviewed by the Survey Research Center, and asked about their beliefs about police practices and their personal experiences with the police. Negroes, especially youth,

---

police chiefs as to whether they would exclude from recruitment individuals with particular ideologies. See U.S. Commission on Civil Rights, *Law Enforcement: A Report on Equal Protection in the South.* Government Printing Office, Washington, D.C., 1965, p. 93. In the published volumes of the censuses of 1940, 1950, and 1960, aggregate data on the racial composition of police forces are presented, although the occupational category is not exactly comparable over the three periods. At each of these points Negro males constituted about 8.5 percent of the employed male population over age 14 in the nation. Among police (plus marshalls and sheriffs), Negroes constituted .9 percent of the force in 1940; 1.9 percent in 1950; and 3.2 percent in 1960. This shows a rising trend, although underrepresentation, relative to their proportion among *all* workers, still persists. A regional break for 1940 shows that recruitment of Negro police is lowest in the South, but since then no breakdown has been published. These few data suggest the potential utility of the sources, but the grossness of the published data, the lack of exact comparability, and the "buried" character of the material suggests how much more could be done. I thank Sophia C. Travis, Chief, Division of Labor Force Studies, Bureau of Labor Statistics, for bringing these data to my attention which can be found in: U.S. Census of Population, 1940, Vol. III, Part I., pp. 88 ff.; 1950, Vol. IV, Part I, Chap. B, p. 35; 1960, PC (2)-7A, p. 29.

[31] See P. Rossi *et al.,* "Between White and Black: The Faces of American Institutions in the Ghetto," in *Supplemental Studies for the National Advisory Commission on Civil Disorders.* Government Printing Office, Washington, D.C., 1968, especially pp. 103–114.

are more likely to believe that the police engage in improper practices than are whites. The proportion expressing such beliefs, however, is substantially larger than the proportion who report that they or their acquaintances have actually experienced such a practice. Thus, it seems to be the case that the belief is not rooted in direct personal experience or even in vicarious experience. But, when asked whether black police treat Negroes better than white police, the great majority do not report that there is any difference in treatment.[32]

Another series of studies, reported by Reiss, notes that what defines an improper practice depends in part on the citizen's definition of propriety and dignified treatment. In a survey of Detroit after the 1967 riot, one-fifth of the Negro sample reported that the police have "talked down to him" and "more than one in ten says a policeman has called me a bad name." Based on observations of police in selected precincts in Boston, Chicago, and Washington, D.C., in the summer of 1966, improper force occurred toward both white and Negro lower-class individuals, was more likely to be focused on youth, but was *more* likely to be manifested toward whites. The rates are computed on various bases but run generally below 5 percent of the encounters, in striking contrast to the prevalence of such practices believed to occur by the samples of individuals in the other studies.[33]

The social environment contains several other groups who affect Negroes in important ways, if not as critically as do the police. Here again the same simple, objective indicators of racial composition would provide the beginnings of knowledge, and special studies would provide deeper understanding. In 1967, the Kerner Commission found that inadequate "welfare programs" and "municipal services" were deeply held grievances, although at the "third level of intensity," and, long before that, Myrdal had remarked that "this whole problem of Negroes' public contacts with all the minor functionaries in private and municipal service would deserve intensive study."[34]

The general category of *functionaries in public agencies* in frequent contact with the Negro population includes various specific groups, but one could certainly make a judicious selection of social workers or welfare workers and begin studying their objective characteristics and their practices toward their clients.

Public welfare workers in major cities were one of the strategic groups chosen for study by Rossi. Differences in attitudes between Negro and white

[32] See Angus Campbell and Howard Schuman, "Racial Attitudes in Fifteen American Cities," in *Supplemental Studies for the National Advisory Commission on Civil Disorders*. Government Printing Office, Washington, D.C., 1968, especially pp. 42–44, 27.

[33] For these and other findings, see A. J. Reiss, "Police Brutality—Answers to Key Questions," *Trans-action*, vol. 5, July/August, 1968, pp. 10–19. Also see Chapter 10 of this volume.

[34] Kerner Commission, *op. cit.*, p. 538.

workers were very small. In general, the group reported little prejudice toward Negro clients but asserted that the Negro clients did not get equally favorable treatment, thus locating the source of the problem not in themselves but in the institutional system.[35]

I omit any reference to indexing the racial composition of schoolteachers. Certainly, the educational system has been a source of grievance and the race of the teacher has been an issue. Such data were recently presented in the Coleman report which estimates for the average Negro child that over 60 percent of his teachers are Negro, and similarly that his school principal is most likely to be Negro. The case of the schoolteacher, however, illustrates the limitations of objective indicators. Such findings might be construed by some as indicators of segregation of school facilities and regarded as likely to provide a basis for grievance. Others might construe the predominance of Negro teachers and principals as a desirable state of affairs, insuring that the Negro child will be receiving sympathetic teaching and will have an appropriate exemplar on which to model himself. The vicissitudes of doctrine and the diverse reactions to an objective datum suggest again the necessity for continuing psychological levels of measurement. In the fall of 1965, Coleman found that the attitudes of school principals on the desirable composition of teaching staffs in schools which have predominantly Negro pupils was that the staff would either be selected without regard to race or be both white and nonwhite. For only 1 percent of the Negro children in such schools did their principals (themselves predominantly Negro) favor an "all nonwhite" staff.[36] What the general finding would be in the 1970's is hard to say and would be nice to know. The "faces of American institutions," to use Rossi's fine phrase, are prominent features of the environment, changes in which should be documented by simple objective indicators. But the environment is also permeated by all sorts of stimuli, more fleeting in character and yet with potential important effects on Negroes, which should be measured periodically. In its entirety, the task is overwhelming. But a selective approach to strategic bits of the total flow of communication which impinge on critical forms of behavior is feasible. These few suggestions are in that spirit.[37]

Patterns of exposure to Negro and/or white media call for careful and

---

[35] Rossi, *op. cit.*, pp. 139–144.

[36] James S. Coleman *et al.*, *Equality of Educational Opportunity*. Government Printing Office, Washington, D.C., 1966, *passim*, especially pp. 180–181.

[37] The Kerner Commission Report presents many findings that bear upon this discussion. It notes the very low representation of Negroes in editorial positions in the media, an occupational group that might well be monitored over time. It notes certain deficiencies in the handling of news about racial problems, and the way *particular* reporting contributed to fear, tension, or violence, although the media in general did not sensationalize the riots. Kerner Commission, *op. cit.*, *passim*, especially Chap. 15. For mid-1968 data on Negro personnel in various mass media and changes in recruitment policies, see the *Columbia Journalism Review*, vol. 7, Fall, 1968, pp. 42–65.

continuing measurement and will be mentioned later as psychological indicators of considerable utility. But even fragmentary data suggest that present-day audiences of the Negro media constitute a very large number, and that the white media are often distrusted.[38] Content analysis of the *Negro media* with special reference to auditing the ratio of appeals for separatism to those for integration and of calls for moderate vs. extremist action would provide valuable and now missing evidence. Juxtaposed with more psychological data on the degree to which representative samples espouse these positions, one might then infer the degree to which the ideological messages have been resisted or accepted. Not knowing these ratios of response vs. exhortation, the susceptibility of the population is an unknown.

It may well be that the Negro mass media—perhaps also the white media—feature the more dramatic reports of spokesmen for extremism, and that much *interpersonal communication* of a more moderate sort does not reach the media, although it impinges on individuals with tempering effects.[39] Perhaps the findings may turn out to be the reverse—exhortations flowing via interpersonal communication may add to the totality of extremist or separatist stimulation. These fugitive forms of communication from pulpits, from various elites, from neighbors, ought somehow to be measured to see the total blend of stimuli and how it is changing.

Although it does not seem possible to measure this from the side of the myriad sources in a strictly objective way, it would be possible to use sample surveys for reports of the types of exhortations the respondents have received from various sources within some interval of time, and their corresponding reactions. What, for example, did their clergymen urge upon them in last week's sermon?[40] It may appear to strain our terminology, but this subjective

---

[38] In his survey in late 1964, sampling Negro adults in metropolitan areas outside the South with oversampling of two Northern cities and the addition of two Southern city samples, Marx obtained data on magazine and newspaper readership. While the marginals are not presented in such a way as to obtain precise estimates of general patterns of selective exposure, one can infer that the Negro print media had larger audiences in this sample than did the white print media. Marx, *op. cit.,* especially p. 189. On the basis of a survey in the Pittsburgh ghetto, the Kerner Commission reports frequent distrust of the white media. *Op. cit.,* pp. 206–207. From a Detroit area survey it was estimated that 65 percent of the adult Negro population read the Negro weekly, *Michigan Chronicle.* For trend data indicating increasing use of television (certainly not a Negro medium) by Negroes, see M. E. McCombs, "Negro Use of Television and Newspapers for Political Information, 1952–1964," *Journal of Broadcasting,* vol. 12, Summer, 1968, pp. 261–266.

[39] A policy statement issued by the NAACP shortly after this passage was written mentions "a tendency on the part of the news media to bypass spokesmen for the majority and to project the minority spokesmen as the authentic voices of the Negro community." *New York Times,* November 22, 1968, p. 52.

[40] In recent surveys of Negro attitudes, little inquiry has been made into the stimulation received interpersonally, and in turn, into the diffusion of the respondents' views. The whole question of a multiplier effect for the attitudes of one particular group rather

avenue may work fairly well to obtain objective data on this important aspect of the immediate environment and could provide trend measures of the changes in such stimuli.

Specialized Methods for the Study of Change

Our basic point should have been made by now. The value of trend data, of periodic, direct measurement of a series of important but neglected variables, should be clear. How one wishes it were now underway. We shall soon propose a list of social-psychological dimensions for which changes in the Negro population should be charted beginning today and on into the future. But apart from such a broad, direct approach, there are a number of specialized approaches to the study of change which deserve brief treatment.

Comparisons between Age Cohorts. The value of comparing the views of the young and the old, as well as those who are "middle-aged," could be argued on practical grounds alone. Within the Negro population, young men have been found most likely to engage in civil disorders; among current militant leaders, the young have been very prominent. And if we try to anticipate the distant future, we must give special attention to the views of younger cohorts, since they are bound to replace the old—given enough time. Yet any comparison between age groups at a *single* point in time plunges us into risky modes of prediction. For example, the militancy that Campbell and Schuman found among Negro youth in 1968, in contrast with their elders, certainly has impact on society. Yet, in projecting the future, it may "have no lasting effect, but subside into middle-aged acceptance."[41]

If only we could trace the life course of enough cohorts, we could determine the degree to which aging and cumulative experience produce regular changes and the degree to which the early experiences of generations leave effects that persist despite aging. Many such analyses might produce sufficiently lawful findings to reduce the risks of prediction. Clearly, trend designs and age comparisons—at least for a while—are not alternative but complementary approaches.[42]

---

than another by virtue of different degrees of diffusion of their own views to others seems to have been neglected. There is some suggestive data in the analysis of the Detroit and Newark surveys conducted for the Kerner Commission, where it is demonstrated that rioters are more likely to engage in frequent civil rights discussions and meetings, but it is not clear whether they are the recipients or the disseminators of such communication. Kerner Commission, *op. cit.,* p. 334.

[41] Campbell and Schuman, *op. cit.,* p. 18.

[42] For a more thorough treatment of the ambiguities of the problem, modes of analysis, and findings of generational differences in attitudes, see H. Hyman, *Political Socialization.* Free Press, New York, 1959, Chap. VI. An alternative to tracing a cohort over time by trend surveys would be to follow the same individuals in a longitudinal or long-term

To be sure, some risk remains. Whatever laws are established from observing the life cycles of previous cohorts may not hold for all future cohorts. A unique historical era may have had a particular and powerful impact on previous generations and never be repeated. Events previously unknown may fall with special force upon a new cohort. "An assassination, a war, a major racial clash," as noted by Campbell and Schuman, "can always alter the direction or speed of change" between generations. But enough such misfortunes may happen over time that the trend study of a fair number of cohorts would permit some generalizations about the role of this *class* of events.

The risk in making predictions may also be less than is feared. Analysts tend to overstate the role of the dramatic, brand-new event in producing generational change, and to neglect more orderly institutional changes which enlarge finally to envelop a whole new generation, but to which some members of earlier generations have also been exposed. Among American Negroes, more of whom are now being reared in the North and fewer being deprived of formal education, this may be especially true.[43] By comparing age cohorts matched in education and region of early socialization, one can estimate the influence of such factors. The residual differences, after such controlled comparisons, provide a sounder measure of the role of events, and the finer comparisons locate more precisely where the changes are occurring.[44] With benefit of data on institutional trends, one might then predict whether generational differences will level out.

---

panel study. Unfortunately, such studies are very rare. In the mid-1950's, a group of investigators restudied Negro adults who had been intensively studied by Allison Davis and John Dollard some 20 years earlier. It was thus possible to examine the effects of aging in this sample of the youth of the 1930's and, as the investigators stress, to see whether the social-psychological patterns were transmitted and perpetuated in the children of this group, or whether they show a generational variability within this relatively homogeneous age cohort, all of whom had spent their teens in New Orleans. The chronicle of the methodological problems and rigorous procedures would make it much easier for the investigators to repeat this unique inquiry, and the parallel youth studies of the 1930's in areas other than New Orleans—Chicago, the upper South, the rural area—conducted by Charles Johnson, Franklin Frazier, etc. provide the strategic baselines and the samples to be empaneled. See John H. Rohrer *et al., The Eighth Generation Grows Up: Cultures and Personalities of New Orleans Negroes.* Harper Torchbooks, New York, 1960.

[43] The census estimates a net migration out of the South of 3.7 million nonwhites between 1940 and 1966. *Social and Economic Conditions of Negroes in the United States.* Bureau of the Census: Series P. 23, No. 24, October, 1967, p. 6. For partial data on increased educational attainment of nonwhites in recent years, see pp. 46–47 of this same report.

[44] In Detroit and Newark, it was the better educated and those reared in the North who were more likely to have participated in the riots, suggesting the importance of these variables for predicting behavior and in possibly accounting for the generational differences reported. Caplan and Paige, *op. cit.*

Table 2 presents age comparisons from the three recent surveys involving large samples of broad universes of American Negroes. Although I have presented only a few of the findings within these major studies, I have exhausted all the major surveys that seem appropriate.[45]

Given the importance of a series of refined age comparisons for understanding social change, it is a stroke of good fortune that we have three elaborate surveys spanning the period from 1964 to 1968. One can begin to examine the consistency of the age differences, and to trace a particular cohort as it ages over the four-year period. But we are tantalized as we try to impose upon these diverse surveys an ideal model for inquiry. Apart from the fact that the sampling designs differ geographically, the coverage of age groups varies. Campbell and Schuman have caught the youngest in their net, but left out those over age 69. Marx has pushed in the other direction to the limit, interviewing individuals over 75 years of age. The continuum of age is cut at different points, making it impossible to trace a cohort from the published data. Although attitudes are cross-tabulated by such characteristics as sex, education, and region of socialization, the three inquiries do not present age groups refined in the same standardized ways on characteristics that may locate and explain the generational differences. Unless independent investigators were to adopt some common framework, order will only come by a unified and continuing approach to the problem.

There is, however, a virtue in the diversity of the attitudes studied. Over a wide range of measures, the youngest group is always the most militant. But the magnitude of the generational gap varies widely from item to item. One could index this gap in various ways. As Campbell and Schuman note, separatist attitudes triple in size among the youngest men, but one may also note in all the surveys over this period that such thinking characterizes only a small minority of even the youngest generation, and that the absolute difference in percentage points between youngest and oldest is small.[46]

An additional risk attends the use of age comparisons for predicting social change. The single survey captures each generation at a point in time

[45] Harris did an earlier survey of a national sample of Negroes in 1963, and repeated some of the same questions in his 1966 survey, to obtain trend data. Thus it would be possible in principle to trace an age cohort, and compare refined age groups. But to underscore one of our suggestions, the earlier book presents no age breaks, whereas the later book presents only the three gross age categories shown. For the earlier publication see William Brink and Louis Harris, *The Negro Revolution in America*. Simon & Schuster, New York, 1964.

[46] Partial data on differences in attitude for age groups matched in education are presented in the Michigan survey and suggest to the writer that the difference shrinks, although it does not disappear. One can only guess as to how much residual difference would remain if sex and region of socialization were controlled. Campbell and Schuman, *op. cit.*, pp. 19, 57.

Table 2. Some Age Differences in Attitudes among Negroes
(In Percent)

Survey	16–19	18–29	20–29	Under 35	35–49	50+	60+	Difference between Extremes
1964 urban:[a]								
Index of anti-white attitudes (males)		27					18	− 9
(Number of cases)		(199)					(182)	
Index of conventional militance		31					15	−16
(Number of cases)		(243)					(211)	
1966 national:[b]								
Civil rights pace is too slow				54	41	35		−19
1968 urban males:[c]								
Discourage whites from participation in civil rights organization	19		12				5	−14
Favor separate black nation in U.S.	11		10				10	− 1
Would join a riot	20		13				3	−17
(Number of cases)	(163)		(259)				(118)	

[a] Recomputed from Gary Marx, *Protest and Prejudice*. Harper, New York, 1967, pp. 53, 185–186.
[b] From William Brink and Louis Harris, *Black and White*. Simon & Schuster, New York, 1966, p. 259. Numbers of specific cases are not reported, although the total sample size is 1,059.
[c] From Angus Campbell and Howard Schuman, *Racial Attitudes in Fifteen American Cities*. Survey Research Center, Institute for Social Research, University of Michigan, Ann Arbor, 1968, pp. 18–19, 56. In the domain of separatist attitudes, I have chosen the two questions which give respectively the biggest and smallest differences by age to show the range within which such differences fall. When the better-educated members of each group are compared, the differences shrink. The numbers for the age groups are the ones reported for these cells and because of nonresponse may vary slightly from question to question.

and describes the net result of all *past* influences. But thereafter, the generations do not go their separate ways, confronting only new events and aging. They also confront each other, and mutually influence one another to some unknown degree. A series of trend surveys and age comparisons, however, would obviate the uncertainty, since the effect the generations have on each other would be incorporated into the net results, although its exact contribution could not be separated.

The relation between generations could also be subject to intensive study, and considering the ease with which survey questions could be couched for various facets of the phenomenon, it is surprising how little we find in past or current surveys. The potentialities are suggested in a secondary analysis by Broom and Glenn of some 32 questions in eight attitude spheres asked of national samples in the 1950–61 period.[47] For each sphere, the difference between Negro and white adults is summarized and then analyzed so as to control for the influence of region, formal education, and age. For the three questions dealing with child rearing and discipline, the Negro-white difference is greater than for any of the other seven attitude areas, and is not accounted for by Southern background or educational disadvantage.

In the 1940's, only a few relevant questions were asked. Although the size of the Negro sample is too small to carry weight, two questions are germane, and I report this flimsy secondary analysis to suggest some of the lines of future inquiry.[48] In that distant past, Negro adults were *more* likely than whites to say that teen-agers were behaving worse than they themselves behaved as teen-agers, and to feel that the then current crop of teen-agers was less level-headed and sensible than they themselves had been. If such strong attitudes of censure still existed today, it seems unlikely that the old would take the young as exemplars of proper behavior. New surveys could provide solid, rather than fragmentary, evidence on the relations between the generations.

Just as Negro youth cannot be considered in isolation from their elders, the predictions also must take into account the younger generation of whites. The two sets of generational processes may work in complementary fashion to accelerate social change, or may work in opposition to slow down change within the larger society. Of necessity, this paper omits a general treatment of white attitudes and behavior. They are indeed relevant to full understanding of race relations, but the scope of such a comprehensive paper is unmanageable. Some comment, however, is required on the generational change that has

---

[47] L. Broom, and N. Glenn, "Negro-White Differences in Reported Attitudes and Behavior," *Sociology and Social Research,* vol. 50, January, 1966, pp. 187–200.

[48] I am indebted to the Roper Center at Williamstown for making these data available to me. A search of their very extensive holdings found only a few questions which appeared germane to the problem of the relations between generations.

seemed to characterize white youth. In the 1950's and up to about 1963, the evidence on the white cohort aged 21 to 24 suggested a growing tolerance in race relations, which seemed attributable to the enlightening influence of education. Such a generational process would add its force to the demands of young Negroes and ultimately accelerate change in the society. In the cohort that reached ages 21 to 24 around 1963, especially in the South, the evidence suggested that the trend toward tolerance had stopped or begun to reverse itself.[49] In the 1968 Michigan surveys, the younger age groups with higher education continue to be found to show much greater tolerance. It should be stressed that the universe was 15 large cities, none of them in the Deep South, in contrast with the National Opinion Research Center surveys. Again, there is one disquieting note. White male teen-agers report that they would engage in counter-rioting to Negro riots more than other age groups.[50] The parallel in these two generations may suggest that the future will be even more conflict-laden, but the parallel also is suggestive of a temporary youthful masculinity, black or white, rather than a generational change that will persist. Only as the trend studies trace both white and black cohorts over time will there be a basis for confident long-term prediction.

Studies of Influentials. In the long run, the young are bound to exert great influence and thus deserve special study. By the same canon, those who *now* are influential are commended to the student of social change as strategic subjects for special study. Their own beliefs, attitudes, actions, political goals and tactics—and the ones they urge upon others—should be measured periodically. But exactly who shall be studied?

That small group who have achieved national prominence may be omitted. No special inquiries need be made to determine their views; perforce they must express their views all the time in order to maintain their prominence and assert their leadership. Thus, the content of their communications is readily analyzed. Admittedly, a problem exists in choosing which notabilities are, in fact, leaders. Some are would-be leaders with no followers; some may be on the rise, others on the wane. Given the competition and the vagaries of publics, the possibility must be entertained that top leadership is in continual flux. Fortunately, the evidence suggests the contrary. The authority conferred on particular national figures by the Negro population has been stable. Each one may feel shaky and may be adjusting his views to maintain the loyalty of his followers. No single one can claim the exclusive loyalty of the total population. The share he gets may shift in some degree but seems fairly secure. Table 3 presents data from various surveys.

Since the universes vary and the questions are not identical, one cannot

[49] H. Hyman and P. Sheatsley, "Attitudes Toward Desegregation," *Scientific American,* vol. 211, July, 1964, pp. 22–23.

[50] Campbell and Schuman, *op. cit.,* pp. 34–35, 58–59.

Table 3. Evaluations of Negro Leaders

	Percent Positive Evaluation[a]		*Percent State Trusted Very Much*[b]	*Percent Approving Stand*[c]
	1963	*1966*	*13 cities, 1967*	*15 cities, 1968*
Martin Luther King	88	88	82	72
Roy Wilkins	69	64	52	50
Thurgood Marshall	65	48	50	[d]
Ralph Bunche	62	53	[d]	[d]
Adam Clayton Powell	51	44	25	[d]
Whitney Young	[d]	33	37	[d]
Floyd McKissick	[d]	19	15	[d]
Stokely Carmichael	[d]	19	20	14
Rap Brown	[d]	[d]	18	14
Elijah Muhammed	15	12	[d]	[d]

[a] From William Brink and Louis Harris, *The Negro Revolution in America.* Simon & Schuster, New York, 1964, pp. 120–122; *idem, Black and White.* Simon & Schuster, New York, 1966, p. 54. The 1963 data are reported in both volumes and there appear to be occasional typographical errors in percentages, but these are so small as not to affect the basic picture. The "don't know" response increases for those who are rated less positively.

[b] *Fortune,* January, 1968, p. 148. On another question asking whether the leader "fights for what people want," the hierarchy is identical.

[c] Campbell and Schuman, *Racial Attitudes in Fifteen American Cities,* p. 21.

[d] Attitudes toward this leader were not measured.

treat the *four* arrays as a true time series. The two Harris surveys may be treated as a trend over the three-year period and reveal considerable stability, and the four surveys, spread through a most eventful five-year period, show various leaders maintaining their relative position in the hierarchy of public support.[51] In another survey conducted by Harris in early 1968 on a cross-section of Negro college seniors, Martin Luther King was mentioned by 56 percent when asked to "choose one leader they would follow," Roy Wilkins was next with 5 percent and Stokely Carmichael next with 4 percent.[52] The educated and young cohort of Negroes has been regarded as unusually mili-

---

[51] In his 1964 survey in metropolitan areas, Marx presented a card listing four leaders, and asked "Are there any persons on the card you don't like or disapprove of?" Only 1 percent expressed dislike of Martin Luther King, Roy Wilkins, and James Farmer, but 48 percent expressed dislike of Malcolm X. Marx, *op. cit.,* p. 27.

[52] These and other findings may appear to be contradicted by journalistic reports which tend to stress the rise of new and militant leaders. For example an article in the *Times* recently stated that SNCC "has lost much of its power and influence to the northern slum-born Black Panthers." Yet, when one searches for the evidence to support such conclusions, one finds no data. The Harris survey was reported in a release dated April 18, 1968. For the *Times* story, see the issue of October 7, 1968.

tant, and this finding is additional, and compelling, evidence on the general phenomenon.

In light of the pattern of enduring loyalties revealed in these data, we can have some confidence that those leaders initially selected for content analytic studies would, in fact, continue to lead and would find responsive audiences for their utterances.[53] But the sample whose statements are analyzed does not have to be frozen for all time. It can be modified in light of new, empirical evidence on the public's support. Conveniently, such measures serve two purposes. They not only validate the selection of a sample of particular national leaders, but they serve more importantly as an index of the ideological leanings of the general population, since the various leaders take identifiable political positions. For this reason, a question on attitudes toward a list of leaders constitutes a simple and useful procedure which should be employed on a trend basis in our charting of social change, and automatically yields the extra dividend of correcting the sampling for content analysis.

The leadership position of national notables could emerge from more subtle, almost whimsical, processes of *pluralistic ignorance*. Many Negroes might feel no bond of loyalty for a particular leader but, in the false belief that many other Negroes support him, might decide to yield to his directives. Also, a Negro leader might wield a great deal of influence if the white community responded positively to him, on the basis of the false belief that the leader had a large following in the Negro population.[54] But the many varieties of pluralistic ignorance can be readily measured. Respondents, both white and black, can be asked whether they themselves have a positive atti-

---

[53] The methodologically sophisticated reader might argue that the data, from trend rather than panel studies, do not establish stable preference. The aggregate stability might come about despite a great deal of intra-individual shifting in loyalty. Whatever the findings of a panel study might show, for the *collectivity,* the general Negro population, the stability of the relative leadership position of various national figures is clearly documented, and this is the relevant datum.

[54] The work of Daniel C. Thompson provides many valuable conceptual distinctions which bear upon this and other facets of research on Negro leadership. See, for example, his distinction between interracial and intraracial leaders and between the leader and the celebrity. Daniel C. Thompson, *The Negro Leadership Class.* Prentice-Hall, Englewood Cliffs, N.J., 1963, Spectrum Book S-55. Also, social distance between Negroes and whites and the lack of intercommunication work to increase ignorance of such support. On the general importance of restriction of communication at various levels of social systems and its effect on negotiations and processes of political change, see Daniel Katz, "Group Process and Social Integration: A System Analysis of Two Movements of Social Protest," *Journal of Social Issues,* vol. 23, January, 1967, especially pp. 7–9. In one of the rare instances where white attitudes toward particular Negro leaders were obtained, Harris found in 1966 that whites showed much less favorable evaluations than did Negroes; but large percentages expressed no opinion rather than a negative view. See *Public Opinion Quarterly,* vol. 31, Winter, 1967–68, pp. 661–662.

tude to a given leader and their estimate of how widespread is the support for him.

At the pinnacle, national leaders are few in number, readily identifiable, and volunteering of their views. Below that level there must be hundreds of individuals who exert influence informally on small groups of loyal followers. Their views must be solicited, not just monitored. Since their notability is limited, they must first be located. Drawing such a sample may be difficult, but it is a most strategic target universe for study.

To identify public leaders, some half dozen different approaches have been developed, each tested for its merits by empirical studies of communities. Many of these studies dealt with the general power structure of the community and focused on the white population. Thus, they may provide dubious principles for selecting those who are influential within the Negro community. Perhaps the bases of leadership are different. But, fortunately, a number of studies which focused specifically on the Negro community leader provide guidance.[55] And what we seek is not perfection, but some efficient procedure that will approximate our target.

What commends itself on both grounds is a "first-stage" sample of Negro teachers and preachers, plus journalists, lawyers, labor-union officials, plus possibly physicians and businessmen. In some of these specific occupations, the role of adviser or communicator to an audience is central and continuous, and Negro leaders have been found to be recruited especially from the ranks of all these occupations.[56] Not every individual in these occupations will, in fact, be a leader of men. But we can hit the target better by screening questions applied to the first-stage sample. They can be asked about their membership and participation in voluntary associations, about their acts of influence. And the process of locating and questioning them can all be part of ordinary surveys of the general population within which they are contained,

[55] For a critical review of the various procedures and the literature, see W. Bell, R. J. Hill, and C. Wright, *Public Leadership.* Chandler, San Francisco, 1961. For a summary of past studies of Negro community leadership, and findings on such leadership in 14 cities and the correlates of styles of leadership, see G. McWhorter and R. L. Crain, "Subcommunity Gladiatorial Competition: Civil Rights Leadership as a Competitive Process," *Social Forces,* vol. 46, September, 1967, pp. 8–21. For a critical and succinct treatment of six studies of Negro leadership, see H. M. Blalock, Jr., *Toward a Theory of Minority-Group Relations.* Wiley, New York, 1967, pp. 19–21.

[56] I rely mainly on Thompson, *op. cit.* In his 1963 study, Harris chose a sample of 100 leaders whose attitudes were compared with the national sample. The procedure for selecting the leadership sample is not clear but it was a blend of the different approaches. See his appendix for the actual list of individuals. In general, the leaders had much more crystallized views than the rank and file, but it is difficult to discern any consistent pattern of ideological differences. Thompson's study was conducted in New Orleans between 1958 and 1962, and some may argue that the bases of leadership have shifted since then.

rather than requiring any specialized undertaking. They simply would be broken out of the larger body of data that becomes available cumulatively.[57] Those same general surveys can yield other evidence which would provide another correction factor. The respondents could be asked about the *type* of individuals whom they seek out for advice or to whom they would respond.[58] Incorporating the studies of local leaders into the continuing surveys of the general population is not merely an economy measure. It builds an ongoing comparison between elite and mass opinion. Perhaps Gandhi's statement will describe the findings: "There go my people, I must catch them, for I am their leader."[59] Or perhaps the followers will be found to change in the direction of the prior position of the leaders. Analysis of the two time series will provide the answer. Our discussion turns to our final and main theme, social-psychological patterns in the larger Negro population.

Dimensions for Describing Social-Psychological Changes in the Negro Population

Choosing a set of dimensions along which change will be charted is a difficult task. If there were no limit to resources, one could adopt the safe strategy of trying to measure an endless number of variables, being sure thereby of including those which would finally turn out to be important. But even if our resources were not taxed too severely—as surely they would be by the necessity of repeating the giant inquiry over time—our respondents would be too severely taxed.[60] Certainly, description must be along multiple dimensions but the number must be limited to those of high priority. And these must have just the right blend of timeliness and timelessness. If they are too abstract

[57] One specialized problem: These individuals would be found in the course of an ordinary survey, and would, in turn, be expressing their attitudes as "ordinary" individuals, since they and the interviewers would not be defining this as an inquiry among leaders. By contrast, their views in their role as leader might be quite different. But perhaps this is not a criticism of the procedure. And one could conduct some experimental work to determine whether the reports differ when the leadership role is made salient, by adding appropriate phrases to the questions. For an illustration of a leadership survey in which the leader responded in terms of his *private* role, see S. Stouffer, *Communism, Conformity, and Civil Liberties.* Doubleday, Garden City, N.Y., 1955.

[58] To be sure, this would yield some leaders who are themselves whites, but who are "functional Negro" leaders. Thompson reports about a dozen such persons in New Orleans. These would be left out of our first-stage sample. Thompson, *op. cit.*, pp. 32–33.

[59] Quoted by Martin Luther King, Jr., in his Foreword to Thompson, *op. cit.*, p. x.

[60] There are various disquieting signs of the difficulty of recent survey research in urban ghetto areas. One notes the relatively high rates of nonresponse. Or, as in a recent Gallup survey in Harlem, evidence of cheating on the part of two interviewers, and two others who did not complete the assignment because of hostile encounters. See *New York Times*, November 1, 1968, p. 33. Certainly, increasing the difficulty and length of inquiry can only operate to aggravate such problems.

and remote, our description may have no implications for the present. But if they are too topical, they may be appropriate to the problems of the moment, only to become meaningless questions to future respondents. Such conceptual puzzles would burden any analyst.[61]

Another type of conceptual puzzle—often ignored—also must be solved. Who shall be included in the universe from which repeated samples will be drawn for trend studies? Some aspects of the question demand careful thought but present only technical problems. For the reasons already noted, Negro youth as well as adults should be included. Although men and residents of the great cities, and within these, the ghetto areas, should perhaps be oversampled, the geographical boundaries should be national. Otherwise, there is the risk of misreading the changing temper of the population which may vary greatly between rural, suburban, and urban areas, and by region of the country. We may be well advised to obtain comparative measures on strata within the white population, so as not to misinterpret findings which reflect class, age, educational, and regional variables as well as color.

Definition of the Universe and Conceptions of Self. A fundamental aspect of the question must be resolved: Who is a Negro? Upon reflection, one realizes that sample surveys as well as censuses have defined those who fall within or outside of the scope of such inquiry merely on the basis of the interviewer's visual observation and classification. To erect a time series on such judgments, without benefit of critical review, methodological checks, and other empirical supports, may be to build on a shaky and unreliable foundation. One may venture the thought that comparisons between "Negro" residents of different areas and over time may be obscured in some unknown way by elements that intrude upon the interviewer's judgment. One might hypothesize, for example, that the same light-colored respondent would be more likely to be adjudged Negro if he lived in a ghetto area than if he lived in a white suburb. One might hypothesize with the rise of certain ideological and cultural currents that respondents will be more likely to use distinctive cues of language and dress and thus be included in the "Negro" population, whereas previously they might have been classified as "white." The consequences of being a Negro are, of course, dependent on the *social* definition given to him

---

[61] A sense of doom touches the white analyst who reads and heeds the warning of Whitney Young: ". . . when white sociology professors *do* study black people they do so with sterile questionnaires developed and designed by, and for, white people, and they do not find it necessary or convenient to associate themselves with black collaborators. Of course, they often use black interviewers and black subjects and black people in other inferior roles but not as equals." Remarks by Whitney M. Young, Jr., prepared for delivery at the American Sociological Association, August 27, 1968, mimeographed. I have based my paper on a careful reading of a large literature, selected for its relevance but without reference to whether the authors were black or white.

by others, and the ensuing treatment. The judgments of interviewer *may* be the microcosmic equivalent of the larger social definition. But certainly we should not let the matter rest on this assumption. The variance in interviewers' ratings of equivalent samples and the agreement in the ratings of the same respondents should be tested.[62]

In addition to the social definition of a person as a Negro, there is also a *self*-definition. Whatever the historical or developmental process that relates these two definitions, the self-concept ought to be measured and then used to refine our classification of respondents. Certainly, it is an intervening variable that modifies the responses that follow from being treated by others as a Negro. And many self-propelled patterns must exist that are initiated simply by a definition of the self as Negro, in the absence of any social stimulation. Perhaps at the heart of recent social change is a heightened sense of self-identity, and the trend data from such a measure would have substantive importance, apart from methodological utility. Surveys that have experimented with an open-ended question exploring how the respondent classifies himself seem non-existent, and this certainly should be incorporated at the beginning of the interview. One might also experiment with a list of labels, such as "Negro," "white," "black," "Puerto Rican," "American," "Afro-American," "African," etc., pressing the respondent to choose the one designation that best describes him.

Such a procedure would serve not only to measure whether the self-perception is "nonwhite" but also to indicate more subtle aspects of group identity and the response to ideological currents. If we were to find that the feedback from such measures did not affect the interviewer rating, we would then have a typological system for classifying respondents into those who are seen by others as Negro and who perceive themselves in that reflected light, those whose definition of themselves as Negro is self-imposed, even though they are not so perceived, and those who do not see themselves as Negro despite the fact they are so perceived.[63]

---

[62] In a recent study, ratings of the skin color of a sample of middle-class Negroes taken twice over a 10-month period and where different interviewers were generally assigned to the reinterview, were found to be highly reliable. See H. Freeman *et al.*, "Color Gradation and Attitudes Among Middle-Income Negroes," *American Sociological Review,* vol. 31, June, 1966, pp. 365–374. In a much earlier study, the rating was dependent on the rater's own color, generally being displaced toward the opposite pole. See Eli S. Marks, "Skin Color Judgments of Negro College Students," *Journal of Abnormal and Social Psychology,* vol. 38, July, 1943, pp. 370–376.

[63] The parallel with studies of subjective class identification is instructive. The predictive power of the subjective measure in that realm has long been established; differences between subjective and objective location have been demonstrated, and the power of the two measures handled in combination documented. The same vista may await us in the realm of racial identification. In studies based on self-administered questionnaires, racial classification would reflect a self-definition. I assume that the comparisons in the Coleman

To use the interviewer's powers of observation merely to rate whether a respondent is "white" or "black" is to neglect other observable data, which may be indicative of the self-concept. The persona, the self he wishes the world to see, is certainly conveyed by such signs as style of hair and dress and by the choice of phrases and words such as "black," "brother," "soul," etc. The self that he may or may not be communicating to the outside world, but at least to intimates, is conveyed by whether pictures, sculpture, ornaments in his house are African in theme. Fruitful modes for enumerating such observables would provide richer data for classifying respondents, and might provide trends of substantive significance.

Although the decision to include a respondent in the universe would not be based on the measure, the interviewer could supplement his usual classification with more refined rating of skin color. Pettigrew and his associates found not only that a six-point scale of shades of color could be used reliably, but also that skin color correlated with anti-white attitudes.[64] If the respondent's self-definition of his own shade of color were also obtained, the discrepancy between the two ratings and its direction could be used as a possible indicator of the attitude toward the self. Perhaps the findings of classic studies of Negro children on the preference for seeing oneself as light would still be replicated among adults of this era.[65] Perhaps a new trend will emerge in which the dis-

---

et al. report between various minorities and whites are based on the question which asked the pupil to check whether he was "Negro," "white," "American Indian," "Oriental," or "Other," and an immediately following question which asked if he was "Puerto Rican," "Mexican-American," or "neither." It is highly relevant that a repeat reliability study of about seven hundred of the students revealed the following agreement on the first racial identification item: Grade 3, 97.6 percent; Grade 6, 99.5 percent; Grade 9, 94.8 percent; Grade 12, 99 percent. Coleman *et al., op. cit.,* pp. 568–570. In the Newark study, rioters were more likely to describe themselves as "black," not "Negro" or "Colored," than were nonrioters, suggesting that simple linguistic cues, and the self-definition, have psychological significance. Caplan and Paige, *op. cit.,* p. 21. To avoid the contamination of the interviewer's rating, it might be recorded before the self-definition question is asked.

[64] Pettigrew *et al., op. cit.* The correlations are modest, but the findings too complicated to present in detail, depending on whether the husband's or wife's color is used as the predictor and whether interaction with class is taken into account.

[65] For a summary of these early studies, see H. Proshansky and P. Newton, "The Nature and Meaning of Negro Self-Identity," in M. Deutsch, I. Katz, and A. R. Jensen, eds., *Social Class, Race, and Psychological Development.* Holt, New York, 1968, pp. 178–218. Most studies were done in an earlier era, and should be replicated now. And with the exception of one current program of research, they dealt with very young children, so that developmental changes with age remain unknown. In a program of research done in the mid-1960's, including college-age students and obtaining semantic differential measures of color names and racial concepts, Williams and his associates found that Negro college students rated the entity "black person" least favorably on the evaluative dimension. See, for example, J. E. Williams, "Connotation of Racial Concepts and Color Names," *Journal of Personality and Social Psychology,* vol. 3, May, 1966, pp. 531–540.

crepancy will become reduced, or respondents will see themselves as darker, as blackness becomes a positively valued trait.

Thus far, our essential concern was to stress that the definition of the universe for continuing inquiries of the Negro population is itself problematic, and some lines of methodological innovation were suggested. As the self-concept and the evaluation of self come under discussion, one is quickly led to the realization that this is a central psychological realm to be explored on a continuing basis for trends of substantive significance. A number of dimensions of high priority for measurement will be suggested. In contrast with other dimensions to be noted below, these do not pose issues of race relations to the respondent. The patterns observed may *reflect* the system of race relations and the treatment of minorities. But their explicit focus is on the person, not the Negro vis-à-vis white society, and they should be matters of separate inquiry or asked prior to questions on race relations and racial identity.

Self-esteem should be measured by some scale that does not make the concept of race salient by its wording. And since self-esteem may well vary with age and class, norms should also be obtained for comparable white groups.[66] The oppressiveness of white society may well have robbed Negroes of self-esteem, but recent attempts to create group pride and the political gains of Negroes may well have restored it. The actual level of esteem resultant from all such forces remains to be measured, and the changes charted over time.[67]

A related dimension has come to be known variously as *powerlessness,*

[66] The need for statistical norms on comparable groups of white subjects is shown by a finding on the self-concept among a sample ·of 688 Negro youth enrolled in the four grades of the predominantly Negro high schools in Atlanta in 1967. The self-administered questionnaire contained a four-part question on the self, and 26 percent were found to have checked either the statement: "I don't like myself the way I am; I'd like to change completely" or "There are many things I'd like to change; but not all." Seventy-four percent checked statements indicating that they would make few or no changes in themselves. In this otherwise admirable study, the investigators then stress the "feelings of self-debasement and sense of personal isolation" and predict that "acting out behavior among youth may be expected to continue at a high level." That one-quarter of the youth have negative self-feelings hardly seems a large magnitude; one might hypothesize that such feelings would be as prevalent among white adolescents. J. E. Conyers, W. J. Farmar, and M. Levin, *Black Youth in a Southern Metropolis.* Southern Regional Conference, Atlanta, 1968.

[67] For one such scale, see Morris Rosenberg, *Society and the Adolescent Self-Image.* Princeton University Press, Princeton, 1965. A small sample of Negro youth were not found especially low in self-esteem. A larger-scale inquiry in self-esteem of the Negro population in Philadelphia commends itself on a number of grounds. The respondent rated his actual performance in each of a series of areas, and then indicated what he would regard as ideal behavior in that sphere. The magnitude of the discrepancy between actual and ideal behavior summed over all areas provides a comprehensive index of self-esteem. Particularly interesting is the "racial sub-identity" scale which measures the departure from ideal behavior in dealing with whites. The functioning of the self in this

fate-control, personal and political efficacy. Depending on its content, the instrument locates the sense of inadequacy in the weakness of the self or in the unresponsiveness and brutishness of the environment, or leaves it unlocatable with respect to these internal and external forces. The duality increases the attractiveness of such instruments since we obtain measures that somehow are a bridge or halfway point between self and society, and the total belief system may well predict types of behavior. Some minimal sense of power, whatever its source, may be the precondition for *conventional goal-directed* behavior, but powerlessness may initiate unconventional acts. The person has nothing to lose and, while he may not have everything to gain, how else can he gain anything?

Perhaps the distinction should be sharpened and two subscales elaborated —one that taps more of the dimension that the self is inadequate and the other tapping the feeling of futility in the face of an overpowering environment, despite confidence in the self. One may venture the thought that real changes in the environment may modify the latter belief, but that the former (perhaps based on the consolidation of many early experiences with a brutish environment) is not so readily changed by new experience.

By way of illustration, one of the dramatic findings of the Coleman *et al.* report is that minority-group children feel less able to control the environment than whites, and that higher school achievement is related to the sense of control, certainly suggesting the importance of measuring this variable and the therapeutic effects that might follow from making the environment more supportive and predictable. But perhaps the inability to control that environment is felt to reside in the self. It would be nice to know, and the items leave unclear whether the lack of control is felt to stem from an oppressive society or personal inadequacy: "Every time I try to get ahead, *something* or someone stops me," and "*People like me* don't have much of a chance to be successful in life," are ambiguous as to where the trouble lies.[68] To be sure, a separate battery of three questions is designed to tap the "self-concept." By multivariate analysis, one might determine how much of the control of the environment ultimately is felt to reside in the self. But the questions on the "self" may also suffer from the same ambiguity. "I sometimes feel that I just can't learn" may focus on the deficiency inside the person, but the rest of the sentence might possibly be completed with the unstated remark, "because they don't give me a chance." Certainly another item, "I would do better in school work if teachers didn't go so fast," straddles both sources of inadequacy. Who's wrong: the teacher or the pupil? On the face of it, the item on "luck" seems a pure

---

special area may well be central to a Negro's sense of self-regard, and one could compare the score in this area with the level in the other areas. Obviously, the racial items could be located *later* in the interview. See S. Parker and R. J. Kleiner, *Mental Illness in the Urban Negro Community.* Free Press, New York, 1966, pp. 170–182.

[68] Coleman *et al., op. cit.,* pp. 281–290, 319–320, italics added.

measure of the unpredictability of the environment, and the item on "how bright they judge themselves in comparison with their classmates" seems a pure measure of self-confidence. At any rate, on the three-item index used for "self-concept," Negro and white children show about the same level of self-esteem, strengthening the inference that the Negro child locates the source of the trouble outside himself.

A brief paper from 1952 anticipates the current problem. From his observations of pupils in the integrated schools of Flint, Michigan, Amos began to focus on "the *power of control* of the teacher and the implications which it seemed to hold for the Negro." He hypothesized that "in the case of the white pupil, this factor was taken as part of the routine of a rigid teacher, but in the case of the Negro this control was more likely perceived as an attempt to subordinate him on a racial basis." What is suggested is that the *apperception* the child brings is critical to the interpretation of the teacher's behavior. Given the fact that the teacher role involves the exercise of some authority, and given his apperception, the Negro child might continue to feel powerless against an arbitrary, hostile authority, even in the face of an objective improvement in the school environment. Amos subjected his hypothesis to empirical test by obtaining the attitudes of samples of ninth-grade Negro and white children and of their teachers, and also obtained the estimates the pupils made of the teachers' attitudes. Both white and Negro children underestimated how favorable the reported attitudes of the teachers were to Negroes, but the underestimate was greater on the part of Negro children. However, when class is controlled, the lower-class pupils, and not a particular ethnic group, see the teacher as more hostile than he is by reference to his own attitude scores.[69]

The scale that Seeman has employed to measure sense of powerlessness, and that Rotter, Liverant, Gore, Seeman, and others have at various times employed to measure the sense of internal control of outcomes vs. the control that external force or fate exercises over the person, may be interpreted almost unambiguously as measuring futility in the face of powerful or mysterious forces, rather than powerlessness because of limitations inherent in the self. Degree of commitment to civil rights activity increased among those who saw themselves as in control of their own fate,[70] But whether the instrument services this practical, immediate purpose is only incidental to its larger value.

In choosing from among these various instruments, one might well de-

---

[69] Robert T. Amos, "The Accuracy of Negro and White Children's Prediction of Teachers' Attitudes Toward Negro Students," *Journal of Negro Education,* vol. 21, Spring, 1952, pp. 124–135, italics added.

[70] P. M. Gore and J. B. Rotter, "A Personality Correlate of Social Action," *Journal of Personality,* vol. 31, 1963, pp. 58–64. But in another study of Negro college students and Negro civil service employees, scores on general powerlessness and a subscale of "civil rights powerlessness" showed no correlation with scores on militancy in civil rights.

cide to suffer some ambiguity in interpretation in return for the information on trends and changes from the past. The items used by Coleman, and by Ernest Campbell *et al.,* yield a baseline on a huge sample of the cohort that was aged 6 to 18 in 1965. Repeating them on a new cohort of children, or on the cohort of adults that correspond to the original group, would document whether changes have occurred in the interim.[71] So, too, the items from the Harris index of alienation yield trends for Negro adults beginning with 1966.

In this light, the scale of political efficacy (vs. powerlessness) developed in the course of the Michigan voting studies recommends itself, since baselines and trends are available for Negro and white adults beginning with 1952 and for a sample of high school youth in 1965. What this may lack in coverage of the total domain within which one could be efficacious or powerless, it makes up in its span of time, and the political realm is certainly not unimportant. Contained within this short, five-item scale, an advantage in itself, are questions that tap the two sources of efficacy or powerlessness. "I don't think public

---

See S. J. Surace and M. Seeman, "Some Correlates of Civil Rights Activism," *Social Forces,* vol. 46, 1967, pp. 197–207. Among Negro male heads of households, sampled in selected areas of Los Angeles, and interviewed shortly after the Watts riot, powerlessness correlated with reported willingness to use violence and with reported violence during the riot, among those with little formal education, but *not* among those with college education. See H. E. Ransford, "Isolation, Powerlessness, and Violence: A Study of Attitudes and Participation in the Watts Riot," *American Journal of Sociology,* vol. 73, March 1968, pp. 581–591. In the course of a 1964 study of the correlates of moving into residentially integrated suburbs in the Los Angeles area, Bullough finds that those adults who had childhood experience in integrated schools and neighborhoods were less likely to feel powerless. The finding certainly suggests that there may be long-term trends in the feelings of powerlessness in the Negro population as integration patterns rise or decline. See Bonnie Bullough, "Alienation in the Ghetto," *American Journal of Sociology,* vol. 72, January, 1967, pp. 469–478. An index of alienation developed by Louis Harris includes several questions on the sense of powerlessness for which trend data on the Negro population are available from surveys conducted in 1966 and again in early 1968. "What I personally think doesn't count very much" increased from 40 percent to 61 percent and "The people running the country don't really care what happens to people like ourselves" increased from 32 percent to 52 percent. The level in early 1968 must, however, be seen in comparison with norms for the white population. On the two items, for the white population the early 1968 figures are 48 percent and 39 percent, respectively. The difference would no doubt, be smaller if the norms were presented for whites equated in class position and other characteristics. The trend is clearly a matter of concern, and should be measured in the future for both groups. Harris Release, April 15, 1968. That the trend is worth measuring is underscored by the unexpected finding reported by Harris in a release dated December 16, 1968. On the first item, the evidence suggests that alienation has returned to the lower level of 1966, 44 percent of Negroes endorsing it. On the second item, the percent is 44, suggesting a considerable drop in alienation since the earlier 1968 point.

[71] As William Sewell has noted, if the original sample had been identifiable, a longitudinal or panel study could be designed, but presumably administrative decisions precluded such a possibility. See his review in *American Sociological Review,* vol. 32, June, 1967, p. 478.

officials care much what people like me think," puts the locus of the difficulty outside of the self, whereas the item "Sometimes politics and government seem so complicated that a person like me can't really understand what's going on," puts the problem squarely inside the self. In 1952, Negroes were less likely to score as "efficacious" than any other demographic group examined, but the strata in which they were concentrated also scored low: the rural, the uneducated, the South, those of low occupations and incomes.[72] In 1956, a special analysis documented that socialization in the South was an important determinant of the findings for the Negro. Those born and remaining in the South scored lowest; those born and remaining in the North scored highest, and those born in the South who had migrated North scored in-between.[73] If the behavior were completely determined by the *contemporary* experience, the migrants should approximate the efficacy level of those with whom they now share a common environment. If the behavior were completely a product of *early* socialization, the migrants should remain at the level of those they had left behind. The 1956 finding suggests that both early socialization and subsequent experience determine the sense of efficacy. In this light, the dramatic political gains that Negroes have made recently in registering voters, organizing effective political movements, electing candidates—especially in the South—should have increased their sense of efficacy, despite the political culture they may be carrying along from their earlier years. By contrast, recent gains in the North, being smaller and less dramatic, and the initial level of efficacy much higher, one would expect little further growth in efficacy among Northern Negroes. Table 4 presents trend data from 1952 to 1964 on three of the five items in the original scale, separately for Negroes residing in the South and North. The two items on the act of voting are omitted for the reasons already noted. What has been tabled is the *deviation* in efficacy from the level shown by the white population in the same region. Thus, any general gains or losses in efficacy that are common to all residents of the region are deliberately removed from view so as to highlight what has been *distinctive* to the recent experience of Negroes.

In light of the small size of the Negro samples, one must be most tentative in drawing conclusions, and one would expect an occasional inversion in the findings. Certainly, the trend in the South seems clearly to be toward a growth of efficacy, especially on the two items that locate the difficulty in the unre-

[72] Angus Campbell, Gerald Gurin, and Warren Miller, *The Voter Decides*. Row, Peterson, Evanston, Ill., 1954, pp. 187–194. At least one, perhaps two, of the five items may have changed their meaning radically in the 1960's, since they relate to the voting act as a prime avenue of influence, in contrast with new and current modes of political pressure in the Negro community. These items could be examined separately, and certainly the trend in the belief about voting as a political force relates to a major institution and is important in its own right.

[73] Angus Campbell *et al., The American Voter*. Wiley, New York, 1960, p. 453.

Table 4. Trends in Political Efficacy among Southern and Northern Negroes Relative to the White Level of Efficacy in the Region[a]

	Percent Negroes minus Percent Whites Giving Response Indicative of Low Efficacy	
	South	North
Public officials don't care what people like me think:		
1952	28	− 3
1956	27	14
1960	15	13
1964	10	10
People like me don't have any say in what government does:		
1952	33	4
1956	31	21
1960	12	12
1964	− 4	3
Politics and government so complicated that person like me can't understand		
1952	7	3
1956	21	6
1960	10	10
1964	8	− 4

[a] I acknowledge with thanks the special analyses provided by the Survey Research Center, University of Michigan. The *Ns* for Southern Negroes ranged from 52 to 114; for Northern Negroes, from 40 to 62.

sponsiveness of the system rather than in the self. In the North there appears to have been no consistent trend over the entire period 1952 to 1964. The trend since then should be documented.

Another variable which is a halfway point between self and society lends itself to simple measurement on a continuing basis and would have rich informative value. The *ego-ideal*—the person, living or dead, who is most admired —could be determined. The young may be modeling their selves on his image, and for those too old to change, the variable may suggest, remorsefully, the lost self that they would like to have been and the ideal they communicate to the young. And the larger society is also urging a variety of models on the individual, some of whom may be rejected and others idolized. The data could be coded along a variety of dimensions.

As times change, is the Negro's ego-ideal moving toward the heroic man of action and away from the more contemplative or otherworldly type? Is the frequency of choosing *white* personifications of the ideal, a President Kennedy, for example, diminishing?[74] As the African past becomes prominent in literature and school books, and as Negro history is being rewritten, which of the many heroes of diverse type that are presented become internalized as the ideal? How many *white* youth are now selecting as their ego-ideals heroic *Negro* figures? Does the choice of family figures, fathers or mothers, as *ideals* by male and female respondents provide an empirical clue about Negro family structure, a topic much discussed and debated?

On the ideal self, we simply lack information. But on another set of variables in the general area where the self and society intersect, we have a great deal of information, but suffer from confusion. Findings of studies on *occupational aspirations and the plans or expectations* of Negroes are contradictory. Clear evidence, on a large and continuing scale, would be very relevant. What do Negro youth hope and want to become? Are their aspirations for the self scaled down as they inspect the barriers in society in order to protect themselves from frustration? Do they keep their hopes high, but scale down their realistic expectations with consequent embitterment about society?

In the late 1930's, during a period of great unemployment, Charles Johnson reported that rural Negro youth "were overwhelming in their desire for professional occupations." Given the period and the prospects, this was perhaps a fair reading of the finding that 39 percent of the boys and 65 percent of the girls desired to enter professions. But he stressed that "these were not the occupations they actually expected to follow" (26 percent and 48 percent of boys and girls respectively), and for that historic era he concluded correctly, "that the *expectation* itself borders on fantasy."[75] In the 30 years since then, opportunity has certainly expanded. As it continues, will Negro youth show a corresponding heightening of *both* hope and expectation, or will the gap between the two remain as an irritant?

A number of local studies in the 1950's and early 1960's suggest that the gap is still there, aspirations being high, but expectations lower.[76] But Coleman's data apply to the mid-1960's, and are national in scope and huge in size. He finds that Negro youth have high occupational *expectations,* although

---

[74] A dramatic example is provided in a case study of one of the four Negro students who began the sit-in movement in the South in Greensboro. "John" began at age 15 to read stories about Gandhi, and reported "I began to wonder sometimes why couldn't I be a Gandhi myself, doing something for the race. Gandhi was a 'hero of mine' along with Frederick Douglass." See F. Solomon and J. R. Fishman, "Youth and Social Action: II. Action and Identity Formation in the First Student Sit-in Demonstration," *Journal of Social Issues,* vol. 20, October, 1964, p. 38. In this sphere, the interviewer's observations may also provide a neglected source of data. Among the pictures observed in the home, which heroes are displayed—Martin Luther King, Malcolm X, Gandhi, etc.?

[75] Charles S. Johnson, *Growing Up in the Black Belt.* Schocken Books, New York, 1967, pp. 200, 223, italics added.

[76] Proshansky and Newton, *op. cit.* But for proper interpretation the discrepancy scores for equivalent groups of white children should be available.

somewhat lower than their white counterparts in the same areas of the country. He also demonstrates that Negro youth have high educational aspirations.[77] Will the pattern continue, or will it be broken as youth—perhaps both Negro and white—become alienated from the conventional occupational definition of success in American society? There are other possibilities not yet entertained which may emerge and should be documented. In a study of some six hundred white and Negro high school sophomores in a poor rural area of Texas in 1966, the investigators found that Negroes had *higher* aspirations *and* expectations for advanced education than whites, suggesting, in line with Coleman's comments, that education is seen by Negroes as a major avenue of mobility. The most dramatic finding was that the Negro students often expected to go *further* in their education than they desired, a discrepancy with this sign almost never being demonstrated for the white students. What imperative impels this particular subgroup of Negro youth to such a dutiful commitment to something they personally do not want is a fascinating question to be explored, and perhaps an unexpected trend to be watched.[78] The measures appropriate to these problems can be applied directly to the younger cohorts. For the older generation whose careers are firm, the same questions could be put in terms of the occupational aspirations and plans they urge upon the young.

Feelings and Sentiments: Hate, Desperation, and Distrust. The list of variables in the general area of the self-in-society is almost complete, but before we turn to specific attitudes about race relations, we suggest one other set for continuing exploration. Consider the image conveyed by a good deal of

[77] Coleman *et al., op. cit.,* pp. 275–286.

[78] G. W. Ohlendorf and W. Kuvlesky, "Racial Differences in the Educational Orientations of Rural Youth," *Social Science Quarterly,* vol. 49, 1968, pp. 274–283. Using a scale developed by Leonard Reissman, these same investigators found very high scores, sometimes exceeding the white scores, on a scale of intensity of aspiration. The score is based on a series of sacrifices which the respondent indicates a willingness to make to reach his goal. In another study where this same instrument was given to 700 Negro college freshmen at a Southern college, Harrison observed interesting patterns in the particular sacrifices the subjects were willing to make or not make to achieve their occupational goals. The students were rarely willing to go against their parents' views or to leave their parents in order to achieve their goal. In general, however, the total findings are indicative of intensity of drive. See E. C. Harrison, "Achievement Motivation Characteristics of Negro College Freshmen," *Personnel and Guidance Journal,* vol. 38, October, 1959, pp. 146–149. The individual differences found again and again in studies in this sphere call for intensive study. Consider a finding on the perception of barriers to occupational advancement reported for a homogeneous group, Negro medical students at Howard University. The 186 students were asked whether being a Negro would advantage them, make no difference, or disadvantage them in each of nine medical specialties. Forty-three percent were optimists thinking they would be advantaged in some specialties, 41 percent pessimists thinking they would be disadvantaged, and 16 percent believing it would make no difference. See Kurt Back and Ida Simpson, "The Dilemma of the Negro Professional," *Journal of Social Issues,* vol. 20, April, 1964, pp. 60–70.

current commentary and semi-scientific writing: that *hate* is a pervasive state of feeling in the Negro population, ready to erupt at the slightest provocation. There is also an ample literature about whites hating Negroes, and many chronicles of hateful acts on their part. Ironically, now the theme is how much hate flows in the other direction.

To accept this image uncritically would be a mistake, but to reject it out of hand would be equally wrong. Some measurement of this and related variables, of their depth and spread in the Negro population, of their rise and fall, must be attempted. Let us not prejudge the frequency of such states of mind, or their character. Perhaps these strong emotions exist, but have no unitary focus. Perhaps the hate some Negroes feel is focused on other Negroes. Perhaps we have arrived in race relations at a terrible point when hatred of whites has taken on the dimensions of a sentiment. If so, a Negro would not find an individual white man an object of the emotion, hate, as he might take another person as an object of love. Just as the sentiment of patriotism might be aroused in another at the thought of the nation or flag, the Negro's feeling of hatred might have become a sentiment, an enduring state aroused merely at the thought of the idea, "whiteness" or "American society." Perhaps hate has almost become a "value," and is in some circles regarded as desirable and proper.

Whatever the etiology or the just basis for the growth of such feelings of hate, the consequences that flow from their existence, or from the mere belief of whites that they exist, can be dire.[79] Whites may try to allay the hate by actions which reduce the grievances of Negroes, but they may also respond to the belief that they are hated with fear, avoidance, or social distance; resort to arms to protect themselves against the perceived threat; demand law and order; or hate back those who they think hate them. The process then keeps spiraling. A Negro who felt no hate initially now responds to the hateful actions of whites and begins to hate back.[80]

Measurement of the true state of affairs might well break the vicious process, since the strands of evidence do not weave a picture of hate spread through the Negro population, despite the injuries suffered and the grievances

[79] When Katz and Braly did their classic study of stereotypes in 1932, the 12 traits most often assigned to Negroes included no trait that might be described as threatening, although other ethnic groups were described frequently as "cruel," "treacherous," "quarrelsome," or "aggressive." What a replication of this study would reveal now is uncertain, but certainly the threatening aspects of image may have increased. See D. Katz and K. Braly, "Racial Stereotypes of 100 College Students," *Journal of Abnormal and Social Psychology,* vol. 28, October–November, 1933, pp. 280–290.

[80] We could, of course, begin the analysis the other way, with the hatred that may in fact characterize some whites or be imputed to them, which in turn generates a set of responses from Negroes. Certainly, the usage by some Negro leaders of the term "genocide," suggesting that whites plan to exterminate Negroes, could not be better calculated

felt. Perhaps the most striking datum is provided by a study done in the early 1950's in Bakersfield, California, Savannah, Georgia, and Elmira, New York, when only 28 percent of the 665 Negroes interviewed agreed with the statement: "*Sometimes* I hate white people."[81] This is not an inconsiderable number. A few haters can do a lot! But the critic might say that the hatred is lodged deep in many others and simply not elicited by the question asked, I might add, by Negro interviewers. If so, this hardly suggests hate so strong that it spews forth at every opportunity. Whatever the true facts, they should be determined. Certainly, direct questions ought to be tried again, now in the 1970's and hereafter. But we can also develop more subtle approaches, and we should develop open questions to determine whether the focus of hate is all white society, particular categories of whites, or some groups of Negroes. We can also instruct the interviewer to be more sensitive to recording language cues. Words like "honky," "pig," "fat cat," various obscenities, and a specialized lexicon of hate may well be indicators of the tones of feeling that underlie expressed attitudes.[82]

Although hate may not be the predominant note in Negro feelings, other complexes of destructive feeling may be present. Tumin remarks on the "politics of *despair* and anger,"[83] and it may well be that Negroes today are less angry than despairing. Perhaps acts of violence can be seen not as expressions of hatred, but as acts of desperation—taken, not when all hope is lost, but when one senses a last desperate chance before resigning oneself to despair. Yet, a good deal of evidence from recent surveys suggests that many Negroes see the future as hopeful, and thus could not be adequately characterized as in despair.[84] But this still leaves some who may, in fact, have already given up all

---

to produce protective measures and hatred of whites among Negroes. A statement attributed to a Negro militant, Dan Watts: "You tell a white man that you love him and he believes it; but you tell a white man . . . I'm getting ready to slit your throat, he just can't believe it," may well have the situation upside down. Quoted in Brink and Harris, *Black and White*, p. 58. Far more whites may now be anticipating hate, rather than love, as suggested by the survey findings that 49 percent said they were more worried about their safety on the streets than they were a year ago, and 43 percent said this made them feel personally uneasy (p. 220).

[81] Robin M. Williams, Jr., *Strangers Next Door*. Prentice-Hall, Englewood Cliffs, N.J., 1964, pp. 280–281, italics added.

[82] As an illustration, a leader of the Black Panthers recently labeled Justice Thurgood Marshall "an Uncle Tom, a bootlicker, a nigger pig, a Tonto and a punk." *New York Times,* November 27, 1968, p. 28:2.

[83] Melvin M. Tumin, "Some Social Consequences of Research on Racial Relations," *American Sociologist,* vol. 3, 1968, p. 122, italics supplied.

[84] Brink and Harris, *Black and White,* pp. 222–231. Various scales, labeled morale, anomie, or alienation, have a high loading of items that measure hopelessness, the lack of support, loneliness, malaise, confusion, etc. On such an index of "morale" Marx found that only one-quarter of his sample scored at the lowest end. But, as suggested above, those

hope, and others who may be desperate to have a good, but distant, future speeded toward them. Certainly, the balance between feelings of hope vs. despair can be readily measured, and attempts could be made to measure that critical state of desperation as one teeters on the edge of despair.

Another constellation of feelings possibly more widespread among Negroes than either hate or despair may be *distrust* of others and whites in particular. Kenneth Clark puts it well: "In a ghetto community, where the material rewards are hard to come by, the motives of almost everyone are suspect. . . . Any form of altruism appears to be a ruse, a transparent disguise for the 'hustle.' The 'hustle,' the 'cashing in,' the smooth or crude exploiter, seem the realities." Under such conditions, hope is not lost, nor is hate let loose. Strategy may become shrewd and calculating. The sincerity and good intent of whites in future relations may be doubted. Evidence of good faith will be denied, and even a rumored instance of bad faith believed.[85]

In the study of Negro high school students in Atlanta, only 25 percent agreed with the proposition that "white people can usually *be trusted,*" 45 percent disagreeing with the proposition, the rest being uncertain about the matter.[86] The low magnitude of hate reported above, 28 percent of Williams' respondents agreeing that they hate whites *sometimes,* and the high magnitude of distrust reported in this study, suggests that this variable may be the more critical one for measurement and amelioration.

Such feelings are accompanied by beliefs about the bad character, deceitfulness, unfairness, etc., of those who cannot be trusted. Thus, instruments of a cognitive sort, involving moral imputations, could provide a technique of measurement. Scales for the measurement of distrust or "cynicism" have been developed mainly in the political sphere, but ought to be extended in future work to focus on other persons and institutions: various classes of Negroes, Jews and other minorities, the police, and teachers. The generalized distrust of others should be measured prior to making the respondent's Negro identity salient. Norms should be obtained for white as well as Negro subjects in order to interpret the data conservatively. Findings on such items are presented in Tables 5 and 6 based on a 1965 nationwide survey of white and Negro

---

with "zero" morale, truly despairing, were least likely to be militant about civil rights. Marx, *op. cit.,* p. 87.

[85] K. B. Clark, *Dark Ghetto.* Harper, New York, 1965, p. xvii. Any number of "natural experiments" have been reported in the press where a false rumor starts about the actions of whites against Negroes, but is quickly believed and leads to a violent outburst before the truth comes out. An example is provided by a week of demonstrations at the University of Massachusetts following a hoax which had been perpetrated by a white student and his Negro guest that they had been assaulted by four other whites. *New York Times,* November 17, 1968.

[86] Conyers, Farmar, and Levin, *op. cit.,* p. 13.

Table 5. Feelings of Trust among Matched Groups of Southern Negro and White Youth, 1965
(*In Percent*)

	High Socioeconomic Status				Low Socioeconomic Status			
	Male		*Female*		*Male*		*Female*	
	Negro	*White*	*Negro*	*White*	*Negro*	*White*	*Negro*	*White*
Quite a few government officials crooked	33	39	27	40	29	36	26	42
Only trust government some of time	17	14	15	10	14	13	8	12
Government run for benefit of few	24	32	20	24	22	30	18	24
Teachers do not treat everyone fairly	49	56	60	53	54	56	64	56
Most of time, people look out for themselves	43	42	48	34	42	40	37	38
Can't be too careful in dealing with people	60	48	71	39	59	40	56	38
Most people try to take advantage of others	56	43	61	36	64	39	53	33
Number of cases	149	609	208	748	145	1,432	136	1,470

Table 6. Feelings of Trust among Matched Groups of Northern Negro and White Youth, 1965
(*In Percent*)

| | High Socioeconomic Status | | | | Low Socioeconomic Status | | | |
| | Male | | Female | | Male | | Female | |
	Negro	*White*	*Negro*	*White*	*Negro*	*White*	*Negro*	*White*
Quite a few government officials crooked	23	26	28	26	28	25	25	27
Only trust government some of time	12	7	15	7	12	9	10	7
Government run for benefit of few	21	24	19	20	24	23	20	19
Teachers do not treat everyone fairly	46	57	55	58	56	56	54	54
Most of time, people look out for themselves	48	46	44	38	51	44	40	34
Can't be too careful in dealing with people	60	47	60	42	57	41	54	34
Most people try to take advantage of others	56	48	56	38	55	41	52	31
Number of cases	403	1,974	419	2,142	405	4,805	410	4,296

high school youth.[87] At that time there was little evidence in this age cohort that the *system* of beliefs of Negro youth involved more distrust and cynicism than the one characterizing their white counterparts. Distrust of the political sphere was markedly less than found in other spheres or in the general outlook on others. Only on two items expressive of a *general* sense of the exploitativeness of others (the last two in the tables), were the Negro youth consistently, in eight out of the eight possible comparisons, markedly more distrustful. Certainly, it would be valuable to have such measures available for adults, and for various age cohorts in the future.

Beliefs and Attitudes about Race Relations

Estimates of Past and Future Progress in Race Relations and Psychophysical Measures. From our discussion of feelings of despair and our earlier treatment of the problem of deprivation, it is evident that the variables: perceived rate of progress in race relations generally, and in particular spheres, for the respondent himself and for the group in the large, should be measured on a periodic basis. And the level of satisfaction with that rate of change should also be determined for *whites* as well as Negroes, since conflict may arise out of different standards as to what is fast or slow or *too* fast or *too* slow. Here we can certainly build upon the time series that have already been started in various surveys. Some of the aggregate findings are presented in Table 7 and suggest that dissatisfaction with the speed of past progress is considerable. Nevertheless, it has declined in general, and in particular areas of life, and is less than might be surmised.[88] Certainly, one cannot reconcile these aggregate data with an image of pervasive despair, although such despair reaches high levels in particular subgroups.[89]

The data are fragmentary and need updating. The parallel perception

[87] I acknowledge with thanks the courtesy of Kent Jennings and the University of Michigan's Survey Research Center in making these unpublished data available to me. A single, but crisp question in the Michigan survey of adults in 15 cities asked whether the respondent trusted Negroes more than he trusted white people. Twenty-three percent answered that they did, and the differential distrust of whites is most characteristic of the younger age groups. See Campbell and Schuman, *op. cit.*, pp. 25–26.

[88] For a convenient summary of poll data on the perceived speed of integration, see *Public Opinion Quarterly,* vol. 32, Fall, 1968, pp. 513–524. Most of these data are the attitudes of whites, and the occasional datum on Negroes is probably derived from the very small cell of cases obtained in the course of a regular national survey. Table 7 presents data mainly from special, large samples of the Negro population.

[89] The *Fortune* survey of 1967 of some three hundred Negroes in 13 cities provides the most dramatic evidence of hope about the future and the widespread feeling that things have changed for the better in many respects.

Table 7. Some Trends in Estimates and Evaluations of Progress for Negroes among Negro and White Respondents
(*In Percent*)

	1963[a]	1964[b]	1966[a]	1967[c]	1968
Personally better off than 3 years ago in:					
Work situation	45		54		
Housing	43		43		
Pay	55		54		
Being able to vote	31		53		
Being able to eat in any restaurant	36		55		
Being able to have children educated with white	39		58		
All respects	[d]		67	73	
In general things getting better for Negroes:		81			
In past 10–15 years, lot of progress against discrimination (15 cities, Negro)					62[e]
Recent progress has generally been too slow (*Negro* respondents)	51		43		
Negroes have tried to move too fast (*white* respondents)	64		70		
Government pushing integration too slow (metropolitan, non-Southern Negro)		34			
Progress should be speeded up a lot:[f]					
Negro respondents					41
White respondents					13
Progress should be slowed down a lot:[f]					
Negro respondents					2
White respondents					14

[a] Brink and Harris, *Black and White*, pp. 220–230.
[b] Marx, *Protest and Prejudice*, pp. 6, 11.
[c] *Fortune*, January, 1968, p. 148 (13 cities).
[d] Not asked in 1963.
[e] Campbell and Schuman, *Racial Attitudes in Fifteen American Cities*, p. 22.
[f] Louis Harris, *Public Opinion Quarterly*, vol. 32, 1968, p. 523.

and evaluation of the past tempo by whites suggest the potential for conflict, since many feel the pace has been too fast. With respect to the desired speed of *future* change, again one notes a root of conflict: Negroes wanting it speeded up and whites wanting it slowed down. The differentiation in the judgments obtained about progress in different sectors of life suggests that they reflect the realities rather than being global beliefs. *Objective* changes in the aggregate, however, and for subaggregates such as the South vs. North, should be examined in parallel with these subjective trends on the perception of progress for the group.[90]

Objective changes the individual experiences in his own life circumstances can also be enumerated in the interview and compared with the perception of personal progress made. Perhaps the disparities between objective reality and subjective feeling can be understood in some degree by taking into account the two perspectives on progress that the individual may maintain— one where he focuses on the self, and the other where he focuses on the group. Or perhaps the paradox that he may not perceive social change, when it has in fact occurred, may simply be a function of ignorance. Questions of knowledge of the objective changes that have occurred, and quasi-experimental questions involving judgments of the experienced magnitude of certain stimuli, an approach that might be labeled *social psychophysics,* should be tried. Whites and Negroes could be asked what exact percentage of Negro children are in integrated schools; what the increase in that number has been in the last three years; what the average earnings of Negro families are and how much they have increased in a given period; and so forth. Various increments could be presented and subjects asked to appraise whether such changes are small, medium, or large. By such an approach, one might determine whether the judgments of the tempo of change are based on knowledge, and also obtain a better sense of what actual rates of change will seem satisfactory to given parties.

Measures of Specific Grievances and Dissatisfactions. The fact that many Negroes feel their situation has improved and will continue to improve does not mean that they are completely satisfied. Such a sense of progress may blunt the sharp edge of a frustration, but it cannot remove all sense of pain, since all of us, white or black, see events in some longer perspective. Some index of the dissatisfactions being experienced must be obtained, but this presents certain problems when the plan for such measurements should be on a continuing basis, and there are limits to the number of specific variables that can be studied. The psychological variables treated thus far did have immediate relevance, but also had a quality of timelessness and generality simplifying the task of coverage of a domain and the spanning of time. By contrast, the grievance of today may be resolved tomorrow, only to be replaced by another grievance.[91] As one contemplates the variety of situations that Ne-

---

[90] Marx provides some very interesting data and interpretation of differential perception of changes in South and North. Some of these findings suggest that improvement is more visible in the South, since the base point for change is lower to start with. Marx, *op. cit.,* pp. 8–9.

[91] The data from the Harris surveys presented in Table 7 show the way experienced improvement in one section may be offset by dissatisfaction in another sector. Other examples are given in his text. Brink and Harris, *Black and White,* p. 27.

groes face in their different milieux, the possible sources of grievance make a long list. Garbage collection, sewers, sidewalks, parking facilities, street lights, transportation, parks and recreational facilities, shopping facilities and prices have been a focus for dissatisfaction for Negroes—and whites—apart from more obvious grounds for grievance, such as treatment by police and other public officials, and conditions of housing, military service, employment, education, health and welfare, and political rights.

One could develop some system for staggered measurements over time of satisfaction with each of a long list of specific conditions. Or one could develop some omnibus question or summary question on general satisfaction with life conditions. Or one could have an open-ended question to catch a newly emerging focus of dissatisfaction. Some of the conditions are fundamental, e.g., police protection, employment, and should be the core of the battery on satisfactions and grievances, to be supplemented periodically by questions on more peripheral areas of life.

The complexity of measurement and analysis is compounded, however, as one considers the fact that the dissatisfactions of Negroes have two facets. The dissatisfaction is a natural accompaniment of experiencing some unsatisfactory situation, but such dissatisfaction is sharpened, and turned into a grievance, when it is perceived as a disadvantage that Negroes are suffering relative to whites, because of discriminatory treatment. Thus, objectively satisfying conditions can even be experienced as *relative* deprivation, and unsatisfactory objective conditions can be tolerated and not formulated as grievances, if they are seen as universal or personal difficulties rather than as differential treatment of Negroes. Discrimination, substitute *relative* deprivation, implemented legally or informally, is central to the reaction.

In this context, the transformation being worked in the meaning of the terms *racism* or *racist* is a significant datum. So learned a writer as Arnold Rose reminds us of the strict meaning, as he looks back from 1962 at the changes among whites in the 20 years since he and Myrdal collaborated on *An American Dilemma:* "Prejudice as an attitude was still common, but racism as a comprehensive ideology was maintained only by a few."[92] The belief in innate inferiority of Negroes and the justification this provided for discrimination and segregation have been severely undermined as an ideological system among whites. But the term, in its current usage, now provides a ready framework into which Negroes can assimilate all manner of acts and attitudes on the part of whites. This ready categorization provides endless ammunition for the belief that they are and will continue to be treated badly

[92] Myrdal, *op. cit.,* p. xliv. In addition to the other inquiries into language already suggested, the concept of "racism" might be subject to special study to determine what meanings it is now given by whites and Negroes, and to test what classes of acts are categorized under this currently all-enveloping term.

simply because of their color. Understandably, it increases their hostility. Among whites, it produces a burden of guilt for some but a bitter resentment at being misunderstood for others, and the distance then widens.

To some extent, the amount of actual inequality in certain spheres, e.g., housing and employment, can be indexed by objective measures and comparisons of the situation for equivalent groups of whites and Negroes. Comparisons of the dissatisfactions with given conditions reported by whites and Negroes living in the same communities and equated in other respects can reveal whether common felt predicaments need broad amelioration or whether some greater grievance is localized among Negroes. In addition to such questions, one must inquire into the perceptions of Negroes that their circumstances are caused by discrimination. Parallel measures of white and Negro satisfaction as of 1967, and the degree to which the cause is perceived to be discrimination, were obtained in the Michigan surveys and demonstrate that there is much dissatisfaction and a sense of grievance.[93]

The Resolution of Grievances: Measurement of Ideological Positions. At a level of specificity, there are many varieties of attitudinal response that Negroes might have to their situation. A few broader indexes are essential for summarizing a basic ideological position, and providing sensitive measurement of the changes over time in the distribution of scores in the Negro population. Two dimensions provide major coordinates for mapping ideological trends: one that might be labeled degree of militancy, and the other running from separatism to integration.[94] The former may be a more elastic dimension; what once was militant action may shrink to moderation as new levels of aggressive or violent action find their supporters. Such a scale, in the perspective of trend measurement, must be able to register *now* the lack of support for an extreme position, and thus must not be truncated by the narrowness of our present horizons. Otherwise, we will not know whether the support once existed and simply was not measured. We may think of the two dimensions in a typologi-

[93] Survey Research Center, *op. cit.,* pp. 22–26, 39–45. An especially noteworthy point is made in these pages that Negroes may feel dissatisfaction and grievance because of the attitudes they perceive whites as having toward them. The area of interperson perception is certainly of importance for intensive and continuing study.

[94] In a public statement on the Report of the Kerner Commission, Bayard Rustin mentioned a typology of four categories: "the believers in the American system, the moral crusaders"—these two types suggestive of levels of militance—"the alienated reformers who think institutions must be restructured and who seek local control by Negroes, and the alienated revolutionaries who preach a separate black state." The last type is certainly the extreme of separatism, and the third type seems to partake both of a high degree of militance and a quantum of separatism. *New York Times,* April 28, 1968, p. 36. Marx had initially conceptualized his study in terms of a fourfold typology based on the two dimensions, militancy and black nationalism. It is worthy of note that "because of the virtual absence of black nationalist support, it was not possible to proceed in this fashion." Marx, *op. cit.,* p. 109*n*.

cal scheme. Perhaps a man may move to separatism as he finds that militancy seems to be of no avail. But some separatists may be passive, and others may seek separatism by the most militant of actions. And certainly integrationists may vary in militancy.

In developing instruments to measure such patterns of attitudes, we should also obtain collateral reports of behaviors that may accompany such ideologies and thereby strengthen the evidence. For example, trends in the audiences that are *exclusively* for Negro media, in memberships *exclusively* in Negro organizations, in the racial composition of friendships should be enumerated. And we should be thoughtful about the possible correlates of such ideological positions, trying thereby to improve our mapping of the concentrations of the adherents of various ideologies, and our analysis of the causes. For example, studies document that young males have been more disposed to violent forms of action, but the surveys do not examine whether veterans of military service, those who have been trained as "specialists in violence," are most likely to exhibit such acts.[95]

With respect to separatism, a variety of indicators have been employed already which range widely over the entire ideological dimension and which provide baselines for a continuing time series. Some of these data are presented in Table 8 and show that integration is the position espoused until now by the great mass of Negroes.

Other findings from these same surveys, using different indicators, confirm the pattern shown. And a number of other studies give added support. In the 1967 study of Negro high school youth in Atlanta, 12 percent endorsed the proposition that "the more Negroes are separated from whites, the better."[96] And in a study that was a companion piece to the Coleman *et al.* report, depth interviews and prolonged anthropological observations were conducted in eight communities, ranging from very large to small, and from Deep South to North and West in late 1965. The investigators conclude: "Nowhere in the country did we discover evidence to support the idea that most black Americans subscribe to separatism and would prefer black schools for black children."[97]

The very small proportion of separatists found in all these surveys are not an inconsiderable number in absolute terms, but still the rarity of the adher-

[95] In a most interesting study of an "informal police organization" formed for protection of Negroes in a Southern city, it is noted that all recruits must have "served at least six weeks under active war combat conditions." See H. A. Nelson, "The Defenders: A Case Study of an Informal Police Organization," *Social Problems,* vol. 15, Fall, 1967, p. 132.

[96] Conyers, Farmar, and Levin, *op. cit.* In the study by Marx in 1964, 198 adults were sampled in Atlanta and 26 percent favored a separate black nation, the highest estimate I have seen for any survey.

[97] R. W. Mack, "The Negro Opposition to Black Extremism," *Saturday Review,* May 4, 1968, p. 53.

Table 8. Some Data on Ideological Support for Separatism

	Percent Favoring Separatism
Favor black nation:	
1964[a]	17
1968[b]	6
Favor working mainly in nonmixed group:	
1963[c]	11
1966[c]	10
Favor living in all-Negro neighborhood:	
1963[c]	20
1966[c]	17
Favor children not going to school with white children:	
1963[c]	10
1966[c]	11
Integration of any kind undesirable:	
1967[d]	5
Prefer child to have only Negro friends:	
1967[b]	5
Negroes should have nothing to do with whites if they can help it:	
1967[b]	9

[a] Marx, *Protest and Prejudice,* p. 28.
[b] Campbell and Schuman, *Racial Attitudes in Fifteen American Cities,* p. 16.
[c] Brink and Harris, *Black and White,* pp. 232–234.
[d] *Fortune,* January, 1968, p. 148.

ents of this ideology may seem surprising. We are again reminded of the phenomenon of pluralistic ignorance. It may well be that many Negroes overestimate the support for separatism, and thereby feel shaky about their own support for integration. As these measures of the person's own ideology are applied in the future, his estimate of the views of other Negroes ought also to be obtained.

The finding may also be surprising because we confuse the two dimensions, militance and separatism, and do not realize that intensity of drive may be directed toward a variety of goals, in this case, toward integration. And we may also mistake certain attitudes to be indicative of political separatism, which are simply expressive of pride in a cultural heritage, and not incompatible with a pluralistic society. Campbell and Schuman document that favorable attitudes toward Negro history and African languages are widespread in their sample, and argue persuasively that such measures tap a cultural dimension.

But if separatism has not, at least until now, been of wide appeal, militancy with respect to the speed of change and the strength of means to be employed to achieve change has become widespread in the Negro population. Much evidence from these many surveys in recent years is available and will not be presented.

A Methodological Note

A basic list of variables for describing the social-psychological profile of the Negro population, and for charting the changes of the future, has now been presented. The interrelations of these variables, the tracing of their patterns in segments of the large and heterogeneous Negro population, among the young and the influentials, and the parallels between these patterns and objective conditions, may take us a good way toward an understanding of the changes that will unfold. At times there will be illumination. But, no doubt, at other times the data will present puzzles that defy understanding. We cannot prevent such occurrences, but we can plan against such uncertainties. We shall have to dip down into these trends periodically, scooping up smaller samples for deeper studies, selecting groups that exhibit particular patterns—those who deviate from the general trend and those who typify it—for intensive study. Small numbers of individuals with particular initial constellations of attitudes and other characteristics should be empaneled for longitudinal studies so as to trace the processes that emerge from such roots. Trends often cannot explain themselves, but the large-scale studies will create resources for a great variety of more penetrating inquiries.

Some of the trends presented earlier, or rather the absence of a major trend in the direction of extremism and separatism, may already appear to demand explanation. These findings may appear so anomalous to some that they may feel the compulsion to plunge immediately into deep explanatory studies. Before taking that plunge, they might well ask a question: Have they made an unwarranted assumption that the modal pattern would be different simply because they have overgeneralized about the many from the behavior of a few who have been highly visible and vociferous? In fact, there may be nothing problematic at all about the trends described thus far. And before they search for mysterious causes, they should also question the *accuracy* of the findings now being obtained. Intensive studies of a methodological, rather than explanatory nature, should be begun immediately. Three types of inquiry may test the quality of the findings.

The *restriction of the universe* of conventional surveys to the non-transient, non-institutionalized, stable residents of households may not distort the description of many phenomena, but may produce a substantial bias in surveys of the attitudes of Negroes. Young, educated males living in collegiate institutions, or those in military service, may be more militant than others. Those young males now adrift from conventional milieux may be more alienated from society. Members of the latter group who have no stable residences within households are often omitted from our samples and are especially difficult to measure directly or to make estimates about by inferential means. Direct access to those in educational institutions, perhaps even in military institutions, may be possible but indirect approaches are not difficult to develop. The recent graduates of college and the recent veterans are included in our ordinary samples if only we enumerate their histories. Their measured characteristics reveal what such groups are like shortly after they are reassimilated into society.

The second and third suggestions relate to response error. From his studies of Harlem youth, Kenneth Clark warns us that

> the use of standardized questionnaires and interview procedures would result in stylized and superficial verbal responses or evasions. The outstanding finding at this time was that data obtained by these traditional methods did not plumb the depth or the complexities of the attitudes and anxieties, the many forms of irony and rage which form the truth of the lives of the people of Harlem.[98]

Whether the warning applies to studies of other segments of the Negro population remains unknown, but the cautionary note should be heeded, and our next suggestions follow from it.

Long ago it was established that the use of *Negro interviewers* in contrast with white interviewers was more likely to yield answers from Negro respondents that were critical of white society.[99] Nowadays, we might perhaps still rest content once we had assigned Negro interviewers. But as the ideological issues have become intensified and the divisions within the Negro community have grown, we may have to go beyond such gross controls on error. Perhaps the seemingly middle-class, well-educated Negro interviewer also has an inhibiting effect on some Negro respondents. It certainly seems apropos to conduct some experiments on the effects produced by Negro interviewers contrasted in styles that might symbolize different cultural or ideological positions. Such styles could be experimentally manipulated via type of clothing, language cues, and the like.

Apart from problems of interviewing, at least one set of experiments on question wording seems needed. It is ironical that social scientists have now become so sensitized to the two words, *black* vs. *Negro,* that they often go to great lengths to substitute the word *black* in their writings when referring to research findings that were based almost completely on questions where the

---

[98] Clark, *op. cit.,* p. xix.

[99] For a summary of these early studies, see H. Hyman *et al., Interviewing in Social Research.* University of Chicago Press, Chicago, 1954, pp. 159–170.

word *Negro* was used. If the terms have such a distinctive connotation, perhaps denotation, for the audience for which they write, perhaps they have equally distinctive auras of meaning for the respondents. Why then not test it by comparing questions the same in all respects except for which term is used? Perhaps also the questions addressed to whites about their racial attitudes should be tested to see whether they respond differently to the symbols, black vs. Negro.

If our present findings pass these three methodological tests, we can continue our research with confidence. If not, we shall have to improve our instruments and surmount whatever methodological barriers confront us with all the ingenuity and energy at our command.

Conclusion

To embark on a voyage of scholarly discovery, measuring the future course of race relations along specified coordinates, may seem futile in the 1970's. Some may regard it as academic—as the plotting of fine points on a navigational chart to a promised land never to be reached because of the man-made hurricane lying directly ahead. Some may regard it as ideal but impractical. They fear or anticipate so many new currents and landmarks in race relations as to make any chart obsolete before it is printed. Others facing dangerous uncharted seas try as best they can, albeit inadequately, to plot their exact location and progressively to correct their course. Thus oriented, instead of adrift, they move forward with more confidence. Perhaps we cannot see what lies ahead as clearly as Myrdal saw it so long ago. But we can share some of the "sense of hopefulness" that infused his vision of the American future, realizing that knowledge will guide us.

10

Monitoring the Quality of Criminal Justice Systems

Albert J. Reiss, Jr.

Crime is generally regarded as an indicator of the quality of life in a society. So much so that civilized communities invest considerable effort in monitoring the kind and level of criminal activity. Moreover, whenever there is a substantial rise in the level of crime officially monitored in a community or in the society, definitions of a "crime wave" emerge. Considerable effort then may be made to alter an assumed level of criminal activity.

Much has been written about limitations in defining and measuring the quality of life in a society using measures of criminal violations compiled by law-enforcement agencies. Some of the criticism has been directed at the practice of measuring criminal activity seemingly more characteristic of lower socioeconomic citizens while ignoring that of higher status citizens. Sutherland, for example, did much to call attention to white-collar crimes, "crime committed by a person of . . . high social status in the course of his occupation."[1] Official statistics of crime in the United States also have been criticized for their failure to include crimes that go unreported to the police and their compilation as an unweighted index of serious crime.[2]

---

[1] Edwin H. Sutherland, *White Collar Crime*. Dryden Press, New York, 1949.

[2] Daniel Glaser, "National Goals and Indicators for the Reduction of Crime and Delinquency," *The Annals,* vol. 371, May, 1967, pp. 104–126; Marvin Wolfgang, "Uniform Crime Reports: A Critical Appraisal," *University of Pennsylvania Law Review,* vol. 3, April, 1963, pp. 708–738; Stanton Wheeler, "Criminal Statistics: A Reformulation of the Problem," *Journal of Criminal Law, Criminology, and Police Science,* vol. 58, September 1967, pp. 317–324; Leslie T. Wilkins, "New Thinking in Criminal Statistics," *Journal of Criminal Law, Criminology, and Police Science,* vol. 56, September, 1965, pp. 277–284.

No attempt is made in this survey to reassess official indicators of crime. The discussion focuses on subjective indicators or assessments of qualitative features of crime and the criminal justice system. Considerably less effort has been devoted to monitoring the systems that define human behavior as criminal, whether it be the public, legislatures, the police, public prosecutors, or the criminal courts. The quality of life in a society is reflected by what *they* define as criminal, how *they* charge suspects or persons with violating the criminal law, and how *they* label or process them as deviant or criminal. The subjective responses that citizens make to these decisions and events emerge as evaluations. The clamor for "law and order," for "justice," and for "civil rights" by the many, or for "due process" and "equal protection of the laws" by the more literate few are evaluations about our system of criminal law.

Subjective Indicators of Quality. To measure the quality of life in a community or society is no simple matter since what is at stake are human values, human judgments, and subjective perception of social reality. Moreover, indicators of the quality of systems may refer to rather distinct levels of the system. First, there is the quality of the institutional order, for example, the quality of the institutions of freedom and public order. Second, there is the quality of any organized service, for example, the qualitative response of the police to citizen calls for service. Third, there is the quality of the behavior of (public) servants within any system, for example, whether judges dispense justice. And finally, there is the quality of the behavior or responses of those who are served. The level of violence or of hostility to policing in a population is an illustration.

In the section that follows, these major levels of any system serve as a basis for organizing our discussion of subjective indicators of the quality of criminal law, law enforcement, and the administration of justice. The reader should be aware that at any level of the system, populations representing other levels may be considered evaluators. If one is assessing the quality of police behavior, for example, it may be important to secure the evaluations not only of those being served but also of the police themselves. Indeed, any discrepancy in their perceptions or evaluations may be important.

No attempt is made to be exhaustive of types of subjective indicators, nor is much effort devoted to discussing how any indicator may be improved. Rather, the purpose is to review some major qualitative features of crime and criminal justice and the subjective assessment of them. Since in recent years qualitative aspects of law enforcement have been subject to measurement more often than other levels of the criminal justice system, examples are drawn disproportionately from studies of police and law enforcement. The reader must bear in mind that such indicators normally are equally appropriate for other levels of the system.

Quality of Criminal Law Institutions

Even a casual observer of the American scene is aware that institutions of the criminal law are challenged and changed. Challenges to the legitimacy of police authority and their discretion to search, seize evidence, or obtain confessions eventuate in new procedural criminal law. Challenges to abortion as a criminal violation eventuate in the repeal of criminal abortion statutes. And challenges to the quality of justice in the juvenile court leads to the introduction of adversary proceedings to handle juvenile offenders. At the same time one is aware that the disruption of public order of universities can eventuate in laws making it a criminal offense to disrupt a college classroom. Opposition to the limitations on police powers to search persons has given rise to "stop and frisk" laws. And cries of leniency in releasing suspects awaiting trial has led to demands for "preventive detention."

Such changes in the institutions of criminal law, whether in defining matters as criminal, delimiting the discretionary authority of public officials, or limiting freedom in the interest of public order, are aspects of the quality of life in any society. The toleration for deviance by the public, the respect for law or police authority, and the belief that justice has or has not been done are qualitative responses. Although many of the indicators for other levels of the criminal justice system are in some sense qualitative features of institutions of criminal law, the discussion in this section is restricted to aspects of institutional integration in the criminal law.

The Rule of Law

A major stabilizing institution in modern societies is the development of institutions of legality. The "rule of law" expresses the idea that legal institutions are the legitimate basis for ordering the behavior of *all* people in a society. Since this abstraction encompasses diverse interpretations about legality and order, it is no simple matter to operationalize the rule of law for scientific investigation. Popularly, the rule of law is regarded as *"respect* for law."

Divergent interpretations of the rule of law can be illustrated in recent writings on law enforcement and the rule of law. Jerome Skolnick, after noting that the police in democratic societies are ". . . required to maintain order and to do so under the rule of law," goes on to say that the rule of law ". . . emphasizes the rights of individual citizens and constraints upon the initiative of legal officials," a *due process* interpretation of the rule of law.[3] By contrast, a staff report of the National Commission on the Causes and

---

[3] Jerome H. Skolnick, *Justice without Trial: Law Enforcement in Democratic Society.* Wiley, New York, 1966, p. 6.

Prevention of Violence emphasizes ". . . the willingness of a people to accept and order their behavior according to the rules and procedures which are prescribed by political and social institutions . . . and enforced by these bodies or other institutions."[4] The "legitimacy" of legal institutions is emphasized in their treatment of the rule of law.

Lawrence Friedman emphasizes that an aspect of any rule-making system is its *penetration*. "Penetration refers . . . to the number of actors and spheres of action that a particular rule, legal institution, code, or system of law actually reaches."[5] A comparison of the "living law" with "statutory law" is then an aspect of investigating respect for the rule of law.

Friedman suggests that penetration refers to the degree to which government is successfully imposed. Its twin is *participation* in making and carrying out the law.[6] Willingness to participate as a juror, in efforts to make matters crimes, or in efforts to repeal criminal law, are instances of participation under a rule of law.

Some major indicators, then, of accepting the rule of law are respect for law as a means of ordering behavior, the penetration of given laws and codes in populations, the granting of legitimacy to legal institutions and organizations, concern for due process, and willingness to participate in roles in the legal system.

Respect for the Rule of Law and Legitimately Constituted Authority. Despite the central position of respect for the rule of law in legal theory and presumptions about its functioning in societal integration, attempts to measure respect are limited. For that reason, we cannot measure whether public confidence or respect for the rule of law varies significantly over time. Few attempts have been made to measure general respect for the rule of law and legitimately constituted authority. It is more common to measure respect for some legitimately constituted authority, for example, the police or the Supreme Court.

Given changes in the public's awareness of crime and public order, the confidence or respect for the rule of law may be expected to vary as well. Bayley and Mendelsohn found that, in 1969, three of every four Denver citizens agreed that "respect for law and authority is declining."[7] This question unfortunately combines measuring the idea that law orders behavior with

---

[4] James S. Campbell *et al.,* "Law and Order Reconsidered," in *Report of the Task Force on Law and Law Enforcement to the National Commission on the Causes and Prevention of Violence.* Government Printing Office, Washington, D.C., 1969, p. 8.

[5] Lawrence M. Friedman, "Legal Culture and Social Development," *Working Paper #1.* Center for Law and Behavioral Science, University of Wisconsin, 1968, p. 27.

[6] *Ibid.,* p. 29.

[7] David H. Bayley and Harold Mendelsohn, *Minorities and the Police: Confrontation in America.* Free Press, New York, 1969, pp. 40–41.

that of measuring the perceived legitimacy of constituted authority, but the two could be measured separately.

Of considerable interest in measuring changes in respect for the rule of law is its relationship to perceived changes in the behavior of citizens. Are shifts in challenges to legitimately constituted authority a major precondition for perceptions of diminished respect for the rule of law? What leads to perceptions of an increase in respect for the rule of law? Perceptions of changes in respect for law and authority do not necessarily mean that there is any over-all decline in expressed trust, confidence, or respect in legitimately constituted authority. There is good reason to believe that pluralistic ignorance abounds in such perceptions, if data on public respect for police authority are taken as an indicator. Public expression of respect for police authority runs high. A 1965 cross section of the population of the United States, for example, found that 70 percent of the population said they had a great deal of respect for the police in their area and 22 percent said they had some; only 4 percent reported they had hardly any respect.[8] For the same question in June, 1967, the proportion of citizens saying they had a great deal of respect was 77 percent. Again only 4 percent said they had hardly any respect.[9]

Perceptions of change in respect for law and authority must have at least a moderate correlation with perceptions that respect of others for law and authority is declining. Reiss found that only a minority of 7 percent of all residents in high-crime-rate areas of Boston, Chicago, and Washington, D.C., said they had little or no respect for the police.[10] A majority of 54 percent said they had great respect for the police, while a substantial minority of 37 percent said they had mixed feelings about them. Nonetheless, among those reporting that the public had changed, a majority of the 71 percent who regarded public opinion as changing negatively toward the police held positive opinions of the police.[11] Perhaps what shapes perceptions that disrespect for law and authority is growing among others is the behavior of a minority that is perceived as consciously flouting authority. Such perceptions of disrespect in others may at the same time reinforce one's own respect for law and authority.

Nowhere is respect for the rule of law more crucial than among the agents of criminal justice. Especially crucial are the perceptions of the police. Studies by McNamara of changes in opinions of police from recruitment

---

[8] American Institute of Public Opinion Poll (AIPO), April 25, 1965.

[9] AIPO, June, 1967.

[10] Albert J. Reiss, Jr., "Public Perceptions and Recollections about Crime, Law Enforcement, and Criminal Justice," in the President's Commission on Law Enforcement and Administration of Justice, *Studies in Crime and Law Enforcement in Major Metropolitan Areas, Field Surveys III*, vol. I, sect. II. Government Printing Office, Washington, D.C., 1967, p. 54.

[11] *Ibid.*, p. 56.

through training and experience in the field show that police training, and particularly experience, in New York City weakens the officer's sense of authority appropriate to his position.[12] At the beginning of police training, only 24 percent of all officers agreed or strongly agreed with the statement: "The present system of state and local laws has undermined the patrolman's authority to a dangerous extent." At the end of training, 34 percent were in agreement, and the proportion rose to 76 percent of all patrolmen by the end of the first year. Likewise, while 76 percent of all patrolmen agreed at the beginning of training that "Generally speaking, patrolmen today have enough legal authority to get their jobs done efficiently," only 35 percent thought so at the end of two years' experience in the field.[13]

Officers not only saw their general authority undermined by law, but they regarded the courts as undermining their authority as well. Police recruits generally believed that the courts would accept them as reliable witnesses to crime events. Only 19 percent agreed with the statement: "The courts have tended in recent years to discount the testimony of patrolmen where there are other witnesses or there is no other proof regarding an alleged crime, offense, or violation." By the end of training this had risen to 45 percent of the cohort, and to 60 percent after two years in the field.[14] Whatever the effects of training and experience in police work, there appear to be strong effects on a police officer's sense of authority.

A measure of the quality of authority in the system is the *trust* that citizens are willing to place in authority and its exercise. Although respect and trust are closely related properties of authority, they may be separable aspects. To my knowledge, only The Netherlands measures trust in police authority. A 1966 poll in The Netherlands showed that 92 percent of the Dutch citizens "trusted" the Dutch police force.[15] The degree of trust Dutch citizens expressed in their police is roughly the same as the degree of respect American citizens have for their police.

An aspect of the respect for legitimately constituted authority is the prestige accorded occupations and offices in the criminal justice system. The surveys of occupational prestige in the United States have consistently shown that lawyers are among the top prestige occupations in the United States and judgeships are a top office. Indeed, the position of U.S. Supreme Court Justice ranks highest among the offices included in studies measuring prestige of

[12] John H. McNamara, "Uncertainties in Police Work: The Relevance of Police Recruits' Backgrounds and Training," in David Bordua, ed., *The Police: Six Sociological Essays.* Wiley, New York, 1967, Table 8.

[13] *Ibid.,* Table 8.

[14] *Ibid.,* Table 8.

[15] Nederlands Instituur voor do Publieke Opinie Poll (NIPO), Mar. 28, 1966.

occupations and offices. There has been remarkably little change in the prestige of these occupations and offices since 1925. A correlation of .99 was observed between prestige scores derived from the 1947 National Opinion Research Center (NORC) study of occupational prestige and a 1963 replication.[16]

Given this remarkable stability in the prestige rating of occupations from 1946 to 1963, one of the few occupations to display an increase in prestige was that of policeman. There was a sharp rise in the percent rating it excellent or above average, from 31 percent in 1947 to 54 percent in 1963.[17] Moreover, compared with other occupations in the legal system, the public was more inclined to regard as "too high" the social standing of lawyers than they were that of the police: 2 in 10 thought the social standing of lawyers was "too high" but only 1 in 10 thought this of the police.[18] The public also affirms that "people who take on the job of policing deserve a lot more thanks and respect than they get from the public," as 85 percent of persons surveyed in Washington, D.C., high-crime-rate areas in 1966 agreed.[19] There undoubtedly is considerable variation in the prestige of various police occupations and offices, though comparable measurement has not been undertaken. A Gallup poll in 1965 found that 86 percent of the college, 81 percent of the high school, and 65 percent of the grade school educated said they would be pleased if their son decided to become an FBI agent.[20] One doubts that it would be quite that high for line police officers, or would one expect the same variation by education.

Despite this "favorable" regard that the public shows for policing, police officers believe that the prestige of police work has been declining. McNamara found that only 12 percent of the police recruits he surveyed in New York City believed that the respect that citizens have for a patrolman has been steadily increasing over the years[21] and Reiss found that 59 percent of all police surveyed believe that the prestige of policing is lower today than

---

[16] Robert W. Hodge, Paul M. Siegel, and Peter H. Rossi, "Occupational Prestige in the United States, 1925–63," *American Journal of Sociology,* vol. 70, November, 1964, pp. 286–302.

[17] *Ibid.,* Table 1.

[18] Robert W. Hodge, "The Public, the Police, and the Administration of Justice," unpublished manuscript, National Opinion Research Center, University of Chicago, December, 1965, p. 7.

[19] Albert D. Biderman *et al., Report on a Pilot Study in the District of Columbia on Victimization and Attitudes toward Law Enforcement, Field Surveys I.* President's Commission on Law Enforcement and the Administration of Justice, Government Printing Office, Washington, D.C., 1967, p. 135.

[20] AIPO, Aug. 8, 1965.

[21] McNamara, *op. cit.,* p. 198.

20 years ago.[22] Police officers, of course, overrate the prestige of their occupation relative to other raters, as do members of most occupations. Yet, the police regard their work as having much higher professional status than the public would grant. McNamara found that 75 percent of the police officers in New York City with two years' experience on the force thought that "police work should be ranked alongside that of doctors or lawyers."[23]

An aspect of the prestige of any occupation is the willingness of persons to enter the occupation. Negroes have both accorded the police less prestige and have been less willing to consider it an occupational choice. Reiss found this was true for both the general public and police officers.[24] Particularly striking is some evidence that young people are less likely now to consider police work a future occupational choice. Bouma found that only 8 percent of the white youth and only 3 percent of the Negro youth "would like to be a policeman when they grow up."[25] Such willingness, of course, provides a sufficient pool of manpower, assuming qualification for police work. But occupational prestige surveys would do well to measure the prestige of occupations and willingness to enter them for persons under age 21. Indeed, for many of the measures of quality of the criminal justice system, persons at least 14 years and over, rather than persons 21 and over, are the relevant population.

Penetration of Norms, Laws, and Sanctions. The extent that given norms penetrate populations is one indicator of moral integration in a society. Demands for legalizing behavior or proscribing it under the criminal law similarly penetrate populations in varying degrees. Monitoring issues that may be controversial in repeal of the criminal law or in introducing matters to be considered criminal is an essential adjunct to the legislative process in modern societies. A comparison of the penetration of several norms across countries provides some indication of the potentiality for making previously civil matters criminal.

Prior to legislation to stop motorists or to have compulsory breathalyzer tests, 59 percent of the English population approved of the proposal and only 28 percent disagreed.[26] An even larger proportion (78 percent) agreed that it

---

[22] Albert J. Reiss, Jr., "Career Orientations, Job Satisfaction, and the Assessment of Law Enforcement Problems by Police Officers," in President's Commission on Law Enforcement and the Administration of Justice, *Studies in Crime and Law Enforcement in Major Metropolitan Areas, Field Surveys III,* vol. II, sect. II. Government Printing Office, Washington, D.C., 1967, pp. 91–94 and Table 43.

[23] McNamara, *op. cit.,* p. 218.

[24] Reiss, "Career Orientations, Job Satisfaction, and the Assessment of Law Enforcement Problems by Police Officers," pp. 7–22, and "Public Perceptions and Recollections about Crime, Law Enforcement, and Criminal Justice," pp. 53–56.

[25] Donald Bouma, *Kids and Cops: A Study in Mutual Hostility.* Eerdmans, Grand Rapids, Mich., 1969, p. 47.

[26] Social Surveys (Gallup Poll) Ltd. (SOC), January, 1966.

should be an offense to drive after drinking "more than the equivalent of three whiskies."[27] Although the question was worded somewhat differently, 76 percent of the Australian population favored laws such as making driving after drinking a criminal offense and instituting a compulsory breathalyzer test; only 18 percent were against these measures prior to legislation.[28] Although the data are not strictly comparable, at a later date only 40 percent of the U.S. citizens were in favor of such laws, while 54 percent were against them.[29] Undoubtedly, the "drink but don't drive, and drive but don't drink" norm has a lower penetration in the United States than in these other countries. This lower penetration may inhibit legislation and enforcement similar to that in parts of Europe and the Scandinavian countries.

A more controversial issue is that of consenting adult statutes relating to homosexual behavior. Again, the contrast between Great Britain and the United States is of interest in comparing the penetration of norms that could eventuate in the legalization of behavior formerly regarded as criminal. In 1965, 63 percent of the English population agreed that homosexual acts between consenting adults in private should be regarded as a noncriminal matter; only a minority of 36 percent thought it should be continued as a criminal matter.[30] The U.S. population was far more split in July, 1966, with 39 percent believing it should not be a criminal act and 44 percent regarding it as a criminal matter.[31]

If one is monitoring norms for changes in them that could lead to legislation repealing criminal laws, or vice versa, one may also be interested in investigating whether the stand a legislator takes on controversial issues affects voting behavior toward him. During the public debate over consenting adult statutes in England, the polls attempted to measure whether one's position as a Member of Parliament would be in jeopardy were one to vote for a consenting adult statute. While opinion is not a necessary condition for behavior, it is of interest that three out of four citizens said that, were their M.P. to vote for a consenting adult statute, it would make no difference in their voting for him at the next general election; 4 percent said it would make them even more likely to do so. Only a minority of 21 percent said it would make them less likely to vote for him at the next general election.[32]

Some of the conflict between citizens and law-enforcement officials undoubtedly comes about because of differences in the penetration of norms and laws in their respective populations. Monitoring of the penetration of such

---

[27] SOC, October, 1965.
[28] Australian Public Opinion Polls (APOP), April, 1966.
[29] AIPO, 1968.
[30] National Opinion Polls (NOP), October, 1965.
[31] AIPO, July, 1966.
[32] NOP, October, 1965.

norms may facilitate police handling of these matters, particularly if ways are sought to relate the police more effectively to the public in the formation of policies to govern their discretionary authority to arrest.

Although there may be near unanimity in the public over matters that are to be made criminal at law, there may be a substantial difference in consensus about their seriousness and the sanctions to be imposed for their violation. An indicator of the penetration of law and of sanctions is the extent to which statutory and law-enforcement definitions of "a crime" and of "seriousness of crimes" corresponds with those of various publics. Durea, Sellin and Wolfgang, and Biderman report such comparisons.[33] Discrepancies may occur in such scales, however, if they are monitored and compared over time.

Another indicator of the penetration of the law is the "complaints" the public makes by calling the police to handle matters they regard as "criminal." Such lay definitions do not always correspond with those of police or other officials. What the public regards as "criminal," the law may treat as a "private" or "civil" matter, as is the case with many disputes that arise in common affairs. Wilkins observes that probably "the threshold value of disapproval for a constant event will change with time and from place to place, that complaints will reflect the public expectation of behavior, and that this will provide a relative rather than an absolute measure of 'crime.' "[34]

Discretionary Authority and Due Process. The system of criminal justice grants enormous discretionary authority to the police to arrest, to the prosecutor to issue warrants, and to judges over matters of "justice." Such discretionary authority may be challenged within the system in a series of appellate proceedings, by legislation restricting or granting discretionary authority, and by the power of citizens to make their views effective.

The quality of the exercise of discretionary authority is an essential aspect of the quality of life in a civilized society. Evaluations of the "openness" of a society to deviation and the "freedom for individuals" from "state intervention" should be monitored in the assessment of the quality of discretionary authority. In the United States, attempts have been made to develop indicators of the willingness of citizens to grant authority to the police when "constitutional rights" may be at issue. Here our interest focuses on the assessment the public makes of "police rights" to discretion, in contrast to the citizen's rights to freedom from police authority and intervention.

By custom and by law, the police in modern democratic societies pos-

[33] Mervin A. Durea, "An Experimental Study of Attitudes toward Juvenile Delinquency," *Journal of Applied Psychology,* vol. 17, October, 1933, pp. 522–534; Thorsten Sellin and Marvin Wolfgang, *The Measurement of Delinquency.* Wiley, New York, 1964, Chap. 19; Albert D. Biderman, "Surveys of Population Samples for Estimating Crime Incidence," *The Annals,* vol. 374, November, 1967, pp. 23–24.

[34] Wilkins, *op. cit.,* p. 281.

sess a virtual monopoly over the internal exercise of force. Although there is some variation among the states regarding the circumstances under which the police may legitimately use force, generally it is limited to the maintenance of public order and in sustaining the power to arrest. Studies in Washington, D.C., showed that a substantial majority of the citizens (73 percent) agreed that the police ought to have leeway to act tough "when they have to," a grant of considerable legitimacy to their use of force.[35] More precise measures of the conditions under which the public "legitimates" the use of force are necessary, however, if opinion is to serve as a guide to policy.

The discretionary power of the police to arrest hinges upon their having reason to believe that a crime has been committed, the doctrine of probable cause. An NORC study found that 42 percent of the U.S. population thought that the police should risk arresting an innocent person rather than letting the criminal get away, while the majority of 58 percent thought that the police should be sure they are getting the right person before making an arrest.[36] The level of certainty expected by the majority undoubtedly is greater than that ordinarily granted the police.

Appellate decisions are not always regarded as legitimate by segments of the public, particularly when the decision extends "rights" that the public believes endanger their safety and the authority of the police to prevent and control crime. The legitimacy granted by the public to such appellate decisions can be monitored, as the constitutional decisions with respect to criminal procedure and police practice have been in a number of surveys conducted during the 1960's. Some of these questions should be asked at periodic intervals to assess the extent to which such decisions become legitimated over time.[37]

Consideration of one aspect of the discretionary authority of the police may provide an example of this kind of evaluation. Studies for the National Crime Commission measured the conditions under which citizens legitimated the right of the police to "stop and question" them. Studies by Reïss in high-crime-rate areas of several major cities showed that 69 percent of the citizens were willing to have an officer question them "about a lot of things to find out if he thought you committed a crime." An even larger majority thought the police should be able to stop citizens and ask them to give their name and address (79 percent). An absolute majority of 56 percent set no conditions

---

[35] Biderman *et al., op. cit.,* p. 146.

[36] Phillip H. Ennis, *Criminal Victimization in the United States: A Report of a National Survey, Field Surveys II.* President's Commission on Law Enforcement and the Administration of Justice, Government Printing Office, Washington, D.C., 1967, p. 65.

[37] Biderman *et al., op. cit.,* pp. 148–151; Jennie McIntyre, "Public Attitudes toward Crime and Law Enforcement," *The Annals,* vol. 374, November, 1967, pp. 43–44; Ennis, *op. cit.,* pp. 64–72; Reiss, "Public Perceptions and Recollections about Crime, Law Enforcement, and Criminal Justice," pp. 78–90.

for being stopped and asked to identify themselves and to give information about what they are doing, where they have been, and similar matters.[38] Correlatively, however, almost 2 in 10 citizens did not believe the police had a right to stop and question them under any circumstances.

Other constitutional questions of rights of the criminally accused have been surveyed similarly, following decisions by the Supreme Court. Among them are procedures for interrogation of the criminally accused,[39] reasonableness of search procedures,[40] stop and search and search and seizure,[41] the right to counsel,[42] and the admissibility of confessions.[43] Some of these issues also have been investigated in other English-speaking societies. Citizens of Great Britain, for example, are more likely to approve of search of the premises and seizure of evidence than are citizens of the United States.[44]

Many survey questions that try to measure public evaluations of appellate court decisions show an inadequate understanding of legal issues. To fault them on their understanding of legal issues is not to suggest that survey questions must be phrased in legal jargon. Rather, it is to argue for accuracy in the statement of legal issues. Consider, for example, a 1966 NORC survey question: "The Supreme Court has ruled that in criminal cases the police may not question a suspect without his lawyer being present, unless the suspect agrees to be questioned without a lawyer. Are you in favor of this Supreme Court decision or opposed to it?"[45] The phrasing of the question suggests that under no circumstances may the police question a suspect without a lawyer being present. Although Miranda failed to make clear whether such rights pertained only to questioning when placed in custody (indeed, whether in the station house), the failure to limit the question to interrogation of suspects in custody renders it less useful for evaluating public agreement *with* the Miranda decision (*Miranda v. Arizona,* 384 U.S. 436, 1966).

Willingness of Citizens to Accept Roles in the Criminal Justice System. The criminal justice system involves citizens in a rather large number of roles. Our system of law enforcement is organized for citizens to serve as complainants in mobilizing the police and in seeking warrants from the public

[38] Reiss, p. 87.

[39] Ennis, *op cit.,* pp. 64–65.

[40] Angus Campbell and Howard Schuman, "Racial Attitudes in Fifteen American Cities," in *Supplemental Studies for the National Advisory Commission on Civil Disorders.* Government Printing Office, Washington, D.C., July, 1968, p. 42.

[41] Reiss, "Public Perceptions and Recollections about Crime, Law Enforcement, and Criminal Justice," pp. 89–90; Joel Aberbach and Jack Walker, "The Attitudes of Blacks and Whites toward City Services: Implications for Public Policy," University of Michigan Institute of Public Policy Studies, Discussion Paper No. 10, 1969, p. 13.

[42] Ennis, *op. cit.,* pp. 65, 69.

[43] Minnesota Poll (MINN), December, 1965.

[44] SOC, August, 1967.

[45] Ennis, *op. cit.,* p. 65.

prosecutor. Their role as witnesses to criminal violations is integral to the functioning of law enforcement, the prosecution of crimes, and trial proceedings. The courts also make provision for citizens in the role of juror. Even when charged with an offense, the "accused" is expected "to tell the truth" and to cooperate in the trial proceedings. Disruption of a trial proceeding is a breach of contempt. Over and above these roles that are formally provided in the criminal justice system, citizens are expected to serve in yet other ways when the situation arises. Thus, the police expect citizens to aid them in their time of trouble or to serve as informants about criminals.

The willingness of citizens to assume formal roles in the criminal justice system indicates both the extent to which they will participate in the rule of law and the quality of their participation in the system. Several measures of the willingness of citizens to participate in the criminal justice system have been used in survey research. They are discussed here as measures that can be developed further as indicators of citizen participation in the system. They are: (1) the role of citizens as mobilizers of the police in their status as victims; (2) the role of citizens in their formal roles of complainant, witness, juror, and related roles; (3) the role of citizens in cooperating with policemen in police work; (4) the willingness of citizens to become formally registered in a criminal justice system.[46]

The crime-victim surveys for the National Crime Commission made abundantly clear that at least half of all criminal victimization of citizens is not reported to the police.[47] Apart from the importance of monitoring crime by sample surveys of victimization from specific types of crime, investigation of their reasons for not mobilizing the police are important in understanding crime and law enforcement in a society.

Previous investigations show that several factors appear important in motivating persons to mobilize the police when they are *victimized* by crime. The more serious the crime, the more likely a citizen is to report it.[48] The reporting of property losses is enhanced if the loss is covered by insurance, as it generally is for automobiles.[49] The single most important reason for *not* reporting crimes to the police is a citizen belief that the "police can't do anything about it."[50] A substantial proportion of citizens fail to report some

[46] *Ibid.*, Chaps. 2–5; Biderman *et al.*, *op. cit.*, Chap. 2; Albert J. Reiss, Jr., "Measurement of the Nature and Amount of Crime," in President's Commission on Law Enforcement and the Administration of Justice, *Studies in Crime and Law Enforcement in Major Metropolitan Areas, Field Surveys III*, vol. 1. Government Printing Office, Washington, D.C., 1967, pp. 143–171.

[47] Biderman, *op. cit.*, pp. 28–32.

[48] *Ibid.*, pp. 23–24; Ennis, *op. cit.*, p. 41.

[49] Biderman *et al.*, *op. cit.*, p. 54; Ennis, *op. cit.*, p. 41.

[50] Biderman *et al.*, *op. cit.*, pp. 153–154; Ennis, *op. cit.*, pp. 43–48; Reiss, "Public Perceptions and Recollections about Crime, Law Enforcement, and Criminal Justice," p. 67.

crimes because they do not consider the crime a police matter.[51] Among their specific reasons are that they consider it a "private" matter, they regard it as too trivial for the police to be bothered, and they do not want to bring harm to the offender.[52] Only a very small proportion mention fear of reprisal or of punishment by the police as a major reason for not reporting crimes to the police.[53]

The data on reporting of crimes to the police strongly suggest that citizens mobilize the police when they expect a gain from their act of reporting. Generally the gain is one where they expect to recover their loss, as is the case for reporting crimes covered by insurance. A part of this gain in reporting victimization from crime to the police appears to arise from moral indignation over their victimization—though additional investigation seems necessary to confirm this finding.[54]

The willingness of citizens to call the police when they *witness* a crime in which they are not victims is apparently low.[55] This may seem somewhat surprising, given their belief that law enforcement is the most effective means for controlling crime. The major reason citizens give for their not notifying the police about crimes they witnessed is that they "do not want to get involved."[56] For some citizens, this means no more than that they do not want to take the time, recognizing that talking to the police and going to court takes time away from work and may actually involve some loss of income. For others, it appears to arise from a genuine sense of disengagement from responsibility. "I am not my brother's keeper" was a typical sentiment.[57]

It is a surprising fact that citizens give relatively few reasons for failing to report crimes to the police that imply negative images of the police. Indeed, they seem more likely to hold negative images of the cost of being a citizen when the case may be prosecuted in the criminal justice system than they do negative images of the police.

The surveys of criminal victimization have focused far more on reasons why citizens do not call the police than on why they call the police to report crimes. To understand the basis for mobilizing the police and other levels of the criminal justice system, we shall need to measure more carefully what motivates citizens to participate by calling the police as well as why they fail to fulfill these roles.

Few studies have investigated the willingness of citizens to participate in

[51] Ennis, *op. cit.*, Tables 24 and 25.

[52] *Ibid.*

[53] Biderman *et al.*, *op. cit.*, pp. 154–155.

[54] Albert J. Reiss, Jr., *The Police and The Public,* Yale University Press, New Haven, 1971, pp. 68–70.

[55] Biderman, *op. cit.*, 1967, pp. 154–155.

[56] *Ibid.*, Tables 3-24 and 3-25.

[57] *Ibid.*, p. 154.

other formal roles in the criminal justice system. Investigation of excuses from jury duty suggest that fear of financial loss or unwillingness to deprive oneself or others for a period of time are factors motivating withdrawal from participation as jurors. Similarly, the unwillingness to serve as a witness is affected by the degree of intimacy in the relationship of complainant and offender. Young people, particularly, seem unwilling to report they witnessed a criminal violation when the offender is their friend.[58]

The role of witness in a civil or criminal proceeding is fairly common; almost one in four persons in a major metropolitan area such as Detroit report they have served as a witness.[59] It is difficult to estimate what proportion of citizens have participated as a witness in a criminal proceeding, however. For citizens in high-crime-rate areas of three major metropolitan areas, 11 percent reported such participation.[60] Citizens who report participating in criminal trials as witnesses were more than twice as likely to appear for the prosecution as for the defense.[61] This is a not unexpected result since, in the adversary system of justice, the citizen is expected to fulfill the role of complainant-witness. Unfortunately, no estimates are available for estimating citizen participation in trial proceedings, using the trial as a base, though official court records of proceedings might readily provide such information.

The extent of participation in court proceedings as reported by citizens is in keeping with the widely documented "delay in the courts." While about 4 in 10 witnesses report they appeared in court only once, 2 in 10 said they appeared twice, and 4 in 10 had to appear three or more times.[62] The modal time witnesses reported spending in court was half a day, although almost one-half of all respondents said they spent a day or more in court.

Participation as a witness in either a civil or a criminal proceeding is not altogether a satisfactory experience for citizens. More than 1 in 4 in the Detroit study of civil and criminal trials[63] and almost 1 in 3 in criminal trials report dissatisfaction in some way with the proceedings.[64] The most common response is a personal reaction to the outcome as unfair. Yet 2 in 3 Detroit witnesses reacted negatively to some feature of the proceeding. Roughly one-fifth objected in some way to the conduct of court officials (judges and lawyers). For the most part they regarded them as "officious" or "bureaucratic."

---

[58] Bouma, *op. cit.,* pp. 61–63 and p. 70.

[59] Leon Mayhew and Albert J. Reiss, Jr., "In Search of Justice," University of Michigan, Detroit Area Study, April, 1967.

[60] Reiss, "Public Perceptions and Recollections about Crime, Law Enforcement, and Criminal Justice," Appendix A, p. 18.

[61] *Ibid.*

[62] *Ibid.*

[63] Mayhew and Reiss, *op. cit.*

[64] Reiss, "Public Perceptions and Recollections about Crime, Law Enforcement, and Criminal Justice," Appendix A, p. 18.

An additional one-fourth found the adversarial nature of the proceeding disturbing, particularly the interrogation procedures. Minorities of 1 in 20 acknowledged they were disturbed by their ignorance of the proceedings and a similar minority (all women) said they were frightened in the courtroom.[65]

These studies are for selected metropolitan populations and, therefore, pose problems of generalizing on a national basis. They strongly suggest that a substantial minority of the population that has participated as a witness in the adversary system of proceedings is disturbed by either the "quality of justice" or the "quality of the proceedings." An important research undertaking would be to determine whether those who have had any contact with criminal or adversary proceedings are less favorable to an adversary form of proceeding than those who have not had such experience. The Mayhew and Reiss study opens the possibility that a major objection to one's role as witness is the "interrogation" procedure which follows participation in the adversary system. Citizens who are interrogated as witnesses may be no more favorable to the procedure when used in the courtroom than when used in the interrogation room of the police station.

The role of witness was further explored in studies for the National Crime Commission. Citizens were asked whether they had ever refused to serve in the role of witness when asked. Roughly 1 in 20 said that at some time they had refused.[66] Of those who saw themselves as having information to serve as a witness, roughly 2 in 10 said they would not volunteer to be a witness.[67] Exploring the reasons why one accepts the role as witness and why one refuses it, the major factors citizens cite as motivating them to be a witness are a sense of "civic obligation" and a sense of "loyalty" to some person. Only a minority of citizens saw their role as that of helping to enforce the law, punish criminals, or aid the police in their work.[68] Those that reported they would not serve as witnesses in court emphasized that they felt there would be serious "repercussions," or that they did not want to get involved in what was "not their business."

Jury service is far less common than serving as a witness, although reliable information on the extent (much less quality) of participation as a juror is lacking for the U.S. population. Sample surveys of witnesses and jurors in trial proceedings seem a more appropriate way to investigate both the quality of the proceeding and citizen reaction to it, given their low frequency in the general population.

Considerably more investigation of the factors involved in participation

[65] Mayhew and Reiss, *op. cit.*

[66] Reiss, "Public Perceptions and Recollections about Crime, Law Enforcement, and Criminal Justice," Appendix A, p. 19.

[67] *Ibid.*

[68] *Ibid.*

out of a sense of "civic duty" or obligation should be undertaken in studies of witnesses and jurors if one is to understand better what leads citizens to fulfill their formal roles in the system of justice. Additional investigation is also necessary to understand the reactions of citizens to the quality of the proceeding, particularly to treatment in the courtroom. Among the matters that should be investigated is citizen determination of whether "justice is done." One is impressed with the substantial proportion of citizens who participate as jurors and report they thought the outcome was unfair.[69] Although a similar response is obtained from persons who serve as witnesses, the dissatisfaction of witnesses with the outcome is more reasonable to expect as they are cast in adversary roles for the state or for the defendant. Such is not the case, however, for the role of juror.

The major informal roles in the criminal justice system arise in connection with the law-enforcement system and the system of prosecution and defense. What is surprising is how little is known about *any* roles in the system of criminal prosecution in the United States—an unexplored terrain in the sociology of law that may soon be regarded as the turf of some sociologist.

The greater visibility cast upon informal roles in the law-enforcement system through appellate decisions on the role of informants (the protection of the police officer's right to protect the identity of his informant, for example), or the startling failure of citizens to fulfill a helping role to citizens in distress (the Kitty Genovese type of case), or of citizens to aid policemen when in trouble provide us with some information on these citizen roles in the law-enforcement system.

Studies of crimes against businesses and other organizations for the National Crime Commission disclose that businessmen, managers, or heads of organizations are particularly cooperative as informants with the police. More than one-third of all these people helped the police at some time by providing information the police sought.[70] Skolnick has analyzed the way police employ deviants as informants, although his study provides no way of estimating the extent of that participation.[71] It might be worthwhile to estimate the extent of citizen participation in police informant roles, defining such roles as ones where the police solicit information from the citizen on criminal matters, but the citizen is not directly involved in its production.

The police seem far more interested in citizens' providing information by cooperating in the "investigation" of a criminal matter than in their special role as "informant." Nothing is known about how citizens respond to this role, although police-officer satisfaction with citizen participation in the role

[69] Mayhew and Reiss, *op. cit.*

[70] Reiss, "Public Perceptions and Recollections of Crime, Law Enforcement, and Criminal Justice," p. 14, 16–17.

[71] Skolnick, *op. cit.*, Chap. 6.

has been investigated. James Q. Wilson found that a majority of police sergeants in Chicago do not agree that "civilians generally cooperate with police officers in their work."[72] McNamara found that experience with police work substantially alters the perception officers have of citizen cooperation with the police in their work. While at the end of their police training only 1 in 5 patrolmen believed they would never receive the cooperation from the public that is needed in their work, at the end of two years, 1 in 2 believed that was the case.[73] What is more, 6 of every 10 patrolmen felt at the end of two years' experience that "it is difficult to persuade people to give patrolmen the information they need."[74] Police officers assigned to high-crime-rate areas of major metropolitan cities are even less likely to conclude that the public is cooperative in giving information, with white officers particularly skeptical of help from Negro citizens.[75]

Police officers, of course, may exaggerate the unwillingness of citizens to cooperate with them in their work. When Bouma compared the willingness of inner-city youth to cooperate with the police with police officer expectations about cooperation from youth in the same city, he concluded that, even though inner-city youth are less willing to work with the police in the reporting of a crime than are other youth, the amount of cooperation they are willing to give the police is greater than the police expect.[76] Perhaps the fact that the police do not encounter a random set of the citizens in their work is important in explaining this discrepancy. Police work is disproportionately concentrated among persons who have had or are in trouble. The way that the police co-opt citizens in police work also may affect these reciprocal evaluations. When police departments actively encourage citizens to provide anonymous information on crimes, they report a substantial increase in such information. A Gallup poll in 1968 reported that 87 percent of the U.S. population said they would be "willing to work with local police in a community anticrime operation and report on any suspicious activity in the neighborhood." This willingness varied with the education of the citizen; 79 percent of those with a grade school education and 93 percent of those with some college reporting such willingness.[77]

Police officers commonly complain that the public will not come to their aid when in trouble. McNamara found that roughly 6 in 10 New York City

---

[72] James Q. Wilson, "Police Morale, Reform, and Citizen Respect: The Chicago Case," in David Bordua, *The Police: Six Sociological Essays,* Wiley, New York, 1967.

[73] McNamara, *op. cit.,* p. 221.

[74] *Ibid.*

[75] Reiss, "Career Orientations, Job Satisfaction, and the Assessment of Law Enforcement Problems by Police Officers," p. 79; Bouma, *op. cit.,* pp. 124–127.

[76] Bouma, *op. cit.,* pp. 124–126.

[77] AIPO, 1968.

officers did not agree that "most citizens would try to help a patrolman who is being attacked on the street."[78] Officers in high-crime-rate areas were even less likely to believe they could count on citizen aid when in time of trouble, as 87 percent expressed that belief.[79] Officers believe that citizens fail to aid them because they don't want to get involved, fear retaliation from other citizens, or dislike the police.[80]

It is unclear whether or not citizens in Continental democracies are more willing to accept what specialists on civil liberties consider prohibitive restrictions on freedom than are citizens in the United States. Practice in the Continental democracies where national registration systems, systems of registration on movement, and other citizen intelligence and bookkeeping systems prevail suggests that may be the case. The extent to which citizens support, or fail to support, controversial proposals such as citizen registration or identification is rarely investigated in the United States. A May, 1966, Social Surveys poll of the British public included the statement: "The Home Office is examining a scheme to introduce compulsory fingerprinting of adults as a method of combating crime. Do you think this is a good idea or a bad idea?" It found that 64 percent thought it a good idea, and only 23 percent a bad idea. Moreover, 72 percent said that, if the scheme were a voluntary one, they would be fingerprinted. But 19 percent said they would not.[81]

Accountability and Quality of Criminal Justice Organizations

A central problem of democratic societies is how public officials and agencies shall be held accountable to the citizens they serve. Accountability exists as a structural feature of organizations as well as in the moral conduct of men. Little is known about how citizens evaluate the *quality* of the service received from public officials or of their knowledge and beliefs about how organizations are to be held accountable to them. Much investigation is necessary to determine what leads citizens to complain, or fail to complain, when they are dissatisfied with law-enforcement and criminal justice services.

A gap arises in our knowledge about the quality of service in the criminal justice system because our indicators generally specify "professional" rather than "client" criteria of quality. What is more, we know little about how the clients who are arrested, jailed, bailed, bonded, charged, tried, and convicted or treated, view these processes distributively and collectively.

There are a number of salient features about the nature and quality of

---

[78] McNamara, *op. cit.,* Table 15.

[79] Reiss, "Career Orientations, Job Satisfaction, and the Assessment of Law Enforcement Problems by Police Officers," Table 41 and p. 90.

[80] *Ibid.*

[81] SOC, May, 1966.

public services that should be monitored on a continuing basis. They include: (1) public perceptions of the problems and the quality of the operating service offered; (2) the quality of sanctions employed for failing to conform with the system; (3) the quality of "justice"; and (4) the effect of the operating system on its agents. Each of these is discussed below in terms of some current indicators. The need for others is explored.

Assessment of Criminal Justice Services. We shall consider two kinds of assessment of criminal justice services. First we shall examine perceptions of the need and demand for them and then the evaluations of the quality of these services will be considered.

The demand for a service may be measured in several quite different ways. One may base demand upon some reasonably objective assessment of matters that give rise to the demand. Demand for police service, for example, could be based on an assessment of the "actual" level of crime activity in the society, whether or not that level is accurately perceived by the public. Or, one may base the demand level simply upon actual public requests for a service. Actual demand for police service may depend, of course, as much upon citizen perceptions of reality as upon any objective conditions. Thus, citizens may demand that the police come for matters that are not bona fide crimes if they either perceive that is a role of the police or they define the matter as a "crime problem."

Citizen perceptions of the need or demand for services are basically of two kinds. The assessment may be made for one's *own* need or demand for a service, or it may be an evaluation of the *public* need or demand for that service. Similarly, one's evaluation of the quality of any service can be in terms of one's own experience or the perceptions one has of the experience of others. As we shall see, much evaluation of police service is based on hearsay rather than one's own experience with the police.

The "objective" demand for police service is measured in a number of ways. Police departments generally maintain at least two measures: they record all calls for service or "complaints," and then determine which represent bona fide crimes known to the police.[82] Household surveys of victimization[83] and observation of police and citizen transactions are other ways to estimate actual demand.[84]

Little attention has been given to polling the general public for judg-

[82] Reiss, *The Police and the Public,* pp. 70–114.

[83] Biderman, *op. cit.,* pp. 16–33; Albert D. Biderman and Albert J. Reiss, Jr., "On Exploring the 'Dark Figure' of Crime," *The Annals,* vol. 374, November, 1967, pp. 1–15.

[84] Donald J. Black and Albert J. Reiss, Jr., "Patterns of Behavior in Police and Citizen Transactions," Report of a Research Study submitted to the President's Commission on Law Enforcement and the Administration of Justice, *Studies in Crime and Law Enforcement in Major Metropolitan Areas,* vol. II, sec. 1. Government Printing Office, Washington, D.C., 1967, pp. 13–16.

ments about its need, as well as its demand, for a particular service, although the victimization surveys provide evidence on the conditions under which citizens will regard their experiences as necessitating police service. More commonly, the extent to which citizens perceive crime as a problem has been monitored. Over the past 10 years, for example, the Gallup polls have shown substantial shifts in the public assessment of crime as a major problem in the United States and England. In 1960, the English and U.S. public did not list crime among the major problems confronting the respective countries. By the spring of 1966, crime was considered the major problem in England and in the United States.[85] Yet, in the United States by the summer of 1970, crime virtually had been replaced as a major problem. Matters such as campus unrest and the war in Vietnam were the most frequently mentioned major problems with crime dropping to sixth place among mentions of major problems.[86]

Such public perception of problems perhaps presents as much a measure of what is at issue in the society, as it does an evaluation of the need for a service. Nonetheless, it is worthwhile to measure levels of "issue politics," particularly if one pays attention to what generates civic awareness of the issues. For example, what effect does experience with victimization from crime, reports of others about victimization, or media reports about victimization have upon one's sense of crime as a "major" issue?

Demands for Service. The extent to which demands for existing services are met, complaints about the way that demand is handled, and demands for service that go unmet are ways of monitoring the quality of existing services. Surprisingly little is known about demands for services that are not formally provided for or met by organizations. Indeed, police service to a substantial degree is characterized as meeting demands for service unrelated to any criminal activity. The poor are more likely to perceive the police in a general service role than are the well-to-do. Knowledge of such unmet demands is important information for public policy makers.

Evaluations of existing services all too often are made by monitoring a single service, for example, satisfaction with the police. It is less common to assess such service in comparison with other services. Yet, comparative judgments are useful as indicators of the quality of service in a system. Aberbach and Walker had Detroit citizens express their satisfaction with five municipal services: schools, police, garbage, parks, and teen centers.[87] Despite generally lower satisfaction of Negroes than whites with any municipal service, satisfaction with the police service was high relative to satisfaction with parks and teen centers and almost the same as the satisfaction with the public schools. Such asssesments of satisfaction with services should generally be

[85] SOC, March, 1965, and AIPO, 1965.
[86] AIPO, June, 1970.
[87] Aberbach and Walker, *op. cit.,* p. 6.

monitored for communities since communities generally are responsible for them.

One way to evaluate the quality of any public service is to assess complaints about it and how they are met. This necessitates developing measures for particular services. It is no simple matter to assess the quality of and satisfaction with a particular service such as police service. Citizens often are satisfied with some elements and not others. For example, they may be satisfied with the quality of the police behavior or the quality of the outcome of their handling a matter. If one is to assess the quality and satisfaction with criminal justice services, considerable effort must be expended in defining and measuring such appropriate indicators.

Apart from monitoring citizen perceptions of the quality of service rendered, little is known about the quality of enforcement and service actually desired in a community. Information on the quality of enforcement desired in a community is essential to the formulation of policy about levels of law enforcement to be practiced in a community. John Clark has made the interesting observation that the police and the public tend to regard enforcement matters alike. Measuring the appropriateness of police intervention in six hypothetical situations where police could intervene (Sunday blue laws, prostitution, racial prejudice, gambling, handling drunken bums, obscene literature), he found that the distributions for the police and the public were not significantly different. At the same time, he found that the police did differ significantly from other social control agents such as prosecutors, clergymen, and social workers in their views of the appropriateness of intervention in one or more of these situations.[88]

Clark's method of investigation could be adapted to actual community problems of enforcement rather than the hypothetical ones he selected. Particularly worthy of investigation is whether there are significant foci of minority opinion in the community. For example, do the opinions on enforcement of young people, businessmen, ethnic or racial minorities, and deviants differ substantially from those of other segments in the community? Such difference could be monitored in residential space as well, if one is interested in differential enforcement policies in a community.

Attempts to measure the quality of police service have led to several prototype measures. One of these is assessment of the over-all performance or job that the police are doing. American police on the whole are rated more favorably in their performance in enforcing the law than are the French police.[89] Actually, 33 percent of the French public evaluated the performance of their

[88] John P. Clark, "Isolation of the Police: A Comparison of the British and American Situations," *Journal of Criminal Law, Criminology, and Police Science,* vol. 56, September, 1965, pp. 307–319.

[89] Ennis, *op. cit.,* p. 53; Institut Français d'Opinion Publique (IFOP), March, 1966.

police as rather poor (27 percent) or very poor (6 percent) whereas only 8 percent of the American public saw their police as performing poorly. The questions unfortunately are not strictly comparable since the French generally evaluate the performance of all police in France while the American polls focus on local police.

A second type of measure focuses on some specific function that the police perform and evaluates it, such as protection of citizens from victimization, enforcing the law, or catching criminals. Ennis found, for example, that most Americans are convinced that their police do a good job of giving *protection* to people in the neighborhood while smaller proportions found them doing an excellent or good job of enforcing the law.[90] The practice, by the way, of measuring different police functions with different rating scales in the same poll should be discouraged in the interest of comparability among measures. It is unclear why the NORC poll just mentioned should measure the public's assessment of the job police are doing in enforcing the law on a scale ranging from excellent to poor and their job of protecting people on a scale from very good to not so good.[91] What is surprising is how stereotypically survey research has treated police functions and services, focusing almost exclusively on crime services which comprise less than half of all citizen requests for police service!

The efficiency with which a service operates is always important for citizens. This is particularly so when matters become defined as emergency, although what is emergency to the citizen is rarely emergency to the police. Citizens expect, for example, that when they call the police to report a burglary that has taken place in their absence, the police will come. The police may well consider it a "cold" matter, one of "taking a report." Hence, in evaluating the citizen's satisfaction with police response, it is not clear how much of the dissatisfaction stems from slow response when quick response, for example, might pay off, and how much does not. Response time to the operating agency is not response time to the citizen.

Citizen perception of the response time of the police to their calls for service can vary considerably, as the Campbell and Schuman survey in 15 cities shows. They found that Negroes were far more likely than whites to believe that people in their neighborhood did not receive prompt police service. One in four Negroes as compared with one in six whites said they had experienced poor service, and Negroes were twice as likely as whites to say they knew someone who had experienced poor response to a call for service.[92]

Any casual inspection of attempts to assess the specific attributes of a service makes apparent that indicators are not developed on the basis of an

[90] Ennis, *op. cit.*, p. 53.
[91] *Ibid.*
[92] Campbell and Schuman, *op. cit.*, p. 42.

analysis of the functions and how they are related to citizen groups but, rather, arise out of particular administrative concerns or public issues. Below is a report on indicators of the quality of police behavior, an aspect of police service that has been evaluated extensively because of its controversial nature over the past few years.

The Quality of Sanctions

Despite the fact that one of the most important elements in the criminal law and its administration is the imposition of sanctions, surprisingly little investigation has been undertaken of criminal sanctions and their imposition. The major exception has been the investigation of public support for capital punishment, the rarest sanction in the system and, undoubtedly, the least consequential for offenders in the aggregate. Perhaps this says more about the concerns of nonviolators than it does of violators in such systems.

Several indicators of the quality of sanctions are discussed below. They include subjective perceptions about the imposition of sanctions attached to behavior, evaluations of various forms of punishment and treatment, and the evaluation of the performance of sanctioning agents, particularly in jails, courts, and prisons.

Risk in Behaving as a Function of Perceived Sanctions. Generally we assume that decisions to violate social norms are more a function of subjective probabilities that sanctions will be imposed than they are of ignorance. Yet, little is known about how subjective probabilities are estimated. Edwards, among others, argues that people will overestimate probabilities associated with favorable consequences and underestimate those associated with unfavorable consequences.[93] One speculates whether the type of violation, the objective probability of sanctions, and the type of penalty also are factors in decisions to violate laws. Few studies are directed toward these questions. But they would seem to be among the more important ones to understand how citizens perceive risk in the system of crime and criminal justice.

Contrary to Edwards' hypothesis, Claster found that delinquents and nondelinquents tend to overestimate the probability of being caught and convicted for a number of crimes when he took the official clearance by arrest and conviction rates as measures of actual probability.[94] Despite the difficulty in

[93] Ward Edwards, "Information Processing, Decision Making, and Highway Safety," in *Driver Behavior: Cause and Effect,* Proceedings of the Second Annual Traffic Safety Research Symposium of the Automobile Insurance Industry. Insurance Institute for Highway Safety, Washington, D.C., 1968, pp. 165–180.

[94] Daniel S. Claster, "Comparison of Risk Perception between Delinquents and Non-Delinquents," *Journal of Criminal Law, Criminology, and Police Science,* vol. 58, March, 1967, pp. 80–86.

finding objective probabilities, the extent to which subjective probabilities accord with objective ones may be among the most important indicators to assess propensities to violate the law in populations. Similarly we need to investigate how citizens evaluate the current penalty structure in the United States. These remain among the more promising areas for investigating social-psychological aspects of crime.

Assessment of Specific Sanctions. There may be considerable change in public support for a sanction when it is monitored over a period of time. This is particularly true when the sanction becomes a matter for public discussion and controversy. Only a few sanctions have been monitored over a period of time, the most noteworthy being the penalty of capital punishment. There has been substantial change in American society in support for the death penalty since public opinion on that issue was first measured in 1953, as Table 1 shows.[95] Even were the death penalty to be eliminated, one might continue to monitor sentiment for and against it. In England, a similar trend was observed prior to repeal of the death penalty for most crimes. Yet, sentiment has shifted recently in the direction of re-imposition of the penalty, at least for some crimes.

Table 1. Changes in Attitude toward Capital Punishment
(*In Percent*)

Favorable to Capital Punishment	Year of Poll			
	1966	*1965*	*1960*	*1953*
Yes	42	45	51	68
No	47	43	36	25
No opinion	11	12	13	7

No other sanction unfortunately has been monitored over as long a period of time, although examples of questions on a specific sanction are not uncommon. For example, in Denmark citizens apparently found the sentences for car theft too lenient[96] and the English public was almost equally divided on prison sentences for homosexuality.[97] The Australian public favors whipping for serious robbery.[98] The American public is moving toward supporting lesser penalties for conviction on possession of marijuana.[99]

Evaluation of Official Behavior in Sanctioning. Rather than assess the penalty structure attached to offenses, it has been more common to assess the behavior of judges in imposing sentences. Indeed, there is good reason to be-

[95] *Polls,* vol. II, Spring, 1967, p. 84.
[96] Gallup Markedsanalyse (GMA), April, 1965.
[97] NOP, October, 1965.
[98] APOP, February, 1966.
[99] AIPO, 1970.

lieve that the public is quite unaware of the sentencing structure followed by judges. Most of the evidence supports the view that the general public assumes a punitive position, charging the judicial system with sanctioning criminals too leniently. That there can be rather sharp shifts in such assessments seems apparent from two American Institute of Public Opinion (AIPO) polls in 1965. In April, 48 percent of the American public said they thought "the courts in this area did not deal harshly enough with criminals";[100] by September the proportion was 60 percent.[101]

The Quality of Justice

Perhaps the concept of justice is more difficult to operationalize than any other, whether distributive or retributive. Most surveys measure perceptions of whether "standards" of justice are applied universalistically. "Fairness" or "discriminatory" treatment in decisions are the most common indicators. Generally speaking, in the United States a substantial minority of citizens regard the police as discriminatory toward minorities in enforcing the law. Police standards are to favor the rich over the poor;[102] whites over Negroes;[103] old over young;[104] conformers over people with a record for trouble.[105]

Few attempts have been made to measure the quality of discretionary justice for other than the police in the United States. A survey for the National Crime Commission measured how victims of crimes see justice in the way their victimization is handled in the criminal justice system. Ennis found that people who did not call the police were most dissatisfied with the outcome.[106] If the police are called and come, the rate of satisfaction increases and it is increased if the police make an arrest. The substantial differences occur, however, when judicial behavior is assessed. When the victim regards the penalty as "unjust" (in this case too lenient), he is very dissatisfied. Satisfaction is highest when the victim believes that the offender is given the proper penalty. Such are victim views of justice. Offender views might be quite different. Yet, no attempt is made to measure systematically their views or to compare them with those of others.

[100] AIPO, April, 1965.

[101] AIPO, September, 1965.

[102] Bouma, *op. cit.,* pp. 53, 63, 68–69; Reiss, "Public Perceptions and Recollections about Crime, Law Enforcement, and Criminal Justice," pp. 43, 45.

[103] Aberbach and Walker, *op. cit.,* p. 16; Biderman *et al., op. cit.,* pp. 143–145; Bouma, *op. cit.,* pp. 53, 68; MINN, December, 1965; Reiss, "Public Perceptions and Recollections about Crime, Law Enforcement, and Criminal Justice," pp. 41–50.

[104] Bouma, *op. cit.,* pp. 53, 69.

[105] *Ibid.,* p. 53; Reiss, "Public Perceptions and Recollections about Crime, Law Enforcement, and Criminal Justice," pp. 41, 43, 45.

[106] Ennis, *op. cit.,* pp. 50–51.

A Louis Harris poll in the District of Columbia found that substantial minorities of whites and Negroes thought the jails treated prisoners unfairly and that the district courts did not administer justice fairly.[107] Equally noteworthy, however, were the substantial number of minority respondents that said they could not assess how prisoners are treated in jail or how justice is administered in the courts. This latter is an important methodological problem in assessing citizen perceptions of the quality of justice in the system. While assessments are important as information regardless of origin, how such assessment are formed and their basis in knowledge also is important, particularly when perceptions change over time.

A Netherlands poll has attempted a more direct measure of justice, beginning with: "Some people feel that judges in The Netherlands do not measure all persons by the same standard; others feel they do. What is your opinion?"[108] Such a question includes the idea of a standard of justice so that respondents who answer "by a different standard" are questioned about that standard.

One of the few attempts to measure justice in decisions by prosecutors occurred in studies on the police for the National Crime Commission. Reiss found that a substantial minority of police officers thought prosecutors based their decisions more on whether a case could be won than on their interest in equity or justice.[109] They also regarded prosecutors as too quick to reduce charges or to fail to press charges without any apparent standard for doing so.

All in all, however, the most important quality imputed to the criminal justice system—justice—is not operationalized satisfactorily, or is measurement undertaken for those responsible for dispensing justice.

Quality of the Servants and Those They Serve

Citizen encounters with public services occur primarily through bureaucratic channels and contacts. There are notable exceptions, of course. The use of many public parks, for example, rarely requires contact with any member of the Parks Department. When contact occurs with someone in the agency, it may occur largely in impersonal ways, as through paper communication.

The police are one of the few remaining bureaucracies where the citizen's use of the service occurs principally through personal contact and interaction. Policing also is one of the few remaining bureaucracies where the citizen mobilizes the officer to the citizen's territory. Contact with police officers

---

[107] Harris Poll, October, 1966.

[108] NIPO, 1968.

[109] Reiss, "Career Orientations, Job Satisfaction, and the Assessment of Law Enforcement Problems by Police Officers," p. 106.

occurs primarily outside organizational settings controlled by the police. Contacts with other agencies and officials in the criminal justice system, such as the public prosecutor, jail personnel, or officials of the court, also are largely personal. As a matter of fact, there is surprisingly little paper communication between citizens and officials in the bureaucracies of the criminal justice system. A citizen may look in vain for *his* copy of the arrest record or the warrant issued (unless the warrant is served); even the transcript of *his* trial and the decision in *his* case are not given him as a matter of record. What paper there is on any case is exchanged among the officials in the system, not between officials and citizens. Such a public system of contact and interaction therefore must inevitably revolve around the assessment of the behavior of individuals in interaction.

Despite the fact that the bulk of the contacts between citizens and officials in the criminal justice system are personal, little attempt is made to measure the quality of their behavior in interaction. Generally, only the evaluations one of the parties has to the behavior of the others is measured. Citizens are queried about police behavior and vice versa. Rarely are they queried about the same interaction. Exceptions are the work by Toch where the parties to conflicts in police and prison interaction setting were interviewed, and the observational studies by Reiss of police and citizen transactions.[110]

Failing to consider a model of interaction between public official and citizen as the basis for measuring the quality of their behavior, most studies neglect important data not only on the quality of interaction but on how the behavior of one group is related to that of another. Moreover, the behavior of citizens is generally not measured; only measures of the behavior of public officials, such as the police, are obtained. Yet the quality of citizen behavior must affect in some way the quality and manner of handling citizens shown by public officials. One need only be reminded that jurists may lose their cool in the courtroom when citizens fail to display the demeanor ordinarily expected of them. Clearly, too, the model of measuring qualitative features of the behavior of citizens and public officials is one where primarily negative rather than positive aspects of interaction are evaluated. The interest lies in measuring violence between police and citizens, not civility. Were one to monitor the quality of any service, one should measure positive as well as negatively evaluated characteristics of interaction.

There are problems, of course, in adapting the sample survey to studies of interaction between citizens and public officials. Most of these problems arise because of choices about a universe and what sample is to be drawn from it, rather than to other elements in the survey such as soliciting information by

---

[110] Hans Toch, *Violent Men: An Inquiry into the Psychology of Violence.* Aldine, Chicago, 1969, pp. 1–33; Black and Reiss, *op. cit.*

interview. As Toch shows, it is possible to interview all parties to conflicts.[111] Observation is not necessary to "construct" interaction. Often what is at stake in sample surveys is that one wants to estimate for a population of citizens, e.g., how many have had a negative experience with the police, not for a universe of encounters.

Several qualities of the behavior of police and citizens are examined in this section. Similar indicators should be developed for other public servants and citizens in the criminal justice system. The major topics considered are the personality of men recruited to the police; the quality of police behavior in police and citizen transactions; the conduct of police apart from these transactions; the morale of the police; and their participation in community life.

Personality of Police. A substantial clinical literature suggests that police officers are a special type of personality—authoritarian, aggressive, and sadistic. Yet, surprisingly little investigation exists of the extent to which police are made up of distinct personality types or characterized by particular personality structures. Two studies tested the hypothesis that the police are authoritarian personalities. Both studies conclude that policemen are less likely than the dominant population to score high on the F scale.[112] Indeed, McNamara found that policemen score lower on the F scale than non-police people of the same class and in the same occupations.[113]

Some social clinicians also suggest that police culture coerces officers to withdraw from identification with the public and the community into an officer subculture. Policemen are represented as alienated. Reported below are studies on some specific aspects of alienation of the police from the community. Here it should be noted that on the Srole anomie scale, policemen in Denver, Colorado, were less likely than the dominant population to be despairing and fatalistic about life's possibilities.[114]

Such investigations, of course, do not prove that some police are not authoritarian, fatalistic, and so on; indeed, they show that some are. But, taken at face value, they suggest that police officers are not a random set of the general population in these characteristics but are, on the average, less authoritarian and less likely to experience anomie. To be sure, given questionable validity to the F scale and Srole scale, the hypotheses require further investigation. Yet it should be apparent that, if personality differences exist between the police and the public, they are unlikely to be large, given the variability within the population of police officers.

Quality of Police and Citizen Transactions. The quality of police and citizen transactions can be assessed by observing them in interaction. Al-

[111] Toch, *op. cit.*
[112] McNamara, *op. cit.*, p. 194; Bayley and Mendelsohn, *op. cit.*, pp. 17–18.
[113] McNamara, *op. cit.*, p. 194.
[114] Bayley and Mendelsohn, *op. cit.*, p. 16.

though there are several observational studies of the police, only those by Black and Reiss provide a basis for estimating the frequency with which any behavior occurs in police and citizen transaction systems.[115] Observational studies are important as they provide a basis for evaluating citizen and police officer reports of one another's behavior in their transactions.

Problems exist in making data on police and citizen behavior from the population surveys comparable with those from observation studies, particularly since their sampling base is different. Observation of the police in the Reiss studies occurred for units of transactions between citizens and officers; it is the quality of behavior in the transaction that is reported. Surveys generally sample citizens or officers. Thus, to know that the police behaved with civility in a majority of the transactions with citizens does not permit one to conclude that a majority of police behave with civility in their transactions with citizens. Indeed, the prevalence rate of incivility in at least one transaction may approach unity for any officer cohort.

Any "error" or "mistake" by police toward citizens may never be erased by police behavior that is positively evaluated by citizens. Similarly, given repeated encounters with the police, negative experiences may cumulate across citizens much as they do for the police. How these experiences are subjectively evaluated and counted is important in assessing the quality of any service. A single act of misconduct by the police may generate a complaint against the officer and place at least one citizen in the count of those experiencing misconduct from the police. "Once ever" measures of experience with police behavior appear to have consequences for police organizations that do not occur for many other types of high-volume transaction systems.

A number of propositions about police and citizen conduct emerge from observational studies of their transactions. In only a minority of encounters are either citizens or the police antagonistic to one another, and indeed, civility on the part of one is generally coupled with civility on the part of the other.[116] Furthermore, Negroes apparently are no more subject to discriminatory treatment by the police than are whites; class is more important than race in explaining police behavior toward citizens. Most police transactions with citizens are routine and "businesslike."[117]

Although these observational studies clearly show that the probability of civil or deferential treatment from the police is very high in transactions with citizens, each day a minority of 4 to 6 percent of all transactions involve antagonism between officers and citizens. Such antagonism sets the stage for a substantial proportion of citizens to report unfavorable encounters with the police, particularly if one assumes that from day to day there is little overlap

[115] Black and Reiss, *op. cit.*
[116] *Ibid.*, Table 5.
[117] *Ibid.*, p. 37.

in contacts of police and citizens. A substantial proportion of citizens who encounter the police in the long run may experience at least one encounter in which they define the police as antagonistic. Similarly, an officer is more likely than not in the short run of a week to have one or more encounters with antagonistic citizens. Nevertheless, on the average, positive contacts between citizens and their police are far more probable than negative ones, even in repeated encounters with the police.

The quality of behavior in transactions at other levels of the criminal justice system also needs investigation. What is the behavior of the prosecutor toward the police and complainants during the charging process, and vice versa? Or how does the judge treat police officers when they testify, and what is their response? Indeed, since at least part of the transactions in the criminal justice system are public, the opportunity for observing them without awareness on the part of anyone is quite good, particularly in large urban jurisdictions.

Quality of Police Behavior Toward Citizens. Most recent surveys of the police measure the *negative* experiences that citizens have with the police— their use of force unnecessarily (the police brutality issue), the use of abusive language, or their lack of courtesy and respect for citizens. Surprisingly one finds few measures of "proper" police behavior toward citizens. What is more, I have been unable to find any surveys seeking information from citizens on antagonistic or hostile behavior of citizens toward the police. Surveys readily ask whether citizens have seen police behave improperly toward citizens but not whether they have seen citizens behave with incivility or hostility toward the police. There appears to be an ideological bias in the measurement of the police and citizen behavior toward one another in sample surveys, such that the positive aspects of the behavior of either party goes unmeasured. Only the negative aspects of police behavior are generally investigated. Measures of civility, courtesy, respect, and special treatment are rare in sample surveys evaluating police and citizen behavior.

1. *The use of force.* At law, police are permitted to use such force as is necessary to sustain an arrest and, under certain conditions, to maintain public order. The use of deadly force is more restricted. In many states its use in arrest is limited to felony arrests and, in many jurisdictions, its use to maintain public order should occur only on command of a superior officer. The fact that, at law, the police may *legitimately* use force against citizens poses problems of measuring when force is "unnecessary." Or correlatively, when is force necessary to sustain an arrest? When is more force than necessary exercised? These are no simple problems of judgment, even in observational studies of the police, much less when their definition varies from citizen to citizen.

The question of whether citizen perceptions of the use of force are valid is germane, to be sure, only if the validity of their perception is under consideration. If citizens believe matters to be real, there may be real consequences from their beliefs. Whether we are measuring belief or reality is difficult to know for any aspect of police and citizen behavior, but particularly so for the use of force.

A number of surveys use the term "police brutality" to elicit citizen reports of experience with the police.[118] Yet Reiss and Chevigny have shown that citizens, particularly Negro citizens, do not always equate brutality with unnecessary use of force.[119] Abusive language and other forms of mistreatment also are considered brutality. Surveys, therefore, might well avoid the measurement of "brutality," if the object is to measure the use of force unnecessarily by the police. Some form such as "Some people say that policemen use 'unnecessary force' . . ." is closer to what one seeks to measure. A few surveys that use this terminology add "in making an arrest,"[120] The Campbell and Schuman survey limits their questions to "when they are arresting them and afterward," thereby eliminating the situation where there is force without arrest, a not unlikely situation if observation of police and citizen encounters are taken as a measure.[121] Clearly such phrasings do not cover all cases where the police use force unnecessarily. It would be worthwhile to investigate whether citizens ever report that force is used "legitimately" against them.

The surprising result from comparing polls that measure citizen beliefs about "police brutality" is the similarity in evaluations across rather different police systems. The Denmark poll found that 10 percent of Danish citizens believe their police behave "brutally," varying from a high of 24 percent of young persons aged 15 to 17 to a low of 4 percent of those aged 61 and over.[122] Conservative Party members in Denmark were far less likely than Social Democrats or Radicals to believe the Danish police are brutal, and of course those residing in Copenhagen were four times as likely (16 percent) as those residing in the country to believe in the brutality of policemen. The AIPO poll reported that 9 percent of U.S. residents believe in police brutality.[123] Comparable figures for urban whites are reported by Campbell and Schuman and Aberbach and Walker.[124] The figures for urban Negroes are considerably higher with roughly one-third in major cities believing that police-

---

[118] Iowa Poll, 1968; GMA, 1968; Bouma, *op. cit.,* p. 110; AIPO, April, 1965; Harris Poll, 1966.

[119] Albert J. Reiss, Jr., "Police Brutality—Answers to Key Questions," *Trans-Action,* vol. 5, July/August, 1968, pp. 15–16, and "Policemen's Lot," *Yale Law Journal,* vol. 78, May, 1969, pp. 1103–1106; Paul Chevigny, *Police Power: Police Abuses in New York City.* Pantheon, New York, 1969.

[120] Aberbach and Walker, *op. cit.,* p. 13.

[121] Campbell and Schuman, *op. cit.,* p. 43.

[122] GMA, October, 1967.

[123] AIPO, April, 1965.

[124] Aberbach and Walker, *op. cit.,* p. 13; Campbell and Schuman, p. 43.

men use force unnecessarily.[125] Although much smaller proportions of citizens claim they themselves have experienced force unnecessarily at the hands of the police, or that people they know have had that experience, this difference between Negroes and whites prevails. Survey findings on citizen reports of police use of force are at odds with the observational data showing that whites are as likely as Negroes to experience excessive use of force.[126] The discrepancy between Negro and white self-reports, their reports about the experiences of others, and their beliefs about the police from surveys and observation studies of police behavior is not easily resolved. Class differentials, if any, play a minor role in accounting for the discrepancy.[127] Further investigation seems necessary to explain the discrepancy.

Hans Toch, through extended interviews with police who were charged with using force unnecessarily and with their complainants, concludes that the improper use of force by the police is the outcome of an *escalation of conflict*.[128] Moreover, in almost all encounters in which police use force improperly against citizens, both the officer and the citizen have a history of the escalation of conflict to the point where force is used by both. Toch concludes that they are "violence-prone" persons. Just how one might develop an operational measure of "proneness" to violence is not clear, intriguing as is his hypothesis about the escalation of conflict between violence-prone persons.

Some surveys construct a "police abuse" index based on two or more measures of police "misconduct" toward citizens.[129] Such indexes seem no more defensible than the common Uniform Crime Reports (UCR) crime index and risk misinterpretation as easily. This is particularly so since the behavioral referents in survey questions about police behavior often are "unclear." Quite commonly, a "sentiment" or "Gestalt" is tapped more than a precise description of the behavior of police or citizens. Consider, for example, the question used in National Crime Commission studies in which citizens were asked: "How many police do you think there are in Boston/Chicago/Washington, D.C., who just enjoy pushing people around or giving them a hard time?"[130] Conceivably the question aims at tapping "sadistic" behavior (the enjoy referent), or/and the improper use of force (pushing people around), or harassment (in giving them a hard time). Not only are there far

[125] *Ibid.,* pp. 43–44.

[126] Reiss, "Police Brutality—Answers to Key Questions," pp. 15–18.

[127] James R. Hudson, "Characteristics of Police-Citizen Encounters That Lead to Altercations," unpublished manuscript.

[128] Toch, *op. cit.,* pp. 34–67.

[129] Aberbach and Walker, *op. cit.,* pp. 18–20; Howard Schuman and Barry Gruenberg, "The Impact of City on Racial Attitudes," *American Journal of Sociology,* vol. 76, September, 1970, pp. 213–261.

[130] Biderman *et al., op. cit.,* p. 136; Reiss, "Public Perceptions and Recollections of Crime, Law Enforcement, and Criminal Justice," pp. 44, 51.

too many behavioral referents (pushing people around, giving people a hard time, and enjoyment) but judgments are implied about the behavior (sadism, impropriety, harassment). Clearly a different structure of questioning should be adopted for precise evaluation of these aspects of police behavior.

2. *The use of language.* Campbell and Schuman investigated the extent to which citizens in their 15-city survey believe that the police "don't show respect for people and use insulting language."[131] Setting aside the possibility that people might regard "respect" as not quite synonymous with "the use of insulting language," a pronounced race difference was observed with Negroes far more likely than whites to report it happens to people in their neighborhood, that it has happened to them and others they know. This was, in fact, the most pronounced race difference in perceptions of police treatment of citizens. "Courtesy" similarly implies more than the use of language. Ennis found that the most pronounced race difference in citizen perception of police behavior occurred for "courtesy."[132] These two studies suggest that monitoring the more common day-to-day qualities of face-to-face interaction is worthwhile, given marked difference by race and age.

3. *Deference and respect for officials.* It is difficult to separate empirically the qualities of deference and respect in behavior. Both are subjective qualities attached to behavior. Both exist as "expectations" in interaction between officials and citizens. An interesting question arises as to the relationship between one's appraisal of deference or respect and satisfaction with one's transactions in interaction.

The Black and Reiss study of police and citizen transactions concluded that paradoxically:

> The citizen who treats the officer with civility not infrequently regards civility in the officer as a sign of disrespect. And the officer who meets civility in the citizen not infrequently perceives it as a sign of disrespect. The paradox arises because of their reciprocal expectations. The citizen wants the officer to behave with more than civility; he wants to be treated as a "person." . . . The officer wants the citizen to behave with more than civility, to show deference toward his authority.[133]

Rossi and his associates note that while only a minority of 30 percent of the police perceive the average citizen as failing to accord them respect, a majority of 54 percent of the police are dissatisfied with the respect they receive from citizens.[134]

[131] Campbell and Schuman, *op. cit.,* p. 42.

[132] Ennis, *op. cit.,* p. 58.

[133] Black and Reiss, *op. cit.,* p. 48.

[134] Peter H. Rossi *et al.,* "Between Black and White: The Faces of American Institutions in the Ghetto," in *Supplemental Studies for the National Advisory Commission on Civil Disorders.* Government Printing Office, Washington, D.C., 1968, p. 105.

These discrepancies in expectations and perceptions of behavior merit further investigation. The policeman's dissatisfaction with citizen behavior toward him may arise not from his perceptions of the "average" resident but the fact that many of his contacts are not with "average" residents. Contacts with juveniles, offenders, or simply those who call the police about trouble are not generally from the average resident. Yet, those may be the ones that are crucial in forming police images about respect, deference, and support from the public. There is some support for this in studies by Reiss in which it is shown that officers do differentiate among the public in terms of "those who give you a hard time." Youth and known criminals are particularly selected in these categories and regarded as "belligerent," "flouting authority," and "hostile."[135] Correlatively, citizens may form their images primarily from expectations about the behavior of public persons rather than in terms of conceptions of bureaucratic contacts or as the result of their own contacts with public officials.

4. *Selecting qualities of behavior in transactions for monitoring.* There are almost as many ways to measure the behavior of officials and citizens as there are adjectives in the English language. Some studies, for example, measure whether police are "nice guys"; others how they "get along with people"; and still others with whether they regard police as "enemies or friends."[136] What is important if one is to develop indicators to monitor the quality of police and citizen behavior are models that specify indicators so that standardized variables can be developed that are valid over time.

Two such models have been implicit in the foregoing discussion. One is a model of the civil service and the civil society based on the rule of law. This is a model of the legal bureaucracy. The other is a model of citizen and official expectations of one another's behavior. Insofar as possible, such models should not be specific to a given bureaucracy such as the police, but should be applicable to others as well. The specification of models of behavior in organizations does not make the problem of operationalizing behavior less difficult since to measure civility in behavior in the model of the legal bureaucracy or deference in the model of expectations is no simple matter.

Morale. The morale of groups or officials in organizations in the criminal justice system is rarely measured. This is true of police morale, perhaps surprisingly so since military morale has been studied so extensively. Research on morale in organizations has not yielded very well to measurement, however, so that questions can be raised as to whether it is worthwhile to monitor morale in organizations in the criminal justice system. One answer is that, at least for police organizations, officers speak about "morale." James Q. Wilson notes

---

[135] Reiss, "Career Orientations, Job Satisfaction, and the Assessment of Law Enforcement Problems by Police Officers," p. 121.

[136] Rossi *et al., op. cit.,* p. 156.

that morale is especially difficult in organizations such as the police where it is dependent upon factors external as well as internal to the organization.[137] Management is in a far more difficult position to affect morale when it cannot directly control such external factors. Then it must either find indirect ways of doing so, or produce some internal substitute. Indeed, Wilson found that, when Chicago police sergeants perceived a heightened animosity of the citizenry toward them, they responded by attaching less importance to citizen attitudes. Professionalization of the Chicago police brought with it less concern for public views.[138]

One substitute for measuring morale in organizations is to measure characteristics of work in organizations believed important in morale, for example, satisfaction with one's job. Studies for the National Crime Commission explored the measurement of job satisfaction among police officers. Negroes, as expected, perceived fewer opportunities for promotion than whites.[139] Like all workers, the police expressed far more dissatisfaction with day-to-day working conditions (e.g., shift work), the financial rewards that go with the job, and the conditions of promotion (e.g., merit exams), than they did with the effect of appellate court decisions or the behavior of the public on their discretionary authority.[140] In short, internal conditions of work were more important than external ones in job satisfaction, regardless of the level of professionalization of the department.

Police Participation in Community Life. The work of the police in handling mobilizations by citizens, maintaining public order, and preventing crime is believed to depend substantially upon their knowledge of a territory and its residents, and upon their participation in its common life. Arguments about the advantages of "foot" compared with "mobile" patrol, for instance, are made to rest upon it. So far as we know, the effects of the quality of patrolmen's knowledge of and participation in a territory on the quality of policing are undemonstrated. Surprisingly, more is known about their informal than their formal knowledge and participation.

Informal as well as formal procedures determine the quality of any operating system. The formally prescribed transactions between police and citizens are but one aspect of the relationship between citizens and the police; many informal ties may develop as well. Some of these may enhance police status and help to implement the formal goals of law enforcement, such as the participation of police in the community. Others may subvert it, as may be the case when citizens bribe the police or persuade them to bear false witness.

---

[137] Wilson, *op. cit.*

[138] *Ibid.*, p. 155.

[139] Reiss, "Career Orientations, Job Satisfaction, and the Assessment of Law Enforcement Problems by Police Officers," Tables 2, 3, 13.

[140] *Ibid.*, pp. 22–38.

The quality of legal systems depends heavily upon the quality of informal systems. Yet, their quality is not easily measured since both citizens and the police often have an investment in protecting information about their existence. Not only is it difficult to measure when individuals are involved in "misconduct" or "corruption," but it is exceedingly difficult to develop such measures for organizations. What is the extent of corruption in a given police department or police precinct? How extensive is false witness in criminal trials? How many juries are manipulated? What is the probability of "fair trial"? Important as these questions are for the quality of life in any society, they are most difficult to measure.

Observation has proved to be the principal means that sociologists use to investigate "informal" systems, particularly those that subvert organizational goals. This has been true as well for studies of police misconduct.[141] Data collected in the observational studies of police and citizens for the National Crime Commission show that at least one-fifth of all officers engaged at least once in a violation of the criminal code that could be regarded as a misdemeanor or a felony. Moreover, 4 officers in 10 were observed in serious violations of the rules and regulations of the department. "Serious violations" meant engaging in behavior that affects the quality of policing, for example, drinking on duty, falsifying reports, or neglect of duty altogether in sleeping or remaining off post. Such estimates based on observation are necessarily minimal estimates. Besides, given the basis of sampling for observation, it was difficult to establish either an incidence or a prevalence rate with high reliability.

To secure valid and reliable observations about informal systems, the cooperation of participants generally is essential. In studying the police, such cooperation is not readily obtained and "covers" are easily penetrated. The other means for gathering information on informal systems that depend upon citizen reporting also present major problems of cooperation, validity, and reliability. Asking citizens to report on police misconduct, for example, when the citizen is implicated in the illegal act, should be investigated nevertheless, even though attempts to monitor the extent of organized crime may be useless. Such questions as: "Have you bought a number within the past week?" or "Is there a bookie in your neighborhood?" may bring valid responses.

Despite problems in obtaining valid citizen perceptions of police misconduct, opinion polls provide some useful information on the quality of law enforcement. Almost half the citizens of India believe their police are corrupt.[142] The National Crime Commission studies asked citizens to report

---

[141] Reiss, "Police Brutality—Answers to Key Questions," 10–19, and *The Police and The Public,* pp. 141–150, 156–167.

[142] The Indian Institute of Public Opinion (IIPO), March, 1964.

whether they thought "most," "some," or "no" policemen take bribes or pay-offs. Although one-third of all citizens queried said they could not say, another third believed the police could be bribed or paid off. Of these, one-third thought *most* police in their district could be bribed or paid off.[143] A related question was asked in the NORC poll for the Commission: "Some people say that most policemen are honest and others say that most policemen take bribes and payoffs. Do you think the police around your neighborhood are almost all honest, mostly honest with a few who are corrupt, or are they almost all corrupt?" A minority of almost 3 percent believed all were corrupt.[144] Unfortunately, the characteristics of citizens who regard police as corrupt is not investigated in any of these studies, although such analysis may help in determining the value of such questions for monitoring police conduct.

In the NORC study, twice as many whites (63 percent) as Negroes (30 percent) thought the police were "almost all honest."[145] Such race differences in perception could reflect less about the quality of police honesty in Negro and white areas of cities (or for that matter of the level of honesty of the police) than they serve as measures of general "hostility" toward the police.[146] A generally "hostile" respondent may opt for any negative expression about the police. Where there is some public support for police officers engaging in behavior that is officially proscribed, information about conduct is more readily obtained. Reiss found that owners and managers of businesses were quite willing to report they did "favors" for the police.[147]

An aspect of the quality of police participation in a community is the level of contact and communication officers have with various segments of the community that are believed important in policing the territory. Studies for the National Advisory Commission on Civil Disorders by Rossi and his associates asked the police how many persons they knew in various subgroups in the community. Since there are quite different numbers of people in any subgroup within a police territory, as, for example, fewer youth leaders than businessmen, it is difficult to assess reported differences among subgroups in numbers with whom the officer is acquainted. Their data lend support, however, to the notion that policemen are more oriented toward the business community than they are toward other segments.[148] To avoid some of the prob-

---

[143] Reiss, "Public Perceptions and Recollections about Crime, Law Enforcement, and Criminal Justice," pp. 69–70, 76–77.

[144] Ennis, *op. cit.,* Table 33.

[145] *Ibid.*

[146] President's Commission on Law Enforcement and the Administration of Justice, *The Challenge of Crime in a Free Society.* Government Printing Office, Washington, D.C., 1967, p. 99.

[147] Reiss, "Public Perceptions and Recollections about Crime, Law Enforcement, and Criminal Justice," p. 18.

[148] Rossi *et al., op. cit.,* pp. 112–114.

lems in comparison evident in these measures, other ways to measure knowledge of various persons and groups in the community and estimate the size of various subgroups in the population should be developed.

The level of contact and communication between police and citizens in a community can be measured also by sampling various subgroups within the population. Studies of businesses and other organizations in high-crime-rate areas show that 6 of every 10 businessmen knew one or more police officers well enough to converse with him.[149] Similar measures were developed for surveys of the resident population.[150]

One other measure of the quality of police participation in the community is their participation in the life of the community not directly connected with their police work. Rossi and his associates developed four such measures of informal participation: (1) officer lives in the same area where he works; (2) officer has relatives in area where he works; (3) officer frequently sees friends from neighborhood socially; (4) officer attends meetings in neighborhood "often" or "sometimes."[151] The difficulty with such indexes is the presumption that each is somehow important in the quality of police work. They are based on causal presumptions that are largely untested. Perhaps they are more closely related to some aspects of police work than others. It may be that, when police contact with a subgroup in the community is high, the officers are evaluated more highly than when it is low. Yet, such contact may have little to do with the prevention or solution of crimes unless it could be shown, for example, that it increases the voluntary reporting of information to the police.

Police work, it is believed, isolates policemen from extensive contact with others in the community. Banton notes this is particularly true in England, but that the American police are less set apart from participation in the community.[152] Data from the Royal Commission Studies on the English Police and from Clark on some American police lend support to Banton's observation.[153] Just how being a policeman limits one's participation in the life of the community is not clear, although the presumption that policemen must be more sensitive to their reputation as guardians of the moral order may limit their

[149] Reiss, "Public Perceptions and Recollections about Crime, Law Enforcement, and Criminal Justice," p. 10.

[150] Biderman *et al., op. cit.,* pp. 142–143; Ennis, *op. cit.,* Appendix A, "Attitudes and Experience Questionnaire: Victimization Study," Items 30, 31, p. 9; Reiss, "Public Perceptions and Recollections about Crime, Law Enforcement, and Criminal Justice," pp. 58–66.

[151] Rossi *et al., op. cit.,* p. 113.

[152] Michael Banton, *The Policeman in the Community,* Basic Books, New York, 1964.

[153] Clark, *op. cit.,* p. 313; R. Morton-Williams, "The Relations between Police and the Public," *Royal Commission on the Police,* Appendix IV to the Minutes of Evidence, H.S.M.O., London, 1962, pp. 41–43.

participation; 75 percent of the police officers in one study reported that, when off duty, they acted in such a way as to keep up their reputation as a police officer.[154]

Effects of the Criminal Justice System on Clients and the Public

Numerous attempts have been made to assess the effectiveness of each level of the criminal justice system in reaching its "goals." There are studies of the effect of police in preventing crime, of the deterrent effects of punishment, and of the effects of probation and parole in reforming offenders, to mention but a few examples. None of these studies is reviewed here, but it is worth noting that, as yet, none of these effects is reliably measured. The problem arises in large part because the indicators for concepts such as crime prevention and reform of an offender are poor. It seems doubtful that we can measure such general concepts well. Work on indicators in this area, therefore, should rely on developing more specific indexes, perhaps primarily behavioral in nature. Thus, concepts such as criminal recidivism are more easily measured than "reformed offender."

In this final section, some recent attempts to develop behavioral and social-psychological indicators of the consequences of crime in a community are reported. Such indicators are of special importance in assessing the quality of life in the community. We focus especially on the level of victimization and offending in a community and its effects on a citizen's way of life.

Estimating Victimization from Crime. A major qualitative aspect of life in any community is the extent to which one is free of victimization by others and, correlatively, whether one conforms in such a way as to bring no harm to others. Sociologists have made much of this distinction, pointing out that some crimes are "victimless" and thus of less consequence in the life of a community.

Until quite recently, it was commonly assumed that the majority of the population did not experience crime directly as a victim or as an offender. It also was assumed that one therefore had very limited contact with the criminal justice system, particularly if traffic offenses were eliminated from consideration. Although estimates of the incidence and prevalence of criminal victimization or offending and its corollary, contacts with the criminal justice system, are only partial, such estimates indicate that much of the U.S. population will experience at least one such contact during their lifetime. For a substantial minority, the likelihood of repeated contact is high.[155]

---

[154] Reiss, "Career Orientations, Job Satisfaction, and Assessment of Problems of Law Enforcement by Police Officers," Table 20.

[155] Ronald Christensen, "Projected Percentage of U.S. Population with Criminal and Arrest Records," in *Task Force Report: Science and Technology.* Government Printing Office, Washington, D.C., 1967, Appendix J, pp. 216–228.

Consider the ways that a citizen may encounter crime and the criminal justice system. He may experience it directly as a victim, an offender, or a witness to a crime event. These, in turn, may lead him to contact with agencies in the criminal justice system such as the police, the prosecutor, or lawyers for the defendant, the jails, courts, probation officer, correctional institutions, and their auxiliary agencies. One can also participate indirectly in the system by serving as a juror or in some capacity as a witness, other than testifying to the event. Quite clearly the criminal justice system works so that one is far more likely to be a victim or an offender than, for example, an arrested person, a convicted offender, a parolee. What remains unclear is whether one is more likely to be a victim of a crime than an offender, given the high probabilities attached to both. This question of whether victimization or offending is greater within a population cannot be answered without incidence and prevalence measures on both. Unfortunately, there are no good prevalence measures for victimization in the general population. Recent work for the National Crime Commission provides means of estimating the incidence of victimization in the population using sample surveys of the resident population.[156] Nonetheless, there are types of victimization from crime that were not measured in these surveys. As Biderman and Reiss point out, the choice of crime indicators and their measurement depends upon some organized system of knowing, no one of which is uniquely qualified to measure all kinds and levels of criminal activity.[157] The sample survey, for example, provides information on victimization of persons or their organizations where the reporting of victimization is socially acceptable. It is a relatively poor way to measure other aspects of crime such as its professionalization or organization.

Sample survey estimates of victimization show that, within a given period of time, at least twice as much victimization occurs as is officially recorded by the police.[158] Such estimates are conservative. Given how recall affects measurement, a single sample survey will give a poor estimate of the prevalence of victimization in a population.[159]

Estimating Criminal Offenders in a Population. Attempts to estimate the percentage of the future U.S. population that will have a criminal arrest record resulting from at least one nontraffic arrest, and the percentage that will have a criminal conviction record resulting from such an arrest were made by Christensen for the National Crime Commission.[160] Making such estimates requires assumptions about populations, crimes, arrests, and conviction trends. Christensen's model of estimation assumes a "steady state," that is, that the state of the mid-1960's would continue into the future.

---

[156] Biderman, *op. cit.,* pp. 16–33.
[157] Biderman and Reiss, *op. cit.,* pp. 1–15.
[158] Biderman, *op. cit.,* pp. 30–32.
[159] Biderman and Reiss, *op. cit.,* pp. 11–13.
[160] Christensen, *op. cit.,* Appendix J.

As Christensen's estimates in Table 2 show, the lifetime probability of a nontraffic arrest is 50 in 100 for males but only about 1 in 10 for females.[161] The probability is more than 6 in 10 for city men as contrasted with 2 in 10 for rural men. Nonwhite men and women have much higher chances of arrest than white men and women, particularly in the cities.

Table 2. Lifetime Probability of a Nontraffic Arrest

Males	*Percent*	*Females*	*Percent*
U.S. Males	56	U.S. Females	12
City	62	City	15
White	58	White	14
Nonwhite	90[a]	Nonwhite	25
Suburban	32	Suburban	7
White	30	White	7
Nonwhite	55	Nonwhite	12
Rural	22	Rural	4
White	21	White	3
Nonwhite	38	Nonwhite	7

[a] The data used were not sufficiently accurate to justify making other than general estimates of percentages exceeding 80 percent. In this case, effects such as differential survival probabilities between males and females and whites and nonwhites, which were not taken into consideration, as well as the basic uncertainties in the virgin arrest ratios, can produce distortions with greater absolute magnitudes.

These estimates are for all nontraffic offenses. Experience with major crimes against the person, such as homicide, aggravated assault, rape, or armed robbery, or with major offenses against one's property are less likely. Whether experiences in the more serious offenses affect one's evaluations of the criminal justice system differently than if one is involved in the less serious offenses is not known, a matter, however, that certainly requires investigation.

Conviction on an arrest is about 1 in 5 for men, but only 1 in 20 for women, as the Table 3 data from Christensen disclose.[162] These estimates may seem exceptionally high—a probability of 50 in 100 that a male will be arrested at some time in his life for a nontraffic arrest and a probability of 1 in 5 that he will be convicted following arrest. Such estimates, of course are no more valid and reliable than the assumptions in the model and the data on which they are based. The utility of such models for planning in a criminal justice system and for constantly monitoring the quality of life in a society make their continued development a high priority in research.

[161] *Ibid.*, p. 224.
[162] *Ibid.*, p. 225.

Table 3. Lifetime Probability of Conviction on Arrest

	Percent Arrests	Convictions per Arrest	Percent Corrected Lifetime Convictions
Males			19
City	62	.40	25
Suburban	32	.32	10
Rural	22	.33	7
Females			5
City	15	.39	6
Suburban	7	.36	3
Rural	4	.52	2

Effects of Victim Experiences. Without examining the data on victimization, it often is assumed that experiences with victimization are influential in shaping one's attitudes toward the evaluations of crime and the criminal justice system. The assumption is a difficult one to test, since too little is known about how to measure the effect of any given experience on evaluative processes, particularly their long-run effect.

Several recent studies provide a basis for concluding that there is no appreciable effect of experiences as a crime victim on one's attitudes about serious crimes, one's own safety, or attitudes toward law enforcement and the criminal justice system.[163] The NORC survey for the National Crime Commission showed that victims were somewhat more concerned about burglary and robbery.[164] But, as in the precinct profile studies, no differences were found between victims and non-victims in measures taken to protect their home and persons against crime. For the national survey 58 percent of the victims and 57 percent of the non-victims took measures to protect their households from victimization.[165] Moreover, measures of victimization showed no relationship to one's stance on civil rights,[166] or most attitudes about crime and criminals. In the Washington, D.C., studies for the Commission, Biderman developed indexes of exposure to crime and of anxiety about crime. The index of exposure to crime was based on whether oneself, family, or friends had been victimized by crime or whether one had personally witnessed crimes.[167] This index showed no significant relationship to the measure of anxiety about crime or toward their attitudes about crime and law enforcement in their areas.

[163] McIntyre, *op. cit.,* pp. 34–46.
[164] Ennis, *op. cit.,* Tables 48 and 50.
[165] *Ibid.,* Table 1.
[166] Biderman *et al.,* pp. 150–151.
[167] *Ibid.,* p. 161.

That victimization bears so little relationship to one's evaluations about crime and criminals and one's personal reaction to crime and criminals is surprising. Investigation should be continued, since it is generally assumed that experiences are important in forming attitudes and actions.

Measures to Reduce Risk as Response to Perceptions about Crime. The quality of life in a community is measured in part by the degree to which residents are free of fear as they go about in public. Regardless of the objective probabilities of victimization, which vary considerably among American communities, subjective estimates of victimization may be of greater consequence in determining one's behavior. In monitoring the quality of life in a community, therefore, one should develop a measure of the extent to which the individual feels personally safe in public and private places or, correlatively, fears being victimized by criminal activity in public and private places.

Several indicators have been developed to measure the perceptions that citizens have of their likelihood of victimization. The most general ones are those measuring perceptions about the crime problem in their area. Some measures ask residents to compare the present crime situation with that some time ago (whether crime has been increasing or decreasing, for example).[168] This can be asked for specific types of crime, such as crimes of violence. But the major measures developed to the present time are those that measure actions to reduce the risk of victimization from crime.

Personal Safety. It is a striking fact that in their evaluations of the environment, persons often regard themselves as well or better off than others. Only a small proportion of all citizens see themselves as living under "less than average" conditions. Such seems to be the case also with perceptions about crime and safety in one's own area. Studies for the National Crime Commission showed that a substantial proportion of persons living in high-crime-rate areas see crime as a serious problem and are alarmed by the rising crime rate. Yet, at the same time, a majority regard their own neighborhood as "average" or "very safe" as compared with other neighborhoods.[169] A significant minority saw themselves as less safe near home than in other parts of the city, however.

One way that citizens reduce the risk of victimization is to fail to act because they wish to ensure their safety. Indeed, information on failure to act generally can be secured only from reports of persons. Failure to act occasionally can be measured in other ways. This is true for market activity, for example, foregoing attending the movies may show up in reduced motion-picture theater attendance. On the whole, however, failure to act out of a fear of personal safety cannot be measured except from personal reports.

[168] *Ibid.,* p. 132; Reiss, "Public Perceptions and Recollections about Crime, Law Enforcement, and Criminal Justice," p. 95.
[169] Biderman, *op. cit.,* pp. 120–121; Reiss, "Public Perceptions . . .," pp. 28–34.

Several measures of desired action or failure to act have been utilized to measure fear of personal safety because of crime. One of these developed in surveys for the National Crime Commission asked respondents whether they would like to move because of crime in their neighborhood.[170] Others asked whether there is any area where the respondent is afraid to walk alone at night.[171] A Gallup poll asking this question in 1965 and 1967 showed that there was no significant change in the proportion expressing the view that there was such an area close by (about one-third of all residents).[172]

Another way that citizens can reduce risk of victimization is to change their way of living, opting for lower-risk patterns of behavior. Most indicators of change in risk measure *avoidance* behavior in public places such as "stay-in off the streets at night," "avoiding being out alone at night," or "avoiding talking to strangers."[173]

A third way that one can reduce risk of victimization is to take steps to increase one's personal protection and security. Some actions are designed to secure oneself in public, such as carrying a weapon or taking taxis rather than walking. Other activity is designed to protect oneself and property in a private place. This includes such actions as buying or installing protective devices, hiring protection (e.g., securing guards), or keeping weapons to defend oneself. Concern with violence in the United States has resulted in our monitoring the extent to which citizens have guns and are purchasing them. Without additional information, it is difficult to assess whether the motivation for their acquisition is violence or self-protection. In any case, if one is interested in ways that citizens express their fear by taking protective measures to reduce their risk of victimization, the gun is only one such measure.

A fourth way that citizens may reduce their risk is to take steps to reduce the consequences of victimization. One such measure to protect oneself against losses is to spread the risk by sharing the losses. Insurance is one way to collectivize risk. The monitoring of citizen behavior with respect to the acquisition of insurance for protective purposes is certainly one means of measuring the quality of life in an area.

There is considerable evidence that, on the average, the losses that citizens actually experience by victimization from crime are small. At the same time, it is evident that citizens may pay very high opportunity costs for feeling safe. Such opportunity costs may indeed be greater economic burdens for citizens than direct costs of victimization.[174] Better measures of such "oppor-

---

[170] Biderman, *op. cit.,* p. 121; Reiss, "Public Perceptions . . .," p. 31.

[171] Biderman, *op. cit.,* p. 129; Reiss, "Public Perceptions . . .," p. 103; Ennis, *op. cit.,* pp. 74–75

[172] AIPO, April, 1965 and August, 1967.

[173] Biderman *et al., op. cit.,* pp. 128–131; Ennis, *op. cit.,* pp. 77–78; Reiss, "Public Perceptions . . .," pp 102–112.

[174] McIntyre, *op. cit.,* pp. 38–39.

tunity costs" might be developed in assessing the effect of crime on a community.

Community Variation in Law Enforcement and Criminal Justice

Several years ago I wrote the following remarks in commenting upon the failure of American sociologists to develop a viable theory about community:

> Mention has been made of the fact that communities are a microcosm of the larger society. In a most important sense, however, the American community is the arena where the value and organizational conflicts of the larger society are played out.
>
> It is in the community that violence erupts and where rioting must be dealt with. Under these circumstances it is the local police who first are called upon to enforce the law and it is the local courts that are usually called upon to administer justice—even though in some cases they are under a more general jurisdiction. A local community, too, has considerable power to legislate— legislation that affects people's rights and opportunities. For in the United States much of the law in relation to land use, traffic, housing, health, education, and welfare is developed and enforced at the local level. The community is likewise a major political unit in either stabilizing or changing these conditions. It is not surprising, therefore, that one is most likely to encounter conflict and violent outburst in the context of a governing community in the United States. Indeed, it attests to the fact that communities are perhaps more autonomous and viable as units in the American social system than much of the literature of American sociology suggests.
>
> Geared, as it has been for much of its recent history to investigating the current structure and functioning of American communities, sociology in the United States has neglected the investigation of the community as the arena within which value conflicts of the society are often engendered, frequently carried on, and usually resolved. The sociology of the next years may well redress these omissions.[175]

To redress these omissions, more effort should be concentrated on selecting those indicators that are particularly indicative of differences among communities. Schuman and Gruenberg have found, for example, that attitudes toward law enforcement, discrimination in employment and housing, and other attitude variables in the Campbell and Schuman study for the National Advisory Commission on Civil Disorders are explained either by city variation or by attributes of individuals, not both. One of the few instances they observed where both city and individual variation explain attitudes, however, is for belief in police abuse.[176]

[175] Albert J. Reiss, Jr., "Some Sociological Issues about American Communities," in Talcott Parsons, ed., *American Sociology: Perspectives, Problems, Methods.* Basic Books, New York, 1968.
[176] Schuman and Gruenberg, *op. cit.,* pp. 227–229.

Schuman and Gruenberg's analysis provides us with some criteria for assessing which variables are more likely to be explained by city differences and which by individual characteristics. Questions that deal directly with city officials and city services not unexpectedly had a high variance accounted for by city, while questions that were more personal or had a personality reference had more variance accounted for by individual attributes.[177] Although the finding seems obvious enough, it suggests that one will find city effects on individual opinion and attitudes where city differences exist. Moreover, their examination of the independent power of city as a predictor and the type of variables it best predicts showed that the explanatory power of city lies in the cognitive perceptions of social reality rather than in its conative or motivational side.[178] What this means, perhaps, is that community variation in citizen assessments of the reality of crime, law enforcement, and criminal justice systems generally will be explained by attributes of cities rather than attributes of individuals and, correlatively, that opinions about punishment or treatment of criminals, anxiety about criminal victimization, or the seriousness of criminal offenses are more likely to be explained by individual attributes.

If one of our goals is to develop indicators that are appropriate for community action as well as for national action, then clearly they should be investigated in terms of the independent power of variation among cities as an explanatory variable.

Summary and Conclusions

Our treatment of subjective indicators of the quality of criminal justice systems has brought forth a rather large number of measures, even though our catalogue is not exhaustive. It has occurred to the reader, I am sure, that not all of these are equally important for a given purpose. In conclusion, I should like to suggest that some are more important than others for the evolution of theory, the development of policy and practice, and for the measurement of social change.

There are several types of theory that have been implicit in our discussion of indicators of the quality of criminal justice systems. There is general behavioral theory of decision and action, some general theories about social change, and somewhat more explicit propositions about bureaucratically organized systems of discretionary authority.

Interest in behavioral theory should lead us to investigate some of the relations among perceptions of rewards and punishments as determinants of decisions. Mention was made earlier that, generally, people will overestimate probabilities associated with favorable consequences and underestimate prob-

---

[177] *Ibid.*, p. 230.
[178] *Ibid.*, pp. 230–231.

abilities associated with unfavorable consequences. Such may not always be the case where criminal violations and sanctions are at stake. In point of fact, we know very little about how various values, probabilities, and combinations of value and probability affect decisions to violate norms or to impose sanctions. Since for major norm violations there is a high negative value to violation but a fairly low probability to detection, this combination is of special interest.

Both for sociological theory and policy, special interest attaches to investigating the relationship between experience and action. We observed that there seems to be little relationship between one's experience as a victim of crime and one's attitudes and opinions about the criminal justice system, or the steps one takes to deal with crime. This remains one of the unexpected findings of the surveys on victimization and invites investigation.

Special attention should be given to whether there are not substantial media effects producing differences in attitudes and opinion where actual experience seems negligible. Some years ago Robert Hodge pointed out to the staff of the National Crime Commission that one of the effects of a growing population is that, even without any increase in the crime rate, there are simply *more* sensational and violent crimes to be reported in the mass media.[179] Reporting, in turn, may have unintended effects such as high opportunity costs created by reduced social interaction that comes about as the result of induced fear. Indeed, any substantial reduction in the public habits of persons may itself be an important factor in victimization from crime. For nothing may inhibit most crimes of violence in public as much as the presence of others. All of this needs to be moved beyond speculation, however, by more careful investigation.

Following work for the National Crime Commission on victimization of citizens, the Law Enforcement Assistance Act (LEAA) has contracted with the Bureau of the Census to develop periodic surveys of the criminal victimization of households, businesses, and government organizations. It is of considerable importance to continue such surveys as a means of monitoring the level of crime in the society. Such surveys, however, should determine how the behavior of citizens in reporting crimes may be more effectively linked to the police as an organization for monitoring crime. This means that any interest in changing citizen behavior requires that we pay attention not only to reasons citizens give for failing to cooperate with or mobilize the police, but also of reasons why they do so.

Despite the lack of fit between experience and attitudes on crime and law enforcement, it is important that we continue to monitor selected attitudes and opinions toward victimization because of their immediate relevance to public policies. Of particular importance is continued measurement of the level of fear or anxiety that persons have about being victimized by crime and the actual

---

[179] Hodge, *op. cit.*

behavior they engage in as a result of their attributions. Whether or not their fears are "real," the consequences in higher opportunity costs may be so.

Increasingly, there is a concern in American society for the quality of discretionary authority and a desire to hold such authorities accountable. This interest means that we must try to develop indicators of the quality of the exercise of discretionary authority at all levels of the criminal justice system and of how citizens may (or could) hold authority accountable. Not only must we have indicators of the quality of police discretion but of that exercised by prosecutors, judges, and others in the system as well. Special interest should attach to developing indicators of the positive features in the exercise of discretion. Thus, we need measures not only of dissatisfaction with particular forms of official behavior, but also of satisfaction.

Although there is often theoretical or even practical interest in some matters of quality in the criminal justice system, it is apparent that significant portions of the population cannot reasonably be expected to have an informed judgment on the matters. Although there are ways of separating persons who are capable of making informed judgments from those who are not, there are nevertheless good reasons to reject such indicators for monitoring on a regular basis, particularly with general population samples. The quality of "justice" to the "poor" may be assessed more appropriately by studies of how the organizations process them than by any survey of relatively uninformed opinion.

In conclusion, given the many qualitative features of crime and criminal justice systems that might be investigated, our efforts should be concentrated in a few domains because of their theoretical, methodological, and policy interest. These domains are those of victimization by crime, the quality of discretionary authority and service for citizens, and the accountability of public servants.

11

Aspiration, Satisfaction, and Fulfillment

Angus Campbell

In the United States during the past decade, official rhetoric in high places has demonstrated an increasing concern with the quality of the American way of life. On revealing the first indistinct image of the Great Society in his speech at the University of Michigan in May, 1964, President Lyndon Johnson spoke of advancing "the quality of American civilization." Subsequently, Senator Walter F. Mondale introduced into the Senate a bill designed to create a Council of Social Advisers which would report on "the state of the nation's social health." In 1969 President Richard Nixon announced the establishment of a National Goals Research Staff which was to have among its functions "developing and monitoring social indicators that can reflect the present and future quality of American life, and the direction and rate of its change."

Social commentary of all kinds is now replete with references to the quality of modern living. The meaning of this phrase obviously differs a good deal as it is variously used but, in general, it is intended to refer either to the conditions of the environment in which people live or to some attribute of people themselves. The first case includes concern with pollution of the air and water, overcrowding in the cities, poor housing, the inadequacy of recreation areas, and similar aspects of living. The second typically includes references to health, family stability, educational achievement, artistic and cultural concerns, and other such dimensions on which people differ.

One does not ordinarily speak of the quality of life without implying a comparison of what exists to some more or less explicit standard of what ought to exist. Thus, it is clear in all of the examples given above that things ought to be better than they are. There should be less pollution and better housing; people should have less sickness and more education. Bertram Gross has proposed that there be an annual Social Report to the President in which an accounting be given the nation of how well or badly it is doing in meeting standards of quality in these measures of "social well-being."[1] The purpose of this Social Report would be "to make America more conscious of the factors involved in enriching the quality of life and moving toward something that might be termed a 'great society.'"

Our purpose in this essay is to approach the concept of quality of life at a different level than that implied by the kinds of measures we have been discussing. We will be concerned with the quality of personal experience, with the frustrations, satisfactions, disappointments, and fulfillment that people feel as they live their lives in our changing society. Ultimately, the quality of life must be in the eye of the beholder, and it is there that we seek ways to evaluate it. This is regarded as dangerous ground by some, specifically by Professor Gross, who observes "Since satisfactions and dissatisfactions are almost impossible to observe directly, we must use a wide variety of 'surrogates,' that is, indirect indicators that serve us as quantitative substitutes or representatives of the phenomena we want to identify or measure."[2]

Without questioning the value of these "surrogates" as social indicators in their own right, I cannot feel satisfied that the correspondence between such objective measures as amount of money earned, number of rooms occupied, or type of job held, and the subjective satisfaction with these conditions of life, is close enough to warrant accepting the one as a replacement for the other. Indeed, I will undertake to demonstrate that the correspondence is in some instances rather weak. The attraction of "factual data" that can be readily counted is certainly strong, but in my view the possibility of assessing the direct experience is more appealing than accepting the surrogates which may be highly reliable but not entirely valid.

In focusing attention on satisfactions and dissatisfactions, I do not wish to imply that perceived satisfactions can be equated in a simplistic way with quality of life. Satisfactions and frustrations depend jointly on objective reality on one side and aspirations and expectations on the other. Concern over the quality of life must include a hope for personal development beyond the individual's present limits of vision. Upgrading the quality of life implies progressive liberation from the constricting limits of modest aspiration levels and increasing fulfillment of the human potential.

An attempt to map all of the goals to which people aspire would be a discouraging undertaking; an attempt must be made to reduce the almost infinite variety of human goals that might be identified into some system of categories.

[1] Bertram Gross, "The Social State of the Nation," *Trans-action,* vol. 3, November/December, 1965, pp. 14–17.

[2] Bertram Gross, "The State of the Nation: Social Systems Accounting," in Raymond A. Bauer, ed., *Social Indicators.* M.I.T. Press, Cambridge, Mass., 1966, p. 221.

We will take as the basis of the ensuing discussion Abraham Maslow's theory of a hierarchy of human needs.[3] Maslow proposes that the basic physiological needs of hunger and thirst and the maintenance of homeostatic mechanisms of the body are the most primitive and prepotent of all needs and that other higher needs cannot emerge until these are satisfied. Assuming the gratification of these needs, the need for safety must be met, meaning security in the surrounding environment and protection from physical dangers. If these underlying physiological and safety needs are reasonably gratified, the need for love, affection, and belongingness emerges, the need for fulfilling interpersonal relations. At the next level is the need for self-respect, self-esteem, and the esteem of others. This divides into the desire for prestige, status, and dominance. Finally, if all these needs are satisfied there remains the need for self-actualization—the desire for self-fulfillment—to become everything that one is capable of becoming.

This set of need categories provides a simple map on which we can plot an individual's aspirations, satisfactions and frustrations. We must recognize at once that society is divided into subpopulations which differ greatly in the degree to which they find their worlds satisfying, and the profile of need satisfaction which we might find for one such segment of the population may have quite a different contour than that of another. Even taking account of these differences, we will inevitably oversimplify the status of need satisfactions in American society, both in reducing the range of needs to the Maslow pattern and in dividing a highly heterogeneous population into a limited number of contrasting categories.

It is evident at the outset that satisfaction and deprivation are psychological concepts and that we cannot assume that levels of living that are objectively equal or similar will have the same meaning to everyone. People evaluate their achievements in relation to their levels of aspiration, and what may be entirely gratifying to one person may be intolerably frustrating to another. Moreover, levels of aspirations change through time, and what may be satisfying at one point in a person's life may become dissatisfying at another time. Satisfaction is an entirely personal experience, and the input required to produce this experience varies greatly from person to person.

It is no doubt the highly individual quality of the experience of satisfaction that has raised doubts as to whether it can ever be successfully assessed directly. Is it reasonable to equate experiences which depend on such contrasting objective conditions? Can it be said that the satisfaction of a college student who has been elected captain of his football team is equal to that of a candidate who has been elected to the United States Senate? In some sense, no; for example, the one achievement may be thought to represent a more important

---

[3] Abraham H. Maslow, *Motivation and Personality*. Harper, New York, 1954.

goal than the other. But in the sense that specific aspirations are fulfilled, they are equally fulfilled. The satisfactions are equal in the sense that two bottles may be equally full even though one holds much more than the other.

In the discussion which follows we will assume that satisfaction and dissatisfaction are experiences that most people can report with reasonable validity. We will undertake to review those research findings which seem important and suggest additional measurements which might be desirable to provide a fuller documentation of the quality of life as Americans experience it.

Basic Physiological Needs

A nation of affluence should not have great trouble in providing its people the essential food, clothing, and shelter necessary to maintain life. Americans have become used to believing that "no one starves in this country," and they are shocked to discover that pockets of serious malnutrition exist in some of the poorer areas of the nation. Our housing has more electricity and plumbing than that of any other country, but our large cities all contain slum areas which are an affront to the eye. It is apparent that in affluent America the soaring national income is leaving a good many people far behind.[4]

It is easily possible to establish an objective standard of an adequate diet, and attempts have been made on the basis of household surveys to estimate the proportion of the population that actually meets or falls below this standard. Recent studies of the national population by the Survey Research Center estimate that, in 1967, 12 percent of the families of the United States spent less on food than would be required to meet Department of Agriculture (USDA) standards of minimum food needs.[5] Impressive as this figure is, its full impact is not apparent until we take into consideration the fact that these families account for almost one-fifth of all the children under 18 years of age. Nineteen percent of American children live in families whose food expenditures are below the level necessary to support a diet that the USDA classifies as minimally adequate. An incredible 50 percent of black children live in such families.

These studies make clear that the American diet falls far short of satisfying objective measures of adequacy, but they do not tell us to what extent these shortcomings are translated into personal dissatisfactions. It may be that most people whose food intake is objectively substandard are subjectively satis-

[4] A recent statement of the nature of poverty in the United States is presented in the report of the President's Commission on Income Maintenance Programs entitled *Poverty Amid Plenty*. Government Printing Office, Washington, D.C., 1969.

[5] John B. Lansing and Katherine Rogin, "Consumption Patterns of the Poor." Unpublished manuscript, Survey Research Center, Institute for Social Research, University of Michigan, Ann Arbor, 1969.

fied with it. How does a person raised in poverty learn to expect something more than a poverty diet? Presumably some do. It would be desirable to know how many such people there are and who they are. How many people if asked: "Do you think your children are getting all the food they need to be healthy and strong?" would answer "No"? How do these people differ from other parents of similar social and economic circumstances who answer this question "Yes"?

There has probably been a long-term upgrading of the aspirations of the general public regarding what they eat and drink. The substantial rise in educational levels and the diligent propaganda of the nutritionists can hardly have failed to have raised public concepts of what is an acceptable diet. There may also be a rising unwillingness among poverty-level families to accept as inevitable a diet that does not satisfy; the discrepancy between inadequacy and subjective dissatisfaction may be narrowing. These speculations are entirely without empirical support, however, and will remain so until greater interest is shown in this very basic aspect of human needs and satisfactions.

The need for shelter translates in modern society into the need for housing. No doubt, for most people, housing fulfills needs that go far beyond simple protection from the elements. One's home is the locus of family life, a refuge from an intrusive world, in a word, one's castle. It remains, however, a shelter in both an elemental and a derived sense, and the individual's evaluation of this aspect of his environment must contribute substantially to his sense of the quality of his life.

The growing crisis in the cities has greatly increased interest in the importance of housing as a factor in the current national malaise. It is not uncommon to find housing referred to as the heart of the urban problem; Robert C. Wood, former Undersecretary of the Department of Housing and Urban Development (HUD), in 1968 spoke of "the nation's most pressing urban problem, which is housing."[6] Statistics regarding the state of the nation's physical plant are systematically collected, and it is easy to draw the inference that bad housing has contributed substantially to bad tempers in the cities.

The physical conditions in which people live in this country certainly vary tremendously, in square feet per person, in age and state of repair, in light, heating, kitchen and bathroom facilities, and in the quality of the surrounding environment. But it is doubtful if we can assume that satisfaction with housing is closely associated with these physical characteristics. Figure 1 shows the proportions of people in a large-scale urban survey who described themselves as "very satisfied" with their housing.[7] If satisfaction with housing

[6] Robert C. Wood, "Rediscovery of the American City," *Technology Review*, vol. 70, January, 1968, p. 47.

[7] Angus Campbell, "White Attitudes Toward Black People." Survey Research Center, Institute for Social Research, University of Michigan, Ann Arbor, 1971.

were closely associated with the physical quality of housing, we would expect to find progressively rising curves in Figure 1, since people with higher income live in better circumstances than those with less. In fact, the differences in levels of satisfaction expressed by people of different income are rather modest. High-income people of both races are clearly more pleased with their housing than are less affluent families, but through the low and middle ranges of the income scale the differences are small.

Figure 1. Satisfaction with Housing by Level of Family Income in 15 American Cities

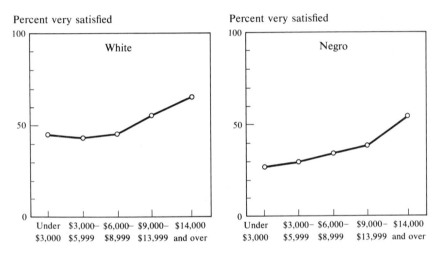

Figure 1 provides a reminder that satisfaction is a subjective experience, and it is better understood in relation to another subjective fact, level of aspiration, than it is to objective reality. Upper-middle-class urban planners may find it hard to believe that anyone could be "happy" with the blighted housing in which the urban poor live, but the answers to survey questions make it clear that, among the white poor at least, nearly half describe themselves as "very satisfied" with their lodgings. No doubt they would be pleased to have something better, but their perception of discrepancy between their achievement and their aspiration is not strong enough to produce an acute sense of deprivation.

The distribution of Negro attitudes in Figure 1 gives an additional indication of the fact that satisfaction with housing depends on psychological as well as physical considerations. If people feel that they must, because of social prejudice, live in houses or in neighborhoods which are not their choice, their frustration with this involuntary quality of their housing may transcend any other feeling they may have about it. The fact that Negroes of all income levels express more dissatisfaction with their housing than white people of comparable rank suggests that these people are moved by the common problem of racial discrimination in housing. If this in fact is a major contributor to Negroes' dissatisfaction with their housing in the inner city, the replacement of their present homes with what has been called a "gilded ghetto" may not greatly improve this aspect of the quality of their lives.

A question asking merely for satisfaction or dissatisfaction with housing undoubtedly oversimplifies a rather complex experience. To provide an adequate measurement of the evaluation people put on their housing would require readings of the kinds described in detail by Peter Rossi in Chapter 3. He prescribes measures of satisfaction with the interior characteristics of the dwelling unit, with its exterior characteristics, with its location in physical space, and with its location in social space. If we were to ask a series of questions covering these various dimensions of the quality of a person's housing, we might find differences by status level that do not appear in Figure 1. A single global question may serve to disguise important differentials and to cover up dissatisfactions that a more detailed inquiry would reveal.

Although little direct evidence of a longitudinal character exists that would tell us what people of various statuses and locations consider desirable and satisfactory in their housing, it seems most probable that their aspirations and expectations have been rising. Whether these expectations are being fulfilled more adequately now than they were at an earlier time is another unanswered question. We know that the physical quality of housing in the cities has improved substantially since the Second World War, but we do not know whether the people who live there are more or less satisfied with what they have. We assume that much of the mobility that characterizes the American population is motivated by a search for more satisfactory housing. Those who move to the suburbs seem in large part to be searching for a single-family house. The single-family house appears to have become a cultural ideal in this country, even among those of modest circumstances. It is an ideal that has been realized by a very sizable proportion of suburban residents, but it will clearly not be achieved by most people in the inner city.

Rising affluence has undoubtedly made it possible for an increasing proportion of the population to acquire housing that fulfills all or most of the dimensions of satisfaction enumerated. Affluence is very unequally distributed, however, and for many people, especially urban Negroes, housing is evidently an unsatisfactory and frustrating experience. The extent to which this experience can be improved by the vast programs of public housing now contemplated by the federal government remains problematic; satisfaction with housing involves more than simply numbers. As research tells us more about what people value in their housing, we may find that space and physical condition are not the primary factors and that such psychological considerations as familiarity with the neighborhood, proximity of friends, and the appropriateness of location to one's social status make a greater contribution to the satisfaction or dissatisfaction that a person feels about the place in which he lives.[8]

Safety Needs

In 1954, Abraham Maslow wrote, "the healthy, normal, fortunate adult in our culture is largely satisfied in his safety needs. The peaceful, smooth-running good society ordinarily makes its members feel safe enough from wild animals, extremes of temperature, criminal assault, murder, tyranny, etc. Therefore, in a very real sense, he no longer has any safety needs as active motivators." Had Maslow been writing in 1970, he might not have made such a confident statement.

One of the psychological changes that has surely accompanied the shift in the pattern of American life during the past decade is an increase in the sense of insecurity and apprehension at being abroad in the streets of our cities. The lack of public concern with this problem at the time Maslow was writing his book is demonstrated by the fact that polling agencies did not see fit to ask questions about it. Recently, however, the issue has become far more salient, and Dr. Gallup reports that one-third of his national sample tell him that there are areas within a mile of their home where they would not feel safe walking at night. They are not greatly disturbed by the danger of wild animals, but they are frightened by the possibility of assault by their fellow citizens.

No doubt some individuals in our society are far more sensitive to threats to their safety than others. The reports in the media of middle-class white women being instructed in the use of firearms by their local police gives something of the flavor of the degree of threat these people feel. Individuals will differ in their sensitivity to insecurity as a reflection of their own underlying personality structure, but they will also differ according to their location in the social order. This is demonstrated in rough terms by comparing the reports of whites and blacks in the cities and whites in the suburbs in their satisfaction with the police protection they receive. In a sample study of populations of 15 major cities, the following proportions expressed themselves as generally satisfied:

46 percent of black people in the cities
67 percent of white people in the cities
84 percent of white people in the suburbs.

[8] A recent study finds, for example, that satisfaction with one's neighborhood is related to the compatibility of the neighbors and how well they "keep up" their property but not to dwelling unit density. See John B. Lansing, Robert W. Marans, and Robert B. Zehner, *Planned Residential Environments*. Institute for Social Research, University of Michigan, Ann Arbor, 1970.

We also find that, within each race, those people of high income are more likely to express satisfaction with their police protection than people of low income.

The striking increase in crimes against the person reported in recent years reverses a long-term trend toward the reduction of such crimes and compels a reassessment of the "peaceful, smooth-running" quality of our society.[9] Violence is certainly on the increase and public insecurity must also be growing. Documentation of this change is almost entirely lacking; social scientists obviously did not anticipate such a trend and did nothing to plot its movement. Consequently, we find ourselves confronted by what appears to be a profound change in public attitudes which we do not understand. This, alas, seems to be our characteristic situation during this period of far-reaching social change.

It would not appear to be beyond the scope of survey methods to provide a continuing measurement of the sense of physical security Americans feel in their everyday life. Such an inquiry might begin with an identification of those elements in the life space that appear threatening to one's sense of safety. Personal assault is a dramatic example, but there may be other, less obvious experiences which frighten. Does the noise and rush of metropolitan crowds and traffic disturb people who live in this environment? Or the necessity of submitting to mechanical devices such as subway trains, elevators, automobiles, and the like? Does the persistent news of public disturbances and disorders create a general sense of unease? Is the threat of natural disaster such as earthquakes, floods, windstorms, and such more than an occasional disturbance? How many people feel insecure at the prospect of nuclear war?

Who is afraid, and of what? As Maslow points out, "Some neurotic adults are . . . like the unsafe child in their desire for safety." They react to "unknown, psychological dangers in a world that is perceived to be hostile, overwhelming and threatening." Presumably most adults do not have such generalized fear of the world around them, although they may feel unsafe in particular situations. It would appear, for example, that some white people are afraid of Negroes, and with the recent rise in black assertiveness, this number may be growing. No doubt part of the Negro response to white people is compounded by fear. The police may create fear in some parts of the community and their own situation may be fear inspiring. Old people may have special reasons for apprehension and insecurity. We have only plausible guesses as to where in our society people feel unsafe, what is the source of their fears, and what is the long-term trend.

No better example of the discrepancy between the objective quality of life and the psychological quality could be asked for than the apparent rise in

---

[9] The National Commission on the Causes and Prevention of Violence reports a 100 percent increase in the rate of violent crime (homicide, forcible rape, robbery, and aggravated assault) between 1958 and 1968. See *To Establish Justice, To Insure Domestic Tranquillity*. Government Printing Office, Washington, D.C., 1969, p. xiv.

public insecurity at a time of rising public affluence. Whatever the physical attributes of a community may be, a place in which people are increasingly in fear of their lives can hardly be said to be improving in quality.

Belongingness and Love Needs

The need for human acceptance and affection has been noted at various points in this volume. Relationships in marriage, in the larger family, in the work group, and elsewhere provide, in greater or less degree, the psychological support and reward which gratify this need.

Research interest in the love need appears to have been more concerned with failure in its fulfillment than in success. Since a large fraction of the population who come to the attention of clinical psychologists and psychiatrists are suffering from some sense of deprivation or conflict in this area of their lives, it is not surprising that the frustration of this need commands more attention than its gratification. The gratified person does not present such a dramatic image, and therefore he tends to go unremarked.

If we were concerned only with those members of society whose failures in love relationships are so severe as to lead them into contact with medical or paramedical personnel, we might attempt to follow through time the total number of such people, their social origins, and the nature of the situation that produced their difficulties. It is doubtful if the availability of medical records and the varying standards of diagnosis would make this enterprise entirely satisfying, but it might be possible over time to develop aggregative data of some validity. Of course, our interest includes the entire population as well as this extreme segment, and medical statistics, however accurate, would tell us only part of what we want to know.

We do not know how Americans would respond if they were asked to describe their need for love and belonging or whether, indeed, this question would make sense to the ordinary person. Some period of development would be necessary to refine this concept into more specifically defined dimensions and to develop measures which could be used with the general population. The national survey of Gurin, Veroff, and Feld provides a background of information concerning the satisfactions and problems associated with marriage, parent-child relationships, and the job.[10] These data do not deal specifically with satisfactions and dissatisfactions associated with the affectional aspects of these relationships, but they suggest ways in which such an inquiry might be developed.

A national reading on the extent to which people feel their need for

---

[10] Gerald Gurin, Joseph Veroff, and Sheila Feld, *Americans View Their Mental Health*. Basic Books, New York, 1960.

affection fulfilled or deprived would not in itself be as interesting or as important as the identification of those segments within society that feel themselves
loved or unloved and the study of how these segments change in their sense of
satisfaction or dissatisfaction as changes in the larger society or their situation in it occur. A variety of such special studies suggest themselves.

Youth. It is commonplace at the present time to hear young people spoken
of as alienated. Youth are widely described as "turned off" by the society in
which they live, detached from their families and lacking in sense of social
belonging. It is very difficult to know how accurately these terms describe
contemporary young people, and even more difficult to know how the present
generation of youth differs from preceding generations. It is apparent that
some young people, especially those on college campuses, are prepared to engage in open conflict with local authority, but they appear to be a very small
fraction of the age cohort to which they belong, and their motivation seems
very mixed.[11] The additional small percent who have "dropped out" give a
different, and, in some respects, more convincing image of alienation, despite
the fact that "love" figures prominently in their rhetoric.

Because of our past failure to study the values and attitudes of the nation's youth, we are unable to say whether the apparent changes we now see in
some young people express a failure to give and receive love from their families and from broader social entities or whether they spring from entirely different motivation. It is doubtful if college students ever felt any great affection
for the Board of Regents; perhaps because of a more permissive experience in
their own homes, they are simply less respectful of authority. Perhaps the
turmoil among young people owes its major dynamic to the Vietnam War and
the threat it poses for young men. The fact that the "rebellion" of the young is
being waged largely by the offspring of affluent families suggests that there
now exists a basic sense of economic security among those people which
makes possible contumaceous behavior that, at an earlier time, might have appeared to have more dangerous consequences.

Since we know so little about the motivation that underlies the behavior
of present-day youth, we can only speculate as to how it has been influenced
by changes in the larger society. If mass alienation is in fact growing within
the coming-of-age generation, the implications are serious enough to warrant
a major effort to monitor this movement and to understand its origins. The
only continuing study of American youth at the high school level is the Purdue
University poll which has provided a great deal of information over the years
but has not probed very deeply into questions of this nature. There has been
a plethora of studies of college students, some of them detailed analyses of in-

---

[11] Joseph Katz *et al., No Time for Youth: Growth and Constraint in College Students.* Jossey-Bass, San Francisco, 1968.

dividual cases (Keniston),[12] others using larger populations and more impersonal forms of data gathering (Gurin, Newcomb, and Cope).[13] There is at present only a beginning of a program of research which seeks to describe the entire population of youth, college and noncollege, alienated and nonalienated, to follow its psychological changes from adolescence into adulthood, and to identify the associations between these changes and the circumstances of life that these people experience.[14] We have apparently come to the end of the period when youth could be taken for granted in this country, but we have made only a small start in developing an informed understanding of the relationship which now exists between the various segments of the 15- to 25-year-old generation and the rest of society.

The Inner City. The murder of Kitty Genovese in the stairway of her apartment house in Brooklyn within the hearing of some 38 unresponsive neighbors illustrates the extent to which the quality of common humanity has been strained in the metropolis. The refusal of these witnesses to involve themselves in defending this unfortunate woman from attack, or even to call the police, testifies to how little these people felt themselves bound by any sense of community or human brotherhood. The metropolitan press carries frequent reports of similar incidents, usually not as dramatic but equally impressive of the unwillingness of city dwellers to concern themselves with the troubles of their fellow man.

The iniquities of the city have been a popular theme for many years.[15] The anonymous quality of urban living in contrast to the *"Gemeinschaft"* of the smaller communities has been described and deplored by countless critics of urban life. Whether or not the life of the average city dweller is becoming more dehumanized is a question we cannot answer.[16] It seems beyond dispute that the incidence of interpersonal violence in the cities has increased sharply during the past decade, but it is difficult to attribute this change to any specific

---

[12] Kenneth Keniston, *The Uncommitted: Alienated Youth in American Society*. Dell, New York, 1967.

[13] Gerald Gurin, Theodore M. Newcomb, and Robert G. Cope, "Characteristics of Entering Freshmen Related to Attrition in the Literary College of a Large State University." Report to the Office of Education, Department of Health, Education, and Welfare, 1968.

[14] Jerald G. Bachman *et al., Youth in Transition*, vols. I and II. Survey Research Center, Institute for Social Research, University of Michigan, Ann Arbor, 1967.

[15] A review of the literature on this argument is provided by Morton White and Lucia White, *The Intellectual Versus the City: From Thomas Jefferson to Frank Lloyd Wright*. Harvard University Press, Cambridge, Mass., 1962.

[16] We note, however, that Inkeles and Smith conclude from their study of six developing societies that "Exposure to the impersonality of urban life, to its plethora of stimuli, to its frenzied pace, and to its crowded conditions does not unmistakably induce psychosomatic symptoms." Alex Inkeles and David H. Smith, "The Fate of Personal Adjustment in the Process of Modernization," *International Journal of Comparative Sociology*, vol. 11, June, 1970, pp. 81–114.

aspect of the city environment. On the contrary, it may be caused in large part by the circulation of population elements within the cities, the replacement of middle-class whites by lower-class whites and blacks of rural and Southern origin.

It should not be too difficult to develop measures that would give some assessment of the extent to which city people feel anonymous and unloved. Axelrod's study of social relationships among families in Detroit suggests one method of plotting the network of affectionate connections that the individual city dweller has in the society around him.[17] This might be extended to the enumeration of a larger sociometric map, including people whom one addresses by name (storekeeper, policeman, bus driver) but does not socialize with, or a still more remote ring of people whom one recognizes as familiar but cannot identify. Personal relationships in the work situation provide an important element of the city dweller's total sociometry, for some perhaps the most important element. The extent to which the neighborhood network overlaps that of the work situation is a question of interest.

Plotting these personal relationships would provide a reasonably objective basis for the comparison of the range of affectional associations experienced by different segments of the population and, over time, should give dependable readings of changes in the breadth and depth of these networks. It would not, however, give any direct reading of the extent to which people identify with their community, feel any sense of friendliness with their fellow citizens, or feel themselves supported or threatened by them. Robert Angell demonstrated in 1947 a variety of ways in which measures of this kind could be obtained from an urban cross section, but his pioneering studies have not been followed up.[18] Recently the Survey Research Center has been experimenting with an adaptation of Rosenberg's misanthropy scale, a series of questions intended to measure "trust in people," asking its respondents whether they think most people can be trusted, generally try to be helpful, or try to take advantage of you.[19] This scale needs to be refined and additional measures are needed which will give better information than is now available regarding the positive and negative meanings the surrounding community has for the individual citizen.

Older People. The plight of the unwanted and unloved aged person has been a problem for society since antiquity. American society has never countenanced any of the procrustean devices by which some preliterate societies have

---

[17] Morris Axelrod, "Urban Structure and Social Participation," *American Sociological Review,* vol. 21, February, 1956, pp. 12–18.

[18] Robert C. Angell, "The Moral Integration of American Cities," *American Journal of Sociology,* vol. 57, Part 2, July, 1947, pp. 1–140.

[19] John P. Robinson and Phillip R. Shaver, *Measures of Social Psychological Attitudes.* Survey Research Center, Institute for Social Research, University of Michigan, Ann Arbor, 1969, p. 529.

lightened this burden but it has found its own ways to ameliorate it. These ways have changed over the last 50 years, and it is questionable whether these changes have increased the sense of loving support older people feel as they live through their terminal years.

During the last half-century, this country has become urbanized, the number of large families has declined, affluence has become widespread, and the ideal of the nuclear family has displaced that of the extended family. As a consequence, the younger generation find it increasingly inconvenient and disagreeable to devote themselves to an aged parent or grandparent. The older person, through his retirement income or with the help of his more affluent children, may be able to arrange for more impersonal care of an institutional kind. He is likely to find himself physically removed from those whom he would ordinarily look to for love and must look elsewhere for affectional support.

Despite the greatly increased interest in the economic, social, and psychological problems of older people that we have witnessed in this country since the Second World War, it cannot be said that an adequate program of study of their psychological situation currently exists. The inexorable increase in the numbers of people of retirement age has compelled a concern for research on the national economic implications of aging, but no comparable activity can be seen on the psychological side. Many local studies of restricted populations have been done, but they have not been expanded to a national base. For example, the measures of "life satisfaction" developed by Neugarten, Havighurst, and Tobin in studies of older people in Kansas City have not been carried beyond the developmental stage.[20]

It may well be that the lugubrious stereotype of the old person who feels rejected and unloved is a gross misrepresentation of fact. It may be more stressful for an old person to live in the household of his children than to live with other people of his age in an old-age community. We have no way of knowing whether the older generation of an earlier day felt their needs for love and belonging more fully realized than are those of the current generation of old people because no evidence of any consequence exists from that earlier day. There is also very little evidence of the feelings of old people in the present day; consequently, there is very little basis of knowing how they are changing as social conditions change around them.

Esteem Needs

"All people in our society," writes Maslow, "have a need or desire for a stable, firmly based, usually high evaluation of themselves, for self-respect, or self-esteem, and for the esteem of others." They desire achievement and recognition.

[20] Bernice Neugarten, Robert Havighurst, and Sheldon Tobin, "The Measurement of Life Satisfaction," *Journal of Gerontology,* vol. 16, April, 1961, pp. 134–143.

The psychological importance of self-esteem has been recognized by personality theorists for many years, and concern with it has undoubtedly filled many a psychiatrist's hour. Numerous attempts have been made to develop scales intended to measure this variable, but as a recent review observes, it "has been difficult to operationalize well." It is arguable as to whether people typically have a single, over-all evaluation of themselves rather than various evaluations of different personal attributes. There is question whether one's self-esteem does not vary from day to day as experiences of success and failure follow each other. There is great difficulty in establishing the validity of a measure which purports to reflect an experience known only to the individual concerned. There is the underlying problem of whether a person who esteems himself highly in relation to a relatively low level of aspiration should be equated with a person whose estimate of himself is based on a much higher aspiration level. Despite these complexities, Robinson and Shaver's review lists 16 different studies concerned more or less directly with the dimension of self-esteem.[21] They vary greatly in definitions and techniques and some of them have been developed for specialized populations (Negro sixth-graders, grade school children, college students). Relatively few studies of the general public have been reported.

A great deal of initiative has been shown by the authors of these various studies, but there appears to have been very little coordination or replication. There has been no agreement on standardized measures; each new entry into the area invents his own scales. This is inevitable perhaps in working with a concept as slippery as self-esteem, but if longitudinal studies of change are to be developed, measures which can be repeated through time must be agreed upon, even though in the long term they will almost certainly prove to be less than perfect. The work that has been done provides the background from which such measures will come and their development will open the way for a variety of significant analyses.

The first comparison to be made would be between objective status and subjective self-esteem. Are those people who occupy positions of power and prestige more satisfied with their own achievements than people whose situation is more modest? Are the esteem needs of people in the occupations that rank high in the Occupational Ranking more fully met than those in the lower-rated occupations? Are people whose economic and educational achievements exceed the average more than ordinarily satisfied with themselves, or does the sense of self-esteem become more difficult to fulfill as one attains higher levels of objective achievement?

The present evidence on this question is conflicted and demonstrates the difficulty of trying to represent self-esteem as a single dimension. In what is probably the most sophisticated study of perceptions of the self done with a

[21] Robinson and Shaver, *op. cit.*, p. 45.

national sample, Gurin, Veroff, and Feld report that college-educated people are less likely than people of less achievement to show a positive self-image and more likely to acknowledge shortcomings in their social skills, achievement orientation, and general adjustment.[22] On the other hand, surveys of personal competence (also called ego strength and internal control) have repeatedly shown this variable to be positively related to education, income, and other status indicators. There are obviously differences in what these scales are measuring and the relationship between objective status and perception of the self is probably far from simple.

Another particularly interesting aspect of the relationship between social position and self-esteem is the situation of those segments of society subjected to influences which might be expected to be especially damaging to the self-image. Prominent among these would be minority groups who have experienced discrimination and humiliation from the majority society. Is it true, as sometimes theorized, that many Negroes are filled with self-hate because of the negative images of them held by white people? Are other minorities, Jews and Chinese, for example, similarly afflicted? Does the experience of being on welfare destroy the self-respect of people who find themselves in this situation? Maslow's hierarchical theory of needs would suggest that needs for self-esteem would not develop in people who are struggling to fulfill the more primitive physiological and security requirements. It is certainly true that individuals within each derogated group differ in their esteem needs and in their fulfillment, and it is probably true that the groups themselves differ also. The attributes of personality that make it possible for persons whose objective circumstances seem to be the same to differ in this quality of their lives are, unfortunately, largely unidentified.

Moreover, the unavailability of standardized measures of self-esteem has meant that we have no dependable evidence of the impact recent social changes may have had on this aspect of human experience. It is particularly regrettable, for example, that there has been no program of measurement of the self-image of black people in this country. The current campaign in the black community to create pride of race and to strengthen the sense that "black is beautiful" may or may not be reaching its mark. It may be that feelings of personal worth cannot be changed in such a short period, except perhaps among the very young. In any case, this campaign will almost certainly continue in one form or another, and a program of measurement of response to it would be most valuable.[23]

[22] Gurin, Veroff, and Feld, *op. cit.,* Chap. 3.

[23] A baseline of measurements of Negro attitudes toward various aspects of black nationalism was taken by the Survey Research Center in 1968. See Angus Campbell and Howard Schuman, "Racial Attitudes in 15 American Cities," in *Supplemental Studies for The National Advisory Commission on Civil Disorders.* Government Printing Office, Washington, D.C., 1968, pp. ix–67.

Other changes in the way people evaluate themselves may also be going undetected. Does the relative anonymity of urban life or the bureaucratization of the work situation lead to loss in the sense of personal worth? Are increasing levels of education raising the sense of self-respect in the general public? Is the movement of women out of the household into work situations rewarding to their need for self-esteem? Are there changes associated with the life cycle; are young people more or less concerned with their self-image than people in their middle years? Does old age with its disabilities lead to a loss of self-esteem and feelings of incompetence and lack of worth?

In describing the esteem needs, Maslow distinguishes between self-esteem (which we have been discussing) and the esteem of others. This latter he elaborates as "the desire for reputation or prestige (defining it as respect or esteem from other people), status, dominance, recognition, attention, importance or appreciation." Although he warns of "the dangers of basing self-esteem on the opinions of others rather than on real capacity, competence, and adequacy to the task," one must assume that the opinions of others, especially respected others, serve as one of the primary criteria for many or most people in assessing their own worth. This in itself is a research problem of considerable significance and we might find that there are more "inner-directed" people than we might expect in a society that is sometimes described as primarily concerned with conformity to the expectations of other people.

There appear to be two methods of assessing the amount of recognition an individual receives from the world around him: (1) by counting the actual evidences of recognition he has received (prizes won, offices elected to, promotions received, deference shown), or (2) by eliciting his own report of the extent to which he feels recognized and appreciated. Neither of these procedures has been developed to the degree one might wish. There have been numerous inquiries about group membership that include a question as to offices held, but no serious effort has been made to conduct a complete enumeration of the objective signs of recognition people receive. Subjective measures of the experience of recognition are also very primitive. A small-scale study by Fey developed a scale of "acceptability to others" which suggests one aspect of the perception of approval with which we are concerned but leaves the major problem untouched.[24]

Assuming that suitable measures of objective and subjective recognition can be developed, it should be possible to identify those strata of society in which the need for recognition is strong and is typically gratified and those in which one or both of these conditions are not met. Over time, an account could be developed of the extent to which satisfaction growing out of recognition of this kind contributes to the quality of life in this country.

[24] William F. Fey, "Acceptance by Others," *Journal of Abnormal and Social Psychology,* vol. 50, March, 1955, pp. 274–276.

Need for Self-Actualization

The ultimate need in the Maslow hierarchy is "man's desire for self-fulfillment, namely, the tendency for him to become actualized in what he is potentially. This tendency might be phrased as the desire to become more and more what one is, to become everything that one is capable of becoming."

It is not surprising perhaps that a human need as esoteric as self-actualization has not been the subject of much research. If we assume, as Maslow does, that this need emerges only after the lower needs have been satisfied, we can still only guess as to what proportion of the population we are considering. As Maslow suggests, people aspire to fulfillment in very different forms, as artist, author, athlete, salesman, or perfect mother. But presumably many, or most, people do not dream about what they might be, are not motivated to reach a potential that they have not attained, and are not frustrated by a sense of failure to fulfill their potential or rewarded by the feeling that they have done so.

We know from studies of achievement needs that people differ a great deal in the extent to which they feel motivated to expend energy to attain various kinds of payoffs. High achievers are not necessarily motivated toward self-fulfillment, but it seems unlikely that low achievers would be characterized by a high need for fulfillment. A clear understanding of the relationship between these two kinds of needs would provide a firmer grasp on the meaning of self-fulfillment.

It should be possible through an appropriate program of development to find methods of identifying people who are motivated by a vision of their own ultimate potential. Some of them presumably will be satisfied that they have or will attain their full actualization; others, perhaps a larger number, will be unhappy that life is not everything it might be. One can anticipate great problems in attempting to evaluate the significance of these satisfactions and dissatisfactions. Is the unhappiness of the college professor who never got asked to Harvard comparable to the dissatisfaction of the young housewife who would rather go back to school than take care of children? We assume that the experience of failure to fulfill oneself is important to the individual, however exalted or modest the personal aspiration may be. The simple location of dissatisfaction is not as instructive as the measurement of it, but it is a first step.

It may appear that concern with the need for self-fulfillment might reasonably play a smaller part in a general program of research on public aspirations and satisfactions than interest in those needs that motivate the entire population. It surely seems more urgent to know how many people feel themselves deprived of the basic physiological requirements of life than to know how many feel they have not attained their full potential. In the long term, however, this ordering of priorities may change. If educational levels continue to rise and economic affluence is extended more broadly in the population, the numbers of people who are motivated by the higher needs (in Maslow's sense) will increase. The revolution of rising expectations will go beyond the demand for better housing and cleaner air to the requirement of a fuller life. There are indeed confused indications, particularly among the younger generations, that this point is already being reached.

Desire to Know and Understand

As Maslow points out, although psychologists have devoted a certain amount of attention to the phenomenon of curiosity in white rats and other lower animals, they have shown scant interest in this type of need among human beings. Frustration of the need to know seldom sends the sufferer into the hands of a psychiatrist.

On the other hand, one cannot fail to be impressed by the apparently insatiable demand for learning of every variety in this country. The flood of young and not-so-young people into post-high school education of one kind or another constitutes one of the major social changes in American society during the postwar period. It would certainly be naive to assume that these people are primarily motivated by a desire for learning for its own sake. National surveys have repeatedly shown that the majority of the population see the major advantage to be gained from a college education as "training for a good job after graduation."[25] There is a significant minority, however, who see the primary value of college as "increasing one's understanding of the world and oneself," and this turns into a majority among those whose own educational and economic status is high.

The love of learning for the simple satisfaction of knowing and understanding would be difficult to dissect from the many other motivations that impel people into learning situations, but it no doubt exists, and in a nation with rising educational achievement, it may be growing. It may not be possible at the present state of the arts to locate those individuals within the population who are moved by a pure need to know, but it should be possible to identify those who aspire for whatever reason to more learning than they have. These people may fall into quite distinct categories; there may be, for example, a category of people who were forced to terminate their education before they wished and now are hoping to make up lost ground; there may be a class of late bloomers who dropped out of school because of disinterest and later find

[25] A. Campbell and William C. Eckerman, *Public Concepts of the Values and Costs of Higher Education.* Survey Research Center, Institute for Social Research, University of Michigan, 1964.

their everyday lives unfulfilling. Maslow reports from his own practice observation of many upper-middle-class women who had developed "symptoms of intellectual inanition" for which he counseled immersion in "something worthy of them." If it were possible to ascertain in individual cases the situation from which the search for learning comes, it should then be possible to infer the major motivation that impels it.

There is a second and quite different way in which people need to know. This is not concerned with learning a new skill or a new form of expertise but with understanding the immediate flow of public events. Many surveys have shown that people differ greatly in their concern with the world outside their immediate surroundings: many have very little interest but some have a great curiosity about the larger world.[26] These surveys also show that incidence of this curiosity does not appear to be growing in the general population. The increase in the number of college-educated people might have suggested that it would; the advent, and near universal adoption, of television might also have been expected to have a stimulating influence. These plausible expectations are apparently erroneous, however; there is certainly little evidence that interest in political affairs has increased during the past 20 years.[27]

Nevertheless, a large number of people do show a strong need to be informed about these matters, and they exploit the various media to fulfill this need. The failure of the others to inform themselves apparently comes more from a lack of interest than from any difficulty in access to the information. In a democratic society which derives legitimacy from the general electorate, this aspect of the need to know has more than simply intellectual interest.

Aesthetic Needs

It is difficult to define precisely what the need for aesthetic experience implies, and Maslow is not very explicit on the subject, beyond observing that some individuals "get sick from ugliness and are cured by beautiful surroundings." And yet it is impossible to speak of "the quality of life" without implying something about the aesthetic aspects of human experience.

Traditionally, the aesthetic experience has been closely associated with the arts, music, painting, dance, and drama. Thirty years ago, Thorndike undertook to measure the "goodness" of cities with a collection of indicators which included measures of the interest of the citizenry in these "cultural" activities.[28] More recently, Berelson has attempted to estimate how much time the average American spends "in the presence of culture," including various

[26] Angus Campbell *et al.*, *The American Voter.* Wiley, New York, 1960.
[27] Angus Campbell, "Has Television Reshaped Politics?" *Columbia Journalism Review*, vol. 1, Fall, 1962, pp. 10–13.
[28] Edward L. Thorndike, *Your City.* Harcourt, New York, 1939.

forms of artistic performance.[29] The Department of Health, Education, and Welfare (HEW) bulletin, *Toward a Social Report,* comments on the importance of "artistic creativity and its appreciation" to the national life.[30] It notes the increasing accessibility of art to the general public but observes that the audiences for the performing arts are not increasing with the increase in population.

There is, however, a larger sense in which the need for aesthetically gratifying experience is important in modern life and that is in the quality of the surrounding environment. There are growing indications that the tolerance of the public and of their elected representatives for various forms of despoliation of the environment is decreasing. This applies not only to those types of pollution (of air and water) that threaten human life, but also to pollutants such as billboard advertising and the sonic boom, which are simply intrusive. Man-made ugliness in the environment, which was accepted as an unfortunate but inevitable by-product of progress in an earlier generation, is now being aggressively resisted. Part of the "revolution of rising expectations" appears to be an increasing demand that the heedless desecration of the natural environment which has characterized this country for generations should now be reversed.

It cannot be said that social scientists have devoted very much energy to the study of man's aesthetic experiences and, as a result, they have relatively little to say about them. As long as we measure the need for the experience of beauty through the arts by the effective demand at the box office, we will undoubtedly grossly underestimate the total public interest in these forms of aesthetic expression. Our failure to anticipate and monitor the rising aspirations for a natural and beautiful environment has been almost complete. Social scientists have avoided this area of experience partly because of the difficult problems of definition and measurement that it involves, but if they seriously mean to evaluate the psychological quality of the lives people lead, they must undertake to find out what the experience of beauty means to people and what people find in their lives which gratifies or is repulsive to their aesthetic needs.

Pursuit of Happiness

If we were to assess the degree of satisfaction an individual feels with each of the types of need we have now reviewed, we would certainly know a good deal about the quality of his life. It may be, however, that his evaluation

[29] Bernard Berelson, "In the Presence of Culture," *Public Opinion Quarterly,* Spring, 1964, vol. 28, pp. 1–12.

[30] Department of Health, Education, and Welfare, *Toward a Social Report.* Government Printing Office, Washington, D.C., 1969.

of his general state of well-being cannot be inferred from these separate satisfactions but as a whole quality that is not the exact sum of the parts. There may be a single over-arching dimension of satisfaction with life on which people place themselves consistently and realistically.

The concept of the happy life has been debated by philosophers since the time of the Greeks, and the term "happiness" has many meanings. During the past few decades, psychologists and others have made repeated attempts to measure the happiness of various populations. For the most part, they have avoided the difficult problem of definition by accepting "avowed happiness," the subject's own estimate, as the ultimate measure of happiness. This may not be an altogether satisfactory procedure since it raises serious questions of comparability. Boswell records an exchange with Johnson which states the problem directly:

> I mentioned Hume's notion that all who are happy are equally happy; a little miss with a new gown at a dancing school ball, a general at the head of a victorious army, and an orator, after having made an eloquent speech in a great assembly. Johnson—"Sir, that all who are happy are equally happy is not true. A peasant and a philosopher may be equally satisfied but not equally happy."

Samuel Johnson's pronouncement on the quality of happiness does not appear to have had great influence among American psychologists. Wilson's recent review presents the findings of the increasing number of happiness studies now in the literature.[31] He finds that avowed happiness is typically reported with rather convincing reliability over short time periods; tests of validity are "meager." There is also a good deal of consistency in the results from various studies concerning the distribution of happiness scores in different segments of the population. The two major studies, Gurin, Veroff, and Feld[32] and Bradburn and Caplowitz,[33] both find more self-described happy people among the young, married, better-off, and better-educated.

Robinson and Shaver describe a series of recent studies in which respondents were asked: "How satisfying do you find the way you're spending your life these days?"[34] Answers to this question were found to correlate in the .4 to .5 range with avowed happiness. The measures obviously have something in common, but they are far from identical and they show interesting differences in their distribution in specific groups. Widowed men and women, for example, are more likely to call themselves "not too happy" than divorced

---

[31] Warner Wilson, "Correlates of Avowed Happiness," *Psychological Bulletin*, vol. 67, April, 1967, pp. 294–306.

[32] Gurin, Veroff, and Feld, *op. cit.*, Chap. 2.

[33] Norman M. Bradburn and David Caplovitz, *Reports on Happiness.* Aldine, Chicago, 1965.

[34] Robinson and Shaver, *op. cit.*, Chap. 2.

people but less likely to say they are "not very satisfied" with their lives. Reported unhappiness increases with age, but dissatisfaction with life does not.

In a recent publication, Bradburn has developed a measure of what he calls "psychological well-being" based on the number of positively and negatively toned feelings experienced by the respondent during a reporting period of "the last few weeks."[35] Although, surprisingly, the scores of positive experiences do not correlate with the scores of negative experiences, a combination of the two, the "affect balance scale" relates quite strongly with a simple single-question measure of avowed happiness. The measures of positive and negative affect relate rather differently to other commonly used indicators of mental health, such as anxiety, worry, psychosomatic symptoms, social involvement, and varied experience.

The self-anchoring scale devised by Cantril has also been used in survey research to assess satisfaction with "your own personal life."[36] This procedure asks the respondent to imagine a person who is entirely satisfied with his life and a person who is extremely dissatisfied and to place himself on an 11-step ladder in relation to these extremes. According to Cantril, this technique overcomes the limitations of questionnaires using preconceived classifications by asking the respondent "to define on the basis of his own assumptions, perceptions, goals, and values the two extremes or anchoring points of the spectrum." The Cantril procedure has been adapted in various ways to inquiries regarding the "best possible life," and it lends itself to open-ended exploration of the aspects of their lives people find satisfying or dissatisfying.

These attempts to represent happiness or life satisfaction with a single question seem pretentious and meaningless to some critics who are not enchanted with empirical studies of attitudes, and they have given rise to charges that "the sociologist seems to pretend to define the undefinable and to measure the unmeasurable."[37] Since the authors of such protests would probably find most of the measurements proposed in this essay beyond the pale, we do not take this point of view too seriously. Nevertheless, it must be admitted that happiness is a many-faceted concept, and one can readily imagine that different people might interpret a question about happiness in quite different ways. It may be that happiness or satisfaction with life does not have a global quality but has meaning only at the level of specific aspirations.

Of course, the great attraction of global measures of this kind is that they can be introduced into survey questionnaires with relatively little commit-

[35] Norman M. Bradburn, *The Structure of Psychological Well-Being*. Aldine, Chicago, 1969.

[36] Hadley Cantril, *The Pattern of Human Concerns*. Rutgers University Press, New Brunswick, N.J., 1965.

[37] Joseph W. Krutch, "Through Happiness with Slide Rule and Caliper," *Saturday Review,* November 2, 1963, pp. 12–15.

ment of time and effort. This is certainly an important advantage, especially if one is attempting to put together a multipurpose survey in which the pressure for space is severe. It would appear desirable to develop a scale of manageable length which could be used for such purposes, preferably including an open-ended probe that would permit the respondent to reveal those aspects of his life situation which contribute to his happiness or satisfaction, unhappiness or dissatisfaction. This would not take the place of more detailed questioning regarding specific needs, but it would be more satisfactory than the single-question measures of avowed happiness now in the literature.

If it can be demonstrated that happiness-satisfaction has a unidimensional quality, and if a satisfactory measure of it can be developed, an interesting program of research would emerge from its use. Social scientists have had very little opportunity to study the impact of national events on collective attitudes, particularly on a short-term basis. In this respect Katona's 20-year program of study of consumer optimism is almost unique.[38] A great deal needs to be learned about the relative effectiveness of various kinds of stimuli, the responsiveness of different parts of the population to different kinds of events, and the predictive value of short- and long-term fluctuations in these attitudes. It will no doubt be a long time before any future Council of Social Advisers turns over to the President an annual reading on the national happiness in the way the Council of Economic Advisers now reports on the national income. But it would be at least as important for the President to have the former as the latter.

Commentary

In January, 1969, the Department of Health, Education, and Welfare issued a publication entitled *Toward a Social Report*. Although this report recognizes the importance of knowing whether people have satisfying jobs, what the satisfactions that income brings are, and whether group relationships in our society are harmonious and satisfying, it is primarily devoted to the more familiar categories of health, income, crime, and education. Indeed, the term "social indicators" has come to refer, for the most part, to these and related measures.

It is reasonable perhaps in the early overtures toward a description of what a Social Report to the President might look like to emphasize those kinds of measurement that are produced as by-products of established reporting procedures, that are based on total populations rather than on samples, and that raise the least question of reliability and validity. This is the strategy under which the Council of Economic Advisers has operated successfully, and it continues to recommend itself. However, social scientists should not deceive

[38] George Katona, "Anticipations, Statistics and Consumer Behavior," *American Statistician,* vol. 21, April, 1967, pp. 12–13.

themselves as to what such measures actually tell them and what they do not. The HEW report points out that "economic indicators have become so much a part of our thinking that we have tended to equate a rising national income with national well-being." It is the argument of this essay that, valuable as the various social indicators are and much as they should be refined and expanded, they cannot be taken uncritically to represent the quality of life as the people of this country experience it.

It cannot be said, however, that social scientists are fully prepared to provide the kinds of data regarding aspirations and satisfactions which this essay has discussed. The preceding chapters of this volume have made clear that some areas of inquiry have been the subject of continued research interest from which reasonably well-standardized measuring instruments have emerged. In other cases, there has been a good deal of uncoordinated thrashing about, with each investigator devising his own procedures with little cumulative result. The entire development of psychological measures of the kind with which we are concerned has been greatly handicapped by the inability of the investigators to reach broad populations. Unavailability of funds and some lack of enterprise have resulted in a great many studies of college undergraduates and other captive audiences which represent a very small part of the total range of human experience. The measures devised for the study of these specialized and relatively sophisticated groups are often quite unusable in the larger population since they presume a familiarity with vocabulary and concepts which many people of modest background do not have.

The fact is, however, that the techniques of sampling large populations without bias are now well developed both theoretically and practically. Social scientists clearly have the capacity to obtain data from the national population or any important segment of it; they cannot be so confident about the quality of the data they obtain. It is time for a major investment of effort into the development, refinement, and standardization of the kinds of scales and other measures needed to carry forward a program of documentation and analysis of the dimensions of human experience which we have reviewed in the preceding pages.

One of the consequences of the scatteration of effort in the study of public aspirations and satisfactions is the fact that, at this point, we have relatively few substantial bench marks against which to measure change. As we have pointed out in the opening chapter of this volume, an essential feature of a program of research on psychological change is measurement over time. A sequence of studies must begin with one against which subsequent ones are compared. Unhappily, in a number of the areas we would want to see monitored, the first study has not yet been done. There are some exceptions. The Gurin, Veroff, and Feld study, conducted on a national sample with a sensitive and sophisticated interview schedule, provides a valuable array of baseline data, and this 1957 study should now be replicated. In other areas of inquiry we are not so fortunate, and in those cases the task is to develop, with as much foresight as possible, a primary study that will serve as the basis of a series of studies to follow.

Comparisons through time provide the basis for the study of causal relationships. While it is seldom possible to exercise effective experimental controls in the study of large populations, it is possible to document the sequential relationships that exist between various kinds of social change and changes in public attitudes. Inferring cause from such relationships is admittedly hazardous, and under different circumstances such an inference may be more or less convincing. Comparisons through the various strata of society demonstrate the differences which exist and the contrasting movements which occur as different segments of the population are affected differently by changes in social structure, institutional prescriptions, and economic and political circumstances. Such comparisons are of particular significance in a society with our equalitarian pretensions since they show the extent to which our aspirations to an equal, or at least a minimal, level of living for everyone fall short of reality.

Comparisons through the world raise serious questions of comparability, and those that have been done seem rather superficial. Cross-national studies of life satisfactions belong on the social scientist's agenda, however, even though the present methodologies may not be adequate to the task. We have argued that the economic and other external conditions of an individual's life may have a very imperfect relationship to his internal evaluations of the quality of his life, and we suspect that the same may also be true of nations.

In his State of the Union address in January, 1970, the President of the United States made the following statement, "In the next ten years we will increase our wealth by 50 percent. The profound question is: Does this mean that we will be 50 percent richer in any real sense, 50 percent better off, 50 percent happier?" Who will answer this question for the man who is President in 1980? There will be no answer unless social scientists accept responsibility for developing appropriate measuring instruments and for generating data necessary to monitor psychological changes in American life. If, for reasons of failure of enterprise or lack of financial support, we do not accomplish this, we will have no better understanding of the quality of life in 1980 than we have today.

12

Alienation and Engagement

Melvin Seeman

The idea of alienation has shown remarkable endurance and an embarrassing versatility. It survives despite recurring invitations to abandon the concept on varied grounds, including the fact that it explains too much by far. The invitation seems especially tempting when it is invoked to explain particular troubles and their opposites: alienation accounts, at once, for conformity and deviance, for political passivity and urban riots, for status-seeking and social retreat, for "other-directed" styles of life and the "hippie" phenomenon, for suburban malaise and do-it-yourself activism.

The list of phenomena explained is ultimately discouraging. The critics may be right; to explain everything is to explain nothing, and if that is the best we can do we should, indeed, abandon the notion of alienation. We should recognize that we seem unable to escape an array of mutually reinforcing troubles involved in its use: hidden ideological commitments about the good society, romantic assumptions about human nature, confusions between alienation and related concepts, plus some plain vagueness for good measure.

Yet, I do not think that this state of affairs warrants either hopelessness or surprise. We are dealing with an idea that has been both an instrument of social action and of theory, and one that has a uniquely modern application and a distinguished history. It is a striking fact that the language of contemporaries—Erich Fromm, Herbert Marcuse, Paul Goodman, and others—echoes so closely the accents in Schiller's pre-Marxian complaint about the division of labor: "Gratification is separated from labor, means from ends, effort from reward. Eternally fettered only to a single fragment of the whole, man fashions himself as a fragment . . ."[1] The congruence across more than a century reflects the strength and the weakness of the idea of alienation. Its history makes a more than ordinary claim on its use so that the evocative and the critical sentiments predominate over clarity of conception or the demands of demonstration. In a sense, while much of the material and social world around us becomes secularized, the world of alienation remains sacred.

As a consequence, the debate concerning alienation has often remained sterile, however valid the critique of contemporary society and however proper and humane the values involved. My aim, in effect, is to further a new debate in which the central interest lies in clarity and demonstration. The demonstration, in this chapter and in the discipline, goes on at two levels: first, and most evidently, in the accumulating studies that seek to test specific propositions about alienation, but also in the collateral, more difficult, and long-term demonstration that such studies can be carried out without compromising either the intellectual scope or the humanistic concern that generated and sustained the idea of alienation.

Indexes of Alienation: Their Variety and Significance

The intellectual scope and humanist concern that characterize the alienation tradition, and its special relevance in any discussion of large-scale social change, are seen in the fact that the idea of alienation is customarily associated with both a view of history (either Marxian or mass-society persuasion) and an attitude (generally negative) about the effects of this historical drift on the individual. Perhaps the most common way to cast the matter is in terms of what has come to be called mass-society "theory," a theory that has two interesting qualities: (1) it generates considerable debate and, despite its demonstrated survival powers (e.g., in the tenacious dichotomies that span from Durkheim's mechanic-organic to Redfield's folk-urban types), appears currently to have more critics than adherents; and (2) the sense in which it is, in fact, a theory (rather than a perspective or a thesis) remains elusive.

Some clarification of the matter, and especially of the role of the alienation concept in it, can be derived from an analysis similar to the material summarized in Table 1. Mass theory, in which the major theme is that the passing of the old community has had powerful and frequently destructive consequences, is a theory in the sense that it specifies three major elements in the transition process. It becomes a theory—at least in the sense that it can produce testable propositions through a set of independent, intervening, and dependent variables—by combining (1) a historically oriented account of con-

---

[1] Franz Neumann, *The Democratic and the Authoritarian State*. Free Press, Glencoe, Ill., 1957, p. 271.

temporary *social structure,* (2) assertions about the *psychological effects* of that structure, and (3) predictions about the resulting *individual behavior.* In this schema, alienation is the crucial intervening variable: it is produced by the social structure and, in turn, produces distinctive behavior.[2]

Table 1. A Schematic Summary of Mass-Society Theory

(A) *Contemporary Structural Trends*	(B) *Forms of Alienation*	(C) *Behavioral Consequences*
1. Kinship to imperson- ality	1. Powerlessness	1. Political passivity (e.g., nonvoting)
2. Traditional to rational forms	2. Meaninglessness	2. Wildcat strikes
3. Homogeneity to heterogeneity	3. Normlessness	3. Mass movements
4. Stability to mobility	4. Value isolation (cultural estrangement)	4. Ethnic prejudice
5. Enlargement of scale	5. Self-estrangement	5. Mental disorder
	6. Social isolation	6. School absenteeism
		7. Low information level
		8. Suicide

NOTE: The table implies that the factors in Col. A lead to the development of one or more forms of alienation (B) with the illustrative behavioral consequences in Col. C; but the table is not constructed to be read line by line (e.g., powerlessness is not necessarily tied to kinship-impersonality).

The social structural features that constitute the independent variables in this scheme are quite standard ones, depicting what happens in the modernization process. Five postulated historical trends form the core of this part of the argument:

1. The decline of kinship as an important criterion of place and of decision-making, and the consequent increase of anonymity and impersonality in social relations.

2. The decline of traditional social forms and the rise of secularized, rationalized forms, which includes (a) the emergence of bureaucracy as an *organizational* form, (b) the growth of mechanization and standardization (in

[2] For an excellent review of the history of the idea of "mass society," see E. V. Walter, "Mass Society: The Late Stages of an Idea," *Social Research,* vol. 31, Winter, 1964, pp. 391–410. Like myself, Walter is not a grand partisan of the mass-society thesis, but finding it "heuristically rich and suggestive" argues that its defects and ambiguities can be overcome. The discussion here, centering around Table 1, seeks to further such revision and precision.

work and elsewhere) as a *technical* form, and (c) the secularization of beliefs and values, an *ideological* form of secularization involving the weakening of "given" standards of behavior.

3. Increased social differentiation involving an increased specialization of tasks for persons and institutions, with increased division of labor and interdependency (along with, of course, the increased homogeneity implied by standardization in other spheres—e.g., in mass culture and consumption).

4. Increased mobility, both spatial and social, which implies the waning of locality ties and immediate interpersonal bonds.

5. Enlargement of scale, referring to the fact that the bases of action (e.g., communication, transport, politics, urbanization, etc.) have become massive in the literal sense that big corporations, cities, and nations make decisions that affect large populations.[3]

All this should sound quite familiar (though, to be sure, it is only one way to distill a notoriously discursive literature), and little in it seems controversial. The five historical trends, of course, are not measurable variables in themselves; rather, they are guides to such variables. Thus, the kinship-impersonality trend requires the specification of related indexes, for example, the number and/or intensity of primary ties, the presence of extended family networks, or the individual's engagement in an occupational community. Similarly, each of the major trends suggests specific variables congenial to mass theory: (1) membership in mediating organizations (e.g., labor unions), (2) frequency and recency of migration, (3) degree of specialization or automation in work, (4) degree of formalization of rules and procedures, (5) heterogenity of social backgrounds in a given population, (6) level of consensus regarding values or conduct, (7) homogeneity of consumption patterns or leisure styles, and (8) rates of social mobility and related patterns of class identification.

With respect to some of these variables, we already know enough to be cautious about ready assumptions; for example, we are wary about the folk wisdom which asserts that geographical and social mobility necessarily attenuates either family visitation or extended family orientations.[4] Nevertheless, when the other elements are added (i.e., the imputed intervening psychological

---

[3] The significance of enlargement of scale is captured in Edward Shils, "The Theory of Mass Society," *Diogenes*, vol. 39, Fall, 1962, pp. 45–66, where he comments, "The inclusion of the entire population in the society, or a pronounced tendency towards that inclusion, is what makes the mass society" (p. 52). For another view of the importance of social scale, cf. Godfrey Wilson and Monica Wilson, *Social Change*. University Press, Cambridge, 1945.

[4] Morris Zelditch, "Family, Marriage and Kinship," in R. E. L. Faris, ed., *Handbook of Modern Sociology*. Rand McNally, New York, 1964, pp. 680–733.

derivations and the behavior predictions), we get the sharpest debate about mass theory, for it is here that explicit and implicit assumptions about human nature, social process, and the good life are brought into play. Thus, the assertions go:

1. The decisive processes of mass society are those of atomization which lead to the individual's increasing sense of powerlessness, anxiety, and tension that finds release in direct and extremist political involvement or in the search for charismatic faiths and alternative "community."

2. The loss of traditional values occasioned by the secularization process has not been balanced by the development of new, central, and unifying values; hence, individual opportunism, moral confusion, and highly fluid tastes.

3. The destruction of the classic public in the interest of mass-scale, but diffuse, opinion leads to an unsatisfying equalitarianism where the individual is likely to be highly conformist and at the same time impressed by his own insignificance and weakness, an unstable mixture at best.[5]

4. The mobile, impersonal, and bureaucratic life style cannot satisfy intrinsic human needs for meaning or for craftlike rewards in work; hence, the intensification of substitute status striving, inadequate self-images, and the frenetic search for leisure-time fulfillment.[6]

The list of propositions could be extended a good deal, each of them postulating an association between social change and alienation, each of them debatable and debated.[7] But our interest here is not so much in mass theory itself (for one thing, the problem of alienation can be treated outside the mass-society framework), but in the alienations that are central to that theory. Some 10 years ago, I stressed the need to be clear about two things concerning

[5] Alexis de Tocqueville, *Democracy in America*, vol. II, Philip Bradley, ed. Knopf, New York, 1945, especially p. 261.

[6] C. Wright Mills, *White Collar*. Oxford University Press, New York, 1951.

[7] See, for example, Laurence Wylie, *Chanzeaux: A Village in Anjou*. Harvard University Press, Cambridge, Mass., 1966: a study of a French village, where he argues against the standard view of change and its supposed impact on the sense of community. ". . . disunity seems to have characterized Chanzeaux for as long as we have been able to study its history. The expressions frequently used to describe rural life—stability, simplicity, homogeneity—have never applied to Chanzeaux at any point in its history. To our eyes, more characteristic expressions have been flux, conflict, diversity." And later: "Some observers may conclude that the sense of community which they insist on attributing to traditional, rural communities has still further deteriorated. But we find the opposite to be true. There is probably a greater sense of community in Chanzeaux today than there has ever been" (pp. 334, 346). The criticism of the romantic element in mass theory has been common enough; Wylie's work details some of the empirical basis for such criticism. Romanticizing the old order often goes along with underplaying the liberating aspects of the new order (on the latter, cf. Daniel Bell, "America as a Mass Society: A Critique," in *The End of Ideology*. Free Press, Glencoe, Ill., 1960, pp. 21–36).

alienation: (1) the variety of meanings that have been attributed to that term, and (2) the utility of defining each variant of alienation in such a way as to produce a specific and unique social indicator (rather than global indicators of the individual's feelings of happiness or despair, well-being or discontent, futility or optimism).[8] The latter, indeed, are often what are meant when alienation is discussed, but useful as these may be for some purposes, they are not analytical enough to serve as indicators in systematic investigations of the human impact of change.

A more telling construction of alienation can be based (as suggested in Column B of Table 1) on the view that alienation refers to six related but distinguishable notions, and that these six varieties of alienation can be rather sharply defined in terms of the person's *expectancies* or his *values*.[9] Thus, to be alienated means to be characterized by one (or several) of the following:

1. A sense of *powerlessness:* a low expectancy that one's own behavior can control the occurrence of personal and social rewards; for the alienated man, control seems vested in external forces, powerful others, luck, or fate.

2. A sense of *meaninglessness:* a sense of the incomprehensibility of social affairs, of events whose dynamics one does not understand and whose future course one cannot predict (more formally, a low expectancy that satisfactory predictions about future outcomes can be made). This is the alienation that Mannheim saw as the consequence of "functional rationalization" in modern organizations, and that Adorno saw as the source of anti-Semitism in post-Weimar Germany.[10]

3. A sense of *normlessness:* a high expectancy that socially unapproved means are necessary to achieve given goals; the view that one is not bound by conventional standards in the pursuit of what may be, after all, quite conventional goals (e.g., position, wealth).[11]

---

[8] Melvin Seeman, "On the Meaning of Alienation," *American Sociological Review,* vol. 24, December, 1959, pp. 783–791.

[9] The two terms ("expectancy" and "reinforcement value") are central to the social-learning theory developed by Julian B. Rotter, *Social Learning and Clinical Psychology.* Prentice-Hall, Englewood Cliffs, N.J., 1954. In this theory, the potential for the occurrence of a given behavior is a function of the expectation the individual holds that the behavior (or class of behaviors) will result in the achievement of a valued reinforcement (in a specified situation). The theory is useful not only in defining alienation, but also in the specification of hypotheses relevant to mass theory (cf. Melvin Seeman, "Alienation, Membership and Political Knowledge: A Comparative Study," *Public Opinion Quarterly,* vol. 30, Fall, 1966, pp. 353–367).

[10] Karl Mannheim, *Man and Society in an Age of Reconstruction.* Harcourt, New York, 1940. Also T. W. Adorno *et al., The Authoritarian Personality.* Harper, New York, 1950.

[11] This version of alienation derives from Durkheim via Robert K. Merton, *Social Theory and Social Structure,* rev. ed. Free Press, Glencoe, Ill., 1957. It should be noted

4. *Value isolation* (or cultural estrangement): the individual's rejection of commonly held values in the society; in the language of social learning theory, the assignment of low reward value to goals or behaviors that are highly valued in the given society. The typical image invoked here (but not the restricted application, by any means) is that of the alienated artist or intellectual who rejects the going standards of success or attractiveness.

5. *Self-estrangement:* this is perhaps the most difficult to define with any clarity, though numerous efforts have been made in that direction (including two versions not employed here—the individual's sense of a discrepancy between his ideal self and his actual self-image, and the failure to satisfy certain postulated inherent human needs). For present purposes, borrowing heavily from classic descriptions of the worker who is estranged when carrying out unfullfilling and uncreative work, to be self-estranged is to be engaged in activities that are not rewarding in themselves.

6. *Social isolation:* the individual's low expectancy for inclusion and social acceptance, expressed typically in feelings of loneliness or feelings of rejection or repudiation (found, for example, among minority members, the aged, the handicapped, and various kinds of less visible "strangers").[12]

In sum, this exercise in definition is not only and academically an exercise; it is also a way of furthering the development of clear indicators of the kind and degree of alienation which characterize American life (or its Western, or underdeveloped, co-societies) in the context of a theory of consider-

that the notions of "normlessness" and "meaninglessness" as given here make a distinction in what is often treated together, namely, the question of whether the norms no longer govern behavior (however clear they may be), and the question of whether the norms are unclear or confusing (the latter being "meaninglessness," or what Jessor *et al.* speak of as "uncertainty about what behavior is appropriate in various social situations." Cf. Richard Jessor *et al., Society, Personality, and Deviant Behavior.* Holt, Rinehart & Winston, New York, 1968, p. 102).

[12] This version of alienation was not included in my earlier treatment: (Seeman, "On the Meaning of Alienation"); indeed, it was explicitly abandoned, chiefly because a good deal of what is called "social isolation" refers, in fact, to facets of alienation that are already captured in the other five variants. I think now that the exclusion of social isolation was a mistake, but the caution bears repeating. When one speaks of "feelings of social isolation in the sense of lacking commonalities with others, absence of shared values" (Jessor *et al., op. cit.,* p. 300), the alienation in question may correlate with loneliness or with a sense of rejection, but in principle it seems much closer to what is here called "value isolation." Often, what is called the sense of "community" refers to the normlessness problem; cf. James Q. Wilson, "The Urban Unease," *Public Interest,* vol. 12, Summer, 1968, pp. 25–39 ("When I speak of the concern for 'community' I refer to a desire for the observance of standards of right and seemly conduct in the public places . . ." p. 27). For further comment on these distinctions, and an effort to implement them empirically, cf. Russell Middleton, "Alienation, Race and Education," *American Sociological Review,* vol. 28, December, 1963, pp. 973–977.

able scope. Moreover, it is a way of being explicit about the impact of alienation on some quite important, and notably American values. For it becomes
quite clear that the alienations described above are the obverse of values central to American society: the sense of powerlessness goes counter to the values
of mastery and autonomy; value isolation undercuts the goal of consensus;
normlessness threatens the stable development of order and trust; meaninglessness and self-estrangement are the alienative counterparts of understanding
and engagement; social isolation (especially in relation to the minority problem) implicates the values of egalitarianism and individual worth. These are the
positive values that are at stake when the evidence concerning alienation is
assessed. The analysis suggests (in keeping with the spirit of Table 1) that (a)
the indicators of alienation can be *in themselves* measures of national achievement in some important degree (i.e., indicators of our extent of achievement of
values relevant to democratic institutions), and (b) to the degree that it can
be shown that alienation has *consequences,* these consequences in turn become
matters that a democratic society would find important in its accounting of
the personal meaning of social change.

Distribution and Correlates of Alienation

There is very little news in the view of alienation that I have presented—
although, hopefully, there is some improved order and clarity, allowing improved attention to demonstration. The bulk of the available evidence concerns
three of the forms of alienation—powerlessness, normlessness, and self-
estrangement—on these, at least, one can make a start toward a proposi-
tional inventory summarizing some major lines of inquiry (the bulk of it being relevant to the theoretical view of mass society sketched earlier). Despite
its length, the following inventory remains essentially illustrative.

Powerlessness. The most solid evidence concerns the sense of powerlessness. Obviously, how powerless people will feel, as well as the level of correlation with other variables, will depend upon the way in which the question is
asked, hence a methodological word is in order. Two ways of asking about
powerlessness have been common:

1. The most systematic measure is the so-called I-E (internal vs. external control) scale, developed chiefly by Rotter.[13] It is, in strict accord with the
definition given above, a measure of the individual's *expectancy for control;*
and it is systematic in several senses, not least of these being (a) its effort to
focus on expectancies without building in a host of other sentiments (mistrust,
hopelessness, rebellion, complaint, etc.), and (b) the effort to pose choices

---

[13] Julian B. Rotter, "Generalized Expectancies for Internal vs. External Control of
Reinforcements," *Psychological Monographs,* vol. 80, 1966, pp. 1–28 (whole No. 609).

that are relatively equal in their social desirability. In the following items, by way of example, the respondent may find both alternatives "nice" enough, but he must opt for one:

A. ———— Most people don't realize the extent to which their lives are controlled by accidental happenings.

———— There really is no such thing as "luck."

B. ———— Becoming a success is a matter of hard work; luck has little or nothing to do with it.

———— Getting a good job depends mainly on being in the right place at the right time.

2. Several Likert-type measures have been developed under various names (depending partly on their domain of reference) but sharing similar content and an agree-disagree format. Thus, there are measures of: (a) "political efficacy"—the best-known scale being that of Campbell, Gurin, and Miller asking, in effect, whether people feel that they have any say in what the government does;[14] (b) generalized "powerlessness"—as in Dean's 9-item scale (sample item: "We are just so many cogs in the machinery of life");[15] or (c) "political alienation"—a recent and very typical version being the one employed by Aiken *et al.* in a study of the effects of economic deprivation (sample item: "In my opinion, important political decisions in the U.S. today are made more by political machines than by voters").[16]

The difference in format (forced-choice vs. Likert) is not nearly so important as the difference in intention, which translates into a difference in definition. Thus, regardless of format, "powerlessness" as measured by the I-E scale is quite close to the "sense of civic competence" measured by Almond and Verba through relatively open-ended questions.[17] They asked the respondent to suppose that an unjust or harmful law were being considered (at both the local and national level of government), and to indicate (a) what the respondent thought he could do, (b) how likely he would be to succeed in an effort to change such a law, and (c) how likely it was that he would actually try to do something about it. These questions all refer to what Almond and Verba call the "input" dimension (political efficacy or influence); but, as

[14] Angus Campbell, Gerald Gurin, and Warren E. Miller, *The Voter Decides.* Row, Peterson, Evanston, Ill., 1954.

[15] Dwight G. Dean, "Alienation: Its Meaning and Measurement," *American Sociological Review,* vol. 26, October, 1961, pp. 753–758.

[16] Michael Aiken, L. A. Ferman, and H. L. Sheppard, *Economic Failure, Alienation and Extremism.* University of Michigan Press, Ann Arbor, 1968.

[17] Gabriel A. Almond and Sidney Verba, *The Civic Culture.* Little, Brown, Boston, 1963.

Gamson has recently noted, the idea of political alienation often includes a trust (or output) dimension as well.[18]

Whether trust ought to be included along with efficacy in a measure of alienation is a question that cannot be settled simply by definition. It requires, at the very least, some attention to (a) correlation between these sentiments, (b) the empirical difference it makes when they are treated independently and jointly, and (c) the theoretical purpose for which the measures are employed.[19] Methodological excursions may make dull reading, but the warning at least is clear: In what follows, although "powerlessness" is the main theme, the propositions are based on measures and constructs that are far from coordinate and reflect differences in conceptions of alienation (to which we will ultimately be forced to return).

Proposition 1. *Membership and participation in control-relevant organizations is associated with low alienation (powerlessness).* A good deal has been said in the mass-society literature concerning the need for organizations that can mediate between the individual and the state or corporation. The implication is that such organizations provide the individual with an instrument for control over his affairs, hence the prediction that participation will be associated with low alienation (i.e., with a relatively high sense of mastery).

Studies over a wide range of countries, times, and measures support the mediation hypothesis. The most direct demonstration for the United States is found in the study by Neal and Seeman, where (especially for the manual workers) those who reported membership in a work-based organization were consistently lower in powerlessness (as measured by a variant of the I-E scale).[20] The consistency of the results is suggested in Table 2, which presents the data for manual workers with income controlled.

That such results are probably stable, and not a function of the American situation (e.g., our special attitudes about "joining"), is suggested by a parallel study conducted in Malmö, Sweden, where a random sample of the male work force was interviewed (using a Swedish version of the I-E scale).[21] For both manuals and nonmanuals, the organized workers were distinctively high in powerlessness, and these differences were sustained with education controlled. That such results override differences in method as well as differences

[18] William A. Gamson, *Power and Discontent.* Dorsey, Homewood, Ill., 1968.

[19] For an initial effort showing the utility of treating these dimensions—trust and powerlessness—independently, see J. Herbert Hamsher, Jesse D. Geller, and Julian B. Rotter, "Interpersonal Trust, Internal-External Control, and the Warren Commission Report," *Journal of Personality and Social Psychology,* vol. 9, July, 1968, pp. 210–215.

[20] Arthur G. Neal and Melvin Seeman, "Organizations and Powerlessness: A Test of the Mediation Hypothesis," *American Sociological Review,* vol. 29, April, 1964, pp. 216–226.

[21] Seeman, "Alienation, Membership and Political Knowledge: A Comparative Study."

Table 2. Mean Scores on Powerlessness for Unorganized and Organized Manual Workers in the United States, with Income Controlled (N = 241)

Income	Unorganized	Organized
Under $3,000	2.50	2.20
	(14)	(5)
$3,000–$4,999	3.20	2.81
	(46)	(52)
$5,000–$6,999	3.20	2.55
	(25)	(75)
Over $7,000	3.00	2.65
	(4)	(20)
Total: Mean	3.08	2.64
	(89)	(152)
Standard deviation	1.5	1.8

NOTE: Scores on the powerlessness scale ranged from 0 to 7. High scores equal high powerlessness.

SOURCE: Arthur G. Neal and Melvin Seeman, "Organizations and Powerlessness," *American Sociological Review,* vol. 29, April, 1964, pp. 216–226.

among countries is further demonstrated in Almond and Verba's study of political attitudes and democracy in five nations, using the measure of "sense of civic competence" discussed above.[22] For the better-educated portion of their sample, they report the results shown in Table 3 showing nonmembers in each country to be relatively low in subjective competence. They show further that degree of participation ("active" vs. "passive" membership) is also related in the expected way to competence, and they conclude that their findings "strongly support the proposition associated with the theory of mass society that the existence of voluntary associations increases the democratic potential of a society."[23]

Some caveats, however, are in order. First, none of these studies demonstrates the "impact" of organizational membership on attitudes concerning control, since the data are entirely cross sectional and suffer alternative interpretations (e.g., that the sense of powerlessness is a *determinant* of membership). Second, the evidence is not firm concerning the *kinds* of organizational membership that are related to higher competence. Work and political organizations involve, almost by definition, control-relevant interests; but social clubs, athletic organizations, and all those "other" memberships that are part of social involvement and isolation may be quite another thing. The argument can be made that such groups have latent political functions or that, irrespective of such latent functions, the alienation sentiments of loneliness, powerlessness,

[22] Almond and Verba, *op. cit.*
[23] *Ibid.,* p. 262.

Table 3. Percentage of Respondents Who Scored Highest in Subjective Competence among Members of Political and Nonpolitical Organizations in Five Nations (Secondary Education or More Only)

Nation	Member of Political Organization		Member Nonpolitical Organization		Nonmember	
	Percent	*(N)*	*Percent*	*(N)*	*Percent*	*(N)*
United States	87	(137)	81	(160)	68	(116)
Great Britain	74	(86)	77	(112)	62	(148)
Germany	94	(32)	65	(63)	57	(55)
Italy	85	(31)	55	(85)	48	(183)
Mexico	64	(24)	58	(36)	46	(67)

NOTE: The percentages are based upon the *N*'s in parentheses, and refer to those who "received the three highest scores on the subjective competence scale."
SOURCE: Derived from Gabriel A. Almond and Sidney Verba, *The Civic Culture*, Little, Brown, Boston, 1963, Table X.6, p. 253.

etc. are so closely bound together that membership of any sort is likely to have an effect on powerlessness.[24] But neither the argument nor the data seem very persuasive, and there is certainly no need to assume that the mass-society argument concerning mediation holds for any kind of membership (or any kind of social participation, including involvement in primary group relations).

Proposition 2. *The alienated (powerless) person is not likely to engage in planned, instrumentally oriented action.* The "action" these days is in the area of Negro integration into American life, hence it is no surprise that this is one of the major arenas for demonstration of the tie between social action and powerlessness. One of the early studies was carried out by Gore and Rotter at a Southern Negro college which had featured prominently in the protest movement.[25] They sought to show that low generalized expectancies for control (high powerlessness) would be associated with reluctance to commit oneself to social action, even when the goal involved represented a highly desired change in civil rights and desegregation.

The procedure was quasi-experimental in character. Four weeks after a set of questionnaires (including the I-E scale) had been administered, a student confederate addressed three psychology classes asking their cooperation in a fictitious "Students for Freedom Rally." The students were asked to complete a slip indicating their interest in: (A) attending a rally for civil rights;

[24] *Ibid.;* Scott Greer and Peter Orleans, "The Mass Society and the Parapolitical Structure," *American Sociological Review,* vol. 27, October, 1962, pp. 634–646.
[25] Pearl M. Gore and Julian B. Rotter, "A Personality Correlate of Social Action," *Journal of Personality,* vol. 31, March, 1963, pp. 58–64.

(B) signing a petition addressed to local government and/or to news media calling for full and immediate integration of all facilities in the state; (C) joining a silent march to the capitol to demonstrate for full and immediate integration; (D) joining a Freedom Rider's group for a trip during the semester break; or (E) indicating no interest in participating in these activities.

Evidently, categories A and E represent the lowest commitment to social action, while C and D represent high commitment, with B being intermediate. The mean scores on powerlessness, as shown in Table 4, follow the predicted pattern: "those individuals who were more inclined to see themselves as determiners of their own fate tended to commit themselves to more personal and decisive action."[26]

Table 4. Mean Scores on Internal vs. External Control, by Categories of Commitment to Social Action for a Sample of Negro College Students

Action Category	Mean Powerlessness	Standard Deviation	(N)
A (Attend rally)	10.3	3.1	(20)
B (Sign petition)	9.2	3.4	(20)
C (Silent march)	7.4	2.9	(24)
D (Freedom Rider)	8.1	3.8	(20)
E (No action)	10.0	3.9	(32)

NOTE: The difference between category C and both A and E was significant at the .01 level; the categories of relatively high commitment (B, C, and D) differ as a group from both no commitment (category E) and little commitment (A) at the .05 level.

SOURCE: Scores are based on the 23-item I-E scale; from Pearl M. Gore and Julian B. Rotter, "A Personality Correlate of Social Action," *Journal of Personality,* vol. 31, March, 1963, pp. 58–64.

One might also view powerlessness as playing more of a mediating role in the determination of civil rights action as, for example, in mediating the effect of interpersonal black-white contact. That contact is a determinant of tolerance seems well established; but civil rights activism might be quite another matter. Here, a commitment to action is involved (rather than simple attitude change), and contact may correlate less strongly with activism for those who are high in powerlessness, since they believe that their own action is not likely to be efficacious. Data on this point have been reported for a sample of both blacks and whites; though these data are only suggestive, the results (a) go in the anticipated direction, and (b) show a distinctly different pattern for

[26] *Ibid.,* p. 62; see also Bonnie R. Strickland, "The Prediction of Social Action from a Dimension of Internal-External Control," *Journal of Social Psychology,* vol. 66, August, 1965, pp. 353–358, for comparable results.

blacks compared with whites.[27] As predicted, the effect of contact on reported civil rights activity is greater for whites who scored low in powerlessness, but this pattern does not hold for the Negro sample (and tends, indeed, to be reversed). One may suspect that not only contact but powerlessness as well have different meanings for the two samples; in any event, powerlessness as a mediating factor certainly appears to work differently in the two groups.

Quite another kind of minority-related social action is involved in Bullough's study of segregated vs. integrated Negroes in the Los Angeles area.[28] Her concern was with the factors that make for willingness to move out of the ghetto and into integrated areas of the San Fernando Valley, the hypothesis being that, beyond the well-known barriers to such movement (e.g., education or income), there were the psychological barriers, among which the sense of powerlessness was a relevant variable. Two samples of middle-class Negroes were interviewed, one living in the traditional black ghetto and the other in a predominantly white suburban area. As indicated in Table 5, the integrated group expressed the anticipated low powerlessness, the inference being that their relative sense of mastery encourages them to take the action that leads to integrated housing.

Table 5. Mean Powerlessness in the Valley-wide (Integrated) and Ghetto Areas, with Education Controlled

	Valley (Integrated)		Ghetto	
Education	Mean	(N)	Mean	(N)
College graduate	2.14	(43)	2.88	(32)
Some college or technical	2.74	(42)	3.15	(39)
High school or less	2.75	(16)	2.97	(34)

NOTE: The over-all ghetto mean was 3.01, while the "outsider's" mean was 2.48 ($t = 2.07$; $p < .05$).

SOURCE: Scores are based on a 10-item I-E scale; from Bonnie L. Bullough, "Alienation in the Ghetto," *American Journal of Sociology,* vol. 72, March, 1967, pp. 469–478.

At each level of education, the integrated sample has the lower powerlessness score, but perhaps the most intriguing fact is that, among the college graduates, where the objective barrier to movement is minimal, the largest difference in powerlessness occurs. A further intriguing fact is revealed in Bullough's analysis of the life styles *within* the two samples—meaning by "life

---

[27] Samuel J. Surace and Melvin Seeman, "Some Correlates of Civil Rights Activism," *Social Forces,* vol. 46, December, 1967, pp. 197–207.

[28] Bonnie L. Bullough, "Alienation in the Ghetto," *American Journal of Sociology,* vol. 72, March, 1967, pp. 469–478.

style" the degree to which these respondents lead a relatively integrated or segregated way of life (in church affiliation, newspaper reading, school attendance, close friends, etc.). A summary measure of integrated vs. segregated life style was developed, and it is instructive to note (see Table 6) that, *within the ghetto,* those who are characterized by a more integrated life style—who, in effect, are acting as though they are candidates for moving out of the ghetto—have a significantly lower powerlessness score than the more ghetto-oriented respondents.

Table 6. Mean Powerlessness Scores in the Valley-wide (Integrated) and Ghetto Areas, for Respondents Divided at the Median on the Index of Life Style

Life Style	Valley (Integrated)	Ghetto
Integrated orientation	2.38 (N = 49)	2.63 (N = 57)
Ghetto-oriented	2.75 (N = 52)	3.45 [a] (N = 48)

[a] The difference in powerlessness for those with integrated vs. ghetto orientation was significant at $p < .05$; cf. Bonnie L. Bullough, "Alienation in the Ghetto," *American Journal of Sociology,* vol. 72, March, 1967, pp. 469–478.

Congruent results concerning powerlessness and political participation have been reported with considerable reliability, most notably by the Michigan group using the "political efficacy" scale. They show, for the 1956 election, that "the rate of voting turnout was found to increase uniformly with the strength of the individual's sense of political efficacy"—more than 40 percentage points separating those who feel that their action has an impact upon the political process as compared with those who doubt their effectiveness.[29] A more generalized measure of participation than simple turnout has also been significantly associated with efficacy scores, and this association tends to hold with educational level controlled.[30]

Thus far, the discussion of action-taking and powerlessness has concerned some standard forms of action in civil rights and politics; but the evidence suggests, as well, that less standard instrumentally oriented action can be predicted. Two quite different studies of Peace Corps trainees, for example, report data that are consistent with the proposition at stake. Rotter shows that 155 such trainees (from three combined programs) achieved *the most internal* mean score of the 10 groups on which normative data for the I-E scale are

[29] Angus Campbell *et al., The American Voter.* Wiley, New York, 1960, p. 105.

[30] Campbell, Gurin, and Miller, *op. cit.*

presented.[31] These results may, of course, be a function of the testing conditions (the I-E scale being part of an assessment battery). Yet the data are consistent with the spirit of Ezekiel's study of Peace Corps competence.[32] He sought to show that trainees' "fictional autobiographies of the personal future" could be used to predict style and quality of later overseas performance. The most interesting feature of these autobiographies was a score developed ("agency" score) indicating the degree to which the subject saw himself as a prime agent in determining the course of his future life. The "agency" score is obviously a close kin to "internal control," and it correlates with ratings of later performance in the expected way.[33] Those who were low in "agency" (effectively, high in powerlessness) were characterized in the field as showing "limited commitment" (i.e., "Peace Corps duties limited to teaching; teaching only a '9 to 5' affair; other items of personal agenda compete successfully with Peace Corps duties for central commitment"), and "passivity" (i.e., "conventionality and low energy; lack of zeal, activity or inventiveness").

As before, a general demurrer is in order concerning the proposition at issue here. The alienation (powerlessness) variable may contribute very little independent understanding of participation and social action when the proper (and multiple) controls are applied. Thus, Erbe has examined the correlates of political participation, seeking to determine whether alienation continues to have an effect when both socioeconomic status and involvement in organizations is held constant (meaning both "social" organizations and "issue-interest" organizations such as the Parent-Teacher Association, veterans organizations, political parties and clubs, business and professional organizations, etc.).[34] Using Dean's alienation scales (including a 9-item powerlessness measure), Erbe found that although alienation "is of some importance at the zero order, higher-order partialling raised grave doubt as to whether alienation affects political participation independently of socioeconomic status and organizational involvement."[35]

Proposition 3. *The powerless are characterized by their readiness to participate in relatively unplanned and/or short-term protest activities.* Two

[31] Rotter, *op. cit.,* p. 15.

[32] Raphael S. Ezekiel, "The Personal Future and Peace Corps Competence," *Journal of Personality and Social Psychology, Monograph Supplement,* vol. 8, February, 1968, pp. 1–26.

[33] *Ibid.,* p. 21.

[34] William Erbe, "Social Involvement and Political Activity," *American Sociological Review,* vol. 29, April, 1964, pp. 198–215.

[35] *Ibid.,* p. 213. "Organizational involvement" includes some directly political participation, as well as quasi-political interest groups, hence the control for such activity—where the dependent variable is itself political participation, and where the alienation score includes some highly political attitudes—raises some interesting questions about the exact meaning of the control in question.

things are implied in this proposition: (1) the powerless outlook encourages a short-range view—the inability or unwillingness to plan, to defer gratification or to coordinate steps toward a future state of affairs; and (2) this short-range view is expressed in particular kinds of protest. In a variety of ways, the tie between powerlessness and a narrow time perspective has been demonstrated. For example: (1) in his intensive interview study of alienated college students, Keniston discerns "short-range personally centered values" as a feature of the alienated outlook; (2) Ezekiel finds that the Peace Corpsmen who were rated as high in the "agency" dimension were significantly more often characterized (by raters making an independent judgment about their field work two years later) as having "long-term goals"; and (3) Jessor *et al.* report a correlation of − .20 between a measure of future time perspective and I-E score— high externality goes with restricted perspective.[36]

More important for present purposes, this short-range perspective apparently coincides with the temper of contemporary direct-action forms of protest, and one finds in these protests—in urban riots, student demonstrations, and local community conflicts—the evidence of a "powerlessness" factor. The Negro's powerlessness is hardly surprising. Kenneth Clark refers to "the psychology of the ghetto with its pervasive and total sense of helplessness," and the Kerner report makes the obvious tie to urban violence: "The frustrations of powerlessness have led some Negroes to the conviction that there is no effective alternative to violence as a means of achieving redress of grievances . . ."[37]

What "some" means in empirical terms, and what the complexities of it are, can be suggested by a glance at the data provided in the Kerner report and in a recent study by Ransford.[38] The latter obtained interviews concerning the Watts riot of 1965 and found that powerlessness was related to "willingness to use violence"—41 percent of those high in powerlessness expressed such willingness, compared to 16 percent of the "lows," and this trend held both for the immediate riot area (South Central Los Angeles and Watts) and for the surrounding higher-income Crenshaw area. Ransford also shows that the powerlessness-violence tie is not merely a function of social isolation from whites or degree of dissatisfaction concerning one's treatment as a Negro: each of

[36] Kenneth Keniston, *The Uncommitted: Alienated Youth in American Society.* Harcourt, New York, 1965, p. 80; Ezekiel, *op. cit.;* and Jessor *et al., op. cit.*

[37] Kenneth Clark, *Dark Ghetto: Dilemmas of Social Power.* Harper, New York, 1965, p. 156; Kerner Commission, *Report of the National Advisory Commission on Civil Disorders.* Bantam, New York, 1968, p. 11.

[38] H. Edward Ransford, "Negro Participation in Civil Rights Activity and Violence," unpublished doctoral dissertation, University of California, Los Angeles, 1966; H. Edward Ransford, "Isolation, Powerlessness, and Violence: A Study of Attitudes and Participation in the Watts Riot," *American Journal of Sociology,* vol. 73, March, 1968, pp. 581–591.

these variables makes its own contribution, and it is among the "ideal type alienated" who combine low contact, high powerlessness, and high dissatisfaction that violence approval was notably high, 65 percent of this group expressing willingness to use violence (as against 12 percent for the unalienated).

Such findings are consistent with the evidence we have on powerlessness and social-distance attitudes. Ransford's data show that those who feel more powerless express more hostility to whites ($r = .38$)—a fact which takes on considerable significance in light of the findings concerning social distance reported by Murphy and Watson in their post-riot study in the same Watts area.[39] They interviewed 585 residents of the area and found that social distance does not correlate in quite the expected way with riot participation. The expected way would be to find that those in *low* socioeconomic positions with high social distance would be the most bitter and resentful toward whites and thus most likely to have participated in the riot. "Instead," they write, "we find that the highest levels of riot activity appear when high social distance is coupled with *high* socio-economic position."[40] Apparently "distance" (which is correlated with powerlessness) makes a bigger difference at the higher socioeconomic level, which recalls the "intriguing fact" observed earlier in Bullough's study of housing integration: it is at the higher level of education that the greatest difference in powerlessness occurs (the well-educated who have stayed in the ghetto are notably high in powerlessness).

The point is that education, and high socioeconomic position generally, may work in a rather more complicated way for alienated minorities than one is accustomed to think (especially in relation to the violence issue). The data in the Kerner report encourage one further in that expectation. Their data on Detroit and Newark show that the rioters (as compared with the "non-involved") were *better* educated, *more* involved in organizations concerned with civil rights, and *more* knowledgeable about politics—but also more powerless in that they attribute their employment troubles to "external" sources (69 percent of the rioters perceive "discrimination" as the obstacle and only 18 percent refer to "lack of training," while among the noninvolved, 41 percent choose the latter, more "internal" explanation).[41]

All this concerns Negro protest. The relevant data for whites are of a somewhat different order, but consistent with the over-all thesis. With respect to social distance, the powerlessness variable repeatedly, but moderately, cor-

---

[39] Raymond J. Murphy and James M. Watson, "The Structure of Discontent: The Relationship between Social Structure, Grievance and Riot Support," in N. E. Cohen, ed., *The Los Angeles Riots: A Socio-Psychological Study*. Praeger, New York, 1969, pp. 140–157.

[40] *Ibid.*, p. 103.

[41] Kerner Commission, *op. cit.*, especially pp. 174–178.

relates with anti-ethnic (including anti-Negro) prejudice. Among Swedish manual workers, the obtained r was .24; for American manual workers, .21.[42] Obviously, such prejudice measures are only indirectly and imperfectly indicative of social action tendencies; but one might infer that the powerless and prejudiced person would be more strongly and directly resistive in minority matters.

Nor is the proposition, on the white side, limited to minority affairs. The argument concerning powerlessness and protest has been applied in the case of voter response to local political issues, for example, fluoridation, school bond levies, urban renewal, and the like. Thus, Horton and Thompson showed that political alienation (which, in their measure, combines powerlessness, consciousness of potentially menacing power, and mistrust as well) was related not to passivity but to negative voting on a school bond issue in two upstate New York communities.[43] With respect to the fluoridation issue, Coleman has suggested that the rank-and-file opponents of fluoridation are characterized by lack of attachment to community organizations, and in that case one might expect that they would also be relatively high in feelings of powerlessness. Indeed, Gamson has shown that they are.[44] Even among college students, the association between powerlessness and protest holds, as appears in Richard T. Morris and Raymond Murphy's unpublished data showing support for the

[42] Melvin Seeman, "On the Personal Consequences of Alienation in Work," *American Sociological Review,* vol. 32, April, 1967, pp. 273–285.

[43] Wayne E. Thompson and John E. Horton, "Political Alienation as a Force in Social Action," *Social Forces,* vol. 38, March, 1960, pp. 190–195.

[44] James S. Coleman, *Community Conflict.* Free Press, Glencoe, Ill., 1957; William A. Gamson, "The Fluoridation Dialogue: Is It an Ideological Conflict," *Public Opinion Quarterly,* vol. 25, 1961, pp. 527–537. In a later work Gamson also (and I think rightly) makes a case for not confusing powerlessness and mistrust in one's measure of alienation: ". . . a combination of high sense of political efficacy and low political trust is the optimum combination for mobilization—a belief that influence is possible and necessary." Gamson, *Power and Discontent,* p. 48. For evidence that "political cynicism" is correlated with disapproval of urban renewal programs, cf. Robert A. Agger, D. Goldrich, and B. I. Swanson, *The Rulers and the Ruled.* Wiley, New York, 1964. Robert L. Crain, Elihu Katz, and D. B. Rosenthal, *The Politics of Community Conflict: The Fluoridation Decision.* Bobbs-Merrill, New York, 1968, argue, however, that the fate of fluoridation proposals in American cities is not well explained by the alienation thesis, an argument that is consistent with my view that alienation alone (e.g., without attention to the situation, or to alternative values and pathways) is not likely in itself to explain very much (cf. *infra,* especially pp. 506–507 and p. 525). While granting "that the concept of alienation has some relevance to the fluoridation problem" (p. 50), they remark: "Even the most alienated or unhappy individual may be prevented from expressing his personality in extremist behavior if he is in a situation that does not provide an extremist alternative" (p. 37). Thus they argue that the fluoridation decision "depends upon the local political structure more than individual psyches" (p. 10).

Free Speech movement at Berkeley to be significantly higher among those who felt more powerless.[45]

Proposition 4. *Those who feel powerless tend to learn less of the control-relevant information available in the environment.* In a series of studies in varied contexts, it has been demonstrated that poor learning and high powerlessness are associated. The poor learning is not simply a function of such variables as intelligence, test-taking skills, or status background, for the learning in question is differential: it does not occur with any and all information, but occurs especially when the information involved is potentially useful in the planning, management, and control of life outcomes. The most striking and recent demonstration of the proposition is found in the well-known "Coleman Report" where it is noted that the powerlessness variable outranked a set of objective school factors in predicting school achievement: ". . . a pupil factor which appears to have a stronger relationship to achievement than do all the 'school' factors together is the extent to which an individual feels that he has some control over his own destiny."[46]

Earlier, Seeman had shown that the I-E scale can predict learning differences in a variety of settings. For example, tuberculosis patients who differed in powerlessness (but were matched for other variables) showed differential knowledge about health matters—including knowledge about the causes and treatment of tuberculosis.[47] In a subsequent study carried out in an Ohio reformatory, it was shown that inmates who are low in powerlessness had significantly better recall of control-relevant information concerning the parole process.[48] Several kinds of information were offered to the inmates for potential learning, and the differences in the effects of powerlessness were least significant when the information concerned incidental (and presumably useless) facts about the age of the guards, the per capita costs of reformatory life, etc. Finally, in a Swedish setting, a similar demonstration of differential knowledge associated with powerlessness was made, in this case showing that students and workers differing in powerlessness also differed in their level of political knowledge but *not* in their level of general cultural knowledge (i.e.,

---

[45] A typical distribution on the six powerlessness items was as follows (reported here for the item, "Becoming a success is a matter of hard work; luck has little or nothing to do with it"): strongly agree (an internal response), 22% favorable to FSM; agree, 33% favorable; disagree, 43% favorable; and strongly disagree (the most powerless response), 53% favorable to FSM.

[46] James S. Coleman *et al., Equality of Educational Opportunity.* Government Printing Office, Washington, D.C., 1966, p. 23.

[47] Melvin Seeman and John W. Evans, "Alienation and Learning in a Hospital Setting," *American Sociological Review,* vol. 27, December, 1962, pp. 772–782.

[48] Melvin Seeman, "Alienation and Social Learning in a Reformatory," *American Journal of Sociology,* vol. 69, November, 1963, pp. 270–284.

knowledge of music, literature, etc.).[49] That such results can be repeated in a wide variety of contexts is suggested not only by Coleman's nationwide sample of children, but also by Bullough's use of the same proposition in her study of desegregation. She constructed a "housing facts" test (10 factual items concerning the legality of restrictive covenants, the status of discrimination in public accommodations, etc.), and found the expected differences: both within her ghetto and integrated samples, those high in powerlessness scored lower on housing information.[50]

A final word about learning, in this case concerning the learning of powerlessness itself. Studies on the learning of mastery attitudes are rare, but at least one such study suggests that attitudes of powerlessness are responsive to the relevant experiences. Hunt and Hardt conducted a study of "Upward Bound" programs, and included the I-E scale in the pre- and post-test measures.[51] They report an initial mean score of 9.29 and a post-test score of 9.67, the difference being significant at $p < .01$, indicating a trend in the direction of lower powerlessness after the summer experience. The change is small, but occurred with considerable uniformity: In 20 of the 21 programs studied they found less externality in the postmeasure (this despite the fact that the initial mean score was unexpectedly higher than that reported for a national sample of 1,000 high school students in the Purdue Opinion poll, where the mean was 8.57).

Proposition 5. *Negroes and other minorities tend to feel more powerless than comparable whites.* We have already had occasion to note the widespread agreement about the Negro's sense of powerlessness, but it is still pertinent to ask what the evidence looks like and how it compares with data derived from other minorities. Although there are some conflicting findings, the black samples show greater powerlessness regardless of measures (I-E, political efficacy or political alienation) and regardless of populations (children, community samples, prison inmates, or older employed males).

[49] Melvin Seeman, "Status and Identity: The Problem of Inauthenticity," *Pacific Sociological Review*, vol. 9, Fall, 1966, pp. 67–73; *idem*, "Powerlessness and Knowledge: A Comparative Study of Alienation and Learning," *Sociometry*, vol. 30, June, 1967, pp. 105–123. Jack McLeod, "Alienation and the Uses of the Mass Media," *Public Opinion Quarterly*, vol. 29, Winter, 1965, pp. 583–594, a study of mass media use, is relevant here. He found the more alienated (largely, powerless) respondents significantly less likely to offer informational reasons in describing their use of the newspaper (e.g., use it "for interpretation of important events") and more likely to acknowledge "vicarious reasons" (e.g., "to bring some excitement into my life"), a finding which held when education was controlled. The correlation between alienation and expressed interest in political-economic "headlines" was − .28.

[50] Bullough, *op. cit.*

[51] David E. Hunt and R. H. Hardt, "The Effect of Upward Bound Programs on the Attitudes, Motivation, and Academic Achievement of Negro Students," *Journal of Social Issues*, vol. 25, Summer, 1969, pp. 117–129.

Thus, Battle and Rotter found that lower-class Negro children were significantly more "external" in their orientation than lower-class white children (or than middle-class Negroes and whites); and Lefcourt and Ladwig found higher powerlessness among Negro inmates in two correctional institutions.[52] Two community samples not only provide the basis for the racial comparison, but are also suggestive on other counts. Ransford and Seeman's unpublished data yield the expected black-white difference (for a Los Angeles population), but beyond that, the pattern of differences at the item level suggest that the results are not due to generalized response tendencies—rather, they reflect differential social experience. Thus, the item comparisons in Table 7 show no difference between black and white when global political problems are at issue, while the differences in response widen when the question involves control over one's own social outcomes.

Table 7. Black-White Differences on Political and Personal Problems
(*In Percent*)

	Negro Choices (N = 312)	*White Choices* (N = 390)
1. A. Wars between countries seem inevitable despite the efforts of men to prevent them.	69	66
B. Wars between countries can be avoided.	31	34
2. A. Becoming a success is a matter of hard work; luck has little or nothing to do with it.	58	77
B. Getting a good job depends mainly on being in the right place at the right time.	42	23

In another community study, Middleton developed a scale composed of single items measuring each of the six varieties of alienation described earlier.[53] The powerlessness item ("There is not much that I can do about most of the important problems that we face today") revealed clear differences between blacks and whites in a central Florida city (population 18,000). What is of special interest is the result when level of education is established as a control (see Table 8).

Obviously, the black-white differences do not disappear with education controlled; indeed, the *difference* in powerlessness is somewhat greater among

[52] Esther S. Battle and Julian B. Rotter, "Children's Feelings of Personal Control as Related to Social Class and Ethnic Group," *Journal of Personality,* vol. 31, December, 1963, pp. 482–490; Herbert M. Lefcourt and Gordon W. Ladwig, "The American Negro: A Problem in Expectancies," *Journal of Personality and Social Psychology,* vol. 1, April, 1965, pp. 377–380; *idem,* "Risk-taking in Negro and White Adults," *Journal of Personality and Social Psychology,* vol. 2, November, 1965, pp. 765–769.

[53] Middleton, *op. cit.*

Table 8. Black-White Differences by Level of Education

Education	Percent Scoring High in Alienation
Negro:	
Less than 12 years	73
12 years or more	60
White:	
Less than 12 years	57
12 years or more	34

those who are better educated; certainly, the level of powerlessness is high among the well-educated blacks (as high as it is among the poorly educated whites). It is a pattern of large difference among the better-educated that we have had occasion to remark on before.[54] Such differences in attitude at the higher educational level should not occasion great surprise, since they match some very clear objective disadvantages that go with higher education for the Negro. As Siegel shows, increments in education lead to greater gain for whites, so that the earning gap increases with education: ". . . in most occupations the handicap is *accentuated* with increasing education."[55]

With regard to other minorities, the evidence is less plentiful and less clear, although it generally follows the expected pattern. Thus, Jessor *et al.* report significant differences in their tri-ethnic community study: The dominant Anglos scored lowest (most internal) on the I-E scale, and the Spanish most external, with the Ute Indians between the two, a finding which they argue is "in line with data on the ethnic group differences in the socioeconomic opportunity structure in the community, where the Indians occupy a somewhat more favored position than the Spanish."[56]

The Jewish minority, as might be expected, appears not to share this pattern of high powerlessness. Strodtbeck, for example, developed a scale which has a "mastery" component, and found that Jewish subjects were more committed to mastery attitudes than Italians.[57] Much of the variance in this instance is probably attributable to social-class differences, but the weight of the over-all

[54] The same point is even more sharply made in Middleton's data concerning "meaninglessness." On this item ("Things have become so complicated in the world today that I really don't understand what is going on"), there is substantially no difference (76% vs. 80%) for poorly educated Negroes and whites; but among the better-educated, 56% of the Negroes agree, but only 35% of the whites.

[55] Paul M. Siegel, "On the Cost of Being a Negro," *Sociological Inquiry*, vol. 35, Winter, 1965, pp. 41–57, especially p. 53.

[56] Jessor *et al., op. cit.,* pp. 302–303.

[57] Fred L. Strodtbeck, "Family Interaction, Values and Achievement," in D. McClelland, ed., *Talent and Society.* Van Nostrand, New York, 1958, pp. 135–191.

evidence suggests that there are direct cultural teachings regarding mastery, that is, there are systematic differences in beliefs about fate control among Negroes, Mexicans, Jews, Italians, etc., quite independent of socioeconomic considerations. That is certainly the import of Rosen's finding that the Jewish group is significantly high in "achievement values" (and the Italians significantly low) with social-class differences controlled—a finding which is of direct interest here, since the items include a heavy component of passivity and fatalism (and are, in fact, very similar to the standard I-E content; e.g., "When a man is born, the success he is going to have is in the cards, so he might just as well accept it and not fight against it").[58]

One would not need to struggle very hard to make the connection between the facts about minority differences in sensed control and the previous propositions (e.g., regarding learning). That connection is made in the Coleman report:

> The responses of pupils to questions in the survey show that minority pupils, except for Orientals, have far less conviction than whites that they can affect their own environment and future. When they do, however, their achievement is higher than that of whites who lack that conviction. Furthermore, while this characteristic shows little relationship to most school factors, it is related, for Negroes, to the proportion of whites in the schools. Those Negroes in schools with a higher proportion of whites have a greater sense of control.[59]

An important cautionary note needs to be entered on these propositions about powerlessness. As I indicate later, when the future needs in research are discussed (see p. 523 especially), distinctions concerning the domains, brands, or contexts of powerlessness have not been prominent in the literature, and sharper evidence on many points will certainly be forthcoming when the appropriate distinctions are made. The I-E. scale, for example, does not distinguish between attributions about "fate and luck" as contrasted with the powerlessness generated by the action of "powerful others"; and that distinction may be quite important in predicting achievement behavior or protest action, as Patricia Gurin and her colleagues have recently sought to show by

---

[58] Bernard C. Rosen, "Race, Ethnicity and the Achievement Syndrome," *American Sociological Review,* vol. 24, February, 1959, pp. 47–60.

[59] Coleman *et al., op. cit.,* pp. 23, 320–321. Concerning Orientals, cf. also the argument by Caudill and DeVos (William Caudill and George DeVos, "Achievement, Culture and Personality: The Case of the Japanese Americans," *American Anthropologist,* vol. 58, December, 1956, pp. 1102–1126) that their successful relocation in Chicago after the Second World War resulted from a significant compatibility between American and Japanese culture—especially with respect to a middle-class emphasis upon personal achievement and long-range goals.

distinguishing attitudes of "system blame" from "internal control" of the more personal kind.[60] If the distinction holds, it may tell us (in seeming contradiction to what has gone before) the conditions under which *internal* control will be associated with riot participation, or the conditions under which *external* control conceived as system blame will be associated with higher aspiration and achievement.

Normlessness. The previous section sought to demonstrate a degree of empirical consistency concerning one variant of alienation. The propositions involved can all be related to the schema regarding mass theory presented in Table 1: The data bear upon the notion that certain structural attributes (e.g., organization membership or minority position) encourage alienation (the A → B relation in Table 1), or upon the notion that powerlessness has specifiable behavioral consequences (the B → C relation). One could develop a similar set of propositions for normlessness, but it seems wiser to alter the focus somewhat, making the discussion now an occasion for highlighting the difference between the forms of alienation (especially here, between normlessness and powerlessness).

As with powerlessness, there are a variety of ways of measuring the anomic brand of alienation, and a wide range of behaviors has been linked with it—everything from fertility rates to delinquency. The most popular indicator of normlessness has been the Srole anomia scale, which has the advantage of being short (five items) and scalable in a Guttman sense. It has some serious disadvantages as well, especially if one wishes to maintain a clear distinction among the various alienations. Srole indicates that his scale is intended as a measure of "interpersonal alienation," but it is noteworthy that the items include the notion of trust, powerlessness, and various degrees of hope or despair.[61] It is perhaps the latter notion (despair) which best captures the major thread in the scale.[62]

There are numerous variations on the Srole index, for example, Dean's "normlessness" scale, McClosky and Schaar's measure of "anomie," Jessor's

[60] Patricia Gurin, "Motivation and Aspirations of Southern Negro College Youth," *American Journal of Sociology,* vol. 75, January, 1970, pp. 75–91; Patricia Gurin *et al.,* "Internal-External Control in the Motivational Dynamics of Negro Youth," *Journal of Social Issues,* vol. 25, Summer, 1969, pp. 29–53; John R. Forward and Jay R. Williams, "Internal-External Control and Black Militancy," *Journal of Social Issues,* vol. 26, Winter, 1970, pp. 75–91.

[61] Leo Srole, "Social Integration and Certain Corollaries: An Exploratory Study," *American Sociological Review,* vol. 21, December, 1956, pp. 709–716, especially p. 712.

[62] Dorothy L. Meier and Wendell Bell, "Anomia and Differential Access to the Achievement of Life Goals," *American Sociological Review,* vol. 24, April, 1959, pp. 189–202; Edward L. McDill, "Anomie, Authoritarianism, Prejudice, and Socio-Economic Status: An Attempt at Clarification," *Social Forces,* vol. 39, March, 1961, pp. 239–245.

"alienation," and Kornhauser's index of "Personal morale."[63] But a word should be said about two indexes that are, at least theoretically, of a different order. Neal developed a measure of normlessness based on the definition provided at the outset of the present chapter, intended to measure "the expectancy that socially unapproved behavior is necessary for goal attainment." And Rotter has reported some success with a scale to measure "interpersonal trust," an idea that is important in the Durkheimian notion of anomie, and has obvious affinities with the Neal measure (both of the scales, for example, contain an item like, "Most elected public officials are really sincere in the campaign promises").[64]

Since scales can be manufactured and intercorrelated almost endlessly, the question posed above becomes crucial: What is the evidence that the anomic variant of alienation is usefully distinguishable from the powerlessness brand? Although these two (e.g., the Srole and the I-E scales) tend to correlate positively—the r was .33 in the Neal-Seeman study[65]—there are, nonetheless, some interesting differences between them.

1. *Anomia is more highly related to the common indexes of socioeconomic status* (income, occupation, and education). In one of the best-known treatments of the Srole measure, Meier and Bell note that "socio-economic status is the most important predictor of anomia."[66] This tends, however, not to be true for powerlessness as measured by the I-E scale. For example, in a comparison of Swedish manual and nonmanual workers, the respective mean scores were 4.87 and 4.83, and in a recent (unpublished) replication of the Swedish work, a similar pattern was found for American workers. Bullough reports correlations as low as $-.03$ between powerlessness and income, and $-.07$ for powerlessness and educational attainment; the comparable r's for anomia being $-.28$ and $-.31$, respectively.[67]

Apparently, class-based differences are not to be taken for granted so far

[63] Dean, *op. cit.;* Herbert McClosky and John H. Schaar, "Psychological Dimensions of Anomy," *American Sociological Review,* vol. 30, February, 1965, pp. 14–40; Jessor *et al., op. cit.;* Arthur Kornhauser, *Mental Health of the Industrial Worker.* Wiley, New York, 1965.

[64] Arthur G. Neal, "Stratification Concomitants of Powerlessness and Normlessness: A Study of Political and Economic Alienation," unpublished doctoral dissertation, Ohio State University, 1959; Theodore H. Groat and A. G. Neal, "Social Psychological Correlates of Urban Fertility," *American Sociological Review,* vol. 32, December, 1967, pp. 945–959, especially p. 948; Julian B. Rotter, "A New Scale for the Measurement of Interpersonal Trust," *Journal of Personality,* vol. 35, December, 1967, pp. 651–665.

[65] Neal and Seeman *op. cit.*

[66] Meier and Bell, *op. cit.* p. 198.

[67] Bonnie L. Bullough, *Social-Psychological Barriers to Housing Desegregation.* University of California Housing, Real Estate, and Urban Land Studies Program, Los Angeles, Special Report #2, 1969.

as the expectancies for control in the I-E scale are concerned. The situation appears quite different for the Srole scale where the customary finding is that each status variable contributes a significant portion of the variance; for example, even though it seems likely that education is a strong determinant of anomia, Mizruchi shows that, with education controlled, and even among those of college level, income differences are correlated with differences in anomia.[68]

2. *Although anomia, like powerlessness, tends to be associated with organizational affiliation, more discriminating predictions concerning their relation to membership can be made.* Thus, for example, Neal and Seeman argued that, while membership in a labor union—an eminently control-oriented type of organization—may be associated with relatively low powerlessness, there could be no a priori reason to assume that lack of membership would lead to diffuse and generalized disaffection (of the kind tapped through the Srole scale).[69] That is, in fact, what the data revealed, namely, differences in powerlessness but not in anomia between the organized and unorganized manual workers. Whether this is a stable finding remains to be seen, but it illustrates the possibility and necessity of demonstrating how different types of membership relate to different types of alienation.

3. *Anomia and powerlessness in all likelihood make independent contributions to attitude and behavior differences.* Although relatively little effort has thus far gone into demonstrating the independent effects of various types of alienation, the evidence warrants the hope that such additive (and theoretically important) discriminations can be made. Thus, Bullough shows that, with anomia held constant, the powerlessness differences between ghetto and integrated Negroes do not disappear, and the reverse is true as well: with powerlessness held constant, the anomia scores are significantly high in the ghetto and low in the integrated Valley areas.[70]

4. *Despite their correlation, anomia and powerlessness show different patterns of association with predictable dependent variables.* An example can illustrate the point. Jessor's interest lay chiefly in the problem of deviance (especially drinking behavior) in a tri-ethnic community, and, as one might expect, it is the normlessness measure, rather than powerlessness, which more successfully predicts "global deviance" (meaning serious drunkenness or other serious deviance including court-related offenses).[71] Among those who scored high in "alienation" (an anomia-like index), 52 percent qualified as global deviants, while only 32 percent so qualified among the low scorers ($p < .01$), but

[68] Ephraim H. Mizruchi, *Success and Opportunity: A Study of Anomie.* Free Press of Glencoe, New York, 1964.

[69] Neal and Seeman *op. cit.*

[70] Bullough, *Social-Psychological Barriers to Housing Desegregation.*

[71] Jessor *et al., op. cit.*

the difference for those high and low on the I-E scale was an insignificant 6 percent (39 percent vs. 45 percent; cf. p. 343).

5. *Despite the indicated differences between anomia and powerlessness, the two versions of alienation yield congruent conclusions concerning minority status.* Perhaps most important, the pattern of large differences between whites and *more* advantaged Negroes appears to hold for the anomia scale as it does for powerlessness. That is the import, in different ways, of the findings reported by Killian and Grigg and by Lefton.[72] The former showed that, for both rural and urban samples in two Southeastern communities, highly educated Negroes and whites differ far more in anomia than do those with less education (e.g., in the urban area, 32 percent of the highly educated Negroes score high in anomia, as against 19 percent of the whites; the comparable figures for those with low education were 45 percent and 42 percent, respectively). Lefton also found surprisingly high anomia among the *more* advantaged Negroes, in his study of 155 autoworkers who were interviewed prior to a large-scale layoff in the plant. In that case, anomia was significantly *higher* among the Negroes with higher seniority (and stable employment histories), as compared to their lower-status counterparts, while the contrary was found for the whites in the sample (for them, low seniority went, as one might more reasonably expect, with high anomia).

I have not tried to reflect here the full range of studies that have employed some version of normlessness; that would be difficult for the Srole scale alone. I have simply tried to suggest what the difference between powerlessness and normlessness has to do with making predictions about delinquency, desegregation, prejudice, or engagement in organizational life. The relevance of all this for the structure-alienation-behavior model in Table 1 is perhaps nowhere better shown than in the 1968 work by Jessor's group.[73] Theirs is an elaborate effort at demonstration, wedding (a) the structural interest in deviance exemplified by Merton, to (b) a theoretically oriented version of alienation, as a way (c) of predicting deviant behavior. Specifically, this requires them to show how differences in objective access to the "opportunity structure" of the community are translated into individual sentiments (among others, internal-external control and "alienation") that influence conduct.

This model is not in principle different from Stinchcombe's, where again the structure-alienation-behavior sequence is demonstrated. Stinchcombe shows that rebellion among high school students is the product of "expressive alienation" (which includes a negative attitude toward conformity, that is, a kind of normlessness). This is engendered by a disjunctive opportunity or reward structure: "poor articulation" (of post-high school status with present

[72] Lewis M. Killian and C. M. Grigg, "Urbanism, Race and Anomia," *American Journal of Sociology,* vol. 67, May, 1962, pp. 661–665; Mark Lefton, "Race, Expectations and Anomia," *Social Forces,* vol. 46, March, 1968, pp. 347–352.

[73] Jessor *et al., op. cit.*

academic activity) produces rebellion because it produces expressive aliena-tion.[74]

Self-Estrangement. The transition from normlessness to a considera-tion of self-estrangement is easily (perhaps too easily) made, for it is com-monplace to argue that the attitude of distrust for others is simply the other side of estrangement from self (as Smith recently put it, "corresponding to generalized favorable self-evaluation is an attitude of optimistic trust").[75] There is, in the mere statement of this truism, enough to make us wary of the great morass of work on self-conception and self-esteem (in clinical and social psychology, social psychiatry, and sociology) that can be invoked in an examination of self-estrangement.

The definition of self-estrangement offered earlier can be helpful, I think, in establishing a firmer footing; namely, the view that to be self-estranged is to be engaged in activities that are not intrinsically rewarding. That defini-tion clearly represents a departure from two prevalent alternatives: (1) that self-estrangement consists of the nonfulfillment of certain innate human needs;[76] and (2) that self-estrangement involves some degree of rejection of one's self—some sense of discrepancy between what one is and what one would like to be.[77] What the definition does not depart from, however, is the scope and amenability to demonstration required in the secularization of alienation.

Concerning scope, I have argued elsewhere that Marx's view of alienated labor embodies the "intrinsic satisfaction" version of self-estrangement (and other elements, of course, not least of all a philosophy of human nature); what constitutes the alienation of labor is that it is *"external to the worker"* who *"does not fulfill himself"* in work which is *"only a means."*[78] Marx develops what Kaufman has called the "principle of the sufficiency of unalienated labor" —the belief that "the chronic and remediable ills of society will disappear once the alienation of labor has been ended."[79]

In that broad scope, the proposition can hardly be tested, but the theme embedded in it (what I have elsewhere called the theme of "generalization") can be tested. The thesis is that alienation in the work place generalizes out of

[74] Arthur L. Stinchcombe, *Rebellion in a High School.* Quadrangle Books, Chicago, 1964, p. 12.

[75] M. Brewster Smith, "Competence and Socialization," in J. A. Clausen, ed., *Sociali-zation and Society.* Little, Brown, Boston, 1968, pp. 271–320, especially p. 282.

[76] Erich Fromm, *The Sane Society.* Rinehart, New York, 1955; Amitai Etzioni, *The Active Society.* Free Press, New York, 1968.

[77] Carl R. Rogers, *On Becoming a Person: A Therapist's View of Psychotherapy.* Houghton Mifflin, Boston, 1961.

[78] Seeman, "On the Meaning of Alienation"; Erich Fromm, *Marx's Conception of Man.* Frederick Ungar, New York, 1961, p. 98.

[79] Arnold S. Kaufman, *The Radical Liberal: New Man in American Politics.* Ather-ton, New York, 1968, p. 5.

the work sphere into a broad range of "remediable ills"; for example, frustration in work breeds hostility which overflows into intergroup antagonism; the lack of engagement at work leads to similar disengagement in politics and social life; the overwhelmingly extrinsic character of work life is reflected in extrinsic, status-minded styles of life.

These are not easy propositions to test, but the evidence on hand is not resoundingly supportive of the generalization thesis. My own Swedish data were quite negative about generalization; and recent (unpublished) American replications, with both Negro and white workers, go predominantly in the same direction.[80] The scores on alienation in work (sample question: "Is your job too simple to bring out your best abilities or not?") do not correlate with such variables as ethnic hostility, political awareness, or generalized powerlessness.[81] A variety of explanations may be offered for the fact that work situations that are experienced as extrinsically governed do not have the serious consequences often imputed—among these reasons being the likelihood that such intrinsic rewards are not as highly valued by workers as the intellectual tradition regarding alienation would assume.[82]

The generalization thesis will be recognized as a variation of the "alienation has consequences" portion of Table 1 (the B → C relation). As one might surmise, the structural side of the matter—work rationalization as a source of alienation (especially here, self-estrangement)—has received substantial attention as well. There are, obviously, grounds for concern about alienated labor regardless of the amount of "generalization" (and regardless of the assumption that there are basic human drives toward creativity or self-fulfillment). As Weiss and Reisman put it: "Work which is too dull, which involves a man too little, or which places him under demeaning supervision, is damaging to him . . ."[83]; and if one restricts the meaning of "damage" to include simply one or another variety of alienation, the evidence seems clear

[80] Seeman, "On the Personal Consequences of Alienation in Work."

[81] It ought to be noted that positive evidence concerning generalization has been presented. Thus, McKinley (Donald G. McKinley, *Social Class and Family Life*. Free Press, New York, 1964) has verified the hypothesis that "those individuals who enjoy great autonomy in their work will tend to show less hostility in their families and toward their children in the socialization process" (p. 129). Unfortunately, the data are based largely upon the son's report about all these matters. See also the conclusion by Oeser and Hammond (O. A. Oeser and S. B. Hammond, *Social Structure and Personality in a City*. Routledge & Kegan Paul, London, 1954): "A correlation of .51 (tetrachoric) was found between the husband's dissatisfaction with his job and tension in the home" (p. 248).

[82] John H. Goldthorpe, "Attitudes and Behaviour of Car Assembly Workers: A Deviant Case and a Theoretical Critique," *British Journal of Sociology,* vol. 17, September, 1966, pp. 227–244.

[83] Robert S. Weiss and David Riesman, "Social Problems and Disorganization in the World of Work," in R. K. Merton and R. A. Nisbet, eds., *Contemporary Social Problems.* Harcourt, New York, 1961, pp. 459–514, especially p. 464.

that routinized work does take its toll, as reflected, for example, in the elaborate rationalizations developed to explain one's lack of success and maintain one's self-regard.[84]

Put most simply, what the evidence says is that differences in the work situation *are* associated with attitude differences that serve as indicators of alienation—a conclusion that hardly seems surprising in light of the great variety of social-class differences in attitude that have been established. The clearest documentation on the point is seen in the contrast between the negative findings I have just described concerning generalization, and the positive results reported by both Blauner and Kornhauser *using basically the same questionnaire items.*[85] Blauner essentially shows that different work circumstances (i.e., a skilled trade such as printing, a machine industry such as textiles, the assembly-line auto industry, or automated chemicals) produce job-related attitudes, that is, feelings of freedom on the job, of monotony, of meaningless work and the failure to use one's abilities. These measures reflect the *fact* of self-estrangement defined as nonintrinsic attachment to work (and predictably, assembly-line and textile workers are more estranged). Similarly, Kornhauser demonstrates that differences in jobs (e.g., skilled, high semiskilled, or repetitive semiskilled) are associated with differences in the worker's sense of well-being; for example they differ on numerous items measuring "personal morale." These items are akin to the Srole anomia scale in the worker's sense of job satisfaction and in their feeling that their abilities are being used. But there are evidences that the generalization to nonjob attitudes has its limits, as, for example, in Kornhauser's conclusion that "even routine production workers have overall feelings of life satisfaction only slightly lower than other groups and not at all commensurate with their relatively great job discontent."[86]

Much of the above is based, of course, on a particular definition of alienation in work, and on a measurement process suitable to that definition. It would be hard to make a strong case for the measurement process in question (consisting essentially of asking workers whether they find their work monotonous, strongly paced, creative, etc.), though there is some evidence that expressing "alienation" by these questions is not the same thing as expressing "satisfaction" with one's job—a distinction that seems theoretically meaningful.[87] Still, there are other ways to go about measuring self-estrangement in

[84] Eli Chinoy, *Automobile Workers and the American Dream.* Doubleday, Garden City., N.Y., 1955.

[85] Robert Blauner, *Alienation and Freedom: The Factory Worker and His Industry.* University of Chicago Press, Chicago, 1964; Kornhauser, *op. cit.*

[86] Kornhauser, *op. cit.,* p. 266.

[87] Kornhauser reports, for example, that ". . . almost half of the men for whom the job is not interesting and who do not find use for their abilities, nevertheless feel well

work, among which two in particular deserve mention, namely, the work of Dubin and Wilensky.[88]

Dubin examined the degree to which work appeared as a "central life interest" for workers in three industrial plants in the Middle West. To do so, he developed a questionnaire (CLI) to determine the "expressed preference for a given locale or situation in carrying out an activity."[89] Each activity presumably had an approximately equal likelihood of occurring in connection with the job or work place, or at some definite place in the community outside of work (and a third choice was added to represent an indifferent or neutral response): For example, "I would hate (a) missing a day's work; (b) missing a meeting of an organization I belong to; (c) missing almost anything I usually do." The most crucial finding in Dubin's study was the low percentage of workers who chose the work-related responses: Only 24 percent of all workers ($N = 491$) could be labeled as being job-oriented in their life interests. Dubin concluded that "work and the workplace are not central life interests for a vast majority" of industrial workers, a way of saying that the level of alienation in work is high.[90]

Wilensky comes to a different conclusion through a procedure based on the notion of "prized self-image." For him, alienation consists in the enactment of role obligations incongruent with the individual's conception of himself with respect to five basic attributes which could be validated or violated in the work context: sociability, intelligence, conscientiousness, independence, and ambition. Later in the interview, six features of the individual's work situation were examined, each of which could be related to these attributes of self-image (e.g., chances to talk sociably on the job, to use one's own judgment on the job, opportunities to work well, chances for promotion). Two major conclusions emerge from Wilensky's data: (1) "By our stringent measures, relating work role to prized self-image, the incidence of alienation is low: only 177 of our 1,156 employed men score 'alienated' on even one of the six possible attributes of the work situation; only 51 are alienated on two or more attributes; 11 on three or more"; and (2) "High economic, occupation and educational status together form a leading predictor of strong attachment and

---

satisfied with the job" (p. 172). For a sample of Negro workers in Los Angeles the obtained *r* between an index of job satisfaction and of work alienation was −.18; and for white workers, −.34. Crozier (Michel Crozier, *Le Monde des Employés de Bureau*. Le Seuil, Paris, 1965) has shown that clerical workers frequently express satisfaction with the job despite its monotonous character.

[88] Robert Dubin, "Industrial Workers' Worlds," *Social Problems,* vol. 3, January, 1956, pp. 131–142; Harold L. Wilensky, "Varieties of Work Experience," in H. Borow, ed., *Man in a World of Work*. Houghton Mifflin, Boston, 1964, pp. 125–154.

[89] Dubin, *op. cit.*, p. 134.

[90] *Ibid.*, p. 140.

the absence of alienation."[91] Wilensky remarks: "I am inclined to take the amount of alienation uncovered as the minimum that exists,"[92] and though he finds predictable differences among categories of occupation (e.g., more alienation among blue-collar workers and engineers than among lawyers or university personnel), the task of discovering the utility of the index for testing propositions about sources and consequences of self-estrangement at work remains to be done.[93]

Even more remains to be done on an aspect of self-estrangement that is not so strictly work-centered. I refer to the notion of inauthenticity—a notion that is hardly recent in origin although it has become increasingly popular, especially in existentialist writing and among "new left" activists whose revolt against the establishment is often couched in terms of the search for a more authentic political style.

The idea of inauthenticity, and its contribution to a systematic notion of self-estrangement, are not easy to define. Certainly it does not seem adequate to discuss the matter in terms of moral rectitudes or of false appearances (e.g., feigning pleasure when distaste is the true sentiment; or pretending to be a friend while being, in fact, a con man). I have tried elsewhere, beginning with Sartre's provocative analysis of the inauthentic Jew, to elaborate three forms of inauthenticity that share an important aspect of self-estrangement.[94] In each case, the inauthentic person bases his behavior on a distorted view of himself—he is self-estranged at least in the sense that he does not fully know himself in the given situation. The three types are taken from research instances and they concern, respectively, (1) black children who claim lighter skin color than objective raters assign, (2) academic intellectuals who defensively hide their status as intellectuals, and (3) school leaders who claim an ease in decision-making which other evidence suggests they do not actually possess. The key idea that ties these forms of inauthenticity together and makes them of interest in connection with self-estrangement is the idea of self-deception. The Negro child is pressed by society to delude himself into a false conception of his color; the intellectual, in his overdefensiveness, misreads what

[91] Wilensky, *op. cit.*, p. 143.

[92] *Ibid.*, p. 146.

[93] There is a useful literature on occupational *choice* which is of interest in connection with alienated work though not reviewed here (cf. Morris Rosenberg, *Occupations and Values*. Free Press, Glencoe, Ill., 1957, especially for the distinction between intrinsic and extrinsic values sought in jobs). Note also the demonstration by Liberty, Burnstein, and Moulton (Paul G. Liberty, Jr., Eugene Burnstein and Robert W. Moulton, "Concern with Mastery and Occupational Attraction," *Journal of Personality,* vol. 34, March, 1966, pp. 105–117) that preference for a job that emphasizes an extrinsic value (prestige) over the intrinsic value of "competence" is greater among those who are high in powerlessness.

[94] Seeman, "Status and Identity: The Problem of Inauthenticity"; Jean Paul Sartre, *Anti-Semite and Jew.* Grove Press, New York, 1960.

others in the non-intellectual community think of him; and the leader, like the mother who is oversolicitous about the child she unconsciously dislikes, protests too much about his leaderly decisiveness. In all these cases, too, there is a stereotype (of Negroes and whites, intellectuals, and leaders) that is at the root of the self-deception; in their different ways, the three types of inauthentics accept the stereotype as a valid image of themselves.[95]

In another way—from a societal rather than an individual standpoint—the idea of self-deception is crucial also for Etzioni.[96] He uses the notion of inauthenticity to diagnose the contemporary Western situation and, in the process, distinguishes between alienated and inauthentic societies. The distinction, which is also roughly a distinction between industrial (alienated) and postmodern (inauthentic) society, rests upon the idea of deception: "When both the appearance and the conditions are nonresponsive, we deal with outright alienation . . . when the appearance is responsive but reality is not, with inauthenticity,"[97] a good example of the latter being decision-making forms that are in fact shadow processes of decision (as in high school student organizations, or manipulated industrial decisions about productivity). Obviously, conceptual and measurement troubles abound in these efforts concerning inauthenticity; yet the attractive thing is that they are of the order sought when we are trying to bring clarity and demonstration to the kinds of large-scale and meaningful problems that are traditionally put in the language of alienation.

Some Congruences in Psychology

In the foregoing treatment of three varieties of alienation, I have concentrated on the sociological literature, but the approach adopted makes it easier to discern the fact that recent developments in psychology—where the idea of alienation has hardly been popular (especially in social psychology)—are nonetheless coordinate with sociological interests. Indeed, one of the virtues of the definitions outlined earlier is that they make that coordination more explicit and feasible.

That this is so has already been foreshadowed in the discussion of "internal vs. external control"—a construct (and a measurement device) useful both

---

[95] This view of self-estrangement as self-deception has some obvious affinities with the "discrepancy" approach discussed earlier (sensed discrepancy between ideal and real self) though it is not precisely the same thing—for one thing, because it does not depend upon an awareness of such a discrepancy. It also has an affinity with Buford Rhea's "interactionist" conception of alienation as "a process or experience of disowning a 'Me' which has not measured up to one's standard for oneself" (cf. "Measures of Child Involvement and Alienation from the School Programs," 1966, p. 12, mimeographed).

[96] Etzioni, *op. cit.*

[97] *Ibid.*, p. 621.

as a variant of alienation (powerlessness) and as a generalized expectancy (for control of reinforcements) that is important in Rotter's social learning theory. Among other things, the importance lies in the fact that such a construct can be useful in making traditional learning theory more responsive to the specifically human features of the learning situation. Prominent among these features is the attribution that persons make concerning the causal texture of their circumstances. Along that line, Rotter and his colleagues have shown that such differences in causal attribution make a very large difference in the pattern of learning in laboratory settings.[98] The pattern of extinction is quite different under "chance" vs. "skill" circumstances, and subjects are generally less responsive to success and failure cues in the "chance-luck" situation than in a situation defined as being dependent on individual skills. In a sense, they learn less from their past experience in the situation when they feel they have low control.

There are three things that ought not to be missed in this example from psychology. First, in challenging the experimental paradigm of traditional learning experiments—where perceived experimenter control, hence low subject control, is the rule—Rotter is, in effect, employing a small-scale version of the structure-alienation-behavior model in Table 1. The structure of the situation (e.g., the chance vs. skill task) encourages the development of high or low expectancies for control, and these expectancies in turn are shown to govern behavior (in this instance, learning and extinction). Second, these findings regarding learning lend themselves to propositions and implications of considerable scope going well beyond their application to laboratory tasks. That is what I have sought to show in the several field studies of learning already reviewed (concerning, for example, health, politics, and reformatory learning), and that also is the import of Coleman's remarks based on these studies.[99] Based on the demonstrated tie between powerlessness and low control-relevant learning, Coleman suggests that such findings may illuminate the difficulties experienced by Negro migrants coming to the city from feudal social structures of the rural South (difficulties going considerably beyond sheer discrimination, just as Bullough's findings go beyond socioeconomic barriers to integration) and, more generally, that the findings may be relevant for the behavior of ethnic groups who occupy "precarious" positions in the social structure and who may consequently develop "a high sensitivity to the cues of the social and economic environment."[100] Third, this example concerning Rotter's social learning theory

[98] Julian B. Rotter, Shephard Liverant, and Douglas Crowne, "The Growth and Extinction of Expectancies in Chance-Controlled and Skilled Tasks," *Journal of Psychology,* vol. 52, July, 1961, pp. 161–177.

[99] James S. Coleman, "Implications of the Findings on Alienation," *American Journal of Sociology,* vol. 70, July, 1964, pp. 76–78; and vol. 70, January, 1965, pp. 479–480.

[100] *Ibid.,* p. 480.

is but one instance of a trend in psychology that has led to formulations that are considerably more congenial for those with an interest in alienation.

Two major lines of work can illustrate these more congenial formulations. One stems from the growing unhappiness with the narrow behaviorism (emphasizing drive or tension reduction, and the search for equilibrium) that typified the psychological literature on motivation and learning for a long period. That unhappiness was well reflected in the influential paper by White on "competence motivation."[101] In addition to seriously questioning the adequacy of the going model based on drive satisfaction and the quest for quiescence, White proposed that there is an intrinsic motivation toward competence —toward effective mastery of the environment—which leads the individual to seek and to process information about the effect of his own behavior upon the environment. In much the same way, Koch has called for a reconsideration of the prevalent instrumental ("in-order-to") versions of motivation (the view that persons act to satisfy some extrinsic need beyond the act itself) in the interest of developing a more intrinsic language of description.[102]

These interests in "intrinsic" rewards recall the definition of self-estrangement outlined above, where the key feature is the individual's engagement in activities that are intrinsically rewarding. In neither White's nor Koch's case can it be said that they have offered a truly viable alternative. The idea of instrumentalism dies hard, and the idea of "intrinsic reward" is a more difficult theoretical problem than it may initially seem. The critics of instrumentalism have suggested a path more than a clear program, but my point is that the path has obvious affinities to the interest in alienation, whether or not one accepts the specific definitions offered here. The sociological interest in competence (and in the individual's sense of control) was evidenced some years before the White-Koch proposals in the work by Foote and Cottrell where interpersonal competence is the major focus (meaning by "competence" the individual's skill in controlling the outcomes of social interaction).[103]

The second line of development in psychology owes its inspiration to

---

[101] Robert W. White, "Motivation Reconsidered: The Concept of Competence," *Psychological Review*, vol. 66, September, 1959, pp. 297–333.

[102] Sigmund Koch, "Some Trends of Study I: Epilogue," in *Psychology: A Study of A Science*, Vol. III. McGraw-Hill, New York, 1959, pp. 729–788. In the recently published *Encyclopedia of the Social Sciences*, Birney (Robert C. Birney, "Motivation: Human Motivation," in David Sills, ed., *Encyclopedia of the Social Sciences*, Vol. 10. Macmillan and Free Press, New York, 1968, pp. 514–520) emphasizes ". . . the severe limitations of reducing the study of motivation to those behavior sequences which focus on action 'in order to' at the expense of action for its own sake of 'being'" (p. 515). For a similar point of view concerning the intrinsic motivation of tasks carried out for their own sake, see T. A. Ryan, "Drives, Tasks and Rewards," *American Journal of Psychology*, vol. 71, March, 1958, pp. 74–93.

[103] Nelson M. Foote and Leonard S. Cottrell, Jr., *Identity and Interpersonal Competence*. University of Chicago Press, Chicago, 1955.

Heider's work on "phenomenal causality," which is concerned with the question of how the naive observer attributes causes, properties, and dispositions to the persons and objects in his world; that is, how he grasps reality and learns to predict or control it.[104] In good part, that is what the sociologist's interest in powerlessness and the mass society is all about as well. Although we may talk a very different language about apparently different problems, for example, about attitudes of fatalism in underdeveloped countries, about conspiracy theories among the masses in developed countries, or about the discrepancy between rising expectations and low present capability in changing societies, the fact is that we, too, are talking about the attribution process (and, in all three of my instances above, about attributions concerning the locus of control).

One example from the attribution literature can perhaps help make the congruence of interest clear. One of the basic problems in that literature is to specify the conditions under which there will be an external attribution of causation (to the environment or external object) or an internal (self) attribution. Obviously, this is a variant of the problem of internal vs. external control (powerlessness) already reviewed at some length. Kelley describes three essential criteria that are employed in making such attributions, for example, in deciding whether (let us say) a given movie was itself really good, or whether the person himself simply was "in the mood." They are: (1) *uniqueness* (if the individual doesn't have the same response to all movies, it's more likely that this movie will be judged responsible for his reaction); (2) *consistency* (the movie draws the same reaction each time it is present, although it may be presented under somewhat different circumstances of time or place); and (3) *consensus* (other observers have the same reaction to the movie).[105]

Could all this have anything to do, either in principle or in fact, with what we know about the externality of Negroes and other minorities? It would seem so. They experience a world with a telling kind of uniqueness, consistency, and consensus. As to uniqueness, certainly the efficacy of one's efforts are quite distinguishable, for minority members, in different domains (e.g., in the streets vs. in the school); the inefficacy of "trying" is relatively consistent in the conventional domains (of education, jobs, or housing); and if there is any consensus it is on the fact that you never really know whether a given effort will succeed, there being just enough randomness in the pattern to make it simulate a game of chance.

One would expect relatively high generalized powerlessness under such circumstances. One would expect that even when there is interest in achievement, such interest would not be readily translated into effective action. One

---

[104] Fritz Heider, *The Psychology of Interpersonal Relations.* Wiley, New York, 1958.

[105] Harold H. Kelley, "Attribution Theory in Social Psychology," in D. Levine, ed., *Nebraska Symposium on Motivation.* University of Nebraska Press, Lincoln, 1967, pp. 192–240.

would expect that a generally or vaguely favorable self-image would not be as important for getting such goal-oriented and future-oriented action as would an internal attribution of causation (i.e., low powerlessness). And one would expect that being in school with others who do have such an internally oriented view of things would be a favorable circumstance for learning and achievement. Coleman's data are consistent with all of these expectations.[106]

A number of recent researches on the psychological side have employed the Heider framework on problems that are similar to those reviewed in the previous section on powerlessness, normlessness, and self-estrangement. De Charms and his colleagues, for example, sought to operationalize the distinction between "origins" and "pawns"—between those who are seen as independent agents of their own action, and those who are constrained by external forces.[107] The distinction is clearly similar to that between internal and external control in the sense measured by the I-E scale. The question for DeCharms was that of determining (1) whether there are consistent tendencies for given persons to see others as either origins or pawns, and (2) whether there are specifiable characteristics of an individual or situation which leads others to judge an action as being more like an origin or pawn. The results show that those who feel themselves more in control of their own destinies (i.e., the low scorers on powerlessness, using the I-E scale) tend to see the characters in constructed stories more as "origins" than do those who are high in powerlessness but, more interesting in light of our discussion immediately above concerning intrinsic motivation, "an intrinsically motivated character was seen as the epitome of an origin"—which is to say that the attribution of powerlessness and of self-estrangement (in our terms) are coordinate.[108]

The general point is that studies stemming from attribution theory are hardly irrelevant for those interested in alienation, despite the fact that they do not typically speak the language of estrangement or normlessness. Their relevance is very nicely suggested by the fact that studies of the attribution process very quickly lead to investigations bearing on the kinds of questions about

---

[106] Coleman *et al., op. cit.,* especially pp. 23, 320–321.

[107] Richard DeCharms, Virginia Carpenter and Aharon Kuperman, "The 'Origin-Pawn' Variable in Person Perception," *Sociometry,* vol. 28, September, 1966, pp. 241–258.

[108] *Ibid.,* p. 241. They also found a relation between the attribution of causality and attractiveness of the persuader: Doing something on the persuasion of one who is seen as attractive makes one appear more an "origin" than does following the suggestion of an unattractive source. Good events and good persons tend to attract "internal" explanations (Gwynn Nettler, "Using Our Heads," *The American Sociologist,* vol. 3, August, 1968, pp. 200–207). For related studies on the perception of locus of causality employing the Heider viewpoint, cf. John W. Thibault and Henry W. Riecken, "Some Determinants and Consequences of the Perception of Causality," *Journal of Personality,* vol. 24, December, 1955, pp. 113–133; Albert Pepitone, "Attributions of Causality, Social Attitudes, and Cognitive Matching Processes," in R. Tagiuri and L. Petrullo, eds., *Person Perception and Interpersonal Behavior.* Stanford University Press, Stanford, 1958, pp. 258–276.

the moral order that sociologists assume to be important and that should sound familiar in the present chapter: questions about trust and deception, responsibility, self-determination and freedom.[109]

Seven Deadly Sins

No one imagined that the wedding of scope and demonstration would be easy, and there are a set of recurring questions that have arisen in connection with that effort in the study of alienation. We ought at least to take cognizance of these problems, sketching some lines of argument without anticipating that a discussion in depth is possible here. Although there is a reasonable doubt whether Marx in fact abandoned the idea of alienation or merely transformed his interest in it in his later works, there is a good chance that we will have to abandon it if we cannot do better than we are now doing at solving, or being clear about, the seven problems discussed below.

1. The problem of *subjectivity*. The view of alienation embodied in the definitions employed here is social psychological: Alienation is defined in individual terms, using the person's expectations or values as the basis for discriminating the kind of alienation involved. There are those who are unhappy with such a view, who wish, rather, to treat alienation as a fact of society determinable without reference to individual states of consciousness, and the customary appeal for the objectivists is Marx.

Whatever else may be said on this hoary objective-subjective argument (which has appeared in many guises, and on many topics other than alienation), it cannot be said that the appeal to Marx is very secure, certainly not the appeal to the early Marx so much concerned with alienation. It is not only that one finds there clear evidence of the subjective concern—for the worker who "has a feeling of misery rather than well being" and who "feels himself at home only during his leisure time"[110]—it is more than that. Tucker has made the larger point quite strongly: "Marx's first system is openly subjectivistic . . . its pervasive idea is the idea of the self (and) the evil is alienation."[111] Indeed, Tucker argues that the later Marxian system is a reflection of the same subjectivist concern, a massive and effective "myth" about an inner struggle projected onto society: ". . . the reality that Marx apprehended and portrayed was inner reality. The forces of which he was aware were subjective forces,

[109] Kelley, *op. cit.,* notes, for example, how the idea of freedom is involved in the standard cognitive dissonance study—how the "illusion of freedom" is generated under conditions of essentially forced compliance, since the trick is to induce subjects to "freely" cooperate in completing an unpleasant task. It can be added that the large literature on need achievement is also deeply involved in attribution problems, e.g., attribution concerning the sources of success and failure.

[110] Fromm, *Marx's Conception of Man,* p. 98.

[111] Robert Tucker, *Philosophy and Myth in Karl Marx.* Cambridge University Press, Cambridge, 1961.

forces of the alienated self—conceived, however, and also perceived as forces abroad in society."[112]

This hardly settles the matter of subjectivity, although at the very least it suggests how much room for debate there is about Marx's use of alienation. More important, there are three problems related to the objectivity question that arise (and are treated in points 2 to 4 below).

2. The relevance of the *objective situation.* To opt for a social-psychological definition of alienation is not equivalent to dismissing objective circumstances, a point I made in my conceptual paper some ten years ago. There is some truth to the complaint recently made by Aiken and Hage to the effect that often "alienation has been defined, measured and discussed as if it represented some 'free floating' human condition irrespective of specific social contexts which produce such mental states."[113]

If this means, however, that those who define alienation in subjective terms should be sensitive to "contexts" in something like the following ways, it would be easy to agree (and such sensitivities have already been demonstrated):

a. The objective situation will usually need to be specified as part of the process of discovering whether or not the given brand of alienation works differently in different circumstances, for example, showing whether the sense of powerlessness has different consequences when the individual is subject to a highly stratified vs. a less stratified organizational setting.[114] In this instance, the "context" is treated in the way that is now customarily called "contextual analysis" (a variety of statistical interaction, in which the objective situation serves as the conditional variable affecting the relation between alienation and some correlates of it).

b. The idea of alienation—in each of the six forms defined earlier—can be defined over a wide range of contexts: in relatively miniscule and fleeting situations of interaction (Goffman); in specific organizational settings (Clark); or in broader society-wide contexts (Nettler).[115] Thus, the "context" needs to be specified simply as a matter of clarity concerning the social field that is under review.

[112] *Ibid.,* p. 219.

[113] Michael Aiken and Jerald Hage, "Organizational Alienation: A Comparative Analysis," *American Sociological Review,* vol. 31, August, 1966, pp. 497–507, especially p. 497.

[114] Seeman and Evans, *op. cit.*

[115] Gwynn Nettler, "A Measure of Alienation," *American Sociological Review,* vol. 22, December, 1957, pp. 670–677; Erving Goffman, "Alienation from Interaction," *Human Relations,* vol. 10, February, 1957, pp. 47–60; John P. Clark, "Measuring Alienation within a Social System," *American Sociological Review,* vol. 24, December, 1959, pp. 849–852.

c. There is no reason to assume a strong correlation between *feelings* of powerlessness (or other alienations) and *circumstances* of powerlessness (indeed, as we have noted earlier, Etzioni uses the discrepancy between feeling and fact as a way of designating what he calls the "inauthentic" society). Thus, it is surely a good and fair question to ask whether apparently alienative objective circumstances actually produce alienative sentiments—to ask, for example, as Rhea proposes: "Does the bureaucratic organization of the school alienate students?" The question has several distinct parts referring to different kinds of alienation. Do the students in such an objectively defined bureaucratic system *take pride* in the school; do they feel *intrinsically engaged* in the work they do (as against simply fighting for marks and success); and, more important for present purposes, do they *feel powerless* in it. Rhea finds that the sense of powerlessness is not characteristic of the students he studied—that through the operation of a "paternalistic" ethic, they adjust remarkably well to their bureaucratic circumstances (but neither are they very much engaged intrinsically in what they do); in short, they are alienated in some senses but not in others under the given structure.[116]

Although there is no reason to assume high correlation between objective structure and subjective sentiment, there *is* reason to assume that situations and feelings will generally not be independent. A small-scale example of that is found in the demonstration by Lippitt *et al.* that the perception of one's power within the group corresponds fairly closely to both the power attributed by other group members and the objectively observed influence patterns.[117] In brief, whether the objective context and individual sentiments are congruent or not, attention to the context can be effectively used to force a careful examination of theoretical assumptions, of the respondent's rationalization processes, of failures in prediction, and the like.

3. The problem of *normative judgment*. Those who emphasize the objective aspect of alienation often have quite different interests than those described immediately above. They would not be content to see the objective situation included simply as a contextual variable in any of the three ways outlined. What is wanted is a *judgment*. Thus, as Lipsitz wrote, in his review of Blauner's work on *Alienation and Freedom:* "It is not adequate to the nature of this concept to substitute the worker's measure of his own satisfaction for a normative judgment made by an observer."[118] Among other things, this normative approach achieves two purposes: (1) it retains the tradition of radi-

[116] Buford Rhea "Institutional Paternalism in High School," *The Urban Review,* vol. 2, February, 1968, pp. 13–15, 34.

[117] Ronald N. Lippitt, N. Polansky, and S. Rosen, "The Dynamics of Power," *Human Relations,* vol. 5, no. 1, 1952, pp. 37–64.

[118] Lewis Lipsitz, "Review of Blauner, *Alienation and Freedom,*" *Public Opinion Quarterly,* vol. 19, Fall, 1965, p. 519.

cal criticism so essential to Marx, and (2) it makes it possible to see the deepest form of alienation in *non*awareness—in Mills' "happy robot" or Marcuse's "one-dimensional man" who have capitulated to the objectively alienated system yet believe that they are free and satisfied.[119]

It is hardly possible here to do more than signal this problem and to offer some cryptic notes on it. First, there is no doubt about the critical power originally tied to the concept of alienation, or about the critical power shown by the more recent advocates of the normative approach (Marcuse, Goodman, Fromm, and others). But what is gained in critical force is often lost in repetition and unanalytical pronouncement—which is why the latter-day improvement on Marx (or on Schiller or Rousseau, for that matter) in this recent critical literature is often hard to catalogue. Second, the decision to "secularize" the varieties of alienation (as in my 1959 paper) is a calculated risk to be sure, aimed ultimately at achieving greater clarity and demonstration without loss of intellectual scope.[120] But certainly it does not entail a loss of moral concern or unwillingness to examine the moral order: Why else would anyone be interested, as I have been, in how the individual's sense of powerlessness encourages ignorance in critical matters of health and politics; why else try to find out how the person's sense of mastery depends upon objective opportunities for control in his organizational life; or try to show what difference it makes in one's sense of mastery (and all the other consequences thereof) if minorities are excluded from participation in economic and social life; or try to separate the lack of intrinsic fulfillment in work from its supposed evil consequences (prejudice and the like); or try to demonstrate the inauthenticities that develop when people are subjected to strongly stereotypic and generally negative images of themselves? The secularization of the concept of alienation is a strategic enterprise that does not restrict our interest in, or our competence to talk about and examine, the full range of problems that are captured in words like justice, evil, trust, ignorance, or personal development.

4. The "givens" of *human nature*. Etzioni writes: "The concepts of alienation and inauthenticity assume the concept of basic human needs."[121] And that is certainly historically true for Marx, and true as well for a number of contemporaries. Etzioni's list of such needs is not remarkably different from Fromm's list in *The Sane Society*.[122] The advantage of such an assumption is that it gives an extra-societal and universal basis for criticism—a basis beyond mere personal preference or cultural prescription in which to root one's criti-

---

[119] C. Wright Mills, *White Collar*. Oxford University Press, New York, 1951; Herbert Marcuse, *One-Dimensional Man*. Beacon Press, Boston, 1964.

[120] Seeman, "On the Meaning of Alienation."

[121] Etzioni, *op. cit.*, p. 120.

[122] Fromm, *The Sane Society*.

cism of status striving, of the "happy robot's" adjustment to routine labor, and similar alienated states.

Such lists of basic needs, however, have some very serious disadvantages, a fact which Etzioni does not fail to note. They have proved to be exceedingly elusive and obscure both from the standpoint of the concrete evidence for them and from the standpoint of a philosophic defense of them that takes account of situational complexities and logical coherence. In the contemporary Marxist literature, the allegiance to such a notion is notably mixed, as is reflected in Titarenko's critique of Fromm: "What capitalism crushes is not various characteristics alleged to be eternally inherent in man, but those possibilities that man himself constantly formulates as demands and inquiries."[123]
It need hardly be said that the formulation proposed here, both for alienation and inauthenticity, does not rest on the assumption of universal and basic needs whose lack of fulfillment constitutes the core problem.[124]

5. The problem of *redundancy and triviality*. I am tempted to say that what the empiricist on alienation really faces is the risk of tautology; although that stretches the point, the thrust of the criticism is correct. The problem is not new or obscure, but it persists. Suppose we show, for example, that the anomic brand of alienation (normlessness) correlates with certain other variables—let us say with personal rigidity or with low ego strength, as McClosky and Schaar have shown.[125] It is difficult to know what to make of the correlation between rigidity and anomie when the illustrative item measuring the former variable is: "It bothers me when something unexpected interrupts my daily routine," and items in the anomie scale read: "People were better off in the old days when everyone knew just how he was expected to act," or "With everything in such a state of disorder, it's hard for a person to know where he stands from one day to the next." The perplexity is not helped by the authors' assurance that "clearly there is no connection between the face content of the items in the (rigidity) scale and that of the anomie items."[126] The same difficulty holds when we correlate "political alienation" and "anomie" with political participation, as McDill and Ridley have done, seeking to show that these variables (and education as well) are additive in their effects on

[123] A. I. Titarenko, "Erich Fromm in the Chains of Illusion," *Science and Society,* vol. 29, Summer, 1965, pp. 319–329, especially p. 323.

[124] For some earlier and well-placed doubts about such lists of needs cf. Foote, *op. cit.* As Lichtheim (George Lichtheim, "Alienation," in David Sills, ed., *Encyclopedia of the Social Sciences,* vol. 1. Macmillan and Free Press, 1968, pp. 264–268) has recently remarked, in a somewhat different context, "The alienation of labor as the self-alienation of man from his essence is a concept that presents considerable intellectual difficulties," p. 267.

[125] McClosky and Schaar, *op. cit.*

[126] *Ibid.,* p. 29.

participation—the difficulty being that the two alienation measures are hard to distinguish conceptually when political alienation is conceived to be "a reflection of a general feeling of social alienation or anomie" and the two measures correlate at the .6 level.[127]

These are rather straightforward measure overlaps, but even the better demonstrations concerning alienation suffer from similar troubles. Where is the surprise, for example, in Blauner's demonstration that people in a skilled trade (like printing) are more inclined to feel that their skills and abilities are being used than are those in an assembly-line or machine-tool occupation? Where is the surprise in Pearlin's evidence that work alienation (by which he largely means a sense of low control at work, but also "an overtone of resentment" at being deprived of greater control) is correlated with the "inability of subordinates to act back upon their superordinates," and is higher when one "evaluates his monetary rewards negatively."[128] In the first instance, one could say that we are talking about two ways of indexing the sensed low control of the nurses on the ward, and in the second instance (regarding pay) we are talking about two ways of capturing a portion of their resentment in the work situation. There is even less news in learning, in the Aiken and Hage study, that "lack of participation in agency decision-making is strongly related to alienation from work $(r = -.59)$" when the latter includes dissatisfaction with the authority (independent decision-making) allowed to workers by boards of directors and supervisors.[129]

Most generally, the problem of triviality and redundancy is encouraged by the common practice of building alienation scales that incorporate a strong evaluation component; they are indexes of unhappiness if not despair, of mistrust mingled with powerlessness, of negativity and complaint ("things are tough all over" indexes). Some would argue, of course, that this component of evaluation (the strong judgmental character of the items, which often gives them an extreme quality as in the Srole scale) captures the very essence of alienation, and I am not inclined to argue the matter of definitions at the moment. The point, rather, is that the definitional alternatives impose restrictions on the kinds of demonstrations that can be made. If one chooses to define powerlessness in expectancy terms (as in the forced-choice I-E scale), that is one thing. It is quite another to define powerlessness in terms of a sensed discrepancy between what is, and what is desired (*unhappiness* over one's control), for then the measure easily becomes an index of resentment, discon-

[127] Edward L. McDill and J. C. Ridley, "Status, Anomia, Political Alienation and Political Participation," *American Journal of Sociology,* vol. 68, September, 1962, pp. 205–213, especially 206.

[128] Leonard I. Pearlin, "Alienation from Work: A Study of Nursing Personnel," *American Sociological Review,* vol. 27, June, 1962, pp. 314–325.

[129] Aiken and Hage, *op. cit.*

tent or the like—and in the latter case, dependent variables that are also (in one way or another) measures of resentment, despair, or mistrust become unpersuasive as correlates of the alienation index. The point holds, too, for the third common way of defining alienation—there are *expectancy,* sensed *discrepancy,* and *objective* definitions—for with the latter too, redundancies enter, as is well argued by Bordua when he notes the danger of tautology in treating delinquency as a *product* of anomie when, in fact, it can be treated as an (objective) *index* of anomie.[130]

6. The problem of *priorities:* the concentration on attitudes. A great deal of effort in the past 10 years has gone into the measurement of attitudes—not only with respect to alienation, of course, but certainly in that domain the effort has been substantial. The aims and styles of research on attitudes have been different, yet the essential similarity remains. Thus, Keniston provides a detailed and subtle portrait of the syndrome of attitudes that constitutes the alienation of cultural estrangement; McClosky and Schaar seek to show the wide range of personal and social attitudes that underlie and correlate with "anomie"; Davids develops an alienation syndrome composed of five dispositions (egocentricity, distrust, pessimism, anxiety, and resentment); various efforts are made to determine the association between powerlessness and its cousins—need achievement, authoritarianism, inner-direction and the like (cf., for example, Crandall *et al.*); and there are numerous efforts to factor analyze the disparate domains of alienation (e.g., Neal and Rettig).[131]

It comes as no surprise that all this attitude-centered activity generates disaffection. Some are simply unhappy about the quick and uncreative retreat to attitude measurement (and a corollary underattention to the situation) when social behavior should be the critical test, and others are unhappy with the very definition of alienation in attitude-like terms, since they have grave doubts about the theoretical status of the concept of attitude itself. Given the fact that the theoretical status of "attitudes" cannot be settled here, it remains simply (a) to plead guilty on some counts (e.g., to the overconcentration on attitudes, an example of which can be found in my own recent paper on work alienation)[132] and (b) to insist that there is no solution to be found simply in rejecting the notion of attitude in any form. There is no solution, for example,

[130] David J. Bordua, "Anomie: An Attempt at Replication," *Social Problems,* vol. 6, Winter, 1959, pp. 230–238.

[131] Keniston, *op. cit.;* McClosky and Schaar, *op. cit.;* Anthony Davids, "Alienation, Social Apperception, and Ego Structure," *Journal of Consulting Psychology,* vol. 19, February, 1955, pp. 21–27; Vaughn Crandall, W. Katkovsky and A. Preston, "Motivational and Ability Determinants of Young Children's Intellectual Achievement Behavior," *Child Development,* vol. 33, September, 1962, pp. 643–661; Arthur G. Neal and S. Rettig, "On the Multidimensionality of Alienation," *American Sociological Review,* vol. 32, February, 1967, pp. 54–64.

[132] Seeman, "On the Personal Consequences of Alienation in Work."

in dismissing the idea of "alienation" in favor of the concept of "exploitation" (as Pierre Naville, among others, recommends)[133] since they do not serve the same purpose, and no solution in calling certain attitudes by other names (like "ideology" or "role expectations"). The solution, rather, lies in making the attitudes in question as explicit as possible both in theory and in measurement so that their status is clear—whether as an expectancy construct within the terms of Rotter's social learning theory, as a descriptive feature of the "attitude of everyday life" as described by Garfinkel,[134] or within other schema. Beyond that, there *are* ways of putting the imagination to work so that we are not left with merely and only a set of intercorrelated attitudes—ways, for example, of building designs that incorporate the quasi-experimental methods recently described by Campbell and Stanley for use in natural settings.[135]

7. The problem of *unity*. Alain Touraine has remarked that the conceptual treatment embodied here has the merit of breaking the "false unity" of the idea of alienation,[136] but the difficulty remains that the six variants of alienation proposed here are a theoretically unintegrated lot—simply six variations derivable from classic usages. Critics have not been slow in noting the bare typological character of these definitions, and have sought in various ways to restore unity. The reader will have to evaluate these efforts toward recapturing a general construct of alienation; for the present, I am interested only in establishing that at least four major ways of restoring unity have been recommended:

a. Unity through a conception of *social process*. Browning *et al.* argue that the varieties of alienation are bound together by the fact that they appear in typical sequences; for example, one begins with a sense of powerlessness, from which meaninglessness develops, with the ultimate development being self-estrangement.[137]

b. Unity through a conception of *societal prerequisites*. In one way or another, this view suggests that a theory of society is the only orderly guide to the needed varieties of alienation. Thus, Scott bases his analysis on Smelser's version of the fundamental components of social action—values, norms, role or organization, and situational facilities—and derives from this four

[133] Pierre Naville, "Alienation and Exploitation," *Cahiers d'Etude des Sociétées Industrielles et de l'Automation,* vol. 6, no. 2, 1964, pp. 161–164.

[134] Harold Garfinkel, "Studies of the Routine Grounds of Everyday Activities," *Social Problems,* vol. 2, Winter, 1964, pp. 225–250.

[135] Donald T. Campbell and J. Stanley, "Experimental and Quasi-Experimental Designs for Research on Teaching," in N. L. Gage, ed., *Handbook of Research on Teaching.* Rand McNally, Chicago, 1963, pp. 171–246.

[136] Alain Touraine *et al.,* "Debate on the Sociological Utility of the Idea of Alienation," *Sociologie du Travail,* vol. 2, April, 1967, pp. 180–209, especially p. 195.

[137] C. J. Browning *et al.,* "On the Meaning of Alienation" (Letter to the editor), *American Sociological Review,* vol. 26, October, 1961, pp. 780–781.

types of alienation (e.g., powerlessness represents the individual's alienation from facilities). Presumably, one could make a similar approach through attention to "the functional prerequisites of society" or through the "system problems" (pattern maintenance, integration, etc.) specified by Parsons.[138]

c. Unity through *statistical coherence*. There are various ways to show the coherence (or lack of it) among scales, the most popular at the moment being factor analysis and Guttman scaling. Both of these have been used on the alienation problem. Thus, Middleton has presented evidence that items representing five of the six varieties of alienation (all, that is, except cultural estrangement) form a Guttman scale (the intercorrelation among the five items—one for each brand of alienation—ranging from .46 to .81).[139] The factoring procedure, of course, can be guided by the hope of finding either a large general factor of alienation or numerous independent factors (more or less paralleling the six types discussed here), and one can find evidence on both sides. Thus, McDill finds a rather general "despair" factor; Streuning and Richardson present a factor analysis of 68 items that yields nine factors (with the major factor, however, being a variant of Srole's anomie that is labeled "alienation via rejection"); and Neal and Rettig find some support for both the "single factor" and "multiple dimension" viewpoint.[140]

d. Unity through identification of a *core theme*. The tie in this case is a loose conceptual one. What ties the alienations together is that they partake of a common element, a thread of similarity. Thus, for Blauner, what the dimensions have in common is that "basic to each one is the notion of fragmentation in man's existence and consciousness."[141] For example, powerlessness represents a split into subject and object; meaninglessness reflects a part-whole split; and self-estrangement is a rupture of "temporal wholeness."

There are those, however, who find none of these solutions very satisfactory (I include myself in that category), and who would continue to insist upon the lack of unity. One ground for insisting in that direction lies in the recognition of the difficulty involved in blending an essentially conservative (and

[138] Marvin Scott, "The Social Sources of Alienation," *Inquiry*, vol. 6, 1963, pp. 57–69; Neil J. Smelser, *Theory of Collective Behavior*. Free Press of Glencoe, New York, 1963; David Aberle *et al.*, "The Functional Prerequisites of a Society," *Ethics*, vol. 60, 1950, pp. 100–111, Alex Inkeles, "Society, Social Structure and Child Socialization," in John Clausen, ed., *Socialization and Society*. Little, Brown, Boston, 1968, pp. 73–129; Talcott Parsons, *The Social System*. Free Press, Glencoe, Ill., 1951.

[139] Middleton, *op. cit.*

[140] McDill, *op. cit.*, Elmer L. Streuning and Arthur H. Richardson, "A Factor Analytic Exploration of the Alienation, Anomia and Authoritarianism Domain," *American Sociological Review*, vol. 30, October, 1965, pp. 768–776; Neal and Rettig, *op. cit.*

[141] Blauner, *op. cit.*, p. 32.

pessimistic) Durkheimian notion of normlessness with the radical (and optimistic) Marxian perspective on alienation. What some might call the "deterioration" of the unity of alienation need not be overly disconcerting. I hold only a minimal conception of their unity from the outset: They are bound together only by the historical interest in them as likely products of given social conditions (especially those of modern industrial society as depicted in Table 1).[142] While recognizing the need for a better theoretical conception than that, for the moment I am content to consider the various categories as representing a variety of "alienation" in much the same way that one might speak of varieties of "creativity" (painting, dance, musical composition, etc.), without expecting to find empirical unity among them or having an over-all theory about them.

Some would propose, in that case, that we dispense with the word "alienation" altogether.[143] I would have little objection to that, so long as it were not forgotten that the questions at stake in the investigation of powerlessness, normlessness, self-estrangement, and the like are easily recognizable in the sociological tradition that goes by the name of alienation. That word is absent from Silberman's index, but that fact does not prevent him from asserting: ". . . what is crucial is that Negroes never have had the sense of controlling their own destinies; they have never had the feeling that they were making, or even participating in, the decisions that really counted . . ."[144]

A summary remark: The seven deadly sins sketched above certainly present serious problems, but they are not as deadly, in my judgment, as some make them out to be. The social-psychological view embodied here is not restrictive in the way that some have argued.[145] It involves no commitment to the status quo nor inhibits criticism of it (just as measuring prejudice presumably involves no implicit approval of such attitudes); it does not commit us to the respondent's view (e.g., to believe that people in fact have power because they express low powerlessness); nor does it disallow speculation and imagination

---

[142] For a related view, but one which appears to see greater unity, see Glazer's comment: "If we approach alienation in this way, it becomes less a description of a single specific symptom than an omnibus of psychological disturbances having a similar root cause—in this case, modern social organization" (Nathan Glazer, "The Alienation of Modern Man," *Commentary,* vol. 3, April, 1947, pp. 378–385).

[143] J. M. Domenach "Pour en finir avec l'aliénation," *Esprit,* vol. 344, 1965, pp. 1058–1083. That is Kaufman's (Arnold S. Kaufman, "On Alienation," *Inquiry,* vol. 8, 1965, pp. 141–165) recommendation, but for somewhat different reasons; namely the desire to distinguish between alienation as a moral concept, and the various brands described here (powerlessness, etc.) as technical social scientific concepts.

[144] Charles E. Silberman, *Crisis in Black and White.* Vintage Books, New York, 1964, p. 193.

[145] John E. Horton, "The Dehumanization of Alienation and Anomie," *British Journal of Sociology,* vol. 15, December, 1964, pp. 283–300.

about as yet unrealized ways of achieving greater mastery, better work circumstances, or less deceptive social practices (as well as contemplating the ways in which some alienations may be productive or sought). We are free to entertain as many utopian visions (in the best sense) as we like, while forced to recognize that the ideas of alienation and inauthenticity are not terribly useful if they simply become words that refer (inversely) to a consortium of all virtues. In the lexicon established here (and in my inauthenticity paper referred to earlier), there can well be *un*alienated Babbitts who misread the constraints on their power and feel themselves in control (at least, they are unalienated so far as the sense of powerlessness is concerned), just as there can be *authentic* villains who do evil and know fully what they do.

Some Directions for Research

The reader who has come this far, through the detail that is essential to demonstration whatever the scope, will be in a position to establish his own priorities for future research. I have tried to present a theoretical background in mass theory, some definitional guides for empirical application, a substantive review of some tested propositions, and a sense for the strategic decisions that recur for those who try to deal with alienation.

The following, it seems to me, are some of the more evident general conclusions about the present state of affairs:

1. Change is regularly an implication, not a direct focus of investigation. Although the idea of alienation is frequently discussed in the context of social change, as in the present volume, the evidence concerning change is minimal —which suggests both the need for, and the difficulty of, longitudinal studies.

2. The structure-alienation-behavior triad has rarely been incorporated in a given work. The preceding substantive review shows that the typical investigation concerns either structure and alienation (including the customary "age, rank, and serial number" correlations between social status and alienation), or alienation and its consequences. But, like change, the sequences implied in the structure-alienation-behavior model remain largely inferential.

3. The emphasis is heavily weighted toward the "problem" theme: alienation, not engagement, is the focus. The best parallel, perhaps, is found in the psychological literature that dwells on mental disorder without a corollary interest in health. We seem to take it rather much for granted that engagement is easy, natural, or unproblematic, and turn our attention to the "disengaged." Yet, we hardly have a clear image, much less understanding of, the authentic or unalienated man, or of how the "normal" state of coordinated everyday action is achieved. Indeed, my own work teaches me that it is a good deal easier to talk about alienation and inauthenticity than their inverse—for one reason, it is tempting to let the comfortable catalogue of positive values

(e.g., autonomy, integrity, belonging) hide the hard conceptual and theoretical work of understanding authenticity and engagement. An example of that hard work can be found in the shaggy edges that surround the idea of "intrinsic" rewards (or intrinsic motivation) which has been left so unsatisfactorily advanced by Koch, White, and others, and is so central to old interests in both sociology (e.g., unalienated labor) and psychology (e.g., the functional autonomy of motives).[146]

4. The "indicators" of alienation have not been well developed; they have largely been approximated and "ad hoc"-ed. The most concentrated attention has gone into measurement of the sense of powerlessness, but if we are serious about a comprehensive scheme of social accounting concerning alienation, we need to do a great deal better on the other varieties of alienation.[147]

5. The simple designs that have led to such a concentration on the intercorrelation of attitudes (or correlations with background factors) will have to be improved. Since it is not likely that the sociologist interested in alienation will find the experimental laboratory very congenial, the improvement must be sought through refinements applicable to data derived from natural situations. Two examples come readily to mind: (a) the use of mathematical procedures (e.g., path analysis) for making causal inferences from non-experimental designs, as described by Blalock and Duncan, and (b) the use of quasi-experimental designs in natural settings, in the way described so effectively by Campbell and Stanley.[148] The latter, too, represents a point of methodological convergence with psychology (paralleling the substantive congruences described earlier), for there are signs in that discipline of unhappiness with the deficiencies (both moral and practical) of exclusively laboratory-oriented work in social psychology.[149]

These general directions of future development established, it remains but to illustrate some of the specific types of problems that seem vital for the

[146] John P. Seward, "The Structure of Functional Autonomy," *The American Psychologist,* vol. 18, 1963, pp. 703–710. The problem has recently arisen in connection with the idea of "need achievement," where the question concerns the mix of intrinsic and extrinsic elements in Nach—intrinsic interest in task achievement, and extrinsic interest in competitive success; see, for example, John W. Atkinson and Norman T. Feather, *A Theory of Achievement Motivation.* Wiley, New York, 1966.

[147] Of the three types not treated extensively here (meaninglessness, social isolation, and cultural estrangement), "meaninglessness" is probably least developed; for measures of the other two, see Dean, *op. cit.,* and Nettler, "A Measure of Alienation," respectively.

[148] Hubert M. Blalock, *Causal Inferences in Nonexperimental Research.* University of North Carolina Press, Chapel Hill, 1961; O. D. Duncan, "Path Analysis: Sociological Examples," *American Journal of Sociology,* vol. 72, July, 1966, pp. 1–16; Campbell and Stanley, *op. cit.*

[149] William J. McGuire, "Some Impending Reorientations in Social Psychology: Some Thoughts Provoked by Kenneth Ring," *Journal of Experimental Social Psychology,* vol. 3, April, 1967, pp. 124–139.

near future. These fall naturally into the mold provided by the three columns of Table 1: questions about the sources, the patterns, and the consequences of alienation.

Concerning sources, three lines of inquiry recommend themselves: (1) the learning of alienation in the socialization process; (2) historical studies of alienation; and (3) longitudinal studies of change. The question of socialization is one of the most neglected areas of work, but, not unexpectedly, there is enough to know that the different varieties of alienation attract different theoretical explanations about their genesis. Thus, Keniston hinges his account of the "uncommitted" (culturally estranged) on the Oedipal struggle: the estranged college youth is the "victor who lost," who has learned that men are weak, women are possessive, and the struggle ends in a Pyrrhic victory.[150] In defeating their fathers, these men have learned chiefly about the phony and fraudulent rather than about respect and emulation; in effect, they transfer family disrespect into estrangement from the culture represented in it. More recently, Keniston has described the opposite portrait, namely the committed young radicals, finding there a related but different family scene, namely, basic identification of these radicals with the values of their parents along with disrespect for the violation of these fundamental values that conventional American life encourages. His conclusion is that alienation and the current phenomenon of student protest are two quite distinct, if not opposed, phenomena.[151] It seems to me more likely that cultural estrangement is, indeed, involved in both cases; both his "uncommitted" passives (who appear to resemble the students of the 1950's) and his committed radicals of the 1960's are alienated in that they find American culture tasteless and shoddy, although they may very well differ in other respects—not necessarily in their Oedipal resolutions or failures, but in the other alienations they manifest (e.g., their sense of powerlessness).

As for the genesis of that powerlessness, the more popular line of attack is not through Freudian psychodynamics but through one or another version of reinforcement theory. Thus, one might argue that a difficulty with the rigid child-rearing practices of another day was that they rarely provided for those small occasions in which the child could experience his own competence by "winning" against the parents' rules and schedules. That is certainly consistent with Coopersmith's evidence that high self-esteem goes with a family life in which parents are "willing to allow the children a voice in the making of family plans." That is also the import of Katz's findings concerning Negro boys, whose low achievement and negative self-regard were related to reinforcement his-

---

[150] Keniston, *op. cit.*

[151] Kenneth Keniston, *Young Radicals: Notes on Committed Youth.* Harcourt, New York, 1968.

tories characterized by parental punitiveness and disinterest in matters involving effort and successful accomplishment.[152]

Turning to the historical studies, they are notoriously difficult but they can do two quite important things. First, they provide insight concerning the putative changes brought about in the course of the development of modern society—not least of all by way of correcting the romantic assumptions we are wont to make about the simplicity, coherence, stability, and meaningfulness of the pre-industrial community. In subtle and not so subtle ways, this assumption (what Amiot has called the postulate of "lost paradise.")[153] is built into the ethos of the mass-society literature. I have already noted how Wylie's historical study leads him to doubt that what has happened to Chanzeaux can be interpreted in this "romantic" way, although that community is hardly a strong example of industrialization.[154]

Second, the historical perspective can illuminate the "causes" of alienation in quite another sense, namely, in the sense of keeping the sources of the interest in alienation a matter of constant awareness. We are, for example, very much aware of two elements that help to make up an explosive contemporary situation—the heightened demand for real access to power by new groups (largely blacks and college students), and the civil-disobedience ideology that has developed in the interest of that demand. Their claims are cast in terms of a currently fashionable variant of alienation (self-estrangement): authenticity, identity, conscience, and personal fulfillment are the language in common use. The language (not "exploitation," but "fulfillment") is one feature that distinguishes the "new left" from the old. Two historical interpretations throw some light on this development, both of them focusing on the outmoding of traditional liberal-democratic conceptions. Turner, following Mannheim, argues that we are seeing the emergence of a new conception of justice (a claim to the right to be respected as a person) which serves the interests of a new group making a claim to power (namely, the young).[155] What is being superseded, in his view, is the old liberal-humanitarian conception of justice (emphasizing the right of political participation) which served the

[152] Stanley Coopersmith, "Studies in Self-Esteem," *Scientific American,* vol. 218, February, 1968, pp. 96–106, especially p. 104; I. Katz, "The Socialization of Academic Motivation in Minority Group Children," in D. Levine, ed., *Nebraska Symposium on Motivation.* University of Nebraska Press, Lincoln, 1967, pp. 133–191.

[153] Touraine *et al., op. cit.*

[154] Wylie, *op. cit.* It ought to be explicitly said that the utility of the perspective and the variables implied in the schema of Table 1 does not depend upon the existence of some idealized pre-industrial totality that has been dismembered. Its utility hardly depends upon demonstrating that we are now more alienated than we once were.

[155] Ralph H. Turner, "The Theme of Contemporary Social Movements," *British Journal of Sociology,* vol. 20, December, 1969, pp. 390–405; Karl Mannheim, *Ideology and Utopia,* trans. by L. Wirth and E. Shils. Harcourt, New York, 1946.

middle class in their struggle for power, and the socialist conception of justice that followed (emphasizing the right to material welfare) which served in the worker's struggle for power. In another historical interpretation, Lichtheim argues that "the contemporary form of debate" in the language of alienation shows the effects of the overpowering recent experience with totalitarianism which "upset the traditional equilibrium between the individual and society" and at the same time raised serious questions among intellectuals concerning their own role in furthering the state's capability against the individual.[156]

As to longitudinal studies, these could be particularly productive in two areas: studies of developing societies, and studies of the effects of mobility. It is not the case, at present, that such studies often include direct measurement relevant to alienation. That such studies might be very productive (and in keeping, I might add, with the requirement of intellectual scope) can be suggested by two examples with disparate interests and samples.

Concerning the experience of modernization, Feldman and Hurn have reported on a re-interview study in Puerto Rico (involving 104 heads of household originally interviewed in 1954 and again in 1965).[157] It was possible to compare nonmobile groups with those who had experienced mobility from traditional (mostly rural) occupations to modern urban occupations. What is of most interest here is that the modernizers (as expected) alter their aspirations for their children (revising them upward), but they do not, as a coherent modernizing thesis might suggest they should, assign greater value or importance to education. What this might have to do with powerlessness is revealed in Feldman and Hurn's conclusion that the mobile has learned about the relative unimportance of education from his own successful experience (and has learned to be optimistic about his chances, or his son's): "The case studies frequently report phrases like, 'it takes luck and the breaks, not education.' . . . The tradition-to-modern mobile sounds a good deal like the successful blue-collar worker in industrial societies."[158]

If this says, in effect, that the experience of modernization can validate rather than eliminate one kind of alienation (powerlessness), Hamilton's study suggests how rural-to-urban mobility can be important for another type of alienation: cultural estrangement.[159] His problem was to explain "the persistent leftist character of French working-class politics," using data obtained in a series of surveys conducted from 1952 to 1956.[160] The basic question is

---

[156] Lichtheim, *op. cit.,* p. 267.

[157] Arnold S. Feldman and C. Hurn, "The Experience of Modernization," *Sociometry,* vol. 29, December, 1966, pp. 378–395.

[158] *Ibid.,* pp. 394–395.

[159] Richard F. Hamilton, *Affluence and the French Worker in the Fourth Republic.* Princeton University Press, Princeton, 1967.

[160] *Ibid.,* p. 275.

whether increasing affluence conservatizes or not. Hamilton finds (in a comparison of "before affluence" and "after," made possible by the trend data) that the agrarian radicalism of French workers who move to the urban setting is not diminished but enhanced, which is to say that their preference increases for "basic institutional changes in the character of the society."[161] They are less deprived and more culturally alienated (which sounds familiarly like the situation of the American Negro).

Given the limitations on space and the reader's patience, I will limit my comment on future studies of the "patterns" and the "consequences" of alienation to a brief remark in each case. Much of what has gone before already suggests some needed work in studying patterns—e.g., the discussion of unity among the brands of alienation (or lack of unity); the implication that "powerlessness" (input) and "trust" (output) ought to be distinguished in studies of political alienation, and the suggestion that alienation has itself become an ideology whose distribution in society needs to be examined (to understand, for example, the ecology of "alienation" as an explanation of action or as an excuse for passivity—a "fashionable way of being overwhelmed," said Mills; an "intellectual folk term," said Graña).[162]

The more general point concerning patterns, however, relates directly to the social changes now underway in the sphere of work. I refer especially to three interrelated phenomena which center around the trend toward professionalization: (1) automation and its likely impact on the professionalization of work skills; (2) the increasing interdependence of specialized personnel (e.g., in the military);[163] and (3) the development of professional organizations and ideologies.

What is of interest concerning this thrust toward professionalization is that it can be conceived as a thrust toward the unalienated state. If one asks for an ideal-typical description of the unalienated man, following the sundry meanings of alienation that have been specified, the image evoked bears a remarkable resemblance to what we mean when we speak of the professional. The criteria for the professions have been variously put, but the core features are rather clear.[164] There must be: (1) some procedure for guaranteeing the individual's competence in a *skill;* (2) a recognizable body of knowledge and theory, i.e., an intellectual *understanding* of the technical skills; (3) a proced-

---

[161] *Ibid.,* p. 5.

[162] Mills, *op. cit.;* César Graña, *Modernity and Its Discontents.* Harper, New York, 1964; Melvin Richter, "Intellectual and Class Alienation: Oxford Idealist Diagnoses and Prescriptions," *European Journal of Sociology,* vol. 6, 1966, pp. 1–26.

[163] Morris Janowitz, *The Professional Soldier.* Free Press, Glencoe, Ill., 1960.

[164] The list that follows is based on, but does not literally follow, the discussion in Talcott Parsons, "Professions" in David Sills, ed., *Encyclopedia of the Social Sciences,* vol. 12. Macmillan and Free Press, New York, 1968, pp. 536–546.

ure for regulating the *socially responsible use* of the member's talents, preferably by self-regulation in terms of an ethical code, but also by professional
organization; (4) the existence of a *cultural tradition* to which the professional
is committed, which includes a sense for the history of the profession, the
autonomy of its members, and its further development; (5) the sense of
service-centered work, i.e., work which is valuable "for itself" and not dependent upon extrinsic rewards; and (6) a sense of *colleagueship* which involves
loyalty to others and the duty of professional exchange.

Perhaps some unity of a kind concerning alienation can be found in the
fact that, when we seek to professionalize someone, we try to accomplish
these six tasks, and these tasks have a striking parallel to the varieties of
alienation: competence is the obverse of powerlessness; understanding vs.
meaninglessness; trust and social regulation vs. normlessness; cultural commitment vs. value isolation; intrinsic work orientation vs. self-estrangement; and
colleagueship vs. social isolation. Obviously, professionals differ greatly in the
degree to which these qualities are actually learned, and some may feel hope-
lessly unskilled in relation to their own high standards of competence. The
sense of control is hardly the same as the *level* of skill (as measured by an
objective test, for example), and self-regulating adherence to norms may fail
as often as it succeeds; but the process of professionalization is, in principle, a
process formally dedicated to the development of competence, understanding,
engagement, and the rest—both as a matter of professional behavior and of
professional attitude.

This is not an argument for the professionalization of everyone, but rather
an argument for seeing the broad relevance of professionalization to research
on alienation.[165] That relevance can be seen in an application to recent work
on professionals, for example, Miller's study of the alienation of professionals
(scientists and engineers) working in bureaucratic settings.[166] He found (1)
that work alienation (meaning essentially the lack of "intrinsic pride in work")
is high when organizational control over the professional's activities is greater
—i.e., where professionals were either working for a directive supervisor or
were not free to choose the types of research projects in which they were to be
involved; and (2) this relationship between work alienation and organizational
control was strongest for professionals having more advanced training. There
are various ways to view such findings, among them the view that what is being
described is simply the pattern of non-alienation that constitutes one as a professional. If to be professional consists (among other things) of being trained in

[165] Harold Wilensky, "The Professionalization of Everyone?" *American Journal of Sociology,* vol. 70, September, 1964, pp. 137–158.
[166] George A. Miller, "Professionals in Bureaucracy: Alienation among Industrial Scientists and Engineers," *American Sociological Review,* vol. 32, October, 1967, pp. 755–768.

a skill whose use is dictated by one's own understanding, in the interest of a task that is valued for itself, there surely ought to be coherence among these elements. Pride in work does not go with control that violates use of one's own understanding, and that violation is all the more serious when the person is more professionalized in his training. In a sense, the results tell us that these men *are* professionalized because their alienations fit the pattern (just as the set of rules that are followed tell us what game is being played).

I have highlighted the approach to "patterns" of alienation by way of professionalization because I think it has a good deal of promise in a discussion of social change, but there are numerous other questions about pattern that deserve attention. To illustrate, Table 3 tells us that organization membership goes with subjective competence in the five countries studied by Almond and Verba, but it does not tell us two things further about the pattern into which this subjective competence fits. First, it would be valuable to know whether this sense of political competence is part of a generalized competence syndrome or not; that is, is it the case that experiences of competence in politics generalize into (or at least, are congruent with) a range of nonpolitical competencies? Present evidence would suggest that, in the United States at least, the pattern of powerlessness appears to be more generalized than one might have supposed to be the case (cf., for example, Franklin's factor analysis using a national sample of high school students and Rotter's 1966 study).[167] It seems likely, nevertheless, that important distinctions can be made between, let us say, sensed low "personal control" as against "social control"—the former being powerlessness with respect to various personal goals (love and affection, job achievement, family independence, etc.) and the latter being powerlessness with respect to broad-scale social goals (international peace, intergroup harmony, problems of inflation). This difference appears in an unpublished factor analysis of Swedish data, and it may well be important in a case like American student activism, where social powerlessness may be high (i.e., the students reflect their relative removal from effective participation) but their personal powerlessness relatively low: in effect, the latter becomes a basis for acting to remedy the former brand of powerlessness.

Second, one might ask to what extent the Almond-Verba evidence concerning competence holds as well for the other variants of alienation; that is, is there relatively high coherence in the pattern, and does it hold on a comparative basis? The logic and the importance of such a coherence has already been nicely suggested in Inkeles' effort to show that there is cross-cultural consistency in the correlation between one's status position (occupation, in-

[167] R. D. Franklin, "Youth's Expectancies About Internal Versus External Control of Reinforcement Related to *N* Variables," unpublished doctoral dissertation, Purdue University, 1963; Rotter, "Generalized Expectancies for Internal Versus External Control of Reinforcements."

come, and education) and a set of attitudes and values (satisfaction with one's job, qualities desired in a job, general feelings of happiness in life, child-rearing values, etc.).[168] Inkeles found the same status-value associations re-appearing in various Western countries despite wide differences in their cultural base. For our purposes, the most interesting portion of this demonstration concerns what Inkeles calls the "mastery-optimism complex" which involves questions concerning personal competence, dependence on external sources of authority and power (including "trust in God"), and belief in the efficacy of one's own effort—all recognizable components of the sense of powerlessness. The data then available were suggestive (but far from persuasive) on the key point: People more highly placed in the objective status order of a given indus-trialized country differed from those lower in the system, and these differences tended to hold across countries (high-status groups, of course, tending to show greater mastery). Inkeles' way of putting the matter explicitly raises the ques-tion of pattern and coherence in such results: ". . . to the degree a nation's social structure approximates the model of a full-scale primary industrial so-ciety, to that degree will it more clearly show the differentiated structure of response we have delineated, *and do so over a wider range of topics, prob-lems or areas of experience.*"[169] It remains to be seen whether the experience of industrialization goes in this way, whether the process generates a "bundle" of unalienated beliefs that include a rather generalized sense of mastery, plus trust, plus commitment to intrinsically work-centered values, and the like. To doubt that such a pleasantly coherent pattern will emerge would not be diffi-cult in light of the empirical literature already canvassed, and in light of what we know about our unwitting tendency to gather all our hopes into our "scien-tific" concepts (cf. on the latter, Kecskemeti's critique of the concept of "au-thoritarianism").[170]

Finally, a word about consequences, where three brief remarks will have to suffice. First, all of the theses that link social structure and alienation to particular consequences (illustrated in Table 1) do so by employing certain theoretical principles or "mechanisms" of behavior, and often enough, these principles and mechanisms are left implicit, much less tested. In a recent paper, I identified three mechanisms commonly found in the literature on alienated labor.[171] Such labor is said to have generalized effects through the operation of either (1) the principle of *frustration-aggression* (e.g., alienated work builds frustrations which find release in ethnic hostility); (2) the principle of *substi-*

---

[168] Alex Inkeles, "Industrial Man: The Relation of Status to Experience, Perception and Value," *American Journal of Sociology,* vol. 66, July, 1960, pp. 1–31.

[169] *Ibid.,* p. 29.

[170] Paul Kecskemeti, "The Study of Man—Prejudice in the Catastrophic Perspective," *Commentary,* vol. 11, March, 1951, pp. 286–292.

[171] Seeman, "On the Personal Consequences of Alienation in Work."

tution or compensation (e.g., since alienated work fails to provide the requisite intrinsic satisfaction, workers are driven to seek substitute, and generally shallow, satisfaction in status, display, and power); or (3) the principle of *social learning* (e.g., through alienated work people learn that they are the objects of control by others, and this learning is applied to their other affairs, for example, in politics, where powerlessness is displayed in nonvoting, ignorance, etc.).

Second, as such mechanisms are specified and tested,[172] we will have to come to terms with the contradictory predictions they often generate (the kinds of contradiction noted at the outset of the present chapter). Recall, for example, that there are signs of both activism and passivity among the powerless, and it becomes obvious that predictions about consequences cannot readily be made without a clear specification of situational variables. Thus, if the studies of voting in local referenda and of ghetto violence (and possibly campus activism as well) tie activism to powerlessness, while powerlessness is also associated with non-participation, retreat from knowledge, and unwillingness to act (as in the Gore-Rotter evidence), then clearly some distinctions have to be made concerning *kinds* of action, *kinds* of knowledge, and the like. The findings encourage the distinction, for example, between two kinds of "actives" differentiated by their conceptions of causality: the "instrumental" action-taker who is also a knowledge-seeker, a planner, and a strategist; and the "symbolic-expressive" action-taker who is engaged on a more spontaneous, direct-action basis—as a way of saying "No" to the authorities, or making a choice among highly limited alternative pathways to protest.[173] The general point is that different processes may be operating in different situations or in different phases of a given social movement, as Pinard has recently argued in suggesting that mass-society theory has paid too little attention to the fact that secondary organizations can serve to *mobilize* discontent rather than restraining it (hence the effect of social isolation is not uniform: it depends on this stage of the process, the degree of social strain, etc.).[174]

Similar contradictory predictions are easily generated by applying the

[172] For a similar set of mechanisms, developed in connection with a test of propositions about participation in community associations, see Robert Hagedorn and S. Labovitz, "Participation in Community Associations by Occupation: A Test of Three Theories," *American Sociological Review,* vol. 33, April, 1968, pp. 272–283.

[173] Such relatively unplanned action may, of course, have quite specific and not undesired consequences for the participants, as in the case of violence in the ghetto which has clearly been considerably less "senseless" than is often imagined; cf. T. M. Thomlinson, "Ideological Foundations for Negro Action: A Comparative Analysis of Militant and Non-Militant Views of the Los Angeles Riot," *Journal of Social Issues,* vol. 26, Winter, 1970, pp. 93–119.

[174] Maurice Pinard, "Mass Society and Political Movements," *American Journal of Sociology,* vol. 73, May, 1968, pp. 682–690.

"social-learning" mechanism and the "frustration-aggression" mechanism to alienated labor. Is it the case, for example, that "the more power the individual wields in the work situation the greater the likelihood that his behavior as father and socializer will be less hostile"?[175] One might think so, if the frustration-aggression mechanism is dominant, and those with less autonomy at work must displace their aggression at home. But it is equally arguable, via the social-learning principle, that those who have both their power and their relative freedom "to express hostility or its psychological equivalents"[176] validated every day at work will find it easy to generalize that learning to the family situation. That people do generalize in this way was the burden of Miller and Swanson's evidence that "bureaucratic" and "entrepreneurial" fathers teach their children differently, in conformity with the different demands that characterize their work life.[177] In short, one could predict that low control at work produces *either* low control at home or high control, these contradictory predictions requiring further specification about the situation (at work and/or at home) or about the person (e.g., his typical style of causal attribution), if the seeming contradiction is to be resolved. The third general point concerning consequences flows easily from the foregoing; namely, it is not likely that very many successful predictions can be made from the construct of alienation alone (and, as implied above, the contradictory and sweeping character of the customary predictions flow from just such efforts). This would hold both on theoretical and methodological grounds. Theoretically, both sociological requirements and the requirements of Rotter's theory (in terms of which the definitions of alienation are given) agree that, with respect to powerlessness, for example, very little would be predictable from expectancies alone. Social-learning theory is consistent with sociological interests in this matter, at least in the degree that it insists that three major elements are required to make effective predictions: a characterization of the situation, as well as a depiction of individual expectancies and personal values. I have tried to show elsewhere how the specification of values sharpens the predictions that can be made from the powerlessness scale (prisoners who are committed to the value of rehabilitation show different powerlessness-learning patterns than do those who are not committed), and also how the prisoner's situation (the objective prison term remaining to be served) affects the relation of learning to powerlessness (that relation is strongest where parole is most imminent, and very weak for the long-termers).[178] These are small-scale and modest examples, but they help to make the general point concerning the required range of variables.

[175] McKinley, *op. cit.,* p. 145.

[176] *Ibid.,* p. 146.

[177] D. R. Miller and Guy E. Swanson, *The Changing American Parent.* Wiley, New York, 1958.

[178] Seeman, "Alienation and Social Learning in a Reformatory."

Methodologically, too, one ought not expect very much from alienation alone. That is the import of Campbell and Fiske's insistence on demonstrations that use multiple measures of a given variable *and* include variables other than those which are the prime focus of attention.[179] It is an argument which holds that we are required to show (a) what powerlessness does *not* correlate with, (b) that powerlessness measured in different ways produces similar results, and (c) that variables that are not indexes of powerlessness (other forms of alienation, for example) produce a different pattern of correlation. It is as important, in this view, to show what *isn't* the case as it is to demonstrate significant associations, and this requires multiple measures and variables. These requirements for future work make severe demands on time and money, but they should sharply cut the intellectual costs of contradiction.

Coda

There is a revolution under way in the universities around the world, one that has been only lightly touched upon in this discussion; yet surely both alienation and the study of alienation are not lightly involved. Students now actively recognize their traditional powerlessness; they reject the old system and its values (as in France only recently); they want no more of the alienated labor of working for points and prestige on irrelevant substance; and many are prepared to get what they want by means that are outside the normative proprieties. It is as though their rebellion is meant to deny the validity of Jacques Ellul's description of technological society: "The human being is no longer in any sense the agent of choice . . . all men are constrained by means external to them to ends equally external."[180]

One may think that Ellul's pessimism, or Marcuse's,[181] is too one-dimensional by a good deal, but recent uprisings such as the French "events of May" show how deeply the strains of contemporary social change run and how slow we really are to understand and respond to them. Touraine contends, indeed, that the French revolt revealed a new form of class struggle powered by "the new alienations" which our postindustrial programmed society generates for professionals, technicians, students, and others. Whether consciously or not, the movement constituted the effort of a new coalition to achieve substantial control over the course of social change in France.[182]

[179] Donald T. Campbell and D. W. Fiske, "Convergent and Discriminant Validation by the Multi-Trait Multi-Method Matrix," *Psychological Bulletin*, vol. 56, March, 1959, pp. 81–105.

[180] Jacques Ellul, *The Technological Society*, Knopf, New York, 1965.

[181] Allen Graubard, "One-Dimensional Pessimism: A Critique of Herbert Marcuse's Theories," *Dissent*, vol. 15, May–June, 1968, pp. 216–228.

[182] Alain Touraine, *Le Mouvement de Mai ou Le Communism Utopique*. Editions de Seuil, Paris, 1968.

It is not so clear that "new" alienations are involved; but it seems quite likely that the old ones reviewed here—powerlessness, cultural estrangement, and work alienation, in particular—are key elements in the current rebellions. If that is truly the significance and force of alienation, it simply will not do for us to avoid the magnitude of the research task by getting bored with the word itself, by arguing endlessly in exegesis about its "true" meaning,[183] by escaping into a narrow scientism that is a form of alienation in itself (overly bound by technical rules, devoid of personal involvement, and largely oriented to careers), or by escaping into critiques that are more a moral claim to an identity (as "radical," or "humanist," or "realist," etc.) than an analysis. My hope is that the secularization of work on alienation can go beyond all that to illuminate the fundamental changes underway in the modern world.

[183] For a recent and comprehensive review of the idea's history and its variations, see Richard Schacht, *Alienation,* Doubleday, Garden City, N.Y., 1970.

Subject Index

Author Index